RELATING EVENTS IN NARRATIVE:
A CROSSLINGUISTIC DEVELOPMENTAL STUDY

RELATING EVENTS IN NARRATIVE:
A CROSSLINGUISTIC DEVELOPMENTAL STUDY

RUTH A. BERMAN
Tel Aviv University

and

DAN ISAAC SLOBIN
University of California at Berkeley

in collaboration with

**Ayhan A. Aksu-Koç, Michael Bamberg, Lisa Dasinger,
Virginia Marchman, Yonni Neeman, Philip C. Rodkin,
Eugenia Sebastián, Cecile Toupin, Tom Trabasso,
and Christiane von Stutterheim**

1994

LAWRENCE ERLBAUM ASSOCIATES, PUBLISHERS
Hillsdale, New Jersey
Hove, UK

The cover illustration is based on a "frog-crossing" road sign in the Austrian Alps, first noted by Nini Hoiting, and photographed by Dan Slobin.

Lawrence Erlbaum Associates, Inc., Publishers
365 Broadway
Hillsdale, New Jersey 07642

Cover design by Kate Dusza

Library of Congress Cataloging-in-Publication Data

Berman, Ruth Aronson.
    Relating events in narrative : A crosslinguistic developmental study / Ruth A. Berman and Dan Isaac Slobin, in collaboration with Ayhan Aksu-Koç...[et al.].
        p.   cm.
    Includes bibliographical references (p.) and index.
    ISBN 0-8058-1435-3.
    1. Discourse analysis, Narrative. I. Slobin, Dan Isaac, 1939-.
II. Title.
P302.7.B44   1994
401'.41—dc20   93-39190
                                                                         CIP

Printed in the United States of America
10 9 8 7 6 5 4 3 2

If we cannot end now our differences,
at least we can help make the world safe for diversity.

-John F. Kennedy
(Address at American University,
Washington, D.C., June 10, 1963)

CONTENTS

Part V. CONCLUSIONS

APPENDICES

Preface

You are about to join us in a quest for a runaway frog. That is, the many analyses of child and adult language in the following pages are all based on the ways in which speakers provide words to a wordless picturebook devoted to that quest (*Frog, where are you?*, by Mercer Mayer). Our own quest, however, is for a better understanding of the complex of linguistic, cognitive, and communicative abilities that underlie the human ability to capture and convey events in words. In that quest we have been immeasurably helped by good colleagues and students and by generous institutions.

The book itself is the result of a decade-long project which included many of the students and former students whose research papers and dissertations have contributed to the following chapters — from Berkeley: Ayhan Aksu-Koç, Michael Bamberg, Lisa Dasinger, Aylin Küntay, Virginia Marchman, Tanya Renner, and Cecile Toupin; from Tel Aviv: Yonni Neeman and Ziva Wijler; and from Madrid, Eugenia Sebastián. In addition, we have benefited from the contributions of colleagues — from Heidelberg: Christiane von Stutterheim, and from Chicago and Harvard: Tom Trabasso and Philip Rodkin. Except for the last two Chicago/Harvard contributors, who were invited to contribute their independent analysis of some of our materials, the group of us have worked together through the years, on every stage of the project — from planning, through execution and analysis, to writing. In addition, we have been joined by researchers from other countries carrying out related projects: Edith Bavin from Australia, Aura Bocaz from Chile, Hrafnhildur Ragnarsdóttir from Iceland; and Berkeley students have gone on to gather comparable data elsewhere: Guo Jiansheng in China, Aylin Küntay in Turkey, Yana Mirsky in Russia, and Keiko Nakamura in Japan. Various subgroups have met together for workshops at the Max-Planck-Institute for Psycholinguistics in Nijmegen, at Tel Aviv University, and at the University of California at Berkeley. More recently, we have benefited from the wider crosslinguistic and crosscultural insights of the Cognitive Anthropology Research Group in Nijmegen, headed by Stephen Levinson.

As the two main authors, and co-principal investigators of the project, we have worked over many drafts of all of the chapters in this book. Chapters with no author listed are the sole products of the two of us; the remaining chapters represent the joint efforts of the research team, with the responsible author(s) listed for each. In every instance, the final version has been reworked in detail by the two of us. Because this was a long and mutually interactive endeavor, we have agreed to list all of the co-authors from our project in alphabetical order in their chapters.

We are deeply grateful to Wolfgang Klein, Co-Director of the Max-Planck-Institute, for meticulous reading of the final manuscript. We have tried to incorporate his many useful and detailed suggestions. Overall responsibility for the entire volume, of course, rests with the two of us.

In order to bring the culmination of this long project to the public as soon as possible, we have undertaken the task of preparing camera-ready copy on our own, with technical support from the Max-Planck-Institute and from the Institute of Cognitive Studies of the University of California at Berkeley. In the process, we gained deep respect for the work of professional book-producers, and we wish we could have matched their skill.

This project, and the writing of the book, owe a debt of gratitude to the Max-Planck-Institute, which, at various times, has hosted the two of us and some of our co-authors and has sponsored workshops — in a setting which offers both rich intellectual stimulation and remarkable technical facilities — from computers and printers, to xerox machines, to a competent and dedicated support staff, and a superb library. In our home institutions, we have been supported by the facilities and staff of the Faculty of Humanities of the University of Tel Aviv and, in Berkeley, by the Department of Psychology, the Institute of Cognitive Studies, and the Institute of Human Development. Jane Edwards, at Berkeley, contributed her time and skills to creating the computer capacities for coding and analyzing our data, with continuing support from Michael Robinson. Lisa Dasinger, Guo Jiansheng, Virginia Marchman, Tanya Renner, and Cecile Toupin systematized and organized vast amounts of quantitative and qualitative data and carried out numerous analyses. Lisa Dasinger formatted the tables for the book and kept our growing list of references organized. And finally we thank the granting agencies which supported us: the U.S.-Israel Binational Science Foundation (Grant 2732/82, to R. A. Berman and D. I. Slobin), the Linguistics Program of the National Science Foundation (Grant BNS-8520008, to D. I. Slobin), the Sloan Foundation (to the Institute of Cognitive Studies, University of California, Berkeley), Boğaziçi University (to A. A. Aksu-Koç), the Mellon Foundation (to the Center for Middle East Studies, University of California at Berkeley, for D. I. Slobin with R. A. Berman and A. Küntay), and University of Chile (Grant H2643-8712, to A. Bocaz).

It is a pleasure to acknowledge what we have learned from many colleagues, too numerous to list here. We are especially grateful to Melissa Bowerman, Seymour Chatman, Esther Dromi, Susan Ervin-Tripp, Suzanne Fleischman, Julie Gerhardt, Maya Hickmann, Wolfgang Klein, Iris Levin, Stephen Levinson, Magdalena Smoczyńska, Sidney Strauss, and Liliana Tolchinsky-Landsmann.

This is a long and complicated book. It is hard to think about five languages and five age groups, and to simultaneously situate the findings in the fields of linguistics, psycholinguistics, developmental psychology, cognitive science, narratology, rhetoric, and others. Perhaps few readers will want to read each and every chapter. We have tried to organize the book so that readers with special interests can dip into it at various places. (As a consequence, the thorough reader will find some redundancy across the chapters.) Chapter IB gives a road map for the prospective traveler through our study.

In spite of the crosslinguistic scope of our endeavor, we are only at the beginning of understanding the roles played by individual languages and cultures in the development and use of language. The particular picture storybook that we have used in this study is fast becoming a worldwide research tool, and we are eager for the results of more broad-ranging typological and cross-cultural comparisons. Appendix III lists all of the studies that we know of that make use of *Frog, where are you?*. Much to our surprise, and delight, we know of at least 150 researchers, collecting "frog-stories" in 50 languages — not only in the field of standard spoken language development, but also in the development of sign languages, in a range of language-impairments, in various bilingual combinations, and in both spoken and written modes. We offer this book, then, as a systematic part of a larger quest. And we also offer it as an example of human diversity within a framework of universal patterns of human thinking, feeling, and speaking.

Ruth A. Berman
Dan I. Slobin

Nijmegen
November 1993

Contributors

Ayhan A. Aksu-Koç
Department of Psychology
Boğaziçi University
P.K. 2 Bebek
80815 Istanbul
Turkey
e-mail: koc0@trboun.bitnet

Michael Bamberg
Department of Psychology
Clark University
Worcester, MA 01610
USA
e-mail: mbamberg@clarku.bitnet

Ruth A. Berman
Department of Linguistics
Tel Aviv University
Ramat Aviv,
Israel 69978
e-mail: rberman@ccsg.tau.ac.il

Lisa Dasinger
Department of Psychology
University of California, Berkeley
Berkeley, CA 94720
USA
e-mail: dasinger@cogsci.berkeley.edu

Virginia Marchman
Department of Psychology
University of Wisconsin
Madison, WI 53706
USA
e-mail: marchman@merlin.psych.wisc.edu

Yonni Neeman
Center for Educational Technology
Klauzner Street
Ramat Aviv
Israel 69978

Philip C. Rodkin
Department of Psychology
Harvard University
William James Hall
Cambridge, MA 02138
USA
e-mail: pcr@isr.harvard.edu

Eugenia Sebastián
Departamento de Psicología Evolutiva
   y de la Educación
Facultad de Psicología
Universidad Autónoma de Madrid
Cantoblanco
28049 Madrid
Spain
e-mail: eug@emduam53.bitnet

Dan I. Slobin
Department of Psychology
University of California
Berkeley, CA 94720
USA
e-mail: slobin@cogsci.berkeley.edu

Christiane von Stutterheim
Institut für Deutsch als
   Fremdsprachenphilologie
Universität Heidelberg
Plöck 55
D-6900 Heidelberg 1
Germany
e-mail: u87@dhdurz1.bitnet

Cecile Toupin
Department of Psychology
University of California
Berkeley, CA 94720
USA
e-mail: toupin@cogsci.berkeley.edu

Tom Trabasso
Department of Psychology
The University of Chicago
5848 S. University Avenue
Chicago, IL 60637
e-mail: tsqd@midway.uchicago.edu

Part I

INTRODUCTION

Chapter IA

DIFFERENT WAYS OF RELATING EVENTS: INTRODUCTION TO THE STUDY

Our chapter title is deliberately ambiguous, reflecting the interwoven strands of our study. We intend, in the course of this book, to convey several senses of the words **different** and **relate**. The point of reference for these senses is a series of pictures that represent **events** — that is, dynamic interactions, over time, between animate beings, in physical settings. The pictures — 24 of them — were created by Mercer Mayer (1969) to form a story accessible to children. They are bound together in a storybook without words — except for the title, *Frog, where are you?*. This is our "frog story" — the source of our data, which consist of elicited narratives from preschool, school-age, and adult narrators in five languages: English, German, Spanish, Hebrew, and Turkish. We suggest that, at the outset, you turn to Appendix I, where the pictures are reproduced, and "read" the story, since it is the point of departure for the entire course of this study.

The stories that make up our data are told in **different ways** because: (1) the narrators are of different ages; (2) the narrators speak different languages; and (3) there are different ways of talking about the same pictures. We seek to show that each of these factors — age, language, and choice of narrative perspective — systematically contributes to identifiable uses of linguistic means to relate events in the frog story narrative (and, by implication, in narrative generally).

When we speak about **relating events**, we have two sorts of issues in mind. Taking the sense of "relate" that means "tell," we are concerned with the ways in which narrators put into words their conceptions of events — in this instance, events that are visibly displayed in pictures. That is, we are studying the development of the capacity to describe situations. We are also concerned with the ways in which individual events are **related to each other**. That is, we are studying the development of linguistic means to connect events and syntactically "package" them into coherent structures — at the levels of scene, episode, and overall plot. "Relating events" thus includes all of the verbal means for **encoding** and **emplotment** in narrative.

We did not begin our study — in 1983 — with all of these goals in mind. Rather, we were led to them by our data, which made it clear that the development of grammar cannot be profitably considered without attention to the psycholinguistic and communicative demands of the production of connected discourse. We began with a more limited goal: the study of the development of temporal expression in two quite different languages, English and Hebrew. We chose these two languages because one, English, has an elaborate set of verb markings for tense and aspect, while the other, Hebrew, does no more than mark the verb for the basic three tenses — past, present, future — with no grammaticization of aspect. We wondered whether Hebrew-speaking children would attempt to "compensate" for the sparse grammatical marking of temporality in their language by the use of **lexical** expressions for notions that are grammaticized in English. In so doing, we were guided by an approach to "cognitive prerequisites for the development of grammar" (Slobin, 1973) according to which children seek linguistic means of expression for emerging concepts — in this case, supposedly universal concepts of temporality. This approach seemed well established in the child language literature. Roger Brown had defined the goals of study as "the acquisition of knowledge, both grammatical and semantic" (1973, p. 254). In investigating the initial acquisition of grammatical morphemes in English, he had found it possible to objectively define "obligatory contexts" for the use of grammatical morphemes, including contexts for the temporal markers of progressive aspect and past tense — with the proviso that such contexts "should not be dependent on the topic of conversation or the character of the interaction" (p. 255). He had found that, once a child began to use a particular morpheme in 90% of such contexts for several consecutive longitudinal samples, it did not drop below 90%; and so "the 90% criterion" became established as the standard of acquisition. However, Brown dealt with the early emergence of grammatical morphemes. Later, "functionalist" investigators were to find that "topic of conversation" and "character of the interaction" have their own developmental histories, and that uses of grammatical morphemes are, indeed, dependent on learning their contextually situated meanings (e.g. Budwig, 1989, 1991; Ervin-Tripp, 1989; Gerhardt (Gee), 1985, 1988, 1990). And we were to find that many of the morphemes and constructions that we were interested in did not have "obligatory contexts," but, rather, represented **expressive options** that a speaker could take.

In the domain of temporality, the most extensive crosslinguistic surveys have been carried out by Richard Weist (Weist, 1986, 1990). Weist moved the terminology from "obligatory expression" to "conceptualization." Various researchers had found that the inherent semantics (*Aktionsart*) of a verb played a role in determining its tense/aspect marking in early speech (e.g., Antinucci & Miller, 1976; Bloom, Lifter, & Hafitz, 1980; Bronckart & Sinclair, 1973). Brown had already noted that: "Appropriate uses of the past begin with a small set of verbs which name events of such brief duration that the event is almost certain to have ended before one can speak. These are: *fell, dropped, slipped, crashed, broke*" (1973, p. 334). Thus it is not clear if such past-tense forms express anteriority (tense) or completion (aspect), and it became commonplace to claim that it was more probable that very young children were marking aspect, rather than tense, with their early past-tense verb forms. Weist, however, found that Polish children distinguished both tense and aspect, since these two temporal notions are marked separately on the Slavic verb. He proposed that children are able to take two kinds of "perspectives on situations" — "external" and "internal" (1986, p. 365): "When a situation is conceptualized from an external perspective, properties such as 'complete', 'punctual', and 'resultative' are salient, and when conceptualized from an internal perspective properties such as 'ongoing' ('continuative'), 'durative', and 'incomplete' are prominent."

Putting together the functionalists' concern with communicative settings for the choice of linguistic forms, and Weist's crosslinguistic concern with the sorts of conceptualizations involved in such choices, it is evident that the child has to learn much more than whether a particular "objectively definable" situation requires the use of a particular grammatical morpheme. The youngest children in the present study have passed their third birthday, and are well beyond the early stages studied by Brown. They already "know" many of the morphemes under study, but they do not yet know everything about the uses of these morphemes. And, in the following several years, they are learning not only new uses for the forms they know, but they are also acquiring new forms — in our study, both tense/aspect forms and interclausal connectives.

As we mentioned earlier, we were driven to this "functionalist-conceptual" approach by the use of an elicited narrative task. We picked the "frog story" (first used by Michael Bamberg in his 1985 Berkeley dissertation) because it is rich in opportunities for the encoding of temporal distinctions — sequence, simultaneity, prospection, retrospection, ongoing and completed events, etc. We found — at first to our surprise — that English and Hebrew narratives were quite different in their expression of temporality, even though narrators were, in some sense, telling "the same story." Bamberg's dissertation research had been carried out in Germany, and so it became fruitful to add German to our comparisons, leading to new surprises. Later, we were joined by two colleagues who completed the spectrum of languages represented in this book: Eugenia Sebastián, who gathered Spanish data in Madrid, and Ayhan Aksu-Koç, who gathered Turkish data in Istanbul. (The English stories were gathered in Berkeley by Tanya Renner and Virginia Marchman.) Our surprises, insights, and discoveries are documented in this volume.

1. FORM AND FUNCTION

The Leitmotif of our study is that form and function interact in development. Under "form" we include a broad range of linguistic devices — from grammatical morphemes and bound inflections to interclausal connectives and syntactic constructions — along with lexical items encoding notions of temporality, manner, and causation. By "function" we understand the purposes served by these forms in narrative discourse — purposes of constructing a text that is cohesive and coherent at all levels: within the clause, between adjacent clauses, and hierarchically relating larger text segments to one another. The developmental history of any given form reflects the expanding range of functions served by that form, and, at the same time, also reflects the "acquisitional complexity" of that form as determined by local processing constraints as well as the role played by the form in the overall system of the grammar. (By limiting ourselves to monologic narratives we exclude the considerable range of functions involved in the construction and maintenance of dialogue, including such issues as turn-taking, inter-speaker anaphora, question-answer pairs, and the like.)

Progressive aspect in English. As a mini-case-study, consider the development of progressive aspect in English. The present progressive is the first to be acquired of Brown's 14 grammatical morphemes. It is used in its "primitive" form, without a reliable auxiliary, throughout Brown's five developmental stages. He states that it is "almost always [used to name] an action or state in fact of temporary duration and true at the time of utterance" (1973, p. 318), and notes that: "The children did not attain criterion on the full progressive until long after Stage V, and by then the children could speak of remote past and future times, could use modal auxiliaries as well as catenatives, and could move the temporal reference point into the past" (1973, p. 319). The 3-year-olds in our study have reached this point and are exploring additional functions of the progressive, in both present and past tenses.

One function of the progressive (and durative or imperfective aspects in general) is to present the continuing background against which a foregrounded event occurs. This function is evident in the following narrative segment from a child of 3;9, who temporally situates the frog's escape during the period in which the boy was asleep:

(1) *The frog got out, when he's sleeping.* [E3h-3;9][1]

This usage differs in at least two important ways from the early use of the progressive noted by Brown: (1) It is not "temporary duration" that is at issue, but rather the temporal overlap between a durative and a punctual event. (2) The event of the boy's sleeping is not "true at the time of utterance," but rather true at some narrative reference time.

The separation of speech time and reference time is even clearer when the narrator uses the **past** progressive. The following segment, from a child of 3;5, shows an attempt to use the progressive to backtrack in time, describing a state — sitting on the edge — that existed before the boy fell into the water:[2]

(2) *And then he fell over with the dog - into the pond. He **was just sitting** - on the - edge before - with his dog, and pow - into the water.* [E3d-3;5]

Examples (1) and (2) indicate the **backgrounding** function of the progressive. Another way in which 3-year-old progressives differ from earlier uses is that they are not strictly tied to inherent verb semantics or *Aktionsart*. Recall that Brown found that punctual verbs like *fall* at first were used only in the past tense. But 3-year-olds can take either an "external" or an "internal" perspective on such events. For example, Picture 17 shows the boy and dog in mid-fall, while Picture 18 shows them landing in the water. Several 3-year-olds describe the event in the first picture as *falling* and that in the second as *fell*.

Another "liberation" of the progressive from pre-Stage V meanings appears in its use with state verbs. Brown noted that his children made no errors of progressive marking of verbs of involuntary state, such as *want, like, need, know, see,* and *hear*, and he suggested that children, somehow, discover this semantic restriction. He also noted, however, that the restriction is not absolute. He mused about such exceptions (p. 323):

---

[1] Excerpts from the data are followed by a code indicating language, age group, subject indicator, and exact age. Thus [E3h-3;9] indicates the eighth child in the sample of English-speaking 3-year-olds, aged 3 years and 9 months. Adult narrators are all arbitrarily given the age of 20. The languages are: E - English, G - German, H - Hebrew, S - Spanish, T - Turkish.

[2] Transcription conventions: hyphen indicates slight hesitation pause; three dots indicate longer pause; comma is non-final intonation; period is final fall. Words in capital letters indicate heavy stress, while boldface is used to highlight utterance segments that are relevant to the analysis. Some false starts may be omitted in examples for purposes of readability. Deleted clauses are indicated by three dots enclosed in square brackets. Linguistic examples and quotes from the texts are given in italics; glosses are enclosed in single quotes. (See Appendix II for more detail.)

Once upon a time when I was on a plane landing in Austin, Texas, I was thinking about these very verbs and the fact that they could not take the progressive when a gentleman standing in the aisle said to the girl next to me: "Are you wanting your suitcase down?" What will account for this case? The wanting was as involuntary as it is in *I want my lunch* and yet the progressive was used. In circumstances, however, where the states had a definite duration that was clearly temporary. The girl would shortly leave the plane. What seems to have happened is that the exceptionally clear applicability of the meaning 'temporary duration' overrode all else.

Such extended meanings are already accessible to 3-year-olds, as shown in the following explanation of why the boy and dog are returning home at the end of the story:

(3) *I think they swam out so far and they came right back to see their mom cause I think they **were missing** their mom.* [E3g-3;9]

Finally, to complete this mini-case-study, we find that 3-year-olds use the progressive not only on main verbs encoding actions, but also on modal and aspectual verbs that modify main verbs, such as:

(4a) *The dog's **trying** - get out - the window.* [E3d-3;5]

(4b) *He's **starting** to wake up.* [E3g-3;9]

In sum, long after its occurrence in 90% of obligatory contexts in the early stages, the progressive continues to take on new functions — both in terms of discourse structure (backgrounding) and semantics (temporary duration, modality, aspect). At the same time — as we will see throughout this book — such emerging functions motivate the acquisition of new forms. To repeat a familiar truism: "New forms first express old functions, and new functions are first expressed by old forms" (Slobin, 1973, p. 184). Essentially, **our** narrative task is to fill in this formula with crosslinguistic and developmental detail beyond Stage V.

2. TEMPORALITY AND GROUNDING IN NARRATIVE

Our brief overview of uses of the English progressive shows that we are concerned both with the semantics of temporal marking and the use of such marking to background or foreground events in discourse — what has come to be called "grounding" (see papers in Tomlin, 1987). In fact, an initial impetus to our study was Paul Hopper's (1979) suggestion that a major function of tense/aspect distinctions is to differentiate main-line (foreground) events from commentary (background) in narrative. As far back as 1967, Labov and Waletzky had characterized a narrative as a sequence of clauses whose order mirrors the sequence of events they relate. Such clauses contrast with "evaluative" clauses that give the "point" of the narrative as an interactive speech event. Hopper went on to note that the essential sequenced events in a story-line tend to be dynamic, punctual, and completive — contrasting with supportive background information which is frequently descriptive of physical or inner states and of durative situations. He proposed that if a language marks its verbs for perfective aspect (completive, nondurative, punctual), such forms tend to occur in foregrounded clauses; and if it marks its verbs for imperfective aspect (durative, progressive, iterative), such forms tend to occur in backgrounded clauses.

Examples (1-3) are consistent with Hopper's analysis. The progressive clauses depict states of affairs that are not sequential to the clauses which they follow. In (1), *sleeping* is the durative background to the foregrounded event of the frog's escape. In (2), *sitting* is a physical state that preceded the foregrounded event of falling. And in (3), the mental state of *missing their mom* stands outside of the narrative sequence of actions, and motivates those actions. These are discourse-oriented rather than narrowly semantic uses of progressive aspect. Thus a full account of the acquisition of grammar must include the mastery of linguistic devices for grounding — or, more broadly, linguistic devices for guiding **attention flow** — in narrative as well as in other discourse contexts not considered here, such as planning (Gerhardt (Gee), 1985), justifying (Sprott, 1990), demanding (Budwig, 1989), etc.

These issues go well beyond encoding of temporal distinctions. Hopper noted that word order, voice, and topic-focus particles function to mark foreground/background in various languages, and Labov (1972) claimed that subordinate clauses do not serve to advance a narrative. We might expect, then, that the child's task in acquiring "the grammar of narrative" would be to identify the foreground or main plot line of the story (the semantic task) and to acquire the necessary syntactic forms for mapping this foreground onto linguistic expressions (the formal task). The foreground would be mapped onto main clauses with active verbs of perfective aspect, animate subjects, canonical word order and other morphological marking of those subjects as topical, and so forth. In addition, the child would face the narrative task of adding background information by the use of imperfective verb forms in various types of noncanonical clauses (subordinate, passive, reordered, etc.).

However, this definition of the task assumes that there is a single objective series of events, waiting to be encoded in standard form. While this is certainly true to some extent, we have been struck by the different ways in which narrators choose to verbally present the standardized pictured situations in the frog story. **Foreground and background are not given by the pictures, but are constructed by the narrator**.

Compare, for example, the following adult English narrations of the scene in which the dog runs from the bees (Picture 12). There are two events — a running dog and a pursuing swarm of bees — with various conceivable causal relations between the two. The action of the dog can be foregrounded in a main clause with active verb, and the action of the bees can be backgrounded in a subordinate clause, as in (5):

(5) *The dog runs away as bees follow him.* [E20h]

But a similar effect can be achieved by a passive clause, with the dog as topic and the bees in a *by*-clause, as in (6):

(6) *The dog is being chased by the bees.* [E20j]

However, it is also possible to see the action of the bees as the main, foregrounded event, backgrounding the action of the dog in a subordinate clause, which, nevertheless, represents the next plotline event in sequence:

(7) *All the bees start chasing the dog, who runs away.* [E20a]

Catherine Chvany (1984), in an analysis of Russian literary texts, has argued that narrators can manipulate aspect and subordination for dramatic effect. She analyzes a sentence from the end of a story by Chekhov which contains a sequence of two clauses which are temporally ordered — Labov's (1972) criterion for a minimal narrative — but in which the first clause is subordinate and nonfinite (p. 249):

(8) *Zadušiv ego, ona bystro ložitsja na pol...*

'Having smothered him, she quickly lies down on the floor...'

She discusses the oddity of this syntactic arrangement, which seems to background what is obviously a highly important, plot-advancing event in the narrative (p. 250):

> Up to this point in the story, most of the sequential clauses were concentrated in flashbacks that motivate the young nanny's unbearable weariness. By the final segment, her need to sleep overrides all else; the shocking murder of the baby is grammatically backgrounded by subordination and by contrast with the present tense. This example shows that, while a correlation of 'human importance' with foregrounding is the expected *norm*, the two notions are independent. To the reader, smothering a child is a more important, more affective action than lying down, yet the grammar allows Chekhov to *present* it as less important in a dramatic shift to the exhausted nanny's point of view.

She goes on to show various literary effects that are produced in Russian by "backgrounded perfectives" and "plotline imperfectives," breaking the expected alignments of plotline=perfective and background=imperfective.

What is important to us here is that Chvany has made a distinction between "foreground" and "plotline." Foreground is a matter of **perspective**. The narrator chooses which events to highlight by linguistic means — whether the narrator be Chekhov or a child deciding how to present the events depicted in *Frog, where are you?*. In our earlier analyses, we had attempted to find an "objective plotline" — somehow inherent in the sequence of pictures — which would give us an unequivocal definition of foregrounded events. It was our belief that the child, too, would recognize the "foreground of the frog story" and would seek grammatical means to encode it; and that, with increasing attention to background situations, would discover new means for distinguishing background from foreground. However, examples like (4-6) — buttressed by literary analyses such as those of Chvany and also Timberlake (1982) — convinced us that foreground and background are only partially determined by an objective logic of events. They are also the product of creative acts of perspective-taking, by which the narrator guides the listener in a subjective interpretation of the causal/motivational network of events, assigning salience to particular points. With age, the child comes to understand the varying ways that verbal accounts can be structured to bring about desired effects. We propose that this is a major functional motivation for the acquisition of the grammatical forms considered in this study.[3]

3. THREE GUIDING THEMES

All of our discussion thus far can be gathered up into three guiding themes that run throughout the study. These are themes of: (1) the "filtering" of experience through language for purposes of speaking; (2) the "packaging" of event descriptions into larger units for purposes of narrating; and (3) the cognitive and psycholinguistic development that leads to mature "filtering" and "packaging." We discuss each of these themes in turn.

3.1. Filtering

THEME: The world does not present "events" to be encoded in language. Rather, experiences are filtered — (a) through choice of perspective, and (b) through the set of options provided by the particular language — into verbalized events.

---

[3] Much attention has been devoted in cognitive linguistics and pragmatics to issues of perspective; for example, among others: H. Clark's (1992) "choice principle"; Langacker's discussions of "focal adjustments" (1987c) and "construal" (1990); Talmy's discussions of figure/ground (1978) and "the windowing of attention" (in press).

Choice of perspective. Ever since Aristotle's *Poetics*, a distinction has been made between the world of experience (*praxis*) and the selection one makes from experience in constructing a plot (*mythos*). The first act of choice in a narration, then, is the choice of events to be recounted. Aristotle clearly stated the criteria for what we have come to call "narrative" (Labov), "foreground" (Hopper), or simply "plotline":

> [T]he story ... must represent one action, a complete whole, with its several incidents so closely connected that the transposal or withdrawal of any one of them will disjoin and dislocate the whole (*De poetica*, §8; in McKeon, 1947, p. 635).

Beyond this choice — as we have already discussed in terms of grounding — the speaker chooses to highlight or downgrade aspects of experience for rhetorical purposes, and to arrange the narrative to make particular "points." These acts of arrangement represent the next major level of choice. The issue of choice plays a central role in modern approaches to narrative. Seymour Chatman, in his book, *Story and Discourse* (1978), summarizes the distinction made by the Russian formalists and the French structuralists between "the what" and "the how" of narrative:

> The Russian formalists ... made the distinction [between]: the "fable" (*fabula*), or basic story stuff, the sum total of events to be related in the narrative, and, conversely, the "plot" (*sjužet*), the story as actually told by linking the events together. To formalists, fable is "the set of events tied together which are communicated to us in the course of the work," or "what has in effect happened"; plot is "how the reader becomes aware of what happened," that is, basically the "order of the appearance (of the events) in the work itself," (Erlich, 1965, pp. 240-241) whether normal (abc), flashed-back (acb), or begun *in medias res* (bc) (Chatman, 1978, pp. 19-20).

Chatman goes on to speak of the activity of the narrator in selecting and ordering events in the construction of plot — what we refer to as **rhetorical** purposes. He points out that plot:

> exists at a more general level than any particular objectification.... Its order of presentation need not be the same as that of the natural logic of the story. Its function is to emphasize or de-emphasize certain story-events, to interpret some and to leave others to inference, to show or to tell, to comment or to remain silent, to focus on this or that aspect of an event or character. (p. 43)

It is evident, then, that the child must learn how to select and arrange verbalized events to guide the listener towards realization of the "plot" — its temporal/causal sequence and its "evaluation" (Labov). Examples (1) through

(7), above, are exemplary of such narrative choices.

Chatman's concern is to compare how the same story content can be presented differently in novel and in film, demonstrating that each medium constrains the possibilities of selection. Here we would generalize the argument to include the narrative options imposed by the use of one language or another. It is a commonplace that translations from one language to another cannot be fully equivalent, and this fact is at the core of studies of translation (e.g., Catford, 1965; Nida, 1964; Snell-Hornby, 1988; Toury, 1986; Wilss, 1982), contrastive grammar (e.g., Hawkins, 1985; Maslov, 1976), contrastive rhetoric (Bar-Lev, 1986; Kaplan, 1966), and typological discourse analysis (Myhill, 1992). In addition to the fact that narrators can take expressive options in the selection and arrangement of events, and the highlighting or downgrading of event components, each language **requires** or **facilitates** particular choices. This issue is explored at length in Parts IV and V of the book. For now, compare some typical 9-year-old encodings of a single event across the five languages of our study — the event depicted in Pictures 16—18.

English:

(9) *And he starts running. And he tips him off over a cliff into the water. And he lands.* [E9k-9;11]

German:

(10) *Der Hirsch nahm den Jungen auf sein Geweih und schmiß ihn den Abhang hinunter genau ins Wasser.*

'The deer took the boy on his antlers and hurled him down from the cliff right into the water.' [G9d-9;11]

Spanish:

(11) *El ciervo le llevó hasta un sitio, donde debajo había un río. Entonces el ciervo tiró al perro y al niño al río. Y después, cayeron.*

'The deer took him until a place, where below there was a river. Then the deer threw the dog and the boy to the river. And then they fell.' [S9b-9;2]

Hebrew:

(12) *Ve ha'ayil nivhal, ve hu hitxil laruts. Ve hakelev rats axarav, ve hu higia lemacok she mitaxat haya bitsa, ve hu atsar, ve hayeled ve hakelev naflu labitsa beyaxad.*

'And the deer was startled, and he began to run. And the dog ran after him, and he reached a cliff that had a swamp underneath, and he stopped, and and the boy and the dog fell to the swamp together.' [H9i-9;7]

Turkish:

(13) *Ancak önlerinde bir uçurum vardı. Altıda göldü. Çocuk hız yaptığı için, geyiğin başından köpeğiyle birlikte düştü.*

'Just in front of them there was a cliff. Below there was a lake. Because the boy was making speed, he fell from the deer's head together with his dog.' [*T9j-9;1*]

It is evident that these five versions exemplify — once again — the theme of narrator perspective. What is not so evident, however, is that these versions also exemplify differences in **rhetorical style** that seem to be partially determined by linguistic characteristics of these languages. This point is elaborated later in the book. For now, note that the first two languages — English and German — are characterized by compact verbal expressions which trace out the trajectory of the fall by a series of particles attached to a verb: *off over a cliff into the water* and *den Abhang hinunter genau ins Wasser* 'down from the cliff right into the water'. Furthermore, the verb itself — *tips* or *schmiß* 'hurled' — indicates the manner in which the deer's action initiated the fall. The other three versions — Spanish, Hebrew, and Turkish — are similar to each other, and contrast with English and German. Here we find an analysis of the event into phases: the deer does something and the boy and dog fall. There are descriptions of the topographical layout of the setting in which the events occur. And the verbs — 'stop', 'throw', 'fall' — are bare descriptions of changes of state, with no elaboration of manner. These are not random differences between the narrative styles of these five children, but rather show their abilities to convey just those analyses of the event which are most compatible with the linguistic means provided by their languages. English and German provide large sets of locative particles that can be combined with verbs of manner, thereby predisposing speakers toward a dense style of encoding motion events. On the other hand, a different style arises in the other three languages, which rely more on simple change-of-state and change-of-location verbs, thereby predisposing speakers toward more extended analyses of motion events.

These brief examples are intended to demonstrate the theme of **filtering** of experience for the purposes of talking about it — what Slobin (1987, 1990, 1991, in press-a) has called "thinking for speaking." The child has to construct the necessary filters for organizing any experience into a verbal account of that experience — in accordance both with communicative goals and the collection of formal options available in the language.[4]

---

[4] The filters we address here are those involved in selection and linearization of information. As Wolfgang Klein (p.c.) has pointed out to us, the narrator also faces the task of **addition** — that is, providing information from other sources that may aid the listener in interpret-

3.2. Packaging

THEME: A skillful narrative does not simply consist of a linear chain of successive events located in time and space. Rather, events must be packaged into hierarchical constructions.

The simplest narrative is a sequence of clauses whose temporal order is iconic with the order of the narrated events. Very young children are able to produce such narratives. Why, then, do children develop complex syntax, when so much can be done with sequences of simple clauses? The answer is to be sought in another aspect of perspective-taking — namely, the construction of higher-order events, in which event phases are subordinated and interrelated. One of the chief motivations for the acquisition of complex syntax, we claim, is the child's growing understanding of the temporal, causal, and motivational **texture** of events. Consider another frog-story episode — the boy's fall from the tree, depicted in Picture 12. This episode has several components that could be presented in serial order: boy climbs tree — boy causes owl to emerge from hole — owl causes boy to fall. The youngest narrators (3-4 years) rarely mention all of these components. The following is an attempt by a 5-year-old to serialize the three dynamic phases of the episode, with no mention of causality:

(14) *And then he goes up there. And then an owl comes out and he falls.* [E5g-5;9]

Here we see the most minimal event packaging. This child regularly uses *and then* to segment the narration into event-size units — in this instance first presenting the boy's change of location and then more tightly packaging the emergence of the owl and the boy's falling into a complex event conjoined by *and*. Another 5-year-old is able to syntactically package all three components into a single construction:

(15) *And the boy was looking through the tree when a owl came out and bammed him on the ground.* [E5e-5;8]

The clauses maintain the order of the event phases. The emergence and fall are packaged by *and*, as in (13); but this entire sequence is temporally subordinated to the climbing phase by use of *when*.

---

ing and evaluating the narrative. Although such additions are rare in our setting, in which a child narrates to an adult, they are common in narratives constructed by adults, especially those directed to children. For example, in Bamberg's (1985, 1987) original frog-story study, he elicited parental narrations to children, and found such additions as, for example, explanatory comments ('owls sleep in the daytime'). And even our preschool narrators add evaluative comments, such as *The pets think the little boy was proud of them* [E5b-5;2], and occasional explanatory remarks, such as *Dogs can climb trees really good* [E3g-3;9].

Older children combine features of inner state ('frighten') and causality ('make fall'), using syntactic devices to package phases of the event in various ways. For example:

(16) *The owl came out of its tree, and scared the little boy. The little boy fell.* [E9c-9;6]

(17) *Der Junge der sitzt auf'm Baumstamm und kuckt in das Loch rein und da scheucht ihn die Eule runter von dem Baumstamm.*

'The boy, he sits on a/the tree trunk and looks into the hole and there the owl scares him down from the tree trunk.' [G9h-9;11]

Adult narrators are able to syntactically package the entire episode. The following German example is the most elaborate in our collection. It shows an eventual convergence between literary and oral narrative at the most advanced levels of development.

(18) *Der arme Tom hat auch in dem Baum den Frosch nicht gefunden, hat aber eine Eule zu Tode erschreckt, die nun aus dem Baum herausgeflogen kommt und Tom so erschreckt hat, daß er den Halt am Baum verliert und rumms auf den Rücken fällt, herunterfällt auf den Boden.*

'Poor Tom has also not found the frog in the tree, but has scared an owl to death, who now comes flying out of the tree and scares Tom so much that he loses his grip on the tree and falls splat on his back, falls down on the ground.' [G20f]

This segment does more than package an event into one sentence. It elegantly fits that event into both the local time frame and the global time frame of the overall plot. The first clause re-evokes the guiding theme of the search for the frog, and the second gives the immediate cause of the chain of circumstances leading to the fall from the tree. These two clauses are in the present perfect, which both points backward in time to these circumstances and brings them into the present. The third clause switches to 'now' beginning a series of clauses that lay out the sequence of events in slow motion, giving both a motivational ('scares') and physical ('loses his grip') cause for the focal event — falling — presented in present tense. Such density of hierarchical layering of circumstances and happenings in syntactically packaged constructions is found only in our adult narratives. Some school-age children, however, demonstrate considerable skills in event packaging — both in terms of conceptual and syntactic organization.

3.3. Development

THEME: Younger children take fewer expressive options because: (a) cognitively, they cannot conceive of the full range of encodable perspectives; (b) communicatively, they cannot fully assess the listener's viewpoint; and (c) linguistically, they do not command the full range of formal devices.

Cognitive, communicative, and linguistic factors interact in complex fashion in development. In our texts we see instances of children groping to find linguistic means to highlight or downgrade an event phase, to switch topic, to mark an episode boundary, and so forth. In these examples we see old linguistic means pushed to serve new functions and we see the emergence of new forms. A new linguistic device may be used infelicitously or in limited contexts.

These developmental trends can be seen clearly in children's attempts to deal with the conceptually most complex episode in the story — the events in Pictures 13-15 in which the boy ends up holding onto the deer's antlers rather than branches. Cognitively, this situation requires the ability to contrast the narrator's omniscient perspective with the boy's temporary lack of knowledge; i.e., it demands a theory of mind that can separate the boy's state of knowledge from that of the narrator. Communicatively, it requires the narrator to understand that the listener lacks the same information as the boy. And linguistically, the child must command the means to express these contrasting stances. The following examples show a developing ability to cope with these problems. In (19) through (23) we see successively more sophisticated attempts by preschoolers to grasp, and to communicate, the problematic nature of this scene.

(19) *He hops on the deer.* [E4f-4;7] [no understanding of the boy's misjudgment of the "branches"]

(20) *Then he got on a reindeer, because the reindeer was hiding there.* [E5b-5;2] [understanding that the reindeer was not initially visible to the boy, but no attention to boy's state of mind]

(21) *He got picked up by a reindeer.* [E5f-5;8] [use of *get*-passive suggests that narrator is aware that the boy was not an intentional agent]

(22) *He's holding onto some sticks. But they really aren't sticks. When - uh - something came up, and the little boy was on it. Um - it was ... a father deer, I'd call it.* [E5i-5;10] [explicit recognition of the boy's misperception, though from the point of view of the narrator, rather than the boy]

(23) *He - thought it was sticks and - he got on that and - the deer came and - carried him.* [E5k-5;11] [explicit attribution of misperception to the boy; groping for means of encoding the unintentionality of the consequences]

It is not until school age that some (but not all) narrators cope more successfully with the cognitive, communicative, and linguistic demands of narrating this event:

(24) *And then he stands up on the rock and hangs onto some branches. Then it turns out they're a deer's antlers. So - and he gets - he lands on his head.* [E9k-9;11] [the *turns out*-construction provides a means of encoding the switch in perspective, and the interrupted *he gets* - suggests a groping for a passive construction]

Only adults, however, present the ambiguities of this event in their full complexity. Note how the following version demonstrates command of both conceptual flexibility and complex linguistic constructions:

(25) *When he gets to the top of the rock, he holds onto something that he app - thinks are branches, and calls to the frog. [...] And what the boy took to be branches were really antlers of a deer on which he gets caught.* [E20f]

In the various crosslinguistic comparisons in the following chapters, we document numerous common developmental patterns across children acquiring five quite different languages (based, however, only on cross-sectional data). These patterns arise from the interaction of several different types of knowledge and skill. Developmental theory has not yet advanced to match the richness of our developmental descriptions or to account for the complex interactions between cognitive, communicative, and linguistic systems that underlie the production of connected discourse. A major goal of this study is to serve as an impetus for theory-building that takes all three sets of factors into account.

Such theories must also attend to the fact that linguistic forms are multifunctional and that the use of any particular form is multiply determined. This has been a guiding principle of our work — a principle that is borne out repeatedly in the findings presented here.

Chapter IB

RESEARCH GOALS AND PROCEDURES

1. AIMS OF THE STUDY: FUNCTION AND FORM

The focus of our study is **the development of linguistic form in children.** We have chosen to analyze the production of connected discourse because we believe that the uses of language in discourse shape both grammar and the course of its development. There are, of course, many discourse genres that could be studied — but one has to choose. We selected the narrative genre, because it is one which develops relatively early in children, and because we were interested in the expression of temporality, which is critical to the narrative mode of discourse. We have spent a decade with the frog story because it has allowed us to have a measure of control over the content of expression without determining the form. Like all artificial tasks, this one has its strengths and weaknesses. Perhaps the most serious weakness is that we have not been able to control the subject's definition of the task: picture description, picture-supported narrative, colloquial storytelling, bookish storytelling, and so forth. Our texts show us that individual subjects have made different kinds of choices — the youngest subjects more towards the picture description end of the scale, older subjects more towards the model of literary narrative. Chapter IIA shows a clear development in narrative competence, thus demonstrating that all of our subjects are not performing "the same task."

However, this weakness is also a strength when we turn to the investigation of the development of linguistic form. Chapter IIA gives us confidence that we can infer something of the speaker's definition of the task — and these differing definitions have important consequences for the acquisition and use of morphological and syntactic forms. As the child is drawn into more complex communicative tasks, less supported by nonlinguistic context, the ongoing text itself becomes the support for the choice of the next morphosyntactic structure to be added to that text. Thus, for example, the child who is describing a picture has less need for temporal and causal subordination than the child who is situating the depicted situation in a goal-oriented plot. A major contribution of our study, we believe, is to show the interactive development between particular linguistic forms and particular discourse functions. For this aim, we are aided both by the standardization of the elicitation materials and what we take to be the increasing levels of sophistication of children's understanding of the task.

The perspective underlying our endeavor is that the development of linguistic form must be situated in a functional framework. We understand, of course, that many of the forms studied here have prior histories in various types of **interactive** discourse. Susan Ervin-Tripp (1989) has pointed out that the grammatical structures used in narrative are used at earlier ages in conversations and negotiations. In this study, however, we are not interested in the initial emergence of forms or in their earliest uses. Rather, our concern is with the range of different functions which, with age, forms come to acquire in the service of narration. Our framework is the development of the ability to construct a coherent, hierarchically-organized, goal-oriented narrative, to be told to an adult listener. We hope to have shown, in this book, that there are powerful and interesting developmental relations between form and function within this framework.

The **linguistic forms** that we have chosen to focus on are those that play a central role in the construction of narrative. They are the systematic parts of linguistic expressions that make it possible to situate narrative events in time and space, and in relation to one another. We use "form" as an umbrella term for a range of grammatical morphemes and construction types: (1) bound inflectional and derivational morphemes, such as tense/aspect markers on verbs; (2) free grammatical morphemes (functors, closed-class items), such as prepositions, particles, and conjunctions; (3) syntactic constructions, such as relative clauses and complement clauses; and (4) systematic alternations of word order, such as left-dislocation. We also include some lexical items that occur in small sets and interact in special ways with the use of other forms in narrative discourse, such as temporal adverbs and phrases (e.g., *suddenly, later on, in the end*), verbs of motion, and others. At various points in the book, what we here call a "form" is also referred to by terms such as "linguistic device," "expressive device," "linguistic means of expression," "morphosyntax." For our purposes, then, "forms" are the stuff of any "How to Speak Language X" handbook, and are neutral with regard to current models of grammar. At the level of analysis pursued here, we are concerned with the deployment of linguistic forms for the communication of narrative events rather than with an analysis of linguistic structure in itself.

In Chapter III0 we summarize the range of forms that we have chosen to focus on in this study, and the following five chapters in Part III present data on the development and use of those forms in each of the languages in our sample: English, German, Spanish, Hebrew, and Turkish. We have chosen forms that play a role in narrative: those used for the expression of temporal and causal relations, event structure, and the management of information flow. And we have chosen languages that provide typological contrasts with regard to the particular manifestations of these formal categories. We are thus interested in **the relations between form and function, within a typological, crosslinguistic framework**.

TABLE 1

Functional Categories and their Formal Expression

TEMPORALITY: *the expression of the location of events on the time line, temporal relations between events, and temporal constituency of events (contour, phase)* by means of: tense/aspect marking on verbs, lexical marking of aspect (particles, verbs, adverbs), temporal conjunction and subordination

EVENT CONFLATION: *the encoding of components of events in relatively compact or expanded expressions* by means of: verbs and satellites (especially verbs of motion and locative particles), adpositional phrases, nonfinite verb forms (participles, gerunds)

PERSPECTIVE: *the choice of topic and focus, foreground and background, agent-patient relations* by means of: voice alternations of verbs (active, passive, middle), pragmatic word-order variation, reference form (NP, pronoun, zero), topic markers

CONNECTIVITY: *"knitting the fabric" of narrative discourse* by means of: syntactic conjunction and subordination (subordinating conjunctions, relative clauses), nonfinite verb forms, nominalizations, topic ellipsis

NARRATIVE STYLE: *establishing a personal level of discourse (e.g., colloquial, racy, matter-of-fact, literary, poetic)* by means of: all of the devices listed above, plus lexical choice, prosody, tempo, and so forth

---

By "function" we refer to the roles played by forms to convey structured characteristics of events in narrative. We address five functional categories, each with implications for the acquisition and use of particular types of forms.

These categories provide the standard analytic framework for the chapters in Part III, which deal with the frog stories in each of the five languages in our sample. Briefly, the functional categories and associated linguistic forms are summarized in Table 1.

In Part IV we present a collection of studies of relations between form and function. In most instances, we begin with a function and compare the forms that are used in the expression of that function across age and language. In Chapter IVA, for example, Aksu-Koç and von Stutterheim explore the function of expressing temporal connectivity — specifically, linguistic descriptions of two events that overlap in time ("simultaneity"). In other instances, the focus is on a particular form and the range of functions that it can serve, as in the analysis of relative clause functions by Dasinger and Toupin in Chapter IVB.

In the final section, Part V, we bring these various strands together to present two developmental pictures: becoming a **proficient** speaker and becoming a **native** speaker. Every child must become both, of course. We propose that the first process is strikingly similar across the five language communities we have studied, and may well have universal characteristics. The second process, however, is deeply influenced by the **type** of language of which one becomes a native speaker. We attempt to show that children learning each of the five languages in our study end up with particular "rhetorical styles" that are determined, in part, by the available form-function relations in the native language.

2. RESEARCH METHODS

2.1. Materials

As noted in Chapter IA, the study was based on a picturebook without words, *Frog, where are you?* (see Appendix I). The principle underlying the use of a single picture storybook was to provide a common **content** — across age and language — representing a typical children's story with a hero (the boy and his dog), a problem (the boy has a pet frog which runs away), a set of actions which follow from this problem (the boy and dog search for the missing frog), and a "happy ending" (the boy finds his frog, or gets another one in exchange). This type of story is well-known to children in the five countries in which our research was conducted, and the children we worked with were all familiar with picture storybooks (see, further, Chapter IIA).

This particular picturebook proved appropriate to our research aims, since it depicts a fairly long and elaborate series of events, and allows narrators to relate to a variety of topics. These include: (1) expression of temporal contours and the relation between events which follow one another sequentially (e.g., that the frog got out of the jar and then ran away), of events which relate back to prior circumstances (e.g., that the jar in which the frog had been kept was empty), and which concern concurrent or simultaneous events (e.g., that the dog was being chased by the bees while the boy was looking in a hole in the tree); (2) description of locative trajectories, such as the fact that the deer pushed the boy off a cliff into a marsh down below; (3) the possibility to take different perspectives on events (e.g., that the dog is being chased by the bees or that the bees are chasing the dog); and (4) the fact that the story has two main protagonists, the boy and the dog, providing opportunities for expressing the temporal relation of simultaneity in talking about co-occurrent events, as well as for both maintaining and shifting reference from one character to the other. Another useful feature of the frog book is that it allows for different levels of cognitive inferencing between events. For instance, young children had no difficulty in recognizing that the frog had gotten out of the jar in which it was located on one page, and which was empty on the next; but they were unable to grasp what happened to the boy who, climbing onto a rock and clutching onto what appear to be the branches of a tree, then finds that he has inadvertently caught onto the antlers of a deer that was standing behind the rock (Chapter IIA). These different levels of interpretation were of interest to us, since they give rise to quite different types and levels of linguistic expression.

Frog, where are you? is clearly a product of Western culture. An anthropological linguist, David Wilkins, has prepared the following useful orientation to Mercer Mayer's book. We reproduce it here, with his permission, to underline the cultural specificity of our task.[1]

> The pictures conform to the standard semiotic conventions for drawings in Anglo-Western children's stories, and the pictures are presented in a chronological order which precedes from left to right (and front to back) in the book (i.e., one turns through the book, and moves from a picture at left to a picture at right, just as in a typical Anglo-Western book).[2] The story depicted in the pictures is by an Anglo-American author who relies on several culture-specific frames (to use Fillmore's terms) in the pictorial presentation of the story. The most important of these frames are listed as

---

[1] Wilkins and a number of other anthropologists and linguists, at the Cognitive Anthropology Unit of the Max-Planck-Institute for Psycholinguistics in Nijmegen, The Netherlands, are exploring the use of this tool in a wide range of cultures (see Appendix III).

[2] The left-to-right orientation of the book, as well as the corresponding direction of action in the pictures, did not appear to disturb Hebrew-speaking (or Hebrew-reading) children. We have prepared a mirror-image, right-to-left version of the book, with the help of the Max-Planck cognitive anthropologists, in order to explore possible narrative effects of the directionality of pictorial presentation in future research in Israel.

follows:

The frame associated with young children's storybook tales (i.e., they're often not true; they typically have a happy ending; animals can be thought of as acting, thinking, or reacting like people; nothing really bad ever happens to the heroes — i.e., they don't die, they don't sustain permanent damage when they get hit, or fall to the ground, etc.);

The frame surrounding children going into nature to collect different types of small animals or insects, typically in jars, and often collecting the kind of things their mother might find repulsive or slimy;

The frame associated with how dogs behave (i.e., they're curious; they like to chase things; they sniff at things and follow trails; they're loyal to their owners; they love their owners, etc.);

The frame related to our knowledge of frogs (i.e., they live in and near water; they are found only at certain warmer times of year; they are associated with lily pads, etc.);

The frame associated with a widespread "shared" cultural view of "ideal" families, here projected onto frogs (i.e., husbands and wives love each other and their children; a parent would do anything to get back to be with their children; children are a source of pride to their parents, etc.);

The frame encapsulating our knowledge/experience of North American [and Northern European] wooded areas, and the type of animals, plants, and terrain found there.

All of these frames, so insightfully enumerated by Wilkins, are part of the experience of the preschool children with whom we worked in the United States, Germany, Spain, Israel, and Turkey — either through direct experience or through experience with pictures, storybooks, movies, and television.

2.2. Task

The same procedures were followed across different age groups in the five languages which constitute this study. Each subject was interviewed individually, and was given the same instructions (with slight variations for adults, preschool children, and older children). A deliberate effort was made to minimize the burden on memory, and to make children aware in advance that they were being asked to tell a story. To this end, children were first asked to look through the entire booklet, and then to tell the story — again, while looking at the pictures. They were explicitly oriented to the booklet as presenting a "story" in the initial instructions:

"Here is a book. This book tells a story about a boy [*point to picture on cover*], a dog [*point*], and a frog [*point*]. First, I want you to look at all the pictures. Pay attention to each picture that you see and afterwards you will tell the story."

(The title of the book was taped over, so that children old enough to read would not be biased by the author's presentation of the search theme.) The child sat side-by-side with the investigator, who was the sole listener.

Because we wanted to leave the burden of narration on the child, without scaffolding by the adult, our various adult interviewers were instructed to minimize their verbal feedback to neutral comments that would not influence the form of expression chosen by the child. It was especially important that the interviewer avoid prompts that would lead to a particular choice of verb tense, aspectual marking, or perspective on the part of the child. The following prompt types were used, presented below in English, in order of preference (neutrality): (1) silence or nod of head, (2) "uh-huh," "okay," "yes," (3) "Anything else?", (4) "and...?", (5) "Go on."

As noted above, we are not claiming that the "same" task was performed by all our subjects across ages and across countries. Clearly, children's ideas of what is expected, and of what is involved in storytelling, will differ from those of adults. Children in the younger age groups have a shorter attention span, they are more attuned to interactive situations than to formal settings of language use, and they require more scaffolding than older children in producing an extended speech text. In evaluating our findings, accordingly, we attempt to take into account the differences in task-construal across our different groups. Specifically, we bear in mind that many of the youngest children identify the task as one of picture-description, in which they engage in a shared activity with an adult interlocutor. In this they contrast to our 5-year-olds, many of whom are familiar with more structured story-elicitation settings from their nursery-school or kindergarten experiences. And they, in turn, differ from the 9-year-olds who, typically interviewed in a school setting, tended to treat the task as one of providing a school-like assignment to a teacher-like investigator. The adults, in contrast, showed great individual variation in how they construed what they were supposed to do: Some treated it as though they were being asked to tell a children's story;[3] others as an opportunity to demonstrate their literary abilities or their creative imagination; and yet others as a request to do a favor to a friend or family member (the

---

[3] None of the adults, however, told the story in the same way as they would to a young child. This is clear to us from the earlier study conducted by Bamberg (1985, 1987), in which children were told the story by their mothers. Moreover, a pilot study conducted in Israel shows that 25-year-old college-educated mothers telling this story to their 3-year-old children do so in a very different way indeed (e.g., with numerous repetitions, rhetorical questions, labeling of objects and animals in a word-teaching fashion, personal digressions and affective commentary) than did a parallel group of Hebrew-speaking women asked to tell the story to an adult friend. (Also see Harkins, 1992.)

investigator) in need of research input.

Throughout the book, we refer to the materials which constitute our data-base as "texts." We have adopted this neutral term in preference to "narra-tives," because, as discussed in Chapter IIA, many of the younger children do not present a full plotline in their productions. We reserve the term "story" for the contents of the picture book as depicted by its author, rather than for the verbal expression given them by the subjects of our sample, whom we refer to as "narrators."

By taking "texts" as the basic material for analysis, we have abstracted away from the task of actually **performing** this story. This means, in fact, that we are considering the texts in an artificially frozen state. That is, as is commonly the practice in discourse analysis, we are disregarding the actual task of text construction: how speakers produce texts in acoustic and visual form, through time. Thus, we overlook such important features of storytelling as gesture, facial expression, prosody, and other paralinguistic — often affec-tive and evaluative — accompaniments to the verbal component of the task. In fact, each written "text" which remains for analysis is only a trace of a full performance.

Another factor which we bear in mind in evaluating our research metho-dology is the special nature of picture-description tasks in general, and reli-ance on this storybook and our elicitation procedures, in particular. Certain of these problems are noted in Chapter IIA. Despite our many caveats, we feel confident that our findings are robust, because they are consistent with the experience of researchers in diverse cultures who have discussed their endeavors with us, and because we find common developmental patterns across languages. Our findings are also well in line with what has been found by researchers using different procedures for eliciting connected narratives from children on the basis of shorter sets of pictures or of moving films. Before around age 5 years, children tend to focus on the contents of individual pictures or spatial frames, rather than connecting them up together as extended sequences of related events.

Our procedure has a major feature of potential importance for the form and content of the elicited texts: The story was always told to a listener who (a) already knew the story and (b) was able to see the pictures. It is quite likely that this situation heightened the tendency of young children to engage in a good deal of pointing — both in gesture and in the use of deictic expres-sions. After the completion of the present project, Dan Slobin and Aylin Küntay devised a procedure aimed at overcoming the problem of shared knowledge and perception. In the new procedure, after the child has gone through the picturebook with the aid of the experimenter, a familiar adult (usually the mother) enters the room and sits opposite the child, without being able to see the pictures. Küntay gathered Turkish stories from children of ages 3, 4, 5, 7, and 9, using this procedure. A systematic comparison has not yet been carried out between the two Turkish data sets, that of Küntay and the earlier data of Aksu-Koç. However, preliminary analyses suggest two important effects: (1) The development of **narrative ability** does not seem to be influenced by this communicative factor. That is, most preschoolers still do not construct a fully coherent, goal-oriented plot. (2) There is, however, a considerable reduction in deixis, both to protagonists ('this one') and to pictured locations and situations ('here'), using the new procedure. Combining data for 3-, 4-, and 5-year-olds, the percentage of text lines with 'this one' reduced from 12% to 1.5%, and the percentage of text lines with 'here' reduced from 14% to 6%. We do not yet know, however, what effects the two procedures may have on the range of form-function issues analyzed in this book. Kail and Hickmann (1992) have experimented with a similar control, having children narrate the same picturebook to a blindfolded versus sighted listener. They found that in the former context ("no mutual knowledge") children showed better control of reference-maintaining devices, indicating their sensitivity to the needs of the listener. Until much more detailed linguistic work is done, however, we can only remind the reader that our task — as any task — had particular communicative constraints, with as yet unknown effects on the use of linguistic forms in the texts that we elicited. [4]

2.3. Transcription and Coding

Each session was audio-recorded and then transcribed and entered on computer in standard format.[5] Transcription was in standard orthography, except for Hebrew, which was entered in modified phonemic script (Chapter IIID). A certain amount of prosodic information was entered in each transcript (see Appendix II), although this has been only partially taken into account in our analyses. We recognize this as an inadequacy of our study, as is evident from recent research by Reilly (1992). Her meticulous analysis of the use of prosodic and other paralinguistic effects (gestural and facial) compared with overt linguistic expressions of evaluative elements in the frog story narrations of children aged 3 and 4 years versus 7- to 8-year-olds and 10- to 11-year-olds reveals, for example, that preschoolers make far more use of

---

[4] There are several studies comparing children's narratives in response to different task demands (see, for instance, the research of Hicks, 1991, and other studies reviewed there). But these deal mainly with general narrative abilities, rather than with the comparison of linguistic devices across different narrative settings.

[5] The full data sets are available on the CHILDES system, as described in detail in MacWhinney (1991).

paralinguistic means for expressing affect than do school-age children. We recommend that similarly detailed prosodic analyses be attended to in future studies. The use of video equipment to record pointing and gesture would also be valuable (Cassell, 1991; Cassell & McNeill, 1990; McNeill, 1992). Such information, while going beyond the bounds of the aims we set ourselves for the present study, would seem particularly important for crosscultural comparisons.

The minimum unit of analysis, which determined how the speech output was represented in each transcribed text, was what we defined as a "clause" (see Appendix II). This unit was selected as being more linguistically structured than the behavioral unit of an "utterance" but as less determined by syntactic criteria than a "sentence." For our purposes, a clause was any unit containing a unified predication, whether in the form of a verb or adjective. [6] The verb might be finite or nonfinite, e.g., the following were all considered a single clause in English: *running through the woods; taken by surprise; (in order) to help his friends; was angry*. Modal and aspectual verbs were counted together with their main verbs; that is, the following constitute single clauses: *want to climb the tree; goes to look; started running*. This analysis into clauses made it possible for us to compare relative length and propositional complexity of texts (e.g., how many predications are packed together in a single utterance) across the entire sample. Since for each text, we also specified what picture each clause and each utterance referred to (as explained in the transcription procedures in Appendix II), it was also possible to evaluate how many propositions were assigned to each picture in the book.

Texts were analyzed in relation to what we termed "coded clauses." These excluded personal digressions and comments or queries relating to the task (e.g., *Do you want me to go on?*, *That's all I've got to say*) or to object-identification, such as asking the investigator what an animal is called, or saying things like *I can't remember what that's called*, or *It looks like a gopher but I guess you could also say it's a mole*. Digressions and task-oriented comments were particularly common among the younger children, and they also characterized an occasional more personalized adult.

A coding system was developed which related to a variety of analytical dimensions of analysis, including: verb semantics (change-of-state, physical or internal states, causative activities, etc.); grammatical marking of tense-aspect-modality; lexical marking of aspect (by verbs such as those meaning 'begin' or particles like *out, off*); lexical marking of sequential and other

---

[6] Thus our basic unit of analysis is closer to the semantic notion of a proposition, although not as this term is used in describing narrative units in the framework of story-grammar.

temporal relations (e.g., by use of expressions like 'after that', 'meanwhile'); syntactic constructions (simple clauses, complements, relatives, and adverbial subordinates); as well as distinctions between events presented as part of the foreground plot-advancing storyline compared with clauses we defined as specifying different classes of background relations. This detailed set of coding categories and subcategories was adapted for use in all five languages in our sample and applied across the sample by members of the project team working singly and in consultation. It provided us with an invaluable aid in systematizing the data for a variety of analyses.

Much of this great coding effort, however, is not directly reflected in the contents of this book — for two related reasons. First, quantitative analyses proved inadequate in the context of the functionally oriented thrust of our study. For example, the most straightforward, least controversial coding parameter in our system was that specifying morphological marking of tense, aspect, and modality in the different languages (e.g., for English: simple, progressive, or perfect combined with present or past tense, with modal auxiliaries and/or semi-modals listed as such, and specification of finiteness, etc.). Nonetheless, when we started to evaluate use of tense and aspect in our transcripts, it became evident that the quantitative distribution of these forms needed to be evaluated in terms of how they function within a given text, in relation to such factors as overall anchor-tense selected for a particular narrative, and where tense and/or aspectual markings were changed across that text (see the first sections in the chapters on "form" in Part III). Second, where more qualitative evaluation was required — for instance, determining what semantic category we assigned to verbs and other predicates and whether we defined a given clause as foreground or background (let alone what kind of background subcategory it should be assigned), we found that highly proficient, native-speaking psycholinguists were unable to reach agreement sufficient to meet minimal standards of reliability. We therefore decided to replace a standard method of coding across parameters, languages, and age groups by detailed language-particular analysis for the development of **forms** (Chapters IIIA through IIIE), while trying to ensure consistency and hence reliability in the characterization of **functions** through the cooperative efforts of more than one researcher working on each such analysis (Chapters IVA through IVD).

In most instances, we have not performed statistical tests, because the number of subjects in each group are small and their texts vary in length. Numbers become even smaller when groups are subdivided according to criteria such as dominant tense or mention of a particular story event. We have therefore endeavored to present and interpret only those quantitative differences that seem large enough, and consistent enough, to suggest a pattern. In addition, we have as far as possible tried to present quantitative details of forms not only in terms of number and/or proportion of occurrences (say out of the total number of clauses for a given group), but also by specifying the proportion of subjects in a group who used that form.

2.4. Subjects

Three major age ranges were investigated across the languages: preschoolers, school-age children, and adults. Our aim here was to trace the development of narrative abilities from their early, preliterate emergence through to a period when children are already familiar with the book-based traditions of the culture, and on to mature adult capacities. Subjects were all monolingual, from middle-class, literate backgrounds, with differences in socioeconomic status being neutralized as far as possible within and across the groups. The 3- to 5-year-olds generally attended preschool or kindergarten, the 9-year-olds were generally 4th-graders, and adults were college students or graduates, ranging from 18 to 40 years of age. We thus attempted to maximally neutralize the effect of cultural differences, in the aim of focusing on strictly crosslinguistic comparisons. This is, of course, not entirely possible, since storytelling traditions and conventions differ even in the urban, industrialized settings across the different countries in which our data were collected. We are pleased to note that a deliberate effort is now being made to extend the use of these same procedures in populations from very different cultural settings (Appendix III).

Data were collected for English in the San Francisco Bay Area of California, by Tanya Renner (Renner, 1988) with adults added by Virginia Marchman (Marchman, 1989); for German in northwestern Germany by Michael Bamberg; for Spanish in Madrid by Eugenia Sebastián; for Hebrew in towns and villages in central Israel by graduate students of Tel Aviv University; and for Turkish in Istanbul by Ayhan Aksu-Koç.[7] Maximal consistency was provided in methods of eliciting, transcribing, coding, and analyzing data through regular meetings, consultations, and workshops between all participants in the project.

Table 2 shows the breakdown of number of subjects by age group in each of the five languages. The subjects in each group were divided as far as possible between males and females, but this factor was not taken into

---

[7] At some points, we have added, for comparison, Spanish data collected in Santiago Chile and in Argentina by Aura Bocaz (using our original procedure), and the new data gathered in Istanbul by Aylin Küntay, described above.

TABLE 2
Number and Age of Narrators in Five Languages

Language	3 yrs	4 yrs	Age 5 yrs	9 yrs	Adult
English					
N	12	12	12	12	12
age-range	3;1-3;11	4;0-4;11	5;1-5;11	9;1-9;11	—
mean age	3;7	4;7	5;7	9;7	—
German					
N	12	—	12	12	12
age-range	3;3-3;11	—	5;0-5;11	9;0-9;11	—
mean age	3;8	—	5;4	9;7	—
Spanish					
N	12	12	12	12	12
age-range	3;6-3;11	4;1-4;10	5;1-5;11	9;1-9;11	—
mean age	3;8	4;6	5;7	9;7	—
Hebrew					
N	12	12	12	12	12
age-range	3;0-3;11	4;1-4;11	5;0-5;10	9;0-9;8	—
mean age	3;7	4;7	5;5	9;5	—
Turkish					
N	10	—	10	10	10
age-range	3;6-4;3	—	5;0-6;1	9;1-10;0	—
mean age	3;11	—	5;5	9;7	—

account in our analyses. For technical reasons, it was not possible to cover a full range of age groups in each country, and we recognize the need to fill in certain gaps in the number and range of subjects investigated in the different languages. It is important to note, however, that where additional data are available, they tend to confirm and refine, rather than contradict, the findings from the present study. This is shown, for example, in preliminary analyses of the responses of an intermediate group of schoolchildren aged 7 to 8 years old, available in Hebrew and Turkish. In most respects, they are similar to 9-year-olds, while nonetheless constituting a bridge between these older children and the preschool 5-year-olds in both these languages. Similarly, analyses of a larger sample of texts for Hebrew — with 16 subjects in each age group shown in Table 2 plus an additional two groups, of 7- and 11- to 12-year olds — show largely parallel patterns to what we found for the more restricted database of the present study (Berman, 1988; see Chapter IIID). On the other hand, dialect differences are an area which could be profitably studied by comparison of frog stories produced by speakers of variants of these languages — e.g., differences in distribution and use of present perfect in American compared with British English (Chapter IIIA) and in European compared with South American Spanish (Chapter IIIC).

Table 3 shows the range and length of the narrations produced by each age group in the five languages, calculated in terms of the number of coded clauses per text (see Section 2.3). As is to be expected, older speakers produce rather longer texts than the younger children. They also show greater variability, ranging in three of the languages from short texts of around 35 clauses each to well over 100 clauses per narrative. On the other hand, even the 3-year-olds in our sample all proved able to produce connected texts of between 10 to 20 clauses in length, some of them going up to very extensive productions indeed.[8] Children aged 5 to 9 years produce texts of much the same length across the languages, ranging from around 30 to 50, with an average of about 40 clauses per text — a length which provides a sense of some kind of "normative" text for this task: not too lengthy in elaborative detail, nor yet condensed to just a few clauses long. Despite differences in total sample size as well as range and mean number of clauses per text, the figures in Table 3 are similar enough across the languages to give us a sense of having a database which is comparable in quantitative terms. On the other hand, length in itself is not criterial for producing a felicitous narrative based on the frog story picture book, and it is thus not a factor we consider in detail in the analyses which follow.

There are several reasons, both in principle and practice, for this decision. First, the task was such that even very young children could follow the book picture by picture for a fairly extensive length of time and hence production of extended speech output would not be beyond their cognitive capacities, if they so wished. Relatedly, the task did not involve subjects in recall of

---

[8] This is particularly marked in the case of the German-speaking children, and across the sample, the German texts were longer (and often more descriptively elaborate, see Chapter IIIB) than those elicited in the other languages.

TABLE 3
Range and Mean Number of Codable Clauses
by Language and Age Group

Language	3 yrs	4 yrs	Age 5 yrs	9 yrs	Adult
English					
range	11-46	14-44	22-54	39-51	46-122
total	264	319	500	540	903
mean	22.0	26.6	41.7	45.0	75.3
SD	10.7	7.9	10.9	6.3	21.4
German					
range	20-101	—	26-88	47-105	52-133
total	594	—	604	782	1233
mean	49.5	—	50.3	65.2	101.9
SD	21.0	—	19.1	19.7	34.0
Spanish					
range	18-76	22-66	17-69	38-61	30-184
total	494	526	539	609	1096
mean	41.2	43.8	44.9	50.8	91.3
SD	15.1	10.6	13.1	8.1	48.8
Hebrew					
range	19-59	19-56	34-72	41-98	35-91
total	367	451	619	748	734
mean	30.6	37.6	51.6	62.3	61.2
SD	11.3	12.5	15.8	17.8	15.2
Turkish					
range	21-51	—	35-87	10-56	39-117
total	349	—	522	392	819
mean	34.9	—	52.2	39.2	81.9
SD	9.2	—	13.2	14.2	22.1

past events, either of their own experiencing, or which they had heard or witnessed. Again, this seems to render the factor of output length less cardinal as a developmental variable in its own right. For instance, a study eliciting Hebrew narratives based on the "pear-story" film (Chafe, 1980) yielded marked differences in absolute and relative narrative length between children aged 5 to 6 years, compared with 8- to 9-year-olds and then again compared to adults. This was clearly due to the inability of the younger children to **remember** the contents of the film they had just seen as fully, and in as much detail, as older children or adults. Yet in our study, as noted, some adults across the languages produce shorter, more condensed versions than certain of the children. Nor could we correlate the "goodness" of a narrative with its relative length, either in comparing adult narratives with one another, or with the children. Finally, it is not obvious what explanation we could afford within the realms of our present undertaking for the fact that some cultures seem to elicit longer and more elaborate narratives than others, as noted for our German sample. Some reference is made to these issues in Part V, in our discussion of "contrastive rhetoric."

3. GUIDING ASSUMPTIONS AND PREDICTIONS

As the reader will already have noted, we take it as given that form and function develop in complex interrelation. But we also believe that each domain poses problems that can be dealt with separately — both by the analyst and by the child. Thus we expected to find (1) increasing ability to organize a narrative, along with (2) increasing morphosyntactic complexity, and (3) language-specific interactions between narrative organization and linguistic expression.

On the level of **narrative** development — basing ourselves on the considerable literature on cognitive and linguistic development with regard to this domain — we expected to find a number of common patterns across age and language. We predicted that:

1) The youngest children (age 3-4) will produce verbal accounts in response to the pictures, describing not only static scenes and participants, but also events — with only occasional reference to sequential and causal relation between successive pictures.

2) By the end of the preschool period, some children will tell stories with plots, in which there is goal-directed activity, organized around a problem and attempts to solve the problem, and they will refer more often to sequential and, occasionally, causal relations between adjacent events.

3) Across the 5-9 age range there will be an increase in hierarchical organization of the narrative, in which segments are marked off as episodes,

and in which actions in one episode are related to those in other episodes — eventually non-adjacent episodes.

4)   Older preschool, but more particularly school-age children will make causal attributions to events in the story — both internal (emotional, cognitive) and external (physical) causes.

These predictions form the basis for discussion of findings presented in Chapter IIA.

On the level of general **linguistic** development, we expected a number of consequences in this domain as a result of developments such as those sketched out above. We predicted that:

5)   Most generally, it will be the case that individual forms take on more functions with development. That is, as new functions emerge, they will recruit existing forms, and also stimulate the acquisition of relevant new forms.

6)   More specifically, linguistic devices such as the following will develop in connection with increasing narrative proficiency: flexible use of tense and aspect to distinguish foreground and background, voice and word-order alternations to express topic and focus, and a range of syntactic constructions that allow clauses to be expressed as subordinate, nonfinite, or nominalized — in order to manage information flow in narrative.

7)   As such devices are acquired, narrative texts will move from a series of separate clauses to "packages" of clauses of increasing syntactic dependence. The number of clauses packaged together will increase, as well as the diversity of types of interclausal connections.

These predictions are addressed in Chapter VA.

On the level of **particular languages**, we expected typological differences to have an influence on development in the following directions.

8)   The most accessible linguistic means for the expression of discourse functions are found in the obligatory, grammaticized component of the morphosyntactic system of the language. Narrative functions that are expressed by obligatory devices — for example the distinction between simple and progressive aspect in English and between perfective and imperfective forms in Spanish — will appear early in a given language.

9)   To the extent that such devices are easily acquired in a language, children may be stimulated to discover some of their more advanced uses at an earlier age than in other languages. For example, children speaking languages with transparent relative clause structures — as Spanish and Hebrew — may use relative clauses in adult-like fashion by school age.

10) If a language lacks obligatory grammatical expression of a notion that seems to be important for narrative, children may compensate for this lack by the use of lexical means to express that notion. For example, children speaking languages without an inflectional progressive aspect — as German and Hebrew — may use adverbial means to indicate an event as durative or ongoing.

Finally, Chapter VB deals with these issues.

4. PLAN OF THE BOOK

We needed to be selective in presenting the many facets of a complex endeavor such as this. (Readers are referred to the listing in Appendix III to get an idea of the many other perspectives from which, and other languages in which, this story can be told.) Besides, the nature of our undertaking is such that some readers will be interested primarily, or exclusively, in certain aspects of it: narrative, developmental, typological, or language-particular. We therefore decided to organize the book, proceeding from the general orientation provided in Part I (Chapters IA and IB), around the two pivots of form and function. Part II concerns "function" in the sense of the narrative task involved in telling the frog story, and how this was performed by children of different ages compared with adults; Part III deals with "forms" in the sense of the linguistic devices used by speakers of different ages and languages in telling the frog story; while Part IV considers how linguistic forms interact with narrative functions such as temporality, perspective, and segmentation. Part V concludes the book by looking at both form and function from the two perspectives encoded in the subtitle of the book: developmental trends, on the one hand, and crosslinguistic differences, on the other.

In brief summary, then, the two chapters in Part II analyze the development of narrative competence in preschoolers compared with school-age children and adults, generalized across different languages, with detailed examples from English and Hebrew (Chapter IIA), and abstracted away from linguistic form (Chapter IIB). Part III analyzes the distribution and deployment of linguistic forms for each of the dimensions outlined in Table 1 of this chapter. It starts with a general typological orientation to each of these dimensions by comparing the range of forms available in the five languages in our sample (Chapter III0). Then follow descriptions of the relevant forms and grammatical systems and how they are distributed in each of the five languages, ordered in increasing genetic and typological distance from English: English (Chapter IIIA), German (IIIB), Spanish (IIIC), Hebrew (IIID), and Turkish (IIIE). Each of these chapters ends with a brief summary of its main findings.

Part IV attempts to tie together several strands which have emerged separately in Parts II and III, by relating the use of linguistic forms found at different age levels and in different languages to particular narrative functions. Chapter IVA concerns the development of temporality marking within a narrative framework, focusing on the expression of simultaneity for describing co-occurrent events or states; it starts out with a detailed analysis of these phenomena in German and Turkish, supplemented by briefer discussion of relevant findings for the other three languages. Chapter IVB discusses the narrative and general discourse functions of relative clauses, as a particular set of syntactic forms, which are quantitatively and qualitatively compared across children of different ages compared with adults in all five languages in our sample. Chapter IVC considers the discourse functions of "packaging" and "filtering" as defined in Chapter IA in relation to four particular events in the frog story, to demonstrate developmental and typological differences in perspective-taking across the sample. And Chapter IVD examines how English- and German-speaking narrators perform the narrative functions of "foreshadowing" and "wrapping up" different facets of the frog story to express such notions as instantiation and reinstantiation, continuation and completion.

In Part V we attempt to summarize the key findings and major implications of our study in the light of the guiding themes and predictions set out at the beginning of the book. First, we consider the factors involved in developing from an immature to a fully proficient speaker and frog-story narrator in terms of the interplay between linguistic forms and narrative functions from a developmental perspective (Chapter VA). And we conclude by discussing what it means to become a proficient speaker of a particular language, and to tell a mature frog story as constrained by the linguistic forms and rhetorical options of one type of language compared with another (Chapter VB).

Part II

DEVELOPMENT OF FUNCTIONS

Chapter IIA

NARRATIVE STRUCTURE[1]

1. INTRODUCTION: THE NARRATIVE TASK

In this chapter we are concerned with the developing ability to "tell a story." In Chapter IA we argued that there is no single "objective" story, because narrators are free to choose perspectives on events. We also suggested that our texts differ considerably according to both the age and

[1] Thanks are due to Irit Katzenberger and Yeshayahu Shen of Tel Aviv University for their helpful comments on a draft of this chapter.

language of the speaker. Nevertheless, every adult "reader" of *Frog, where are you?* is certain to extract a plotline which goes from loss of the frog, through searches, to recovery. And every adult narrator is certain to add details of the thwarted attempts along the way, with some commentary on the inner states that motivate and respond to some of the events. Thus, there is a sense of "well-formed" story type as the developmental target, although there is an infinity of potential well-formed versions of the frog story. Here we are concerned with what those versions have in common: **linguistic cohesion** on the micro-level of individual clauses and adjacent clauses, and **thematic coherence** on the macro-level of plot organization.[2] It is our finding that — across languages — there is a common developmental pattern towards increasing cohesion and coherence.

The outlines of this pattern are already familiar from the rich literature on the development of children's ability to produce narrative texts (reviewed, for example, in Bamberg, 1987; Peterson & McCabe, 1983; Toolan, 1988, Chapter 6).[3] A variety of methods have been used to induce children to produce narratives.[4] One class of procedures relies on verbal input alone to elicit

---

[2] The literature on narrative and other types of discourse has recourse to a rich range of terminology, reflecting a plethora of related distinctions. For example, some discuss the linguistic or "semantic" content at the "textbase" level of propositional content compared with narrative categories such as "episodes" and "discourse topics" which apply at the level of macro-structure (e.g., Kintsch, 1977; van Dijk, 1972, 1980; van Dijk & Kintsch 1983). Rather different definitions are given to the notion "coherence" by researchers such as de Beaugrande (1980a, p.191, 1980b, p. 290); Brown (1976, p. 265-266), Giora (1985a, 1985b), and Langleben (1981, p. 280). Some of these explicitly distinguish coherence from "cohesion," where the latter applies to overt linguistic markers of text connectivity, particularly Halliday and Hasan (1976, p. 10), and see also Giora (1983), Grimes (1978, p.113), and Hickmann (1991). Relatedly, some but not all researchers draw an explicit distinction between coherence and/or cohesion as properties of discourse structuring in general (what is sometimes termed "textual coherence") compared with their functioning in the particular discourse mode of narrative.

[3] Since this study discusses only narratives **produced** by children, we take relatively little account of the rich literature on developing abilities at processing narrative texts from the point of view of such tasks as: comprehension (Stein & Glenn, 1979; Stein & Trabasso, 1982), recall (Mandler & DeForest, 1979; Mandler & Johnson, 1977; Nezworski, Stein, & Trabasso, 1982; Poulsen, Kintsch, Kintsch, & Premack, 1979), evaluation (Stein & Salgo, 1984), and summarizing (Johnson, 1983; McConaughy, Fitzhenry-Coor, & Howell, 1983).

[4] We refer here only to procedures aimed at deliberate elicitation of narrative texts. Another branch of narrative analysis concerns those which children produce spontaneously when on their own (Nelson, 1989, 1991) or in the course of conversation — a methodology applied mainly in the case of young children from as early as 18 months of age (McCabe & Peterson, 1991; Miller & Sperry, 1988; Nelson & Gruendel, 1981; Ninio, 1988; Sachs, 1983; Sachs, Goldman, & Chaille, 1984), and occasionally with somewhat older preschoolers in different situations (Snow & Dickinson, 1990; Umiker-Sebeok, 1978). These are not relevant to

narratives about personal experiences — either one-time occurrences (Kemper, 1984; Peterson & McCabe, 1983; Roth & Spekman, 1986) or familiar "scripted" events (Fivush & Slackman, 1986; French, 1986; Hudson & Nelson, 1986). In applying these methods, the investigator has little external control over the real-world (or fantasized) events which the narrator is referring to. Another class of procedures aims to overcome this particular problem by providing a shared nonverbal — typically visual and typically fictive — basis for narrative description. This may be done by showing a film without words (Chafe, 1980; Hickmann, 1980, 1982; Sleight & Prinz, 1985; Warden, 1981) or else, as in the present case, by using pictures.[5]

Picture-based narrative elicitations typically use series of from four to ten pictures, often aimed at examining children's ability to introduce, maintain, and shift reference to protagonists — in this case, the characters shown in the pictures (Hickmann, 1980; Hickmann & Liang, 1990; Karmiloff-Smith, 1980, 1981; McGann & Schwartz, 1988). This design has an advantage over the memory burden entailed by film viewings, which vary in degree of retention of the material which they present. Moreover, the small sets of short picture series most typically adopted in such designs differ from the picture booklet used in the present study. The former impose far less of a burden on a child's processing capacities, particularly when presented all together, not in book form. In contrast, the structure of *Frog, where are you?* requires speakers to recall the progression and the outcome of the plot as represented in pictures other than the one(s) they happen to be describing at any given moment. On the other hand, there is evidence that even young children understand that wordless picturebooks are meant to be "read" or that they are the basis for a story to be told in sequential order (Hough, Nurss, & Wood, 1987).

Picture sequences of all kinds impose on children a particular kind of cognitive demand by requiring them to translate spatially static visual sequences into temporally dynamic verbal output. Despite the difficulties involved in such tasks, pictures have proved a reliable means of tapping children's narrative abilities from both a cognitive and a linguistic point of view (Bornens, 1990; Katzenberger, 1992) — at least in cultures where children have experience with pictures. Most importantly from our point of view, use of a single set of pictures as a narrative prop provides a shared point of

---

our concerns, although conversational interactions may well provide the context for initial emergence of narrative production (Bruner, 1986).

[5] Yet another method which bridges these two extremes is to have children retell a story told them by the investigator (Geva & Olson, 1983; Kozminsky, 1986; Merrit & Liles, 1986). This procedure tests children's ability to **recall** narratives, rather than to produce them for themselves, and so is less relevant to our present concerns. (See references in footnote 3.)

departure and a common external basis for comparing the narrative productions of children and adults speaking different languages. The elaborated series of events depicted in the picture-booklet used in this study means that "the narrator is constantly faced with the problems of deciding ... how to make references to each [of the protagonists] clear to the listener, and how to handle the task of ordering the reporting of parallel activities while advancing thematic progression" (Preece, 1992, p. 482). It has the further advantage of allowing narrators to describe a complex network of temporally sequenced events, while prompting them to attend to each scene in turn. This potential duality in "reading" the contents of a fairly lengthy story-in-pictures has definite implications for our study. Respondents can treat the task as either one of picture-description or of story telling — or both construals may be mixed within a single narration.

Several interrelated patterns emerge from the narrations we elicited. On the one hand, even the youngest children, aged 3 to 4 years old, prove able to produce pieces of discourse which are both intelligible and relevant to the task at hand. They typically relate to dynamic events rather than to static entities. And they are occasionally capable of providing "minimal" narrative sequences (Labov, 1972) by relating two or three events to one another in a temporal chain — e.g. *The dog was on top of his head. **And then** he fell over with the dog into the pond [E3d-3;5]; And then some bees came out of the tree, and then he tried to get the bees, but he couldn't [E3f-3;9]*. But these children still need to learn how to integrate different facets of a well-formed piece of discourse, at the interrelated levels of what Bamberg and Marchman (1990) refer to as "referential activity" — how the events are ordered along the sequential axis of an unfolding plotline — and "discourse activity" — how events are organized in narrative according to their thematic relevance.

Our analyses reveal striking age-related differences between the young preschoolers and older, school-age children, and between these latter and adults, from both points of view. At the most global level of narrative structure, young children generally fail to organize the texts they produce in terms of an overall action-structure, i.e., as an explicitly motivated plot — a prerequisite for overall text coherence (Section 2). At the more local level of individual scenes, they are not consistently capable of setting foregrounded, plot-advancing events, e.g. that the frog ran away, within a network of associated circumstances, e.g. that he did so without the boy noticing, because it was at night and he and the dog were sleeping (Section 3). These trends are largely in keeping with the findings of other studies on the development of narrative production (such as those reviewed by Trabasso and Rodkin in the next chapter). The ability to produce extended narratives which are well-formed in terms of hierarchical thematic structuring and global organization emerges relatively late, well beyond the period when children produce sentences which are syntactically impeccable.

This chapter characterizes children's development of **narrative discourse competence** as background to consideration of the development and use of expressive devices available in particular native languages in Parts III and IV. It is based on independent analyses conducted separately for each of the five languages — in English by Marchman (1989) and Renner (1988), in German by Bamberg (1985, 1987) and von Stutterheim (1986), in Hebrew by Berman (1988), in Spanish by Sebastián (1989), and in Turkish by Aksu-Koç (1991). The claims made here apply to all five languages in our study, but they are illustrated in detail in this chapter for only two: English, as the language shared by our readers, and Hebrew as a non-Indo-European language which differs markedly from English in several respects relevant to the crosslinguistic focus of our study (see chapters in Part III).

Our concern in the present chapter is not with what distinguishes children in these different languages, but rather with the common threads which can be discerned across the population. Where these findings can be related to particular age groups, we have a basis for suggesting that general cognitive and expressive development is responsible, over and above the demands and constraints of acquiring a particular native tongue.[6] The broad similarities discernible across the 3-year-olds irrespective of their native tongue, and how distinct they are from the 5-year-old preschoolers, combined with how markedly 9-year-old schoolchildren differ both from them and from the adult narrators suggest that this is in fact the case.

The complexly elaborated series of events depicted in *Frog, where are you?* required that we establish criteria for "narrative competence" beyond what might be relevant in analyzing short texts based on individual personal experiences, on the one hand, or more tightly packaged sets of only four or six pictures, on the other. These criteria needed, moreover, to suit the language-based motivations for our study. The findings described in this chapter are, accordingly, analyzed from three distinct but related points of view. First, we analyze reference to core **plot components** to evaluate whether narrators make explicit reference to the story as having a beginning, middle, and end

---

[6] We have insufficient grounds for claiming that similar trends will necessarily be manifested in the development of narrative discourse abilities in cultures far removed from the Western, urban background of the subjects of our study (Slobin, 1990). Besides, the frog story itself is an instance of a canonically constructed Western fairytale narrative genre (Propp, 1968). As indicated in Appendix III, however, the frog picturebook has recently been used to elicit stories in settings as diverse as New Guinea, aboriginal Australia, and Mayan Central America. It remains to be seen whether similar trends can be found crossculturally.

(Section 2); we then analyze the ability to describe individual scenes and series of scenes in terms of explicitly related **event components** (Section 3); while in the bulk of the chapter we delineate general developmental profiles for four different age groups — 3-year-olds, 5-year-olds, 9-year-olds, and adults (Section 4).

At the outset, a word about terminology is in order. In the present chapter we distinguish between **plot** or **plotline** intended by the author of the booklet, the **story** represented by the pictures, and the oral **narratives** or **texts** produced by the children and adult respondents in our study. The term **narration** is used to describe the process or act of producing a narrative.

Our analyses were motivated by developmental hypotheses concerning narrative abilities, viewed within the framework of developmental phases that have been shown to characterize the acquisition of other types of linguistic knowledge — morphological, syntactic, and lexical (Berman, 1986a, 1986c, 1987a, 1990) — as well as the reorganization of knowledge in other cognitive domains (Karmiloff-Smith, 1984, 1985, 1986a, 1986b, 1987, 1992). We assumed, first, that the ability to construct narrative discourse in the context of the frog story task would manifest the following developmental path. Initially, children will tend to treat each scene as an **isolated event**, with narrative organization restricted to the most local level of the contents of individual pictures; in the second phase, children will **chain** events sequentially, giving evidence of a temporal organization of more extended, though still locally organized, series of events (Berman, 1988); at the next developmental phase, narratives will be **causally** structured in terms of a hierarchically organized goal plan of action (Trabasso & van den Broek, 1985; Trabasso, van den Broek, & Suh, 1989; and see, too, analyses of the frog story in English in Trabasso & Nickels, 1992; Trabasso and Stein, in press; Trabasso, Stein, Rodkin, Munger, & Baughn, 1992 — reviewed by Trabasso and Rodkin in Chapter IIB). These causal interrelations may initially be quite local; mature narrations, in contrast, will be motivated by an integrated construal of events in terms of overall **action-structure** (Giora & Shen, in press; Shen, 1988, 1990), in which factors of importance, thematic coherence, and evaluative commentary are coordinated within the causal structure of an initial goal, attempts to reach this goal, and the final outcome of these attempts.

The distinction between these two latter types of causal structure can be illustrated by how people could describe the events shown in the same series of four pictures about a child picking flowers. A 5-year-old might say, "A little girl picked some flowers in the field. Then she came home and put the flowers in a vase so they wouldn't dry up." A thematically-motivated narrative, organized around an initial goal and action-schema, would go as follows: "A little girl wanted to bring flowers home for her mother's birthday, so she went out and picked them in a field nearby." The two versions differ in their causal structure, since the first encodes local causality (why she put the flowers in a vase), while the second refers to an overall goal at a more global level of organization (why she picked the flowers in the first place). Even more importantly, they differ in **temporal** structure as well. The first shares the chronological sequencing of narratives typical of children still at the previous phase of "chaining," whereas the second account restructures the sequential order in which the events in fact occurred — as reflected in the spatial ordering of the pictures on which these two accounts are based — and mentions bringing the flowers home before their being picked. An example from our sample is provided by immature compared with narratively motivated use of the causal conjunction, Hebrew *ki* 'because' in the frog story. A 3-year-old describes the scene where the boy falls from the tree by saying: 'And here he fell **because** the owl pushed him' [*H3c-3;5*]; a 9-year-old narrator, in contrast, uses the same form to introduce the resolution of the story interwoven with evaluative commentary: 'The boy fell into the river, and he was pleased **because** he heard the croaking of frogs and he was sure that it was his frog' [*H9e-9;6*].

A second assumption underlying our analysis was that this developmental progression from picture-description to thematic organization would be manifested linguistically in several ways. In this chapter, we focus on two types of linguistic expression: **temporal anchoring** in use of inflectional markings of verb tense, and **connectivity** through use of lexical and other overt markers of the relationship between events.[7] Third, we assumed that young children would focus mainly on description of events and activities, whereas older narrators would provide more **background** information relating to the attendant circumstances in which the unfolding plotline events are embedded. This assumption is analyzed below in relation to **evaluative** commentary provided by narrators concerning the mental states and emotional reactions of the boy-protagonist.

---

[7] Another important type of linguistic marking of narrative structure concerns the ability to introduce, maintain, and shift **reference** to the participants in the events described, through such anaphoric devices as definiteness and pronominalization. These abilities have been the subject of much linguistic analysis of developing narrative skills (e.g. Bavin, 1987; Hickmann, 1980; Hickmann & Liang, 1990; Karmiloff-Smith, 1980, 1981; Wigglesworth, 1990), including analyses of narrations based on the frog story in English (Martin, 1983; Wigglesworth, 1992), French (Kail & Hickmann, 1992), German (Bamberg, 1987), and Japanese (Nakamura, 1992). Since the focus of our study is on description of **events** in an unfolding narrative, this set of issues is marginal to our present analysis. It does, however, figure in discussion of the issue of "connectivity" in subsequent chapters.

2. GLOBAL STRUCTURE: OVERALL PLOTLINE

All the children proved able to describe the contents of at least some of the pictures in the book. And they nearly always present them as **events**, rather than merely noting the existence of objects without any dynamic predication (see further, Section 3). In this, they meet at least one criterion of narrative compared with descriptive discourse, which children clearly distinguish by age 5 years (Tolchinsky-Landsmann & Sandbank, in press).[8] However, the younger children fail to produce narratives which can be defined as thematically coherent in the sense of being organized around an overall plotline. In order to evaluate this impression in quantitative terms, we stipulated three elements of the story as criterial of the ability to relate to the contents of the picturebook as an integrated whole. These core components are: I — **the onset of the plot**: the boy's realizing that his frog has disappeared; II — **unfolding of the plot**: the boy's search for his missing frog; and III — **resolution of the plot**: the boy's finding the frog he has lost (or one to take its place).[9]

The texts were scored for these three elements as follows. I: required explicit mention of the boy's noticing that the frog is missing; a child who merely refers to the jar as empty without relating it to the boy's discovery was not credited; II: explicit mention must be made of searching (or looking, or calling) **for the frog**, and this must go beyond beyond the initial start of the search inside the bedroom;[10] and III: the frog that the boy takes home at the end of the story must explicitly be described as being the same as or substituting for the frog the boy has lost.

These three criteria are illustrated from 5-year-old English texts in (1) through (6) below. The first three excerpts **fail** to meet these criteria, while

---

[8] The distinction between these two types of discourse is elaborated in Chapter IVA. See, too, Giora (1990).

[9] These three components of plot structure are taken from the pioneering work of Labov and Waletzky (1967), and correspond broadly to the units defined in different versions of the "story grammar" approach to narrative construction (reviewed in Mandler, 1982; Shen, 1988) as follows: (i) initiating goal: the **problem** that motivates the action; (ii) **elaboration** or complication: the development of the action in terms of the protagonists' attempt(s) to solve the problem; and (iii) the **outcome** of these endeavors: the resolution of the problem. See, further, Chapter IIB and the analyses of narrative functions in Chapters IVA through IVD.

[10] The initial search inside the bedroom constitutes a secondary or "local" goal, while sustained search outdoors in the forest and beyond constitutes a major, global-level goal which needs to be identified as the motivating basis for the story as a whole. The causal network model underlying Trabasso and Rodkin's analysis in Chapter IIB characterizes a "goal-plan hierarchy" such that there is a higher-order goal (to find the frog) which motivates subordinate goals (to search in particular locations) and then gets reinstated to meet "yet another inferred, higher order goal" (to get back his pet). See, too, Chapter IVD.

those in (4) to (6) rated positive scores. Thus the 5-year-old excerpt in (1) was **not** credited for component I — the discovery scene.

(1)   *And then they wake up and he's gone. And then the dog sticks his head in and gets caught. [E5h-5;11]*

Nor did the excerpt in (2) qualify for a positive score on component II — the search motif.

(2)   *The boy's angry [with the dog]. And then the ... dog is trying to eat the fly, and the boy - is calling. And on this ... the boy's digging a hole and looking at it. And in this one - the dog tried to climb - a tree. And the boy found a underground squirrel ... The marmot's out of his hole. The boy's climbing a tree. And the - the dog is ... up on the tree. And then the bees' thing fell down. Now the dog's running, and the boy got knocked over from all the bees. And this time, the boy's going to climb the rock. And this time - a male deer got the um - the boy and threw him over a cliff into a pond. [E5j-5;10]*

And the excerpt in (3) from a third 5-year-old fails to meet the criteria for component III — the recovery scene.

(3)   *So they looked into the hole ... And they saw a family of frogs. First they saw two frogs, and then they saw a family. A whole family! "Come with me! Come on!" There's a frog. [E5i-5;10]*

In contrast, the first part of the story told by the child excerpted in (3) **was** credited for components I — discovery that the frog has gone, and II — searching for the missing frog beyond the confines of the bedroom. These are shown in (4) and (5), from the same child.

(4)   *So in the morning the little boy said "Where is my frog?" [E5i-5;10]*

(5)   *And then he looked and - it was only his dog. "Frog, frog, are you in here?" But there was no ribbit ribbit sound. So they went on to look. "Is that you in there? Is it? Is it?" But it was only a squirrel - or a beaver -* [5 clauses later] *The dog looked in the beehive. It was only bees!* [3 clauses later] *And the bees started running after the dog, but it was only an owl in the - hole in the tree. Then he looked in a rock. "Is - Oh frog, frog! Are you here?" [E5i-5;10]*

Excerpt (6), from another 5-year-old, rated positively on component III — recovery of the frog.

(6)   *And then they go over and they meet a - a family of frogs. And then they say ... And he takes - one of - them. And they [= the boy and the dog] said: "This one - used to be ours ... Can we take one?" [E5f-5;8]*

Table 1 gives the percentages of narrators out of our total sample who made explicit reference to these three core plot components.

TABLE 1

Percentage of Narrators across Five Languages Making Explicit
Reference to Each of Three Core Components, by Age

Component	3yrs (N=58)	4 yrs (N=36)	5 yrs (N=58)	9 yrs (N=58)	Adult (N=58)
I	17	50	78	94	100
II	15	20	52	98	100
III	10	28	41	62	92

The figures in Table 1 show a clear age-related increase in proportion of mention of the three core components, from under 20% for each of them at age 3 years, up to around 50% or more at age 5 years, with an "endstate" ceiling among the adults. Second, they show an increasing level of difficulty for each of the three components: component I achieves a high level of mention (over 75%) by age 5 years, component II by age 9 years, and component III only by the adults. Moreover, analysis of crosslinguistic differences reveals considerable consistency across narrators in the five languages from age 5 years and up. The main source of between-language variability occurs among the 3- and 4-year-olds. For example, 10 of the 12 English 4-year-olds mention component I, compared with only 3 out of 12 Hebrew 4-year-olds. And half of the Spanish 3-year-olds, but only one each of the Hebrew and Turkish children, and none of the English 3-year-olds, make explicit reference to the search for the missing frog.

Nine-year-olds approximate the adult level of 100% on the first two components — the discovery scene and the search motif. On the other hand, one-third of the 9-year-olds, but only an occasional adult, fail to make explicit "closure" by explicitly referring the end-of-story frog back to the one mentioned at the beginning. An adult example of this failure is illustrated by an English text which ended as follows: *The boy and the dog ... crept up on the log, where they heard the noises of frogs. Behind the log, he saw two frogs and to his amazement, even MORE frogs, baby frogs! The boy left the family of frogs with one of the baby frogs and the dog and said good-bye. [E20d]*

The 5-year-olds do much better than the younger children on all three counts, but are much below the level of the 9-year olds in explicit reference to cardinal elements of the plotline. The 4-year-olds again form a bridge between the maturing abilities of the 5-year-olds and the almost total lack of explicit reference to the major plot motifs of the youngest children in our sample.

The same trends are confirmed when we compare the proportion of respondents at each age group whose texts manifest global narrative structure, defined as explicit reference to all three cardinal elements of the plot. These figures are shown in Table 2.

TABLE 2
Percentage of Narrators across Five Languages Making Explicit
Reference to All Three Plot Components, by Age

	3 yrs (N=58)	4 yrs (N=36)	5 yrs (N=58)	9 yrs (N=58)	Adult (N=58)
Percentage	3	14	34	66	92

Table 2 reveals a clear age-related rise in explicit reference to the three critical plot components, with the gap between one age group and the next decreasing proportionately with age (4-year-olds mention all three components five times as often as 3-year-olds, the next group three times as often, 9-year-olds do so around twice as often as 5-year-olds, and adults one and a half times as often as the oldest children). We take this as strong evidence for development of the ability to relate to an overall hierarchical theme or storyline.

Only one of the 3-year-olds, out of nearly 60 in this age group whose stories we analyzed in five different languages, meet these criteria. Interestingly enough, this child tells a story which in other respects is quite impoverished in linguistic expression and in descriptive detail, as shown by the translated version of her Hebrew story given in (7).[11]

(7) 'She ... was inside a can. Again [=here, too]. And then ... he slept, and she decided to go.out. He saw that the can was empty, and then he lost her [literally: she got-lost to-him]. So he searched and searched, and did not find (her). [Here the child skipped over several pictures.] Called to her, she did not lis ... she did not hear him. And then he couldn ... he didn't find her. And then he climbed up a tree, searched in the hole, and he did not find her. And then he fell ..., and he saw the ... him [=owl] and he got out of the hole ... And then he did not see her, and she hid in

---

[11] The pronoun 'she' refers to the frog, since the Hebrew word *cfardea* is in feminine gender, and 'he' refers to the boy. Hebrew uses a different verb for 'search' than for 'look (at, inside)', which is quite everyday and colloquial in register. Items in square brackets in the example are explanatory comments.

the water. And then he decided to look for her for a long time. [The child skipped several more pictures.] And ... he fell. And the ... dog sat in the water, and he nearly drowned. And then he also hid away quietly, and found two she-frogs and then he found a friend - mommy and daddy frogs and then he decided that THAT ONE was her!' [Points to a baby frog in the last picture.] [H3b-3;4]

This 3-year-old has produced a well-constructed narrative at the global level of overall thematic plotline. Her text contains an onset, a clearly articulated elaboration, and an explicit coda. On the other hand, it is juvenile in the limited linguistic devices it uses and in the paucity of its descriptive detail — all short, clipped, clauses, all verbs in the past tense, no lexical specification of other participants such as the owl or the deer, no explaining of **why** the boy fell from the tree or into the water. This combination of impoverished linguistic and descriptive detail with well-structured plot construction is exactly in accord with what Karmiloff-Smith (1984, 1985) characterizes as the middle period of "top-down" processing in narrative abilities as in other domains of cognitive development. And it contrasts with the texts of most 3-year-olds in our sample: They may manifest considerable richness of expression at the level of the individual clause or groups of adjacent clauses, while failing to relate explicitly to critical plot-motivated components. The child who produced the Hebrew text translated and excerpted in (8) uses rich lexicon and complex syntactic structures, but he fails to make explicit reference to any of the three major plot components.

(8)   'Once there was a boy who was very cute. One time he went with his friends to the forest, and he met a frog. So he lay down on the ... he was on the couch, and he didn't feel like going for a walk. So ... so suddenly the idea popped into his head to go ... and take a look at the moon. [several clauses later] And in the end he didn't manage to take (it) out, and in the end, in the end they went for a walk. And the dog jumped from here to here outside. Now he licks [=is licking] him, and he put on the big shoes [=boots] which I saw.' [H3h-3;8]

Thus, as predicted, command of an array of expressive devices in itself does not suffice for children to construct a narrative which has an explicit motivating onset, an elaborated reaction of the protagonist to this realization, and a final resolution to the problem. Rather, narration in general, and of this picture story in particular, is a "**joint process** of event comprehension and language production," as noted in the next chapter, and it is contingent on knowledge of narrative structure and what constitutes a story.

3. LOCAL STRUCTURE: EVENT COMPONENTS

Three- and 4-year-olds speaking different native languages thus appear lacking in the abilities necessary for building up a complete narrative which is thematically motivated at a global level. Yet their performance on our task displays more than direct "reading off" of pictures in the sequence dictated by the visual impact of the book itself, from several points of view. In the first place, the children in our sample only occasionally merely list the contents of a picture as a static array of objects. For example, in response to the investigator's urging the child to tell her what he can see, one child starts listing: *a dog, a frog... a person, a boot, a shoe, a can of water, rubbers ...*, but after warming up a little goes on to say *Next one - alright, he trying to jump out the window. And the dog's trying to get out - the window* [E3d-3;5]. Or a Hebrew child says: *Ze kelev, ve magafayim, ve kise* 'This is a dog, and boots, and a chair' [H3k-3;10]. Such listings typically occur at the **outset** of 3-year-old accounts, suggesting that the children producing them have not yet gotten into their narrative flow. But even these are relatively rare.

Nor do the youngest children rely much on purely static descriptions such as *And here there's bees* [E3c-3;4], or *Hine yanshuf* 'Here's (an) owl' [H3d-3;6]. Such descriptions are rare across the sample, and suggest that these children conceive of the pictures as events, taking a dynamically motivated perspective on what they could in principle have interpreted in purely static terms. This is revealed by analysis of 3-year-old accounts of the contents of Picture 4, where the dog has its head stuck in the jar of the frog: Of the 10 Hebrew 3-year-olds who refer to this situation, eight describe it in dynamic terms of what the dog did, or what happened to the dog, and only two use stative descriptions such as 'The dog's head is in the jar' (Berman, 1993). At this "local" level, all the children, from the youngest age, relate to the pictures as showing **events** — as predications of activities or happenings rather than as descriptions of objects or states. In this they give evidence of a grasp of the most basic element of what's involved in "narrative."

Another ability which all the children evidence to some extent is that of making inferences about what is **not** visible on the printed page. For example, the first three pictures show (1) a jar with a frog in it, (2) a frog climbing out of a jar, and (3) an empty jar. Certain inferences need to be made in order for a child to be able to say of Picture 3, *cause his frog's not in it* [E3b-3;4]; or *And he - the frog got away* [E3f-3;9]. This is even clearer in the example excerpted in (9).

(9) *Oh - oh, he's climbing out and he - and he's and he's starting to wake up and I think he's try - I think he's getting out of the glass* **so he can run away**. *I don't know - if the frog - Oh! the frog's gone! guess he ran away at night.* [E3g-3;9]

Similarly, in order to describe Picture 12, which shows the boy lying on his back with his legs up in the air, the narrator needs to understand that it relates to the previous picture, which shows the boy climbing the tree and peering into a hole. The narrator must make the inference that the appearance of an owl in front of this hole in Picture 12 is related to the boy's position — namely, that he fell. This kind of relation between pictures is reflected, for example, in 3-year-old comments such as: *Owl, owl in there, fall, fall him down* [*E3c-3;4*]; 'And he ... and SUDDENLY he fell on his head' [*H3a-3;0*]. This is an event which nearly all the 3-year-olds describe in the relevant terms, rather than merely describing the boy as lying on the ground with his arms and legs up in the air.

However, the ability to infer beyond what is overtly represented in the pictures themselves is a necessary but not sufficient condition for appropriate narrative construction. Although 3-year-olds show the ability to talk about **events** and to infer **relations** between situations in linking them together, they are not yet proficient storytellers. This was demonstrated at the global level discussed in Section 2. It also applies at the more local level of making explicit reference to different components which make up a single event and different facets of a complex chain of events. We tested this claim in relation to two scenes which require somewhat higher levels of inferencing.

The first of the two scenes appears in Picture 3, which shows the boy lying on his bed with the dog on top of him, looking at the empty jar. Adult accounts of the contents of this scene reveal a maximum of five component parts: the **background** elements of (1) the precursor change of state event (the boy has woken up) and (2) temporal location (in the morning, the next morning); the **plot-advancing** elements of (3) inferencing that the protagonist learns something (the boy sees, discovers, realizes) (4) the state of affairs which is depicted (the jar is empty) or inferred (frog has gotten lost, disappeared, run away); and the **attendant circumstances** or **motivation** of (5) the protagonist's response — either subsequent action (get out of bed to look for the frog) or affective reaction (feeling surprised, concerned, curious). A clear development is revealed by analysis of the English and Hebrew references to this scene across age groups, as shown in Tables 3a and 3b. The 3-year-olds most often mention **none** or only one of the relevant components, e.g. *He's* [= boy] *in the bed* [*E3d-3;5*] or *He's looking for the frog* [*E3j-3;10*], although a few of the younger children include as many as three components, e.g. *When he waked up he saw nothing wasn't there* [*E3h-3;9*]. The 9-year-olds, like the adults, typically encode as many as four or five components, and these include inferences about the boy's internal response to his discovery that the frog has gone in terms such as amazement, surprise, curiosity, or worry. Moreover, closely similar patterns are shown by narrators in two quite different languages, English and Hebrew. This indicates that the choice of components to be expressed is governed by a quite general development of shared perceptual and cognitive abilities, rather than by the dictates of language-particular forms of expression.

TABLE 3a
Number of Component Parts Referred to by English Speakers on
Picture 3 (Discovery of Empty Jar) out of Those Mentioning
this Picture, by Age[a]

	3 yrs (N=12)	4 yrs (N=12)	5 yrs (N=12)	9 yrs (N=12)	Adult (N=12)
Relevant No. of Mentions	7	10	11	12	12
COMPONENTS:					
zero	**3**	—	—	—	—
1	2	—	—	—	—
2	2	**6**	4	2	2
3	—	4	**7**	4	3
4	—	—	—	**6**	**6**
5	—	—	—	—	1

a. Figures in bold are favored number of components for that age group.

Five-year-olds differ from younger children in the number who explicitly make a connection between the jar being empty and the boy's cognizance of this, using predicates like *see* and *find*. The 9-year-olds differ from the preschoolers in two ways: Many of them make overt temporal reference to 'the next morning', inferred from the facts that there is no moon and the boy is awake; and one-third of them describe that the boy feels 'worried', 'concerned', 'curious', or 'surprised', whereas only one 5-year-old noted that the boy was 'sad'. The 9-year-olds construe the picture contents in the same way as the adults in this case, although they use different verbalizations. Not only do the adults use more lexically specific verbs such as 'discover' and 'notice', but some of them also select a more tightly packaged syntactic means of expression, e.g. *When he woke up in the morning, he saw that the frog was gone [E20i]*, or 'Next morning Yoram arose and behold the-jar (is) empty' [*H-20f*].[12] School-age children are much like the adults: they relate to

___
[12] Adults do **not** always make explicit reference to all five or even four of these com-

TABLE 3b
Number of Component Parts Referred to by Hebrew speakers on
Picture 3 (Discovery of Empty Jar) out of Those Mentioning
this Picture, by Age[a]

	3 yrs (N=12)	4 yrs (N=12)	5 yrs (N=12)	9 yrs (N=12)	Adult (N=12)
Relevant No. of Mentions	4	9	12	12	12
COMPONENTS:					
zero	2	1	—	—	—
1	2	2	—	—	—
2	—	**5**	1	—	—
3	—	1	**9**	2	4
4	—	—	2	**8**	7
5	—	—	—	2	3

a. Figures in bold are favored number of components for that age group.

this scene as a necessary component of the overall plotline (Section 2) **and** they refer to its various components as a complex event, involving a change of inner cognitive state on the part of the protagonist at a certain time and with a certain consequence.

Yet 9-year-olds do not display fully mature abilities with respect to a more complex cluster of events. The second scene we analyzed, Pictures 16 and 17, on two different pages of the storybook, imposes a more difficult task, both conceptually and linguistically, than the "realization that frog is missing" scene. The first picture depicts the boy climbing to the top of a rock to call for his frog. It represents a precursor or background event to what happens next and in fact involves a misperception on the boy's part, since in Picture 16 he grabs onto what he thinks are branches behind the top of the rock, but in Picture 17, over the page, these turn out to be the antlers of a deer hidden behind the rock. Picture 17 shows the boy caught in the antlers, and the deer carrying him along in a wild gallop. What needs to be inferred is that the event in 17 is a consequence of the ill-conceived or at least unintentional act in 16. Mature rendering of the contents of these related pictures imposes a considerable burden in terms of perceptual interpretation of the pictures,

ponents, reflecting the **selectivity** referred to by Chatman (1978), in explaining how narrative accounts are not photographic in nature. See, further, comments on adult stylistic differences in Section 4.4.

conceptualization of the link between two apparently distinct events, and linguistic formulation of the initial event and its unforeseeable consequences.

TABLE 4
Relation between Two Events in Pictures 16 (Climbing Rock)
and 17 (Carried Away by Deer)
Noted by English and Hebrew Speakers Combined, by Age

	3 yrs (N=24)	4 yrs (N=24)	5 yrs (N=24)	9 yrs (N=24)	Adult (N=24)
One or no event mentioned	19	13	2	1	1
Unrelated sequence of two events	5	8	17	10	3
Mistake implied	—	3	2	10	8
Misperception explicit	—	—	2	3	12

Table 4 gives figures for how English and Hebrew speakers relate to the component parts of this complex interrelation of two events. The table shows that very few of the youngest children (5 out of 24) make explicit mention of both events, and the few who do so treated them as two distinct events which are either totally unrelated or merely in chronological sequence (e.g. *He went on a rock and the dog was not on a rock. He slipped onto ... a deer [E4b-4;4]* or 'And he climbed up, he climbed on a big stone. Afterwards he climbed on that [=deer]' *[H3j-3;9]*). The few preschoolers (7 out of a total 72 in these three age groups) who demonstrate some further inferencing do so mainly by relating to the fact that the boy's getting caught in the deer's antlers was **accidental**, without explicitly referring to a mistaken identity on his part, as in the examples which follow.

(10) *And then the owl - he hid ... And he got on a deer.* [screaming, laughing] *I think they have to put a danger sign on that thing cause a deer's underneath it.* *[E4c-4;6]*

(11) 'And here he jumped from the rock, and got caught on that, on the deer, he [=deer] took him with its horns.' *[H4l-4;11]*

(12) *And he - climbed - on a - big rock and ... and called out for him ... And then the - reindeer - is that a reindeer? The reindeer - then - then he got on a reindeer - because the reindeer was hiding there.* *[E5b-5;2]*

Only two of the 5-year-olds relate overtly to the boy's misperception. But this is also in terms which are far from giving explicit expression to all the relevant features of this chain of events, as illustrated in (13) and (14).

(13) *Then he - looked in a rock. "Is - oh! Frog! Frog! Are you there?!" But he's holding onto some sticks. But they really aren't sticks ... when - uh - something - came up, and the little boy was on it. [E5i-5;10]*

(14) *And they start calling. And they think that's sticks, but it's a d - um - an antler. [E5d-5;6]*

Even the school-age children do not always make overt reference to the misperception. However, when they do so, it is in terms much like the adults: They make a clear connection between the branches the boy was holding onto and the antlers he got entangled in, as shown in (15) through (19).

(15) *And then he stands up on the rock and hangs onto some branches, then it turns out they're antler - a deer's antlers, so - and he gets - he lands on his head and he starts running. [E9k-9;11]*

(16) 'He got up on a big rock and saw two antlers. He thought it was a plant, and he climbed up on it.' [H9l-9;8]

(17) 'He shouted, and leaned meanwhile on on the ... on kinda branches, but he was wrong, they were the antlers of a deer.' [H7h-7;6]

(18) *Um - while the boy was leaning on the branches, it turned out that the branches weren't really ... branches, they were the ... the horns of an elk.* [E20c]

(19) 'And while he held onto what he thought that it [sic] was branches, he continued to call for the frog. The branches were the horns of a deer ...' [H20g]

The connection between the rock-climbing event in Picture 16 and the deer-carrying event in Picture 17 represents perhaps the most complex network of relations between different components of an event sequence in the frog story. It is not surprising, then, that nearly all preschoolers as well as some older children fail to make any connection between the two events — beyond a straightforward temporal contiguity. The sequence involves a complex kind of "backtracking" at all three levels of processing of information: perceptual, conceptual, and online production of verbal output. The narrator, like the boy-protagonist, must go back and retrace his or her steps to reidentify the branches as antlers, and so to re-evaluate the connection between the boy being on top of the rock and then on top of the deer. This reorganization has linguistic as well as conceptual consequences. In talking about these two pictures, speakers evince a great deal of disfluency in the form of hesitations and pauses as well as numerous false starts, rewordings, repetitions, paraphrases, and other types of repairs, more so than at other places in the story (see Chapter IVc). Competent verbalization of this sequence requires both perceptual attentiveness and conceptual awareness of what is implied in the passage from Picture 16 to 17, and also the ability to plan ahead and prepackage information in ongoing linguistic output. These tasks are clearly beyond the capacities of younger children.

We noted at the outset of this section that young children **do** relate to individual pictures as representing dynamic events, not merely as static arrays. They can also make inferences about situations that are not directly shown in the pictures (e.g. between the jar being empty and the frog leaving it, between the boy lying on the ground and his having fallen from the tree). And they can express relations between such events by syntactic linking of adjacent clauses, e.g. *I think he's getting out of the glass so he can run away* [E3g-3;9]; *Owl push the boy while the dog was be chasing by the bees* [E4b-4;4]. What preschoolers cannot do is embed individual events within a network of associated circumstances that constitute the background events and internal motivations which lead up to a given event and the situations which follow from the event in question. Thus their stories emerge as inadequate not only at the global level of plot-organized action-structure but also, and relatedly, at the more local level of interrelating the relevant component facets of a single event complex. In our sample, this ability becomes manifest from late preschool age, and is consolidated during the early years of schooling in the cultures represented by these children.

4. DEVELOPMENTAL PROFILES

A major finding of this study has been the fact that despite the impact of native-language grammar and rhetoric on the texts produced by the children in our sample (see Chapter VB; and also Slobin, 1991), our texts are identifiable by age group across the five languages. Texts produced by all 58 children aged 3 to 4 years old are recognizable as typical of 3-year-olds and as distinct from those of the 5-year-olds, which in turn differ markedly from the 9-year-olds, while all of these differ again from the mature narratives of our adult respondents. Further, the narratives of the 4-year-olds in the languages for which these are available (English, Hebrew, and Spanish) demonstrate a developmental transition between the younger 3-year-olds and the older 5-year-old preschoolers. Similarly, narratives produced by 7-year-olds (available in Hebrew and Turkish) form a bridge between late preschool age and our oldest group of children, the 9-year-olds.

In this section we delineate properties characterizing the texts produced by members of four different age groups — 3 years, 5 years, 9 years, and adults — generalized across the five languages. Different features are focused on in each of the four group profiles. For instance, individual style and variability are noted particularly in relation to the youngest children (Section 4.1) and the adults (4.4), while use of evaluative devices applies mainly to the oldest children (4.3) and adults (4.4) in our sample. Nonetheless, each of the four profiles is analyzed along a single developmental continuum representing four phases which we identified in the evolution of narrative capacities: (a) spatially-motivated linking of utterances as picture-by-picture description (3-year-olds), (b) temporal organization at a local level of interclausal sequential chaining of events (most 5-year-olds), (c) sequential and/or causal chaining of partially elaborated events (most 9-year-olds), and (d) global organization of entire texts around a unified action-structure (some 9-year-olds, and the adults).

Analyses of the role of temporal and locative "referential frames" in narrative construction have benefited from the insights of Christiane von Stutterheim's largescale research into text construction of second language learners (von Stutterheim, 1987; see also von Stutterheim & Klein, 1989). Many of the conclusions summarized in the developmental profiles presented in this chapter echo independent findings focusing on acquisition of discourse structure in relation to **temporality**, as delineated in Chapter IVA. There, detailed analysis is provided mainly with respect to the German and Turkish texts, whereas this chapter relies largely on English and Hebrew for examples.

The notion of "action-structure" adopted here is anchored in analyses of "degrees of narrativity" in which (adult) subjects were required to evaluate and to state the main idea of narrative texts structured in various ways (Shen, 1990, in press). Those authors distinguish three principles of narrative organization, based on the types of connective relationships manifested within a text. Each of these three levels of narrative structure — temporality, causality, and action-structure — precedes and entails the other, in that order. Their analysis provides a totally independent motivation for the **developmental** progression evidenced by our sample of narratives produced by children at different ages, as discussed here and in Chapters IIB and IVD.

4.1. The 3-Year-Olds

In Section 2 we noted that only one out of nearly 60 3-year-olds in our sample produced an account which meets our criteria for expression of narrative structure in terms of global plotline. In general, although 3-year-olds have considerable command of the lexico-syntax of their native tongue, they fail to demonstrate knowledge of narrative structure. In this, as in other ways detailed here, the youngest group of children differs quite dramatically from all the rest.

Of all the children we approached, 3-year-olds were the only ones who in many cases found the actual task of telling such a long and complicated story beyond the limits of their powers of attention and interest. As a result, in different countries, large numbers of 3-year-olds were interviewed who were not included in our database, since they either refused or failed to talk about the picturebook at all. Tanya Renner (1988, p. 83) describes her experience with the American 3-year-olds as follows:

> In fact it took some 60 sessions with 60 different 3-year-old children to obtain 12 usable stories. About half of the stories that were not usable were either too minimal and/or too unintelligible to transcribe. The other half had to be left out because the children succeeded in obtaining inappropriate prompts from the investigator (i.e., prompts that included temporal and/or causal information).

The children in this age group whose accounts we analyzed all produced texts which relate to the contents of at least some of the pictures in the book. And, as noted, they all relate to them as depicting dynamic events, not merely combinations of objects. These abilities are evident in the 3-year-old English texts reproduced in (20) and (21). (Across these profiles, two English texts are used to illustrate each age group, the first no more than 20 clauses long, relating to only part of the pictures, the other longer, containing more elaborative detail. The texts are reproduced for referential content, with prosodic features of stress, intonation, and emphatic articulations as well as disfluencies [pauses, hesitations, false starts and other repairs] largely edited out.)

(20) *It's a bee. There's a dog. And there's a frog, and slippers, and another slipper, and there's boots. He's wake up! They put her head in the pot. Going down. The dog barked, and here they calling frog. There's bees. And the hole in the tree. Ack! A owl. And he's running through there and he fell off. Look, oh he's up there! He's awake. He fell off, and he fell off of - in the pool. And there's no head! Then there's a frog. See, he caughted a frog. [E3e-3;8]*

(21) *This dog is looking into the bowl. And then the frog is still in there. And now, look what happened. And now, he got away. The frog got away, and then, look what happened. He tried to go in, but, see, he didn't, couldn't go in! And then, he licked the boy, and he was mad! And then, some bees came out of the tree, and then he tried to get the bees, but he couldn't. And then he looked into the hole, and see, there's a mouse coming! And then he climbed a tree - he tried to climb the tree, but look what happened. Owl came out. See, he - and then the bees, he waked up the other bees, and then they chased after the dog! And then he got on top of here, and of these. But look what happened! A reindeer! And then ... they all splash into the water! See, and look it. And then - he got out of the water, and he looked over it. And then there was frogs! Just like the thing, the frog have. His friend! And oh, just like them! And*

then the frog jumped, and then the other frog, while he say "Yah!" And then the end. [E3f-3;9]

4.1.1. Interactive and personalized 3-year-old accounts

One feature of the 3-year-olds which distinguishes them from the other children is their tendency to personalize their accounts, as in exhortations to *look* and *see!* in (20) and (21). They also often digress from the contents of the pictures. For example, one child says: 'I see that the boy and the dog look at the frog. He lies on the small bed. But I've got a big big bed! Bigger even than my sister. And I've got a ...' [*H3d-3;6*]. Some of them preface their statements by first-person hedges or comments, for instance, *I know that the boy took the top, I hope he doesn't fall down, I think that's the baby owl* [*E3g-3;9*]. Others make comments about how they are progressing with the task at hand, e.g., *I'm not gonna tell you this one* [*E3d-3;5*]. In general, the 3-year-olds treat the task as interactive and personalized, and require far more confirmatory prompts and interviewer encouragement than other age groups. Tanya Renner (1988) notes that the American 3-year-olds' descriptions "were almost exclusively conversational ... and their use of conversational strategies to engage the listener in a speechtime-oriented turntaking interaction was overwhelming. It was virtually impossible for the listener to remain silent while 'listening' to a child in this group 'tell the story'."

This thrust to an interactive discourse mode among the 3-year-olds is consistent with the way in which adults in these cultures provide young preschoolers with rich conversational scaffolding. An ongoing study of children's accounts of a personal experience (Berman, in press-c), asked to tell about a fight or a quarrel they had taken part in, reveals that even 3-year-olds are capable of producing a short "storylike" text, but that they need constant prompting from the interlocutor, often in a one-to-one question-answer kind of interchange (and see, too, Hoppe-Graffe, Schoeler, & Schell, 1981). Moreover, Reilly's (1992) analysis of affective elements in the frog-story narrations produced by English-speaking 3- and 4-year-olds compared with 7- and 8-year-olds reveal that the younger group rely significantly more on paralinguistic accompaniments to their accounts, in the form of facial expressions, gestures, and most particularly prosodic features such as pitch contouring, vocalic lengthening, and phonological stress. Three-year-olds in different settings, and ones whose "frog stories" are analyzed for paralinguistic effects as well as linguistic content, like the ones in our crosslinguistic sample, clearly have expectations of what is involved in child-adult interchange which are rather different than those of schoolgoers and even of the 5-year-olds we investigated (typically attending kindergarten or its equivalent in the different countries). One result of the younger children's tendency to personalize their accounts, and to treat the request to "tell a story" as an interactive communicative undertaking, is that the 3-year-old texts are more variable and idiosyncratic than those of the older children.

4.1.2. Picture saliency versus narrative importance

Another source of intersubject variability among the 3-year-olds is the individual choices of each child as to what to talk about. These differ more than among the older subjects, since the immature 3-year-old narratives are not bound by considerations of relevance to overall plotline (Section 2) or relative "importance" of a given picture to the ongoing plot in terms discussed by Marchman (1989).

Marchman investigated the organizational structure of the story in the frog book, isolated from the task of telling the story. She used respondent judgments to identify the "importance units" in the story and to see which series of pictures cluster together. Sixty-four adults were presented with the book and asked to consider how "important each picture was to understanding the overall story" and "whether the story could be understood without this picture" (p. 25). The following definition of episodes results from this analysis, giving mean importance ratings on a scale from 5 for "very important" to 1 for "not so important" across the pictures: Pictures 1 to 3, which Marchman termed **Setting**, rated 3.6; Pictures 4 and 5, labeled **Instantiation**, rated 2.4; Pictures 6 and 7 — **Dog/fall** — 2.4; Pictures 8 to 10 — **Gopher/bees** — 2.4; Pictures 11 to 13 — **Owl** — 2.4; Pictures 14 to 18 — **Deer** — 3.1; Pictures 19 to 21 — **Pond** — 3.1; and Pictures 22 to 24, termed **Resolution**, rated 4.3. That is, highest ranking was accorded to pictures that correspond largely to what we defined in Section 2 as component I — onset or initiating goal — and component III — plot resolution or outcome. (See Chapter IVD, and also Bamberg & Marchman, 1990, 1992).

Marchman's findings are largely consistent with those of Shen (1985), who had subjects read a short folktale and then specify what they considered to be its central topic, yielding an importance hierarchy which he defines in terms of the factors of evaluative focus, poetic preferences, and causal organization. Quite different considerations motivate young children's decisions as to what they find noteworthy enough to talk about in relation to this picturebook story. For instance, Marchman's adult subjects rated the "owl" episode relatively low in importance from the point of view of overall plot development. Yet **all** of the 3- and 4-year-old English- and Hebrew-speaking children refer to this episode, and nearly all of them explicitly describe the boy's falling from the tree, while several of the adults fail to even mention this. The younger children always find the boy's fall from the tree "interesting" enough to talk about, even though it makes little contribution to development of the plot, and so can be treated as dispensable in mature accounts of how the plot unfolds. That is, for young children, the salience of **individual pictured scenes** is what counts, rather than a structurally motivated hierarchy of narrative importance.

4.1.3. Lack of temporal anchoring: Tense mixing and shifting

Further evidence for the fact that, across the languages, the 3-year-olds produce descriptions based on individual picture frames and/or isolated events rather than thematically organized narratives is the way they use **grammatical tense**. An oral text related from a picturebook story allows the narrator to select either present or past as the tense in which to anchor the narrative.[13] This is shown by choice of dominant tense (defined as 75% of all finite verbs in a text) by the adults in our sample: Approximately one-third choose the past tense, the rest select present tense. In view of the tendency of young children to relate to events in the here and now, and the assumption that they might treat the pictured events as concurrent with their telling, we had predicted that the younger children would prefer to anchor their narratives in the present, whereas older children might observe the narrative convention of using past tense throughout.

But in fact, half of the 3-year-olds across the languages manifest "mixed" tense usage, veering back and forth from present to past, as illustrated in the English text in (20). The 3-year-olds quite generally fail to establish a single grammatical tense as a means of temporal anchoring for their account as a unified whole (with the marked exception of the German sample, nearly all of whose texts are restricted to present tense; see Chapter IIIB). We interpret this as indicating that they are unable to remain anchored within a consistent narrative mode, but keep moving into and out of the picture-describing mode. Moreover, their **shifts** from one tense, or from one grammatical aspect, to another is typically not thematically motivated. Rather, it is based on local considerations, such as the move from describing a static to a dynamic situation, or from a durative activity like calling or running to a change-of-state event like having fallen or being caught. This lack of a clear and consistent "anchor tense" among many of the 3-year-olds is another reason for the variability noted in their narrations — both within individual texts and across different children in this age group. It shows that they have not yet established a unified narrative thread, in which grammatical tense serves to establish text cohesion and coherence, providing a temporal anchoring which

---

[13] This option in fact exists for a wide variety of narrative discourse, including literary texts (Fleischman, 1990).

is consistently distinct from time of speech. This contrasts, as we shall see, with the older children who, from age 5 years up, largely favor one tense, either present or past.

4.1.4. Inter-utterance connectivity

The 3-year-olds are distinct, too, in how they express links between the different parts of a text. Their markings of text connectivity are typically **utterance-initial**, specifying that something more is about to be added to the discourse, rather than syntactically **clause-introducing** or thematically **text-embedded** (Berman, in press-c). And they typically rely on **spatial co-presence** rather than on temporal sequencing as the principle of text-structuring (see, further, Chapter IVA). A favored type of utterance-initial connective in the 3-year-old texts is a deictic pointer, such as English *here, here's, in here* and equivalents in the other languages: German *da, hier*, Spanish *aquí*, Hebrew *po, kan, hine*, and Turkish *burda*. These expressions occur substantially more in the 3-year-old texts, per subject and per group, than elsewhere in our sample. They show that the 3-year-olds tend to focus on the spatial arrangements of the pictures rather than on an overall temporal frame of reference.

This descriptive, picture-to-picture mode is also reflected in the tendency to **enumerate** events or states if they occur in contiguous picture frames. The children use expressions like English *again, another, this one too*, corresponding to Hebrew *od pa'am* 'again', *gam* 'also', or German *weiter* 'further', *auch* 'also' in a way that shows they construe the pictures as separate items rather than as parts of an integrated narrative. These "additive" expressions go beyond the locative focus of the deictic connectives, by explicitly relating to **recurrence** — of the same event such as falling or climbing or of the same participant in different pictures. But the effect, again, is of a discourse structure in which individual utterances are added to one another as pieces of information, each of which has equal weight, rather than as temporally, causally, or thematically related.

Some 3-year-olds rely on 'and' to show that, at the very least, something more is about to be said or, at most, that two or more pieces of information somehow hang together (Berman, in press-c), as in the examples in (22). (As discussed in Chapters IIIE and IVC, 'and' is, for typological reasons, not an option for young children in Turkish.)

(22) **3-year-old uses of 'and' for describing pictures** (from Slobin, 1989):

(a)   *A owl. Flew out of here. And he's running away. [E3a-3;1]*

(b)   *Da kommt ein Vogel. Und da rennt er.*

'There comes a bird. **And** there he runs'. *[G3l-3;3]*

(c) *Salió un pájaro inmenso. Y un niñito se cayó de cabeza así.*

'A huge bird came out. **And** a little boy fell on his head like this'. *[S3-3;3]*

(d) *Hine yanshuf. Ve hine hayeled nafal.*

'Here's an owl. **And** here the boy fell (down)'. *[H3d-3;6]*

Other 3-year-olds reflect a sense of narrative sequentiality through use of temporal connectives such as *and then, afterwards.* The English text in (21), above, is a typical example: Even though the child's account is not thematically coherent, it is rendered textually cohesive through the opening use of deictic *now* and the subsequent repeated use of sequential *and then.*

A few 3-year-olds also occasionally make a syntactically explicit distinction between foregrounded events and associated background circumstances within the scope of adjacent clauses, as in the following examples.

(23a) *He was just sitting on the edge with his dog and pow! Into the water!* *[E3d-3;5]*

(23b) *They came right back to see their mom cause I think they were missing their mom. [E3g-3;9]*

(23c) 'And here he fell because the owl pushed him.' *[H3c-3;5]*

But these, as noted, are few and far between; they are often not overly indicated by conventional linguistic markers of coordination or subordination, and they are restricted to a very local level of two or at most three clauses.

The emergence of a more globally organized temporal structure is heralded in several ways. First, as noted, one child in this sample *[H3d-3;4]* does organize her account around the three major plot components (Example 7). Also, at a local level, all of these children can talk about events and they can refer to them as having taken place by appropriate — although not always consistently sustained — use of past-tense forms. Moreover, several 3-year-olds use utterance-initial connectives which show that they recognize they are engaged in producing an extended discourse, as a basis for emerging textual cohesion. But their accounts are as yet far from being thematically coherent. By age 5, children prove far better able to coordinate these two facets of the narrative task.

4.2. The 5-year-olds

The 5-year-olds do not form a homogeneous group — not because of the idiosyncratic perspectives and individual variation from one child to the next noted for the 3-year-olds, but because they produce types of narrations which differ from two orthogonal points of view. In terms of **narrative structure**, some 5-year-olds, as shown in (25), construct globally structured and thematically motivated narratives, whereas others relate to only one or at the most two of the major plot elements, and fail to organize their accounts around the continued search for the frog, as in (24). In terms of **linguistic expression**, some 5-year-olds use elaborate syntax and rich lexicon, whereas others produce juvenile-sounding texts with impoverished linguistic devices.

The three examples we selected from the English-speaking 5-year-olds illustrate some of this variety: Text (24) is linguistically **and** structurally nonelaborated; (25) manifests juvenile linguistic expression but is thematically well-constructed; (26) is excerpted from a long text and demonstrates a third combination: rich linguistic means serving the purpose of picture description, but not an organized narrative.

(24) *And then he - they were going to sleep, and then he's gonna go out the window. And then he had a jar stuck on his head ... And then they were calling for the frog, and then he breaks the jar. There's a beehive and a gopher. And the beehive fell down, and they look in the tree, and they start calling. And they think that's sticks, but it's a - an antler. And then they run, and then they go in the water. And behind that log is frogs. There's some more frogs, and there's another frog. The boy goes in the water, and they look and watch. Oh, there's one! He can't get up. [E5d-5;6]*

(25) *When the boy and the dog were asleep the frog jumped out of the jar. And then the boy and the dog woke up. The frog was gone. Then the boy got dressed, and the dog stuck his head in the jar. And then the boy opened up his window and called out for his frog, and the dog still had the jar on his head. Then the dog fell, and the boy was scared. And then the boy was mad at the dog, and picked him up. And then he called for his frog again. He called in a hole, and the dog called in the beehive. And the dog got some bees out of the hive. And then the dog made the beehive fall, and all the bees came out of the beehive. And the boy looked in the tree. And then the boy fell out, and the owl was flying, and the bees were flying after the dog. And the boy got up on some rocks, and the owl flew away. And the boy was calling for his frog on the rocks. And a deer ... the boy got caught on the deer's antlers. And then the deer carried him over a cliff and threw him. And the boy and the dog fell, and they splashed in some water. And they looked, and they saw a log. And the boy said "shh" to the dog. And they looked over the log. And they saw the frog, and some baby frogs too. And the boy said goodbye to the frogs, and brought a baby frog home. [E5l-5;11]*

(26) *Well, there was a little boy, he liked his pet frog and his pet dog very much. The pets think that the little boy was proud of them. And then he*

was sleeping one night, and when he woke up, then the frog got out of the bowl and he went somewhere else. So he looked in his boots, dog looked in the jar, and he was very worried about him. So the boy called out for the frog, and the little dog was stuck in the jar. And then the dog ran out of the window and broke the glass, and the boy came out in his big boots and carried the dog inside. [E5b-5;2]

4.2.1. Temporal anchoring

Unlike the younger children, most of the 5-year-old texts show clear signs of a temporal organization, and the structural principle underlying them is temporal, or temporal and spatial combined, rather than nontemporal. One such indicator is choice of grammatical tense as a linguistic marker of a narrative perspective on the task. The breakdown for this is quite consistent among the 5-year-olds in English, Spanish, Hebrew, and Turkish (the German narrations are predominantly in present tense from age 3 years to adults). Two or three children in each language group are like the 3-year-olds in having unstable use of tense. However, where they switch back and forth, it is generally across larger segments of text than in the case of the highly variable usage of the younger children — as in the English example in (24). The rest of the 5-year-olds are like the older children (and the adults) in each language. They anchor their narratives consistently in past or present tense — as in the highly typical English past-tense narratives in (25) and (26). In this, they show that they can relate the events depicted in the pictures to a fictive world that is not concurrent with the time of speaking.

4.2.2. Interclausal connectivity: The development of chaining

Temporal organization is also reflected in the linguistic means which children at this age across the languages use to express the idea that events occur in **sequence** or **simultaneously** (Chapter IVA). Evidence of this development is provided by the type of sequential connectives which occur across the 5-year-old texts, taking over from the deictic markers used by 3-year-olds. Even the globally inadequate text in (24) manifests sequential chaining of one utterance to the next, and of one event to another, by means of the form *and then*. And in (25), nearly every clause opens with one of the three connectives *and*, *then*, or *and then*, which serve to chain one event to the next in ongoing narrative sequence. This is typical of most of the 5-year-olds in the different languages (see, for example, the ubiquitous *axarey ze* 'after that' in Hebrew as discussed in Berman, 1988, in press-c; and further examples are provided in the sections on connectivity in Part III, as well as in Chapter IVA).

The 5-year-olds use these overt markers of connectivity for the purpose of **chaining clauses** within extended discourse, going well beyond the **utterance linking** functions of connectivity markings noted for the 3-year-olds. These children in general use a variety of different temporal expressions — e.g., **when** *they're asleep* / **and after** *went out looking for the frog* / **while** *the dog was running away from the bees [E5e-5;8]*; 'and **after that** the boy slept / and **then** he called to the bees / and the dog **meanwhile** looked at the hive / **now** they're coming out' *[H5e-5;3]*. These all indicate that 5-year-olds are relying on a more narratively motivated temporal schema of one event following another rather than the predominantly spatial framing of one picture after another favored by 3-year-olds.

On the other hand, the textual cohesiveness provided by these overt markings of connectivity is generally confined to a narrowly **local** level of organization. There are few indications that the 5-year-olds are relating to larger units of discourse beyond two or three adjacent utterances. And they use syntactic subordination as a means of event-packaging far less than the school-age children in the different languages (Chapter IVC).

4.2.3. Organization of narrative segments

A final indicator of the mixed or transitional nature of the 5-year-olds is the variation they show within and across texts in description of individual scenes. Some children demonstrate an ability to produce well-constructed segments of narrative. That is, they organize chunks of discourse so that background scene-setting is explicitly set off from foreground plot-advancing events by a combination of segment-marking connectives such as *so, and, then,* choice of dynamic versus stative predicates, and explicit temporal anchoring of events by expressions such as *one day, in the morning.* This is clear from the opening lines of the two 5-year-old texts in (27) and (28), below.

(27) *Once upon a time there was a little boy who had a frog and a dog. And it was time to go to sleep, so he went to sleep.* **And in the middle of the night** *his frog creeped out of its jar, so* **in the morning** *the little boy said "Where is my frog?" [E5i-5;10]*

(28) 'Once there was a boy and he had a dog and he had a frog. **So one day in the night** the frog went out of the jar that she had and **in the morning** the boy and the dog looked ...' [H5d-5;3]

These 5-year-olds show a high level of discourse organization; they are able to make a clear functional distinction between the scene-setting background (of Pictures 1 and 2) with the onset of the plotline in Picture 3. But these two children, and other 5-year-olds like them, are generally unable to sustain this level of complexity across their texts. As noted in Section 2, the 5-year-olds also do far worse than 9-year-olds in verbalizing the complex situations involved in the boy's discovery that the frog has gone, and in the boy's landing up on the deer's antlers. And they are generally unable to make explicit the causal relationship between these events and subsequent plot development. Analysis of other episodes in the story — the dog getting his head stuck in the jar, the owl emerging from the hole and the boy falling from the tree, or the dog being chased by the bees — shows that 5-year-olds for the most part describe what happened without relating to the associated causal circumstances surrounding the events. For example, a child might say *The dog went into the glass and he couldn't get it off [E5f-5;8]* without relating to the glass as the object where the frog had been kept. And a string of event descriptions such as *And the boy looked in the tree, and then the boy fell out, and the owl was flying [E5l-5;11]* suggests that these children are still constructing parts of their texts utterance by utterance, rather than within a hierarchically-organized global framework.

4.3. The 9-Year-Olds

The 9-year-old children are 4th and 5th graders who know how to read and write. They have had several years of formal schooling, and have been exposed to narrative texts in the context of classroom study and home reading. In this, they differ markedly from the 5-year-olds.

In terms of overall narrative structure, almost all the 9-year-olds across the five languages make explicit reference to the two key plot components of the plot: the boy's discovery that his frog is missing and his extended search for his missing pet (Table 1). These children all produce texts which give evidence of what we have characterized as a sustained narrative mode. For one thing, they overwhelmingly select a specific grammatical tense as a consistent temporal anchor to their narratives. Past tense is favored by most English and Hebrew 9-year-olds, and present tense by most German, Spanish, and Turkish 9-year-olds, and only one 9-year-old out of nearly 50 idiosyncratically moved from present tense in the initial and final segments of her text to past tense for the rest *[H9a-9;0]*.[14]

---

[14] There is no obvious explanation for this difference in the preference for past tense among American and Israeli schoolchildren compared with their German, Spanish, and Turkish peers. Favored storytelling styles in children's literature and in classroom contexts in the different countries might have some impact in this connection. Katrin Lindner (University of Munich) and Cornelia Müller (Free University of Berlin) have carried out an unpublished survey of 77 German children's books, written for children between 3 and 8 years of age. They found that 51% of these books are in the past tense, and that these were either "stories about something extraordinary outside the real world" or "stories that deal with everyday

Examples (29) and (30), below, are of English 9-year-old texts in present and past tense, respectively. They exemplify the two later developmental phases across the narrative continuum noted in the introduction to Section 4: (a) spatially-motivated utterance linking of picture-by-picture description (3-year-olds); (b) temporal organization at a local level of interclausal sequential chaining of events (most 5-year-olds); (c) sequential and/or causal chaining of partially elaborated events (text 29), like most 9-year-olds; and (d) global organization of entire texts around a unified action-structure (text 30), like some 9-year-olds, and all the adults.

(29) *There's a boy who has a pet frog and a pet dog, and one night after he goes to bed the frog sneaks out. And he wakes up and it's gone. So he and his dog look all over the place for it. So then they go outside and start calling for it. The dog falls out of the win - the dog had got the jar stuck on his head, and he falls out of the window and it breaks and the little boy picks it up. And they start calling after the frog, and the dog starts sniffing some bees. And then he looks in a hole, and the dog's looking at this beehive. Then some little gopher comes up and then the dog's still looking at that beehive. So then the beehive falls and all the bees are - they start chasing after him, and he um - the little boy climbs up a tree and looks into a hole, and an owl flies out, and he falls off the tree. And the bees are chasing after the dog. So the owl flies up and then he stands up on the rock and hangs onto some branches. Then it turns out they're antler - a deer's antlers, so he gets - he lands on his head. And the deer starts running and he tips him off over a cliff into the water, and he lands. But they're both okay, so then he says to his dog "shhh," and they peek over the log and there's two frogs. And then there's a little family of frogs and I guess one frog is his, so he gets one of the little baby frogs, and that's it. [E9k-9;11]*

This is a well-organized narrative from the point of view of plot initiation (*So he and his dog look all over the place for it. So then they go outside*

---

events/activities that are of a pedagogical nature." The frog story is certainly like the first category, indicating that there is a model in German children's literature for past-tense narratives, although they hardly ever occur in our sample. On the other hand, the 43% of books in the present tense (ignoring 6% with mixed tense usage) included, among various real-world topics, stories "that provide solutions to problems" and stories "that contain dreamlike events that could be part of children's everyday life." It is also of interest that parents and shopkeepers believe that books written in the present tense are "easier" for younger children. (We are grateful to Katrin Lindner and Cornelia Müller for sharing these findings with us.) It appears, then, that German children's experience with literature written for this age range would give them models for both present and past tense versions of stories such as *Frog, where are you?*. This topic warrants further investigation.

and start calling for it) and plot resolution (*I guess one frog is his, so he gets one of the little baby frogs*). But the middle section, where a series of goal-oriented activities is elaborated, is characterized by **sequential event-chaining** much like that associated with younger, 5-year-old narratives. [15]

The 9-year-old narrative in (30), which is anchored in past tense, reveals a more explicitly global structure organized around the onset and elaboration (*So they went off to find his pet frog ... and he stood on the rock and called the frog*) as well as resolution of the search for the missing frog (*and so the frog let them have one of his babies, instead of him*). Moreover, on a more local level, there is (sometimes exaggeratedly) explicit reference to **causal** and not merely temporally sequential connections between series of events (for example: *So they went off to find his pet frog / The bees started to chase him, 'cause the beehive fell / And then the dog was running away because the bees were all chasing him, and he had fallen down because an owl poked him out of the tree*).

(30) *Once there was a boy who had a pet frog and a dog. And that night he was watching it. And when he went to sleep, the frog got out of his jar and got away. The next morning, when he woke up, he saw that the frog was gone. So he put on his clothes, and the dog accidentally got his head stuck in the jar which the frog was kept in. They called out the window, and the dog fell down, and the glass jar broke, and the boy was mad at him. So they went off to find his pet frog. And he looked in a hole, and the dog was chasing the beehive. It was a home to a ground squirrel. And he got his nose scratched. And the dog was still over playing with the bees. The bees started to chase him, 'cause the beehive fell. The boy was calling the frog in this tree. And then the dog was running away, because the bees were all chasing him, and he had fallen down because an owl poked him out of the tree. And the bees chased the dog, and the dog chased the boy to a rock, and he stood on the rock and called the frog. But a deer was on top, and it got him by his horns, and carried him to the edge of a cliff, with his dog chasing after, and threw them both into the lake, that was down below, and they both fell in. And then they heard some frogs chirping on the other side of the log. So they went to the log, and they went over and saw his pet frog with a mate. And when they climbed over they saw that he had babies, too, and so the frog let them have one of his babies, instead of him. [E9a-9;1]*

---

[15] Moreover, the referential distinctions between the various participants being talked about are often less than clear, indicating that this is not yet a fully mature narrative text (Bamberg, 1987; Karmiloff-Smith, 1980, 1981; Wigglesworth, 1990, 1992).

4.3.1. A twofold temporal structure

Like the other 9-year-old accounts, these two texts reflect a narrative structure in which the time axis of events, and in some instances the causal relation between them, serve as organizing factors. They demonstrate an ability for quite elaborate backgrounding and indication of temporal transitions well beyond what was evident in the 5-year-old texts. (Consider the complex thread evidenced by the description: *and then the dog's still looking at that beehive* in (29); or: *the dog was still over playing with the bees* in (30).) The sequence of pictures has been transformed into an abstract representation of a temporally sequential chain of events, embedded into particular situational contexts. In terms further delineated in Chapter IVA, in other words, the temporal thread of discourse — the adventures of the boy and his dog in search of their missing frog — has become independent from the time axis of perception — the pictures in the storybook.

On the other hand, the dual nature of picturebook narrations is reflected in occasional shifts into the descriptive mode, as in the following:

(31a) *And **over here** there's a mole.* [E9b-9;3]

    *And the beaver, I mean ... the gopher, **looks like** he bit him on the nose or something.* [E9f-9;8]

    *And then a mole ... or a ... **looks like** a gopher, a gopher popped his head out.* [E9i-9;10]

(31b) *Ve **po** hem amru lahem shalom.* 'And **here** they said goodbye to them'. [H9l-9;8]

    Po ha-karpada she hem mac'u. '**Here** (is) the-toad that they found.' [H9i-9;7]

    Kan hu kore, hu kore la-cfardea. '**Here** he calls, he calls to-the-frog.' [H9f-9;6]

4.3.2. Temporal and causal chaining

These deviations from the temporal thread of narrative to picturebook description are rare in the 9-year-old narratives. On the other hand, the 9-year-olds typically fail to reveal a fully-developed ability to organize their accounts in terms of an overall **action-structure** which goes beyond temporal or even causal interrelating at the local level of contiguous events, hence of adjacent clauses. This difference is shown in the more mature structure of text (30) compared with (29), which is more typical of the 9-year-olds. Most narrators of this age persist in presenting one event after the other in a series, with the events both linked and separated by heavy reliance on temporal shifters such as those meaning *then* or *afterwards*, to a lesser degree by causal connectives such as *because, so*. Over two-thirds of the English 9-year-olds introduce the bulk of the clauses in their narrative by the coordinator *and* or the sequential marker *(and) then*, while Hebrew 9-year-olds favor clause-initiation either by *ve* 'and' or sequentials such as *az* 'then', *axarkax* 'afterwards', or *pit'om* 'suddenly'. This gives the effect of each episode being assigned equal weight, even though these episodes are both more elaborated and more thematically-motivated than the utterance-by-utterance or picture-by-picture basis of the younger children's narrations.

4.3.3. Local and global backgrounding

The 9-year-olds' tendency to refer to **causal** as well as sequential and other temporal relationships is consistent with a more general development in the ability to relate the happenings shown in the pictures to background circumstances. This is shown by the increased use of relative clauses and nonfinite verbs forms as syntactic means for differentiating between contiguous events so that one is backgrounded with respect to the other (e.g., *hu histakel al ha-dvorim **she afu me ha-kaveret*** 'he looked at the-bees **that flew out.of the-hive**' [*H9f-9;6*]; *and the boy stuck his head in a hole **looking for the frog*** [*E9i-9;10*] — and see, further, Chapters IVA and IVB).

A related development is the ability to provide thematic unity through prospection ahead to events which have not yet occurred and through retrospection back to events which took place earlier in a way not found in any of the preschool accounts. Half of the English 9-year-olds provide **prospective summaries** of the search which the boy is about to initiate, a theme which then recurs at other points further along in the text, e.g., *So they went off to find his pet frog ... [E9a-9;1]; And then he goes looking for him in the woods [E9b-9;3]*. These provide thematic background to reinstantiations of the search theme across their stories and constitute summary statements not found among the younger children (see Chapter IVD).

As an instance of **retrospection**, note that half of the Hebrew 9-year-olds, but none of the preschool children, describe the jar which the dog stuck its head into (Picture 5) as the one which the frog had been kept in or had escaped from (Picture 2), e.g., *ha-kelev hixnis et harosh shelo letox ha-cincenet **mimena barxa ha-cfardea*** 'the-dog inserted its head into the-jar **from.which escaped the-frog**' [*H9a-9;0*], *ha-kelev hixnis et harosh letox ha-kli **she ha-cfardea hayta bo*** 'the-dog inserted its head into the-dish **that the-frog was in**' [*H9f-9;6*]. These show the beginnings of an overall "action-structure" based thematic organization, moving out of the purely sequential chaining of more immature accounts of these events.

4.3.4. Evaluative references to states of mind

The 9-year olds also differ considerably from the younger children in the extent to which they attribute inner states and affective responses to the protagonists — as in relation to the boy's discovery that his frog has run away (Section 2). This is consistent with findings for the English narrators, in which 9-year-olds and adults use evaluation devices in general, particularly with reference to "frames of mind," far more than younger children (Bamberg & Damrad-Frye, 1991). The few times that 4- and 5-year-olds characterize the boy (and/or the dog or even one of the other animals) as being 'sad' or 'angry', they typically do so in relation to states which are visible in the pictures. Only half of the English 5-year-olds and even fewer (3 out of 12) Hebrew 5-year-olds refer to the protagonists as having emotions. The repertoire of such states is also very limited, mainly describing the boy as being 'angry' or 'mad' at the dog when the jar broke (Picture 7) while two English 5-year-olds describe the boy (or dog) as being *scared* by the owl, bees, or deer and one Hebrew 5-year-old says they were 'happy' (*samxu*) to find a frog. In contrast, nearly all the 9-year-olds in these two languages (80%) attribute emotions to one or other of the protagonists. In addition to frequent reference to the boy (and/or dog) as being *scared* or *afraid* (Hebrew *nivhal, paxadu*), English 9-year-old children describe the boy as *concerned, worried*, or *excited* and the dog as *curious, interested*, or *whimpering*, while Hebrew 9-year-olds commonly describe the boy (and/or the dog) as being pleased or happy and occasionally as sad.[16]

Evaluative commentary attributing inner states to the protagonists demands a level of inference abstracted away from what is shown in the pictures beyond the abilities of the younger children in our sample. Compare, for instance, the following introduction to a 9-year-old narrative:

(32) 'A little boy caught a frog, and at night he watches his frog. He **thinks that it is happy** but **actually it does not want** to be kept a prisoner.' [H9i-9;7]

In cognitive terms, this ability to attribute feelings, intentions, and states of mind to one being (the frog) as conceived of mentally by another (the boy-hero) represents a high level of development in the domain of what has come to be known as "theory of mind" (see, for example, Astington & Gopnik, 1991; Gopnik, 1993; and, in relation to the English-language texts in our

---

[16] Aylin Küntay and Keiko Nakamura (1993), in a study carried out at Berkeley, have found that Turkish and Japanese narrators, of all ages, rarely make observations about the emotional states of protagonists in the frog story. This, then, is another area which warrants crosscultural examination, in addition to the crosslinguistic analyses we have undertaken.

sample, see also Trabasso & Stein, in press). From the point of view of narrative development, this ability is critical for achievement of a rich interplay between foregrounded plot-advancing events and backgrounded plot-motivating comments — and it is far removed from the associative digressions of the 3-year-olds.

These interpretative comments scattered across the 9-year-old narratives give them an elaborated evaluative flavor lacking in the more picture-bound descriptions of the younger children. Nine-year-olds who make no such comments tend to tell stories which are highly condensed and tightly organized around the central theme, with quite complex syntax. But their stories are dry and businesslike, with no personal flavor. These rather boring, yet proficient 9-year-old stories are very much in keeping with the explanations given by Karmiloff-Smith (1983, 1984) for evolution of narrative as well as other cognitive abilities. She suggests that in the middle phase of development, top-down organization may be at the expense of descriptive detail and lexical elaboration. These children have not yet reached the point where they can integrate their top-down thematically motivated narrative productions with bottom-up stylistic felicity at the local level of event description.

4.3.5. Stereotypical construal of narrative conventions

The 9-year-old narratives are remarkable in how similar they are to one another, across and within languages (and in this they differ strikingly from the adult samples). True, 9-year-olds adopt two somewhat different levels of usage: Some adhere quite closely to a classical "fairytale" tenor (with the past tense as temporal anchor), while others use less self-consciously literary language and adopt a more conversational style. Yet a highly stereotyped format is evident in these school-age texts, as evidenced, for example, in the way that nearly all start out with classical storybook openings. Both the English and Hebrew 9-year-olds use only one of four fairly formulaic opening expressions, as shown in (33).

(33) **Existence:**
   "(Once (upon a time)) there was ..."
   [*E9a, E9c, E9e, E9k*] [*H9c, H9d, H9e, H9h, H9k, H9l*]

   Entry on scene:
   "The boy finds/caught/owned a frog ..."
   [*E9b, E9f, E9g, E9h*] [*H9b, H9g, H9i, H9j*]

   Temporal setting:
   "It's nighttime, One dark night, One day ..." [*E9d, E9j*] [*H9a, H9f*]

   Narrative theme:
   "It's a story about ..." [*E9i*]

Only one out of these 24 9-year-olds plunged directly into picture description in the way that nearly all of the younger children did, starting out with: *The boy's looking at his frog [E91-9;11]*.

Indeed, what generally sets the school-age stories apart from those of both the preschoolers and adults is how stereotyped they tend to be. It is as if these 9- to 10-year-olds have a set idea of what is expected of them — perhaps because they are used to responding to adult requests for verbal performance in their school setting. They also have a firm idea of what a suitable rendering of a children's picturebook would be like, with a set beginning, middle, and end. The children are cognitively well able to describe the events in sequence, even to provide some background comments on motivations and reactions. But they differ markedly from the adults in the lack of variety they demonstrate with respect to the particular rhetorical styles they prefer and the range of expressive options they feel free to select in response to the task at hand.

4.3.6. Summary of 9-year-old profiles

The 9-year-olds present a different kind of bridge between immature and fully-developed narrators than the 5-year-olds. They construct well-organized accounts, and demonstrate good command of complex syntax, which they employ to elaborate on the descriptions both of individual events and of the relationship between one event and another. And they manifest some properties not at all typical of the younger children — particularly in their reference to causal connections and to internal states. However, by and large, their accounts are far from fully mature. They do not generally manifest narrative organization at a level subservient to the overall plot; they fail to consistently characterize backgrounded associated states and circumstances as distinct from foregrounded plot-advancing events; and their perception of the narrative task is stereotypical, rather than constituting a vehicle for individual style and self-expression. These findings thus support the observations of Labov (1972) and others who have noted that pre-adolescents still have a long way to go in the development of narrative skills.

4.4. The Adult Narratives

Our motivation in having adults perform the same task as the children, was to have a standard of comparison that would provide some theoretical "endstate model" which children should achieve in narrating the contents of a pictured story. And indeed, all the adults went beyond the 9-year-olds in the overarching thematic organization they assigned their texts. That is, as we had predicted, a mature narrative demands a global "action-structure." However, there proved to be no "standard profile" characteristic of the adult narratives. Instead, they differ considerably in several ways: how they construe the task, how they construct their narratives, and what particular expressive or rhetorical options they favor.

4.4.1. Different narrative stance and style

These differences are reflected in the two English adult narratives reproduced below. The first, in (34), is told in present tense; it is long and elaborated, and uses syntactic constructions and a level of lexical register not found in any of the children's texts. It also meets our criterion for an adequate account of this story, since it makes explicit mention of all the elements we stipulated as evidence of thematic plot structure. But this adult English narrative is reminiscent of some of the children's stories in its constant use of deictic *now* and chaining *and* as clause-introducing elements, indicative of the picture-by-picture progress guiding this piece of discourse.

(34) *This is a story of a little kid, it is just before he goes to bed one night and he looks in this jar, and he's checking out his frog. And his dog is there, and they both check out the frog. Then they both go to sleep, and the frog, unbeknownst to the two sleeping people in the bed, crawls out of the jar. The next morning the boy and the dog wake up and find the empty jar. The boy looks in his boots while the dog looks in the jar for the frog. They look out the window for the frog. The dog falls out the window, breaks the jar ... The kid goes down out the window as well, picks up the dog. The dog's, happily, rescued from having his head stuck in the jar, but the kid's a little angry - probably because he's lost his jar and his frog. The little boy and the dog go outside looking for the frog. The boy is calling for the frog and the dog is sniffing for the frog. But actually the dog is sniffing at a trail of bees coming out of a beehive. The boy sticks his - is looking down a hole to see if the frog is in the hole, and the dog is intrigued with this beehive. The boy gets his nose either bitten or sniffed at by some little animal living in the hole, and the dog is still intrigued with the beehive. Now the beehive has been knocked down out of the tree by the dog, and the bees are intrigued with the dog, while the boy is sitting in a tree looking in the hole in the tree, thinking maybe the lost frog is there. At this point an owl pops out of the hole in the tree and a bunch of bees start following the dog, probably angry that the dog has knocked their hive out of the tree. Suddenly the owl, oh no! Now the boy is running away from the owl and the boy is climbing up on a rock, and now the owl is gone for some reason and the dog is coming back. Looks like he's either stunned or is just very frightened and ashamed that he was outdone by the bees. The owl is looking at the boy, and the boy is calling for the frog. Now the boy has*

been picked up by some antlered beast, looks like a deer, and the deer is running to a cliff and the dog is barking at the deer. This dog is pretty useless, all he does is cause trouble and bark at things. Now the deer has thrown the dog - no, the boy over the cliff into - it looks like they're heading for a pond, and the dog goes too as the dog has throughout the entire story, and they both fall in the water. Then they sit up in the water and it seems like they both hear something coming from behind the log. And the dog is looking behind the log, and the boy tells the dog to be very quiet. And they crawl over the log, and they find on the other side of the log two happy frogs, one of which was the frog in the jar. And then they see that there was not only two happy frogs, but there is an entire family of little frogs there and one would wonder how long - what the gestation period is for frogs and how come they're so big, when they know they have to go through a tadpole stage first. However it seems that they've raised this happy family and maybe the boy was looking for these frogs for an entire six months to a year, who knows. Now the boy grabs one of the frogs, and leaves with his frog, leaving the two big frogs and all the tiny frogs. So it looks like he has NOT taken away his big frog that was in the jar, but he has taken away one of the sibling frogs... perhaps, one really can't tell. The end. [E20b]

The narrative in (34) is both elaborate and very straightforward, it is both adult and juvenile, it uses both syntactically complex packaging and simple clause-chaining by *and*. On the one hand, it is clearly thematically well-motivated, making explicit reference to the major plot components. On the other, it follows the pictures very closely in chronological sequencing. This is typical of one adult genre of frog stories across the sample, one which slips in and out of narrative to picture-description mode across the text.

Compare this to the shorter, more compact adult story in (35), told in the past tense. It appears totally removed from the picture-description mode, although it makes recurrent use of a self-consciously interactive element not found in the 9-year-old stories. This adult constantly punctuates the course of the narration with an exclamatory sound of surprise, *oops!*, remindful of German and Hebrew children's use of their words for 'suddenly' to set off high-point events in the narrative.

(35) *Once upon a time there was a little boy who had a frog and a dog. And after he and his doggie went to sleep one night, the frog got out of the jar and escaped. When he woke up in the morning, he saw that the frog was gone, and he was very sad. He looks in his boots and the doggie looked in the jar. Oops! The doggie got his head caught in the jar. They looked out of the window and the doggie fell out of the window, but the jar broke off his head, so he didn't have his head stuck in the jar*

anymore. The boy and the doggie went looking for the froggie all OVER the place. The boy found a beehive and the little boy went and looked in a hole for the frog. The boy found a gopher, and the dog played with the beehive some more. That was a really dangerous thing to play with. And pretty soon, well, the little boy went and looked in the hole in the tree, he better be careful, looking in all those holes. Oops! An owl flew out of the hole in the tree and knocked him down out of the tree, and the bees chased the dog. (That boy better let those bees alone.) But the owl kept bothering the little boy, but then he left him alone. The little boy went and climbed up on a big rock and called his froggie. And the dog was really sad and he didn't like all those bees bothering him. But oops! The little boy was holding onto a branch which turned out to be the antlers of a deer, and then the deer went running off with the little boy, and the doggie ran alongside because he didn't want to get separated from his master. And THEN the deer threw the doggie off the edge of a tiny cliff and the doggie fell off too, because he didn't know the cliff was coming, and they fell in some water. And when they looked up they were fine, and they heard some FROGS chirping. And they were very quiet so they could sneak up on the frogs and catch their froggie. But when they looked over the log trying to catch the frog, they found two frogs and they found some little baby frogs. They took one of the froggies away from his family of frogs and they went home. [E20i]

Unlike the adult in (34), here the narrator has entered fully into the mode of children's fairytale. The story opens in classic fairytale fashion (just about the only English adult story which does so), the hero is "the little boy" and his dog is treated throughout as the boy's companion, sometimes personalized as the "doggie" along with the "froggie." The contrast between the two texts in (34) and (35) is typical of what one finds across the adult texts. Each adult selects a particular stance for dealing with the task of telling a children's story from a children's picturebook "as naturally as possible" to an adult acquaintance thoroughly familiar with the contents of the book (Chapter IB). Once embarked on the narrative, adults feel free to recruit their own individual stylistic and rhetorical devices suited to the stance they have selected. As a result, in contrast to the narratives of the 9- and 5-year-old children across the languages, the adult narratives manifest considerable individual variation.

The adult texts in each language differ from each other along a number of dimensions, as suggested by the contrast between the English examples in (34) and (35). This is because adults make highly individual choices in availing themselves of the full repertoire of linguistic forms and of stylistic options appropriate for (a) their mother tongue, and (b) the narrative mode of discourse. As a result, we cannot pinpoint a particular type of narrative as an adult "model." Rather, the adults' accounts range from complexly elaborated narratives that provide fine details of background and attendant circumstances to short, concisely encapsulated, and closely packaged narratives. Some adults prefer the paratactic, nonembedded option as a style suited to informal, nonexpository discourse (Givón, 1979; Ochs, 1979; Tannen, 1982). Others create more densely packaged clusters of clauses with rich syntactic subordination and heavy reliance on nonfinite verb forms. As a result, several different profiles emerge across each group of adult texts. Each such "profile" represents a cluster of different rhetorical options and expressive means chosen by the narrators from a mature repertoire of linguistic forms and anchored in a mature conception of the narrative genre. And each achieves a distinct narrative rhythm by such means.[17]

4.4.2. Plot-motivation and elaboration

A major difference between adult and children's accounts is that adults embed each event within an elaborated network of background circumstances and narrator evaluations. Consider, for example, the **background** event of the boy going to sleep and the **plot-initiating** event of the frog getting out of the jar. Over half the English and Hebrew respondents across the age groups mention both events, but typically on a local level, conjoined through *and* or

---

[17] By way of example, consider the 12 Hebrew adult narratives, broken down into four types (Berman, 1990). (1) Two narrators adopt a "chaining" *and then, and then* type of style similar to that of school-age children. They manifest little subject ellipsis, and use overt pronoun subjects to establish topic maintenance. Their sentences tend to be short and clipped, and they typically coalesce no more than two or three clauses into a single "package." Their narratives are of medium length (around 65 clauses each), one in past tense, the other in present (*H20g, H20j*). (2) A slightly different profile which is also remindful of the 9-year-olds is provided by two other narrators. They also favor clauses with full SVO structure and no word order variation for pragmatic effect. However, they do hardly any chaining through coordination, but package each event-sequence together into a single cohesive unit. Choice of past tense keeps their accounts strictly within the narrative mode. But their style is very matter-of-fact, and they avoid elaborating on attendant circumstances or speculating about the protagonists (*H20a, H20l*). (3) A very compact and tightly cohesive rhythm is achieved by several Hebrew adults through different means: One (*H20k*) makes rich use of syntactic subordination together with numerous evaluative modifiers such as *be'ecem* 'actually', *kolkax* 'so very much', *sof kol sof* 'at long last'. The others (*H20e, H20f, H20h,* and *H20i*) rely heavily on subject ellipsis as a means for achieving textual cohesion, in some instances combined with rich syntactic subordination and nonfinite verb forms. (4) The last group adopt a more clearly "narrative" style. They combine use of these various devices for text connectivity interspersed with deliberate reiteration of key expressions across the narrative (e.g., the equivalent of *they continue to search ...*). They also adopt a self-consciously literary style, by means of higher-register, slightly archaic vocabulary usage and/or heavy reliance on Biblical sounding VS word order (*H20b, H20c, H20d*). (See Chapter IIID.)

temporally related by *when* or *while*. Overt reference to the relationship between these two events as one of **enablement** — hence as plot-motivated and plot-motivating — is rare among the children, even at age 9 years (17% compared with about one-third of the adults). Only adults explicitly relate the two events, e.g., *Then they both go to sleep, and the frog,* **unbeknownst to the two sleeping people in the bed,** *crawls out of the jar* [E20b]. Further examples of the impact of global, macro-level structure on mature expression of local, micro-level components of the narrative are provided from various perspectives in Chapters IVA through IVD.

Relatedly, there is a marked change in the elaborateness and degree of detail with which adult narrators refer to inner states, a difference which goes well beyond the quantitative finding that over half the adults make some mention of such attributes. None of the children provide anything like the following adult ascriptions at the outset of their accounts, in the critical initial **setting** to the story.

(36a)*They [=boy and dog] are both curious, and the frog seems to be happy. Well, eventually the boy and dog grow tired.* [E20c]

(36b)*The boy was obviously very fond of the dog, and the dog was very curious about the frog. And the frog seems to be happy in his little jar, under the boy's attention and care.* [E20k]

(36c)'Once upon a time there was a little boy that loved animals. He had a dog and a frog that he put in a jar. The boy and the dog and the frog were very good friends.' [H20e]

(36d)'Before they [=boy and dog] go to sleep, they are all excited about it [=frog], they're sort of feeling good.' [H20l]

Several adults, then, although no children, found it necessary to comment on the protagonists' frame of mind right at the outset of their accounts, setting the scene for the listener to relate to these protagonists as having thoughts and feelings — and hence to motivate their actions in what ensues.

4.4.3. Mature deployment of forms and functions

Certain other features set the adult narratives apart from those of even the more advanced 9-year-old texts in our sample. First, adults avail themselves of a richer range of expressive options. In each of the languages, the adults used certain kinds of linguistic forms and constructions which did not occur in any of the children's texts. These include lexical markers of plot-advancing sequentiality, e.g., English *eventually the boy and dog grow tired* / *where the dog was* **originally** *located* / *and he* **finally** *got the jar off his head* [E20c]. This is not merely due to a larger and more learned vocabulary, which is true for trivial reasons of the adults compared with children across the sample. It reflects a level of thematic cohesiveness — by explicit crossreferencing to protracted **clusters** of events — not evident in the children's stories. A similar example is provided by the locative terms found in adult Hebrew texts which are not used by any of the children (Hebrew adults averaged 13 different locative prepositions per text, as against an average of 10 different ones in the 9-year-old texts; see Chapter IIID.) This reflects not only a more varied, higher-register vocabulary; it also enables speakers to achieve an event-packaging which is at once both more condensed and more elaborated than the children's (e.g., talking about the fall from the cliff scene discussed in Chapter IVC).

Moreover, in each of the languages, adults deploy some forms with different functions than the children. For example, adults use forms that have a **deictic** sense in the usage of the young children with a nondeictic, discourse-anchored function, e.g., *this* in the context *the dog is intrigued by this beehive* in the sample text in (32), or *now* in a sentence like *now that the owl has been disturbed.* Grammatical constructions not found among the children include: German adults' use of present perfect verb forms as a bridging device, marking prospection towards the next episode (Bamberg, 1987; Chapters IIIB, IVD); Turkish adults' stringing of a number of nonfinite gerunds, with some joined by *ve* 'and' (Chapter IVC); and Hebrew adult use of nominalizations where children use infinitival forms of verbs (e.g., 'they continue with their pursuit' compared with 'continue to pursue') and occasional full syntactic passives (e.g *hu hutkaf al ydey shneyhem* 'he was.attacked by both of them' [*H20i*]). (See Chapters IIIA to IIIE.) These are constructions which school-age children "know," and which they can produce in other contexts. But they fail to avail themselves of these expressive options in the context of the narrative task challenging them in the present study.

At the level of global organization, several adults across the languages provide "encapsulations" of an entire series of events, again in a way not done by any of the children. Thus, adults sometimes generalize over all the different adventures and mishaps that befall the protagonist(s) in the search for the missing frog. These may be summary recapitulations of previous material (as in 37) or prospective summations of what is still to be detailed (as in 38). Thus, an English adult sums up all the various encounters (which she has already described) prior to the denouement as follows:

(37) *And oddly enough, after looking in all these, you know, strange places where other animals have their homes, and obviously not finding their frog, these animals chase them into water - which happens to be the home of the frog.* [*E20e*]

A Hebrew adult provides an encapsulating summary **before** reporting on each individual incident.

(38) 'They continued to search, continued to wander around in the forest, climbed on trees, asked animals they met on the way, fail to find the frog. On the way, when they searched, so all kinds of things waited for them in ambush on the way. Suddenly a hive of bees fell upon the dog ... and after that some kind of large bird of prey tried to attack the boy ... ' [H20e]

The following example reveals adults' tendency to stack more than one encapsulation after another.

(39) 'Right away he went out to search for it. He went out into the forest to search for it. In the forest all kinds of strange adventures befell him. He found a beehive, found a mole, and was attacked by both of them.' [H20i]

The linguistic forms employed in these excerpts are in no way beyond the ability of schoolchildren speaking these languages. They have command of the relevant syntactic constructions and they know the relevant vocabulary items. What our 9-year olds prove unable to do is organize their narrative output retrospectively as in (37) and prospectively as in (38) to generalize across whole sets of isolated episodes which share a common thematic thread. Not only are they all part of the search — a fact most of the 9-year-olds did mention quite explicitly; they also all constitute one in a chain of mishaps which befell the boy as a consequence of the animals he encountered in his search. This seems beyond the capacities, or the inclinations, of the school-children to express.

5. CONCLUSIONS

Our database differs from much of the other material examined in the rich body of psycholinguistic investigations of narrative structure over the past few decades. It concerns narrative **production** rather than comprehension or recall; it is based on a **lengthier** and more elaborated sequence of pictures than those customarily used in picture-elicitation tasks, one which goes well beyond the single-episode structure of typical personal-experience accounts; it focuses on **temporal** organization and the expression of relations between events rather than on anaphora and reference; it covers subjects from the young age of 3 years through school age with comparable groups of **adult** narrators in each language sample; and it generalizes across speakers of five **different languages**. As such, the trends delineated above for four levels of narrative structure and narrative expression complement and go beyond other profiles noted in the literature with respect to children's storytelling abilities. Such profiles include Applebee's (1978) Vygotskian-based analysis of six developmental stages in the fantasy narratives of preschoolers (collected by Pitcher & Prelinger, 1963), Peterson and McCabe's (1983) characterizations of personal experience accounts of children aged 3;6 to 9;6 in terms of Labovian high-point analysis, and Wigglesworth's (1992) analysis of stages in the use of anaphora in English-speakers' narratives based on the same picturebook as ours. [18]

Our findings for the development of storytelling abilities moreover, dovetail remarkably with other narrative research undertaken from very different perspectives. These include Shen's (1990) characterization of different levels of narrative organization, and Giora and Shen's (in press) study of adult subjects' evaluation of the action-structure of precast stories. To their identification of three levels — local temporal, local causal, and global action-structure — corresponding very largely to what we found for the 5-year-old, 9-year-old, and adult profiles in our study, we need to add the initial, 3-year-old level of the individual event. The insights from Karmiloff-Smith's (1984, 1985) psycholinguistic studies on the development from bottom-up via top-down and then integrated solutions to linguistic and other types of cognitive tasks can explain the difference between well-formed text construction at the local level, followed by a superficial dip among somewhat older children as a result of internalization of narrative schemata, culminating in expressive proficiency combined with structural competence. Von Stutterheim's (1987) analyses of second language discourse as first spatially and then temporally organized provide further independent evidence for the results of the present study, as valid beyond the specific picturebook task applied in our study. Our findings also support Hickmann's (1991) observations regarding the emerging ability, after age 7, to "rely on presuppositions established within discourse." Moreover, as will be evident from Chapter IIB, our findings are compatible with the studies of Trabasso and his associates on the conceptual basis for narrating this frog book story within a causal network model of narrative structure.

Analyses taking into account prosodic and other paralinguistic accompaniments to the "frog story" in examining the development of both "story structure" and "the activity of storytelling" (Reilly, 1992) suggest an

---

[18] Wigglesworth (1992) concludes her detailed study of discourse-based anaphora by delineating five stages in narrative development, as follows: (1) **clausal** organization, confined to the clause level, with reference to the story pictures needed to make output comprehensible; (2) **page** organization, with each (double) page described without reference to previous or following pages; (3) **episodic** organization, with episode reference organized globally, generally with a thematic subject (in the sense in which this term is used by Karmiloff-Smith, 1981, **not** as used here to refer to the global plot-structure); (4) **simplified narrative** organization at the narrative level, with each narrative cohesively and coherently organized globally, either with a thematic strategy or an anaphoric strategy, although the storyline is simplified; and (5) **narrative** organization, globally structured around an anaphoric strategy.

interesting re-evaluation of our findings. Young children, whose storytelling is still "pregrammatical" (in the sense of Berman, 1986c, 1987a, 1990) rely on extralinguistic means in performing a task they construe as interactive and communicative in essence. With the development of higher levels of "structure-dependent" narrative organization, late preschoolers and young school-age children become adept at "telling a story." At this phase, they focus on conveying the information in the story in what Reilly characterizes as a rather flat or stereotyped fashion, similar to Berman's (1988) findings for several groups of Hebrew-speaking schoolchildren. Eventually, cognitive maturity, sensitivity to discourse-setting, and knowledge of narrative structure combine in older speakers to enable them to "tell a good story" in what Reilly (1992, p. 374) defines as "an affectively interesting and engaging manner," accomplished by what we have characterized as adopting an individual narrative stance.

Finally, the fact that a common developmental pattern emerges across the five languages in our study shows that, with age, speakers learn about "relating events in narrative" in ways that are only partially explained by the constraints imposed, and the options afforded, by a particular native tongue. Knowledge of a range of grammatical forms and lexical items for describing individual events develops relatively early, and is manifested by all the 3-year-olds in our study. Knowledge of narrative structure and of how to recruit linguistic forms for elaborating on events and the relations between them emerges rather later, from around age 5. School-age children are able to use an array of linguistic means to organize their narratives more rigorously, and to achieve a higher level of narrative coherence. They also manifest greater familiarity with the storytelling norms of their culture. Only later, however, are speakers able to organize entire narratives around a common thematic thread and to generalize across entire sets of events by prospective summations or by retrospective flashbacks. As discussed time and again in the following chapters, only the adults in our study display full rhetorical flexibility in the range of expressive devices which they employ and in the narrative functions realized by these devices.

Chapter IIB

KNOWLEDGE OF GOAL/PLANS: A CONCEPTUAL BASIS FOR NARRATING *Frog, where are you?*[1]

Tom Trabasso & Philip C. Rodkin

1. PLOT STRUCTURE

If asked to summarize the story depicted in Mayer's (1969) picture book, *Frog, where are you?*, an adult narrator might reply with something like the following:

"This is a story about a little boy who had a pet dog and frog. One evening, the boy, dog, and frog were in the boy's bedroom. The boy and the dog went to sleep and while they were sleeping, the frog escaped from its jar. The next morning the boy and the dog woke up and found the empty jar. The boy was upset and tried to find the frog. But in each place he searched, he found nothing or encountered a different animal.

[1] This research was supported by grants to T. Trabasso from the Smart Foundation on Early Learning and from the National Institute of Child Health and Human Development, Grant HD 17431 to T. Trabasso and Grant HD 25742 to T. Trabasso and N. L. Stein. Gratitude is expressed to Dan Slobin, Tanya Renner, and Virginia Marchman for granting us permission to analyze, and for providing us with, the 58 protocols of the American English sample of the Berkeley study [lacking the final two adult texts, which were added later]. We thank Judy DeLoache for providing us with the protocols of 14 mother-child dyads from the DeLoache, Cassidy, and Carpenter (1987) study. We are particularly indebted to Camille Baughn, Margret Park Munger, Margaret Nickels, and Nancy L. Stein for their several contributions to the research that is summarized in this chapter. We also wish to thank Mark Lepper and Gordon Bower of the Department of Psychology, Stanford University, and Shirley Feldman of the Family Studies Center, Stanford University, who generously lent their facilities to the first author during the writing of this chapter while on a sabbatical leave from The University of Chicago.

Finally, a deer accidentally carried the boy to a pond where he found the frog with a family of frogs. The story ended with the boy taking home a baby frog."

This summary follows a plot structure. There is an onset, an unfolding, and a resolution (Labov & Waletzky, 1967). Berman (1988) and Berman and Slobin (Chapter IIA) have analyzed the narrations by English and Hebrew speakers from this rhetorical perspective. The components of the plot were operationally defined in terms of the boy's realization that the frog has disappeared, the boy's search for the missing frog, and the boy's finding of the frog.

The notion of "plot" is an abstract schema for the organization of a story. To have psychological validity, however, "plot" must be instantiated as a process of interpretation of the events that are depicted in the pictures. In effect, one has to decompose "plot" as did Berman and Slobin in order to analyze the narrations of the pictures.

Stein and Glenn (1979), in their analysis of stories, showed how one could decompose "plot" into a structure that consists of a setting and a set of episodes. The setting specifies the characters and the space and time circumstances in which the story occurs. These circumstances enable a series of episodes involving action to take place. An episode is structured around goal-directed action and outcomes and is itself a mini-plot. It has a beginning (an initiating event), an unfolding (internal responses, goals, plans and actions), and an end (outcomes of success or failure in goal attainment, and evaluation of, or reaction to, these outcomes).

An important aspect of the Stein and Glenn (1979) representation of a story was the assumption that the categories of information could be related by causal, temporal, or logical relations. The categories and their relations were what defined both the content and structure of the story according to Stein and Glenn (1979). In the above summary, the setting is the introduction of the boy, dog, and frog and their relationships in the bedroom at night. The initiating events are the frog escaping, the empty jar, and the boy's discovery that the frog is missing the next morning. The goal/plan is the attempt to find the frog in various locations. The outcomes are various failures followed by a success. The causal relations are between the event and the goal/plan, the goal/plan and the renewed attempts, the attempts and the outcomes, and the outcomes and renewed attempts. Thus, the summary is highly structured and its plot can be decomposed into a set of categories of information that imply a process model for understanding the pictorial events.

Trabasso and his colleagues (Warren, Nicholas, & Trabasso, 1979; Trabasso, Secco, & van den Broek, 1984; Trabasso & van den Broek, 1985;

Trabasso & Sperry, 1985; Trabasso, van den Broek, & Suh, 1989) adopted the episodic categories of Stein and Glenn (1979) and Mandler and Johnson (1977), but focused on the conceptual and logical basis for relating their information content in understanding stories. In particular, they followed the lead of Schank (1975) in focusing on causal inferences that link the states and actions of a story. The causal relations were identified between a pair of events when logical criteria of necessity in the circumstances were satisfied (Mackie, 1980). That is, an event A was said to be the cause of an event B if the negation of A (not-A) led to the negation of B (not-B). In the above summary, the frog escaping from the jar would be viewed as necessary for the jar being empty. If the frog had not escaped, in the circumstances of this story, the jar would not have been empty.

Trabasso and van den Broek (1985) and Trabasso, van den Broek, and Suh (1989) showed that one could link the categories of episodes, and the episodes themselves, by causal relations in such a way as to produce causal network representations of a wide variety of stories. Trabasso and Suh (in press) offer a process model by which events are interpreted and integrated into a mental representation of the story during the course of comprehension. For a given picture, the contents are interpreted and encoded as clauses in working memory. How this information is interpreted, however, is constrained by what one can infer or already knows about the goal/plan of the protagonist. Goals are inferred from settings and events. Actions are encoded and interpreted as attempts to achieve inferred goals. Outcomes are evaluated in terms of success or failure to achieve a goal. These inferences thus unite events, goals, attempts, and outcomes into episodes through operations in working memory as one tries to understand a series of clauses or events. The integration is accomplished by mental operations of inferring, maintaining, accessing, or retrieving the goal/plan and relevant knowledge, and using this information to explain or evaluate actions and outcomes. When accomplished, the result is a coherent representation of the sequence of events.

In our view, the narration of events such as those in *Frog, where are you?* requires that the person first interpret what is happening. In this interpretation, a conceptual basis is formed for narrating the pictured events in language. In short, the narration of the picture story is a joint process of event comprehension and language production. Viewing the narrations as comprehension as well as production leads one to believe that the analysis of the narrations as causal networks is possible much in the same way as narrative texts taken from folk tales, myths, and other simple stories, all of which have been successfully analyzed by story grammars (Mandler & Johnson, 1977; Rumelhart, 1975, 1977; Stein & Glenn, 1979) and causal network discourse models (Trabasso et al., 1984; Trabasso & Sperry, 1985; Trabasso

& van den Broek, 1985; Trabasso et al., 1989).

On this view, what Berman (1988) and Berman and Slobin (Chapter IIA) regard as "plot" is the result of the use of the kind of knowledge about goal-directed action that is embodied in these discourse models. Plot is a structure that results from interpreting and integrating event content, i.e., a setting and a set of categories of information that are causally related within and between episodes. What is narrated depends upon the narrator being able to interpret the characters and their relations in time and space, to understand how the initiating events impact on the main protagonist and lead to the formation of a goal and goal plan, how the protagonist enacts this plan over time, whether the attempts to achieve the plan fail, how the protagonist reacts to the failures, and finally, how the attempts succeed and end the story. In short, knowledge of goal/plans or planning is required. Such knowledge, of course, is acquired and develops and underlies the ability of the narrators of the several studies in this volume to narrate the sequence of events of *Frog, where are you?* into a coherent narration.

The story pictures provide the narrator with an opportunity to describe the actions of a protagonist in terms of a **hierarchical** goal plan. The plan is hierarchical because a superordinate goal, namely to retrieve a lost goal object (the frog), motivates subordinate goals, namely to find the frog by searching for it in various locations. Moreover, the goal of finding the missing frog is maintained despite several failed search attempts. Finally, the lost object is found and repossessed by the protagonist. Since the narrators observe and encode the events as they unfold in the picture sequence, the content that is inferred and encoded by the narrator, on-line, allows a direct test of the assumption that children can **selectively encode actions as relevant to a goal plan**. The sustained encoding of these relevant actions, along with marking them with purposes or goals, and the encoding of outcomes as they unfold over time, constitute evidence for the use of knowledge of a hierarchical goal plan.

Trabasso and Nickels (1992) and Trabasso, Stein, Rodkin, Munger, and Baughn (1992) applied the Trabasso et al. (1989) discourse analysis to the American English corpus presented in this volume. In this chapter, we draw heavily upon these reports to indicate how one can analyze the narrations of the *Frog, where are you?* story as embodiments of planning knowledge, how one can then use the analysis to infer the use of such knowledge, and how children of different ages differ in their ability to access and use goal/plans to understand events that they witness.

2. DISCOURSE ANALYSIS

The causal network model of Trabasso et al. (1989) is shown in Figure 1. The content of each clause in the narration may be classified into one of six categories: S (setting), E (event), IR (internal response), G (goal), A (attempt), and O (outcome). Outcomes are marked as successful (+), unsuccessful (-), or neutral (o) with respect to goal attainment. These categories together constitute an episode. In Figure 1, the arrows connecting the letters reflect the causal relations between the categories. The connecting relations between categories are inferred and can be either causal or enabling conditions. Settings can enable all categories. Events can physically cause other events or they can psychologically cause internal responses or goals. Internal responses (cognitions, emotions, beliefs) can psychologically cause other internal responses or goals. Goals (desired or undesired states, activities or objects) can motivate goals or attempts to achieve or avoid them. Attempts can enable other attempts or physically cause successful or unsuccessful outcomes. Outcomes can physically cause other outcomes or, like events, can psychologically cause internal responses and goals. Outcomes can also enable attempts. When faced with a failed outcome on a goal, the protagonist can reinstate the failed goal and attempt once more to achieve it, generate a new, subordinate goal to achieve the failed goal, or abandon the failed goal. The reinstatement, generation, or substitution of goals and subordinate goals organizes the narrative into a goal/plan hierarchy.

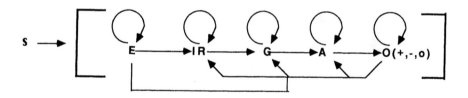

Figure 1. Causal network model of Trabasso, van den Broek, & Suh (1989).

It will be argued below that the story in *Frog, where are you?* follows a hierarchical goal plan with unanticipated goal failures and success. Figure 2, generated from Figure 1, shows a representation of a such a goal/plan hierarchy. This particular representation has three hierarchically ordered goals with attempts that lead to unanticipated goal failures, goal reinstatements, and goal success. The plan begins with a setting (S) that is followed by an event (E) that happens to a protagonist. These, respectively, enable and psychologically cause an internal reaction (IR). The reaction leads to a goal (G1). This goal

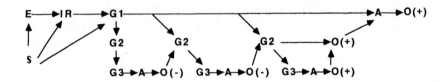

Figure 2. Causal network representation showing a goal hierarchy
with unanticipated failure outcomes and success.

motivates a subordinate goal (G2) to obtain it. The subordinate goal (G2) in
turn motivates another subordinate goal (G3) to obtain it. Together these three
goals constitute a plan. Here, the plan is carried out through actions motivated
at the level of the third goal in the hierarchy (G3). This goal motivates an initial attempt (A) that fails as indicated by an outcome (O(-)). This failure is
monitored and psychologically causes the reinstatement of the second goal
(G2) that is motivated by the first goal (G1) that controls the overall plan. The
cycle of the superordinate first goal (G1), motivating the subordinate second
goal (G2), the second goal then motivating its subordinate, the third goal
(G3), and the third goal (G3) being followed by an attempt (A) and a failure
(O(-)) is repeated. Finally, an attempt (A) leads to a successful outcome
(O(+)) for the third, most subordinate goal (G3). This outcome enables
another successful outcome (O(+)) at the level of the second goal (G2). This
outcome enables an attempt (A) that causes a successful outcome (O(+)) for
the first goal (G1), completing the hierarchical goal plan.

   Filling in the content of the categories in Figure 2 demonstrates why we
suggested that Berman and Slobin's notion of plot may well be a reflection of
what is produced by the access and application of a hierarchical goal plan to
interpret the events portrayed in the pictures of the *Frog, where are you?*
story. In the sequence of pictures, the boy has a pet frog (S), loses it (E), and
shows concern over its loss (IR). His concern initiates a series of goals (G)
and attempts (A) that enact a plan to get the frog back (G1). The plan is to
find the frog (G2) by searching in particular locations (G3) for it. The boy
searches by looking or calling (A), but is met with a series of failures (O(-))
where the frog is not found and where animals other than the frog suddenly
and unexpectedly appear. The boy, however, resumes the search in particular
locations for the frog (G3) in order to find it (G2), and finally does find it
(O(+)) and takes it (A) back home (O(+)).

Trabasso and Nickels (1992) analyzed the 58 protocols of the American English corpus (see footnote 1) with the model depicted in Figure 1. The main question was: Would the resulting representations of the narrations in the protocols show hierarchical goal/plan structures like that depicted in Figure 2, and if so, how would these representations develop with age?

In analyzing the clauses in a narration, Trabasso and Nickels found it necessary to assume the point of view of a given character. In the picture sequence, there are 10 possible points of view: boy, dog, boy and dog together, frog, gopher, bees, owl, deer, other frogs, and narrator. For each point of view, a causal network representation for each narration in the corpus was derived. This analysis resulted not only in a representation of the point of view of each character, but also in a representation of a set of interacting plans for the boy and/or dog with the other animal characters. From this representation, the main protagonist was identified to be the boy since his network was the longest and was the only one that was connected from the beginning of the story until the end.

For purposes of illustrating the method of analysis of Trabasso and Nickels, the interacting networks derived for the text of Subject E20b are shown for clauses 10 through 15 in Figure 3.

A clause is coded by a letter that denotes its category in the causal network model. Each category belongs to an episode and the number after the letter corresponds to the level of that episode's goal in the goal/plan hierarchy. The number in parentheses is the ordinal number of the clause in the narration. Thus, A3(12) refers to an attempt at goal level 3 for clause 12. At the bottom of the figure is a numbered picture line; the brackets mark the clauses in the narration that were made to that picture. Causal relations between pairs of categories are indicated by labeled arrows between categories. The labels **e, psi, m,** and **phi** stand for enabling, psychological-, motivational-, or physical-causal relations, respectively. Enabling relations are those where the conditions or change in conditions allow something to occur. Psychological relations are those between events and outcomes and internal states. Motivational relations are those between goals and attempts. Physical relations are those between actions and outcomes in the physical world. Thus, for example, an attempt, A3(14), enables (e) an outcome, O3(15).

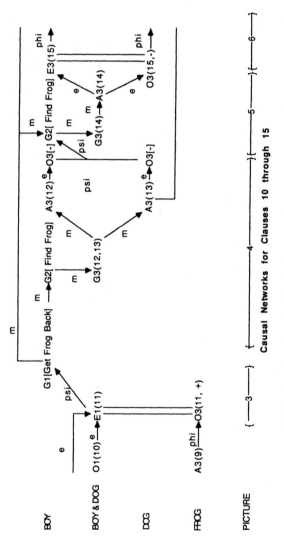

Causal Networks for Clauses 10 through 15

10. The next morning, the boy and the dog wake up
11. and find the empty jar.
12. The boy looks in his boots
13. while the dog looks in the jar for the frog.
14. They look out the window for the frog.
15. The dog falls out the window.

Figure 3. Causal network representations of four characters derived
from clause 10 through clause 15 narrated to Picture 3 through Picture 6 by E20b.

Explicit categories are shown by parentheses around the clause number; implicit categories are shown by brackets and a description following the letter and goal level. Explicit categories are those that correspond to clauses in the narration. Explicit goals are marked by use of modal verbs such as *want, desire, need, had to*, etc., or by a prepositional phrase or an infinitival joined with an action such as *look for the frog* or *went to get on top of the rock*. Implicit categories are goals inferred from explicit outcomes and actions, or outcomes inferred from explicit actions and goals.

A successful outcome is denoted by a plus sign in the parentheses or bracket; a failed outcome is denoted by a minus sign. Since the same clause can be categorized from the perspective of more than one character, it may be represented in more than one causal network and its category membership may change. Clauses that are in two networks have the same number and their equivalence is depicted by vertical, parallel lines between them. For example, an outcome, the empty jar in O3(11, +), that was enabled by the frog's attempt of leaving the jar (A3(9)) from the frog's point of view became an event, E1(11), from the boy's and dog's points of view.

In the series of clauses 10-15 in Figure 3, the boy and dog wake up and see the empty jar. The dog looks in the jar for the frog. Then they both look out the window for the frog. The dog falls out the window. The narration contains an outcome in clause 10, an event in clause 11, two purposeful attempts in clauses 12 and 13, another purposeful attempt in clause 14, and a failed outcome or an event in clause 15. Purposeful attempts were separated into two categories: a goal and an attempt that together make up a local goal plan. The goal is based upon the purpose of the action and is expressed frequently as a prepositional phrase (e.g., *for the frog*) or as an infinitive phrase (e.g., *to see if the frog is in there*). The presence of the frog in the phrase indicates that it is the desired goal object. We assume that the goal exists prior to the attempt and motivates it. Thus the action of looking in the boot, A3(12), is motivated by the goal of looking for the frog in certain locations, G3(12). The purposeful attempt in clause 14 is another local goal plan. Here the goal is to look for the frog in another location, namely out the window in G3(14), and is carried out as an attempt in A3(14).

Why do the boy and the dog look for the frog out the window after looking for the frog either in the boots or in the jar? Apparently, they did not find the frog in the first locations. A failed outcome was therefore inferred from each of their points of view, O3[-]. This outcome was enabled by the initial attempts and it contributes psychologically to another, local goal plan. What motivates these two local goal plans of searching for the frog in specific locations? These local plans are best understood as motivated by an inferred, higher-order goal, labeled G2[Find the Frog]. This higher-order goal of finding the frog motivates local goal-directed actions to search in particular locations for the frog, and it is reinstated each time the local goal plan fails. Why does the goal of finding the frog get reinstated? The answer is that the boy has developed yet another inferred, higher-order goal, namely to get back his pet, labeled G1[Get Frog Back]. Together, these inferred and explicit goals constitute a goal/plan hierarchy, where the top-order goal, G1[Get Frog Back], motivates a second-order goal, G2[Find the Frog], that, in turn, motivates a local goal plan, G3[Search in Particular Locations], that then motivates attempts at this third level. One can now understand why levels 1, 2, and 3 were assigned to the categories. Finally, what caused the goal/plan hierarchy to arise? The answer lies, in part, in the Event E1(11), where the boy discovers the empty jar, indicating that the frog is lost and that psychologically causes, in the circumstances of the story, the boy's goal of wanting to get the frog back, G1. Note that E1(11) is not sufficient to cause this goal. Rather, it is necessary to know that the boy values and desires the frog as a pet, inferrable from the setting in the first picture and often encoded explicitly as "his pet frog." It is the loss of a valued goal object that results in the desire to reinstate the relationship with the frog. The relation between goal states and changes in goal states as determinants of emotions and goals is central to Stein and Levine's (1987, 1989, 1990) theory of emotional understanding and is consistent with the present analysis.

In the analysis, episodic structures emerge when the narration permits identification of a set of categories that depict goal-directed action. A complete episode would contain one or more of each of the categories in the causal network in Figure 1, namely, an event, a goal, an attempt, an outcome, and a reaction. Figure 3 shows partial goal-attempt-outcome episodes in the boy's network. For example, clauses 12 and 13 contain a local goal and an attempt that are followed by a failed outcome for the boy. Similarly, for the dog, clauses 14 and 15 contain another local goal and an attempt followed by a failed outcome. The main action sequence in the narrative occurs at level 3, where the boy is trying to find the frog in particular places.

In order to compare the narrations to the extent that they indicate a goal/plan hierarchy, Trabasso and Nickels (1992) extracted the boy's network from each analyzed narration. It is not convenient to show the complete network of the boy for any one narration. However, to motivate the data analyses below, part of the episodic structure of the boy's network is shown for Subject E20b in Figure 4. The corresponding clauses for the explicit categories are presented in Table 1 to assist in the reading of the notation.

Figure 4 shows evidence that E20b's narration is structured according to a hierarchical goal plan strikingly similar to the idealized plan in Figure 2. The network begins in the upper left with an event in which the boy finds the jar empty (E), causing his desire to get his frog back (G1) in episode 2. This goal generates a goal plan to find the frog (G2) and entails a subordinate goal plan to search in particular locales (G3). The first realization of the local goal is in episode 9 where the boy wants to search for the frog outside [G3] and so he calls for the frog (A) but fails to find it [O-]. The boy's goal plan is reinstated in episode 10 where there is a hole in the ground (S) and the boy wants to see if the frog is in it (G3). He looks (A), but a small animal that lives there (S) bites him on the nose, a failed outcome (O-).

The goal plan (G2) is reinstated once again in episode 11 where the boy is sitting in a tree (S) and there is a hole in the tree (S). The goal plan to find the frog [G2] psychologically causes the boy to think about these two conditions as a <possible> location where the frog might be searched for and found (IRC). This cognition (C) psychologically causes the activation of the goal to look in the hole (G3). This goal motivates an attempt to look (A) that is disrupted when the owl pops out and is consequently a failure to find the frog (O-). Later, in episode 14, the boy finds himself sitting in the water, an outcome from episode 13 where the deer had thrown him over a cliff into the pond. An event occurs where he hears (IRC) some sound coming from the other side of the log (E). This cognition, in conjunction with the reinstatement of the goal plan (G2), causes the local goal of wanting to see if the frog is on the other side of the log (G3). This motivates him to crawl over the log (A) where he finds some frogs (O+), one of which was the frog that had been in the jar (0+). This outcome completes episode 3 in that it finally satisfies the goal of finding the frog. The finding of his frog completes our criteria for inferring a second-order goal (G2), and enables the boy to attempt (A) to achieve his top-order goal of getting the frog back home (G1). The attempt of taking the frog back home (A) constitutes part of the second episode. This explicit attempt supports our inference that there is a top-order goal (G1) of wanting to have the frog back. Once again, we require an antecedent (the initiating event of the frog leaving the jar empty, E), and a consequent, the attempt to bring it back (A), for the inferred goal. The inferred goal/plan hierarchy is anchored by explicitly narrated clauses, either an event that causes a goal and an attempt to achieve it or by failed outcomes and instances of goal plans to search in particular locales.

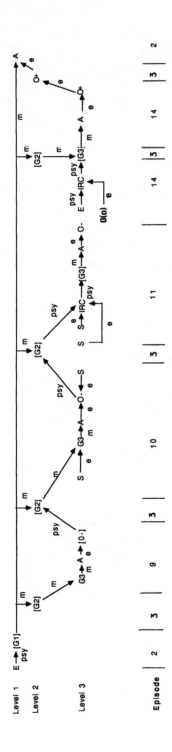

Figure 4. Selected episodes showing a goal hierarchy with
unanticipated failure outcomes and successes taken from the
boy's perspective in the causal network representation of E20b's narration.

TABLE 1
Selected Episodes (Boy's Perspective) of E20b's Narration[a]

Episode 2
The boy finds the frog's jar empty. (E)
He wants his pet frog back home. [G1]
   Episode 3
  The boy decides to search for his frog. [G2]
      Episode 9
     He wants to search for his frog outside. [G3]
     So he called for the frog. (A)
     But the frog did not come. [O-]
   Episode 3
  The boy decides to search for his frog. [G2]
      Episode 10
     There is a hole in the ground. (S)
     The boy wants to see if the frog is in there. (G3)
     The boy is looking in the hole. (A)
     Some little animal is living in the hole. (S)
     The boy gets his nose bitten by the animal. (O-)
   Episode 3
  The boy decides to search for his frog. [G2]
      Episode 11
     The boy is sitting in a tree. (S)
     There is a hole in the tree. (S)
     The boy thinks that maybe the lost frog is in there. (IRC)
     He wants to see if the frog is in the hole. [G3]
     So he looks into the hole. (A)
     But at this point an owl pops out of the hole in the tree. (O-)
   Episode 3
  The boy decides to search for his frog. [G2]
      Episode 13
     A deer threw the boy over a cliff. (O)
     The boy fell into a pond. (O)
      Episode 14
     The boy sits up in the water. (O)
     Some sound is coming from behind the log. (E)
     The boy can hear the sound. (IRC)
   Episode 3
  The boy decides to search for his frog. [G2]
      Episode 14
     He wants to check if there are frogs behind the log. [G3]
     So he crawls over the log. (A)
     And he finds on the outer side of the log two happy frogs. (O+)
     One of which was the frog in the jar. (O+)
Episode 2
Now the boy leaves with his frog (A)

The letters correspond to the content categories of the general causal transition network. The numbers on the goals refer to their level in the hierarchy. The positive and negative signs for outcomes indicate goal success or failure. The bracketed goals and outcomes are inferred.

3. EPISODIC STRUCTURING OF EVENTS

An episode's basic structure is a goal-attempt-outcome sequence. In order to find out when children began to interpret the *Frog, where are you?* story episodically, Trabasso and Nickels (1992) counted the number of such goal-attempt-outcome (GAO) units in each network for each narrator. These were contrasted with those categories of information that were not connected into episodes (non-GAO units). Figure 5 summarizes their findings on these units.

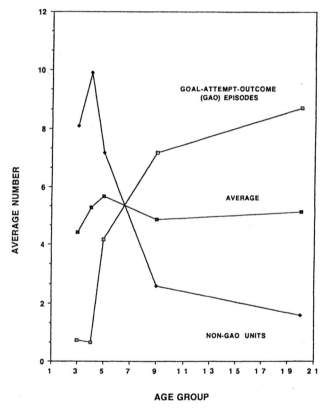

Figure 5. Average number of Goal-Attempt-Outcome (GAO) episodes and non-GAO units for each age group.

In Figure 5, the number of GAO units increases sharply between the fourth and fifth year. This means that at about age 5, the children became more explicit in marking attempts with purposes and in including obstacles as failed outcomes in their narrations. Many 5-year-olds used planning knowledge to integrate information more fully into episodes. The episodes are, in turn, causally and temporally related and are organized hierarchically into an overall plan. This organization of the narration increases at age 9 and continues to increase slightly into adulthood.

Of interest in Figure 5 is the relative constancy of the average number of units. If one thinks of GAO and non-GAO units as "chunks" of information (Chi, 1978), then the children encode the same number of chunks per story (about 4.5 on average). The ability to use planning knowledge to interpret and encode actions as attempts to attain a goal and to evaluate the outcomes of the attempts in terms of goal success or failure enables the child to "chunk" greater amounts of information. For 5-year-old children, who begin to evidence the clearest use of planning knowledge, this means that they should also encode more categories per episode and more relations between episodes. Trabasso and Nickels (1992) found that the number of categories per episode and causal relationships both within and between episodes increased substantially after age 4, precisely when goals and outcomes began to be increasingly added to the narration.

4. PLANNING COMPONENTS

To understand how a plot may be decomposed into a goal plan, and how it may follow that plan, Trabasso et al. (1992), on the basis of an analysis of planning components by Scholnik and Friedman (1987), supposed the following: A child is asked to narrate a sequence of events; the child has knowledge of planning; and the child uses this planning knowledge to encode events into a coherent narrative. Then, they asked: How might this child's narrative proceed? How might one verify that the narrative produced by the child follows the goal plan? In answer, for a narrator to encode a temporal sequence of events as a coherent narrative organized around a hierarchical goal plan, the narration should include the following content: (1) The protagonist has a relation to an object, state, or activity (e.g., the protagonist possesses an object of value). (2) The protagonist undergoes an undesirable state change relative to the valued object that initiates a goal and goal plan (e.g., the protagonist loses the object of value). (3) The protagonist carries out actions relevant to the goal of altering the undesirable state change (e.g., the protagonist attempts to repossess the lost object through carrying out a plan to search for it). (4) The protagonist continues attempts to attain the goal in the face of failure (e.g., the protagonist makes repeated search attempts). (5) The protagonist's attempts finally result in the successful attainment of the goal (e.g., the protagonist finds and repossesses the lost object).

Table 2 summarizes the main findings of Study 1 of the Trabasso et al. (1992) article in terms of the proportion of narrators in each age group who included a particular planning component in narrating *Frog, where are you?*.

If the child uses knowledge of a plan, the child should encode the opening events (setting) that establish the boy's possession of a valued object. Then, the child should narrate the necessary information for inferring the goal(s) of the main protagonist by encoding the chain of occurrences (initiating events) that result in the establishment of the protagonist's goal and goal plan. These interpretations in a narration together underlie what Berman and Slobin (Chapter IIA) refer to as the "opening of the plot." They report data that correspond to what we term "initiating events."

TABLE 2

Proportion of Narrators Who Include Planning Component

Component	Age				
	3 yrs	4 yrs	5 yrs	9 yrs	Adult
Setting					
Introduce Frog	1.00	1.00	1.00	1.00	1.00
Possession	0.17	0.25	0.58	1.00	0.90
Initiating Events					
Boy Asleep	0.58	0.58	0.92	0.83	1.00
Frog Leaves	0.67	0.83	1.00	1.00	1.00
Boy Wakes	0.08	0.50	0.67	0.58	0.90
Boy Finds Jar	0.00	0.25	0.25	0.42	1.00
Frog Gone	0.33	0.83	0.83	0.92	0.90
Boy Sad	0.00	0.00	0.08	0.08	0.80
Average	0.28	0.50	0.63	0.63	0.93
Attempts					
A1 Room	0.00	0.58	0.50	0.58	0.90
A2 Window	0.08	0.33	0.58	0.75	0.90
A3 Outside	0.08	0.25	0.50	0.92	1.00
A4 Hole in Ground	0.00	0.25	0.67	0.75	1.00
A5 Hole in Tree	0.00	0.17	0.58	0.75	1.00
A6 Rock	0.00	0.25	0.58	0.67	0.90
A7 Log	0.08	0.25	0.33	0.83	0.90
Average	0.03	0.30	0.53	0.75	0.94
Proportion Attempts Marked with Purpose	0.00	0.21	0.35	0.47	0.55
Outcome					
Find or Take	0.16	0.42	0.42	0.75	1.00
Higher-Order Goals					
G1 [Get the Frog Back]	0.00	0.00	0.25	0.83	0.90
G2 [Find the Frog]	0.00	0.17	0.33	1.00	1.00

Table 2 shows that all the narrators encoded the presence of the frog for Picture 1 but possession increased markedly with age. The largest increases are between ages 4 and 5 and between 5 and 9. The data on encoding initiating events parallel those on possession except that the largest increases are between ages 3 and 4 and between 9 and adult. Four-year-old children show signs of taking the boy's perspective in encoding the initiating events by including the cognitive states of the boy: waking and finding. Few children of any age include emotion, whereas the vast majority of adults include an emotional reaction on the part of the boy.

To encode subsequent events according to the protagonist's goal plan, the child, as an ideal narrator, must have inferred the goal, and must anticipate possible courses of action open to the protagonist. The child narrator should then encode the protagonist's actions in a manner that indicates the relevance of the actions to the attainment of the goal. Which particular actions are encoded is crucial. To make it clear that the attempts are related to the plan, the narrator should also conjoin the relevant actions with purposes. Furthermore, if the narrator is monitoring the goal plan of the protagonist, the narration should feature renewed attempts and purposes or outcomes. Each time the protagonist tries and fails, the ideal narrator should encode actions as attempts that indicate a reinstatement of the goal, and mark them with purposes. A narrative produced in this fashion would show the clearest evidence of following a sustained goal plan of action. The encoding of renewed attempts under the same plan, given goal failure, is what defines the "unfolding of the plot" in the analysis of Berman and Slobin (Chapter IIA). The explaining of attempts with goals would constitute the best evidence that the child is using a goal plan to interpret and encode attempts.

Table 2 shows the seven pictures in which narrators could encode a goal-relevant action, and indicates that the ability to encode such attempts increased with age. Looking down a column for the attempts indicates that the children tended to sustain their encoding with two exceptions: over the first three attempts, the 4-year-olds tend to decline over time while the 9-year-olds showed an increase.

Attempts were marked with purposes about half the time by adults. One reason why this is the case is that there is a distinct tendency to trade off marking of attempts with purposes and narrating an outcome. Outcomes are more informative than purposes since they allow one to infer whether or not an attempt succeeds. Trabasso and Nickels (1992) found that they had sufficient information to infer a purpose because of this tendency to alternate attempts marked with purposes with unmarked attempts and outcomes. In this sense, then, the narrators were following Grice's (1975) principles of being informative and not redundant. Against the adult standard, the rate of marking attempts with purposes is greater than 50% by age 5. The lower rate for 4-year-olds contributed to the smaller number of GAO units found by Trabasso and Nickels (1992), shown in Figure 5.

The ideal narrator should conclude the story by encoding the successful attempts of the protagonist. Successful goal attainment can also be hierarchical: The attainment of one goal (finding the lost object) is necessary for the attainment of another goal (possessing the object). These goal attainments are what, for us, define "resolution" of the plot. In Table 2, it can be seen that the rate of including finding or taking the frog increased substantially between ages 3 and 4, and between 5 and 9.

Trabasso and Nickels (1992) inferred goal G2 if the narrator's representation had two GAOs. They inferred the operation of a hierarchical goal plan with goal G1 if the narrator marked the possession in the setting statement, had two or more G2s indicating a sustained search, and concluded with the finding or taking of the frog. Two GAO units indicate the goal of reinstating the search (G2); more than two G2s indicate the reinstatement of the goal of repossessing the frog. Table 2 also summarizes the proportion of narrators who provided sufficient evidence in their narrations for Trabasso and Nickels to infer either G1[Get Frog Back] or G2[Find the Frog]. These criteria, while stringent, show that evidence of beginning to structure hierarchically the narrations is clearest at age 5.

The data on initiating events, sustained search, and finding or taking from Trabasso et al. (1992) correspond closely to those reported in this volume by Berman and Slobin and by Berman (1988). The data on introducing characters, possession, marking attempts with purposes, and providing enough information to allow one to infer a hierarchical plan add to this analysis. Berman and Slobin, summarizing across all five languages, conclude that the largest developmental differences occur between 3 and 5. Our analyses indicate that, as Berman (1988) and Berman and Slobin (Chapter IIA) conclude, children as young as 5 access and use their knowledge of goal plans to encode narrative events. Four-year-old children are, as Berman (1988, p. 490), Berman and Slobin (IIA, Section 4), and other cognitive developmentalists (e.g., Nelson, 1992; Perner, 1992) claim, a "mixed" group. We have found that 4-year-olds are in transition from describing isolated states, actions unrelated to the plan, and neutral outcomes — all characteristics of 3-year-old narrations — to taking the perspective of the main protagonist, encoding initiating events, encoding attempts without purposes, and encoding the ending. These latter qualities suggest to us that 4-year-olds have amassed at least some knowledge of others' goal plans. In this light, it is the relative omission of goals by the 4-year-olds that is intriguing. Both Trabasso and Nickels (1992) and Trabasso et al. (1992) interpreted the 4-year-olds as not following another Gricean principle (Grice, 1975) of orienting the listener to new information by explaining actions when the scene shifts.

5. WHY DO THE 4-YEAR-OLDS TEND TO OMIT PURPOSES?

Trabasso et al. (1992) followed up the findings on the 4-year-olds by another study (their Study 3). Over half of the 4-year-olds encoded attempts at the beginning of the initiating event sequence, but only 25% sustained the encoding of attempts beyond the third scene. Furthermore, these children linked attempts to purposes infrequently. This omission may arise from the implicit nature of the goal plan in this particular story. The frog as a goal object is materially absent throughout the sequence of attempts. Four-year-olds might explicitly narrate the relationship between attempts and a goal if the object was materially present in each action scene, thus making it visually more obvious towards what end an action is addressed. To explore the importance of having the goal object present, Trabasso et al. (1992) chose an additional frog picture story, *A boy, a dog, and a frog* (Mayer, 1967), where the boy tries repeatedly to capture the frog. Here, the goal object and attempts are always pictured together in the story.

If the child does not encode an attempt or does not explicitly link a purpose with an encoded attempt, we cannot be sure that the child lacks knowledge of the goal plan. Therefore, the results of analyzing only what the speaker says may underestimate what the speaker knows. As communicators, children need not narrate everything they know (Bamberg, 1987; Bamberg & Marchman, 1990). In order to find out whether 4-year-olds understand the purposeful nature of actions, contingent questioning procedures were used. The children were asked to narrate the pictures in a book as in the last study. Then, they narrated the book a second time. During the second narration, the experimenter intervened and asked descriptive (What is happening?) and/or explanatory (Why?) questions for action scenes. The question asked (cf. Trabasso et al., 1992, Fig. 4) was contingent on what the children spontaneously narrated.

The key findings were that the 4-year-olds spontaneously encoded attempts in both stories at nearly the same rate (65 and 70%, respectively, when the frog was present or absent). With prompting by questions, these rates rose to 86 and 82%. However, when the frog was present as a goal object, they encoded purposes at the high rate of 64 percent; when it was absent, they encoded purposes at the low rate of 20%. Asking why-questions on attempts revealed that the 4-year-olds knew the reasons for the actions. Adding the answers to the why-questions increased the percentages of attempts encoded with purposes to 77% and 73%, respectively. Thus, the 4-year-olds could, with prompting, conjoin attempts with purposes at a very high rate. There is no question that they could access the relevant goal plan. They clearly had less of a tendency to orient the listener as to the goals of the story when the goal object was not present. It may be the case that they are less aware of the necessity to orient listeners in this way. They may also assume that the listener knows about the frog since, in the original study, the child knew that the experimenter could see the picture book. As discussed in Chapter IB, it is important to collect narrations of picture books where the listener does not see the book and the task more closely approximates one of storytelling to a naive listener.

6. WHAT DO THE 3-YEAR-OLDS DO AND KNOW?

The 3-year-old children exhibited little use of knowledge of plans in encoding action in the *Frog, where are you?* story. Rather, their narrations were focused on identifying objects and animate beings, and on describing states and actions unrelated to the theme of finding the frog. They required a lot of intervention and prompting by the experimenter and seemed to treat the picture book task as one of communicative interaction rather than cooperative storytelling (cf. Hausendorf & Quastoff, 1992). The narrations may have reflected the 3-year-olds' assumptions about the communicative roles of adults and children in interaction with experiences such as "reading" books.

DeLoache, Cassidy, and Carpenter (1987) used the *Frog, where are you?* book to study how mothers label animals' genders while interacting with their children in this kind of communicative context. Trabasso et al. (1992) received permission from Judy DeLoache to analyze 13 protocols of the DeLoache et al. (1987) corpus of interactions, and report this as Study 2 in their article. The children ranged in age from 18 to 38 months (median age = 30 months). Their mothers were asked "to act naturally" in their interaction with their children over the picture book.

In Trabasso et al.'s (1992) analysis of these interactions, the mothers told the story to their young children more or less as a background to the conversation. In the foreground were the mothers' attempts to engage the child throughout the telling. A mother asked her child an average of 30 questions over the course of telling the story.

Of interest is the fact that the mothers reduced what they told as a story to approximately that of the 5-year-olds of the study reported in this volume. This shows a sensitivity to the competencies of the child, but at a more advanced level that served as a kind of scaffolding experience (Vygotsky, 1934/1978). The majority of the mothers' questions asked the child to identify or locate objects, and to describe or elaborate actions. A minority of questions focused on what happened, why it happened, and what the consequence was of what happened. However, these questions, central to learning about causes, consequences, and plans of action, increased with age. Thus, mothers also adjusted and scaffolded their questions as their children became more conceptually and linguistically adept at answering and at asking their own questions. The mothers' questions began to focus more upon agents and actions, requiring children to tell what was happening, why some event happened, and to speculate on what may happen in the future. The mothers clearly fostered understanding of the causes and consequences of actions by asking children of age 30 months or older to relate the past to the present to the future.

The children's answers and questions, in turn, showed an increase in goals, outcomes, and taking on the role of the animals in speech as they grew older. The children in the DeLoache et al. study were learning to describe and identify events dynamically by encoding actions and state changes, and to relate and explain events with the aid of the mothers' scaffolding. What mothers asked for and what their children answered corresponded well with what and how the 3-year-olds in the Berkeley study narrated the picture stories. The mothers' questions took into account the linguistic and cognitive skills of their children and fostered the children's descriptive and identification skills. The 3-year-olds in the Berkeley study may well, then, have reflected in their attempts to tell the picture story a history of interactive, communicative contexts with adults.

7. CONCLUDING REMARKS

The results of the analyses of Trabasso and Nickels (1992) and Trabasso et al. (1992) presented here support the claim that the narrators of *Frog, where are you?* increase their use of planning knowledge as they approach school age. The clearest use of such knowledge occurs by age 5, but there are many signs of its use by a minority of 4-year-olds. The children, from 3 to 5 years, move from description (identification and naming) of isolated objects, states, and actions to encoding and temporal sequencing of relevant actions as attempts related to a plan to the full use of a plan to encode and explain action within its context. This access and use of goal/plan knowledge leads, along with linguistic development, to the creation of coherent narrations of a series of pictorial events.

These results also indicate that the conceptual knowledge underlying "plot" is that of goal/plans. The selective interpretation of events within the context of a goal/plan gives rise to the structural units of a plot, not vice versa. The goal/plan is a kind of situation model that is inferred from the events themselves, and constructed from knowledge about search for lost objects, etc., and then is used to interpret and evaluate subsequent events. The inferred plan and its application depend upon the child's processing of the data that are observed and upon the child possessing knowledge of a loss-search plan. The inferring and using of a plan to understand and narrate a sequence of events is the result of interactive processes between conceptual structures and perceptual data. The beginning happens to be those events that cause changes in the goal states of a person or protagonist. The unfolding happens to be the carrying out of a goal/plan to undo or restore the states that were changed. The resolution happens to be the successful attainment of goals that restore the changed states. The structure of a plot is a conventionalized categorization imposed on what may be regarded as a particular application of knowledge of goal/plans to interpreting or generating a set of events.

Part III

DEVELOPMENT OF LINGUISTIC FORMS

Chapter III0

OVERVIEW OF LINGUISTIC FORMS
IN THE FROG STORIES

1. Typological Characteristics
2. Tense/Aspect
2.1. Inflectional Morphology
2.2. Other Means of Expressing Aspect
3. Event Conflation
4. Perspective
5. Connectivity

This part of the book is concerned with the development of linguistic **form** in child language, as reflected in the frog stories. In the following five chapters we describe the relevant grammatical structures in English, German, Spanish, Hebrew, and Turkish and present summaries of the development of linguistic forms in each language. As an orientation to the issues raised in those chapters, it is necessary to lay out the types of linguistic forms that are considered. By "form" we include grammatical morphology, syntax, pragmatic word-order patterns, and lexicon.[1] Since the focus of the study is the description of **events**, we limit ourselves to forms of predicates and clauses that are involved in the temporal unfolding and interrelation of events in time and space, excluding detailed examination of the language of reference to protagonists (names and nouns, pronouns, anaphora, etc.).

1. TYPOLOGICAL CHARACTERISTICS

Each of the five languages represents a unique cluster of typological characteristics. A major claim of this study is that children — from early on — are sensitive to such characteristics in acquiring and using their native languages. This claim has three aspects: (1) Even quite young children will

---

[1] We recognize that prosody (stress, intonation, pausing, etc.) is a critical part of the structure of oral narrative. However, given limitations of time and labor, we have not been able to include prosody in our analyses. Perhaps if standard writing systems reflected prosodic distinctions, as they do phonological ones, linguistics would have long since treated prosody as part of grammar. Such treatments are beginning to emerge, and we hope, someday, to return to our tape recordings to study the developing levels of linguistic organization that are not visible in our written transcripts.

exploit the range of structural options offered by the language within a given domain. For example, Spanish-speaking children will make many tense/aspect distinctions and German-speaking children will make many locative distinctions — because these are semantic domains which receive rich grammatical elaboration in their languages. (2) The child will treat the native language as a **system** of interrelated formal options. We suggest, for example, that one reason for the abundance of relative clauses in our Spanish and Hebrew stories is that they are compatible with the general direction of information flow in those languages, since both adjectives and relative clauses follow the noun that they modify. (3) The child will also treat the native language as a system of interrelated **expressive** options. For example (as discussed below), Spanish, Hebrew, and Turkish have limited means for the grammatical encoding of paths of movement. As a consequence, it seems that children have to learn to devote more narrative attention to locative description in these languages than in languages like English and German, which have an elaborate system of verb satellites encoding path distinctions.

Table 1 shows the dimensions of typological variation that are most relevant to this study. We discuss these dimensions below with regard to four broad issues pertaining to narrative discourse: (1) **Tense/aspect**: What temporal distinctions are grammatically encoded in the verb phrase in each language? (2) **Event conflation**: How does the language grammatically array the components of events — location, movement, manner, temporality, causation? (3) **Perspective**: What morphological and syntactic devices are available for varying the order and semantic roles of nounphrase arguments with respect to the verb? (4) **Connectivity**: How are event descriptions syntactically "packaged" into multiclause constructions?

2. TENSE/ASPECT

2.1. Inflectional Morphology

In all five languages, the morphology of the verb can be adjusted to indicate temporal characteristics of the event referred to. In Table 1 we use the general term "grammaticized" to refer to a variety of such adjustments, including: (1) affixation (e.g., *play* — *played*), (2) stem change (e.g., *fall* — *fell*), (3) periphrasis (e.g., *fall* — *will fall*), and (4) combinations of the above (e.g., *was falling, had fallen*). The languages vary in the number and diversity of such devices and in their expression of temporal notions. For the purposes of this overview, the specific morphological forms of grammaticized temporality will not concern us. (These are dealt with in the following chapters.) What is important is that each of these languages requires the

TABLE 1
Typological Characteristics of the Five Languages

	English	German[a]	Spanish	Hebrew	Turkish
TENSE/ASPECT					
grammaticized tense	+	+	+	+	+
grammaticized aspect	+	(+)	+	-	+
tense/aspect categories					
progressive	+	-	+	-	+
perfective/imperfective	-	-	+	-	-
past perfect	+	+	+	-	+
present perfect	+	+	+	-	-
EVENT CONFLATION					
verb-/satellite-framed	sat	sat	verb	verb	verb
PERSPECTIVE					
dominant main-clause order	SVO	(SVO)	SVO	SVO	SOV
prepositions/postpositions	prep	prep	prep	prep	post
noun/adjective order	AN	AN	NA	NA	AN
noun/genitive order	NG/GN	NG/GN	NG	NG	GN
relative clause/head position	post	post	post	post	pre
word-order variability (5=high)	1	2	4	3	5
case-inflectional	-	+	-	-	+
passive voice	+	+	+	+	+
CONNECTIVITY					
clause combining	conj	conj	conj	conj	converb
subject ellipsis	-	-	+	+	+

a. As discussed in Chapter IIIв, grammaticized aspect is marginal in German. Also, the characterization of dominant main-clause word order as SVO only applies to clauses in which the subject is not preceded by any other element ("verb-second rule").

speaker to grammatically express **some** temporal notion(s) in each and every clause that has a finite verb (main or auxiliary). In other words, the grammatical expression of temporality is, to some degree, **obligatory** in these languages. For example, in English one cannot say (as one can, for example, in Chinese), *Last night I go to bed early and sleep when the phone ring.* Rather, one must (however redundantly) indicate for each verb that it took place before the current time of speaking. **Tense** — in this instance past tense

— is obligatory in English. Furthermore, we are obliged in English to note grammatically that particular sorts of events progress in time, using the appropriate form of *be* and the suffix *-ing*, that mark the progressive **aspect**. Thus, the grammar of English obliges one to say, *Last night I **went** to bed early and **was sleeping** when the phone **rang**.* In the terms of Table 1, English has both grammaticized tense and grammaticized aspect. To use Comrie's definitions, **tense** is the grammaticized "expression of location in time" (1985, p. 9) while **aspects** "are different ways of viewing the internal temporal constituency of a situation" (1976, p. 3). This English example demonstrates the grammatical marking of past tense (*went, was, rang*) and progressive aspect (*sleeping*).[2] It is important to bear in mind that aspect does not encode objective event characteristics, but rather the speaker's chosen perspective on an event. As Fleischman has emphasized (1990, p. 19): "Unlike tense..., aspect is not a relational category, nor is it deictic; it is not concerned with relating the **time** of a situation to any other time point, but rather with how the speaker chooses to profile the situation."

Our five languages all use some formal means to indicate that an event can be located before the moment of speaking. This is, furthermore, the **only** grammaticized temporal distinction that they all share. In a sense, the past is the most "objective" of the range of possible temporal distinctions: An event is either in memory or it is not. The present passes during the act of speaking. In English we can enter into an ongoing dynamic event by use of the progressive aspect (*you're reading*), but we use the so-called "present tense," without aspectual marking, for ongoing states (*you **believe** what you're reading*) as well as unbounded, "timeless" conditions (*intelligent readers **question** what they **read***). Projections into the future are less certain, and we can use the present tense and various periphrastic forms (*you leave/will leave/are going to leave/will be leaving for New York tomorrow*). Each of our languages varies in the set of grammaticized options for adding dimensions of aspect onto the location of events along a timeline.

For purposes of the frog story, reference to future tense is less relevant, since narrators either describe what they see in the pictures, using present-tense forms, or project the story into the narrative past. But we do need to attend to the narrator's choice to present events as past or present, and to the

---

[2] The above-referenced works of Comrie provide useful basic orientations to the crosslinguistic study of tense and aspect. Other valuable overviews are provided by Chung and Timberlake (1985) and Dahl (1985). Klein (in press) presents a comprehensive and innovative approach to "time in language." Fleischman (1990) insightfully explores tense and aspect in the framework of narrativity. The present chapter is intended only as a schematic introduction to the language-specific details taken up in the following five chapters.

ways in which events are "contoured" in time by means of aspectual marking of various sorts. Hebrew presents the most limited grammaticization of temporality in our sample. As shown in Table 1, it inflects the verb only for tense (past, present, future). The other four languages make more distinctions — of aspect, relative tense, and modality.

First consider aspect. Turkish and Spanish, like English, mark progressive aspect. However, the commonality of the label masks distinctions. The Turkish progressive, unlike its English and Spanish counterparts, is used with stative verbs (e.g., *bil-iyor-um* 'know-PROG-1SG' [=I know]). In the present-tense it contrasts only with a generic/habitual tense, and so is not truly "progressive" in the English or Spanish sense. However, the same form does mark progressivity in the past tense. The Spanish progressive is part of a larger set of aspectual distinctions which includes **perfective** and **imperfective** aspect. Imperfective and progressive both mark durativity, but with different perspectives (discussed in more detail in Chapter IIIC). And, in the past, both contrast with the perfective, which takes a non-durative perspective. In Dahl's definition (1985, p. 78):

> A PFV [perfective] verb will typically denote a single event, seen as an unanalyzed whole, with a well-defined result or end-state, located in the past. More often than not, the event will be punctual, or at least, it will be seen as a single transition from one state to its opposite, the duration of which can be disregarded.

For example, if one says *El perro corrió de las abejas* 'The dog **ran:PFV** from the bees', one is concerned only with the fact that the running took place and is now over and done with. The corresponding imperfective treats the event as unbounded, extended in time, typically in contrast to a parallel punctual event: *El perro corría de las abejas y el niño se cayó del árbol* 'The dog **ran:IPFV** from the bees and the boy **fell:PFV** from the tree.' The Spanish progressive makes it possible not only to treat an event as unbounded, but also as in progress. Furthermore, the auxiliary of the past progressive can, itself, be perfective or imperfective, thus rendering two perspectives where English has only one (compare *he was running* with *estaba corriendo* 'was:IPFV running' and *estuvo corriendo* 'was:PFV running'). Thus although all three languages have means of marking progressive aspect, they differ with regard to the range of contrasting tense/aspect forms, the types of verbs that can be marked as progressive, and the tenses in which such marking occurs. As a consequence, the meaning of a given form cannot be fully determined without regard for the entire system of grammaticized tense/aspect forms of which it is a part, in a particular language. However, for the purposes of this typological overview, it is sufficient to note that Hebrew and German do not grammaticize either progressive or perfective/imperfective; that English and Turkish grammaticize progressive; and that Spanish attends to both kinds of aspectual distinctions.

Up to this point, we have dealt with **absolute tense,** that is, the relation of a referent event to the moment of speaking. Four of our languages (all except Hebrew) also grammaticize **relative tense** by means of the past perfect. This form allows the speaker to relate an event to a reference time prior to speech time, as in the following possible statement in a frog-story narration: *When the boy woke up he saw that the frog **had escaped**.* Here the narrator takes the moment of the boy's realization as reference time, with a retrospective view of the frog's escape from that time point.

Table 1 also shows that English, German, and Spanish have a **present perfect** construction. The range of uses of this construction vary across languages, but there is considerable overlap in functions for purposes of the frog story.[3] In all three languages the grammatical form of the present perfect combines a present-tense auxiliary with a past participle (e.g., *The boy **has fallen** from the tree*), clearly showing the Janus-like quality of this form, which simultaneously points to the past and present. This dual nature makes it awkward to treat the present perfect simply as another tense. Yet it is not quite an aspect, since it readily combines with other aspects and does not clearly provide an aspectual meaning of its own. (Compare *he has worked* and *he has been working,* both present perfect, but differing in aspect.) For our purposes, it is sufficient to note that English, German, and Spanish use this form to relate a past event to speech time with some sense of "continuing relevance" of the event or its consequences.

Turkish presents an additional dimension of grammaticized temporality, lying outside of tense and aspect as discussed above. In that language there is an obligatory distinction in the past tense between events that the speaker has experienced first-hand and events that are known through inference or hearsay (Aksu-Koç, 1988b; Slobin & Aksu, 1982). The latter form is also used for some kinds of narratives, typically folktales, and is chosen by some narrators as the tense of the frog story. The two past tenses both combine with progressive and with resultative, allowing for parallel past progressive and past perfect forms in the "direct experience" and "nonwitnessed" modes, indicated by D and N in Tables 2a and 2b. (For a more detailed discussion of Turkish

---

[3] Anderson (1982) provides a crosslinguistic overview of the range of meanings encoded by forms of the present perfect. Dahl (1985, Chap. 5) has a valuable discussion of "the Perfect and its relatives." Detailed examinations of the English perfect can be found in Brinton (1988) and McCoard (1978), and a valuable recent analysis is offered by Klein (1992). Bamberg (1990) examines uses of the German perfect. Recent analyses of the Spanish perfect are presented by Schwenter (in press).

tense/aspect/modality, see Chapter IIIE, where the two past-tense forms are represented by D and M.)

Table 2 summarizes the variety of tense/aspect distinctions discussed above. (Table 2a presents the grammatical forms and Table 2b presents examples of each form.) It is clear that the five languages lie on a cline, with Spanish presenting the greatest diversity and German the least, while Hebrew has no diversity at all. English and Turkish lie somewhere in the middle of this cline. They both mark progressive and perfect in the past, and English has a present perfect. Turkish does not have a distinct present perfect form (but see Chapter IIIE), however it has twin versions of each of the past forms, depending on mode.

TABLE 2a
Tense/Aspect Forms by Language

Spanish	English	Turkish	German	Hebrew
PRES	PRES	HAB		
			PRES	PRES
PRES.PROG	PRES.PROG	PRES.(PROG)		
PRES.PERF	PRES.PERF	—	PRES.PERF	
PAST.PERF	PAST.PERF	D.PAST.PERF/ M.PAST.PERF	PAST.PERF	
PFV				
	PAST	D.PAST/M.PAST		
IPFV				PAST
			PAST	
PFV.PROG				
	PAST.PROG	D.PAST.PROG/ M.PAST.PROG		
IPFV.PROG				

TABLE 2b
Examples of Tense/Aspect Forms

Spanish

PRES *escapa*

PRES.PROG *está escapando*

PRES.PERF *ha escapado*, PAST.PERF *había escapado*

PFV *escapó*, IPFV *escapaba*

PFV.PROG *estuvo escapando*, IPFV.PROG *estaba escapando*

English

PRES *runs away*

PRES.PERF *has run away*, PAST.PERF *had run away*

PAST *ran away*

PAST.PROG *was running away*

Turkish

HAB *kaçar*

PRES.(PROG) *kaçıyor*

D.PAST.PERF *kaçmıştı*, M.PAST.PERF *kaçmışmış*

D.PAST *kaçtı*, M.PAST *kaçmış*

D.PAST.PROG *kaçıyordu*, M.PAST.PROG *kaçıyormuş*

German

PRES *läuft weg*

PRES.PERF *ist weggelaufen*, PAST.PERF *war weggelaufen*,

PAST *lief weg*

Hebrew

PRES *boreax*

PAST *barax*

2.2. Other Means of Expressing Aspect

In addition to the typologically varying means of temporal expression reviewed above, all languages have means of encoding aspect that go beyond the restricted set of grammatically obligatory devices. Essentially, there are four major categories of such optional devices: (1) morphological marking on the verb, such as English particles (*eat **up**, cool **off**, slow **down***, etc.), (2) aspectual verbs (*start, stop, keep on*, etc.), (3) adverbial words and phrases (*already, all the time, again and again*, etc.), and (4) repetition (*run and run, searched and searched*, etc.). Table 3 lists the major aspectual categories available for such extended expression, with examples from English frog stories.

TABLE 3
Categories of Extended Aspectual Expression

Achievement: a goal is reached
   (*manage to, at long last, after many attempts, succeed, after all*)
Cessive: termination or coming to an end of a process
   (*stop, in the end*)
Completive: endpoint of a process
   (*finish, crack open, knock over, all the way*)
Cumulative: adding to a series of events
   (*even, end up by, go so far as to*)
Generic/Habitual: timeless without implying inception or completion
   (*always, used to*)
Imminent: about to happen, on the point of occurring
   (*about to, nearly, almost, just gonna*)
Inceptive/Inchoative: entering a state
   (*begin, suddenly, get* + PARTICIPLE)
Iterative: repeated individual events
   (*again and again, look in all kinds of places, jumped and jumped*)
Lative: moving/changing location in order to do something
   (*go out to search, come to see, run to meet*)
Perfect: relevance to time of speech or to some other reference time
   (*already, still, not any more*)
Protracted: process is drawn out continuously, extending over time
   (*go on doing, keep on, run and run and run*)
Prospective: looking forward to when an event will take place
   (*until*)
Recurrent: non-iterative repetition of an activity or state by the same protagonist
   (*again, once more, another time*)
Retrospective: looking back to when an event occurred
   (*since*)

3. EVENT CONFLATION

Leonard Talmy (1985, 1991) has proposed that there are basically two distinct ways in which languages allocate information between the main verb and supporting elements ("satellites") in a clause. Consider, for example, the description of movement. In languages like English, the verb simply indicates the fact of movement — e.g., *go*, with possible specification of manner, using verbs that conflate movement and manner — *walk, run, swim, fly*, etc. It is the job of the satellites to the verb — in English, verb particles — to specify direction e.g., *walk in, run up to, swim across*. Talmy suggests that if we take the basic message of a movement-event communication to be that an entity has moved along a path in a specified direction, we can say that English is a **satellite-framed language**, since it is the satellite that conveys this core information. By contrast, Spanish is a **verb-framed** language, because the core information is generally conveyed by the verb alone — e.g., *entrar* 'enter', *salir* 'exit', *subir* 'ascend', *bajar* 'descend'.[4] The encoding of manner is optional in Spanish, and is expressed by a satellite — typically a gerund or prepositional phrase serving an adverbial function. Compare, for example, English *the owl flew out of the hole* and Spanish *el buho salió volando del agujero* 'the owl **exited flying** from the hole'. (Note that both languages allow additional path specification in prepositional phrases, *of the hole* and *del agujero*.)

As shown in Table 1, English and German are satellite-framed languages while Spanish, Hebrew, and Turkish are verb-framed languages. (The contrasts are evident in the examples in Table 2b.) This typological division has important consequences for the frog story, in which there is much movement from place to place. Satellite-framed languages allow for detailed description of paths within a clause, because the syntax makes it possible to accumulate path satellites to a single verb, along with prepositional phrases that add further specification (e.g., *the deer threw them off over a cliff into the water*). (Although both types of languages allow for phrasal path descriptions, as indicated above, our data suggest that satellite-framed languages make more

---

[4] Notice that the English glosses use Latinate terms available to serve in verb-framed constructions in English. These do not, however, constitute the dominant, productive system of movement description in the language. In this regard, the registers of English that use these terms can be considered to represent a "mixed type," in comparison with the relatively pure type of satellite-framed language represented by German. However, children's English frog stories use the Germanic vocabulary exclusively. Although any language may have expressive options that go beyond its typological characterization, here we are concerned with the dominant forms used in colloquial speech, as reflected in these oral narratives. **As a general caveat, it should be remembered that typological characterizations often reflect tendencies rather than absolute differences between languages.**

abundant use of this option than verb-framed languages, perhaps reflecting the typological tendency to specify path outside of the verb.) The satellite-framed languages in our sample also tend towards greater specification of manner, probably because the lexicon provides a large collection of verbs that conflate manner with change of location (*crawl, swoop, tumble*, etc.), often conflating cause as well (*dump, hurl, shove*, etc.). In verb-framed languages, such elaboration is more of a "luxury," since path and manner are elaborated in separate expressions, which are generally optional, and which are less compact in form. As a consequence of these differences, it seems — at least in our data — that English and German narrations are characterized by a great deal of dynamic path and manner description, while Spanish, Hebrew, and Turkish narrations are less elaborated in this regard, but are often more elaborated in description of locations of protagonists and objects and of endstates of motion (as shown in examples (8-12) in Chapter IA; also see Chapter VB and Slobin, in press-c).

It is of interest that this typological division groups the languages differently than the classification of tense/aspect forms. Here we find German grouping with English in terms of relative elaboration, and Spanish grouping with Hebrew and Turkish in terms of minimal elaboration. Thus, as noted at the outset, each language must be treated as a special constellation of characteristics varying on a collection of typologically specified dimensions or parameters.

Talmy's binary typology goes well beyond the encoding of motion events, continuing the division with regard to aspect and causation. Consider the categories of extended aspectual expression summarized in Table 3. Like verbs of motion, some of these are expressed by satellites (e.g., *crack open, knock over*) and some by verbs (e.g., *begin, keep on, stop*). Talmy (1991, p. 13) proposes a "conceptual analogy" between space and time, based on evidence

> that the organization of conceptualization for linguistic expression sets temporal contouring [i.e. aspect] into analogy with Motion as part of a broader cognitive analogy by which temporal structuring is conceptualized as paralleling spatial structuring. This conceptual analogy motivates a syntactic and lexical analogy: to a great extent in a language, aspect is expressed in the same constituent type as Path ..., and often by homophonous forms.

The analogy may be grounded in situations in which motion in space and "motion" in time are inseparable, as in the verb+satellite construction *they walked on and on*. The temporal component seems predominant in *they searched on and on*, and it is the only interpretation of *they slept on and on*. The comparable constructions are verb-framed in Spanish, all with the main verb *seguir* 'continue' plus a gerund of what would be the main verb in a satellite-framed language: *siguieron andando / buscando / durmiendo* '(they) continued walking / searching / sleeping'. Talmy notes that English is a mixed type (possibly under Romance influence), also allowing for constructions like *they went on searching* and *they kept on sleeping*. He compares German and Spanish as fairly "pure" types: Where German has a variety of prefixes marking extended aspect, Spanish makes use of aspectual verbs. The following examples are illustrative of the two patterns:

(1a) **German.**

Sie haben den Frosch weiter-gesucht.

they have the frog further-searched

(1b) **Spanish.**

Siguieron buscando la rana.

they.continued searching the frog

'They went on searching for the frog.'

(2a) **German.**

Sie haben ihn wieder-gesehen.

they have him again-seen

(2b) **Spanish.**

Lo volvieron a ver.

him they.returned to.see

'They saw him again.'

The language types differ more sharply in the lexicalization patterns for change of state verbs. Consider, for example, the transition from sleeping to waking. English and German append a satellite to the verb — originally a locative particle: *wake up, auf-wachen*. The other three languages inflectionally mark the verb 'wake' or 'arise' as reflexive, thus using verb-framed means to indicate entry into a state.

The typological contrast is again reflected in expressions of caused change of state or location. English and German can combine a verb of action with a path particle to encode caused change of location in a particular manner. Spanish, by contrast, tends to encode manner optionally, in a separate clause. Compare the following adult descriptions of the scene in which the deer throws the boy from its antlers into the water: **English:** *knocked them off, dumped them off*; **German:** *schmeißt den runter* 'hurls him down', *hat den runtergeschuppst* 'has shoved him down'; **Spanish:** *le da un empujón y le tira* 'he gives him a shove and he throws him', *frenó* *violentamente y el niño cayó* 'he braked violently and the boy fell'.

In general, then — as Talmy's terms suggest — verb-framed languages rely on the inherent semantics of verb roots that encode simple change of state/location, inflectional modification of such roots, and optional encoding of manner in adverbial phrases or separate clauses. Satellite-framed languages make use of verbal particles that add meanings of change of state/location, often in combination with verbs of manner. They place such verb complexes into transitive frames to encode change of state/location in a particular manner. These differences have pervasive effects on narrative style in our five languages, as documented in the following chapters.

4. PERSPECTIVE

The five languages differ in terms of the available morphological and syntactic means for taking perspectives on events. By "perspective" we understand such issues as foreground/background, topic/focus, highlighting/downgrading, and the like. For example, a narrator can choose which participant to encode as topic and whether to present the event in active or passive voice, as shown by the following perspectives taken on the same event:

(3a) **agent-patient, active:** *The deer lifted the boy up. [E5c-5;3]*

(3b) **patient-agent, passive:** *He got picked up by a reindeer. [E5f-5;8]*

(3c) **patient-agent, active:**

    Le cogió un ciervo.

    OBJ.PRO picked.up a deer

    'Him picked up a deer.' *[S3j-3;11]*

Here we examine means for ordering or deleting arguments of the verb **within** the clause, rather than across clauses. From a typological point of view, our languages vary in terms of both syntactic and pragmatic word order. Table 1 presents the orders of subject, object, and verb in simple, affirmative, declarative sentences.[5] Turkish stands alone in being an SOV language. Furthermore, it exhibits a high degree of what Hawkins (1985) calls "cross-category harmony" — the tendency of operators to be consistently preposed or postposed across constructions. In Turkish, just as the verb is final within the clause, the adposition is final within its phrase (i.e., the language has

---

[5] Language-specific details are not considered here — for example verb-second and verb-final orders in German, under varying syntactic conditions; varying positions of Spanish clitic pronouns; etc.

postpositions rather than prepositions), and nouns follow their modifiers (adjectives, genitives, relative clauses). Spanish and Hebrew present an opposite, but consistent pattern. Adpositions are phrase-initial (i.e., prepositions) and nouns precede adjectives, genitives, and relative clauses. English and German are also prepositional, but are not as consistent in their orderings of nouns and modifiers.[6] All of these factors are important in guiding the direction of information flow in narrative, and have particular consequences for the use of relative clauses, as discussed in Chapter IVB, and passives, as discussed in Chapter IVC.

More important for information flow in narrative is the degree of pragmatic word-order variability in a language. In Table 1 we have placed the five languages on a cline with regard to the flexibility of placement of nounphrase arguments within the clause. English lies at one end, with minimal variability, and Turkish lies at the other (although in our data Turkish narrators make less use of word-order variability than they do in natural conversations). Several factors contribute to the possibility of flexible word order (MacWhinney & Bates, 1989; Slobin, 1982). Essentially, if there are morphological indicators of the syntactic role of a nounphrase the pragmatic relocation of that nounphrase is facilitated. Three types of such indicators are at play in our languages: (1) inflectional casemarking (German articles, Turkish noun suffixes), (2) casemarked pronouns (Spanish, Hebrew), and (3) extensive subject agreement marking on the verb (German, Spanish, Hebrew, Turkish). Note that English, with its nearly inflexible word order, lacks these indicators almost entirely. German case inflection is not reliable, since there are many homophonous forms (e.g., *der* is the definite article for singular masculine nominative, singular feminine genitive and dative, and plural genitive for all genders). This factor limits word-order flexibility in German in comparison with Turkish, where all nounphrases are clearly casemarked.

In addition to possibilities for reordering nounphrases in clauses with active verbs, all five languages have passive constructions which allow for fronting of patients and for elision of agents (optional in English, German, Spanish, and Hebrew; obligatory in Turkish). However, as discussed in Chapter IVC, passive constructions are relatively frequent in a language like English, which lacks other means of reordering, while they are relatively infrequent in a language like Spanish, which has simpler morphosyntactic means for accomplishing similar purposes. Compare the following options for topicalizing the role of the dog in the scene where the bees set off after

---

[6] In both English and German adjectives precede nouns, and relative clauses follow (except for preposed relative clauses in some more formal registers in German). And, in both, two orders of genitive and noun are used (e.g., *the jar of the frog/the frog's jar*).

him. The English and German examples use passives, while the other three
languages left-dislocate 'dog' in active verb clauses.

(4a) **English.**

  The dog's getting chased by the bees. [E4k-4;10]

  German.

  Der Hund wird von den Bienen verfolgt.

  'The dog is chased by the bees.' [G20h]

(4b) **Spanish.**

  Al perrito le persiguen todas las avispas.

  OBJ:DEF dog:DIM CL.PRO chase:PL all the wasps

  'To the doggie him chased all the wasps.' [S51-5;8]

  Hebrew.

  Axarey ha-kelev radfu milyon dvorim.

  after the-dog chased:PL million bees

  'After the dog chased a million bees.' [H9l-9;9]

  Turkish.

  Köpeği de arılar kovalıyormuş.

  dog:ACC TOPIC bees were.chasing

  'As for the dog, him the bees were chasing.' [T9j-9;1]

Note, also, that Turkish is unique in our sample in having a topic/focus
particle, *de*, as shown in (4b).[7] This particle plays an important narrative role
in shifting perspective from one protagonist to another, often implicitly linking two clauses where a temporal conjunction would be called for in other
types of languages. (The role of this particle in indicating simultaneous
actions of two protagonists is examined in Chapter IVA.) Compare, for
example, the following two segments from 5-year-old narratives:

---

[7] A typologically similar, language, Japanese, is well known for its use of such particles.
Indeed, at least one book is devoted to this issue: *Perspectives on topicalization: The case of
Japanese 'WA'* (Hinds, Maynard, & Iwasaki, 1987).

(5a) **English.**

A owl came out and bammed him on the ground while the dog was running away from the bees. [*E5e-5;8*]

(5b) **Turkish.**

Baykuş düşürüyor onu, köpek de kaçıyor.

owl fall:CAUS:PRES him dog **TOPIC** run.away:PRES

'The owl knocks him [=boy] down; and as for the dog, he runs away.'
[*T5f-6;1*]

5. CONNECTIVITY

The five languages have various means of conjoining and subordinating clauses and tracking referents across clauses. Part of the development of narrative capacity in any language involves learning how to syntactically package clauses into larger constructions in which some clauses play structurally and discursively subordinate roles. Two typological dimensions of cross-clause relations appear in our sample: the syntax of clause-combining and the grammatical marking of subjects.

Our Indo-European and Semitic languages have a familiar array of coordinating and subordinating conjunctions that combine finite clauses — that is, clauses with full verb-marking for person/number and tense/aspect — such as *and, when, while,* and so forth. A verb-final language like Turkish, by contrast, relies on nonfinite forms, referred to as **converbs** in Table 1. In constructions with converbs, the stem of the verb of the first clause receives a suffix that indicates the relation to the second clause, and only the second-clause verb indicates tense/aspect and person/number. Consider, for example, how the Turkish converb suffixed by *-ip* functions like the English conjunction *and* in linking the two clauses in (6a) and (6b).

(6a) **English.**

*He stood on the rock **and** called the frog.* [*E9a-9;1*]

(6b) **Turkish.**

Çocuk taşın üstüne çık-ıp bağırmış.

boy rock's top:DAT climb-***ip*** called

'The boy climbed to the top of the rock and called.' [*T91-9;5*]

(Note that Turkish-like nonfinite constructions are available in the other languages as well, where they are literary, rather than colloquial forms of expression — e.g., *Having climbed the rock, the boy called for his frog.* In Turkish, however, these constructions are the most natural, everyday means of clause combining.)

Finally, our languages differ in the possibilities they provide for subject ellipsis (or what has come to be called "pro-drop" or "null subject" in one area of the technical literature). (6a) shows that a "null subject" is allowed in conjoined clauses in English, as it is also in German, Spanish, and Hebrew — that is, the second clause has no overt subject. (The issue does not arise in Turkish, because the converb is nonfinite.) However, these four languages differ in the syntax of subject expression. In English — as in German and Hebrew — a redundant third-person subject pronoun can be added to the second clause, with no change in meaning — e.g., *The boy stood on a rock and he was calling for his frog.* In Spanish, though, the equivalent construction entails a shift in subject: **This** boy stood on a rock and **some other person** was calling.

These crosslinguistic differences are part of the overall grammar of subject ellipsis (much of which goes beyond the aims of this study). In our sample, Spanish and Turkish have rich person/number marking on verbs and are the most thoroughgoing in subject ellipsis, relying on third-person pronouns primarily for contrastive reference. In successive clauses with same subject, verb-marking is sufficient to indicate continuity. This is generally true of Hebrew as well (with some restrictions, discussed in Chapter IIID). English and German, by contrast, show much less person/number marking on the verb and require an overt subject in each independent clause. The following two 4-year-old narrative segments give a graphic example of this major typological difference. Note the repetition of the English pronoun *they* in contrast to the subjectless Spanish verbs with their repeated third-person-plural endings, *-eron/-aron.*

(7a) **English.**
and then they fell backwards
they climbed on a log
and they met a frog
they met ... seven frogs [E4g-4;7]

(7b) **Spanish.**
*ca-**yeron** a un lago ...*
*se escond-**ieron** en un tronco ...*
*salt-**aron***
*salt-**aron** otra vez por aquí*
'fell-3PL to a lake
hid-3PL in a trunk
jumped-3PL
jumped-3PL again over here' [*S4h-4;7*]

* * *

The dimensions briefly reviewed above represent major formal differences between the five languages from the point of view of the developing ability to relate events in narrative. The following five chapters document the development of these formal means in detail. The final section in each chapter summarizes the course of development in terms of the four topic areas presented here. In addition, an overall view of the development of temporality across languages is given in Chapter IVA.

Chapter IIIA

DEVELOPMENT OF LINGUISTIC FORMS: ENGLISH[1]

---

[1] This chapter is based on materials collected by Virginia Marchman and Tanya Renner as part of their doctoral research at the University of California, Berkeley (Marchman, 1989; Renner, 1988). We are grateful to them for making these data and their valuable analyses available to us. Responsibility for the contents of this chapter lies with the authors.

0. INTRODUCTION

The English frog stories were collected in California from children and adults of middle-class background, monolingual speakers of American English. Except for occasional higher-register vocabulary used by some adults, their style is colloquial, spoken English. For example, gerundive *-ing* forms are preferred to Latinate nominalizations (Section 1.2.1); Germanic verb-particle combinations are used rather than more formal, Latinate monolexemic locative verbs — e.g., *go up* vs. *ascend*, *run after* vs. *pursue* (Section 2.1); and everyday connectives like *and, so, also* are preferred to expressions like *moreover, therefore, furthermore* (Sections 4.2, 4.3).

The English preschool narrations — all the 3-year-old texts, most of the 4-year-olds, and around half the 5-year-olds — are rather juvenile in form and content compared with the other languages. Not one of the English-speaking 3-year-olds, an occasional 4-year-old, and around half the 5-year-olds make overt reference to the search theme, and these 5-year-olds are also the only ones who refer explicitly to all three major plot components (Chapter IIA, Section 2). Most 3-year-old texts switch between present and past tense and fail to establish a unified temporal anchor. Only around half the clauses they produce have lexically specific verbs, the rest being static descriptions with *be*.[1] Many of the 3-year-olds also make errors in the grammatical forms of verbs — e.g., regularizations like *falled, keeped, runned*, ill-formed complex strings like *he's wake, were go, was take*, and agreement errors like *it have, they cames*. Their texts lack cohesiveness, except for one child who chains

---

[1] In contrast, 80% of the clauses produced by children from age 4 years and up include verbs other than the copula.

clauses by *and then* (*E3f-3;9*) and another who uses causal connectives like *so* and *because* (*E3g-3;9*), while two others make mechanical use of *and* to indicate that another utterance is to follow (Section 4.2). The 3-year-old transcripts reveal many prompts and encouragements on the part of the investigator (Chapter IIA, Section 4.1), and these 3-year-olds produce far more interactive comments and digressions than their contemporaries in the other languages.

This discrepancy between the level of the 3-year-old English texts compared with some of the 4- and 5-year-olds and all the older children is reflected across the different linguistic devices and grammatical constructions surveyed in this chapter: tense-aspect usage (Section 1), descriptions of the component parts of a situation (Section 2), perspectives encoded by different verb-argument arrays (Section 3), and markers of textual cohesiveness (Section 4).

1. ENGLISH TENSE/ASPECT/MODALITY

English has an elaborate system of grammatical marking of tense, aspect, and modality.[2] The forms include (1) **bound suffixes**: *-s* for 3rd person singular in the present tense — e.g., *jumps, falls*; *-ed* for past tense and regular past participles — e.g., *jumped, climbed*; *-en* for irregular past participles — e.g., *fallen, gone*; and the *-ing* ending of present participles and gerunds — e.g., *jumping, falling*; (2) **internal stem-change** — e.g., *fall ˜ fell, come ˜ came*; (3) **auxiliary verbs** — *be, have, do*; (4) **modal verbs** — *can, may, must, shall, will* followed by an uninflected form of the main verb; and (5) **semi-modals** used with some form of *be* and followed by an infinitival *to* — e.g., *be going to* = *gonna, able, about, used*. These different forms are used in combination with one another to constitute complex tense and aspect marking (and also passive voice, Section 3.1). Perfect aspect is formed by *have* combined with a past participle — e.g., *has jumped, had fallen*, and progressive aspect is formed by *be* combined with the *-ing* present participle — e.g., *is jumping, was falling*. (Verbs with none of these overt aspectual markings are referred to in this chapter as "simple aspect" forms.) These complex auxiliary constituents can cooccur, with the modal element (if there is one) first, followed by perfect aspect, and/or by progressive aspect (and/or by passive voice) — e.g., *may have jumped, may be jumping, has been jumping, may*

---

[2] The rich linguistics literature on these systems is concerned mainly with their form and/or function in sentences, not connected text. General background on tense and aspect are provided in Comrie (1985) and Comrie (1976). The English forms are surveyed in Joos (1964) and Palmer (1974), with attempts at semantic generalizations in King (1983) and McCawley (1971), and see, particularly, Declerck (1991).

have been jumping.

Finite verbs are marked for either present or past tense — e.g., *jumps / jumped, fall / fell, is / was.* In complex verbal strings, tense is marked on the first element — modal, or *have* or *be*, compare *may / might have fallen, has / had been falling, is / was falling.* Forms traditionally termed **future** tense have the structure of a modal (or semi-modal) plus main verb — e.g., *will / would fall, will / would have fallen, will / would be falling* and also *is / was going to fall, is / was going to have fallen.*

Nonfinite verb forms are not marked for tense. They occur in simple clauses, with complex verbal strings, preceded by tense-marked auxiliaries and modals or else by modal or aspectual verbs. They may stand alone as main verbs, but may also modify the modal or aspectual contour of another verb. Examples of modal modification in our English sample are: *The boy **tried** to climb up it [E3d-3;5], The dog **decided** to go away [E9e-9;7].* Examples of extended aspect are: *They **keep** going around [E4f-4;7], They **went** looking for it [E4e-4;7], And they **start** calling [E5d-5;6].* Nonfinite verb forms also occur in multiclause sentences, and then their temporal reference is relative to the tense of the verb in the main clause, e.g., *(The deer) carried him to the edge of the cliff, with his dog **chasing** after [E9a-9;1]; The little boy just watches him **fall**, still **wondering** where the frog is [E20h]; The dog is rescued from **having** his head stuck in the jar [E20b].*

Our analysis focuses on the facets of tense and aspect which proved most relevant to the English frog stories (Sections 1.1 to 1.3). Reference to the future with *will*, and irrealis mood in general, is relatively marginal to these accounts and is not treated here.

1.1. Present and/or Past Tense

Findings for different languages show that by age 3, children are able to mark distinctions between past and present tense as stipulated by the grammar of their native language (Aksu-Koç, 1988b; Weist, 1986). This is supported by evidence from children acquiring both American and British English (Brown, 1973; Fletcher, 1979, 1981). We therefore assumed that the youngest children in this sample, aged 3 years, would be able to make appropriate use of one or both of these tenses in formulating their narrations. This in fact turned out to be true in a rather limited sense. Most of the younger children, as noted, make **errors of form**. They sometimes regularize "strong" or irregular past tense forms (Bybee & Slobin, 1982), e.g., *falled [E3a-3;1], caughted [E3e-3;8],* and *catched [E4a-4;0], keeped [E3g-3;9], comed [E4e-4;6], taked [E4f-4;7],* now and then even in 5-year-old texts, e.g., *flied [E5b-5;2], creeped [E5i-5;19].* Children occasionally add a present-tense suffix to a past-tense stem — e.g., *cames [E3g-3;9], gots [E5g-5;9];* and quite a few 3-year-olds, although few older children, omit the *-s* suffix and use an unmarked stem form with a 3rd-person singular subject — e.g., *He cry, and it fall down* [E3c-3;4], *The owl come* [E3d-3;5]. Another common omission is of the tense-marking auxiliary *is* or *are* with verbs in progressive aspect (Section 1.2.1).

Where correct, the younger children's use of grammatical tense reflects structural well-formedness within the confines of individual clauses, not at the level of more extended discourse. Examples of grammatically correct tense usage in 3-year-old English texts include "strong" past tense forms — e.g., *A owl flew out of here* [E3a-3;1], *The jar broke* [E3i-3;9], *The dog fell down* [E3j-3;10]; regular past tense — *The dog barked* [E3e-3;8], *And then he climbed a tree* [E3f-3;9], *He knocked them off of the cliff* [E3j-3;10]; and an occasional simple present tense — *What if he steps in the glass!* [E3g-3;9], *The mouse wants to eat the boy* [E3h-3;9], *He sees two frogs* [E3j-3;10]. However, and this is the burden of our argument, the younger children fail to use grammatical tense or aspect in a discourse-appropriate fashion, in keeping with the demands of a well-organized narrative text.

1.1.1. Dominant tense

Choice of a consistently favored tense throughout the narration was taken as criterial for a well-formed narrative (Chapter IIA). As noted there, narrators can select to anchor their accounts in either present or past tense. Past tense in English as in other languages is the unmarked or most typical temporal setting for the recounting of chronologically sequential events in narrative. But speakers may choose to depart from this norm by adopting the more marked "narrative" or historic use of present tense for the main thread of their narrations (Casparis, 1975; Herring, 1985; Silva-Corvalán, 1983; Wolfson, 1982). In such instances, the text is generically anchored in simple present-tense forms, as illustrated by the following excerpt from an adult English story.

(1) *And then all the bees start chasing the dog, who runs away, and this owl comes out and the boy falls, and then he climbs a rock, climbs to the top of the rock, and he screams for the frog again, calls for the frog, and then he gets stuck in a reindeer's antlers, and the reindeer takes off with him, on him, and they go over to a cliff.* [E20a]

The picture-based nature of our narratives makes a present-tense perspective fully appropriate, since the events depicted in the book can be viewed as ongoing, and narrators can choose to treat the pictures as depicting a currently unfolding sequence of events. This is shown in the following excerpt from a 9-year-old text.

(2) *The boy's looking at his frog, and the dog's smiling down, and then he's going to bed and the frog is sneaking out. Then it's morning and the frog is gone. He's looking all over his room, messing it up.* [E9l-9;11]

Reliance on past tense is thus not criterial for evaluating a narrative as well-formed in our study; either present or past can be considered normative as a temporal anchor. And indeed this is what we found for the more mature English narratives, as shown by the English 9-year-old and adult texts reproduced in Chapter IIA: They are told in the present — examples (29) and (34) — or in the past — examples (30) and (35). However, the younger English narrators do not always manage to adhere to a single grammatical tense. Table 1 below compares figures for those favoring either past or present tense in at least 75% of the clauses they produce compared with temporally "mixed" texts, which use both tenses to a similar extent.

TABLE 1
Number of English Texts Favoring Past or Present Compared
with Mixed Tense Usage, by Age [N = 12 per group]

Age Group	Mean Age	Mean No. Clauses	Dominant Tense		
			PAST	PRESENT	MIXED
3 yrs	3;7	22	1	3	8
4 yrs	4;7	27	5	5	2
5 yrs	5;7	42	6	4	2
9 yrs	9;7	45	8	4	0
Adult		75	2	9	1

Table 1 shows that a third of the English-speaking preschoolers (among the 3-year-olds, as high as two-thirds) shift back and forth between present and past tense. In contrast, all the older children and adults (except for one) provide a consistent temporal thread to the texts by anchoring them in either past or present tense — with most 9-year-olds favoring past tense and most adults favoring present tense as dominant. The following 3-year-old text exemplifies the back-and-forth shifting between present and past characteristic of the more juvenile English narrations.

(3) **PRESENT:** *Look at this frog, look when he's sleeping, and ... his frog getting out!*

TRANSITION: *Look what happened to the guy!*

PAST: *Oh no! He licked on his face, and he fell out the window.*

PRESENT: *Bee - er - beehive. He's standing on two toes.*

PAST: *He broke it. A owl flew out of here.*

PRESENT: *And he's running away. Look at the dog, he's sad.*

PAST: *A reindeer - he threw them down.*

TRANSITION: *Now look what happened to the dog. Frogs! A whole family of frogs!*

[Investigator asks: "What about the boy?"]

PRESENT: *He doesn't have a family.* [E3a-3;1]

This child knows how to use present and past tense at the level of the single sentence, but is incapable of maintaining a consistent narrative flow across more than two consecutive clauses. Another juvenile narration, produced by a 5-year-old, contains rather larger chunks of text in each tense. The text in (4) starts out in conventionally narrative vein, anchored in a block of consistently past-tense clauses. The child then shifts to present tense for the rest of the narration, slipping back into past for only two isolated sentences.

(4)   **PAST**: *One day, he woke up from his bed, he seed the doggie looking at the frog. And then, they turn the page. And then in the night, when he was sleeping, and his dog - er the frog tried to get out!*

PRES [+IRREALIS]: *And then he's, oh my gosh! My frog is gone! He couldn't be in the shoe. What if he bangs this? He could get cut easily this way, because what if he bangs on the floor, all the glass breaks and goes into his mouth. That might - er - see, it broke. But he's mad, he thinks that he's happy. Bumblebees coming out of the honeyhive. Oh my gosh! What if he stings me on the nose! Uh oh, he sees the gopher, oh my gosh!*

PAST: *He had an accident. He knocked me down there.*

PRES: *Uh, you know what, you don't know where the deer is. I do. His horns ...* [Child points to picture]. *He's mad, deer's mad.*

PAST: *He fell in the water.*

PRES: *It's very ... he can't swim. Lookit, how deep it is for him, but it's not very deep for him. We're dry.* [Singsong tone of voice]. *Wow! We see a family of frogs! That's the end.* [E5a-5;1]

This veering between past and present coincides with a shift from a narrative to a picture-description mode. The personal comments which the children address to the investigator in examples (3) and (4) also reflect departures from the narrative mode. In contrast, children whose stories demonstrate a well-defined plot structure are typically consistent in their choice of a dominant tense. Thus failure to select either present or past tense for temporal anchoring reflects lack of narrative discourse structure at a developmental phase where children already have command of tense usage at the level of the simple clause — as in (3) and — as in (4) — even in stringing adjacent clauses in more complex sentences.

1.1.2. Tense shifting

All the 9-year-olds and all but one adult demonstrate consistent use of a single dominant tense. This need not entail total avoidance of **tense shifting**, as a legitimate device for switching temporal perspectives within an ongoing narrative (Bamberg, 1987; Schiffrin, 1981). Three of the English-speaking 9-year-olds and no fewer than eight adults shift one or more times out of their dominant past or present tense to its converse. Tense switches are commoner from present-tense anchors to past tense — one 9-year-old and seven adults, compared with two 9-year-olds and only one adult (*E20d*) who shift from past-tense anchors to present tense. These switches perform one of two complementary functions — local and extended. Local tense shifting meets requirements of grammatical "sequence of tense" (Comrie, 1986; de Clerck, 1990). This is the case, for instance, in past tense complement clauses semantically anterior to the dominant present tense of the main clause — e.g., *The dog is coming back, looks like he's either stunned or is just very frightened and ashamed that he **was** outdone by the bees. The owl is looking for the boy ... [E20b]*. Adults also freely shift to past tense in relative and adverbial clauses which describe situations viewed as **anterior** to the main eventline — e.g., *The boy falls out of the hole because an owl **came out** of the hole [E20g]*, *The dog has a jar on top of his head, which **was** where the frog was originally located, and he seems not to be so happy [E20c]*.

The "extended" function of tense shifting is motivated by the thematic organization of the narrative as a whole. For example, a 9-year-old narrative starts out in present tense, to meet the scene-setting function of background to the ensuing events, for a total of nine clauses. The second of these clauses shifts to past with the "local" function of expressing the anteriority of the boy's having found the frog prior to the scene-setting situation of the "exposition" (Sternberg, 1978). The exposition continues in present tense, until the onset of the narrative action, from which point the entire narrative adheres strictly to past tense (see Chapters IVA and IVD). The relevant section is reproduced in (5).

(5)   *It's a story about this kid who **found** a frog, and he has - er, he keeps it as a pet. And overnight the frog gets out of the jar that he's in, and jumps out the window. The next morning they find out that he's gone and they, they look for him.*

*And the dog **stuck** his head in the jar, looking for him, and he peeked out the window. Then he fell, and the glass broke. And they went out the window ... [E9i-9;10]*

Extended tense shifting in the adult English narratives may also function to distinguish between two series of events going on concurrently — one set in the past and another in the present (see Chapter IVA). This is a strategy adopted throughout the single adult narrative which manifests several blocks of past-tense forms embedded in present-tense contexts (the adult assigned to the "mixed" category in Table 1), as excerpted in (6).

(6) *The dog is shaking the tree where the beehive is connected to, while the boy climbs on top of the tree and starts yelling in a hole for the frog. While the dog **shook** the tree so much that the beehive fell down ...*

 *And the dog is being such a loyal dog, he runs after the elk trying to per- suade him to let go of his master. Well, it **was** of no use because the dog ran off the edge of the cliff, while the boy was thrown off by the elk. [E20c]*

Nearly half the adult English narratives shift tense liberally, manifesting a kind of rhetorical flexibility not evident in the children's stories. Moreover, the adults are **selective** in their use of this device. Some avoid it altogether; others use it sparingly for local purposes of temporal and aspectual departures from the main plotline; one adult (*E20e*) uses it to set off the initial scene-setting and the final coda parts of the narrative (in past tense) from the main substance of the story; another (*E20c*) does so to set concurrent blocks of events off from one another. For adult English narrators, tense shifting is an expressive option which they may, but need not use in relating these events.

The 9-year-olds shift tense relatively rarely. The example in (5) is not typical of the English schoolchildren, who tend to adhere more strictly to their chosen anchor tense than the adults (or the younger children). Only three 9-year-olds shift tense, no more than one to three times per narrative, with their shifts typically local in scope, rather than across thematically motivated blocks of text. The school-age children clearly prefer a straightforward, uni-form narrative mode rather than flexible tense switching for purposes of plot-motivated backgrounding or for shifting from current to anterior and from ongoing to generic temporal reference.

The 5-year-olds shift tense more often than either 9-year-olds or adults. Ten of the children in this group switch from one tense to another, between two and seven times per text. Several use local tense shifting felicitously, generally to move from a past-tense plotline to personal digressions or generic descriptions in present tense — e.g., *He was playing with the bees again, he was trying to kid them, and then a rugrat came. **I call them rugrats because***

they go in holes. *And then the dog was still trying to kid the bees* [*E5b- 5;2*]; *Then they fell where there is a stream. But the dog got on his head* [*E5c-5;3*].[3] Temporally well-motivated use of tense shifting to express "relative tense" between a matrix predicate and its associated complement clause is rare among the 5-year-olds, and among the English-speaking preschoolers in general. One 5-year-old text [*E5i-5;10*] manifests an **incipient** reliance on this device, as follows. The narrative is anchored in past tense, starting with *Once upon a time there was a little boy who had a frog and a dog. And it was time to go to sleep, so he went to sleep*; and ending with *And they saw a family of frogs, first they saw two frogs, and then they saw a family, a whole family!* In between are six blocks of present-tense clauses, representing **direct speech**, e.g., *So they went to look. "Is that you in there, is it, is it?" But it was only a squirrel. Then he looked in a rock. "Is, oh - Frog, frog, are you here?"* This is an idiosyncratic means of using tense switching to avoid syntactic embedding by complement clauses and the sequence-of-tense constraints they impose.

The 5-year-olds' uses of tense shifting reflect two extremes of narrative ability. At the more mature end is a 5-year-old narrative told entirely in the present tense, until it shifts to the past tense to describe the boy's mistaken clutching onto antlers in lieu of branches and the entire denouement of the story. The relevant part is given in (7).

(7) *The bees come out of the beehive, and the boy's looking in the hole, and the boy falls. The bees go after the dog, and the boy - he's gonna climb the rock, and then he calls up on the rock for the frog. And then he um - he - um he **thought** it was sticks and he got on that and the deer came and carried him and the dog was in front, and he throwed the boy and the dog into the water ...* [*E5k-5;11*]

The 5-year-old excerpt in (7) is from a narrative which makes explicit mention of all three major plot components; it relies on the connectives *and* and *and then* to chain events sequentially; and it is anchored consistently in present tense until a specific turning point in the narrative, where it shifts to past. At the opposite end of the scale is the juvenile 5-year-old text in (4), liberally sprinkled with erratic switching from one tense to another. Between these two extremes, preschoolers' shifting between the two tenses is locally governed, and lacks the thematic motivation in older narrators' use of this

---

[3] Such "local" tense shifting to generic present is restricted in syntactic scope, yet it reveals a semantically sophisticated distinction between transient or occasional events and generic states. A parallel adult example is *The dog, being the rambunctious animal that it is, found a beehive and decided to have some fun* [*E20d*].

device.

1.2. Grammatical Aspect

This section deals with the grammatical constructions of **progressive** (Section 1.2) and **perfect** aspect (1.3), and how they interact with simple present and past tense. They take the form of an auxiliary combined with the main verb — *be* plus the participial *-ing* form in the progressive and *have* plus the participial *-ed* or *-en* form in the perfect. Morphologically, they are more marked than their simple counterparts. One might thus hypothesize that children would prefer the simplex verb forms; instead, our study reveals a tendency to **avoid** the unmarked simple aspect in the texts of the younger children.

1.2.1. Progressive aspect

Progressives focus on the internal contour of events characterized as having temporary duration. They are used in describing situations which are construed as episodic, hence as less stable or constant, as lacking in the intrinsic permanence associated with simplex predicates (Goldsmith & Woisetschlaeger, 1982; Hatcher, 1951; Langacker, 1987a; Smith, 1983). In present tense, progressive forms thus also serve as the immediate present in English, contrasting with the simple form of the "extended present" used to describe habitual or generic situations. This deictic function of present progressives as anchored in speech time explains the finding that the progressive was identified as the first of 14 grammatical morphemes acquired by the (American) English-speaking children studied by Brown (1973). Initially, children use it in its "primitive" form, without the requisite auxiliary *am, is,* or *are,* and they continue to use the bare *-ing* form of verbs as late as Brown's Stage V.

We analyzed the distribution of *-ing* forms across all clauses in the English frog stories which contain an explicit main verb.[4] Table 2 below shows the breakdown of these *-ing* forms among the different age groups.

---

[4] These account for only 57% of the 3-year-old utterances, as compared with around 80% of the clauses produced by 4- and 5-year-olds. With age, there is a clear tendency to prefer lexically explicit verbs rather than copular constructions with the verb *be* alone, e.g., *And leaves are there, and leaves are everywhere!* [E3d-3;5]; *There's a dog, and there's a frog* [E3e-3;8]; and also *He went somewhere else, cause it wasn't as quiet there* [E5b-5;2]; or *And the boy thinks those are twigs* [E9b-9;3].

TABLE 2
Distribution of -*ing* Forms out of Total Lexical Verb Tokens,
by Age [N = 12 in each age group]

	3 yrs	4 yrs	5 yrs	9 yrs	Adult
Total verbs	252	297	428	500	790
Percent of -*ing* forms	39	25	19	20	25
Total -*ing* forms	99	74	81	99	194
Percent "bare" progressives	31	20	3	0	0
Percent present progressive	60	59	58	29	40
Percent past progressive	7	13	35	33	8
Percent nonfinite -*ing* forms	2	7	4	38	52

Table 2 shows that English narratives make wide use of verb forms with suffixal -*ing* — approximately one-quarter of all lexical verbs across the age groups. The 3-year-olds rely most heavily on -*ing* forms — around 40% of their verb forms, compared with around 20% to 25% from age 4 years up. Moreover, nearly one-third of the -*ing* forms used by 3-year-olds are ungrammatical "bare" forms with no overt form of the auxiliary *be*, as in (8) and (9).

(8) *And that - he floating off, uh - sitting down.* [E3c-3;4]

(9) *And here, he trying to get the bees, trying to get the bees!* [E3l-3;11]

Such tenseless main clauses are rare from age 5 years up.[5]

The distribution of -*ing* forms is affected by choice of tense. Preschoolers, in particular, use progressive forms in present far more than in past tense. There is also a steady decline in proportion of progressive forms out of total present tense forms used with age. Fully two-thirds (66%) of all the present-tense forms used by 3-year-olds take progressive aspect, compared with around half among 4-year-olds (48%), a third (30%) among 5-year-olds, and even less out of all the present-tense forms used by older narrators (22% of 9-year-olds present-tense clauses, 17% among the adults). This suggests that for younger children, progressive aspect is treated as the unmarked, most basic way of describing events construed as applying to the time of speaking.

---

[5] Only one child outside of the 3-year-old group (*E4h-4;8*), consistently favors this "bare" -*ing* form of verbs.

This claim is supported by occasional 3- and 4-year-old extensions of progressive forms from process verbs to **stative verbs** which typically disallow their use. These appear to contradict the findings of Brown (1970, 1973) and Kuczaj (1978) for American-English children's "error-free" acquisition of the progressive, but they are in line with Mapstone and Harris (1985), who found that nearly half of the British 4- to 6-year-olds whom they tested "made at least one generalization of the progressive to a stative verb" (p. 439). The frog story shows such uses mainly with the verb of perception *see* — e.g., *He's seeing if there's honey in there* [E3j-3;10], *He's seeing that the frog got out* [E4h-4;8], *And then he was seeing a lot of frogs* [E3d-3;5]. These "errors" are made by children who favor *-ing* forms across their texts, and who treat them as neutral, rather than as semantically restricted by verb *Aktionsarten*.

Past progressive forms with *was* or *were* are never numerous, and account for only 10% of all past-tense forms across the sample (from 9% among 3-year-olds to 12% among adults), although even 3-year-olds can produce them correctly. Out of the total *-ing* forms distributed as shown in Table 2, those marked for past tense account for only 10% among 3- and 4-year-olds, going up to around one-third among 5- and 9-year-olds. This relative increase in past progressive with age reflects the rise in older children's favoring of past tense in general. Younger children favor present progressive as a means to present events as ongoing at the time of narrating, construed as identical to the time of speaking. For them progressive is largely identified with immediate present tense. Older children, in contrast, rely increasingly on past progressive as a relative tense, for distinguishing different events within the ongoing narrative.[6] They are able to deploy progressive aspect for the backgrounding function of indicating the temporal overlap between events narrated in the past and a clear separation between speech time, narrative time, and reference time.

Another related change in use of *-ing* forms with age concerns the distribution of **nonfinite** *-ing* forms in different syntactic contexts. We defined an *-ing* form as nonfinite if it occurs with a verb in present or past tense, other than the auxiliary *be*, within the same simple clause or in an adjacent dependent clause. These forms are rare among preschool children, but constitute over a third to more than a half of the *-ing* forms used by 9-year-olds and adults (see last line of Table 2). Only 11 out of all 36 preschool children use

---

[6] The relative few past progressive forms in the adult texts compared with the 9-year-olds (8% versus 33% of total *-ing* forms) is accounted for by the fact that most English adults chose the present as anchor tense for their narratives (nine adults versus four of the 9-year-olds).

such forms, never more than once or twice per narrative, compared with nearly all the 9-year-olds and adults (19 out of 24).

Nonfinite -*ing* forms serve different functions at different stages of development. Among the preschoolers, they occur as **complements** in relation to three types of predicates: (a) following presentative *There + be* expressions — e.g., *And see! There's a mouse coming [E3f-3;9]*, *There's a deer hiding up there [E4f-4;7]*; (b) with aspectual verbs — e.g., *Then he started playing around [E4e-4;7]*, *He kept on calling frog [E5h-5;10]* (see Section 1.3);[7] and (c) following clauses with verbs of perception — e.g., *He's looking at all the bees flying out of the honey [E3g-3;9]*, *I see him snoring [E4j- 4;9]*. In addition to complements like these, older narrators also use nonfinite -*ing* in dependent, modifying clauses. Nearly one-quarter of the nonfinite -*ing* forms of 9-year-olds, and well over half those used by adults, have **adverbial** functions, typically in describing two concurrent events or attendant circumstances, e.g., *And the deer carried him to the edge of a cliff, with his dog **chasing** after [E9a-9;1]*, *The three were just sitting around, **doing** nothing [E20d]* (Chapter IVA). Nine-year-olds and adults also use nonfinite participials with the modifying function of **relative clauses**, e.g., *The dog was shaking the tree with the beehive **hanging** from it [E9i-9;10]*, *The dog is curious about some bees **flying** overhead [E20c]*. None of the preschoolers use these forms in syntactic subordination, for purposes of adverbial or relative modification.[8] The figures in Table 2 thus reflect a change in the function of -*ing* forms with age. For the younger children, they frequently constitute the favored verb form within the bounds of the simple clause — from age 4 up, nearly always with the auxiliary *be* carrying marking for present or past tense. For schoolchildren, they may serve as a means of subordinating one event to another, in nonfinite complement or adverbial clauses.

Use of progressive aspect also reveals different ways in which speakers relate to the text as a whole, beyond sentence boundaries. The tendency of younger children to avoid simple present-tense verbs reflects their reliance on the **picture-description mode** adopted by the 3-year-olds across the languages. They treat the events depicted in the storybook as ongoing, and so

---

[7] Older children use these constructions with a wider range of aspectual verbs (e.g., *And the dog came whimpering over [E9i-9;10]*) and also with occasional modal verbs, e.g., *The dog tried running after the deer [E9c-9;8]*.

[8] The single exception is a 5-year-old who uses a nontensed -*ing* form in a dependent adverbial clause, thus: *And he was standing on a stone, calling [E5c-5;3]*. The comma between the main clause and the gerundive *calling* in fact represents a longish pause, suggesting that these two predications are not fully knitted together in a single prosodic or syntactic package.

describe them from the temporal perspective of immediate present rather than the generic or narrative stance of simple present. Compare the following descriptions of the same series of events in a 4-year-old compared with an adult narrative.

(10) *When the boy wakes up, he's gone. Here he's looking in his boot. Now he's looking out the window. Now the dog jumps down, and now he's hugging the dog. Now all the leaves are falling down.* [E4l-4;11]

(11) *The next morning the boy and the dog wake up and find the empty jar. The boy looks in his boots, while the dog looks in the jar for the frog. They look out the window for the frog. The dog falls out the window, breaks the jar. The kid goes down out the window as well, picks up the dog ...* [E20b]

The 4-year-old in (10) clearly knows how to use the simple present, but is incapable of sustaining the narrative perspective which it entails across entire stretches of text. In contrast, the adult relies consistently on the simple present to anchor her narrative. Some of the 5-year-olds, and all those from age 9 years up who select present tense as their anchor (22 out of the 36 in these age groups, see Table 1) favor simple aspect. The few older children who rely relatively heavily on progressive aspect use it as a bridge between picture-description and fully narrative mode.[9]

Shifting from simple to progressive aspect thus occurs across the sample. Every text from age 3 years through adults contains two or more clauses in progressive aspect — except for two 9-year-old texts, both anchored in past tense (*E9c-9;6* and *E9f-9;8*).[10] But these shifts perform different functions across the age groups. Among the 3- and 4-year-olds, either progressive is a favored tense form, indicative of picture-description mode, or it is used to mark local contrast between durative and punctual activities, or between speech time and reference time. The older children use progressive aspect to mark departures from the narrative backbone of the plot, not as the unmarked form across their texts. Adults, in contrast, use progressive forms across blocks of text, for highlighting or backgrounding specific segments of their story. Adults' use of *-ing* forms reveals several different patterns — in line with what we noted for individual preferences (Chapter IIA, Section 4.4). Some adults use them very liberally. Other adult narrators adhere strongly to

---

[9] The only 5-year-old who does so (*E5j-5;10*) is still adhering to more juvenile picture description, with no explicit reference to any of the three major plot-components (Chapter IIA).

[10] And both of these include several nonfinite uses of *-ing* following aspectual verbs like *start, keep on.*

simple aspect, in either present — *(E20g)* — or past tense — *(E20i)*. Unlike the younger children, adults never anchor their narratives predominantly in progressive aspect; but unlike the 9-year-olds, none of them avoid progressives altogether. Rather, they use progressive aspect with a more global, plot-based motivation, for events which form a durative background to the plot-advancing sequentially unfolding course of events described in simple narrative present or past.

1.2.2. Perfect aspect

Unlike progressives, verbs in perfect aspect cannot be interpreted in purely deictic terms of the temporal relation between the time of speaking (or narrating) and the time of the event's occurrence. They involve consideration of some **other** reference point, to which the situation being described has current relevance or to which it is anterior (Klein, 1992; McCoard, 1978; Reichenbach, 1947a, 1947b; Smith, 1980a, 1980b). In our English narratives, verbs marked for perfect aspect serve two related functions, both characterizable as expressing **relative** tense: (1) They express **anteriority**, that is, they mark one event as having occurred prior to another, for which it constitutes a temporally backgrounded event, and so departs from the normal temporal sequence of the unfolding plot — e.g., *The boy, who **had climbed** the tree, looked in it* [E9i-9;10], *The boy **has climbed** a tree and is looking in a hole* [E20h]. (2) They meet the requirements of traditional **sequence of tense** rules (Comrie, 1986), that is, they serve to "backshift the tense forms from direct speech when the introductory verb is in the past tense" (de Clerck, 1990, p. 1), e.g., *They asked the gopher and the bees where ... if they **had seen** the frog [E9b-9;3]* — and, by extension, to the relationship between the introductory matrix verb and the verb in complement clauses in general — e.g., *He's all happy he's **found** his frogs* [E20a], *It seems that **they've raised** this happy family* [E20b], *The next morning they discover that the frog **has escaped*** [E20g].

The frog story provides numerous opportunities for backwards temporal reference to events which occurred at some prior point in the plot. Examples include the scene where the dog gets his head stuck in the jar in which the frog **had been kept** or from which the frog **had escaped**, or the situations illustrated above where the owl pops out of the hole in the tree which the boy **has climbed**, as well as the final scene in which the boy recovers the frog which **had run away** or which he **had lost**. Despite this "objective" reality, we hypothesized that perfect forms would be relatively rare in the young children's narratives, since they are known to be a late acquisition compared to other tense/aspect forms in American English. This delay is more marked in the language acquisition of American compared with British children, since adult American English allows simple past tense in many contexts where British speakers require a perfect form (Gathercole, 1986; Slobin, 1987, in press-b; Wells, 1985).

These predictions are strongly borne out by our findings. Perfect forms are used only twice across the preschool corpus. A 3-year-old uses it as a means of switching from ongoing, durative to a **perfective** perspective on the scene of the boy falling off the deer's back into the water: *He's trying to get off. He's falled off! He falled off!* [E3k-3;10].[11] And a 5-year-old uses it in a typical "sequence of tense" context of a complement clause, thus: *And then they saw - the frog **had married** another frog* [E5c-5;3]. Three 9-year-old schoolchildren use the perfect, only in **past** tense, only once or twice per text (a total of four out of all their clauses, the bulk of which, as noted, are in simple past tense). The vulnerability of this system is revealed, moreover, by an occasional ungrammaticality, e.g., *And then the dog's running away, cause the bees were all chasing him, and he **had fell down*** [E9l-9;11].

In contrast to the children's avoidance of perfect aspect, no fewer than **eight** of the adults use such forms at least once, while three adults use them four or more times in their narratives *(E20b, E20f, E20k)*. The adults use perfect aspect exclusively in **present-tense** contexts. In contrast to the few 9-year-olds we noted, there is not a single instance of past perfect in the adult corpus, no doubt because the bulk of the adults relied on present as an anchor for their narratives (see Table 1). For these speakers of American English, formal "sequence of tense" requirements as well as expression of anteriority with a wider discourse scope are neutralized by reliance on **simple past tense**, as shown in (12). That is, in present-tense contexts, simple past may serve where present perfect is still largely mandatory in British English.

(12a) *The owl **is** angry that the boy **interrupted** his home.* [E20c]

(12b) *The dog's head **gets** stuck in the little bottle that the frog **was** in.* [E20l]

(12c) *He's even happier when he **sees** the frog **had** little kids.* [E20l]

---

[11] A problem arises due to the ambiguity of contracted *'s* as between *has* and *is*. Fletcher (1979, 1981) suggests that this blurring of the distinction between a verb in the present perfect and a copula plus adjective combination may constitute a problem for children in acquiring perfect aspect. This is particularly relevant at one point in our sample. As many as six preschoolers describe the scene where the boy sees the empty jar by some combination of *is* plus *gone*. Among the smaller children, this is always in the ambiguous form of *the frog's gone* [E3g-3;9] or *he's gone* [E3k-3;10] and [E4l-4;11], but the 5-year-olds disambiguate this to some overt form of *be* — e.g., *And then the frog is gone!* [E5e-5;8], *The frog was gone* [E5l-5;11].

The bulk of the 25 adult uses of present perfect do, in fact, observe the local-anteriority, "sequence of tense" requirements between present-tense matrix clauses and their associated dependent clauses describing prior events. The examples in (13) correspond to those in (12), but present perfect is used in place of past simple.

(13a) *He's all happy he's found his frogs.* [E20a]

(13b) *They're probably angry that the dog has knocked their hive out.* [E20b]

(13c) *The next morning they discover that the frog has escaped.* [E20g]

(13d) *He looks in his boots to see if the frog has taken up quarters for the evening.* [E20k]

The contrast between the dependent clauses in (12) and (13) — simple past versus present perfect respectively — is found only in the adult narratives and reflects different expressive options available to fully proficient speakers of American English. They can be more or less conservative, depending on personal choice of style in local tense/aspect shifting and the extent to which they observe the traditional grammar of "sequence of tense" constraints.[12]

1.2.3. Developmental trends

The dominant themes of our book are manifest in how the English-speaking narrators avail themselves of the formal tense/aspect options provided by the grammar of their native tongue. The 3-year-olds reveal incomplete grammatical mastery, with a relatively high rate of "bare" progressives with no overt auxiliary *be*. Their over-reliance on progressive forms shows

---

[12] In general, adult narrators differ in the extent to which they choose to overtly mark perfect and durative event characteristics through recourse to grammatical aspect. Compare the following descriptions of the same sequence — being caught by the deer to the fall from the cliff — in different adult texts. The first is from a highly elaborated text, the only adult with mixed tense as well as progressive and perfect aspect, with much use of nonfinite *-ing*; (b) mixes simple and progressive aspect in the dominant present tense; while (c) remains anchored in simple present. (a) *Now the boy has been picked up by some antlered beast, looks like a deer, and the deer is running to a cliff, and the dog is barking at the deer ... This dog is pretty useless, all he does is cause trouble and bark at things. Now the deer has thrown the boy over the cliff into - looks like they're heading for a pond, and the dog goes too, as the dog has throughout the entire story.* [E20b] (b) *So now they go back to looking for the frog, and the - er - the deer pops out of the rock and - after being disturbed, the deer starts giving him a ride, unintentionally, and the boy and the dog go running with the deer and get thrown off the cliff.* [E20e] (c) *Then these branches turn out to be antlers of a deer. The boy gets snagged on it. The deer runs away with the little boy on its head to the edge of a cliff. The boy falls off into a pond.* [E20l]

that they are not yet liberated from the picture-description mode. On the other hand, children from as young as age 3 do demonstrate knowledge of both present and past tense, in both simple and progressive aspect, and by age 5 years syntactic command of these forms is well-established. And even the younger children show some ability to alternate between durative **states** described by copula predicates, change-of-state **events** with verbs in simple aspect, and durative **activities** marked by -*ing*. This is illustrated by the opening to the following 4-year-old narration.

(14) *The frog and the dog, and the boy's here. The dog's climbing out there, when he's sleeping! And the dog's somewhere else, maybe he must be in his cage, sleeping too, right there.* [Child points] *When he wakes up in the morning, he sees he's not there. And they keep going around, and the table, the stool's knocked over. And he gets dressed ...* [E4f-4;7]

Nine-year-olds use a wider range of forms — including nonfinite gerunds, past progressives, and past perfect constructions. Like adults, they shift more consistently than preschoolers from one tense and/or one aspect to another to mark departures from the narrative backbone and to distinguish foreground events from background attendant circumstances. And they are capable of using these shifts on a less local level, in a more discourse-motivated fashion, than the younger children. Adults go beyond the 9-year-olds in deploying an even wider range of forms — e.g., nonfinite auxiliaries as in *The dog's rescued from **having** his head stuck in the jar* [E20b]; *The boy is very happy **to have found** his frog* [E20k]; ***Being** very worried, they searched in their room* [E20d]. Not only do adults make fuller use of a broader range of formal devices, they each construct their texts in accordance with a personal narrative rhetoric which is expressed, inter alia, by the different ways they deploy the tense/aspect options available to (American) English speakers. And these options, as noted in Chapter IIIo, are far richer than those of Hebrew speakers (Chapter IIID), but narrower than the ones to which Spanish speakers (IIIC) can have recourse in telling this same story.

1.3. Lexical Marking of Aspect

Languages also make use of noninflectional devices for encoding aspectual distinctions. Here we consider three periphrastic means of expressing lexical aspect in English: particles like *down*, *off*, and *on* (Section 1.3.1); verbs like *go*, *start*, and *keep (on)* (1.3.2); and adverbials like *already*, *all over (the place)* (1.3.3). These devices combine to express different types of "extended" aspect in the English frog stories (1.3.4). Focus here is on **inchoative** aspect — expressing inception of activities and changes of state — and **protractive** aspect — continuation of activities and extensions of states, since these are particularly relevant to the frog story narratives.[13]

---

[13] For example, particles like *down*, *up*, and *off* are rarely used for expressing **completive** or perfective aspect in our English texts. Compare, for example, durative *the house burned*

1.3.1. Aspectual particles

The most typical function of particles in the English frog stories is in describing **locative trajectories** — e.g. *And the boy's looking **down** the hole [E5k-5;ll]*, *The dog started jumping **up** toward the beehive [E9h-9;9]*, *They fall **off** the edge [E9b-9;3]* (see Section 2). Particles are used aspectually rather than locatively in two main ways in these texts: (1) with change-of-state predicates, as a means of marking **inceptive** aspect (in contexts favoring the reflexive particle *se* in Spanish [Chapter IIIC] and *binyan* verb-morphology in Hebrew [Chapter IIID]); and (2) with durative predicates — the particle *around* marking **iterativity** and *on* for **protraction**. A verb commonly marked by a particle as inchoative in the English frog stories is *wake up*. It is used by three 3-year-olds, by half the 4-year-olds, and in the great majority of the older narratives, as such or in idiomatic *get up*. Inchoative is also expressed with a verb of stative process — *sit*, *lie*, or *stand* with inceptive *down* or *up*; for example, compare the change-of-state predicate followed by a durative predicate at the beginning of a 4-year-old narration: *He **sat down**. And he **laid** there with this thing [E4a-4;0]*. This usage is not common, and is confined to 3- and 4-year-old texts in picture-description mode, to describe *sitting down*, *lying down*, or *standing up*. Elsewhere in the English texts, the particles *down* and *up* typically mark direction of movement — e.g., *fall down*, *throw down*, *knock down*, and *climb up*, *pick up* (see Section 2).

The particle *around*, which combines temporal and locative connotations, is used with an iterative sense, to describe an activity repeated over and over again and/or to express protraction of an activity over a period of time. Four-year-old texts express this idea in describing the dog jumping at the beehive hanging from the tree — *And he started playing **around** [E4f-4;7]* — or looking for the frog before getting stuck in the jar *Like he was looking **around** [E4i-4;9]*, and the bees swarming out of their hive *Now there's bees going **around** [E4l-4;11]*. A 9-year-old uses a more canonically aspectual combination with a verb specifying manner of motion — *And an owl started flying **around** [E9f-9;8]*, as does an adult — *And the dog sees some bees flying **around** [E20l]*. Adults also use *around* to combine aspectual and locative description, e.g., *One night the three were just sitting around doing nothing [E20d]*, *So they began looking everywhere around the little boy's room*

---

with completive *the house burned **down***, or *he was cleaning the room* versus *he was cleaning **out** the room* and *fill the tank* versus *fill **up** the tank*, where the particle implies that the process of cleaning or of filling will necessarily reach an endpoint. That young children can use particles in this sense is demonstrated by the 3-year-old who on reaching the end of the picturebook, says to the investigator: *We are finished. I think we could close the book **up** [E3h-3;9]*.

[E20f]. Another means of combining temporal with locative color is use of *all over* to express **recurrence**. This occurs from age 5 years up with durative activities like running, e.g., *He [= the dog] was running **all over** the place* [E5b-5;2], and in older texts is designated to the thematic search motif, e.g., *So he and his dog **look all over the place** for it* [E9k-9;11]; *The boy and the doggie **went looking** for the froggie, **all over*** [E20i].

The form *on* also functions mainly in **locative** contexts, e.g. stative *The boy is on the deer* [E3i-3;9] and dynamic *climbing on a log* [E3l-3;11]. It is used as a particle to express continuative or protracted aspect only four times across the English sample, usually with a verb like *keep* which also expresses protraction, thus: *They keep going on and on* [4f-4;7], *He kept on calling "frog"* [E5h-5;10], *They went on to look* [E5i-5;10], and also *Then he kept on calling for the frog* [E9i-9;10]. In the English narratives, grammatical particles are thus not highly favored as means of expressing aspectual phases of situations; rather, their main function is in elaborating locative trajectories (Section 2.2).

1.3.2. Aspectual verbs

These narratives also use tense-marked verbs followed by an infinitival or -*ing* participle to express periphrastic, lexical aspect — for instance, **lative**, *They both **went looking** for it*, or **incipient**, *He **started** playing around* [E4e-4;7]. Again, two kinds of "extended aspect" feature prominently in these narratives: inchoative entry into a state or inception of a process and protractive continuation of a state or durative activity.[14] Inceptive or inchoative aspect is marked by **latives** (mainly the general-purpose motion verb *go* + *to do something*), by the inchoative verb *get*, and by marking initiation of a process with the verb *start*.[15] The verb *start* is used by two children in each preschool age group. The 3-year-olds use it with a punctual, change-of-state verb in the infinitive — *He's starting to wake up* [E3g-3;9], *He started to wake him up!* [E3h-3;9]. The 4- and 5-year-olds, in contrast, use it with durative verbs of ongoing activities, in the -*ing* participle form, e.g., *He started running* [E4e-4;7], *And they start calling* [E5c-5;6]. As noted, these are rare in the preschool texts, but most 9-year-olds and adults use *start* for inception of activities, generally with verbs of movement like *climbing* and *running*.

---

[14] We noted earlier that **completive** aspect is not common in our sample. Nor does the frog story lend itself to **cessive** aspect. There are very few instances of verbs like *finish, stop,* or *end* in either the English texts or the other languages.

[15] The verb *begin* occurs only **once** in this function, compared with 54 instances of *start* plus main verb: *So they began looking everywhere around the little boy's room* [E20f]. Preference for the verb *start* reflects the colloquial, spoken register of our narrations.

Moreover, as distinct from the younger children, older narrators use *start* to mark the inception of plot-motivated activities, most often with *chasing* for the bee's pursuit of the dog, but also to describe the more global search-motif of *calling*, *looking*, and *searching* (Chapter IVD).

The polysemous verb *get* is favored for marking inception of a **state**, rather than higher register terms like *become*, *turn*, *grow*. (The latter occurs only once, in an adult text *Eventually the boy and dog grow tired [E20c]*). The verb *get* is used with an adjective by several preschoolers — mainly *get mad, angry* to describe the boy's reaction to the dog's behavior, or *get wet* for what happens when the boy falls into the pond. Older narrators use *get* with a wider range of adjectives — e.g. *get ready, get scared, get upset* — in around half their texts. The verb *get* also occurs with past participial forms in passive voice — e.g., *The dog's getting chased by bees [E4k-4;10]*, *The dog gets stung on the nose [E9l-9;11]* — and in adjectival passives with a clearly change-of-state sense, e.g., *get dressed* or adult *get interested in*. These are used occasionally by preschoolers and by over half the 9-year-olds and adults (see, further, Section 3.2).

The general motion verb *go* marks inception in the lative sense of moving in the direction of doing something, of going towards an activity.[16] The verb *go* — with or without some directional particle — is used with an aspectual function by two younger children, *And then they both went looking for it [E4e-4;7]*, *And after went out calling for the frog [E5b 5;8]*, and by half the 9-year-olds and adults. From age 4 years, lative aspect is used mainly to mark inception of the **search** as the central plot-motif, with age increasingly with nonparticipial forms of the main verb, e.g., *He goes outside, er - goes and looks for him [E9d-9;3]*, *The little boy went and climbed up on a big rock [E20i]*, *They go call in the woods [E20a]* and, among adults, with adverbial particles, e.g. *They go back to looking for the frog [E20e]*. This mature use of a lative verb of inception with a particle of recurrence is used for the complex plot-motivated notion of **reinstantiation**, and ties together the two distinct aspects of inception and retrospection (Chapter IVD).

Continuative, protractive aspect is expressed by verbs like *go on, keep on*, with one adult using higher-register *continue* — *They continue their search* and *After that, he continues and climbs up on this tree [E20f]*. The verb *keep* is used without another verb from the youngest age — *And I think he keeped his head up [E3g-3;9]*, in a way close to the stative sense of *hold*, as in *He keeps it as a pet [E9i-9;10]*. Aspectual *keep* occurs only a few times

---

[16] We do not count formulaic uses of *go to bed, go to sleep*, used by many narrators from age 4 years for the background to inception of the plot.

across the sample, with a participle-form verb, e.g., *They keep going around* [E4f-4;7], *The deer kept running ahead with the boy* [E9c-9;6], occasionally with double marking of protractedness by the continuative particle *on*, e.g., *He kept on calling frog* [E5h-5;9], *He kept on calling for his frog* [E9h-9;9]. The two adult uses of *keep* apply when the same situation continues across different scenes — *The owl kept bothering the little boy* [E20i], *The dog keeps playing with the beehive* [E20g]. The relatively low use of these and other verbs of protraction (only one text has *go on* in this sense) might be due to the ready availability of grammaticized progressive aspect in English to specify activities as durative, hence inherently continuative.

1.3.3. Adverbials of aspect

Adverbials also function minimally to express aspectual distinctions in the English frog stories. In comparison with the other languages in our sample, adverbs like *meanwhile* (or *meantime*), which could be used to express concurrently ongoing activities, or *suddenly* to express inception of a new event, occur only once each across the entire English corpus, each from an adult, thus: *Meanwhile, the dog is being chased by the bees* [E20j], and in a false start *Suddenly the owl, oh no! Now the boy is running away* [E20b]. Similarly, although, as noted, grammatical marking of perfect aspect is rare in the English texts, the adverb *already* occurs only twice across the corpus, both times from young children. Thus the function of the perfect does not seem to be carried out by alternate means. When the investigator asks the child "And the dog, what about the dog?" a 3-year-old replies *I already said dog!* [E3i-3;9], while another uses it in describing a static array of pictured objects as: *His clothes are already out, at the night time!* [E4g-4;7]. Adverbial expressions of protraction or recurrence are likewise few and far between: The phrase *all the time* is not used at all, while *again* occurs several times in two 3-year-old narrations, and in them alone, evidence of the picture-description mode — e.g. in describing the dog and the beehive as *Now, and then he's trying to eat it again* [E3d-3;5], or *Fell in the water again* [E3g-3;9]. This immature use of *again* is akin to the "additive" sense of quantifying expressions — e.g., *And here's another one* [E3h-3;9] when the child sees another picture (of the same rock) on the next page.

The one aspectual adverb which is widespread in the English corpus is the word *still*. In contrast to the low use of verbs of protraction like *keep*, *go on, continue*, it occurs in around half the texts from age 5 years on. At first it is used only with verbs in progressive aspect, so marking continuativity both lexically and grammatically, e.g., *And the dog's still doing that* [E5k-5;9], *And the dog was still playing with the bees* [E5b-5;3], [E9e-9;76], [E9j-9;10]. Older children and particularly adults use this adverbial to mark the protractedness of **states** as well, e.g., *And the bees are still after the dog* [*E9l-9;11*], *The dog is still intrigued with the beehive* [*E20b*], *The dog still has the jar on his head* [*E20g*].[17]

The English frog stories thus demonstrate a generally low reliance on adverbial expressions — particles like *down* or *off*, words like *already*, *meanwhile*, and phrases like *again and again, all the time* — for encoding aspectual distinctions. The only lexical device favored for periphrastic expression of what we have termed "extended aspect" is verbs of inception such as *get, start*. Elsewhere, particles and adverbials like *around* or *all over* have mixed temporal and locative connotations, confirming the impression that rhetorical elaboration in these narratives centers around locative trajectories (Section 2.1, 2.2). Less attention is accorded to temporal distinctions, beyond those afforded by the morphosyntactic devices of tense and aspect alternations, on the one hand (Sections 1.1 and 1.2) and by lexical markers of temporal sequentiality like *then, later* or *eventually*, on the other (Section 4).

1.3.4. Developmental trends

Several devices for specifying aspectual contours of events cluster together mainly in adult usage. For example, *And then the deer **went running off** with the little boy* [*E20i*] combines a lative motion verb used inceptively with the durative *-ing* suffix on the main verb plus the particle *off* for separative or completive aspect — as in *The reindeer takes **off** with the boy on him* [*E20a*]. This use of *off* is confined to the adult narratives. Yet younger children also use a variety of such devices, sometimes even combining them within a single predicate. One 4-year-old story ends with *And they keep going on and on* [*E4f-4;7*], with extended protraction expressed by combining a verb of continuative aspect *keep* with the durative suffix *-ing* and repetition of the continuative particle *on*. A 5-year-old uses a variety of devices to express protracted aspect in the excerpt in (15).

(15) *Uh- and in this (picture) he's **still** calling frog, he **kept on** calling frog. And then um - a deer pulls him up, and then it **runs and runs** to get the dog.* [*E5h-5;10*]

Adults do this together with syntactic subordination (Section 4). For instance, one describes what the dog is doing as background to what happened to the boy as follows: *The groundhog ... bites the boy on the nose while Helmut [=dog] is **still busy** barking up the tree at the bees* [*E20k*] — combining the durative subordinator *while*, the continuative adverb *still*, the semi-modal of ongoing activity *be busy*, and the durative suffix *-ing* on the verb *bark*.

---

[17] This also has a plot-level function: to return to a participant or scene.

This narrator also uses *still* to describes a continued **state** which serves as background to a series of punctual, plot-advancing events, as follows: *The dog loses his balance and slips and lands right on the glass jar which is, up to the point he hits the ground, still attached to his head.* These passages describe the protracted or continuative aspect of an activity as part of an isolated scene. Less local, **plot-motivated** repetition is characterized by different devices — e.g. the adverbial *all over* is used to describe the search as distributively recurrent by two 5-year-olds, two 9-year-olds, and four adults (Section 1.3.1).

Narrators can thus avail themselves of a rich range of nongrammaticized expressive devices for describing protractively extended activities or states and for specifying aspectual contours like inchoativity and iterativity. Some of these forms of expression are favored across the sample, others are selected as rhetorical options by individual narrators. Many are familiar to even the preschool children, but in general periphrastic markings of aspectual distinctions are quite sparingly deployed in these English narrations.

2. EVENT CONFLATION

This section concerns how information is apportioned between verbs and their associated satellite elements. "Event conflation" applies when in elaborating on events beyond the bounds of a bare verb, speakers choose to compress different facets of the situation within a single clause rather than arranging them linearly across successive clauses. Descriptions of an event may refer to the **manner** or **cause** of its occurrence (Section 2.1) and to composites of locative trajectories like **direction**, **source**, or **goal** of movement (2.2). The excerpts in (16) illustrate five different ways of expressing these components in English adult descriptions of the events depicted in the "fall of the beehive" scene. In Picture 10, the dog is shown looking up at a beehive hanging from a tree which he is shaking; in Picture 11 the dog, still holding onto the tree, has turned around to look at the beehive lying on the ground.

(16a) *And in the meantime, the dog is barking up the tree at the bees ... Then the hive falls.* [E20l]

(16b) *The dog shook the tree so much that the beehive fell down.* [E20c]

(16c) *The dog gets the beehive down.* [E20e]

(16d) *The dog knocks the beehive down.* [E20g]

(16e) *To the dog's amazement, he knocked the beehive off the tree.* [E20d]

In (16a), the dog's action and the beehive's change of state are described by two distinct utterances, linked by the temporal connective *then.* The two clauses in (16b) are also nonconflated, but are more tightly linked by syntactic subordination and the resultative connective *so that.* (16c) expresses tight conflation of cause and direction, to which (16d) adds the element of manner — in place of the all-purpose causative auxiliary *get* there is a lexically specified action verb *knock*. (16e) illustrates the most elaborated path, with cause, manner, and direction plus source encoded in the prepositional phrase *off the tree*. We will see that English-speaking narrators are able from a young age to elaborate on several facets of a predication, along the lines illustrated in (16a) through (16e).

In contrast to its elaborate system of grammatical tense/aspect marking (Section 1.1), English has no inflectional means for specifying either causation, on the one hand, or direction of movement, on the other. Instead, English speakers use distinct verb stems to express the manner and causal source of movement (Section 2.1), or they extend the verb by "satellite" particles or prepositional phrases to elaborate locative trajectories and the path from source to goal (Section 2.2).

2.1. Lexically Incorporated Manner and Causation

One relevant device for conflating composite facets of a situation is by lexical **incorporation**, with a semantic distinction encoded as an inherent part of the verb stem. English, as discussed in Chapter III0, is a satellite-framed language, in which the verb often conflates manner and/or cause. Compare, for example, the vocalizations characterized by *call, cry, howl, scream, shout, shriek, yell, yelp* and the manners of walking by the stems *march, limp, plod, stride, stroll, toddle, totter, trot*, or *trudge*. These lexical distinctions are an important part of vocabulary enrichment and rhetorical expressiveness in English, and their acquisition begins from a young age (Section 2.1.1). Another semantic category often implicit in the verb stem is **causativity** — compare verbs like *throw* or *push* with periphrastic *make fall* (Section 2.1.2). Moreover, manner and causation may be conflated, in verbs like *fling* or *jolt*.

2.1.1. *Manner of movement*

Even the youngest children rely on a fairly differentiated vocabulary of movement verbs.[18] Three-year-olds use from two to as many as 12 different

---

[18] The frog story involves numerous motion verbs which lend themselves to different syntactic and/or semantic classifications (Levin, 1989; Levin & Rappaport, 1990). Here, we distinguish four types of verbs of movement relevant to the events described in the frog story: (1) **activity** predicates in the sense of Dowty (1979) and Van Valin (1990), in which a volitional actor performs a durative activity like *go, walk, run,* or *fly*; (2) change-of-state verbs or **achievement** predicates, where a protagonist shifts to another location, primarily *fall*, and verbs with related semantic content such as *drop, plunge*; (3) the **causative** counterparts of such verbs, in which an agent causes the protagonist to undergo this change, e.g., *push, throw*; and (4) a noncausative category of optionally transitive **interactive** verbs, in which two

such verbs per text. One 3-year-old uses the verbs *climb, fall, fly, hang, jump*, and *run* as well as several "general-purpose" verbs (Clark, 1978, in press) combined with particles to express movement — e.g. *get past, go away, put on*, and *pick up* [E3d-3;5]. Across the English texts, the following motion verbs occurred, including verbs of self-movement and caused movement. A plus-sign following the verb indicates that it was used with one or more satellites (verb particles), and see, too, the examples in (18) in Section 2.2.1 below.

(17) **English verbs**: buck+, bump+, buzz+, carry, chase+, climb+, come+, crawl+, creep+, depart, drop+, dump+, escape, fall+, float+, fly+, follow, get+, go+, head+, hide, hop+, jump+, knock+, land, leave, limp+, make-fall, move, plummet, pop+, push+, race+, rush+, run+, slip+, splash+, splat+, sneak+, swim+, swoop+, take+, throw+, tip+, tumble+, walk+, wander+

There are 47 such verb types in the English frog stories (compared with 27 in Spanish), reflecting the variety of English verbs that conflate motion and manner (*crawl, creep, plummet, splat, swoop*, etc.)

With age, children use a greater variety of lexically more specified motion verbs. They rely less on polysemous verbs and idiomatic VERB + PARTICLE combinations — e.g., *chase* instead of *run away*, *escape* instead of *get out*. And they make increased reference to **manner of motion** — e.g., *The boy splashed into the water* [E4c-4;6], *The frog hopped into the boy's hand* [E4f-4;7].

A scene in which manner of motion verbs are common is where the frog climbs out of the jar (Picture 2) — also described accurately, but statically, as follows: *And the frog's - only one leg's out, the other leg's in* [E5g-5;9]. The event is mentioned by three-quarters of the narrators from 3 years on, most often simply by the predicate *get out*.[19] Yet even 3-year-olds use some verbs specifying manner — e.g., one otherwise juvenile text describes the boy in different contexts as *stepping out of bed* and *climbing over the log* [E3l-3;11]. From age 5 years, children add *crawl out, hop out, creep out*, and *sneak out*, with one adult using *tiptoe out*. The main difference is that adults often use the Latinate verb *escape* which, like *get away*, is ablative in implying movement **from** some source, and also entails an aspectual element of **achievement**. Speakers may use *escape* "linearly" rather than in conflation. But they

protagonists are involved in a durative activity, such as *run after* or *chase, run away* or *flee*. We also consider (5) a nonmotion group of verbs which relate to the **plot-based** theme of *looking, searching*, or *calling* for the frog in various locations (Section 2.2).

[19] From age 5 the **source** is also generally specified, e.g. *The frog got out of his bowl* [E5b-5;2].

also use it as a motion verb, conflated with specification of the source, e.g., *The frog is escaping from his jar right now* [E20c], or else they combine conflated and linear description of the event sequence, e.g. *The frog gets out of the bottle and escapes through an open window* [E20g].

Other scenes of "exiting" yield similar results, e.g., the gopher emerging from a hole in the ground (Picture 10) or the owl from a hole in the tree (Picture 12). Most of the children simply use *come out*, but even preschoolers encode some manner elements — e.g. *flew out* [E3i-3;9], *buzzing out* (of the bees) [E4g-4;7] — and one or two respondents in each group from age 5 up specify the sudden, abrupt nature of these exits by *pop out* or *pop up*. Children and adults thus rely on similar devices for describing emergence of an entity from some source — with encoding of manner elements a function of semantic specificity of the verbs used for this purpose.

Manner is also encoded in verbs describing movement **downward**, most typically by the verb *fall* or a causative verb like *push, throw* — e.g., for the boy and his dog's descent from the edge of the cliff (Picture 17) into the water below (Picture 18). Some preschoolers describe the boy's contact with the water by the verb *splash* — e.g., *He splashing in water* [E3c-3;4], *And they splashed in some water* [E5l-5;11]; and several 9-year-olds combine **causation plus manner** of movement in the same stem — e.g., *The deer bucked him off* [E9j-9;11], *He tips him off* [E9k-9;11], *Then he dumped them into the water* [E9g-9;9]; and two adults specify manner of falling in describing the dog's fall from the window (Picture 6) — e.g., *The dog was plummeting to his fate* [E20d], *The dog tumbles out of the window* [E20f]. English speakers thus have a rich repertoire of verbs with which to color their descriptions of how the protagonists get from one place to another, whether volitionally or by an external agency.

2.1.2. Causation of movement

Reference to event causation applies to three "falling" scenes: Where the deer's abrupt stopping causes the boy and dog to plunge down into the pond below, where the emergence of the owl leads to the boy's falling from the tree, and where the dog brings about the fall of the beehive. English allows different levels of event conflation to express causation. At one extreme, clauses can be stacked linearly, with causation only implicit — e.g., *And this owl comes out and the boy falls* [E20a] or *The owl came out of the hole and scared the boy. The boy fell off the tree and landed on his back* [E20c]; or a causative relation between separate clauses can be explicitly marked as in *The boy falls off the tree because the owl came out of the hollow* [E20l]. At the other extreme, both causation and manner may be conflated within a single verb — e.g., *There's an owl in there who bumps him down to the ground*

[*E20j*], *He had fell down cause an owl* **poked** *him out of the tree [E9e-9;7]*, or *An owl came out and* **bammed** *him on the ground [E5e-5;8]*.

Three-year-old children can talk about causative activities of this kind, even if they have not mastered all the relevant lexical constraints (Bowerman, 1974). The single instance of the kind of overextension of an intransitive verb to a causative context noted by Bowerman occurs when a 3-year-old describes the fall from the tree scene as *Owl in there - fall him down! [E3c-3;4]*. Periphrastic causatives with an auxiliary verb *get* or *make* are used mainly by preschoolers; e.g., to describe the beehive's fall from the tree — *And then the dog tried to* **get** *that thing down [E4c-4;6]*, *The dog* **made** *the hive fall [E4b-4;4]*, *And then the dog* **made** *the beehive fall [E5l-5;11]*; or the fall from the cliff — *And he* **makes** *him fall in [E5g-5;9]*. Older children and adults do **not** use these highly productive means for expressing causation.[20] In these English narratives, causation tends to be lexicalized within the stem of a transitive verb, which may be further semantically specified for manner, and which usually occurs together with an additional satellite element specifying **path** — e.g., *knock down, bam on(to), poke out, tip off over into*.

2.2. Locative Trajectories

Across our sample, the frog story elicits rich allusion to the **location** of protagonists — e.g., *in the jar, on top of the rock, at the edge of the cliff*; and it affords numerous opportunities for narrators to specify **movement** from place to place by such means as *falling, climbing*, or *running*. This section considers how subcomponents of events are aligned in the expression of directional paths or locative trajectories. In expressing these facets of event configuration, English deploys linguistic forms which may be identical to those used for elaboration of temporal contours — most particularly, verb particles and adverbial phrases. The satellite elements which cluster around the verb, rather than the bare verb alone, convey different pieces of information associated with a movement-event. Thus, in specifying **direction** of movement, English typically uses polysemous monosyllabic verbs of Germanic extraction combined with a locative particle, where Spanish, Hebrew, or Turkish rely on simplex verbs which incorporate both movement and direction of movement within the bounds of the verb stem. The English corpus contains not a single instance of the monolexemic, Latinate equivalents used in the 3-year-old Spanish, Hebrew, and Turkish texts (Chapters IIIC, IIID, and IIIE).[21] A related finding for the English narratives is that they contain few

---

[20] One exception is where an adult explains why on reaching the edge of the cliff the boy and dog but not the deer fall into the water, thus: *The deer stops abruptly, which* **causes** *the boy to lose his balance and fall ... [E20f]*.

instances of **bare verbs** used without further specification of the scope of the event. Across the sample, this elaboration is typically **locative** in content.[22] The details of locative trajectories take various forms of expression in English. Several such devices occur in the otherwise immature text of the youngest child in the sample *[E3a-3;1]*. It describes the frog as *getting out* — by a verb plus particle combination; the reindeer *threw them down* — a particle with a transitive verb plus direct object (Section 2.2.1); the dog as *standing on two toes* — a verb followed by prepositional phrase (2.2.2); and the owl *flew out of here* — the verb elaborated for direction by the particle *out* and for source by the prepositional phrase *of here* (2.2.3).

As noted, there are few predicates which consist of the verb alone in the English descriptions of events entailing a locative trajectory, even among the 3-year-olds. Clauses which contain only bare verbs, never more than once per text, are: *A owl's flying [E3d-3;5]*; *And then the deer comed [E4e-4;7]*; *Now the dog's running [E5j-5;10]*; and *The beehive fell [E9i-9;10]*. Where such forms occur, they tend to be followed either in the next clause or one soon following, by an explicit elaboration. This method of **event stacking** is illustrated by the clause *And the boy's falling* followed immediately by *He falled into the water [E3b-3;4]*; *And then they started swimming* and a few clauses later *Then he got to it, then he swam over to the log [E4e-4;7]*; *Then they're about to drop. Then they dropped* and a few clauses later — *And they drop down [E4f-4;7]*; or *And then the boy fell out and the owl was flying, and the bees were flying after the dog and the boy got up on some rocks and the owl flew away [E5l-5;11]*. These strings show that English speakers tend to supplement motion verbs by explicitly specifying the path of motion followed by the protagonist(s). Where clause-internal conflation is beyond the online processing capacities of younger narrators, they will do so by clause stacking.

2.2.1. Locative particles

Semantically, locative particles add a directional element to motion verbs — as in expressions like *go in, climb up, swim over*. In the frog story,

---

[21] English does occasionally lexicalize directionality within the verb stem, often in denominal verbs — e.g. in describing the fall of the boy and dog from the cliff into the water down below, *They're **heading** for the pond [E20a]*, *And he **lands** (in the water) [E9k-9;11]*. These are relatively rare, since English has such a rich assortment of satellite particles for expressing directionality, as well as the source and goal of movement.

[22] The high proportion of locative compared with other descriptive elements may be due to the contents of this picturebook, in which plot progression is aligned to the protagonists' movement from one place to another in their search for the missing frog. In general, a search motif entails detailed reference to **location** rather than to the time or duration of the activity.

the commonest uses are with *down* in the falling scenes and *out* in the emergence scenes (Section 2.1). The forms termed **particles** in English have the following syntactic properties: (1) They can occur alone with a verb, constituting a "two-word verb" predicate, e.g., *The dog jumps down [E4l-4;11], And then a bird comes over [E9b-9;3]*. (2) They can occur with a transitive predicate, taking a direct object, where the particle may be shifted to follow the object noun phrase — e.g., *The deer lifted the boy up [E5c-5;3], The dog knocked the beehive down* [E9g-9;9].[23] (3) Verb plus particle combinations can take oblique objects in the form of prepositional phrases — e.g., *A owl flew out + of here E3a-3;1], He swam over + to the log [E4e-4;7], The boy climbs up + in a tree [E5h-5;10], The dog is running away + from the bees* [E20c].

In our English narratives, 3- and 4-year-olds use a variety of directional particles, including *down* and *up, in* and *out, off* and *on*, as well as *around, away*, and *over*. And they use them in all three constructions defined as providing syntactic contexts for such forms in English — e.g., (1) *the dog's going to fall over [E3c-3;4], he's falled off [E3k-3;10]*; (2) *trying to pick it up [E3d-3;5], knocked all the bees down [E3g-3;9]*; and (3) *fell down in the water [E4a-4;0], climbs up on the log [E4f-4;7]*.[24] Younger children use particles relatively less in contexts (2) and (3), that is with transitive verbs and an object noun or prepositional phrase. But even the 3-year-olds show command of the syntax of these constructions, with no instances of word order or other errors in the grammar of particle distribution.

Initially, particles are used mainly with the general-purpose motion verb *go* or the polysemous inchoative *get*, but with age, they occur increasingly with verbs specifying manner of motion like *step, hop*, or *jump* — e.g. *He splashed right in [E4e-4;7], The frog sneaks out, [E5e-5;8]* or *The owl swooped down [E9c-9;6]*. Older children also use them with verbs which conflate manner and causation — e.g., the owl *pokes the boy out (of the tree), bumps him down (to the ground)* (Section 2.1.2). When the 47 types of motion verbs found across the English frog stories, as listed in (17) above, are

---

[23] This permutation is obligatory if the object is a pronoun, e.g., *The reindeer pushing him down [E4h-4;8], He knocked me down there! [E5a-5;1], The deer lifts him up [E9b-9;3]*.

[24] Several children treat *out* as a preposition rather than as a particle, e.g. *the dog jump out the window [E3d-3;5]*, as is common in colloquial American English in general, e.g., an adult says *And the frog crawls out the jar [E20b]*. Others add the linking preposition *of*, mandatory in British English, e.g., *And here (he's) stepping out of bed [E3l-3;11], He went out of it [E4g-4;7], bumblebees coming out of the honeyhive [E5a-5;1]*. Indicative of the unstable nature of these alternatives in English is a child *[E3a-3;1]* who uses both forms four clauses apart, thus: *And he fell out the window* — clause 6, *A owl flew out of here* — clause 10.

combined with the satellite particles used in the English sample, we arrive at no fewer than 123 types of such expressions, as shown in (18).

(18) **English verbs + satellites**

buck + off
bump + down
buzz + out
chase + after, in
climb + down, on, out, over, up, up in, up on
come + after, down, off, on, out, over, up
crawl + out, over, up
creep + out, up
drop + down, off
dump + in, off
fall + down, in, off, on, out, over
float + off
fly + after, away, off, out, over, up
get + away, down, in, off, on, out, over, past, up, up on
go + down, down out, home, in, off, out, outside, over, through, up
head + for, to
hop + in, on, out, over
jump + down, off, out, over, up
knock + down, down out, in, off, out
limp + in
pop + out, up
push + down, off, off in, out
race + after, away
run + after, along, away, by, from, in, off, out, over, through
rush + out
slip + on, over
sneak + out, over, up
splash + in
splat + in
swim + out, over
swoop + down
take + away, off with
throw + down, down in, in, off, over, over in
tip + off over
tumble + down, out
walk + along, down, over to
wander + out

The satellite particles can also assign directionality to nonmotion activity verbs, both transitive and intransitive — e.g., *He's trying to bite the tree down* [E3d3;5], *the deer pulls him up* [E5h-5;10], or *They looked over to the other side* [E9e-9;7], *The dog's smiling down* [E9l-9;11]. These provide a means for specifying direction of movement which is common across the English narratives, and which is very different from what we find with children speaking languages defined as verb-framing, such as Spanish, Hebrew, and Turkish, with directionality lexicalized within the verb stem.

2.2.2. Prepositional phrases

Many forms that meet the syntactic definition of particles in English also function as casemarking and adverbial prepositions, i.e., as forms which must be followed by a noun phrase (either lexical or pronominal).[25] Prepositional phrases serve two main purposes. (1) They mark case relations between the predicate and its associated nominals — e.g., *to* marks dative recipient in *He gave one of its little frogs to the boy* and *with* marks comitative accompaniment in *They went home with the boy* [E9c-9;6]; and (2) they mark adverbial relations which elaborate on some facet of the relation between an event and the circumstances of its occurrence. Our concern is with their adverbial function in describing properties of the locative trajectories followed by the protagonists in the frog story. Prepositions differ semantically from particles in this respect, too, since they can specify **stative** location as well as directionality, e.g., *The boy's **in the bed** [E3d-3;5], They find the frogs **behind a log** [E4d-4;6], The dog has the jar **on his head** [E5j-5;10].*

The 3-year-old texts include numerous different prepositional phrases describing change of location or movement from place to place, e.g., *out the window, in the can, up the tree, from a tree, over a log, into the bowl, to the frog, onto the deer.* These constructions are readily accessible to the youngest children for locative elaboration. Only two of the 3-year-olds (*E3c-3;4, E3k-3;10*) use no prepositional phrases, although both do use VERB + PARTICLE expressions.[26]

---

[25] English is one of the relatively few languages which allows "dangling" or "orphan" prepositions, separated from their associated noun phrase by processes like question formation ("Where are you going to?," "Who will you go **with**?") or relative-clause formation. Compare the relative clause with *in* + (PRONOMINAL) *which* in *They find a hole into which the boy peers*, and relatives with dangling prepositions used by the same adult [E20f] a few clauses later — *The dog has found something new to look at, which is a beehive which he starts barking at.* In such cases, too, the prepositions still have associated, though not necessarily adjacent, noun phrases. Particles, in contrast, may occur alone in the clause with a verb and no associated nominal.

[26] This supports the assumption that English VERB + PARTICLE combinations are an earlier

Age-related progression in use of prepositions, like particles, is lexico-semantic rather than syntactic, since nearly all the 3- and 4-year-old texts include prepositional phrases, and these are grammatically well-formed. A few prepositions occur in the narratives of 9-year-olds and adults which are not found in those of younger children, e.g. *a deer caught him between his horns [E9c-9;6], with the boy strewed across his antlers [E20f], they're looking towards the trees [E20h]*. A general semantic shift is also evident in the **contexts** in which prepositional phrases are used. The younger children use them almost exclusively for locative elaboration, to describe static locations or dynamic trajectories, whereas older speakers use them for a variety of functions. Nonlocative contexts for prepositional phrases, common in the adult narratives but rare among the children, include (1) oblique objects of verbs which govern prepositions lexically — e.g. *concentrating on his beehive [E20e], interested in this beehive [E20f]*; and (2) abstract nominals specifying circumstances or states — e.g., *in pain [E20f], in a dangerous position [E20g], in full force [E20f], in shock [E20h], under the boy's attention and care [E20k], to the dog's amazement [E20d]*.

This progression is clearly reflected by the preposition *after* in the English texts. The 3- to 5-year-olds use it with movement verbs — mainly in the scene where the dog is chased by the swarm of bees — e.g., *chased after the dog [E3f-3;9], running after the dog [E4h-4;8], flying after the dog [E5l-5;11]*. Among older narrators, this form serves more often to mark **temporal** relations, e.g., as a subordinating conjunction followed by a finite clause *after he goes to bed [E9k-9;11]* or, among the adults, by a nonfinite gerund — *after being disturbed [E20e], after saying goodnight to the frog [E20k]* (Section 1.2.1). That is, children first learn to use prepositional phrases with a spatial function for specifying locative trajectories (Section 2.2.3), only later assigning these forms more abstract semantic content and using them in more complex syntactic constructions.

Structurally, 3-year-olds use prepositional phrases with both intransitive and transitive verbs — e.g., both *hanging from a tree* and *put the boot on his head [E3d-3;5], going up the tree* and *throwing the dog and the boy in the water [E3i-3;9]*. As with particles, the younger children add prepositional

---

acquisition than VERB + PREPOSITION phrases. Prepositions are essentially relational elements, connecting verbs to the argument or adjunct nominals associated with them within the clause, whereas particles can be attached to bare verbs to provide semantic information about aspect or directionality. Particles also have some stress, whereas prepositions are pronounced without any stress, with lax vowels reduced to schwa. Particles like *down* and *off* are used at the one-word stage, and in early multiword speech when children's utterances still lack prepositional phrases (Bloom, 1973; Braine, 1976; Brown, 1973).

phrases to intransitive verbs more often than to transitive verb plus object combinations, reflecting the generally smaller number of arguments included in young children's utterances. The major structural advance with age is an increase in the proportion of "doubly elaborated" locative trajectories. These constructions consist of VERB + PARTICLE + PREPOSITIONAL PHRASE, e.g., *hanging down + from his neck* [*E5f-5;8*], *look down + at a gopher hole* [*E9e-9;7*], and are rare among the younger children, e.g., *some bees came out + of the tree* [*E3f-3;9*], *he climbs back up + on the log* [*E4f-4;7*]. These combine particles specifying directionality of movement — *out, up, down, away,* etc. — with prepositional phrases which specify the **source** or **endpoint** goal of movement. In languages like Spanish or Hebrew, such content is typically expressed by a directional verb plus a prepositional phrase, a construction which appears simpler than their Germanic counterparts (although it occurs only rarely in our narratives in these two languages). Yet young English speakers are able to express relations between major lexical categories — the verb specifying nature of motion and the noun the source or goal of motion — by stringing together two (and sometimes more) closed class formatives like *up on, down into,* and so on.[27]

Prepositions can also be strung together, where a verb is followed by an oblique (prepositional) phrase, e.g., *coming from + behind the log* [*E9f-9;8*], [*E20b*]. Such stringing of particle and prepositional phrases is commoner from age 5 years on. But younger children do not necessarily avoid these forms. On the contrary, they sometimes **overuse** such linking elements, adding a redundant *of* in ablative contexts, e.g. *they're coming off of the tree* [*E3h-3;9*], *he knocked them off of the cliff* [*E3j-3;11*]. This again suggests that these particle and prepositional elements are highly salient and readily accessible to English-speaking children from early on in their development of language structure and language use.

2.2.3. Path, source, and goal

In the locative trajectories relevant to the frog story, the boy or some animal or group of animals move in a certain direction and/or manner along a path from source to goal. Such notions, which are expressed inflectionally in some languages by ablative and purposive case markings, are accessible to children as young as 3 years of age, even though they may not always use the conventional lexical items for expressing them (Clark & Carpenter, 1989, 1991). This is confirmed by the findings for our 3-year-olds, who use the

---

[27] In fact, many of these can be analyzed into even more subparts, if one considers the directional prepositions *into* = *in* + *to,* and *onto* = *on* + *to* — e.g., *climbing onto the deer* [*E3i-3;9*], *slipped onto a deer* [*E4b-4;4*].

formal devices described in Sections 2.2.1 and 2.2.2 for expressing both source — e.g. *fell off the tree [E3h-32;4]*, *jumped out the window [E4c-4;6]*, *hanging down from his neck [E5f-5;8]* — and goal, e.g. *fell over into the pond [E3d-3;5]*, *slipped onto a deer [E4b-4;4]*, *looking down the hole [E5k-5;11]*.

The frog story provides ample opportunity for speakers to describe both ends of the trajectory in the falling, climbing, and emergence scenes which it involves. The degree of event conflation required by specifying both source and goal within a single clause seems beyond the capacities of our younger narrators. In order to test this, we analyzed the "cliff scene" (Picture 17), where the deer is shown standing at the edge of the cliff and the boy and dog are in midair, falling down into the water below with a splash (Picture 18). This provides us with a diagnostic for the expressive options deployed by English narrators in expressing the start and/or endpoints of a series of change-of-location events resulting in a highly salient change of location from up above to down below. Speakers selected four major methods of expression:

(19a) Reference to the endpoint goal alone — e.g. *The reindeer knocked the boy and the dog **in the water** [E5b-5;2]*, *It runs and runs to get the dog, and then they fall **into the water** [E5h-5;10]*, often together with some specification of the downward direction and/or the manner of movement — e.g., *They fell straight down into the water [E4c-4;7]*.

(19b) Reference to both the origin and the endpoint of the movement in two separate utterances, with no implication of any temporal or other relation between them — e.g. *Ah! He [=deer] knocked them off of the cliff. And here he's [= boy] in the water [E3j-3;10]*; *And then there was a cliff. And then they both fell straight down into the water [E4e-4;7]*.

(19c) Reference to both source and goal in two separate clauses, with some temporal adjacency or chronological sequencing either overt or implied — e.g. *And they both fell off the cliff, and the deer didn't. And they fell in the water, and the deer was happy that they fell in [E5e-5;8]*; *Then they're on a cliff, and the elk pushes the boy off, and the dog falls off too. Then they land in a pond [E9d-9;6]*; *Now the deer has thrown the dog - no, the boy - over the cliff into ... it looks like they're heading for a pond. And the dog goes too, as the dog has throughout the entire story. And they both fall in the water [E20b]*.

(19d) Event conflation in which the cliff source and the water-goal are combined in a single clause — e.g., *The deer ran away with him, and dropped him off a cliff, in the water [E9h-9;9]*, *He pushed him off the side of the cliff into water [E9e-9;7]*, *They're both falling off the little cliff into what seems to be a pond [E20c], And (he) deposits the boy off the side of the ravine into the creek [E20k].*

The distribution of these descriptions across age groups reflects the development of quite general expressive abilities. Three patterns emerge — a juvenile form of description typical of the picture-description mode (Chapter IIA); transitional expressions in children who are in storytelling mode, but encounter difficulties at the local level of event packaging (Chapter IVC); and mature choice of extended or conflated forms of expression. **Juvenile descriptions** are provided by nearly all the 3- and 4-year-olds (20 out of 24) and several of the 5-year-olds, in the form defined in (19a); they mention only the endstate point of falling or being thrown *into the water* — sometimes with reference to direction of movement down. The 3-year-olds in particular avoid mention of the cliff as source of the event, even though they express source in other contexts, such as falling *out* of the window or *off* the tree. Nor is the problem one of the the causative link between the events, since three of the youngest children do talk about the deer as *throwing the dog and the boy in the water [E3i-3;9]*. These facts suggest that the younger children encounter a genuine difficulty in relating **both** to the source and to the endpoint of a movement event within the same conceptual frame, and hence they are unable to combine them even in successively sequenced syntactic frames.

Only three of the children in the two youngest age groups show some incipient ability to connect between these facets of the event complex, by adopting a type (b) description, mentioning the cliff-source and the water-goal in two separate and unrelated utterances. Not a single 3-year-old explicitly mentions both in a single syntactic package; the most they do is describe the two events serially, with no explicit syntactic, temporal, or logical linking. One child implies a source by a directional particle, but fails to specify it explicitly: *He fell off. And he fell off of - in the pool [E3e-3;8]*, while another 3-year-old describes the source scene by *He knocked them off of the cliff* and, after a prompt from the investigator, goes on to describe the next picture as *And he's in the water [E3j-3;10]*. Similarly, the goal facet is appropriately described by another 3-year-old in the lone clause *(deer's) throwing the dog and the boy in the water [E3i-3;9]*. Further elaboration is achieved by means of syntactic coordination, with two successive clauses conjoined by "event serialization," as in these 4-year-old excerpts: *He pushed them both off the cliff, and they landed in some water [E4b-4;4]; And then there was a cliff, and then they both fell straight down into the water [E4e-4;7]*.

These two 4-year-olds demonstrate **transitional abilities**, although the transition from picture-description to narrative mode generally characterizes the English 5-year-olds — in this particular scene, as across their texts. Half the 5-year-olds provide only type (a) descriptions of the fall into the water, but almost as as many provide type (b) serial descriptions of both the fall from the cliff and into the water. One 5-year-old even conflates both source and goal into a single clause, but does so, as befits this transitional phase, with much backtracking and hesitation. This is illustrated in (20).

(20) *And this time a deer - or, um - a male deer got the um .. the boy, and threw him over a cliff and th ... and - and on this page, he threw him over a cliff into a pond.* [E5j-5;10]

The last clause in (20) — *He threw him over a cliff into a pond* represents mature event conflation, but it takes the child a long time and much hesitation and repetition to produce this description. Thus the 5-year-olds demonstrate a transitional phase of narrative abilities between the juvenile and mature. This is in line with a more general finding: By age 5, children deploy **different** devices for specifying type and direction of movement and for elaborating locative trajectories. One child differentiates between the frog's exiting from the jar as *crawled out* compared with the dog's exiting from the window as *jumped out* [E5c-5;3]. This child also uses directional adverbs and directional verbs in suitably contrasting ways, thus:

(21) *And there was some bees **ahead**, and then they - the dog barked at them, and then they **headed for** the dog.* [E5c-5;3]

But the 5-year-olds are not yet able to use this rich array of lexical and other devices for purposes of "event packaging" in general, and for conflating different facets of a locative trajectory within a single syntactic frame in particular.

Mature expression is demonstrated by the 9-year-olds and adults, most of whom select **either** type (c) event serialization **or** type (d) event conflation. Only three of the older narrators select the favored juvenile option of not referring to the source at all. Where this is the case, they elaborate on some other facet of the event, typically the manner or nature of the fall — e.g., *The boy was on his horns, and then he **dumped** them into the water* [E9g-9;9], *And the dog falls in that pond with him. My goodness! It's quite a fall!* [E20j]. The fact that 9-year-olds and adults favor equally both expressive options — the serialized Type (c) or the conflated Type (d) — demonstrates a central theme of this book. Mature narrators are free to select from a range of expressive options which their language makes available to them structurally and which their knowledge of the language makes accessible to them in the process of narrating the events depicted in this storybook.

3. PERSPECTIVE

This section considers how narrators organize the surface configurations of predicates and their associated arguments so as to present the information they entail from a particular point of view. These different arrays demonstrate choices available to speakers for verbalizing the same events — in this case, ones depicted in the frog storybook.

3.1. Perspectives on a Chase Scene

The "interactive" nature of chase scenes allows for different perspectives, typically expressed in English through converse pairs of verbs like *chase* versus *flee* or *run after* versus *run away from*. They can be described as pursuits, from the point of view of the actor-chaser who pursues, follows, chases, or goes after the pursued; or as flights, from the point of view of the undergoer-fleer who flees or runs (away) from the pursuer. Or both perspectives can be combined, through use of passive voice, so that the pursued is described as being chased by the pursuer. Compare, for example, the following descriptions of the scene in which the bees are shown flying after the dog or, alternatively, the dog running away from the bees — a scene in which "both participants are animate and highly active, and neither is new" (Slobin, 1993b; see also Chapter IVC).

(22) *The dog is running away.* [E3g-3;9]

(23) *He ran away from the bees.* [E4i-4;9]

(24) *The bees chased the dog.* [E4c-4;6]

(25) *The dog was being chased by the bees.* [E5f-5;8]

(26) *The dog's running away because the bees were all chasing him.* [E9e-9;7]

(27) *Both of them are in kinda chase scenes, running away from the other animals.* [E20e]

As these examples show, speakers can choose to focus on the bees, as the topic of this predication, as in (24), or they can present the scene from the point of view of the dog — either as an actor, the one who is running away, or as a patient, the one who is being chased. From the point of view of event conflation (Section 2), both facets of the situation can be compressed into a single clause, as in (23) through (25), or they can be expressed in two temporally or causally linked clauses, as in (26). A higher level of compression is expressed by the adult in (27), the only one out of 55 English descriptions of this scene which generalizes across the boy and the dog as participants in a global set of chase events.

Over half the 3-year-olds, and two other preschoolers, refer **either** to the dog or to the bees, as in (22), whereas 9-year-olds and adults all refer to both parties. These older, hence "normative" narrators, can select either the dog-undergoer or the bees-perpetrators as grammatical subject, and they can express the interaction between them within a single clause or extended across two clauses. The most favored perspective (over 50% of 9-year-old and adult descriptions) is illustrated in (24): The bees are described as *chasing, racing, going*, or *flying after* the dog. Two other forms of description are selected by narrators in each group from age 4 up: The dog-undergoer is presented as grammatical subject, hence the focus, through use of passive voice — as in (25); or both dog and bees are focused on in turn, through two separate clauses, with the dog as subject in the first and the bees as subject in the second — as in (26).

The perspective most favored for this scene is thus of the bees as the active focus of the situation. This was selected by nearly all the 9-year-olds, highlighting what we noted in Chapter IIA: Across the sample, the school-age children tend to be conservative in their choice of expressive devices. They know the grammar, and can use it to perform the narrative task felicitously, and so differ from the preschoolers, but they fail to vary perspective in an adult fashion. Only the adults elaborate on the protagonists' inner states and the motivational circumstances surrounding this situation. Some add details of **manner**, e.g., *The dog runs howling by with this swarm of bees chasing him* [E20f]; others provide causal motivation, as in (28) to (30).

(28) *The dog is being chased by the bees because he wrecked their hive.* [E20j]

(29) *A bunch of bees start following the dog, probably angry that the dog has knocked their hive out of the tree.* [E20b]

(30) *The dog is running away from all the bees, who seem to be quite angry because the dog broke their beehive.* [E20c]

Younger children are able to encode different, and appropriate, perspectives on this scene — as in examples (22) to (25). This ability is demonstrated by even 3-year-olds in different languages with respect to different scenes (Chapter IVC; Berman, 1993). What older narrators can do **further** is **alternate** perspectives on a particular scene, by switching reference back and forth from one protagonist to another (dog — bees — dog — bees) within a single, plot-motivated syntactic package (Section 4).

3.2. Passive Voice

Simple re-orderings of the linear array of arguments with respect to their associated predicate are relatively rare in English compared with languages like Spanish, Hebrew, and Turkish (and see further, Section 3.3). Instead, in order to vary perspective so that, for example, the patient-undergoer rather than the actor-perpetrator is presented as the topicalized focus of a sentence, some further grammatical modification is required. For example, cleft and pseudo-cleft constructions with embedded relative clauses can serve to topicalize a particular NP; or an indirect object can be given relative focus by dative shifting, which promotes it to a syntactic direct object stripped of its dative casemarker. Passive voice is another example of such a grammatical operation. Passives enable speakers to deviate from identifying surface SVO order with the thematic roles of actor-action-patient, by promoting the patient NP to the status of grammatical subject, hence of sentence-topic, thereby demoting the actor-agent to an oblique prepositional phrase, or else downgrading it even further by not mentioning it at all (Keenan, 1985a). Passives have traditionally been treated as a "late acquisition," as they are in a language like Hebrew, in which patient-topicalizing or agent-downgrading can be achieved by straightforward changes in word order (Berman, 1979a, in press-b). Yet in other languages, children have been shown to use passive constructions from as young as age 2 to 3 years (Demuth, 1989; Pye & Paz, 1988). And there is growing evidence that passives are acquired quite early even in English (Budwig, 1990; de Villiers & de Villiers, 1985; Marchman, Bates, Burkardt, & Good, 1991).

Our findings, too, suggest that English-speaking children do, in fact, make use of passive constructions from early on, in order to focus on a non-agent participant in a situation (Slobin, 1993b; Chapter IVC). Passives are used at least once across the English frog texts by half of the children and all the adults. For example, several children at all ages except 3-year-olds describe the dog getting or being chased by the bees in passive voice (Section 3.1). There is a clear developmental increment in this respect. Only two 3-year-olds but nearly half the 4-year-olds and three-quarters of the 5-year-olds use passives. And full passives with an agentive *by* phrase, like those in (31) to (33) account for as many as one-third of these forms across age groups.

(31) *I think the dog's hiding so he doesn't get chased by that big deer.* [E3g-3;8]

(32) *The dog's getting chased by bees.* [E4k-4;10]

(33) *He got picked up by a reindeer.* [E5f-5;8]

Young children can thus use passives with different verbphrase types: negative (31), progressive (32), and verb particle (33). And they use them correctly and appropriately, with few structural errors, apart from an occasional incorrect auxiliary form, e.g., *the dog was be chasing by the bees* [E4b-4;4], or choice of preposition — *the boy got knocked over from all the bees* [E5j-5;10].

There are, however, age-related differences in use of passive voice. Children use *get* passives far more than *be* passives: 61% of all their passives compared with 31% of the adults' passive constructions. They use passives with dynamic change-of-state predicates, generally in the aspectually perfective past tense, whereas adults use them in other tenses, too — e.g., *the dog is intrigued by this beehive* [E20c], *the dog has been picked up by some antlered beast* [E20b]. In general, the adults use passives in a wider range of semantic and syntactic contexts than the children, including stative predicates like *be disturbed, be frightened* and nonfinite forms — e.g., *An owl pops out of the rock after **being disturbed*** [E20e], *The dog is not real happy about **being disturbed*** [E20j], and *The dog is, happily, rescued from **having his head stuck** in the jar* [E20b]. Moreover, the bulk of children's passive forms occur in the inchoative context of *getting stuck* to describe the dog's entry into the jar (Berman, 1993) and/or of *getting caught* to describe the boy's entanglement with the deer (Berman & Slobin, 1987). These two scenes, which represent accidental entrapments of the protagonists, and the two punctual verbs *stuck* and *caught*, account for 70% of all the passive constructions used by the children. (The chase scene noted in 3.1 accounts for most of the others.) That is, children treat passive as a means of encoding inchoative changes of state with a patient-oriented perspective. The adults, in contrast, use passive voice in describing different situations in the story, with a variety of predicates — e.g., *The hive was **knocked down** out of the tree by the dog* [E20b, E20k], *He got **bit** (in the nose) by a gopher* [E20c, E20d, E20f].

Our findings show passive forms to be available to children from a young age. Claims to the effect that English-speaking children avoid passives until quite late may therefore be biased by being confined the level of isolated sentences rather than relating to extended discourse (see Budwig, 1992, and discussion in Chapter IVC). But older narrators deploy passive constructions both more selectively and more extensively than children. They use them in more syntactic constructions, with more varied semantic predicate types, and with a more flexible range of narrative discourse functions.

3.3. Word-Order Alternations

Departures from the canonical or favored word order of a given language (Payne, 1987) are an important means of marking discourse-motivated shifts in perspective (Giora, 1986). English is a language with severe structural constraints on the ordering of elements, compared with languages like

Spanish or Turkish, in which word order is pragmatically rather than grammatically governed (Thompson, 1978). We therefore predicted that narrators across the age groups would adhere to SVO for ordering of major clause-level constituents, and to the canonical ordering of manner, then place, then time, in ordering adverbial elements following the main verb. And we assumed that the youngest **and** the most mature narrators might show relatively more variability of word order, the former because they have not yet mastered the grammatical constraints on the accepted ordering of elements, whereas adults are able to alternate word order for pragmatic purposes of how information is organized and presented in ongoing discourse.

The English frog-story corpus strongly confirms the favored, unmarked status of SVO word order. Contrary to our prediction, however, there are very few departures from this ordering of major constituents across the sample. Word order plays a marginal role in presenting different perspectives on a particular scene, or in changing topic focus in the ongoing narrative. Rather, narrators treat English as an extreme instance of a "right-branching" language, stacking additional information both within and across clauses **after** the initial subject-predicate core constituents (Van Valin, 1993). Across the texts, there is one single favored ordering of elements. This can be schematically represented as the surface string (C)SVX: "C" stands for markers of clause linkage or syntactic connectivity such as the coordinating conjunctions like *and, but,* markers of sequentiality like *then, later,* or markers of logical and temporal contingencies like *so, however,* and *while, because* (see Section 4); "S" stands for the grammatical subject — pronoun, lexical noun, or noun phrase; "V" is a lexical main verb — with or without preceding modals, auxiliaries, or aspectual verbs; and "X" stands for verb complements and adjuncts, including verb particles, direct objects, oblique objects, and particle or prepositional phrases in simple clauses and also nonfinite phrases and subordinate clauses which follow the main clause.

In line with our observation that the English texts contain almost no instances of "bare verbs," minimal well-formed clauses contain at least some elements to the right of the verb, e.g., *The frog got out [E3h-3;9], He sat down [E4a-4;0].* Moreover, even the youngest children go beyond simple one-place elaboration of the verb — e.g. *He trying to put his whole body in the can [E3d-3;5], They find his frogs behind a log [E4d-4;6].* The younger children make no errors in ordering of elements: Auxiliaries and modals precede the main verb, complements and adjuncts follow it in the correct order, subject-auxiliary inversion is correctly constrained in questions — for example, the same child produces both *Why is he putting the nose in the glass* with the correct subject-auxiliary inversion and *I wonder why he's not swimming out* with no such inversion in an embedded question [E3g-3;9]. Even the most juvenile text, in which the child makes errors of form in a number of grammatical systems — e.g., *He see them fall down, Owl in there, fall him down, He no don't like that [E3c-3;4]* — contains not a single error in word order. The constraint of SVX ordering thus appears strongly internalized by English-speaking 3-year-olds.[28]

The younger children never prepose elements — before the subject or between subject and predicate — to highlight or focus on a particular facet of a situation. This (C)SVX ordering produces a rather monotonous effect in the texts of the older children, particularly when accompanied by constant reiteration of the same "C" element (Sections 4.2, 4.3). The 9-year-old excerpt in (34) is typical of this stacking of clauses with the same internal ordering of constituents over and over again.

(34) *The boy jumped out of the window too, to get his dog.*
The dog started to lick him.
And, so then he went calling for the frog,
and he looked in a gopher hole,
and the dog - nah - the gopher came out
and the dog was chasing the beehive,
and then he knocked it down.
The dog knocked the beehive down.
And then, the boy climbed the tree,
he looked into this hole,
and then an owl came out of the tree,
and the boy fell down
and the bees started to chase the dog. [E9g-9;9]

Some children deviate from this consistent word order, particularly when they move out of the main narrative mode. One such strategy is by locative or temporal reference to the task itself. For instance, nearly every utterance of child *[E5j-5;10]* is introduced by expressions like *and on this page, and this time.* Another departure from (C)SVX order occurs when children move out of the descriptive or narrative mode to address a comment or query to the investigator, as in (35).

---

[28] On the other hand, several 3-year-olds (although almost no children from age 4 years and up) fail to provide a surface subject where it is grammatically required in the context of a lone clause. The same surface phenomenon, of clauses with finite, tense-marked main verbs, but no overt grammatical subject, increases from age 5 years up, particularly among 9-year-olds and adults. But with them it functions as a means of achieving narrative connectivity, not as a violation of sentence-level grammar (see Section 4.5).

(35) *And the boy's looking down the hole and calling in the frog, and the dog is looking at the bees. And then -* **What are those called?** [Investigator says: gophers] *A gopher comes out, bites his nose, and the dog's still doing that.* [*E5k-5;11*]

Another way of breaking up the otherwise uninterrupted chains of (C)SVX strings is by using direct speech for one of the protagonists, as in (36).

(36) *So in the morning, the little boy said "Where is my frog?"* [a few clauses later] *He says "Is that you, frog?" So they went to look. "Is that you in there, is it, is it?"* [*E5i-5;10*]

Such departures from (C)SVX order are commonest among 5-year-olds, suggesting they use it as a transitional device not required by either the younger or the older children. As noted, however, such word-order variations — engendered by a shift from a narrative to an interactive mode of discourse — are not found among the older narrators.

Nor is there much use of **inversion** for pragmatic effect. This is notable, considering that even the 3-year-olds can perform grammatically based inversions, as in the earlier examples of question formation. And older children occasionally use grammatical inversion in comparative constructions, too — e.g., *A boy got a new frog, and the dog was looking at it, and* **so was he** [*E9h-9;9*]. Across the English narratives, there are no more than three instances of pragmatically-motivated inversions.

(37) *And then ... and then, pow!* **Over they went**! [*E3d-3;5*]

(38) *And they were coming to an - end, where the deer was bringing (them). And* **down he went!** *"Help!" he cried. He went right into the water.* [*E5i-5;10*]

(39) **Out of the reeds come some baby frogs** *that obviously are the little baby frogs of his frog and his frog's wife.* [*E20j*]

(37) through (39) are instances of **locative fronting.** In the children's case, a locative particle *over* or *down* is preposed in a highly dramatic context (enunciated with high pitch and exaggerated intonation contours), whereas the adult preposes a locative prepositional phrase followed by a very marked, literary-sounding VS word order.

The forms in (40) and (41), like the example in (39), are **presentatives,** where a new object or participant is introduced into the narrative (see Chapter IVB). Thus:

(40) *And then they go in the water.* **And behind that log is frogs.** [*E5d-5;6*]

(41) *And they're looking over on the other side ...* **On the other side** *are two frogs.* [*E20h*]

Presentatives provide a context where languages with SV / VS alternation may prefer VS order (Chapter IIID), but where English narrators typically retain a surface SV order by means of the expletive subject *there*. Children make broad use of this construction from age 3 years, and they clearly distinguish this introducing, pleonastic subject *there* from the stressed locative use of *there*, as shown in (42) to (44).

(42) *There's a frog in there.* [E3c-3;4]

(43) *Cause there's a top on the thing right there.* [E3g-3;9]

(44) *He's seeing if there's honey in there.* [E3j-3;10]

One or two narrators in each age group use this construction with a verb in the participial form (see Table 2, Section 1.2.1), as a means of highlighting the presentative sense of existence or emergence, as in (45) to (48).

(45) *And see, there's a mouse coming!* [E3f-3;9]

(46) *And there's lots of bees coming.* [E5e-5;8]

(47) *Then there was a deer living behind the rock.* [E9j-9;11]

(48) *Cause there's a gopher looking out of his hole right now.* [E20c]

Once again, the major development in deployment of this form is not strictly structural.[29] Rather, use of *there* to introduce new entities into the narrative, and so depart from the strict SVX order we have observed for English, is increasingly preferred at specific points in the story. The 9-year-olds to some extent, and the adults very markedly, use expletive *there* at the outset of the narrative, to introduce the boy, the dog, and the frog as its protagonists, and at its resolution, remarking on the fact that when they look behind the log, *There was the frog, with another little lady frog and little frogs of his own* [E9c-9;6], or *They see that there was not only two happy frogs, but there is an entire family of little frogs there!* [E20b]. The younger children, in contrast, use *there* to describe entities shown in the pictures, or to mention novel entities and objects unrelated to their role in the story as a whole.

Another device for operating on simplex SV order in English is by means of the expletive or pleonastic subject *it*. This also shows an age-related change in function in the English narratives, but in a rather different way than presentative *there*. The younger English children use it as a pronominal, either deictically in relation to picture content, or as a neuter-gender pronoun referring to entities like the jar or the owl. From 4 years, children also use it as a impersonal or nonreferential pronoun, in copula constructions, e.g., *It was*

---

[29] Adults also use expletive *there* in syntactic contexts not found in the children's narratives: with a modal *He realizes there might be some danger involved here* [E20e] and introducing a relative clause *There's an owl in there who bumps him down to the ground* [E20j].

nighttime [E4c-4;6], *It wasn't as quiet there [E5b-5;2]*. Only older children and adults use expletive *it* with modal and affective predicates antecedent to a postposed proposition, e.g., *It turns out they're a deer's antlers [E9j-9;11]*, *It seems they've raised this happy family [E20b]*, *The frog feels that it's time that it can now get out and explore [E20f]*. This use of expletive *it* relates to an increase with age in use of modal and other devices for **evaluative** commentary (Chapter IIA). In English, this function is served by this particular construction, providing a form-function relation that is rare in the younger children's texts.

Word order can also be alternated by left-dislocation of topicalized nominals with a resumptive pronominal copy in the main clause, as in (49) and (50).

(49) *And poor Ralph, the whole beehive was chasing after him. [E9i-9;10]*

(50) *And then, the um - the beehive falls down. The dog, he probably knocked it down. [E20c]*

But these were the sole examples of this device across the English narratives.

In sum, then, although English has a variety of options for alternating perspectives, our narrators preferred to do this by alternating between agent-actor and patient-undergoer as surface subjects (Sections 3.1 and 3.2) rather than by varying the linear ordering of elements. The availability of alternations such as *The bees chased after the dog* and *The dog ran away from the bees* or between *The deer pushed the boy*, *The boy fell*, *The boy got pushed* and *The boy was pushed* enables English speakers to adhere to the standard SV(O) order of their basic clause structure, while at the same time expressing differing perspectives on the events and situations depicted in the story.

4. CONNECTIVITY

Here we are concerned with the way speakers link parts of their narrations to construct a unified, organized piece of text. These connections are minimally between one predicating clause and another — e.g., *He's getting out of the glass **so** he can run away [E3g-3;9]*; ***When** the boy and the dog were asleep, the frog jumped out of the jar [E5l-5;11]*; *The owl came out of its tree **and** scared the little boy [E9c-9;6]*. They can also be manifested across extended chunks of discourse, as in the following two excerpts.

(51) *Well, a boy got a new frog, **and** the dog was looking at it **and so** was he, **and then**, **while** he's sleeping overnight, the frog got out. **And when** he woke in the morning, he saw the frog was gone. [E9h-9;9]*

(52) ***So what happened overall is that** all the animals **that** they disturbed **looking** for the frog somehow, you know, chased the boy to the frog. [E20e]*

Overt markers of connectivity, like those bolded in (51) and (52), are typically clause-initial in a right- branching language like English, yielding the surface order CSV(X) noted in the preceding section.

Even the youngest children are able to link one utterance to the next, but this is motivated by the shift from one picture to another, rather than by demands of discourse connectivity. Older children chain **clauses** (as distinct from **utterances**) by temporal and causal stringing in sequence. Five-year-olds are, again, a transitional group, since some of them are quite adept at expressing connectivity at a local level of two or more clauses. Older children occasionally, and the adults quite often, use global, plot-motivated markers of connectivity which relate to the narrative as a whole — as shown in (52) by the prospectively introducing phrase *So what happened* combined with the generalizing term *overall*.

4.1. Development of Forms and/or Functions

Devices which express connectivity — in English as in other languages — can be described orthogonally in terms of form or function. For example, the forms *then* and *after* both express **temporal sequentiality**. However, syntactically, one functions to introduce a clause which can stand alone as in independent sentence, as in (53), the other is a subordinator which introduces a dependent clause attached to an associated main clause, as in (54).

(53) *Then the little boy climbed up the tree and said "Hello in there!"* [E5f-5;8]

(54) *After he and his doggie went to sleep one night, the frog got out of the jar and escaped.* [E20i]

The words *but* and *however* share the same adversative meaning, yet syntactically *but* is a coordinating conjunction which joins two main clauses, while *however* is a sentence-modifying connective in a higher register of style.[30] Compare the bolded forms in (55) and (56).

(55) *The dog tried running after the deer, **but** the deer kept running ahead, with the boy on his head.* [E9c-9;6]

(56) *The dog ... hopped onto the ledge, **but** Ø hopped out a little too far. ... The dog was plummeting to his fate, **but** luckily for the dog he was unharmed. **However** the boy was quite perturbed.* [E20d]

Similar forms are used as markers of connectivity across the English sample. However, the same forms function differently at different

---

[30] The corresponding subordinating conjunction *(al)though* does not occur in these English narratives.

developmental phases. This was shown by the distribution of nonfinite -*ing* verb forms earlier in this chapter. Young children use them ungrammatically, in lone clauses — e.g. *And he was - he getting out. And that - he floating off. Uh - sitting down [E3c-3;4]*; older children use them as grammatical complements of modal or aspectual verbs — e.g., *He started climbing up the rocks [E9f-9;8]*, *He went calling for the frog [E9g-9;9]*; in more mature usage, they serve for **clause linkage** by grammatical subordination: in complements of perception verbs — e.g *They both hear something coming from behind the log [E20b]*, *He felt someone playing with his horns [E20c]*; in noun modification — e.g., *The boy gets his nose sniffed at by some little animal living in the hole [E20b]*; and as adverbial clauses of circumstance — e.g., *He's looking all over his room, messing it up [E9l-9;11]*.

Each language has its own particular forms for marking connectivity. For example, there is nothing exactly parallel to English participial and gerundive -*ing* in the other languages in our sample. Yet the language-particular forms for marking connectivity in the English frog stories reflect different levels of textual cohesiveness which apply across the languages we have examined. Three-year-old texts show mainly "utterance connectivity," stringing consecutive utterances in juvenile picture-description mode (Section 4.2); 5- and 9-year-olds demonstrate "grammaticized connectivity," sequential chaining of clauses which form pieces of a linearly unfolding narrative (4.3); mature texts achieve "thematic connectivity," constructing chunks of discourse subordinated to an overall plot-motivated theme (4.4).

4.2. Juvenile Utterance Connectivity

Three-year-old English texts fail to provide any explicit marking of connectivity between one clause and the next much of the time. Nearly half (43%) their clauses are "free" (Dromi & Berman, 1986), in the sense that they are neither lexically nor syntactically related to the following or preceding utterances. The text in (57) shows how such "lone utterances" follow one after another, with investigator prompts in square brackets.

(57) *Bees aren't supposed to come around there. They're coming off of the tree! Off of the tree. These are bees right here.* [Yeah, that's right.] *That's what they eat all up. They like to eat those!* [Right, right you are.] *The dog wants to eat it.* [That's right. What about here?] *The mouse wants to eat the boy.* [Uhhuh. Here, here we go.] *He saw something in the tree! Bees in there!* [Yeah, look!] *A thing come out of there, a dinosaur!* [E3h-3;9]

The large proportion of "free-clause utterances" in the younger children's texts relates to their need for constant verbal prompting and their strong reliance on interactive comment. Expressions definable as "interactive introducers" account for nearly one-third (30%) of all connectivity markers in the 3-year-old texts, but are used by only two of the 5-year-olds, and not at all by the 9-year-olds or adults. These interlocutor-addressed comments, lying outside either a narrative or descriptive mode of discourse, differ from one child to the next. One 3-year-old starts out with *Look! Look at ..., Look what happened* most of the time [*E3a-3;1*]; another introduces around half his utterances by exclamatory *Look what happened!* [*E3f-3;9*]; a third [*E3g-3;9*] hedges over one-third of the utterances by a modal or other mental predicate, including *I wonder, I think, I guess, I hope*; and of the two "interactively" oriented 5-year-olds, one starts numerous utterances by modal *What if* [*E5a-5;0*], the other initiates most utterances by spatial deictics like *On this page, in this picture* [*E5j-5;10*].

Among 3-year-olds, then, markers of discourse connectivity typically serve to inform the interlocutor that "more is to come," either another utterance and/or a new picture. And children select their own favored strategy to signal the progression of their narration. Three-year-olds make little use of standard lexical and grammatical means of clause linkage. Subordinating conjunctions, temporal *when* and *while*, and causal *(be)cause* are used only occasionally, by only half the children. Even the one child (with the highest level of language use among the English 3-year-olds) who uses *because* quite liberally is not subordinating two semantically related events in the unfolding plot, as shown in (58).[31]

(58) *Uh oh, owl again. I think that's the baby owl. I didn't see it **cause** he has a little nose right there. Uh oh, **cause** I think his dog is running away, **cause** I can see his legs are moving.* [*E3g-3;9*]

Coordination is also used in a nonstandard way by 3-year-olds. Around one-quarter of all their "linked" or nonfree clauses are initiated by the word *and*, the only coordinating conjunction used by most of the younger children. (One 3-year-old also uses *so* and another uses an occasional *but*). But *and* only occasionally entails genuine clause linkage by syntactic conjunction with same-subject ellipsis, as in (59).

(59) *I hope he doesn't fall down **and** Ø crack his head with all the glass.* [*E3g-3;9*]

Rather, *and* serves 3-year-olds predominantly as an utterance-initial discourse filler, with no semantic or thematic motivation other than to indicate that "more is still to come," as in (60).

---

[31] This use of *because* to express reasons is its earlier function in children's conversations (Kyratzis, 1991; Kyratzis, Guo, & Ervin-Tripp, 1990).

(60) *A owl's flying. Snow in there.* ***And** the boy tried to climb up it.* ***And** he did.* ***And** the dog is going away. A deer trying, jumping over,* ***and** a dog's running away with the deer.* ***And** the boy on top of the deer.* [E3d-3;5]

Markers of temporal sequentiality like *then* and *after that* are also rare among the the 3-year-olds. Only two 3-year-olds initiate clauses with the words *and then,* and they do so for different reasons: as a deictic marker for shifting from one picture to another, like bare *and,* to indicate that another utterance is about to be produced, or more felicitously, to mark the next event in a series of temporally sequenced events. These alternatives are shown in (61), which reflects a transition between juvenile utterance linking and more mature sequentially marked connectivity.

(61) ***And,** um this dog is looking into the bowl.* ***And then,** the frog is still in there.* ***And now** look what happened!* ***And now** he got away.* ***And then,** look what happened! He tried to go in ...* ***And then** he licked the boy and he was mad!* ***And then** some bees came out of the tree.* ***And then** he tried to get the bees, but he couldn't.* [E3f-3;9]

The sequential marker *then* occurs alone, without a prior *and,* only **once** across the younger children's texts. (62) is from the concluding clauses of a short narration.

(62) *He fell off.* ***And** he fell off of - in the pool.* ***And** there's no head!* ***Then** there's a frog. See, he caughted ... a frog.* [E3e-3;8]

This excerpt reflects how different clause-initial elements — interactive *see,* utterance-introducing *and,* and sequential *then* — function as incipient markers of connectivity in early extended discourse. By and large, as noted, the 3-year-old texts simply juxtapose bare utterances strung together in ongoing picture description, or else they overtly initiate fresh utterances by some signal that they have more to say.

4.3. Grammaticized Sequential Chaining

The middle phase of connectivity marking is strongly "additive" in character. At this phase, children tend to explicitly mark each clause as connected to what follows in a chronologically sequenced chain of events. This is reflected in the low proportion of "free" clauses among the 5- and 9-year-olds: Over 85% of all the clauses they produce carry overt marking of a syntactic, semantic and/or thematic relation to the preceding or following clause (compared with less than half the 3-year-olds').[32] Many of the 5- and 9-year-old

---

[32] Only one of the 9-year-olds [E9c-9;6] departs from this strong tendency. Nearly two-thirds (64%) of this child's clauses are "free"; the rest are combined by subject-eliding *and* or

clauses start with the conjunction *and* (71% and 68% respectively compared with only 40% of the 3-year-olds' — utterances, if not clauses). This reveals a similar functional development in English as in other languages. Among the older children, it serves a dual purpose: between clauses with shared subjects as a means of syntactic coordination (Section 4.5), and with same or different subjects as a means of indicating that another event is about to be described.

The single most favored connective device among these children is *and then*, which is used by every single 5- and 9-year-old. *And then* is evidently a criterial marker of narrative construction in English. It marks a clear distinction between the 3-year-old and 5-year-old texts (26% of the latter's clauses), it falls off somewhat among the 9-year-olds (15% of their clauses), and is marginal among the adults. Most of the adults do not use it even once, a quarter use it no more than once, while the narratives of those two adults who use it more widely (though still more sparingly than the children) are in many other respects also quite similar to those of the 9-year-olds. This "middle-phase" marker of sequentiality contrasts with options available to children in the same age range in the other languages — for instance, the use of expressions meaning *afterwards* and *after that* in Hebrew (Chapter IIID). Not a single English text contains the sequential conjunction *afterwards* or *after that* — although one child does (mis)use *after* in this sense, in (63).[33]

(63) *And then he put his boot on his head, and then his other boot on his foot. And after went out calling for the frog. And then the dog fell out and the boy jumped out.* [E5e-5;8]

Instead, half the 5-year-olds and most of the 9-year-olds use the sequential marker *then* without any prior *and*, as in (64).

(64) **And then** *the little boy hollered in a hole,* **and then** *a mole came out.* **Then, then** *the dog barked up at the hive.* **Then** *it shoo - he shook the tree.* **Then** *they fell down.* **Then** *then the dogs got -* **Then** *he, the little boy, climbed up the tree and said ...* [E5f-5;8]

Several older children rely very widely on these chaining devices, initiating most of their clauses with *and* or *then* alone or in combination. Two highly typical 9-year-old texts which resort to this device are excerpted in (65) and (66).

---

by subordination, with little "chaining" overall.

[33] This contrasts with mature use of *after* as a subordinating conjunction illustrated in Section 1.2.1.

(65) **Well**, *the boy, he finds a frog* **and** *... he's sharing it with his dog.* **Then** *he goes to sleep* **and** *the frogs gets away.* **Then when** *the boy wakes up, he finds that the frog's gone.* **Then** *they're looking for him.* **Then** *the dog, he - he gets stuck in the bowl,* **and** *they're - he's looking for him up there.* **And then** *... the dog falls,* **and** *he breaks the glass,* **and** *the boy gets mad at him.* **And then** *he goes looking for him in the woods.* **And** *he's going down, like in a hole,* **and** *the dog's looking in a tree, over here.* **And then** *he knocks the beehive over,* **and then** *the boy's looking in a crack in the tree,* **and then** *the bees run over it ... [E9b-9;3].*

(66) *The boy's looking at the frog,* **and** *- the dog's smiling down.* **And then** *he's going to bed,* **and** *the frog is sneaking out.* **Then** *it's morning* **and** *the frog is gone. He's looking all over his room,* **messing** *it up.* **And then** *the dog gets caught in the frog's bowl,* **and then** *the frog jumps,* **and** *the bowl breaks,* **and** *the boy gets mad at his dog,* **and** *his dog licks his face.* **And then** *they go out looking for the frog* **and** *the dog gets interested in a beehive,* **and** *∅ gets stung on the nose.* **And** *then the beehive breaks* **and** *the bees are coming after the dog,* **and** *he's looking in an old tree ... [E9l-9;11].*

These children increasingly use other devices for connectivity, mainly subordinators like *when* in (67), nonfinites like *messing* in (66), and a somewhat wider range of introductory markers of sequentiality. These are bolded in the excerpt in (67), taken from the most sophisticated of the English children's texts from the point of view of connectivity marking.

(67) **Once** *there was a boy* **who** *had a pet frog and a dog.* **And that night** *he was watching it,* **and when** *he went to sleep, the frog got out of his jar* **and** *∅ ran away.* **The next morning, when** *he woke up, he saw that the frog was gone.* **So** *he put on his clothes, and the dog, acci - accidentally got his head stuck in the jar* **which** *the frog was kept in. They called out the window* **and** *the dog fell down ... [E9a-9;1]*

But the children use such devices sparingly. They obviously have grammatical command of various forms of coordination and subordination as well as other types of clause linkage. And they can doubtless use them in complex sentences as well as isolated utterances in interactive discourse. Yet they have difficulty in deploying them felicitously to organize longer stretches of integrated ongoing discourse.[34]

---

[34] This might not apply to schoolchildren at the same age as these, when required to give the same accounts in **writing**.

4.4. Mature Thematic Chunking

The adult English texts together can be taken to represent a relatively complete repertoire of connective devices for oral English narratives, even though no one such text illustrates a single, canonical endstate model in this, as in other respects (Chapter IIA). This section considers markers of connectivity which occur in several of the adult narratives and which afford relevant contrasts to those of the children.

First, in terms of linear ordering, adults use connectivity devices in clause-medial and clause-final position, in contrast to the children's tendency to restrict them to the introducing slot in the frame CSV(X). This is illustrated by different kinds of **sequentiality** markers scattered across the adult texts — e.g., *And the dog* **eventually** *does fall, And he* **finally** *got the jar off his head* [E20c]; *The bees are* **now** *coming out in full force* [E20f]. Adults also use far more evaluative and epistemic modal expressions, in the form of clause-internal sentence modifiers which relate one event or state to another — e.g., *He's [=frog]* **apparently** *gone* [E20k].

Adults stack connectivity devices across chunks of clauses, creating longer stretches of event packaging than noted among the children. These yield tightly woven texts constructed of units that are highly cohesive in both syntactic organization and thematic relevance, as illustrated in the following two excerpts.

(68) **In the morning** *the boy wakes up* **and** ∅ *sees that the jar is empty.* ∅ *Decides to look in his big hiking boots, his big wading boots,* **to see if** *the frog has taken up new quarters for the evening.* **But** *he hasn't* ∅. *He's* **apparently** *gone.* **In the meanwhile,** *the boy's dog, Helmut, puts - sticks his head into the glass jar,* **trying** *to get the scent of the frog. The boy is so preoccupied with his frog* **that** *he doesn't notice.* [E20k]

(69) **After a while,** *the boy and his dog went out into the forest* **in search of** *their frog. They looked* **everywhere** *- in the woods and even in the gopher holes. The dog,* **being** *the rambunctious animal* **that** *he is, found a beehive* **and** ∅ *decided to have some fun,* **while** *the boy,* **searching** *frantically for the frog, was bit in the nose by a gopher.* [E20d]

These excerpts show that mature narrators can organize their texts from a thematically-motivated perspective, and they use a variety of expressive options for this purpose. These go far beyond the coordinating and subordinating devices of more linearly sequenced texts, including nonfinite participial and prepositional-phrase adverbials, verb gapping, and noun phrase ellipsis. These forms are also found in the children's narratives, but only occasionally, across subjects and texts. Moreover, children use them with a more local scope of application, rather than over large stretches of hierarchically organized pieces of discourse.

4.5. Null Subjects as a Linking Device

The occurrence of subjectless clauses in the English texts reveals a development which links knowledge of syntax with the narrative function of connectivity, and provides a further example of a single surface form serving different purposes at different developmental phases. In a sentence-based characterization, all simple clauses in English must have a surface grammatical subject, since English is a language which prohibits null subjects (Hyams, 1987). Yet in fact, subject ellipsis is found across the English frog stories, occurring in finite clauses with tensed verbs in nearly all the preschool and in several the 9-year-old and adult texts. Among the 3-year-olds, subjectless sentences occur in one of two contexts: as elliptical isolates, which may appear ungrammatical (70) or as elliptical responses to investigator queries (71) — represented in square brackets.

(70) *Here, bong bong! Ø can't get out right here.* [Child points to picture of hollow log.] *Ø go in there, Ø too big right in there. [E3c-3;4.]*

(71) *What's the dog doing there?* [Well, I don't know, what do you think?] *Ø running away ...* [Wait, let's slow down a bit. What about the dog?] *Ø climbing up the tree. [E3bg-3;4]*

Juvenile usage of null subjects is thus either ungrammatical or interactive, suited to conversational rather than narrative mode.

In contrast, children in the middle age range use null subjects for syntactic linking of strings of clauses with a shared surface subject. This is usually grammatically governed by elision rather than pronominalization of the repeated subject of coordinated clauses — e.g., *He climbed on a big rock and Ø called out for him [E5b-5;2]; An owl comes out and Ø knocks him down [E9d-9;6]*. Only one of the 3-year-olds has such phrasal conjunction, compared with nearly all the 5- and 9-year-olds.[35] Five- and 9-year-olds also use subject elision under conjunction without any surface marker of coordination, as in (72) to (75).

(72) *And then they woke up, Ø decided it wasn't there. [E5f-5;8]*

(73) *And the boy's looking down the hole, and Ø calling in the frog, and the dog is looking at the bees. And then a gopher comes out, Ø bites his*

---

[35] Adults also conjoin clauses with shared-subject ellipsis, but they use the coordinators *or* and *but* as well as *and* — e.g. *The frog feels it can now get out and Ø explore or Ø go home [E20f]; Looks like he's either stunned or Ø is just very frightened and ashamed [E20b]; The little doggie doesn't appear too concerned but Ø sticks his nose in the little jar anyway [E20j]*.

nose, and the dog is still doing that. [*E5k-5;11*]

(74) *And um - then the boy wakes up, Ø puts his clothes on, and Ø goes out-side.* [*E9d-9;6*]

(75) *And the dog fell out of the window. Ø Broke the jar. And the boy ...* [*E9f-9;8*]

Again, children use subject ellipsis as a local grammatical device, whereas mature narrators, in English as in other languages, employ it as a means of organizing chunks of discourse with a shared topic — as in the excerpts in (76) and (77).

(76) *Um, there's this little boy sitting in his room. Ø has a pet frog in a jar, and a dog is trying to get into the jar. Ø wants to be playing with the frog.* [*E20h*]

(77) *The boy sees the boulder, Ø follows the owl, and Ø climbs up on the boulder all the while yelling the frog's name. Ø Leans against what he thinks are ...* [*E20k*]

Comparison of two quite distinct connectivity devices — use of *-ing* forms for nonfinite clause embedding (Section 4.1) and null subjects for topic maintenance (this section) — reveals a similar developmental progression. They start out being used in unconventional, nonfelicitous ways; later they occur more sporadically, but show signs of emergent mastery of grammatical devices; subsequently they function as grammatical means for achieving text connectivity at the level of individual pairs of clauses; and eventually they are used with a thematic, more global motivation.

5. A NOTE ON RHETORICAL DEVICES

A further example of the "same form, different function" phenomenon is provided by use of the lexical item *now* in these texts. It occurs most fre-quently in the texts of the youngest children (five of the 3-year-olds and three 4-year-olds, but only once in the 5-year-old texts and never in the 9-year-old texts), and is again quite common among the adults, half of whom use *now* several times in their narratives. Among the 3- and 4-year-olds, it has a **deic-tic** sense, either in an interactive context, e.g., *Now look what happened to the dog* [*E3a-3;1*] or *Now let's turn the page* [*E3j-3;10*], or in a picture-description mode, moving from one picture to the next — as in the case of one 4-year-old, over a third of whose clauses start with *now* [*E4l-4;11*], e.g., *Now there's bees going around, Now the boy's stuck on a deer; Now there's the frogs*, and when asked by the investigator "How about this one?," the child replies *Now he's climbing down. Now they have little baby frogs.* For some of the preschoolers, *now* is an immature chaining device, and they intermix *and now* with *and then* — e.g., when a 5-year-old says ***And then** the bees'* *thing fell down. Now the dog's running and the boy got knocked over [E5j-5;10].* The adults, in marked contrast, use *now* in sentence-medial or final position nearly half the time — e.g., *But it's all okay now [E20e], Consequently the dog feels that it can now get out and ... [E20f],* rather than as a mechanical means of stringing utterances deictically, or of chaining clauses sequentially. Besides, adults do not necessarily use the term as an isolate; they typically embed it within a context which is lexically and/or syntactically more elaborated, e.g., *Right now, in the beginning of the story, the boy and his dog are ... [E20j]; Now, with the frog busily on his way, ... [E20e]; The boy is also in danger now that the owl has been disturbed [E20e].* For them, *now* serves a discourse- motivated purpose, to mark narrative sequentiality in the sense of "at this point in the story" — e.g., *The dog gets the beehive down and now realizes that ... [E20e]* or to indicate a logical inference — as in *Now the boy has been picked up by some antlered beast ... [E20b].* Unlike for the children, the word *now* is not so much a deictic anchor as an anaphoric means of marking different kinds of narrative connectivity.

A similar pattern is manifested by use of the rhetorical device of **repetition** by the English narrators.[36] The youngest children repeat lexical items mainly because of problems of lexical retrieval and disfluencies in the online production of extended discourse. Children in the middle age range use repetition to express semantically-motivated aspectual distinctions. For example, a combination of protracted and iterative aspect is expressed by a 5-year-old who describes the dog's involvement with the beehive as follows: *He was playing with the bees. He was playing with the bees again, he was trying to kid them [E5b-5;2].* This is then extended to discourse-based reiteration several clauses (and pictures) later, when the child repeats *And then the dog was still trying to kid the bees ....* Another 5-year-old makes similar use of repetition as a rhetorical device, thus: *And then he called for his frog again. He called in a hole, and the dog called in the beehive [E5-5;11].* Adults' use of repetition has similar motivations, but they are more clearly relying on the deliberate rhetorical device of **syntactic parallelism** combined with semantic alternation. For example, two participants in the same scene are counterpoised as: *The gopher seems angry and the boy seems hurt [E20c].* (78) shows a combination of all the different uses of repetition in a mature narrative.

---

[36] Preliminary analyses of this device in other languages indicates that these findings may not be peculiar to English. But it is particularly noteworthy in English, since repetition as such is not an approved rhetorical device in the way that has been noted for Semitic languages (Berman, 1979b; Williamson, 1978).

(78) *The boy is looking down a hole to see if the frog is in the hole* [=disfluent lexical repetition], ***and the dog is intrigued by this beeehive.*** *The boy gets his nose either bitten or sniffed at by some little animal living in the hole.* ***And the dog is still intrigued with the beehive*** *... . Now the beehive has been knocked down out of the tree by the dog,* ***and the bees are intrigued with the dog,*** *while the boy is sitting in the tree ...* [E20b]

Development in the use of forms in the English texts is thus revealed in several interrelated ways over a range of expressive devices, syntactic constructions, and lexical items. Children learn to use them in a wider range of syntactic constructions, in a richer variety of lexical and semantic contexts, and with more globally organized discourse-based motivations.

6. SUMMARY AND CONCLUDING REMARKS

This chapter concludes — like the four which follow in this part of the book — with a short summary of the main trends in the development of linguistic forms along the different dimensions selected for crosslinguistic analysis and comparison (Chapter IIIO): tense/aspect, event conflation, perspective, and connectivity. In this chapter, additionally, we note in concluding some more general themes which emerge very clearly from analysis of these dimensions in the frog stories as told in English, the language in which this book is written.

6.1. Tense/Aspect Marking

Three-year-olds are able to use both present and past tense correctly at the level of the individual clause, although the youngest children occasionally make morphological errors in past-tense forms, or omit the third-person suffix in present tense. However, as many as a third of the English preschoolers fail to anchor their narrations in either present or past tense, with 8 out of the 12 3-year-olds using what we characterized as a mixture of present and past, in a rather unsystematic fashion. All the 9-year-olds anchor their narrations clearly in either present or past tense, reflecting adherence to a consistent temporal frame of narrative. Most children with a clearly dominant tense prefer the past, but the English-speaking adults favor present tense in this particular narrative setting.

As for grammatical aspect, perfect forms are rare across the children's texts, though adults do use present perfect quite commonly in present-tense anchored texts. This reflects the late acquisition of present perfect, and the low reliance on perfect forms in general in American compared with British English or, as we shall see, with a language like Spanish. In contrast, progressive forms are extremely common, being used by young children as a basic present tense, and by older narrators increasingly for the aspectual and backgrounding functions associated with past progressives in English.

Lexical aspect is rarely expressed by particles in the English frog stories, while use of aspectual verbs such as *start* for inception is found mainly among the older children and adults. Aspectual adverbs are also quite rare in the English texts, except for quite common use of *still* which is used to mark protraction more commonly than verbs like *go on* or *keep on*. In general, the English corpus lacks rich elaboration of temporal contours beyond the distinction between simple and progressive markings on the verb.

6.2. Event Conflation

The richest devices meeting this function in the English texts are verbs of movement which incorporate the expression of **manner** within the verb stem, e.g., not only *fall* or *drop* but also *swoop* and *plummet*, and locative particles expressing the source and/or goal of a movement, e.g., *knock something down off a tree*. These devices are richly used from the youngest age groups, although they increase in variety and precision with age, culminating in mature packaging of manner, source, and goal within a single clause, e.g., *deposits the boy off the side of the ravine into the creek*. The younger children, in contrast, while paying considerable attention to locative contours in general, fail to conflate more than one facet of an event within a single lexical or syntactic package.

6.3. Perspective

The English texts rely relatively heavily on use of passive constructions to present a nonagentive perspective on an event, with children favoring *get* passives (although even the 3-year-olds occasionally use *be* passives), to express an inchoative, patient-oriented perspective. Adult use of passive voice occurs with a wider range of predicate types (states as well as changes of state) and in more varied narrative settings.

The English frog-story sample is strongly SVO in orientation, with little variation of word order for marking a change in perspective. Even the youngest children generally elaborate the predicate beyond a bare verb, typically by means of particles or prepositional phrases, so that the clauses out of which the English texts are constructed quite generally have an SVX structure. The major developmental trends are in the tendency of the younger children to precede nearly every clause by some utterance-initial element such as *and* or *and then,* with older children increasingly making use of expletive *it* as a means of varying this stereotyped linear ordering of information, for example with epistemic modals like *it seems* or *it turns out*.

6.4. Connectivity

The youngest children merely string utterances together without any overt markers of interclause connectivity, or else they pick on a particular, often idiosyncratic element to mark each ensuing utterance, such as interactive *Look!* or *I think* or more typically *and* used as an empty discourse filler. The 5- and 9-year-old English narrators, in contrast, rely heavily on *and then* as a means for chaining one clause after another in narrative sequence. Only adults use a variety of linking devices, including nonclause-initial markers of sequentiality such as *finally* or *eventually* as well as nonfinite participial clauses for embedding some events or states as backgrounded to others. Similarly, adult English speakers occasionally use null subjects for topic elision in a discourse-motivated fashion, whereas 5- and 9-year-olds use same subject elision as a grammatical device in conjoining, in a way the 3- and 4-year-olds appear unable to do in our English sample.

6.5. Concluding Remarks

Our findings for the development of forms in the (American) English frog stories highlight two themes central to this study. First, the youngest children in our sample, aged 3 to 4 years old, can in some sense be said to "know" the bulk of the forms analyzed in this chapter. Yet this knowledge is only partial, since with age, these same forms take on different functions within the context of an extended narrative text. This development applies to forms from different linguistic domains, including: a verbal inflection like the suffix *-ing* as an unmarked immediate-present tense, marking progressive aspect, in verb complement constructions, and as a nonfinite adverbial subordinator; closed class function words like the prepositions *in* or *after*, which progress from static and dynamic locative to temporal marking, to adverbial use with nonfinite verbs and abstract derived nominals; a syntactic construction like passive voice, which develops from being used with change-of-state situations to marking shifts in narrative perspective; and subject ellipsis, initially symptomatic of ill-formed simple-clause construction, later serving for clause-linkage through syntactic coordination, eventually to achieve discourse connectivity through a shared discourse topic.

A second theme affirmed by the findings for our English corpus relates to the development of narrative structure and discourse abilities in general (Chapter IIA). The texts of the youngest children in our sample manifest considerable individual variation and idiosyncratic choice of discourse mode. They are largely interactive in tenor, and they combine a fair command of lexical and grammatical forms with difficulty in constructing coherent, well-organized extended texts. Some 4- and 5-year-olds narrations are very similar to those of 3-year-olds, whereas some 5-year-olds tell stories much like school-age 9-year-old children. The latter have well-established command of grammatical constructions and an extended lexical repertoire, and they are familiar with the demands of the narrative mode and plot construction. But their texts tend to be stereotyped, describing, generally in past tense, one event after the other in a linear chaining of clauses from onset to resolution. The adults, in contrast, make use of more expressive options, and they reveal individual predispositions in choice of rhetorical style. We noted that younger children's texts include a large proportion of isolated clauses, whereas older children tend strongly to stack clauses linearly. Adults use both expressive options: The text of E20h consists mainly of isolated simple clauses, with occasional coordination or use of nonfinite verb forms; that of E20f in contrast manifests heavy "chunking," with only some 15% syntactically isolated clauses. Some of the adult texts are similar in most respects to the straightforward accounts of the 9-year-olds (e.g., E20a); others provide long and elaborate, highly detailed narrations with higher register items and self-consciously literary usages (E20c, E20f); yet others are short, concise, almost abbreviated accounts with plot summations, generalizations, and lexical or grammatical ellipsis (E20d, E20i).

In sum, the English texts are peculiarly English in some ways, yet they share features noted across the languages in others. The same duality emerges in the following chapters, which analyze linguistic forms in the narratives of children and adults in four other languages.

Chapter IIIB

DEVELOPMENT OF LINGUISTIC FORMS: GERMAN

Michael Bamberg

0. INTRODUCTION: PERSPECTIVE TAKING ON EVENTS, SCENES, AND CHARACTERS

This chapter, like the rest of the book, is concerned with linguistic forms and how they change over time as put to use by children of different ages compared with adults. On the one hand, the task used to elicit the database — narration of a picture-book — severely restricts this investigation of how linguistic forms are deployed. On the other hand, however, the task shares with other types of narrative (for instance, accounts of personal experiences) the fact that narrators cannot simply rely on the "events," the "spatial scenes," and the "characters" who move and act in these scenes and events as givens. Rather, events, scenes, and characters are "middle-level units" of what I have called "part-whole relationships" (Bamberg, 1993). They are parts of larger units such as episodes, plots, and the overall "drama," though at the same time they are also "wholes," in the sense that they are made up of other parts such as movements, states, internal states, feelings, motives, and the like.

Events, scenes, and characters can thus be further broken down into lower-level units, which can then be analyzed as differentiated and re-integrated into middle-level units in the form of events, scenes, and characters. From this point of view, events, scenes, and characters can be viewed as the products of developmental processes of differentiation and integration. At the same time, middle-level units are also the products of top-down processes, derived from themes which take the form of "plots" and, ultimately, of "the drama" as a whole. From this perspective, events, scenes, and characters gain their contour from culturally given themes that govern the whens, the wheres, and the whos, and how these interact with one another, in light of what is considered "relevant," "good," and "human" (Burke, 1968, 1969).

This view of language as operating to construct part-whole relationships has consequences for the notion of linguistic forms. Forms do not "express" or "reveal" nonlinguistic perspectives; they **are** the perspectives. What forms can in fact reveal is the composition of part-whole relationships, that is, how smaller, lower-level units interact with higher-level units in the constitution of "events," "scenes," and "characters."

This chapter, accordingly, considers an array of linguistic forms that are in one or another way relevant to the task of telling the frog story from the pictures. The chapter is divided into three main sections. Section 1 analyzes how events are constructed by use of linguistic forms that aid in the integration of their temporal and aspectual contours, to construct a so-called time-line, including verbal and adverbial marking of tense and aspect distinctions, and temporal conjunction and subordination. Section 2 examines how linguistic forms function in the construction of spatial relationships, particularly in the scenic layout of movements that can be appropriately integrated only from an overarching plot-perspective. Section 3 considers how the story characters emerge as the products of linguistic form, with special attention to different linguistic means for the attribution of agency, for topic-comment, and for figure-ground relationships, including: word order, voice, Aktionsart, and referential choices.

Before discussing the changes of form-function relationships in the German narratives in more detail, let me briefly describe a few common characteristics of German grammar that will help in the interpretation of what German children, as part of their developing narrative competence, have to come to grips with.

First of all, an important characteristic of German is the variable though rule-governed word order which is best characterized in terms of "the verb in second position rule." This general rule holds that, in declaratives, the finite verb follows the first phrasal element — usually the subject. However, a temporal or spatial prepositional phrase or adverb can take the sentence-initial position, followed by the verb, as in *da geht der Hund rein* 'there goes the dog inside' [G3e]. In subordinate clauses, the finite verb occupies the clause-final position. Furthermore, it should be noted that the past participles and infinitives of compound tenses in declarative sentences occupy the clause-final position, as in *Peter ist inzwischen auf den Baum geklettert* 'Peter has in the meantime up the tree climbed' [G20f], while in subordinate clauses the auxiliary, being the finite verb, comes last, as in *weil der Hund daran geschüttelt hat* 'because the dog on that shaken has' (=because the dog has shaken it) [G20b].

Passives, which are used much less in German than in English (e.g., Hammer, 1971, p. 210), are formed in similar fashion to English, by use of the auxiliary *werden* 'become'/'get', the use of *von* 'by' in front of the agent, and by use of the past participle of the verb in clause-final position. Passive constructions that focus on actions employ *werden* 'get', while passives that focus on the resultant state (also called *Zustandspassiv*) are expressed by *sein* 'be'. An interesting difference between German and English is that datives in German active constructions remain datives in the passive voice (*mir wurde ein Buch gegeben* 'to.me was given a book'), whereas accusative objects typically become nominatives, as in *die Bienen jagten ihn* 'the bees chased him' versus *er wurde von den Bienen gejagt* 'he was chased by the bees'.

In addition to word-order variations as well as varieties of passive constructions, it should be noted that German has an extensive gender, case, and number system marked in complex noun phrase morphology as well as in the article and adjectival inflections preceding the noun. Furthermore, there is subject-verb agreement in person and number, leading to a more complex verb morphology when compared with English. More detailed discussions of the acquisition of German grammar can be found in Clahsen (1988), Mills (1985), and Tracy (1991). Behrens (1993) presents a valuable new analysis of the development of temporal reference in German child language.

1. MOVING THROUGH TIME IN GERMAN

1.1. The Linguistic Creation of Temporal Units

As I have argued elsewhere (Bamberg, 1993), the notion of forming the temporal unit of an event needs to be considered in light of two factors: (1) the contour that the unit receives in terms of its lexical (Aktionsart) and aspectual boundaries, and (2) the contour that the unit receives from the preceding and subsequent event in which it is embedded in discourse. In terms of Aktionsart boundaries, accomplishment (transitive-activity) and achievement (change-of-state) verbs are relatively good candidates for temporally bounded units, in contrast to intransitive activity and particularly state verbs. The temporal contour of units realized as events through these latter two classes of verbs is generally more clearly defined in relation to other, surrounding textual properties. The following analysis of how linguistic forms are deployed to create such temporal units in the frog story considers distinctions marked on the verb through the German tense system (Section 1.2) as well as lexical distinctions and temporal conjunctions (1.3).

1.2. Tense and Aspect

Dialect differences in contemporary German have led to the claim that the simple past is in the process of being replaced by the present perfect (*Praeteritumsschwund*: Eisenberg, 1986; Schmidt, 1967, p. 220), particularly in southern parts of former West Germany. In order to circumvent dialectal variation, narratives were collected well to the north of this region. The northern varieties make use of both the simple past and the present perfect. Narratives were elicited from children in Bokeloh and Meppen, two neighboring communities in northwest Germany, south of Friesland, 25 miles from the border with the Netherlands, and from adults (aged between 20 and 32 years) from the same area as well as from other parts of northern Germany. There were 12 subjects in each of four age groups: 3, 5, 9, and adult. (For statistics on age and story length, see Chapter IB.)

A wealth of literature, both contemporary and less recent, has addressed the German system of tense/aspect, but there is by no means general agreement as to the semantics or pragmatics of the main tense forms: simple present, simple past, present perfect, past perfect, as well as future and/or modality markers.[1] I have proposed (Bamberg, 1990) that an analysis of

---

[1] The present analysis focuses primarily on the simple present, the simple past, the present perfect, and the past perfect, with little note of auxiliary markers of future and modality, since

tense/aspect contrasts requires two basic presuppositions: (1) Tenses in their discursive context should not be taken to "refer" to points or places on a pre-established timeline; rather, verb-tense forms serve as an instruction to imagine — points, durations, events, episodes, plots, and the drama (see, also, Bamberg, 1993). (2) The differential force of these forms derives in part from their compliance to such instructions to imagine and in part from the formal contrasts afforded by the grammar. From this perspective, it turns out, for instance, that the present perfect functions differently when it contrasts with the simple present rather than the simple past (Bamberg, 1990).

In terms of surface constructions, the four forms in question (simple present, simple past, present perfect, and past perfect) reflect the same processes of morphological formation as their English counterparts; however the functions served by these apparently parallel constructions differ considerably between the two languages. In addition, on the syntactic level, a major difference between German and English is that the verb stem in German requires sentence-final positioning in the present or past perfect, as indicated in (2) and (3) by sentence-final *geschneit* 'snowed'. Simple past and simple present follow SVO word order as illustrated by example (1).

(1) *Es schneite gestern fünf Stunden lang.*

   'It snowed:SIMPLE.PAST yesterday for five hours.'

(2) *Es hat gestern fünf Stunden lang geschneit.*

   'It has yesterday for five hours snowed.' [PRESENT PERFECT]

(3) *Es hatte gestern fünf Stunden lang geschneit.*

   'It had yesterday for five hours snowed.' [PAST PERFECT]

Another difference between the two languages is the higher frequency of use of the present perfect in German compared with English, which may be responsible for the much earlier appearance of such forms among German-speaking children. The present perfect, at first without the required auxiliary, but soon afterwards in the correct form, is the first tense form in the acquisition of German, even though it is morphologically more complex than the simple past, which emerges later (for more details on the acquisition of the German tense distinctions, see Bamberg, 1986; Behrens, 1993; Rau, 1979; Stern & Stern, 1928; Szagun, 1976, 1979). These properties of the German tense system presumably affect how these forms are deployed in the context

---

these are extremely rare in our sample, even in the adult texts. Note, also, that there is no marking on the German verb for either progressive/nonprogressive or perfective/imperfective aspects. Valuable recent analyses of temporality in German can be found in Ehrich (1992) and Thieroff (1992).

of our narrative texts from age 3 through to adulthood.

1.2.1. Dominant tense: Temporal anchoring

Forty-four out of the total 48 German-speaking narrators, across four age groups, anchor their narratives in the simple present. That is, the simple present is by far the predominant tense form (80-95%), followed by between 5% to 15% in present perfect, with almost no simple past or past perfect forms at all.[2] Out of the four exceptions, two subjects (both 9-year-olds) anchor their narratives clearly in the simple past, while the two others (both 5-year-olds) mix simple present, simple past, and present perfect, switching back and forth between them. The present analysis focuses on the developmental picture emerging from narratives anchored in the simple present, followed in the next section (1.2.3) by a brief consideration of the remaining four narratives.

1.2.2. Simple-present anchoring: Adults and children

What follows is a summary account first for the adult narratives, and subsequently for those of the three age groups of the German-speaking children. This summary account follows methodologically prior and more detailed analyses conducted for similar data (Bamberg, 1987, 1990, 1993).[3] The focus here is on the form-function relationships expressed by the use of the present perfect in the adult German sample as a form contrasting with the simple present, rather than on a detailed quantitative analysis of the distribution of these forms across the sample. All 12 adult narrators used present perfect forms, contrasting with the simple present in two major functions. First, there is what I have termed the **prospective relevance** function of the present perfect, typically used to begin a new scene or episode, followed by one (or more) subsequent proposition(s) that elaborate(s) the happening mentioned in a sequential or even consequential manner. In this way, use of the present perfect instructs the listener to construct a "new" activity scene, and to hold it open for subsequent information relevant to this scene. At the same time,

---

[2] Hickmann and Roland (1992) have found a similar pattern of tense usage in a study employing different picture-story materials. They report the following percentages of present-tense anchoring in German-speaking narrators: 4-year-olds — 77%, 7-year-olds — 75%, 10-year-olds — 80%, adults — 88%. (See, also, footnote 14, Chapter IIA.)

[3] The data for these earlier analyses came from German-speaking adults recorded while narrating the contents of the frog-book to their own children. Accordingly, the form-function relationships expressed to which the verb tenses were put to use may correspond more closely to what is commonly termed "motherese" or "zone of proximal development" (Snow, 1977a, 1977b; Snow & Ferguson, 1977; Vygotsky, 1962; Wertsch, 1985) in contrast to the elicitation conditions of the present study. However, the two functions of present perfect forms revealed in both narrative settings emerged as identical.

taking the middle of such scenes as their deictic center, the content of a proposition marked by a present perfect is temporally prior to that center and so
points forward to it. This yields a discursive function which, if the deictic
center is taken to be what is "currently occurring," closely resembles the
"current relevance" attributed to the perfect form in other Indo-European
languages (Comrie, 1985; Flier & Timberlake, 1985). The following example
illustrates this use of the present perfect in an adult German narrative.

(4)   *Das Glas ist zerbrochen und der Dackel ist wieder frei.*

    'The jar has broken and the doggy is free again.' [*G20a*]

In the example in (4), the state of being free (from the jar) is viewed as a
consequence of what happened in the first clause. Reversing the order of the
two clauses (*Der Dackel ist wieder frei, und das Glas ist zerbrochen* 'The
doggy is free again, and the jar has broken') would take away their consequential force, and might even be mistaken for an instruction to the listener to
construct a scene in which the two events are unconnected. The only way to
reinstate the consequential underpinning would be by way of an overt marking (*weil* 'because' or *nämlich* 'namely'), as in (4a) and (4b).

(4a)   *Der Dackel ist wieder frei, **weil** das Glas zerbrochen ist.*

    'The dog is free again, **because** the glass has broken.'

(4b)   *Der Dackel ist wieder frei, das Glas ist **nämlich** zerbrochen.*

    'The dog is free again, the glass, **namely**, has broken.'

In these two constructed examples, the use of the present perfect *zerbrochen* 'broken' in the second clauses of (4a) and (4b) takes on a "relative" temporal value which is not signaled when used in initial position, as in example
(4). This temporal value of the present perfect in the constructed examples
instructs the listener to "relate" both events represented in the two clauses in
terms of a reverse order: The breaking of the jar takes place before the dog is
liberated again. This sequence of events mirrors the order of the clauses in
example (4), with an additional marking of the first clause as completed.[4] In

---

[4] The narrator could have used the simple present *zerbricht* 'breaks', thus not overtly
marking the current endstate of the process. But then the inference that the jar's breaking
ends up as a completive state of being totally broken (the only way that the dog can be inferred as being 'free') rests to a larger degree on the listener. Besides, at the level of
discourse organization, the marked aspectual perspective does more than merely lighten
listeners' inferential burdens; it also instructs them in the construction of a deictic center from
which the internal coherence of linearly strung events will become clear. It is unnecessary
and ultimately misleading to first construct the "meaning" of the present perfect (perhaps
decontextually) and then explore how it affects the presentation of discourse. This would involve setting up a barrier between the semantic and pragmatic force of tense-aspect forms. In
contrast, the view presented here is that the way these forms are used is their meaning!

the constructed examples (4a) and (4b), then, the present perfect serves primarily to mark that the event in question took place before the event described in the preceding clause or clauses. This particular way of using the present perfect in German is the **retrospective assessment** function of the present perfect. The examples in (5) and (6), from two different adults, demonstrate even more clearly how the simple present and the present perfect contrast.

(5)   *Als am frühen Morgen dann Hans und der Hund **aufwachen**, bemerken sie zu ihrem großen Schrecken, daß Frau Frosch durch das geöffnete Fenster nach draußen **weggelaufen ist**.*

'When in the early morning then Hans and the dog **wake up**, they **realize** to their great fright, that Mrs. Frog through the opened window towards outside **has run away**'. [G20c]

(6)   *Aber Moritz **ist** 'n bißchen erbost denn er **hat** einen riesigen Schrecken **gekriegt**.*

'However, Moritz **is** a little angry since he **has received** a huge fright.' [G20d]

Use of the present perfect in these two examples clearly serves as an instruction to reconstruct the sequence of events in reverse order. The instruction to construct the order with a consequential underpinning is further expressed by use of *daß* 'that' in (5), and *denn* 'since' in (6). Such instructions to reverse the sequential order are often signaled in a context in which consequentiality and/or causality is at issue and, interestingly, mostly when events are viewed from the perspective of one of the characters in the story.[5] In such situations, the character's mental or emotional state is in focus, and so is expressed first, followed by what is assumed to have led to the state in question.

Consider, next, uses of the simple past in the adult narratives, all of which are, as noted, anchored in simple-present-tense narratives. Five of the 12 German adults do not use any simple past forms at all; another four use only one such form; and only three subjects use it three or more times — a total of 21 uses. These divide up into several uses, as follows. (1) Nine instances are uses of *Praeteritopraesentia*, a class of German verbs that historically lost their present tense morphology, which was replaced by the then strong past-tense morphology (e.g., the modals *wollen* 'want', *sollen* 'should', *können* 'can', *mögen* 'may', *müssen* 'must', *dürfen* 'ought'). Essentially, then,

---

[5] For methodological reasons it is important to distinguish between the narrator's perspective and the perspective of the story characters. However, as I have argued elsewhere (Bamberg, 1992), the boundaries between these two different perspectives are fluid and cannot always be clearly differentiated.

these modals have a single past-tense form, and do not normally contrast with present perfect. (2) One narrator starts with four past-tense forms, then switches to the simple present as anchor tense for the rest of her narrative. (3) Another six cases are of simple past with the verbs *sein* 'be' and *haben* 'have' (as main verbs, not auxiliaries). (4) The single remaining simple past form merits consideration, since it demonstrates nicely how the "pragmatics" of the present perfect in contrast with the simple present can be transformed into a simple past form, so long as other pragmatic means are also employed along with the past-tense form, as in (7).

(7)   *Was steckte hinter diesen Büschen? Ein großer Hirsch.*
      'What hid behind these bushes? A big deer.' [*G20d*]

The use of the simple past in the opening clause of (7) can only take on the prospective-relevance discourse force normally carried out by the present perfect because of its question format, which pragmatically enforces the answer as the upcoming orientation point or deictic center of this sequence.

In sum, all 12 German adult narratives are anchored in the present tense, so that the simple present is the overarching, dominant tense form contrasting with the present perfect. The latter functions in these narratives to relate propositions discursively to each other: either prospectively pointing forward to an orientation point or center towards which the discourse is moving, or pointing retrospectively to previously constructed units, for the purpose of clarifying, tallying, or simply wrapping up. The few simple past forms can all be explained as local deviations, grounded either in peculiarities of the German language (as in the case of *Praeteritopraesentien* and the use of simple past *war* 'was' compared with its present perfect counterpart *ist gewesen* 'is been' [=has been] and of *hatte* 'had' rather than *gehabt hatte* 'had had'), or in particular pragmatic constraints that allow these forms to take on the same discourse function as the present perfect. These German tense contrasts in the adult versions of the frog story reflect a telos towards which children will work in their deployment of tense forms for this narrative task.

Few of the total group of children who anchor their narratives in the simple present use this form exclusively, without any other tense forms. We have already noted that children as young as age 3 seem to recognize the present perfect as the appropriate form to contrast with the dominant anchor tense, the simple present. That is, the formal configuration of tense contrasts in the frog-story task appears to have been figured out relatively early. The question which remains, then, is whether these two forms, simple present and perfect, serve the same functional differentiations from early on as well. Should age-related differences be revealed in form-function matchings, these may provide grounds to argue for a developmental sequence in use of verb tense in our sample.

A closer view of the way the 45 present perfect tokens are used by the 12 3-year-old narrators reveals that in 10 cases the present perfect follows the use of the same verb previously marked by the simple present, thus repeating the action description, but taking a completive stance in the second mentioning. Examples (8) and (9) illustrate this common use of the present perfect.[6]

(8) *und der Hund und Walter - die plumpsen da runter*

'and the dog and Walter - they plop down there'

da sind die runtergeplumpst

'there they have plopped down'

und da sind die im Wasser

'and there they are in the water' [*G3f-3;11*]

(9) *die geben einen kleinen mit*

'they [=frogs] give (them) a little one (to take) along'

die beiden Frösche haben einen mitgegeben

'the two frogs have given (them) one (to take) along' [*G3c-3;11*]

Four further uses of the present perfect appear in the text of one 3-year-old (G3d), marking a completive stance on an action of the frogs in the form of a question-answer sequence. This sequence results in a question about how the endstate of reaching the top of the tree trunk may have been achieved, and from there moves on to take a completive stance on the deer's actions as well, thus:

(10) *und wo sind da die Babyfrösche?*

'and where are the baby frogs there?'

die sind da weggelauft, sind weggelauft

'there they have runned away, have runned away'[7]

da sind se hingelaufen

'there they have run toward'

---

[6] When the forms of individual clauses are at issue, examples are given with one clause per line, as in the transcripts, with interlinear glosses and no punctuation. Nouns are capitalized, following German orthographic conventions.

[7] The form *weggelauft* is an overregularization, similar to *runned away*, as given in the gloss. Note the contrast with the morphologically correct *hingelaufen* in the following clause.

sind da die Frösche, die kleinen?

'are the frogs there, the little ones?'

wie sind die da hochgekommen?

'how have they (managed to) come up there?'

und wo ist der Reh hin?

'and where has/is the deer (gone) to?'

der ist weggelauft

'he has run away' [G3d-3;6]

Four other present perfect forms of the 3-year-olds can be interpreted in terms of a retrospective perspective similar to the retrospective assessment function noted for present perfect in the adult narratives. Another four present perfect forms closely resemble the adult prospective relevance function. This form-function pairing is illustrated in (11).

(11) *Jetzt ist er auf den Baum geklettert und ruft da.*

'Now he has climbed up the tree and calls there.' [G3b-3;11]

The other 3-year-old present perfect forms (around half the total) appear not to cluster around particular patterns. It is not clear whether they reveal a completive aspectual stance or are tied to a particular lexical choice. Though most of the present perfect forms cluster around the action descriptions of falling, breaking, and hiding, it is not clear whether the action itself engendered this perspective or whether the perspective is independently realized, as it were, externally to the action description. The evidence for the existence of an aspectual stance not motivated merely by the type of action in half the 3-year-olds' uses of the present perfect / simple present contrast, as illustrated in (8) through (11), seems to support the notion that children's aspectual stances are discursively motivated at this early age, although, as suggested by the remaining 50% of such instances, this motivation may not always be recoverable from the data. The fact that it was possible to more clearly identify a discursive motivation for choice of the present perfect in the much longer texts of the 3-year-olds in my earlier corpus (Bamberg, 1987) lends further support to this assumption.

Even under such an assumption, however, the form-function match of the simple present / present perfect contrast of these younger children is not the same as among adult narrators. Adults discursively orient the propositions to some past or future deictic orientation point within the universe of discourse, whereas the 3-year-olds adhere to a single action as their center. The younger children can change a previous perspective on this center, using the simple present, to a completed perspective, using the present perfect. However, this tense contrast does not contribute to the development of a center outside those propositions from which a directive for these propositions could be orchestrated.

The 5-year-old texts include only 43 present perfect forms in all (compared with 45 among the 3-year-olds), but the proportion of present perfect forms per narrative is slightly higher than in the younger group, if we discount the two 5-year-old texts that are not anchored in the present tense. In the other remaining 10 simple present anchored narratives, use of the present perfect yields a somewhat mixed picture. On the one hand, it continues to be used in the same limited function as by the 3-year-olds, as shown in (12).

(12) *und da fällt der runter*
'and there he falls down'
und der Hund auch
'and the dog too'
kuck mal jetzt sind se in's Wasser gefallen
'look now they have fallen into the water'
und hier fällt er runter mit dem Hund - siehst du?
'and here he falls down with the dog - see?' [referring back to the previous page] [*G5d-5;3*]

This example demonstrates how the narrator switches back and forth between the taking of an open-ended perspective by use of the simple present (which in English might be expressed by progressive aspect) and the completive stance expressed by the present perfect. However, this kind of restrictedness to a "here-and-now" of the deictic center is relatively rare among 5-year-olds. The example in (13) illustrates a more sophisticated orientation by moving the discourse perspective towards a center from which the sequence of events is viewed as evolving.

(13) *der ist dahin gegangen*
'he has gone there'
und da ist ne Eule gekommen
'and there an owl has come'
und da ist er da schnell runtergefallen
'and there he has there quickly fallen down'
weil er sich losgelassen hat
'because he has let go'
darum kommt das
'that's why this happens' [*G5h-5;1*]

Here, as in several other instances, the center is upcoming in the discourse. In (13), the center from which these activities are viewed (thereby creating the impression that they have been moving towards it) is given with the last proposition in the form of a summary: 'That's why this (one) comes', switching back to the use of the simple present after the previous four propositions have been marked by the present perfect. (13) also demonstrates the child-like quality of this precursor of the prospective relevance function of the present perfect.

Another use of the present perfect occurs several times in the story-setting, where the narrators seemingly give the instruction to catch up on previous happenings that may have led to what counts as the current "here-and-now," as in (14) and (15).

(14) *hier ist der Frosch drin*

    'here is the frog inside'

    den haben die gefangen

    'him they have caught'

    haben die mitgenommen

    'have they taken along'

    und in das Glas gesteckt

    'and put into the jar'

    und der Hund kuckt drin

    'and the dog looks inside'

    ob er noch drin war

    'whether he still was inside' [G5f-5;10]

(15) *da haben sie den Frosch ins Wasser getan*

    'there they have put the frog into the water'

    und der Hund kuckt dadrin

    'and the dog looks inside it' [G5g-5;3]

In (14), the present perfect form is totally framed by simple presents, whereas in (15) it seems to have more of a forward-pointing orientation towards an upcoming deictic discourse center. Both of these examples, and several others from the 5-year-olds, demonstrate that the contrast between simple present and present perfect is increasingly employed from a discursive orientation center. It appears that at this age, perspectives no longer hover around the same event or happening, as in example (12), but they take shape from an "outside" viewpoint towards which or from which events appear in sequence.

The texts of the 9-year-old children, 10 of which are likewise present-tense anchored narratives, reaffirm this general tendency of the emergence of patterns. A number of 9-year-olds start the story with use of a present perfect form, as in (16).

(16) *Also da hat ein Junge einen Frosch gefangen.*

'Well there a boy has caught a frog.' [G9a-9;3]

By and large, the 9-year-olds show a more adult-like use of the simple present / present perfect contrast, with discursive purposes similar to the adults. There are still a few cases where they use the present perfect like the younger children, but these are outweighed by far by the more sophisticated use of relating "past" events to the "here-and-now" of internal states. (17) gives an example of a sophisticated interpretation of causal relations between events resulting in an internal state, viewed from a discourse perspective that posits the internal state as the center from which new strings of action can emerge.

(17) *und der Junge ärgert sich*

'and the boy is angry' [lit. 'angers himself']

weil er runtergefallen ist

because he has fallen down' [G9g-9;10]

In sum, the present perfect in texts anchored in the simple present shows the following development. Early on, particularly among the 3-year olds, present perfect is used to present a completive perspective on an event or chain of events. The vantage point for this perspective originates from "outside" of the event, and as such is motivated in the discourse, but it is not yet motivated by a vantage point that itself is organized in light of some past or future deictic orientation point within the universe of discourse. Over time, children begin to group events together and integrate them into units that are organized from discursive orientation (deictic) centers, spanning a number of propositions, as in examples (13) through (15). In the final phase, the present perfect is differentially employed to point forward to an upcoming orientation center (with prospective relevance), or to point back to a previously mentioned orientation center (retrospectively assessing).

1.2.3. Simple-past and temporally mixed anchorings

As noted, two 9-year-olds anchor their narratives in the simple past, while two 5-year-olds present a mixed pattern of tense usage: One has 53 simple present clauses, 24 simple past, and 8 present perfect; the other, 17 simple present, 37 simple past, 9 present perfect, and 6 past perfect forms. The question addressed in this analysis is whether simple-past narratives are "the same" as present-tense ones, particularly with respect to tense contrasts.

Both "past-tense" anchoring 9-year-olds start their narratives in the same way:

(18) *Es war einmal ein Junge der hatte einen ...*

  'There once was a boy who had a ...' [*G9d-9;11, G9l-9;5*]

The *es war einmal* 'once upon a time' formula, typical of fairy tales in the past tense, may have triggered the past tense in the rest of these two narratives. Child G9d presents a highly sophisticated narrative, exclusively in simple past, except for one past perfect form, corresponding to the prospective relevance function of the present perfect noted for the simple-present narratives, e.g.:

(19) *doch als der Hund mit dem Nest gespielt hatte*

  'however when the dog had played with the nest'

  fiel das Nest auf die Erde

  'the nest fell to the ground'

  und alle Wespen flogen hinter dem Hund her

  'and all the wasps flew after the dog' [*G9d-9;11*]

Child G9l seems to have a harder time maintaining the simple past as anchor tense. In the middle of his report of ongoing events, he refers in an atemporal fashion to the relationship between an emotion experienced by the boy and its script-like cause, as shown in (20).

(20) *aber der Junge war böse*

  'but the boy was angry'

  daß der Hund sowas macht

  'that the dog does something like this'

  daß das Glas jetzt in Scherben liegt

  'that the jar lies now in fragments'

  aber der Hund leckt fröhlich an seine Wange

  'but the dog licks happily at his cheek'

  dann gingen sie in den Wald hinaus

  'then they went out into the forest' [*G9l-9;5*]

The orientation from which this sequence is viewed is marked by the deictic form *jetzt* 'now', but the simple present of *liegen* 'lies' is due to the simple present in the previous clause *macht* 'does', reflecting the ordinary, atemporal, script-like quality of the relationship between action and emotion-evaluation of the type "whenever this happens, the boy gets angry." This example thus demonstrates how the grounding of the picture-book narrative in the simple past may become somewhat problematic at points where narrators try to establish orientation centers from which temporal relationships are viewed as grounding relationships.

The temporally "mixed" narratives of the two 5-year-olds highlight even more clearly the problem of tense consistency in the establishment of orientation centers. Neither child switches randomly back and forth between the simple past and the simple present. Rather, small blocks of discourse are kept consistently in one of the two tense forms, with the present perfect and the past perfect used to signal completive (and often temporally previous) stances on particular events or larger information units.

In sum, the four narratives not grounded in the simple present as anchor tense reveal difficulties in establishment of orientation centers from which events can be viewed as interrelated, difficulties which are more marked in the two 5-year-old texts than in those of the two 9-year-olds. The fact that children as well as adult narrators so generally opt for the simple present as their anchor tense is further evidence that this constitutes "the better choice" option of German speakers in this particular narrative task — an option that has consequences regarding the use of other linguistic devices for the arrangement of temporal and spatial relationships.

1.3. Temporal and Aspectual Relations

1.3.1. Lexical marking of aspect and temporality

This section considers three types of lexical devices for marking aspectual distinctions: by inherent verb aspect or Aktionsart (e.g., activity versus state predicates), by aspectual adverbials (e.g., *noch* 'still'), and by markers of sequentiality (e.g., *dann* 'then').

One determining feature of how events acquire a temporal contour is the actual choice of the lexical item constituting the predicate. Although German differs from other languages in our sample in its very productive use of an extensive particle system, this has little effect on deployment of lexical verb aspect (Aktionsart) in the frog-book task. There is a slight increase with age in use of action verbs (describing what an actor does without affecting a change of state), and a slight decrease in motion verbs (actor-initiated movements toward a goal). One group of verbs in the German sample is, however, quite distinct: those used for describing states. These are typically verbs of location or existence such as *stehen* 'stand' or *sein* 'be' and verbs of possession or attribution such as *haben* 'have' or *kaputt sein* 'be broken'. The 3- and 5-year-olds use a much higher ratio of stative verbs, not only in comparison to action and motion verbs, the next-most common type of verbs in the German data, but also in comparison to the other languages. The high frequency of state descriptions drops considerably by age 9 years, and levels in the adults to the same as adults in the other languages. An explanation of this discrepancy between the younger German children and those in the other languages is suggested in the following discussion of temporal deictic and sequential markers and in a consideration of how spatial scenes are linguistically constructed (Section 2.2) in German.

Consider, next, the use of aspectual adverbs like *noch* 'still' and *wieder* 'again', which represent two of the four categories of extended aspect (of those specified in Chapter IIIo) most commonly elicited by the frog-story narratives: (1) **protraction** of an event or activity, in German mainly by use of *weiter* 'further' and the verb *fortsetzen* 'to continue' + NOUN; (2) **inception**, marking the beginning of an activity or process, for instance by the aspectual phase verbs *beginnen* or *anfangen* 'begin/start' + INFINITIVE COMPLEMENT; (3) **recurrence** or **repetition** of an action or happening, particularly by German *wieder* 'again'; and (4) relating the event or state to some other **reference time** or to the time of the speech event, e.g., German *schon* 'already' and *noch* 'still'. These four categories together account for more than 80% of all lexical aspect marking (apart from Aktionsart) across the German sample. Since special attention is accorded to the first two, continuity and inceptive aspect, in Chapter IVD, this section focuses on the latter two, as exemplified by the terms *wieder* for recurrence and *noch* for relative aspect.

These two terms seem to operate on opposite ends of the aspectual perspective of being or existence. For example, following on from an expression like *da sein* 'be there', **noch** *da sein* '**still** be there' focuses on a state previous to a movement or disappearance, while **wieder** *da sein* 'be there **again**' focuses on the state after the movement has come to full circle, or the disappearance is over. Both forms seem to contribute effectively to the establishment of the theme of the overall narrative, i.e., the frog's disappearance, the search for it in several locations, and its final reappearance. However, *noch* and *wieder* can also be put to use to establish background assumptions of a more general nature, such as in *sich wieder beruhigen* 'to calm down again' (said of the owl in text G20b) or in *sich wieder vertragen/versöhnen* 'to make up with each other again' (as used by several adult narrators), where *wieder* creates an association with a previous state of harmony. Across the sample, *noch* and *wieder* together account for about one-third of all aspectual markings, and as high as three-quarters among the youngest children. That is, these two forms are the most common lexical encodings of aspect (again, apart from Aktionsart).

Noch 'still' is used for different purposes, most often together with other adverbials. *Noch einer* or *noch welche* '(yet) another', are used on the assumption of previous mention of the person or object in question. This is how *noch* is most commonly used by the younger children, together with *nochmal* 'yet another time', 'once more = again'. With age, there is more variety of forms: *noch weiter* 'still continuing', and particularly *immernoch* '(ever) still' and *noch nicht* 'not yet'. The functions of *noch* also differ with age. For example, when an adult describes the dog as *Stuppsi ist **noch** heil und gesund* 'Stuppsi is **still** healthy and well' (G20g) after his fall out of the window, there is an implied reference to the dog's state of health previous to the fall. Thus *noch* is used here for a local narrative purpose. At a later point in the same narrative, *noch* evokes previous activities of calling for the frog: *Peter ruft noch einmal* 'Peter calls yet another time'. A different narrator (G20d) uses *noch* to introduce the entire purpose of the search into the discourse: *den Frosch, den haben sie ja nun **noch** nicht gefunden* 'the frog, him they have not found **yet**' (at this point in the story).

Although *nochmal* or *noch einmal* can be replaced by *wieder*, the latter usually creates more than the image of mere repetition. The cyclic gestalt created by *wieder* seems already fully grasped in the 3-year-olds' use of *wieder da rauf wollen* 'wanting to move back up again' (onto the tree trunk in the last picture) or *wieder nach Hause gehen* 'going back home again'. A three-part schematic cycle is evoked by this use of *wieder*: first, the previous, original location; second, the locale at the "present" time; and third, the orientation from here back to the original source. This holistic cycle is most often evoked by adult uses of *wieder* through such forms as *wiederfinden, wieder komplett sein, wiederentdecken, wiederbekommen, wiedersehen* 'find again, be complete again, discover again, get again/back, see again'. In nine out of the 12 adult texts, narrators use such predicates to express the cyclic nature of the overall narrative theme.

Younger children are usually more locally oriented. Moreover, a few 5-year-olds and several 3-year-olds use *wieder* to create character continuity, as in (21).

(21) *da ist der Hirsch*
'there is the deer'
*da ist **wieder** der Hirsch*
'there is the deer **again**'
*und da sind die **wieder***
'and there they are **again**' [G3e-3;5]

As this example shows, *wieder* as an early means of marking character continuity may actually be a prerequisite for the creation of cyclic images of the kind found in the narratives of older children and adults.

Another kind of temporal distinction concerns marking of interclause relations through sentence-modifying adverbials. Three categories were distinguished for analyzing the German data from this point of view: **deictics**, **sequentials**, and **externally temporal adverbs**. These may occur in different positions within the clause, but sentence-initial position is commonest, since all three types function to shift the temporal (deictic) center of a (spatial) scene (see Section 2). Note that deictic adverbs such as *jetzt* or *nun* 'now' do not necessarily function purely "deictically," that is, to create temporal centers for spatial scenes in the pictures; they also "anaphorically" connect previous and subsequent happenings and as such aid in the creation of a "timeline."

The distribution of sequential compared with deictic adverbs is unexpected in German, compared with the four other languages: German-speaking children at all three age groups make relatively more use of deictics and less of sequentials; the German adults alone use sequentials to the same extent as adults in the other languages. The German forms that are used to give the sense of a sequential arrangement of events are sentence-initial *dann* or *und dann* 'then' or 'and then'. The developmental curve for these two forms is the same in German as in other languages, from rather low frequency at the youngest age group to a peak in the middle age groups with a subsequent drop in the adults. On the other hand, the German forms *jetzt* and *nun* 'now' show the same distribution across the different age groups. The question thus is what motivates German narrators, particularly the younger ones, to overuse deictic *jetzt* and *nun* and to underuse *und dann*. The answer is not a simple one-to-one exchange of deictics for sequential forms, but relates to the broad use of sentence-initial spatial *da* 'there' (as discussed further in Section 2.2). That is, the sentence-initial position in most clauses, particularly in the children's texts, is already occupied by spatial *da*, so ruling out the sequentials *dann* or *und dann*. This does not apply, however, to deictic *jetzt/nun*, which is more likely to be sentence-final. In fact, spatial *da* and temporal *jetzt* are not in competition, since both can be employed in the frame of the same sentence or clause. Thus, as long as *da* occupies the syntactic position of the temporal sequential marker, narrators may be more likely to make use of other temporal adverbs, such as deictic *jetzt* or *nun*. The overall tendency revealed by the German narratives to move the deictic centers by use of (spatial and temporal) deictics rather than sequential adverbials may also be grounded in the fact that nearly all the German narratives are anchored in the simple present, a tense form that more closely signifies the speaker's involvement in the "here and now" of the speech event and the spatial and temporal centers of events and how they figure in higher-order units such as episodes and the plot.

German *mittlerweile, in der Zwischenzeit,* and *inzwischen* 'meanwhile' or 'in the meantime' are used relatively late, first by the 9-year-olds, and more frequently by adults. These markers of discourse sequentiality create temporal and referential continuity, more specifically, when a particular character has been "out of focus" for a while; 'meanwhile' discursively moves back to the last time the character was "in focus." Within this frame of reference, 'meanwhile' is not a simple marker of continuity, nor of co-temporality or even simultaneity with other events, which explains its relatively late acquisition, as shown by its nonuse among the younger children.[8]

The third category of temporal modifiers, temporally external adverbs such as *morgens* 'in the morning', or *nachts* 'at night time', are rare in these narratives. When younger narrators occasionally use them, they typically do so in conjunction with a spatial scene, adding a temporal feature to a locative, as in (22).

(22) *und da ist es mitten in der Nacht*

'And there it is in the middle of the night' [*G3c-3;11*]

Adverbs of external temporality are integrated into the narrative whole relatively late when, mainly in the adult texts, they serve as anchor points for subordinate clauses functioning as backdrops to two events taking place in parallel or in sequence. The following example from a 9-year-old narrator illustrates this kind of ordering relationship.

(23) *Und abends **als der Junge schläft,** steigt der Frosch heimlich aus dem Glas und zum Fenster raus, und morgens **als der Junge aufwacht,** sehen sie daß der Frosch weg ist.*

'In the evening **when the boy sleeps,** the frog secretly climbs out of the jar and out of the window, and in the morning, **when the boy wakes up,** they see that the frog is gone.' [*G9a-9;3*]

The German sample shows similar developmental trends to the other languages in deployment of these types of adverbials.

1.3.2. Temporal conjunction and subordination

Linear ordering of elements in speech (or written language) provides a key to the interpretation of events, episodes, and the plot as sequentially ordered. Additional clues to textual structure are the means by which the information is presented, for instance, the linguistic choice of stative versus active/eventive information. For example, two states, as in (24), are less

---

[8] Terms for 'meanwhile' do not appear before age 9 in any of the languages except for Hebrew, where there are four instances at age 5. For further discussion, see Chapter IVA. Interestingly enough, terms for 'meanwhile' are also used much earlier in Bamberg's 1987 corpus, where the children had been familiarized with the plot, and consequently were able to create characters in their spatio-temporal connectedness at an earlier age.

likely to be understood as following each other in sequence than are two actions, as in (25).

(24) The sun was shining. The moon was in the sky.

(25) The sun set. The moon rose.

A sequential interpretation is particularly likely where the same character or actor is retained across clauses, as in (26).[9]

(26) *He looks in his shoes. He turns the table over.* [E20j][10]

Thus, any use of linguistic means to mark the temporal relationship between two or more propositions works in conjunction with more general, implicit principles of text organization and interpretation. This applies to any temporal marking of interclause relationships, whatever the language-particular means used to mark them.

In German, as in other languages in this sample, the order of MAIN CLAUSE / ADVERBIAL CLAUSE is variable. However, in addition, subordinate clauses differ syntactically from main clauses, since they require final placement of the finite verb. (Consider, for example, the opening clause of (19): *Doch als der Hund mit dem Nest gespielt hatte...* 'However when the dog with the nest played had...') As such, in German, word order in subordinate clauses could be considered "more complex," but so could the splitting of the auxiliary and the nonfinite verb in main clauses by the object and any (additional) adverbial (e.g., *Er hat einen Frosch gefangen* 'He has a frog caught'). The temporal conjunctions most used in this sample to introduce subordinate clauses are *als* 'when' and *während* 'while', which together account for about 80% of overall temporal subordinators, followed by less common *indem* 'as',

---

[9] Sequential coherence is particularly strong in cases of a pronoun following a full nominal, and of an ellipsis following a pronominal expression (Bamberg, 1986, 1987). German and English are similar in this regard: *aber auf einmal schlüpfte der Frosch aus dem Glas raus und hüpfte weg* 'but suddenly the frog slipped out of the glass and hopped away' [G5a-5;7].

[10] 'Looking' into an object (such as a shoe), and 'turning' an object 'over' (such as the table) are "bounded" activities, that is, they are extended in time and have a relatively clear beginning and ending (i.e., they are bounded to the left and to the right). In English, as in German, these boundaries are much clearer if the events are established by means of the simple past, as in *He looked in his shoes, he turned the table over*, which is far more amenable to a sequential reading than the simple present of example (26). Along the same lines, ellipsis in the second clause combined with the connective *and* is even more suggestive of a sequential reading, as in *He looked in his shoes and turned the table over*. That is, the more closely and explicitly the two clauses are tied together, where both events are bounded, the less likely is a simultaneous reading of the two events; and the closer the ties of two conjoint event clauses, the stronger the likelihood of a sequential reading.

wenn 'since', *bis* 'until', and *wie* 'like'.

In general, temporal subordinations are much less common in the German texts than in the other languages in our sample (see further, Chapter IVA), and the form *als* 'when' occurs only once before age 9, in the following 5-year-old text.

(27) *Und als sie aufwachen, ist der Frosch weg.*

'And when they wake up, the frog is gone.' [*G5i-5;2*]

Among 9-year-olds, there are sporadic uses of temporal subordinations of the kind illustrated in (23) above, where *als* is subsequent to the deictic center, so elaborating on a given temporal anchor point. Among adults, there is an equal distribution of temporal subordinations which follow the main clause and so elaborate on the preceding temporal center and of ones which precede it, and so establish a deictic center for the clause to follow. (28) and (29) illustrate these two options.

(28) *Als der Junge und der Hund am Morgen aufwachen, ist der Frosch verschwunden*

'When the boy and the dog wake up in the morning, the frog is gone' [*G20i*]

(29) *Natürlich ist Peter am nächsten Morgen sehr überrascht und sehr enttäuscht als er auf das Glas schaut und keinen Freund mehr entdeckt.*

'Naturally Peter is very surprised and very disappointed the next morning when he looks at the jar and discovers no more friend.' [*G20l*]

1.4. The Emergence of Temporal Movement

A number of potentially interesting interim conclusions can be drawn from this analysis of temporal forms within the German corpus. First, the deployment of a variety of linguistic forms that all in one or another way seem to encode temporality (in its broadest sense) cannot be investigated apart from what they are used for, and apart from other linguistic forms that are used to convey aspects of the spatial arrangement and characterhood/agency. Analysis of lexical choices of verb types indicates that the high proportion of state verbs used by the younger children needs to be viewed as closely interconnected with three other features of the younger children's texts: relatively high use of temporal deictics and low use of temporal connectives, the abundance of sentence-initial spatial deictics — ruling out the use of temporal connectives, and the predominant anchoring of the narratives in the simple present.[11] The interaction of these three factors

---

[11] In my opinion, the lower frequency of temporal subordinate clauses in the overall German corpus (and probably also the lower frequency of relative subordinate clauses, which is

contributes strongly to the impression that the younger the children, the more they adhere to the "here-and-now," coinciding — from an adult viewpoint — with what the pictorial units "represent." Only with increasing age do children learn to connect bounded temporal units (events), thereby contributing to the emergence of the impression of a sequentially progressing timeline.

A second interim conclusion concerns the issue of what it is that is developing across the different age groups. Apart from the development of new forms and the use of old forms for new discursive functions, it seems as if the focus of using forms for local characterizations of the "here-and-now" changes with age to a characterization of discourse units of more than one or two clauses. While younger children order "here-and-nows" (deictic centers) in a serial fashion, older children create a qualitatively different order: The deictic centers become focal points from which previous and subsequent discourse is comprised. In other words, with increasing age, discourse units emerge that gain their organizational orientation "from their middle," as it were. In terms of an underlying strategy, this form of organizing discourse maintains two perspectives at the same time: one that is oriented forward, the other backwards. In consequence, the sequential arrangement of these units contributes to the emergence of a narrative whole, giving "structure" to what holds beginning, middle, and end together.

This is not meant to imply that our 3-year-olds do not tell a complete narrative. Rather, their arrangement of (usually) single deictic centers in a linear fashion is different from that of older children and adults. This kind of linear arranging of states and events appears superficially identical to the genre activity of "describing" the pictures as separate and individual entities. However, "picture descriptions" are of a different genre-type (see Bamberg, 1991b). In order to avoid the developmentally problematic thesis that children first have to learn to describe the picturebook before they can "narrate" the story (see Bamberg, 1991b, 1993; Bamberg & Marchman, 1990, for an extensive critique of this view), I would propose that the younger children resort to a narrative (but not purely "descriptive") strategy that "gets the job done" with an emphasis on the linear order of the part-whole relationships of the frog story. The way the narrative activity at this (relatively) early point in development is structured points to other expressive means and linguistic forms by which a beginning, a middle, and an end are united.[12]

discussed in further detail in chapter IVB) is motivated by the interplay of these three features. Further comparisons with other narrative genres, in particular those that are grounded in past-tense anchored personal narratives, could contribute to clearer hypotheses as to which features contribute more heavily to the relative infrequency of such grammatical constructions in our German texts.

[12] It also should be kept in mind that children at the age of 3 years are very well able to

2. MOVING THROUGH SPACE IN GERMAN

2.1. The Linguistic Creation of Spatial Scenes

I have argued elsewhere (Bamberg, 1993) that sentences in storied discourse are invariably constructed, and interpreted, with a spatial scene in mind. The perspective from which a particular scene is viewed is either overtly stated through spatial expressions (most commonly adverbials) or is inferred by implication. The vantage point from which spatial consistency is created usually does not exist inside the sentence frame, but lies "outside" of it (Langacker, 1985, 1987b). Although the spatial characteristics of a scene do not exist independent of its temporal and referential properties (as explained in greater detail in Bamberg, 1993), for present purposes, spatial relationships are dealt with as a relatively autonomous domain, with the aim of showing how, with age, German speakers create a vantage point for each of the propositions that form their narrative. This account of how spatial scenes evolve in the German narratives is followed by an analysis of how these scenes are connected in terms of actor movement, focusing on certain scenes which require a particular vantage point from which a character perspective is selected, where the character is viewed as a volitional agent engaged in movement that shifts him from one location to another. Both aspects of the telling of the story — the creation of individual scenes in a bottom-up fashion and the interconnection of these scenes from a more top-down plot orientation — are relevant for understanding the linguistic choices characteristic of this task, in particular in young children.

2.2. The Emergence of Spatial Scenes

The earliest and most basic form relating the "here and now" location of the speech event to the location of a narrated event in spoken German is *da* 'there'. This is first and foremost a spatial adverb, but it also occurs in numerous, very common composite forms where it can mark causal, conditional, or temporal relationships between events or happenings, e.g., *dabei* 'thereby', *dazu* 'to that end', *dafür* 'therefore', *davon* 'away from (there)', *damit* 'with (that)' (cf. corresponding English forms with *there*: *thereby, therefore, therefrom*). The creation of spatial scenes in German relies on the differentiation between *hier* 'here' and *da* 'there'. This becomes particularly evident in the narratives of the younger age groups: almost two-thirds (62%)

---

narrate personal experiences or narrate the frog book if sufficiently familiarized with its plot. What earlier studies (Bamberg, 1986, 1987) reveal is not that 3-year-olds simply imitate their parental story input, but that they **create** their own linguistic means to index the binding and unfolding relationships.

of all the 3-year-olds' clauses are marked by use of *da*; with age, this drops somewhat, down to 44% for the 5-year-olds, while even the 9-year-olds have *da* in almost one-third (31%) of their clauses, dropping markedly in the adult narratives (7%).

Consider, first, the difference between clause-initial and clause-internal, preverbal positioning of this very widespread spatial adverb, *da*. (30a) through (30c) are constructed examples that represent variations on how the frog's escape (in Picture 2) can be described using the same subject *er* 'he' and the predicate *ist rausgegangen* 'has gone out'.

(30a) *Da ist er rausgegangen.*

(30b) *Er ist da rausgegangen.*

(30c) *Da ist er da rausgegangen.*

Sentence-initial *da*, as in (30a) and (30c), constructs a general scenario within which all other actions and spatial relationships are framed. In this particular scenario, the preverbal clause-internal *da* in (30b) and (30c) constructs (or reconstructs, if it has been previously mentioned) the jar. Thus, (30a) is best conveyed in English as 'in this scene he stepped out', (30b) as 'he stepped out of there', and (30c) as 'in this scene he stepped out of there'. In view of this distinction, it is relevant that the younger the narrators, the higher the frequency of sentence-initial *da*; with age, there is a relatively greater proportion of clause-internal *da*, particularly among the adult narrators. This suggests that the younger narrators tend to create an independent scene for each clause, so giving the impression that there is no other "spatial glue" holding the clauses together. The following first six lines from a 3-year-old text illustrate this use of *da*:

(31) *da ist der Frosch drin*

    '**there** is the frog inside'

    da kuckt der rein

    '**there** he looks inside'

    der Junge auch

    'the boy too'

    und da schlafen die

    'and **there** they sleep'

    und da schlüpft der Frosch raus

    'and **there** the frog slips out'

    da wachen die wieder auf

'**there** they wake up again'

da ist der Frosch weg

'**there** the frog is gone' [*G3b-3;11*]

Each clause, except for the gapped third clause *der Junge auch* 'the boy too', creates its own spatial scene within which a happening can take place. In this sense, any chain of clauses not marked by sentence-initial *da* can be viewed, in a spatial sense, as inserted into the previously created scene, and as such, as part of a more extended scenario.

In contrast to this stringing along of serially-positioned scenes by the younger children, older children and adult narrators in particular create more integrated spatial scenarios, as in (32).

(32) *der Junge hat immer noch das Problem*

'the boy still has the problem'

den Frosch wiederzufinden

'to find the frog again'

*und kuckt **in einem Baumloch** nach*

'and looks **in a treehole**'

*ob er sich **da** versteckt haben könnte*

'whether he could have hidden **there**'

*aber stattdessen kommt **da** ein Uhu oder eine Eule heraus*

'but instead an owl comes out of **there**'

und der Junge fällt um

'and the boy falls over'

und fällt runter

'and falls down'

und der Junge macht

'and the boy makes'

daß er wegkommt

'that he gets away' [*G20b*]

The scene in (32) is spatially depicted in the third line of this excerpt as *in einem Baumloch* 'in a treehole'. Subsequent activities of the antagonist (the owl) and the boy are viewed within the frame of this scene; that is, the boy does not literally fall out of the treehole, but off of the tree that is created inferentially. Similarly, the movement implied in the last line is no longer away from the tree or the treehole, but away from the implied scene that has emerged fully by now, before a new spatial scenario is created in the following lines. The uses of clause-internal *da* in the fourth and fifth lines of (32) further demonstrate its role for the creation of a fuller scenario.[13]

This analysis has treated the linguistic creations of these scenes in a somewhat decontextualized and idealized fashion. It must be borne in mind that vantage points on spatial scenes always coexist with perspectives on temporal events and on the characters, within the hierarchical levels of the scene, the episode, the plot, and the human drama.

2.3. Movement: A Potential Link between Scenes

This section examines two spatially-constructed scenes: the movement of the frog leaving the jar (Picture 2) and the final scene in the book, when the boy walks off with a frog in hand (Picture 24). Picture 2 depicts the frog with one leg still in the jar, the other leg already outside. In fact, the temporal characteristics of 'still' versus 'already' are used as instructions to connect a previous scene, where the frog is "still" "fully" inside the jar (Picture 1), with a subsequent scene (Picture 3), where he is "fully" and "already" out of it.[14] The sequence of spatial scenes in the Pictures 1, 2, and 3 provides good grounds for construing the frog's activity in Picture 2 as a movement from inside to outside of the jar, even though nothing is visible in Picture 2 itself to yield this interpretation. The (appropriate) construal of the frog's action is based on connecting the interpretation of a state in Picture 1 with the interpretation of a state in Picture 3. From this point of view, the interpretation of movement in Picture 2 is a relatively local task, since it relies on making a connection between the immediately surrounding pictures in terms of a "movement" interpretation. In contrast, the last scene in the book, where the boy is depicted as walking (through the water), waving back to the frogs that have been "left behind," requires a more global construal of the movement component. Here, the movement — if constructed as having started from a source, from where the frogs were on the previous picture(s), towards a goal, most probably back to the place from where the search started out — requires a much more global perspective: It needs to make sense as an integrated movement in space, which demands evocation of the overall plot theme

---

[13] To label this kind of reference "anaphoric" and sentence-initial *da* as "deictic" is misleading and confuses the issue. It is more important to address the question of what a narrator **does** — in terms of creating spatial scenarios within which actors "become alive" — when using such forms.

[14] Pronominal reference to animals in this chapter is based on their gender in German, where the word for frog is masculine, for owl is feminine. (Compare the converse in the other two gender languages in our sample: Spanish — feminine *la rana* 'frog' and masculine *el buho* 'owl', and Hebrew — feminine *cfardea* 'frog' and masculine *yanshuf* 'owl').

holding the narrative together as a whole.

The two spatial scenes analyzed here thus require a different overarching perspective: The first requires a quite local perspective with regard to the movement of the frog, the second requires a more global perspective for the movement of the boy (and the location of the frog) to be meaningfully integrated in relating to the contents of the picture.

2.3.1. The frog's departure (Picture 2)

The first, and in a way surprising, finding is that all narrators of all age groups (except for one 3-year-old) focus on the frog's action in terms of a spatial relationship. One other 3-year-old constructs this relationship in perceptual terms (*da kuckt der Frosch raus* 'there the frog looks out' [*G3f-3;11*]), while the other 10 3-year-olds all construct a spatial movement scene, i.e., the frog as a volitional agent moving away from a source (VERB OF MOVEMENT + *raus* 'out.of'). The source, however, remains unspecified; at best it is constructed as part of the larger scenario established by a sentence-initial *da*, in eight out of the ten cases. One 3-year-old also characterizes the movement in terms of an additional goal-path (VERB OF MOVEMENT + *raus* 'out.of' + *weg* 'away').

Among the older children, all 12 5-year-olds construct the same scene as a movement + source scenario: six in the same way as the 3-year-olds, with the other six all specifying the source, either by *da* or by a nominal expression (e.g., *aus dem Wasser* 'out of the water'). Two of these 5-year-olds also relate to the goal path of the frog's spatial movement. In contrast, only two 9-year-olds construct the scene in the same way as the bulk of the 3-year-olds and half the 5-year-olds: by means of movement + unspecified source. The other ten all specify the source, with four adding a focus with regard to the direction and/or goal path of the movement.

The adults yield a similar picture to the one that emerged in the 9-year-olds with regard to specification of source: Nine specify the source (*aus dem Glas* 'out of the jar'), and five of these double-mark the source by an additional verbal prefix (*heraus-*, *ent-*, and *hinaus-*, all equivalent to English 'out of', adding deictic orientation). In this way, some adult narrators take an **additional** spatial perspective in their construction of the relationship between the source and the character's movement to specify components of the movement scene. In addition, adults describe the movement with less lexical specificity than the children, all of whom use verbs of motion for this purpose, e.g., the highly specific *klettern* 'climb', *hüpfen* 'hop', *steigen* 'mount', or the more general *gehen* 'go'. In contrast, adults tend to perspectivize the movement from a more global stance, by expressions of agentive and volitional (though much more general and unspecific) removal from the scene, e.g., *verschwinden* 'disappear', *sich davonmachen* 'escape, get away', *sich entfernen* 'remove, distance oneself', *abhauen* 'scram, beat a retreat'.

In sum, the construction of the movement in Picture 2 starts out as a movement (of a character) from an unspecified source. Movement and source are grounded in a deictic center that is given, though unspecified at the beginning of each sentence. Gradually, with age, the source becomes specified and a goal-path is added; concurrently, the additional grounding in a sentence-specific center fades, and is replaced by a more integrated and global perspective from which source, movement, and goal path are viewed as forming an episodic whole, along with an intentional act on the part of the character. In other words, the movement that is constructed in Picture 2 connects more than a full jar in Picture 1 with an empty jar in Picture 3. With age, it takes on the function of an integrated link in the construction of a narrative unit spanning over these first three pictures, best identified as the "setting" and the "complication" (see Chapter IIA). As such, the frog's departure becomes the ground for the theme of the subsequent story, the search of the boy and his dog.

2.3.2. The boy's departure (Picture 24)

The last scene in the booklet (Picture 24) again allows narrators to construct a character as moving in space — this time the boy.[15] Note, first, that all 12 adults focus in one or another way on the boy as an actor in this scene, whereas eight (= 2/3) of the 3-year-olds fail to mention the boy as actively involved in this scene. In contrast to the scene in Picture 2, the one in Picture 24 cannot be viewed as connecting a previous and subsequent spatial scene. Rather, the movement of the boy gains its meaningfulness from inferences that span over the search theme as a whole, resulting in the construction of a "return." In other words, the movement of the boy, or what it might imply, requires relating to previous movements in space as motivated by the theme of the story, its result (finding the lost frog), and a "happy" returning home, to the place from where the search started, and where it all began. Thus, the boy's departure is best constructed as a "leave-taking" scene that successfully completes the search and defines a goal path of "back home."

Only three out of the 3-year-olds construct movement scenes here, two in terms of moving away from an unspecified source (*weg* 'away') and two as a movement with a specific goal ('home'). One 3-year-old views the boy as taking leave, and two others view the frogs as giving the boy a little one

---

[15] The dog could be characterized along the same lines, but for present purposes, focus is on the boy's activity alone, with the dog considered only if his and the boy's actions are viewed as a combined entity.

'along' with them (*mit*), thereby evoking an unspecified path of the move-ment. Among the 5-year-olds, five children still fail to construct a movement on the part of the boy, and two others simply note the movement per se, but the other five in this age group do, to varying degrees, all attend to the source or the goal of the boy's movement. This trend towards more differentiation and specification of the movement scene in Picture 24 is more noticeable among the oldest children: 10 of the 12 9-year-olds specify the source or the goal of the movement, and only two fail to provide any spatial relation. Half of the ten, in fact, construct more than one part of the source-movement-path-goal scene, with three children overtly appealing to the theme of the cir-cular movement from home-to-forest and back-home 'again'. Among the adults, all of whom include movement in their characterization of the boy's action-role in Picture 24, five specify the goal ('home') and the remaining seven focus in one way or another on the source. Several adults also note additional aspects of the path of the movement (*davon* 'away.from.there', *fort* 'further', and *mit* 'with'); three explicitly allude to the thematic cycle of the boy's movement.

Construction of the leave-taking scene in Picture 24 thus presents a somewhat different developmental picture compared to Picture 2. Moving through space in the leave-taking scene becomes relevant only in light of a growing appreciation of the story theme. Young children, like older narrators, who construct their narratives in terms of part-whole relationships and so index more aspects of the overall structure of the story, are more likely to view the boy "in motion." Once the motion perspective is chosen, it is cou-pled with a source (away from the group of frogs) and a goal (home), often also with acknowledgment of the cyclical movement throughout the theme: starting from home, to the finding of the frog(s), back home again. Younger children simply do not seem to see the relevance of the motion of the boy with regard to any local or global transformation, and consequently do not take any perspective on his movement. Sporadic notings of the movement per se in the 3- and the 5-year-olds pave the way for an increasing emphasis on the source of movement in the 5- and 9-year-olds, which subsequently can be more fully integrated into the construction of the boy's movement in accor-dance with the theme of the narrative whole, as done in most of the adult nar-ratives. However, as noted, the ability to construct the boy as a moving agent is less dependent on age than on the ability to index aspects of the plot. Although more narrators reveal this ability with age, the fact that even a few 3-year-olds can construct the boy's movement from a thematic plot perspec-tive should not be disregarded.

2.4. The Linguistic Expression of Movement

The linguistic construction of movement in German adheres to the satellite-framed typology discussed in Chapter IIIo. In this regard, German is like English, in contrast to the three other languages of the sample, which are verb-framed. As in English, there is a rich collection of verbs of motion and caused motion, most of them simultaneously expressing manner. There are 37 types of verbs of motion, across the entire age range:

(33) *sich-entfernen* 'distance-oneself', *erklimmen* 'climb', *fallen* 'fall', *fliegen* 'fly', *gehen* 'go', *hoppeln* 'hop', *hüpfen* 'hop', *jagen* 'chase', *klettern* 'climb', *kommen* 'come', *krabbeln* 'crawl', *kriechen* 'creep', *landen* 'land', *laufen* 'run', *plumpsen* 'plop', *purzeln* 'tumble', *rasen* 'speed', *rennen* 'run', *reiten* 'ride', *schieben* 'push', *schleichen* 'creep', *schlittern* 'glide', *schlüpfen* 'slip', *schmeißen* 'hurl', *schubsen* 'shove', *schwimmen* 'swim', *springen* 'jump', *steigen* 'ascend', *sich-stellen* 'stand.up', *stürmen* 'dash', *stürzen* 'tumble', *tauchen* 'plunge', *tragen* 'carry', *treten* 'step', *verfolgen* 'chase', *werfen* 'throw', *ziehen* 'pull'

In addition, each of these verbs can be combined with a large range of path satellites, expressed as verb particles in German. For example, using a simple verb with no indication of manner — *kommen* 'come' — the sample of German texts yields:

(34) *an-kommen* 'arrive', *raus-kommen* 'exit', *rein-kommen* 'enter', *zu-kommen* 'arrive'

Conversely, we can pick a German path satellite and note its occurrences with a range of verbs of motion. For example, all of the following verbs of motion were combined with the particle *raus* 'out':

(35) **raus-** *-fallen* 'fall out', *-fliegen* 'fly out', *-gehen* 'go out', *-gleiten* 'slide out', *-hüpfen* 'hop out', *-klettern* 'climb out', *-kommen* 'come out', *-laufen* 'run away', *-rennen* 'run out', *-schlüpfen* 'slip out', *-springen* 'jump out', *-steigen* 'climb out'

Thus, in fact — when all of these possibilities of combination are taken into consideration — there are far more than 37 types of verbs of motion in the German texts.

Path satellites in German encode directionality, as in English. In addition, they encode deictic viewpoint by means of the particles *hin* 'thither' and *her* 'hither', which can combine with the directional particles. The range of possibilities is thus considerably greater than in English, allowing for expression of viewpoint perspective. Compare, for example, the following two descriptions of the dog's fall from the window. In (36a) the narrator's eye is outside of the house, at ground level, as indicated by the satellite *her* 'hither', while in (36b) the satellite *hin* 'thither' traces a path downward from the viewpoint of the windowsill.

(36a)*Da fiel der Hund zur Erde **her-aus**.*

    'There the dog fell **hither**-out to the ground.' [*G9l-9;5*]

(36b)*Als er sich auf die Fensterbank setzte und **hin**-unter-fiel, zerbrach das Glas in tausend Stücke.*

    'When he got onto the windowsill and **thither**-down-fell, the glass broke into a thousand pieces.' [*G9d-9;11*]

German thus provides rich possibilities for detailed description of motion in a given direction in a given manner. Table 1, on the next page, shows the range of satellites that were combined with verbs of motion by the children in our sample. The translations are only an approximation: Here the richness of German exceeds English. Note that even the 3-year-olds command a large number of verb-satellite combinations.

As discussed in Chapter VB, this range of motion-manner expressions has consequences for the particular "rhetorical style" that characterizes German frog stories (and German narrative generally). Where Spanish, for example, elaborates temporal movement and temporal boundaries by means of its elaborated tense/aspect system, German elaborates spatial movement and location by means of its elaborate verb-satellite and prepositional constructions.

3. CREATION OF CHARACTERS AND AGENCY IN GERMAN

3.1. Characters as Topics

Much of the narrative task consists in picking the appropriate candidates to talk about. From an adult perspective, it is obvious that this story is about a boy, a dog, and a (runaway) frog. While the boy can best be characterized as the protagonist of the story, the dog is better viewed as a fellow protagonist, who at times even gets in the way of the boy's main goal, to recover his frog. The frog is not a protagonist of the story, but he does play a major role, because his actions allow the main goal of the story to emerge. The other characters (the gopher, bees, owl, and deer) all appear at places where the boy or the dog are looking for the frog. As such, they may be characterized as antagonists, since they all block the protagonist's goal of finding the frog at that particular location. But this is by no means a necessary construal, as shown by a German 5-year-old (G5e) who constructs the gopher as a friendly animal who is helping the search by giving directions. Another group of characters enters the story towards the end, when the two protagonists find "their" frog with a number of other frogs, presumably his mate and their baby frogs.

TABLE 1
Particles Used with Verbs of Motion by Children

Particle	3 yrs.	5 yrs.	9 yrs.
her 'hither'		+	
daher 'thence'		+	
hin 'thither'	+	+	+
dahin 'thither'			+
aus 'out'		+	+
heraus 'hither-out'			+
raus 'hither-out'	+	+	+
hinaus 'thither-out'		+	+
rein 'inward'	+	+	+
drin 'therein'	+		
runter 'down'	+	+	+
hinunter 'thither-down'			+
hinab 'downwards'			+
rauf 'thereon'	+	+	+
darauf 'thereon'	+		+
rüber 'over'	+		
darüber 'thereover'			+
an 'to'			+
dran 'thereon'	+	+	
ran 'thereon'		+	
nach 'after'			+
hinterher 'behind'	+	+	+
vor 'in-front'		+	
weg 'away'	+	+	+
davon 'away-from'		+	
lang 'along'			+
um 'around'		+	+
rum 'around'			+
hoch 'high-up'	+	+	+

In general, these characters are linguistically referred to by devices such as a full nominal expression or pronoun, and they may also be referred to by a zero form such as a null subject. In German, nouns are accompanied by articles that are grammatically marked for number, gender, and case. Animals, when referred to by third-person pronouns, particularly in fables and fairytales, are usually marked by the (grammatical) gender of their nominal counterpart. Thus, the owl is referred to as *sie* 'she', the deer by *es* or *das* 'it', and the gopher (*der Maulwurf* or *der Hamster*) by *er* 'he'. Person-marking on the verb in German also clearly differentiates between three different singular person forms and one plural form.[16] Verb inflection thus provides additional information as to the identity of the subject referent, even where the latter is not overtly expressed by a pronoun form. However, German is not a "pro-drop" language: Subject pronouns are required except under specified syntactic conditions that allow for ellipsis.

3.1.1. Creating characters as discourse referents

Prior studies of reference in frog story narratives (Bamberg, 1986, 1987; Kail & Hickmann, 1992; Wigglesworth, 1992) have assumed that the conventional way of introducing characters or groups of characters into a discourse is by means of the least presupposing form that a language offers. In German, this form is the singular indefinite article *ein/eine* 'a' for a single individual and the zero article for more than one individual (e.g., *Bienen* 'bees' or *Frösche* 'frogs'). In this analysis, the bees might also be referred to first by an object noun for 'beehive' (*der Bienenkorb* or *das Bienenhaus*).

A clear developmental picture emerges if we distinguish between three different groups of characters: (1) the boy, dog, and frog; (2) the four antagonists (gopher, owl, deer, and bees); and (3) the group of frogs mentioned towards the end of the story. Three-year-olds create the first group (the boy, dog, and frog) at the discourse level, overwhelmingly by use of the definite article *der* 'the:MASC:SG:NOM, which with age changes increasingly to the indefinite *ein* 'a:MASC:SG:NOM. Note, further, that the younger children tend not to use an ARTICLE + NOUN combination, preferring the third person masculine pronoun *er* or *der* 'he'. Older children and adults sometimes use proper names for the boy-protagonist, occasionally even for the dog and/or frog. However, 9-year-olds and even adults also use the definite article for referent introduction, particularly for the boy, less for the dog, and least for the frog, as shown in Table 2.

The second group of characters that share characteristics in terms of their linguistic realization in discourse are the four antagonists: the gopher, the owl, the deer, and the bees. There is a clear developmental trend with age towards

---

[16] This is true of verbs in the present tense, used for the vast majority of the German sample. Past-tense verbs distinguish between two singular person forms and one additional plural form.

TABLE 2
First References (Character Introduction)[a]

	3 yrs		5 yrs		9 yrs		Adult	
	def	indef	def	indef	def	indef	def	indef
Boy	10	0	6	2	6	5	4	5
Dog	12	0	8	2	6	3	2	4
Frog	10	1	9	2	7	4	1	6
Gopher	0	5	2	6	3	9	0	12
Bees/Hive	8	0	5	5	2	2	1	11
Owl	7	3	6	4	5	6	1	11
Deer	6	2	4	6	5	7	1	11
Frog(s)	4	2	3	1	6	1	5	3

a. Uses of pronouns, possessives, and names for any of these characters are not included in the table.

use of the **indefinite** article for introducing these four characters, to a point where almost all the adults do so. This trend holds more for the three individual antagonists than for the group of bees, but it is marked even from the youngest age group, particularly in comparison to how the first group of characters was introduced (the boy, dog, and frog). Relatedly, an early tendency to introduce these characters by use of the definite article *der, die,* or *das* 'the' + GENDER ASSIGNMENT decreases with age, as shown in Table 2.

No clear developmental picture emerges from analysis of the linguistic forms used to refer to the third group of characters, the frogs mentioned towards the end of the story, where the boy and the dog find "their" frog again. As shown in Table 2, narrators across all age groups use roughly the same distribution of formal devices. This may be because the group of frogs represents a mixed category, one of whose members is "old information" and so has already been introduced before, the others being a number of other characters who need to be introduced. However, closer scrutiny reveals not only formal, but also interesting functional differences between the younger children and the older narrators in this respect. The former use mainly pronouns or a DEFINITE ARTICLE + NOUN to introduce and/or reintroduce the group of frogs, even though there are no other clues in the text to show that they actually intend to convey that this group (or parts thereof) have been introduced into the discourse before. In contrast, the definite forms used by the older children and adults occur in the context of other elaborative means indicating that this group is familiar or has some connection to the protagonists and hence to the listener as well. Use of the indefinite article for the frogs in this scene is even more interesting. As illustrated in (33), the identity of the frog is left open, at least initially, in order to convey how the protagonists entered the scene not knowing the true identity of the characters behind the treetrunk. The point of recognizing the frog as their runaway pet is textually identified, and as such takes greater account of the protagonist's perspective by means of the DEFINITE ARTICLE + NOUN or use of a possessive pronoun, as in *Peter hört das Quaken seines Frosches* 'Peter heard the croaking of **his** frog' [G20l].

(37) *Und was finden sie da, eine ganze Froschfamilie! Hier sitzt Vater Frosch Mutter Frosch und einige Kinder und zur ganz großen Überraschung findet der Junge auch seinen kleinen Frosch wieder.*

'And what do they find there, a whole frog-family! Here sits Father Frog, Mother Frog, and a few children and to their great surprise, the boy also finds his little frog again.' [G20k]

In sum, the use of linguistic forms to introduce referents into the discourse presents a rather complex picture. There is a clear sensitivity to differentiate linguistically between two groups of referents: the boy, the dog, and the frog, on the one hand, and the gopher, bees, owl, and deer, on the other. This sensitivity is manifest at all age groups, though it surfaces differently at different ages. In addition, the linguistic treatment of the boy stands out when compared to that of the dog and the frog, even moreso when compared to the other characters. Although the boy and dog are marked by more definite articles, the boy is linguistically privileged in that he is often given a name and referred to by a bare pronoun. This reveals a possible attempt of narrators at all ages to view events and scenes as being connected from the boy's (i.e., the main protagonist's) perspective. The present database is insufficient for deciding whether this attempt is motivated by the fact that the boy ranks higher on the animacy hierarchy (Comrie, 1981), and as such is the best candidate for being "mapped" onto the corresponding linguistic devices, or whether the linguistic forms are simply available from the child's linguistic environment in conventional clusterings for differentiating between humans and animals in general, and in a similar vein between such categories as protagonists and antagonists. However, the fact that the privileging of certain characters holds across the sample suggests that such notions as "given" versus "new" and/or what is considered as "shared" or "presupposed" might need to be revised. The narrator does not appear to simply take his/her interpretation of what is "given" or "presupposed" as the sole source for deciding how to instruct the listener to view the identity of the characters in question, but presents the information from an involved vantage point. "Involved" in this context implies that the intentions, values, and motivations of the most privileged character, the protagonist, are revealing of the vantage

point from which events and scenes are held together. And it is this involvement between narrator and protagonist that finds its expression in the way the
protagonist is (linguistically) differentiated from other characters.

3.1.2. Grammatical subjects as discourse topics

Another, equally revealing analysis considers how characters are
linguistically encoded after they have been established in discourse. The
three options noted for German are: a full nominal expression, a pronoun, and
a zero form. It is generally assumed that full nominal expressions are used to
reintroduce a character after he/she has been temporarily out of focus; pronouns are used to maintain a character's identity in subsequent discourse that
is not interrupted by other characters' foregrounded activities; and zero forms
can only be used if a character has been clearly established in the immediately
preceding clause (with additional syntactic constraints). Below I first examine the linguistic forms by which the story characters are referred to after they
have been introduced, and then consider whether any distinctive forms are
used to keep particular characters in focus in contrast to others.

TABLE 3

Percentage of References in Subject Position to Story
Characters and Other Story Items, by Age[a]

	3 yrs	5 yrs	9 yrs	Adult
Total Number	665	608	741	1244
Story Characters				
noun/name	35.8	37.5	54.9	37.7
pronoun	41.7	41.8	28.7	28.9
zero form	5.1	3.6	12.9	22.3
Other Story Items	17.4	17.1	3.5	10.1

a. Passives were coded twice, for surface-subject as well as for deep-
subject.

Table 3 reflects two clear developmental trends across the four groups of
narrators. First, there is a clear increase with age in use of the zero form for
the story characters: The two younger age groups rarely use a zero form, 9-
year-olds use it in 13% of all clauses that have a story character in subject
position, and adults use it in 22% of such cases. Second, while 3- and 5-
year-old children rely on nominal and pronominal forms to an equal extent,

there is a radical drop in pronouns among 9-year-olds and adults. Also, 9-year-olds use mainly nominal forms when referring to a character (55% of the time) and they also refer much less to inanimate objects such as the jar or the boy's clothes in the house, or bushes, trees, flowers, and water out in the forest, where the search takes place.

The function served by null subjects increases with age. The following excerpt from an adult narrative shows an abundance of such uses, where Ø represents a null subject or zero form.

(38) *Also ich hätte jetzt damit angefangen daß der durch den Wald zieht* [new referent = boy] *und einen Frosch sucht* [Ø = boy] *und den auch findet* [Ø = boy] *und den mit nach Hause nimmt* [Ø = boy] *und in ein Glas packt* [Ø = boy] *und abends dann garnicht schlafen kann* [Ø = boy], *der Mond ist nämlich schon aufgegangen* [new referent], *und mit seinem kleinen Hund vor dem Glas sitzt* [Ø = boy] *und den Frosch bewundert* [Ø = boy] *und auf ihn aufpaßt* [Ø = boy]. *Aber irgendwann werden die beiden dann doch müde* [new referent], *gehen schlafen* [Ø = boy + dog], *und die Gelegenheit benutzt der Frosch* [new referent] *und entschlüpft wieder aus dem Glas* [Ø = frog].

'Well I would have started now with (saying) that he moves through the forest [new referent = boy] and looks for a frog [Ø = boy] and even finds him [Ø = boy] and takes him along home [Ø = boy] and sticks him into a jar [Ø = boy] and can't sleep at all in the evening [Ø = boy], the moon has namely already gone up [new referent], and sits with his little dog in front of the jar [Ø = boy] and admires the frog [Ø = boy] and watches out for him [Ø = boy]. But at some point the two get tired after all [new referent], go to sleep [Ø = boy + dog], and the frog uses the opportunity [new referent] and slips out of the jar again [Ø = frog].' [G20a]

As shown in this excerpt, use of a zero subject ties activities of the same character together and presents them as "topical packages." These are generally set against each other by use of nominal forms, as in the next to last line, where the narrator switches reference to another character, the frog.

The 9-year-old narrators, in contrast, are much more concerned with differentiating between the characters by mainly nominal forms (note the drop in pronouns compared to the two younger groups, and the increase in nominals in Table 3). This concern with character differentiation in the 9-year-olds is also reflected in the sudden increase of **left-dislocations** in this age group, where a clause-initial full noun phrase is reiterated by a subsequent pronominal copy. While 3-year-olds used no left dislocations at all, and 5-year-olds only sporadically (four occurrences in four narratives), six of the 9-year-olds used as many as 44 left-dislocations, going down to only 11 in four adult narratives. The example in (39), from the opening of a 9-year-old narrative, shows how left-dislocations are used to clearly mark the introduction of a new referent, and so contribute to a clearer differentiation between new topical packages.

(39) *Der Mond steht noch am Himmel und **der Hund der** ist mit der Nase im Glas drinne wo der Frosch drin ist mit dem Wasser und so, und **der Junge der** sitzt und kuckt ihn sich an* [Ø = boy].

'The moon still stands in the sky and **the dog he** is inside the jar with his nose where the frog is inside with the water and such, and **the boy he** sits and watches him.' [*G9i-9;11*]

Right-dislocations — references to characters by means of a pronoun reiterated by a clause-final full noun — do not occur at all in the 3-year-old German texts; 5-year-olds use them four times; and 9-year-olds and adults five times each. In the children's texts, this form of dislocation is better viewed as a false start, that is, the children seem to recognize that the pronoun was not sufficiently clear, and so needed to be replaced by a full nominal expression; adults, on the other hand, use it for more felicitous stylistic purposes. These two different functions of right-dislocations are illustrated by the following examples from a 5-year-old and an adult narrator.

(40) *Und dann ruft er ganz laut aber er kam nicht, **der Frosch.***

'And then he [=boy] calls very loudly but **he** did not come, **the frog**.' [*G5e-5;0*]

(41) *Und da machen sich alle drei, Moritz, sein Hund und der Frosch machen sich auf den Heimweg.*

'And there all three of them start, Moritz, his dog and the frog start to go home.' [*G20d*]

As shown in Table 3, the younger children, aged 3 and 5 years, rely more heavily on pronouns than 9-year-olds and adults. Six children in each of the two younger groups use far more pronouns than nouns in their narratives, deploying what has been termed a "thematic subject strategy" (see Bamberg, 1986, 1987; Karmiloff-Smith, 1981; Wigglesworth, 1992), that is, they match the third person pronoun with virtually all references to the boy as main protagonist, and refer to other characters of the story by a full noun when reintroduced into the discourse, and by a pronoun when reference to the same character is maintained. That is, the pronoun for the boy as the thematic subject of this story collapses two functions, reference maintenance and reference shift. In contrast, a pronoun, when used for any of the other characters in the story, is preserved for reference maintenance only.[17] The following example

---

[17] Bamberg (1987) documents the thematic subject strategy in German children's narra-

illustrates how the pronoun is used for the boy in a 5-year-old's narrative, while the other two characters (the owl in the first and the dog in the last line of the text) are mentioned by a nominal expression.

(42) *und hier sitzt die Eule*

   'and here the owl sits'

   und der sitzt auf'm Schneemann

   'and he sits on the snowman'

   hier ist er auf'm Rehhut

   'here he is on top of a deer's hat'

   und der fällt da runter

   'and he [=boy] falls down there'

   und der Hund auch

   'and the dog too' [*G5d-5;3*]

A more refined analysis, of the sort suggested by Wigglesworth (1992), may reveal additional referential strategies, particularly in the younger age groups. Still, the tendency to privilege the main character of the story by use of particular linguistic devices receives clear support from the German data examined here. In addition, the 9-year-olds' focus on clear identification and differentiation of all characters suggests a streamlining of the referential strategies of the two younger age groups. This overemphasis of the discourse boundaries of topical (character) packages marks a stepping stone in the German-speaking children — and probably children generally — towards the more conventional means available to speakers of their language for switching and maintaining reference.

3.2. Agency

This section brings together three different narrative devices that are quite distinct in surface linguistic form and appear to make reference to rather different aspects of "the world": (1) voice alternations, (2) Aktionsart, and (3) evaluations, i.e., references to psychological states of the characters. These different devices can be considered together if one takes into account, as I

---

tives in more detail. The fact that this strategy was so strongly evinced by even the 3-year-olds in this earlier investigation, was in part because the children were already highly familiar with the story-plot, unlike in the present study. In Wigglesworth's (1992) analysis of frog-book narratives collected from Australian English-speaking children, using the same elicitation procedure as in the present study, a similar trend was found, although it showed up rather later than in my (1987) study. Her more fine-grained analysis revealed various other strategies used by young children in this task.

have suggested elsewhere (Bamberg, 1991b), that passives can serve the same indexical function as references to negative states of existence or to internal states of story characters (e.g., their emotions or evaluative stances). Apart from the description of how these devices are employed in the narrative context of the frog story, I will document how the different devices can be used — at least to some degree — interchangeably; and that different languages may opt for different devices when compared with each other.

3.2.1. Voice alternations

The following two examples from a German adult illustrate the typical way passives are used in these narratives.

(43) *und dann der Junge fällt vom Baum runter*
     'and then the boy falls off the tree'
     *wahrscheinlich weil **er von dem Uhu hier erschrocken wurde***
     'probably because **he got frightened by the owl** here'
     und der Bienenschwarm jagt hinter dem Hund her
     'and the swarm of bees chases after the dog'
     das kriegt der Junge aber noch nicht mit
     'this however the boy does not notice yet'
     *dann **wird der Junge** wahrscheinlich **von dem Uhu angegriffen***
     'then **the boy** probably **gets attacked by the owl**'
     der macht so 'ne Abwehrbewegung
     'he makes such a defensive move'
     und kuckt so
     and looks this way' [G20j]

Both the passives in this text keep the boy in (surface) subject position, and as such contribute to the creation of a smooth discourse flow with the boy as the discursive topic: The passage is mainly "about" him. The next example is something of an exception to the way passives are used in the frog narratives, since a new character, the owl, is inserted into the text line, giving it the clause-initial subject position.

(44) *der Dackel hat inzwischen die Bienen rebellisch gemacht*
     'in the meantime the doggy has made the bees rebellious'
     die hinter ihm her sind
     'which are after him'

und die Eule wird auch aufgeschreckt
'and **the owl** also **gets aroused**'
und der kleine Junge fürchtet sich vor ihr
'and the little boy is afraid of her'
und klettert dann auf einen Fels rauf
'and then climbs up onto a rock'
und ruft nach dem Frosch
'and calls for the frog' [*G20a*]

Note, however, that the passive *wird aufgeschreckt* 'gets aroused' in (44) is a parallel construction, if the issue of agency and its motivating force is taken into account: In the second clause of (44), the bees have become the agents, chasing the dog who was the causal instigator of their action. Now, in line three, the same kind of causal role relationship is evoked for the construction of the interactive relationship between the owl and the boy: The boy had caused the owl to wake up, resulting — supposedly — in some reaction by the owl, which in turn resulted in the boy's internal response (expressed in line four) and the external response (expressed in the two subsequent lines). The use of *auch* 'also' underscores the parallel construction of the two revenge themes. If the narrator had opted for the active construction as in 'and the boy has **also** aroused the owl, and is afraid of her', the underpinning revenge motif would have been lost, and in addition, the use of 'also' would have been highly misleading in so far as it would have instructed the recipient to construct the boy's action (of arousing the owl) as a repetitious act.

In sum, as demonstrated in example (43), in most cases, the passive construction is used to hold the main character in a foregrounded and topical syntactic position, yielding a smooth flow of topical discourse units (Chapter IVC; see also Bamberg 1991b, where I make this point explicitly for American-English speakers). However, occasionally, other motivations for using the passive construction may compete with this general topic-preserving function. In such particular situations, the use of the passive is nevertheless still (motivationally) grounded in the narrator's intent to index reasons for particular happenings or doings, such as the revenge motif in example (44).

A more fine-grained analysis of where passives are used in the German sample (this chapter), combined with the American English sample (Chapter IIIA), reveals an interesting pattern. In 85% of the cases, adult narrators passivize scenes in which one of the four antagonists (the gopher, the bees, the owl, the deer) block the goal of the protagonists, i.e., to find their pet frog. Furthermore, in almost all of these cases, the boy or the dog are kept in topic position, as demonstrated in (43). Rarely are the antagonists passivized as in

(44). Children of both language samples never use passives to topicalize the antagonist. From this we may be able to conclude, in a preliminary way, that passives in the frog narration serve the discursive function of "promoting" the actions of the protagonists and "demoting" the actions of the antagonists. And as such, it can be argued that passive constructions are linguistic means that aid in the construal of "prot-" and "antagonistship."

Further evidence for this kind of argument comes from another level of analyzing the narratives. Almost all passive constructions by all narrators are used to characterize actions from a particular evaluative perspective: They are negative, i.e., they should not have happened, and as such resulted in negative emotional states — at least in a startle or a surprise. Along this line of analysis, all three passive examples in (43) and (44) above fit this pattern. In (43), the main protagonist is characterized as going through two negative experiences, while in example (44) this kind of negative evaluative stance could have been adopted to highlight that the owl actually should not have been disturbed.[18] As a matter of fact, the passive construction in example (44) leads to the impression that a consecutive reaction from the owl is to be expected and potentially even justified; thus, the boy had better be aware.

Building on these analyses of how and where passive constructions are put to use in the frog story, the seemingly different functions of "topic construction," signaling underlying thematic coherence (such as a revenge theme), or indexing a particular "negative" evaluative stance, can all be viewed as operating in concert with what has been termed the **binding** and **unfolding** of part-whole relationships (Bamberg 1992, 1993; Bamberg & Marchman, 1991; see also Chapter IVD).

In terms of frequency of occurrence, German narrators across the age groups make conspicuously infrequent use of passives. Only two children among the 3- and 5-year-olds attempt a passive, both times resulting in an awkward construction. The reason for the relatively low, and relatively late, use of passives in German, particularly when compared to the English narratives, may be in part due to the fact that German presents a more complex problem-solving space in comparison with English (see Chapter IVC, and Slobin, 1990, for supporting arguments for this position). Another way of resolving this puzzle is to look into where in the narratives typical passive constructions are used in the English texts, and compare these uses with how German

---

[18] In parental tellings of the frog book, narrators actually make this point quite explicit to their children: Owls sleep during the day, and they should not be disturbed (Bamberg 1987). See, also, a similar report on the functions of passives in maternal input in American English by Budwig (1990).

narrators solve similar problems linguistically.

In the English adult narratives, we do have a number of occurrences of the type *the boy was frightened by the owl* [E20d] or *the little boy falls off the tree, frightened by an owl* [E20h] or *the dog is intrigued by this beehive* [E20b], all appealing to states of arousal in one of the protagonists, caused by one of the antagonists. In the German narratives, narrators typically do not use passives for exactly the same information value, but rather use reflexive constructions of the following sort: *und Tom hat sich auch sehr erschrocken* 'and Tom has scared himself [=gotten scared] quite a bit' [G20f], *erst mal hat er sich erschrocken* 'first off, he has scared himself' [G20b]. Though it is quite possible to view the action in a transitive way, i.e., the antagonist (e.g., the owl) *erschrickt* 'scares' the protagonist (the boy), German adult narrators as well as the children of the older age groups opt for a perspective that anchors the origins of the scare/fright experience in the self of the protagonist, though not directing the experience outward but rather full circle back to the self. In a similar vein, German narrators are not 'intrigued by something', but rather *interessieren sich für etwas* 'interest themselves for something'.

In general, German reflexives are probably better viewed as middle constructions. Reflexive constructions such as *sich waschen* 'wash oneself', *sich freuen über* 'enjoy oneself', *sich erschrecken* 'get a fright/get frightened', *sich verlieben* 'fall in love', *sich wehtun* 'get hurt', and many others, all signify the source or origin of the action and the goal or recipient as the same person.[19] Some of these actions are by their very nature more agentive than others,[19] that is, they focus more on the source of the action; and this is reflected in their English glosses as active (sometimes even reflexive) constructions. Other actions, however, orient more to the recipient, and so background the agent as actor, as reflected in their English glosses by *get*-passives. Thus, German reflexive constructions of the kind common in everyday conversational usage and in the German frog stories, including those used by 3-year-olds, may in part play a role parallel to syntactic passives in English.

3.2.2. Aktionsart reconsidered

So far, concern has been mainly with how characters are discursively created as separate topics, independent of each other. Yet, story characters are created to relate to each other, and one character's actions have consequences for what others in the story do, think, and feel. Here, I reanalyze the predicates chosen to characterize the actions and interactions of the characters

---

[19] The question arises whether this "nature" is extralinguistic. I believe that it is not, so that my appeal to the "nature" of actions or activities is no more than a figure of speech.

in light of these considerations.

Three-year-olds depict story characters mainly in terms of motion and existential predicates. For instance, the scene where the boy falls out of the tree (Picture 12) or the scene where boy and dog fall off the cliff (Picture 15) are described by 3-year-olds as 'falling' and 'being at a new location'. Analysis of how movements are linguistically constructed (in Section 2) revealed the younger narrators' preoccupation with aspects of the spatial scenery. It is rare for 3-year-olds to elaborate on reasons for events, as in the following example, narrating Picture 8:

(45) *da fällt er*

'there he [=boy] falls'

und dann ist er am Erde

'and then he [=boy] is on the ground'

weil da einer rauskommte

'because someone [=owl] came out of there' [*G31-3;3*]

Five-year-olds are far more likely to characterize the falling scene in terms of an agent who causes the fall; for example, the deer is often described as the one who volitionally *wirft* 'throws' the boy. The 5-year-olds also show the first references to mental states and a few overt causal relationships between events, a trend which is far more marked in the 9-year-old narratives. The older children often characterize the actions of the deer and/or the owl by causatives such as *runterschubsen* 'push down', *runterwerfen* 'throw down', or *runterschmeißen* 'hurl down', and they describe the activities of characters in terms that incorporate telic orientations that affect other characters, e.g., *beschimpfen* 'yell at', *verfolgen* 'follow', and most especially *suchen* 'search'. And 9-year-olds also make more references to internal states of the characters and use more direct speech than the younger children. Nevertheless, there are still long passages that give the impression of parallel-running actions of different characters that are not necessarily viewed as interconnected, even in the narratives of the 9-year-olds, all of whom clearly have a grasp of the overall plot of the frog story.

Adult narratives reveal far more about the characters' inner states and motivations as a basis for expressing complex interactions between characters, as in (44). Adults also very often make references to non-existent states and indulge in extended departures from the storyline to let the listener know how the different characters hook up with each other. Consequently, their descriptions of the characters' actions, though often very similar to those found in texts of 5- and even 3-year-olds, are far more grounded in a network of interpersonal motivations of the story characters. In the mature narratives, in sum, the listener appears to have an easier task in understanding the characters and, hence the narrator as well.

3.2.3. Evaluations and motives to act

The preceding analyses of characterhood and agency have concerned mainly the linguistic means by which characters are introduced and how they acquire a specific contour in the course of the narrative discourse. As a result, the focus of this section has been on the identity and deeds of the story characters. The fact that activities are generally viewed as motivated by thoughts, intentions, feelings, attitudes, and desires — in our Western folk-beliefs at all events — was noted only when narrators explicitly attributed such psychological states to characters of the story. But implicit attributions of psychological states are highly relevant to choice of action descriptions attributed to the characters in the story, and they are ultimately also responsible for how the characters are viewed as moving through time (Section 1 above) and space (Section 2).

As I have discussed elsewhere (Bamberg, 1991a, 1991b, 1992, in press; Bamberg & Marchman 1990, 1991) actions, actors,[20] (spatial) scenes, and (spatio-temporal) events are always viewed from an overarching perspective and as such appear in an integrated relationship.[21] Narrators can try to conceal their integrative perspective, but they cannot run the risk of their narratives becoming fragmented and dissociated, since this might reflect back onto the narrator himself or herself. The integrative perspective from which part-whole relationships are viewed as tied together and at the same time unfolding, is part of an inferential system computed on the basis of linguistic choices. As such, the linguistic means analyzed in this chapter, when viewed as contributing to the constitution of events, scenes, and characterships in the German frog-book narratives, also provide insight into the overall perspectives from which part-whole relationships emerge.

This final subsection briefly considers linguistic devices traditionally viewed as functioning in direct service of signaling the overall perspectives of narratives (and hence of narrators): so-called "evaluative" devices or "evaluations." In the present context, this is done by focusing on two devices that illuminate the development of evaluative stances in the German corpus. The

---

[20] In this chapter, actors and acts (or actions) have been collapsed into the unit of "characters."

[21] This perspective, in line with the work of Burke (Burke, 1968, 1969), originates from the (human) drama (see Bamberg, 1993).

first such device is the linguistic form *wollen* 'want to', by which younger children in particular seem to refer to characters' intentional stances; the second considers use of the adverb *plötzlich* 'suddenly' and overt mention of characters' being scared or startled.

As background, recall some aspects of the overall picture presented in this chapter. The 3- and the 5-year-olds' narratives are clearly shorter than those of the 9-year-olds and adults. One overall characterization of the younger narratives is that they seem to be more "descriptive" (Bamberg & Damrad-Frye, 1991; Bamberg & Marchman, 1990). This, however, does not mean that the younger children's narratives do not contain any evaluative means nor, more particularly, that 3- or 5-year-olds are unable to take a "second" look at the same event to reevaluate it by connecting the "what-is-said" with the "why-it-is-said." Younger children clearly do take evaluative stances in their narratives, but they do so mainly for what we have termed "local" narrative purposes. With age, these "local" stances become more differentiated and integrated into a "global" narrative perspective. Again, this is not to say that younger children do not "have" a global perspective. In fact, there is good evidence to the contrary, particularly in terms of referential strategies as well as aspectual markings used by even 3-year-old children (Bamberg, 1986, 1987, 1993). Thus, even while calling the younger children's narratives more "descriptive" is not really an accurate characterization, it does reflect the overall impression yielded by their texts of a lack of clear evaluative stances, such as stepping out of the narrative clause-line and thereby taking on this second interpretive orientation of "why-it-is-said."

Young German narrators do, nevertheless, overtly express their interpretive stances on characters' perspectives. One clear way they do so is by use of the modal expressions *will*, *wollte* 'wants to', 'wanted to'. Characters' actions are often described in terms of their wishes and/or wants. The 3-year-olds do so 26 times, and the 5-year-olds 23 times, while 9-year-olds in their much longer narratives use this particular device only nine times, and adults in their even longer narratives only seven times. In contrast, other evaluative devices that are only sporadically used by the younger children, occur increasingly in the texts of the older children and the adults.

A second relevant device that differs markedly across the different age groups is the use of questions. Three-year-olds quite often use questions as genuine queries about the underlying motives of participants — e.g., *Und da warum rennt der denn da weg?* 'And there, why does he run away there?' [G3g-3;8], but this decreases with age. Adult narratives show an increase in questions, but these have a clearly rhetorical function to direct the listener's attention and relate his/her local orientation and expectation to the global story thread, e.g., *Sie kucken über den Baumstamm hinweg, und wer sitzt dort? Dort sitzt Frau Frosch* ... 'They look over the treetrunk, and who sits there? There sits Mrs. Frog ...' [*G20c*].

Another development is revealed by comparing two seemingly unrelated linguistic devices, the adverb *plötzlich* 'suddenly' and the overt evaluation of the impact of an event on a character's state of mind by use of terms like *überrascht* 'amazed', *erstaunt* 'surprised', *verdutzt* 'puzzled', and the like, to express surprise, and *erschrocken* 'frightened', *entsetzt* 'disturbed', expressing a surprise turned into a scare. Both *plötzlich* and *erschrocken* take two simultaneously occurring events or situations into account: on the one hand the event that happens (so to speak outside of a perceiver) and on the other hand the mind of a character from whose perspective this event happened unexpectedly — *plötzlich*. The German synonym *auf einmal*, literally 'at one-time', with the connotation of 'all at once' or 'at the same time', demonstrates clearly that a co-temporal perspective is at work in the merging of these two perspectives. The lexical characterization of a character's state of mind as *erschrocken* or *entsetzt* presents the same situation from a slightly different perspective: Only if something has happened unexpectedly — *plötzlich* and *auf einmal* — can this something have the effect of a surprise and potentially cause a fright. Thus, though *plötzlich* and *erschrocken* seem on the surface to be two independent and different characterizations of a temporal and an affective contour respectively at the level of "what-is-said," they are closely related in terms of their discursive value, i.e., at the level of "why-it-is-said."

In contrast to the common characterizations of characters' intentional stances by the 3- and the 5-year-old children, they use few overt references to their states of mind. There is only one reference to the "fright" aspect of an experience, and one to its suddenness by German 3-year-olds. And they make few references to other internal states as well. This changes somewhat in the narratives of the 5-year-olds, some of whom do try to convey the connections between characters' actions more explicitly, though most of their narratives likewise lack reference to an internal state of any kind, or to the suddenness of events. They use *auf einmal* or *plötzlich* and refer to the "fright" factor a total of five times each.

Interestingly enough, the overall samples of narratives of the 9-year-olds, and also of the adults, still include a few narratives that could be characterized as "purely descriptive" in the sense that they fail to make any overt reference to evaluative orientations of the sort under discussion here.[22] The

---

[22] Interviews of the German adult narrators conducted at the end of the session revealed an interesting correlation between story length and use of evaluative devices, on the one hand, and the imagined story recipient, that is, the construction of the interactive situation, on the other. Adults who revealed that they had actually tried to imagine a child recipient construct-

other narratives of the older subjects, however, all in one way or another exploit forms of "suddenness" or the "fright" motif. The 9-year-olds use *plötzlich* or *auf einmal* 26 times, the adults 22 times; the 9-year-olds express a character's surprise 6 times, and the fright factor 10 times; adults do so 9 times and 32 times, respectively.

The marked rise in this particular narrative stance on characters' actions and reactions to events in the German frog stories documents nicely the shift in narrative orientation across the four age groups. Younger children are able to take an evaluative stance on single events, that is, the "here-and-nows" of deictic centers (Sections 1 and 2 above), by revealing characters' volitions and wants; with age, children develop a kind of double-look onto the deictic centers of larger sections or segments of the discourse. In consequence, the evaluative stances taken by older children and adults can take on a signaling function that relates parts of the narrative to the construction of the whole, and as such reveal insights of actors' motivations with regard to the narrative in its entirety.

4. SUMMARY

4.1. Temporal Expression

Almost all of the narrators, across age, anchor their narratives in the present tense, contrasting this with the present perfect. The earliest uses of the present perfect are for marking completion; more developed uses (present in only a few preschoolers) are **prospective relevance**, which points forward from a completed situation to a new activity scene, and **retrospective assessment**, which introduces a prior situation which is relevant to the current situation. A major developmental shift, however, is from early centering on a single action to more developed orientation to a past or future point in a hierarchically ordered narrative structure.

Aspectual adverbs are most commonly used to indicate protraction, inception, recurrence, and relation to another reference time. The variety of forms increases with age. In comparison with the other four languages of the study, German children make more use of deictic adverbs and less use of sequential adverbs in marking interclausal relations. Specific time adverbials are rare. Temporal subordination is a relatively late development. It is proposed that the frequent use of sentence-initial spatial deictics might block the

---

ed longer narratives which included an abundance of overt evaluative stances, whereas those who reported that they simply "wanted to get the job done" for the interviewer, used minimal evaluations in the much shorter texts which they produced.

use of temporal connectives, presenting a narrative sequence from one deictic center to the next.

4.2. Spatial Expression

The younger narrators rely heavily on clause-initial use of the spatial adverb *da* 'there'. Directional prefixes on verbs are used from the youngest age to indicate path in a general way, with specification of source and/or goal becoming more frequent in the later preschool period. A wide range of verbs of motion is used, generally conflated with manner, and combined with path satellites and deictic directional particles. Three-year-olds have almost full command of this complex, satellite-framed system.

4.3. Characters and Agency

The main protagonists tend to be introduced by definite noun-phrases by narrators of all ages, with use of indefinite noun-phrases becoming an equal option only by school-age. Peripheral characters come to be introduced by indefinite noun-phrases more frequently and at earlier ages. Continuing reference is by noun or pronoun, with preschoolers making especially heavy use of pronouns for the boy as "thematic subject"; but there is increasing use of zero pronoun in conjoined clauses by 9-year-olds and adults. Nine-year-olds also make frequent use of left-dislocations in which a clause-initial noun-phrase is followed by a pronominal copy; right-dislocations are rare.

Passives are used by adults to keep a topical participant in subject position, especially when the goal of a main protagonist is blocked. Most passives also focus on a negative consequence for the subject. This construction is rarely used by children; however they do make use of reflexive constructions which often function to downgrade agency. Attention to inner states and motivations develops with age, but even the youngest narrators comment on intentions of the protagonists.

Chapter IIIC

DEVELOPMENT OF LINGUISTIC FORMS: SPANISH

Eugenia Sebastián and Dan I. Slobin

0. Introduction
1. Spanish Tense/Aspect
    1.1. Present/Past Tense
        1.1.1. Dominant tense
        1.1.2. Tense/aspect shifting
    1.2. Grammatical Aspect
        1.2.1. Progressive aspect
        1.2.2. Perfect aspect
        1.2.3. Perfective/imperfective aspect
    1.3. Lexical Aspect
        1.3.1. A particle with aspectual value: The reflexive *se*
        1.3.2. Aspectual verbs
        1.3.3. Aspectual adverbs
2. Event Conflation: Motion and Location
3. Perspective
    3.1. Word Order
    3.2. Valence
4. Connectivity
    4.1. Simple Clause Connection
    4.2. Complex Clause Connection
        4.2.1. Temporal adverbial clauses
        4.2.2. Causal adverbial clauses
        4.2.3. Relative clauses
    4.3. Subject Ellipsis
5. Summary
    5.1. Tense/Aspect
    5.2. Motion and Location
    5.3. Perspective
    5.4. Connectivity

0. INTRODUCTION

The Spanish narratives were gathered in three countries — Spain, Chile, and Argentina.[1] The subjects all came from middle-class, urban environments and all had Spanish as their only mother tongue. All of the analyses in this volume are based on the European Spanish data, but some comparisons are made in this chapter with the Latin American versions. In the Madrid sample there were 12 subjects each in the age groups 3, 4, 5, 9, and adult. The Chilean and Argentinian samples also had 12 subjects per group, including age groups 7 and 11.

1. Spanish Tense/Aspect

Spanish is an interesting language for the study of tense and aspect because it grammaticizes a great deal of information in its verb forms. Verbal inflectional morphemes mark person and number, along with tense distinctions between present, past, and future, aspectual distinctions of perfective/imperfective, progressive, and perfect, as well as imperative, conditional, and subjunctive.

The **perfective/imperfective** (PFV/IPFV) distinction is obligatory in the past tense only (in contrast to languages like Russian, for example, in which this distinction applies in both past and future). This aspectual choice requires the speaker to take a particular stance with regard to a past event. If one wishes to present an event "from outside," without attention to its internal structure (for example, in order to present it as something over and done with), one uses the perfective past (*comió* 'eat:PFV), whereas if one attends to the internal structure of an event, one uses the imperfective past (*comía* 'eat:IPFV'). Thus in Spanish, as in a number of other languages, the perfective past describes a **limited** or **bounded** action — that is, a process that comes to an end, whereas the imperfective past presents the action of the verb as **not limited** or **unbounded** (Demonte, 1991). The imperfective past can be used to indicate the temporal setting in which one or more completed events occurred, marked by the perfective — e.g., *Llovía cuando llegué a Madrid* 'It rained:IPFV when I arrived:PFV in Madrid'. In this example, the action of arriving is presented as completed, whereas the event of raining is not. Some

---

[1] Data were gathered in Madrid by Eugenia Sebastián, who also thanks the Max-Planck-Institute for Psycholinguistics in Nijmegen, the Netherlands, for the facilities which she enjoyed while working on this chapter. Data were gathered in Santiago, Chile, and Buenos Aires, Argentina, by Aura Bocaz, with support from Grant H2643-8712 from Universidad de Chile. We are grateful to her for sharing her texts, and insights, with us. Further aspects of her analyses of those materials can be found in the references under Bocaz and Slobin & Bocaz. Examples from Latin American children are prefixed by *c* (Chile) and *a* (Argentina).

analysts prefer to characterize the perfective as presenting an event as "terminal" (*concluso*) and the imperfective as "nonterminal" (*inconcluso*). This interpretation of the imperfective allows for an openness about the possible realization or conclusion of an action — what Fernández-Ramírez (1986) has referred to as *expectativa*. To take an example from that author, if we are told *No había forma de convencer a Luis* 'There was:IPFV no way to convince Luis', we remain open as to whether Luis was ultimately convinced or not.

Spanish also marks **progressive** aspect, constructed with the verb *estar* 'be' + PRES.PART. The progressive can occur in the past in both imperfective and perfective forms (*estaba/estuvo* 'was:IPFV/was:PFV' + PRES.PART), with the perfect in both present and past (*ha/había estado* 'has/have been + PRES.PART), and further combinations which we will not consider here, since our aim is to compare the progressive with the present, on one hand, and with the imperfective past, on the other. The basic notion that underlies the progressive is that of **duration** or **progress** (Comrie, 1976; Fernández-Ramírez, 1986; RAE, 1982). For example, *estoy comiendo* 'I am eating' indicates that the activity of eating is ongoing at the moment of speaking, with no indication of when the eating started or how long it may continue, and with no attention to either the beginning or end of the activity. The progressive contrasts with the simple present in that it does not mark **habitual** aspect. In the past tense, as well, the progressive indicates only ongoing process — e.g., *(yo) estaba comiendo cuando llegó Miguel* '(I) was:IPFV eating when Miguel arrived:PFV' indicates that Miguel's arrival took place while the activity of eating was already in progress. As various authors have suggested (e.g., Comrie, 1976; Marchand, 1955), the distinction between progressive and nonprogressive forms is not as rigid in Spanish as it is in languages like English, where the absence of a distinction between perfective and imperfective makes it necessary to rely on the progressive to indicate durativity. Consequently, the progressive is considerably "more optional" in Spanish than English.

The **perfect** is formed with the verb *haber* 'have' + PAST.PART. The **present perfect** (e.g., *ha comido* 'has eaten') indicates a continuation into the present of a past situation, thus relating both to the present and the past. In distinction to other languages, the Spanish present perfect permits the specification of event time, as, for example *Hoy me he levantado a las 8* 'Today I have gotten up at 8:00' (Comrie, 1976). (However in many regions of Spain and America such specification is only allowed if the event occurred within the present day. Furthermore, the degree of use of the present perfect varies widely across the Spanish-speaking world, and is almost absent in some parts of Latin America.) The **past perfect** (e.g., *había comido* 'had eaten') functions, as in English, as a relative tense, taking a retrospective stance from a reference point in the past.

Tables 1a, 1b, and 1c summarize the range of tense/aspect forms used by child narrators of the frog story in three dialects of Spanish. It is evident that the forms are acquired early. Almost every combination is attested in the 3-year-old sample from Spain, and comparison with the Chilean and Argentinian data convinces us that we did not chance upon a particularly precocious sample in Madrid. In all three samples, two rare forms are either later acquisitions or are absent: the past perfect (PAST.PERF) and the past progressive with a perfective auxiliary (PFV.PROG). The other striking difference is the absence of the present perfect (PRES.PERF) in the Latin American samples, reflecting the disappearance of this form in colloquial speech. Otherwise, it would appear that the richness of the tense/aspect system stimulates, rather than retards its acquisition.

TABLE 1a
Spain: Number of Children
Using Tense/Aspect Forms at Least Once
(N=12)

Tense/Aspect Form	Age			
	3 yrs	4 yrs	5 yrs	9 yrs
PRES	11	8	7	10
PRES.PROG	6	7	3	5
IFV.PROG	5	5	8	1
PFV.PROG	0	0	0	2
IFV	9	10	7	11
PFV	8	10	9	6
PRES.PERF	9	4	6	3
PAST.PERF	0	3	2	6

1.1. Present/Past Tense

Inflectional errors are rare in our texts, restricted to familiar overregularizations (e.g., *ponió* for *puso* 'put:PFV [S4a-4;1], *caíba* for *caía* 'fall:IPFV [S4d-4;5]). However, the overall correctness of morphological form is a long way from the felicitous use of tenses for purposes of narration. It is important to consider the effect of choice of dominant tense on the selection of tense forms in narrative. For example, a past-tense narration is unlikely to have present-tense verb forms unless the narrator temporarily steps outside of

TABLE 1b
Chile: Number of Children
Using Tense/Aspect Forms at Least Once
(N=12)

Tense/Aspect Form	Age			
	3 yrs	4 yrs	5 yrs	9 yrs
PRES	10	10	8	6
PRES.PROG	10	10	4	2
IFV.PROG	4	10	11	9
PFV.PROG	0	1	0	0
IFV	7	8	12	12
PFV	12	12	12	12
PRES.PERF	0	0	0	0
PAST.PERF	0	1	3	9

TABLE 1c
Argentina: Number of Children
Using Tense/Aspect Forms at Least Once
(N=12)

Tense/Aspect Form	Age			
	3 yrs	4 yrs	5 yrs	9 yrs
PRES	12	8	10	9
PRES.PROG	10	7	8	5
IFV.PROG	5	5	9	6
PFV.PROG	0	0	0	0
IFV2	8	11	11	12
PFV	12	11	12	10
PRES.PERF	0	0	0	0
PAST.PERF	0	0	0	8

narrative time — as in the case of making reference to the general attributes of some depicted object.

1.1.1. Dominant tense

A narration can be carried out in the past or in the present or in an alternation of the two tenses (Silva-Corvalán, 1983). All three possibilities are available in this picture-story type of narration. Table 2 shows the choice of these three options by age group in the Madrid sample. (Dominant tense is defined as that tense used in 80% of the clauses in a text.)

TABLE 2
Number of Spanish Texts with Dominant Present, Past,
or Mixed Tense Forms, by Age-Group (N=12)

| Tense | Age | | | | |
	3yrs	4 yrs	5 yrs	9 yrs	Adult
Present	5	2	3	8	10
Past	2	8	7	4	2
Mixed	5	2	2	0	0

Until age 5 the children oscillate in choice of dominant tense, whereas 9-year-olds and adults tend to use the present tense throughout their narrations. Switches between past and present in the 3-year-old texts often go back and forth from clause to clause, based on picture-description strategies rather than either syntactic or narrative considerations. However, such switching begins to decline at age 4, and — what is more important — longer stretches of text continue in the same tense. Example (1) shows the sort of tense switching characteristic of ages 4-5. This 4-year-old begins to narrate Picture 9 in present tense, switches to past tense for Picture 10, and continues in past tense through Picture 12. At the same time, however, aspect is appropriately used to characterize types of events, distinguishing between processes (PROG, IPFV), states (PRES, IPFV), and completed actions (PFV).[2]

(1) *Éste está mirando por un agujero y el perro quiere coger esto. Éste se puso de rodillas. Aquí se quería subir y aquí salían moscas. Y aquí se subió el niño al árbol. Y aquí se cayó.*

'This.one is looking:PRES.PROG in a hole and the dog wants:PRES to get this.thing. This.one got:PFV on his knees. Here (he) wanted:PFV to climb and here flies came.out:IPFV. And here the boy climbed:PFV the

---

[2] "Null pronouns" are given in parentheses in the glosses. For example, in (1) *se cayó* 'REFL fall:3SG:PFV' is glossed as '(he) fell'. Pronouns are based on Spanish gender; thus *la rana* 'DEF.ART:SG:FEM frog', when referenced with a null pronoun, is glossed as 'she' in this chapter. For consistency, we refer to the frog as *she* in the English text of the chapter as well.

tree. And here (he) fell:PFV.' [S4i-4;7]

Nine-year-olds and adults almost always pick the present as dominant tense. This seems to be the prototypical verb form for telling a story in Spanish. There are no relevant differences between 9-year-olds and adults in their uses of present tense; however these uses differ considerably from those of the younger narrators. Compare the following initial story segments from a 3- and a 9-year-old:

(2a) *Aquí que están viendo la rana. Aquí que están durmiendo y la rana está saliendo. Aquí se está poniendo, y aquí el perro se está metiendo. Aquí a mirar si está la rana. Aquí ha abierto los ojos y no está.*

'Here that they are seeing the frog. Here that they are sleeping and the frog is leaving. Here (he) is putting (on), and here the dog is putting.in. Here to look if the frog is (there). Here (he) has opened his eyes and (it) is not (there).' [S3i-3;10]

(2b) *Esto es un niño y un perro — ¿no? — que encuentran una rana y la meten en un bote. Entonces el niño se va a dormir y la rana se escapa. Al día siguiente el niño y el perro disgustados miran el bote. El niño se levanta, se viste y ve el vaso de cristal que estaba la rana. Se lo pone en la cabeza. El niño mira por la ventana y grita.*

'This is a boy and a dog — right? — that find a frog and put her in a jar. Then the boy goes to sleep and the frog escapes. The next day the boy and the dog, (both) upset, look at the jar. The boy gets up, gets dressed and sees the glass jar that the frog was (in). (He) puts it on his head. The boy looks out of the window and calls.' [S9e-9;6]

Although the 3-year-old consistently maintains present tense, this does not structure his narrative organization in the same way as in the 9-year-old text. Rather, he uses present tense as a means of describing one picture after another, emphasized by the use of *aquí* 'here', and especially by the use of the present tense in the progressive aspect. As discussed in Section 1.2.1, this is the characteristic form of picture description. The 9-year-old, although using present-tense verbs, follows a temporal rather than a spatial organization, segmenting the narration with the use of *entonces* 'then' and *al día siguiente* 'the next day'.

1.1.2. Tense/aspect shifting

Tense/aspect contrasts in narration can be determined by either syntactic factors (e.g., as required in certain types of subordination) or by narrative functions. For example, a characteristic of the present-tense adult texts is an initial stage-setting in the imperfective past, as in (3).

(3) *Esto era un niño pequeño que tenía un perro y una rana que por las noches guardaba en una botella, en un frasco grande. Una buena noche, la rana decide escaparse ...*

'This was:IPFV a little boy that had:IPFV a dog and a frog that (he) kept:IPFV at night in a bottle, in a big jar. One night, the frog decides:PRES to escape ...' [story continues in present tense] [*S20j*]

The past-tense adult texts also begin with imperfective verbs, indicating that this is the characteristic form for stage-setting.

This does not occur, however, in the 9-year-old texts. There is only one instance of a tense shift between the initial stage-setting and the rest of the narration — and, in fact, this shift is produced in the reverse direction: a past tense text begins in the present:

(4) *Un niño un perro y una rana que está metida en un bote, y luego se acuesta y la rana ve que están dormidos los dos y se escapa. Y a la mañana siguiente miran el bote para ver si estaba la rana y vieron que no estaba.*

'A boy a dog and a frog that is placed in a jar, and then (he) goes.to.sleep:PRES and the frog sees:PRES that the two of them are sleeping:PRES.PROG and (she) escapes:PRES. And the next morning (they) look:PRES (at) the jar to see if the frog was:IPFV (there) and (they) saw:PFV that (she) was:IPFV not (there).' [*S9d-9;5*]

As noted above, early tense shifting cannot be explained on discursive grounds. However, it would be incorrect to make the same claim with regard to aspect shifting. A tense shift in Spanish from present to past necessarily requires an aspectual choice — perfective or imperfective. Although we cannot speak of a **systematic** use of these forms for discursive ends until age 5, there are isolated examples at age 3 of well-motivated aspectual contrasts (discussed in more detail in Section 1.2.3). For example, the following narrative segment shows an interesting combination of tense shifts with no obvious justification (from present to past), accompanied by aspectual shifts in the past with apparent discourse motivation.

(5) *Y se sube encima de esto y esto es muy malo ... Y entonces el niño se cayó y éste era muy pequeño. Entonces se cayó otra vez. El niño se cayó al agua y éste le comía el pelo. Se subió a un tronco de un árbol y entonces se bañaba así.*

'And (he) climbs:PRES on top of this.one and it is very bad ... And then the boy fell:PFV and this.one was:IPFV very little. Then (he) fell:PFV again. The boy fell:PFV to the water and this.one ate:IPFV his hair. (He) climbed:PFV a tree trunk and then (he) bathed:IPFV like this.' [*S3e-3;8*]

Here we see a relation between the Aktionsart of the verb and its aspectual marking. Completed events — 'fall' and 'climb' — are given in the perfective, and states and activities — 'be little', 'eat', 'bathe' — in the imperfective. The former are foregrounded events, in that they advance the plot, while the latter are backgrounded, describing ancillary situations.

At age 3, such contrasts in verb form are almost the only means of expressing temporal contrasts that are of narrative relevance. Older children and adults, however, supplement morphological means with additional lexical and syntactic options, as discussed below.

1.2. Grammatical Aspect

In this section we consider the uses made by children of aspectual marking on the verb; the following section (1.3) deals with expressions of aspect outside of verbal inflection. In the subsections below we examine contrasts expressed by inflectional marking of progressive, perfect, and perfective/imperfective aspects.

1.2.1. Progressive aspect

As noted above, the progressive is generally optional in Spanish and is not the only means of expressing durativity. Therefore we expected that it would be used infrequently in our narratives, as Silva-Corvalán (1983) has found with adult subjects. In our adult texts only 2.9% of the total verbs are in the progressive: 1.6% in the present and 1.3% in the imperfective past. (There were no adult instances of perfective past progressives, such as *estuvo buscando* 'was:PFV searching', attested in a few 9-year-old examples.) This tendency is also reflected in the 9-year-old texts, where only 4% of verbs are in the progressive (2.3% PRES.PROG, 0.7% IPFV.PROG, 1% PFV.PROG). However, the progressive is much more frequent at younger ages, both in the present and imperfective past. The present progressive is used at a similar rate by both 3- and 4-year-olds (6.6% and 6.3%). This greater frequency can be explained by the function of the progressive in picture description. For example, the child of 3;8 represented in (6) begins to use imperfective past progressive forms to describe the pictures, switching to the perfective when beginning to tell the story.

(6) *Se va a romper la boca y el niño mirando al perro. Y el niño estaba llamando y el perro estaba mirando. Estaba mirando el niño en ese agujero a ver qué había y el perro estaba mirando ... Se cayó éste.*

'(He) is going to break his mouth and the boy looking at the dog. And the boy was calling:IPFV.PROG and the dog was looking:IPFV.PROG. The boy was looking:IPFV.PROG in that hole to see what was:IPFV (there) and the dog was looking:IPFV.PROG ... This.one fell:PFV.' [S3e-3;8]

As discussed in Chapter IVA, these early contrasts between progressive and nonprogressive are the first linguistic means of expressing a type of **simultaneity**. The youngest children do not yet use subordinate clauses or lexical elements to indicate the temporal overlap of two events or activities.

It is interesting that some preschoolers recognize the durative element of particular situations, using the present participle without an auxiliary, and appropriately contrasting progressive and nonprogressive events in this fashion. This can be seen in the first use of *mirando* 'looking' in (6), as well as in (7), below.

(7) *Y aquí se sentó en el agua y el perro subiéndose a su cabeza.*

'And here (he) sat.down:PFV in the water and the dog climbing on his head.' [S4i-4;7]

Such examples suggest that the element that the child recognizes as basic for marking durativity or progressivity is the present participle. This form is used in several other constructions which may facilitate its acquisition. It is used in combination with "semi-auxiliaries" to express various additional nuances — called **phases** by Coseriu (1976) — such as **continuative phase** (e.g., *sigue buscando* '(he) continues looking' [S9a-9;1]) and **progressive phase**, which seems to take an internal perspective on an event which is, itself, in progress. This construction uses the verb *ir* 'go', bleached of its core meaning of movement, as a semi-auxiliary with the present participle. Compare, for example, the way in which a Chilean child of 4;5 uses progressive aspect in the first clause and progressive phase in the second, in order to place an ongoing event of shorter duration (escaping) within the timeframe of one of longer duration (sleeping):

(8) *Estaban durmiendo y la rana calladita se iba escapando del frasco.*

'(They) were sleeping:IPFV.PROG and the frog very.quietly went:IPFV escaping:PRES.PART from the jar.' [cS4e-4;5]

In addition, the present participle is the verbal form used to indicate **manner**, consistent with the verb-framed typology of Spanish, as discussed in Chapter IIIo. For example, with verbs of motion, the verb conveys the "fact of motion," and manner can be expressed by a present participle, as in *el perro se fue corriendo* 'the dog went.off:PFV running [S3j-3;11]. It is possible that this range of functions of the present participle facilitates the acquisition of its systematic use in various types of periphrasis.

Nine-year-old and adult narrators use progressive forms basically to indicate that something is in progress. Therefore verbs that refer to an activity that is maintained throughout the story, until the final re-encounter with the frog, are almost always in the progressive. These verbs include *buscar* 'search', *llamar* 'call', and *mirar* 'look', as in the following example:

(9) *Y el niño creía que estaba en el agujero y estaba llamándola.*

> 'And the boy thought:IPFV that (it) was:IPFV in the hole and (he) was calling.it:IPFV.PROG.' [S9d-9;5]

Accordingly, we can say that the past progressive marks continuity in these narratives, because the search for the frog has an implicit continuity until the very end of the story, and, as discussed in Chapter IIA, all adult subjects mention this continuity.

One further question that continues to generate a great deal of confusion is the following: As mentioned above, there seems to be general agreement that it is the concept of **duration** that characterizes the periphrastic form *estar* 'be' + PRES.PART (i.e. PROGRESSIVE). However, the picture is somewhat more complex, because there are cases in which *estar* 'be' is used in the perfective (*estuvo*) with the present participle of a verb denoting a continuing action, in order to indicate the **total duration** of a process. That is, it is possible, in the past tense, to form progressives with either an imperfective or a perfective auxiliary. The former is far more frequent, however the latter is used by two 9-year-olds in the Madrid sample, appropriately indicating a continuing action that is also bounded, as in the following examples:

(10a) *Y estuvieron llamándola por la ventana.*

> 'And (they) were:PFV calling her through the window.' [S9d-9;5]

(10b) *Y luego la estuvieron buscando por todas las partes.*

> 'And then (they) were:PFV searching for her everywhere.' [S9g-9;6]

If one substitutes the simple form for the periphrastic in these two examples the notion of **total duration** of the event is lost and only its punctual endpoint is indicated. The reader may ask, then, why the same narrator (S9d) uses the same verb, *llamar* 'call' — which denotes a continuing action in our story — with the imperfective auxiliary in (9) and the perfective auxiliary in (10a). The answer is that in (9) the narrator does not refer to the total duration of the event of calling, but does so (10a).

1.2.2. Perfect aspect

Present Perfect. The present perfect is a complex verbal form, in that it establishes temporal relations with both the present and the past. Although it refers to situations that have already taken place — therefore referring to the past — it maintains a close relation with the present. In Klein's (1992) terms, when one uses the present perfect one "makes a claim" about a particular time: That time includes the time of utterance (present tense) and it is included in the posttime of the situation referred to (perfect aspect). Contextual information allows for various interpretations of the present perfect. For example, if the consequences of the situation persist at the time of utterance, the form is interpretable as resultative. As noted by Comrie (1976), the perfect does not tell us anything about the aspectual contour of a situation in itself, which can be understood as perfective or imperfective, depending on the verb and the situation to which it refers. Thus, for example, the present perfect can indicate the final result of a process (*He encontrado tu libro* 'I have found your book') or can indicate a durative action (*He llorado mucho su muerte* 'I have cried much over his death') (Fernández-Ramírez, 1986).

On grounds of conceptual complexity, Slobin and Bocaz (1988) considered that the present perfect might be a late acquisition. However, as shown in Table 1, it is widely used in the Madrid sample from the youngest ages. By contrast, it is not used by any of the Chilean or Argentinian children of any age, reflecting its marginal and literary usage in those Latin American dialects. (Similar dialectal differences have been noted for the English present perfect, where it is a relatively early acquisition in Britain [Gathercole, 1986], but relatively late in the United States. Again, the factors influencing acquisition seem to be dialectal — reflecting frequency of use and functionality in the grammar — rather than any inherent complexity in either the form or the functions of the construction in itself.)

In the data from Spain, narrators switch into the present perfect when the predominant tense is present, but not past, indicating that this is essentially a form oriented to the present. The switch is found most frequently in 3-year-old stories, but almost always for a single function: to indicate an action that can be inferred from a visible, depicted endstate rather than an action with no immediate pictured support. Thus, in the examples in (11), climbing and breaking can be inferred from the pictured situations of the boy in the tree (Picture 11) and the broken glass (Picture 7):

(11a) *Aquí se ha subido.*

   'Here he has climbed.' [*S3a-3;6*]

(11b) *Aquí se ha roto lo de la rana.*

   'Here the frog's (thing) has broken.' [*S3i-3;10*]

This pattern is repeated in the 4-year-old group, but beginning with age 5, children also begin to use the present perfect for situations which are not depicted but can be inferred from preceding situations:

(12a) *Y el niño se tapa la nariz **porque le ha mordido este bicho.***

   'And the boy covers his nose **because this rat has bitten him.**' [*S5i-5;11*]

(12b) *Y cuando se despierta el niño se encuentra que **se ha ido.***

'And when the boy wake up he finds that **(she) has gone away.**' [*S5c-5;4*]

Neither of these two actions reported in the present perfect actually appears in the pictures, but they can be inferred on the basis of depictions of their consequences (the boy's expression and posture for (12a) and the empty jar for (12b)). These consequences are not obvious endstates, as in (11), but rather require acts of interpretation. We can interpret that the gopher has bitten the boy because in Picture 10 he covers his nose, with a startled expression. Similarly, we can infer that the frog has gone away because it no longer appears in Picture 3. Note that mention of the disappearance of the frog could also be made with a negation of her existence, *no está* '(she) is not (there)', an option that is frequently taken in Spanish. That is, many perfects of completive verbs (*se ha ido/escapado* 'has gone away/escaped') are the equivalent of negated presents of noncompletive verbs. In the opinion of some authors (e.g., Fernández-Ramírez, 1986) this can be taken as additional evidence of the present orientation of the perfect.

Nine-year-olds use the present perfect retrospectively as well, to bring a past action back onto the scene to motivate or explain the current situation, as in the following example, where the action of the bees in Picture 12 is motivated by the dog's actions in Pictures 9 and 10.

(13) *Y luego - entonces se van todas las abejas en busca del perro **porque les ha tirado el panal.***

'And afterwards - then all of the bees go looking for the dog **because he has knocked down their hive.**' [*S9h-9;8*]

What we see developmentally, then, is an expansion of the temporal distance between a completed past situation and the current state of affairs at utterance (=narrative) time, along with more indirect means of linking the two situations into a single time frame "for which a claim is being made."

Past Perfect. The past perfect always plays a clearly retrospective function, beginning with its first uses at age 4. The form is absent in 3-year-old narrations, perhaps due to the fact that it requires attention to three temporal points — speech time, reference time, event time — and, as Weist (1986) has suggested, this poses difficulties for children younger than 4. There are some 4-year-old uses of the past perfect to refer to an immediately preceding change of state in past-tense narratives, parallel to uses of the present perfect in present-tense narratives, as in (14):

(14) *Y el ubo estaba en el agujero que **había subido el niño**.*

'And the owl was in the hole that **the boy had climbed to**.' [*S4k-4;10*]

Towards the end of the preschool period there are more mature uses of the past perfect to indicate **narrative retrospection**, i.e., to refer to a temporally distant prior event that is relevant to the current point in the plot, as in (15):

(15) *El niño buscaba a ver si se **había metido por ahí**.*

'The boy searched to see if **(the frog) had hidden herself over there**.' [*S5h-5;9*]

Switches from the **present tense** to the past perfect are also used for the expression of current relevance of a past event, beginning at age 9:

(16) *Y ve a el perro disgustado **porque se había roto el vaso de cristal**.*

'And (he) looks disgustedly at the dog **because the glass jar had broken**.' [*S9e-9;6*]

Younger children very rarely switch from present tense to past perfect, preferring to switch from present into present perfect or from past into past perfect. However, 9-year-olds are able to switch from present tense into both present and past perfect to indicate past actions whose repercussions are in some way included in the present.

Although the present perfect is absent from colloquial speech in Chilean and Argentinian Spanish, the past perfect is used in those dialects. Table 3 shows the numbers of children using the past perfect once or more in each of the three Spanish language samples, where the Latin American data give us an additional developmental point at age 7. The past perfect begins to make its appearance at ages 4 and 5 in Spain and in Chile, and by age 7 it is frequently used in both Chile and Argentina.

TABLE 3
Number of Children Using Past Perfect at Least Once
(N = 12)

Country	Age				
	3yrs	4 yrs	5 yrs	7 yrs	9 yrs
Spain	0	3	2	-	6
Chile	0	1	3	8	9
Argentina	0	0	0	5	8

The 7-year-old data in Bocaz's Latin American sample show fully mature uses of the past perfect to present a series of activities seen as anterior to narrative reference time in past-tense narratives. In the following example the narrator felicitously switches from an account of the dog's activities in the perfective to relate the activities of the boy in the past perfect, as shown Pictures 9-11.

(17) *De repente el perro subió más, y salieron unas abejas. Claro que le fue peor al niño, **porque le había salido la ardilla y le había mordido la nariz**. Y después al perro se le cayó el panal, y salieron todas las abejas.*

'Suddenly the dog climbed:PFV more, and some bees came.out:PFV. Of course things went:PFV worse for the boy, **because the mole had come.out:PAST.PERF at him and had bitten:PAST.PERF him on the nose**. And then (unhappily for) the dog, the beehive fell:PFV and all of the bees came.out:PFV.' [cS7j-7;6]

Although the activities of the dog and the boy are depicted as simultaneous, the narrator has located reference time with respect to the dog and must backtrack to bring the listener up-to-date with regard to the boy. Clearly, by this age, the story proceeds in narrative time. As Slobin and Bocaz point out (1988, p. 14): "It seems evident that the acquisition of the past perfect reflects an emerging sense of narrative organization. It does not come to be widely used until after age 7, when children show evidence of a sense of plot in their narrations."

1.2.3. Perfective/imperfective aspect

Beginning with the youngest narrators, contrasts between perfective and imperfective are frequent and well-motivated. Three-year-olds use the perfective to indicate completed actions and the imperfective to indicate states or durative events, as in the following examples:

(18) *El perro se **acercó** a la ventana, **descansaba** - no se **levantaba**. Se **cayó**.*

The dog **approached**:PFV *the window*, **rested**:IPFV- **didn't get.up**:IPFV. **Fell**:PFV.' [S3b-3;6]

(19) *Aquí es que **buscaban** a la rana. Aquí que lo **encontraron**.*

'Here it is that they **looked.for**:IPFV the frog. Here that they **found**:PFV it.' [S3k-3;11]

By around age 5, these contrasts begin to serve narrative "grounding" functions, with perfective serving to encode plot-advancing events and imperfective used for various kinds of background. An early kind of backgrounding is already evident in some 4-year-old past-tense narratives, where the imperfective is (correctly) used for enduring physical states, inner states, and conditions of modality, as in the following example:

(20) *El perrito quería coger la piña [=panal] pero como era tan pequeño no la podía coger.*

'The doggie **wanted**:IPFV to get the pinecone [=beehive] but since he **was**:IPFV so small he **could**:IPFV not get (it).' [*S4a-4;1*]

The following example, from a 5-year-old, shows mature use of aspectual contrasts in the past tense, building up a situation by use of imperfective and past progressive and then moving the action forward in the perfective:

(21) *El perro quería coger el tarro de miel que estaba colgado en el árbol. El niño veía un agujero, y estaba llamando por el agujero. Salió la rata, y el niño se puso la mano en la nariz. Dijo "¡uy!"*

'The dog **wanted**:IPFV to get the pot of honey that **was**:IPFV hung in the tree. The boy **saw**:IPFV a hole, and **was calling**:IPFV.PROG into the hole. A rat **came.out**:PFV and the boy **put**:PFV his hand on his nose. (He) **said**:PFV "uy!" [*S5d-5;4*]

By age 5, aspectual marking is no longer determined by the Aktionsart of the verb, as at earlier ages. This child not only uses *llamar* 'call' in the past progressive, as in the above example, but also in the perfective, to indicate a single act of calling:

(22) *Salió de su casa y llamó a la rana.*

'(He) **left**:PFV his house and **called**:PFV the frog.' [*S5d-5;4*]

Especially interesting is aspectual variation of the verb *ver* 'see'. Spanish distinguishes between the bounded seeing of a momentary event, in the perfective, and the unbounded seeing of a state or process, in the imperfective. This child appropriately notes these contrasts. In (21), seeing a hole, the verb is given in the imperfective *veía*. The same form is used for witnessing a process. Picture 6 shows the dog in mid-fall, and both the fall and the boy's perception are appropriately described in the imperfective:

(23) *El niño veía que se caía el perro.*

'The boy **saw**:IPFV that the dog **fell**:IPFV.' [*S5d-5;4*]

However, elsewhere in the same text, the acts of seeing are momentary, and appropriately perfective. In (24) he sees (=realizes) that the frog is gone; in (25) he sees (=catches sight of) the runaway frog:

(24) *El perro miró para abajo, y vió que no estaba la rana.*

'The dog **looked**:PFV down, and **saw**:PFV that the frog **was**:IPFV not (there).' [*S5d-5;4*]

(25) *Se subieron por un tronco del árbol. Allí* **vieron** *a la rana que se escapó, al padre y a la madre.*

'They climbed:PFV over a tree trunk. There they **saw**:PFV the frog that escaped:PFV, the father and the mother.' [*S5d-5;4*]

Thus, by age 5, the Spanish-speaking child can take different perspectives on events described by the same verbs, flexibly using aspect to indicate an event **construal** independent of the inherent lexical semantics of the verb.

An additional function of aspectual contrasts — in both present and past tenses — is to indicate that events with two different temporal contours are occurring simultaneously. This issue is discussed, with a number of examples, in Chapter IVA, Section 5.2.1, and Chapter VB discusses implications for language and cognition.[3] To cite one example here, the following contrast between perfective and imperfective indicates that the two events are to be construed as overlapping in time:

(26) *Se* **cayó** *el niño y le* **perseguían** *al perro las avispas.*

'The boy **fell**:PFV and the wasps **chased**:IPFV the dog.' [*S5f-5;7*]

1.3. Lexical Aspect

In addition to its rich system of aspectual morphology on the verb, Spanish can also mark aspectual distinctions by means of other devices. Here we examine the use of **particles** with aspectual functions, **aspectual verbs**, and **aspectual adverbs**.

1.3.1. A particle with aspectual value: The reflexive se

Spanish, being a verb-framed language, does not have aspectual particles such as English *eat* **up**. However, **reflexive** verb morphology provides an additional means of indicating aspect in Spanish. For example, the reflexive version of various change of state verbs indicates inception of the state, as in *sentar-se* 'seat-self' (=sit down) and *levantar-se* 'raise-self' (=stand/get up). For such verbs, the inceptive reflexive contrasts with the stative participle — e.g., *se sentó* 'REFL sit:PFV' (=sat down) versus *estaba sentado* 'be:IPFV sit:PAST.PART' (=was seated). Note that the nonreflexive forms correspond more to descriptions of pictured situations than of events and, accordingly, these forms are more frequent in the younger texts, whereas older narrators make more use of reflexive forms. The following examples of stative descriptions by means of participles are typical of 3- and 4-year-old uses. Some of

---

[3] Also see Bocaz (1989c) for an analysis of the marking of simultaneity in the Latin American samples.

these uses are verbless, consisting of a "pure description," sometimes even using the participle of a verb of motion such as *subir* 'ascend', as in (27a).

(27a) *Y aquí el niño subido en un árbol.*

'And here the boy **ascend**:PAST.PART (="mounted") in a tree.' [*S3g-3;8*]

(27b) *El niño está ahí sentado en una banqueta.*

'The boy is there **seated** on a stool.' [*S4b-4;1*]

(27c) *Está dormido en la cama.*

'(He) is **asleep** in the bed.' [*S4i-4;7*]

The reflexive has another function in addition to indicating change of state. Some verbs acquire a more perfective or completive sense when they are marked with the reflexive particle. For example, the sentence *Alex se bebió la leche* 'Alex **REFL** drink:PFV the milk' corresponds to the English *Alex drank up the milk*, whereas the nonreflexive version corresponds to *Alex drank (some of) the milk*. This additional nuance has narrative consequences — particularly evident with regard to verbs of motion in the frog story. For most such verbs the reflexive is optional; for example, our texts have instances of both *subir* 'ascend' and *subirse* 'ascend:REFL', *bajar* and *bajarse* 'descend', *caer* and *caerse* 'fall'. In narrative discourse, the reflexive form takes on an additional meaning of "narrative completion," in that the speaker is about to switch to a different topic, phase, or perspective point in the narrative. For example, in the following two segments the 9-year-old narrator uses *subir* in both forms. In (28a) he goes on to evaluate the purpose of climbing, therefore using the nonreflexive form, while in (28b) he switches reference from the dog to the boy, using the reflexive to close off the climbing event as not part of the event reported in the following clause.

(28a) *El niño se protege del buho y sube a unas ramas para llamar a la rana.*

'The boy protects himself from the owl and **climbs** to some branches to call the frog.' [*S9l-9;11*]

(28b) *El perro se sube encima del niño, y el niño escucha un sonido.*

'The dog **climbs**:REFL on top of the boy, and the boy hears a sound.' [*S9l-9;11*]

This is a particularly nice example of a discursively oriented extension of perfectivity, here marked on a present-tense verb, to indicate that one event is — for narrative purposes — "over and done with." Similar oppositions of reflexive/nonreflexive verbs of motion also occur in past-tense narratives, adding a dimension of "super-perfectivity" to verbs that are already inflected in the past perfective. Developmentally, it appears that even 3-year-olds show some differentiated use of reflexive and nonreflexive forms. There are only isolated infelicitous uses of a reflexive form of a verb of motion in a main clause followed by a subordinate clause that adds further information about the event. One might speculate that the central role of perfectivity in the inflectional system makes that notion more available for discourse purposes, attracting additional means of indicating perfectivity even in a present-tense narrative. That is, as discussed in Chapter VB, the language appears to guide the learner's attention to a particular semantic domain, by means of regular grammatical marking of that domain. In addition, because Spanish is a verb-framed language, the means for expressing a salient dimension are drawn from within the system of verbal marking — in this case, extending the use of the reflexive.

1.3.2. Aspectual verbs

Aspectual verbs are not used with great frequency during the preschool period, perhaps due to the richness of aspectual marking in verbal morphology. Children of all ages use **inchoatives** (*ponerse* 'become', *empezar* 'start') and **protractives** (*quedarse* 'remain', *seguir* 'continue'), but only adults use **cumulatives** (*llegar hasta/a* 'reach') and **completives** (*acabar* 'finish'). Table 4 shows that there is a developmental increase in the percentage of verbs that fall into these categories as well as an increase in the lexical diversity of the category.

TABLE 4
Development of Aspectual Verbs

	3yrs	4 yrs	Age 5 yrs	9 yrs	Adult
Percent of aspectual verbs (out of total verbs used)	0.2	0.5	0.9	5.2	8.0
No. of types	2	4	4	7	16

As shown in the table, children younger than 9 rarely use aspectual verbs, limiting their aspectual expression to verb morphology and, as described in the next section, aspectual adverbs. Of the aspectual verbs that are used in the preschool period, 70% are inchoatives, especially *empezar* 'start', along with some instances of verbs that indicate temporal extent of an activity or event, such as *seguir* 'continue'.

Inchoative verbs mark the onset or entry into a state or situation: *empezó a llorar* 'started to cry'. However, the examples of inchoatives in our texts are more frequently used to mark the beginning of a series of events rather than a single event. This is particularly evident beginning with age 5, where an inchoative is first used to indicate the beginning of the search. Marking of episode onset is the major function of inchoatives for the 9-year-olds and adults. Examples from all three ages are given below.

(29a) *Empezó a buscar y a buscar, dijo "rana."*

'(He) started to search and to search, said "frog."' [*S5b-5;2*]

(29b) *Entonces el niño sale al jardín y empieza a llamar a la rana.*

'Then the boy goes out to the garden and starts to call the frog.' [*S9e-9;5*]

(29c) *Salen al bosque, empiezan a llamar a la rana, la rana no aparece.*

'(They) go out to the woods, start to call the frog, the frog doesn't appear.' [*S20b*]

For adults, inchoative verbs are the main means of indicating transitions in the plot, as opposed to the heavy use of sequentials such as *luego, entonces* 'then' in the preschool texts. Furthermore, adults segment the plot into larger units, therefore having less need to mark sequence between what are, essentially, subevents. It is interesting to note that when 9-year-olds begin to use inchoatives in a mature, **prospective** function — pointing ahead to the next series of events in the plot — they often anchor themselves as well in sequential markers, as in the example cited above in (29b): '**Then** the boy goes out to the garden **and starts** to call the frog.'

The other frequent type of aspectual verb, as noted above, marks an activity or event as extended in time. Nine-year-olds begin to use the verb *seguir* 'continue' to refer to activities that span several episodes or even the entire plot, and this verb is used with great frequency in the adult texts. We noted in Section 1.2.1 that 9-year-olds use progressive aspect on verbs whose action is maintained throughout the story, such as *buscar* 'search' and *llamar* 'call'. To this device is added the use of aspectual verbs, as shown in (30):

(30) *Sigue buscando y se sube a una piedra.*

'(He) continues searching and climbs a rock.' [*S9a-9;1*]

The use of *seguir* with an accompanying verb does not appear until age 9, when it is used by seven of the 12 narrators[4]. Eleven of the twelve adults use this construction — with greater frequency and diversity of contexts, indicating more mature narrative organization, as discussed in Chapter IVD.

---

[4] The only preschool uses of *seguir* are as a main verb indicating a continuing condition — e.g., *Y el perro todavía sigue con el cubo en la cabeza* 'And the dog still continues with the block on his head' [*S4f-4;7*].

1.3.3. Aspectual adverbs

The developmental picture is quite different when we turn to the use of aspectual adverbs. These are much more frequent than aspectual verbs in the preschool period, especially the adverb *ya* 'already'. Three-year-olds frequently add this adverb to the present perfect, as if to emphasize the completive aspect of a state or process. This is especially frequent in "blow-by-blow" descriptions of the stages of an event, as in the following examples:

(31a) *Y entonces el perro está encontrando al niño que estaba en las piedras encima y entonces ya lo ha encontrado.*

'And then the dog is finding the boy who was:IPFV up on the rocks and then he has found:PRES.PERF him **already**.' [S3d-3;8]

(31b) *Aquí que se caen los dos al agua aquí ... Aquí que ya se han caído. Aquí que están en el agua.*

'Here that (they) fall:PRES the two of them to the water here ... Here that (they) have fallen:PRES.PERF **already**. Here that (they) are:PRES in the water.' [S3i-3;10]

The 3-year-olds use *ya* more than any other age group, with 21 instances in comparison with only seven for the 9-year-olds and three for the adults. The drop in frequency after age 3 is also evident in comparing the percentage of clauses at each age containing *ya*: 3 — 4.2%, 4 — 1.1%, 5 — 1.0%, 9 — 1.0%, adult — 0.5%. This early overuse of the adverb of the perfect suggests that 3-year-olds, when using the present perfect verb construction, are probably orienting to aspectual rather than temporal characteristics of events, using *ya* to indicate an aspectual contrast between resultant states and ongoing processes (cf. early uses in Turkish of the nonwitnessed past *-miş*, as discussed in Chapter IIIE).

Older speakers use *ya* to indicate the temporal point of view of a **narrator**. These uses are retrospective, bringing the listener "up-to-date" with regard to the result of a past situation. Note also that *ya* is not tied to the present perfect, but occurs in these examples with the present and the imperfective. It is not a redundant reinforcer of the present perfect, but rather serves an independent narrative function.

(32a) *La colmena se cae. Entonces el perro mira hacia atrás, y el niño ya no está en el agujero sino que se ha subido a un árbol.*

'The hive falls. Then the dog looks back, and the boy is **already** not (=no longer) at the hole, but has climbed a tree.' [S9c-9;3]

(32b) *Y miran y ven [...] a la rana que se le había escapado, con un macho y a muchos hijitos que ya tenían.*

'And (they) look and see [...] the frog that had run away from them, with a male and many children that they **already** had:IPFV.' [*S9f-9;6*]

Another frequent aspectual adverb in the 3- and 4-year-old texts is *otra vez* 'again', marking **recurrence**. Its high frequency at this age can be attributed to its use to refer to a situation that appears in more than one picture. This use disappears in the texts of older narrators, who understand that the sequence of pictures represent a continuing situation rather than a series of independent occurrences with new protagonists. Thus, for example, a 4-year-old treats the owl in Picture 13 as a new owl, in contrast to the owl in Picture 12:

(33) *Entonces aquí otra vez sale un buho*

'Then here **again** an owl comes out.' [*S4e-4;6*]

A frequent form beginning at age 9 is *mientras (tanto)* 'meanwhile' (14 instances at age 9, 26 in adult texts). It is used to relate ongoing activities and simultaneous events, as discussed in Chapter IVA. Mature narrators use this form to switch from one simultaneous event to the other, establishing a narrative boundary between the two events, as in the following example from a 9-year-old:

(34) *Y el perro va a la casa de abejas, y le salen todas las abejas y van detrás de él. El niño **mientras** busca por un árbol a ver si está.*

'And the dog goes to the house of the bees, and all of the bees come out at him and go after him. The boy **meanwhile** searches in a tree to see if (she) is (there).' [*S9a-9;1*]

In summary, the youngest children do not seem to have any difficulty in using adverbial constructions with aspectual meanings, especially those that indicate result or repetition. However, the heavy use of verbal aspectual morphology may minimize the need for the use of such adverbs in Spanish. Nine-year-olds seem more comfortable with aspectual verbs, rather than adverbs, and the range and functions of such verbs increase by adulthood. It is characteristic of older narrators to use inchoative verbs, such as *empezar* 'start', to refer to the beginning of a series of events, or episode, rather than to a single event. The segmentation of the narrative into episodes makes it less necessary to link each individual event to the next. As a result, there is a notable decrease with age in elements for "chaining" one clause to the next, as discussed in Section 4.

2. EVENT CONFLATION: MOTION AND LOCATION

As outlined in Chapter III0, Spanish is a **verb-framed** language, along with Hebrew and Turkish, in contrast to the two **satellite-framed** languages in our sample, English and German. This distinction, proposed by Leonard Talmy (1985, 1991), is especially clear with regard to Spanish verbs of motion — indeed, Talmy has used this semantic domain of Spanish to demonstrate prototypical characteristics of a verb-framed language. Consider his example of descriptions of a bottle floating out of a cave, comparing English and Spanish:

(35a) *The bottle floated out of the cave.*

(35b) *La botella salió flotando de la cueva.*

'The bottle exited floating of the cave.'

In English, a satellite to the verb, *out*, conveys the core information of the path of movement, whereas in Spanish it is the verb itself, *salir* 'exit', that conveys this information. Supporting information about the manner of movement is conveyed by the verb in English and by the gerund *flotando* in Spanish. These patterns are quite pervasive in the two languages (with the exception of the use of Latinate verbs of motion in English). Thus English has a large collection of verbs of motion which convey manner, but not directionality (*walk, run, crawl, fly*, etc.), combinable with a large collection of satellites (*in, up to, across*, etc.). Spanish prefers verbs of inherent directionality (*entrar* 'enter', *salir* 'exit', *subir* 'ascend', *bajar* 'descend', etc.). The same typological contrast applies to verbs of caused motion; compare, for example, English *put, push, shove, squeeze* ... + *in* and Spanish *meter* 'insert'.

As a consequence of these typological differences, Spanish has a relatively small set of verbs of motion and caused motion, in comparison with English and German. The following is the total list of such verbs used in all 60 texts from Spain, including periphrastic forms:

(36) *acercarse* 'approach', *alcanzar* 'reach', *arrojar* 'throw', *bajar(se)* 'descend', *caer(se)* 'fall', *correr* 'run', *dar-un-empujón* 'give-a-push', *dar-un-salto* 'give-a-jump', *entrar* 'enter', *escapar(se)* 'escape', *hacer-caer* 'make-fall', *huir* 'flee', *ir(se)* 'go (away)', *llegar* 'arrive', *llevar(se)* 'carry (off)', *marchar(se)* 'go (away)', *meter-se* 'insert-oneself', *nadar* 'swim', *perseguir* 'chase', *poner-se* 'put-oneself', *regresar* 'return', *sacar-se* 'remove-oneself', *salir* 'exit', *saltar* 'jump', *subir(se)* 'ascend', *tirar* 'throw', *traspasar* 'go.over', *venir* 'come', *volar(se)* 'fly (away)', *volver(se)* 'return'.

There are 27 verb types listed in (36), compared with 47 in English (Chapter IIIA) and 44 in German (Chapter IIIB). In fact, however, the number of verb types is considerably greater in English and German, due to the many types of verb+satellite combinations. There are 123 such types listed for English in Chapter IIIA (e.g., *climb + down, on, out, over, up, up in, up on*).

In addition to the small list of rather general verbs of motion, locative prepositions in Spanish are also few and general in meaning. The most frequent in the frog stories are the goal-marker *a*, the source-marker *de*, and the locative *en* — all taking their more specific meanings in combination with particular verbs plus world knowledge. For example, the directional preposition *a* corresponds to motion *to, toward, into, onto*, as in *llevar a un precipicio* 'carry *a* a cliff', *caerse al agua* 'fall *a* the water', *subir a un árbol* 'ascend *a* a tree', *subir a una piedra* 'ascend *a* a rock'.

As a consequence of these typological factors, we find that, overall, Spanish frog stories have less information about the details of paths and manners of motion. Manner is rarely attended to, at any age. Narration of path, however, shows an interesting developmental pattern, characterized by two main phases and a possible intervening phase for some children.

Phase 1. Young children describe a change of location with a simple verb alone, or with the addition of one prepositional phrase, specifying either source or goal, as in the following examples:

(37) **ascend**:

(a) *Se ha subido.*

  'He has ascended' [tree]. *[S3f-3;8]*

(b) *El niño se sube al árbol.*

  'The boy ascends to the tree.' *[S3a-3;6]*

(38) **descend**:

(a) *Se cayó.*

  '(He) fell' [window]. *[S3b-3;6]*

(b) *Se ha caído el perro de por la ventana.*

  'The dog has fallen from through the window.' [Note this child's groping for the appropriate preposition.] *[S3g-3;8]*

(c) *Le tiró.*

  '(He) threw him' [water]. *[S3l-3;11]*

(d) *Le va a tirar al agua.*

  '(He) is going to throw him to the water.' *[S3f-3;8]*

Similar examples could be given for 'enter' and 'exit'. Half of the preschoolers follow such patterns, as do many 9-year-olds and adults as well. Sparseness of path description is characteristic of Spanish generally, as discussed below.

Phase 2. The other half of the preschoolers sometimes add more detail by the use of directional locative adverbs. Although we do not have longitudinal data, we would like to suggest that this phase reflects a U-shaped developmental curve — that is, we propose that some Spanish-speaking preschoolers may attempt to provide more information about paths of motion than is generally found in the language. (It is, of course, possible that these two groups of children represent two different types of individual style, rather than a developmental sequence, or even that locative elaboration is an earlier phase. Further research is needed.)

There are four directional adverbs in our data: *arriba* 'upwards', *abajo* 'downwards', *dentro* 'inwards', and *encima* 'topwards' (=onto an upper surface). Table 5 shows the use of these adverbs by age:

TABLE 5
Number of Locative Adverbs Used with Verbs of Motion,
by Age and Number of Narrators

Adverb	Age				
	3yrs	4 yrs	5 yrs	9 yrs	Adult
arriba 'upwards'		3			
abajo 'downwards'	1	2	3		
dentro 'inwards'	4	6	1		4
encima 'topwards'	8	4	7	5	2
Total occurrences	13	15	11	5	6
No. of narrators	6	6	5	3	5
Mean no. of adverbs/narrator	1.2	1.8	1.8	1.0	1.0

As can be seen in the table, there are somewhat more narrators per age group who use these adverbs in the preschool period than at later ages, and the preschoolers use more types of adverbs and with greater frequency. The fact that 4- and 5-year-olds use a somewhat greater mean number of adverbs per narrator (1.8) than 3-year-olds (1.2) might support our suggestion of U-shaped development. The 9-year-olds use only *encima* 'topwards', most frequently for the unusual situation of the dog climbing onto the boy's head in Picture 19 (a clearly noncanonical kind of ascent, calling for special mention). The most frequent adult use is *dentro* 'inwards', describing the dog's entry into the jar, along with the verb *meter(se)* 'insert (oneself)' (clearly another kind of noncanonical change of location).

By contrast, the preschoolers tend to use directional adverbs redundantly, reinforcing the meaning of the associated verb of motion (just as they make redundant use of the adverb *ya* 'already' along with present perfect verbs forms, as discussed above). The following examples are characteristic:

(39a) *Sube por **arriba** por el tronco.*

'(He) ascends along **upwards** along the trunk.' [*S4c-4;4*]

(39b) *Se cayó **encima** del - de - del - del agua ... **encima**.*

'(He) fell **on.top** of.the - of - of.the - of.the water ... **on.top**.' [Note hesitations and repetition.] [*S5e-5;4*]

(39c) *Entonces **abajo** ... se cayó.*

'Then **downwards** ... (he) fell.' [*S4e-4;6*]

Other uses in this "Phase 2" group are not redundant, but are more elaborate than is typical of the speech of older narrators, e.g.,:

(40) *El perro se cae - por la ventana baja con la cabeza dentro.*

'The dog falls - through the window downwards with his head inside [the jar].' [*S4k-4;10*]

Such uses suggest that these children feel a need to "reinforce" the directional meaning inherent in the verb of motion.

Phase 3. There are two major changes after age 5 in our data, in addition to the decreased use of directional adverbs shown in Table 5. Both of these changes reflect an increasing tendency to provide information outside of the motion descriptions provided by verbs and adverbs. One change is towards increased specification of source or goal, and the other is towards increased static locative description.

As shown in (37) and (38), preschoolers sometimes indicate source or goal by the use of prepositional phrases. About half of the motion descriptions have such specification in the preschool period, whereas 9-year-olds and adults specify source/goal about 62% of the time.[5] Thus there is some increase with age, but this is not the most important development. In fact, Spanish narrators of all ages almost never specify both source and goal with regard to a single verb, by contrast to the frequency of this pattern in English

---

[5] These figures are considerably lower than in English, where 5-year-olds provide source/goal specification in prepositional phrases about 60% of the time, as do 9-year-olds, and adults do so 82% of the time. The development is thus earlier in English and the end point is higher than in Spanish. Even at the mature level of artistic fiction, novelists writing in Spanish provide much less information about paths of movement than do novelists writing in English (Slobin, in press-c). Slobin interprets this striking difference in terms of differing typological constraints on motion description.

and German. There are only two such instances in our entire Spanish corpus of 60 stories, and in the Latin American corpus of 156 stories there is only a single occurrence of a clause that mentions both source and goal in relation to a verb. Such patterns are highly accessible in satellite-framed languages, as discussed in earlier chapters. However, Spanish grammar does not allow compact descriptions such as English *He tips him off over a cliff into the water* [*E9k-9;11*]. (For possible explanations see Aske, 1989; Slobin, in press-c.)

Proficient Spanish narrators make use of other means of presenting paths of motion. Rather than encode every segment of the path itself, the characteristic strategy is to devote more attention to setting the stage, allowing the directional verbs of motion to describe a general change of location. With these two types of information — static and dynamic — the listener can infer the path details that are specified in the satellites of a satellite-framed language. Thus a language like English or German, with rich means for path description, can often leave setting to be inferred, while a language like Spanish, with its sparser path possibilities, often relies on descriptions of settings, leaving paths to be inferred. For example, the English path description quoted above allows one to infer that the cliff is located above the water. This information is often specifically provided in Spanish narratives, as in the following examples, from all three countries.

(41a) *Los tiró a un precipicio donde había harta agua. Entonces se cayeron.*

'(He) threw them at a cliff where there was lots of water. Then they fell.' [*cS7e-7;4*]

(41b) *El ciervo le llevó hasta un sitio, donde debajo había un río. Entonces el ciervo tiró al perro y al niño al río. Y después cayeron.*

'The deer took him until a place, where below there was a river. Then the deer threw the dog and the boy to the river. And then they fell.' [*S9b-9;2*]

(41c) *Lo tiró. Por suerte, abajo, estaba el río. El niño cayó en el agua.*

'(He) threw him. Luckily, below, was the river. The boy fell in the water.' [*aS11k-11;8*]

While only 8% of the Madrid 5-year-olds provide this sort of static description of the location of the cliff and the water, 42% of the 9-year-olds do so (in comparison with 8% at both ages in English). Thus the verb-framed typology of Spanish has implications not only for the use of descriptions of motion but also descriptions of locations. On the level of rhetorical or narrative style, accordingly, such typological factors contribute to differences in the allocation of attention to elements of setting and action (as discussed in a crosslinguistic perspective in Chapter VB).

3. PERSPECTIVE

The main devices available to child narrators for manipulating perspective are variations in word order and in valence, discussed in the next two sections. At the level of the clause, Spanish has considerable freedom in word order, surpassed only by Turkish in our sample, as indicated in Table 1 of Chapter III0. (However, in the frog stories it appears that Spanish is on a par with Turkish in this regard.) At the level of verb-argument structure, reflexive morphology allows for detransitivizing of many of the change of state verbs in the frog story, while past participles allow for stativization. The availability of these two types of perspective shift minimizes the need for passive sentences. Although they are present in some adult texts, they represent a written register and are not considered in our developmental presentation.

3.1. Word Order

Although Spanish has traditionally been treated as a language with standard SVO word order, it allows for a broad range of different orders, especially in connected discourse such as narrative. Although there is no case-marking, person/number marking on the verb generally allows for subject identification and clitic object pronouns allow for preposing of definite and indefinite objects. In syntactic terms, Spanish allows for what Rizzi (1982) characterizes as "free inversion." Nevertheless, inversion is not as free or easy as it might seem. Torrego (1984) has noted that, in addition to free inversion, subject inversion is obligatory in certain *qu-* (wh-) constructions, offering examples such as:

(42) *¿Qué querían esos dos?   *¿Qué esos dos querían?*

      what want:IPFV those two

      'What did those two want?'

      *¿Con quién vendrá Juan hoy?   *¿Con quién Juan vendrá hoy?*

      with who come:FUT Juan today

      'Who will Juan come with today?'

Furthermore, Contreras (1978) has demonstrated that certain sentences that have been treated as stylistic variations of one another are neither semantically nor syntactically equivalent. Thus, although Spanish is a language with a great degree of freedom in word order, there are obviously various types of restrictions. Having pointed this out, we move on to analyze our data with regard to word order.

In the first place, consider syntactically-determined deviations from standard SVO word order. The lack of expletive subjects in Spanish frequently obliges narrators to begin the story with an inverted order. (The only alterna-tive — often taken by the youngest children — is to simply begin by naming the protagonists, with no explicit predicate at all.) The following are typical examples of inversion in introducing protagonists:

(43a) *Estaba el perro con una rana.*

> was the dog with a frog (='There was the dog with a frog.') [*S4l-4;10*]

(43b) *Primero era el amigo de un niño, luego había un perro y luego había una rana*

> first was the friend of a boy, then existed[6] a dog and then existed a frog (='First there was a boy's friend, then there was a dog and then there was a frog.') [*S5b-5;2*]

(43c)*Es un niño y un perro que tienen una rana.*

> is a boy and a dog that have a frog (='It/there is a boy and a dog that have a frog.') [*S9k-9;11*]

Standard formulaic introductions also require inversion:

(44) *Había una vez un niño un perrito y una rana.*

> existed one time a boy a dog and a frog (='Once there was a boy a dog and a frog.') [*S4a-4;1*]

The appearance of a protagonist in the course of a story is often marked with "presentatives" (see Section 3.2 of Chapter IIID for similar constructions in Hebrew). Narrators of all ages make frequent use of the verb *salir* 'exit/come.out' for this purpose. Note that the subject always follows the verb and that the verb can be preceded by temporal and locative adverbs (45b-e) and by clitic object pronouns (45e).

(45a) *Y salen las moscas.*

> 'And come.out the flies.' [*S3b-3;6*]

(45b) *Y luego salió el pájaro.*

> 'And then came.out the bird.' [*S4d-4;5*]

(45c) *Y de aquí salen todas éstas.*

> 'And from here come.out all of these.' [*S5k-5;5*]

(45d) *Del agujero sale como una especie de ratón.*

---

[6] The verb *haber*, formerly a verb of possession and now a grammatical element, functions both as an auxiliary in the present and past perfect and as an existential: *hay* 'there is/are', *había* 'there was/were'. We gloss this usage here as 'existed'.

'From the hole comes.out a sort of kind of rat.' [S9c-9;3]

(45e) *De ese árbol le sale un buho.*

'From that tree to.him comes.out an owl.' [S20g]

In these instances, it would not be ungrammatical to use SVO word order, but the discourse pragmatic function of presentation would be lost.

Similar to the use of *salir* to introduce protagonists, a preposed negative existential "introduces" the absence of a protagonist and a preposed verb of 'escape' "introduces" the disappearance of a protagonist. This is, of course, the motivating element at the beginning of the story, and, again, this sort of inversion is found across the age range:

(46a) *Y vió el nene en el día y no estaba la rana.*

and saw the boy in the day and not was the frog (='And the boy saw in the daytime and the frog was not there.') [aS3g-3;7][7]

(46b) *Y entonces no estaba la rana.*

and then not was the frog (='And then the frog was not there.) [S4e-4;6]

(46c) *Y vió que no estaba la rana.*

and saw that not was the frog (='And saw that the frog was not there.') [S5d-5;4]

(46d) *Un día por la noche se escapó la rana.*

one day at night escaped the frog (='One day, in the night-time, the frog escaped.') [S9g-9;6]

(46e) *Cuando llega la mañana, se levanta el chiquito, ¡qué sorpresa! Estaba el perro pero no estaba la rana.*

when comes morning, gets up the little boy — what a surprise! was the dog but not was the frog (='When morning comes, the little boy gets up — what a surprise! The dog was there but the frog was not there.') [aS20c]

Another syntactically determined deviation from SVO word order is the obligatory preverbal position of clitic object pronouns.[8] This is mastered by children younger than our 3-year-olds and is appropriately used for topic

---

[7] We have used an Argentinian example here because none of the Madrid 3-year-olds referred to the absence of the frog, and those that referred to her escape presented this information in non-inverted order, as a statement about the action of the frog rather than a presentation of the escape (e.g., *La rana salió del bote* 'The frog exited from the jar' [S3b-3;6]).

[8] The only exception is optional postposing of the pronoun in periphrastic constructions with the gerund; e.g., *la estuvieron buscando* 'OBJ.PRO be:PFV:PL searching' / *estuvieron buscándo-la* 'be:PFV:PL searching-OBJ.PRO' (=they were searching for her).

maintenance, as in the following example from the youngest child in the Madrid sample:

(47) *Y entonces el perro se cae con la botella. Y el niño se asoma en la ventana ... y luego aquí, luego le coge el niño.*

'And then the dog falls with the bottle. And the boy appears in the window ... and then here, then **him** picks.up the boy.' [*S3a-3;6*]

This construction also allows for postposing, or "copying" the object NP in an oblique phrase with the proposition *a* 'to', e.g.,:

(48) *Aquí el buho le ha tirado - del árbol al niño.*

here the owl **him** has thrown - from the tree **to.the boy** (='Here the owl has thrown him from the tree, the boy.') [*S3g-3;8*]

Combining these two means of object marking gives Spanish the functional equivalent of the English passive without the morphological complexity of changing the voice of the verb.[9] The use of the pronoun makes it clear that the undergoer argument is a continuing topic. Furthermore, the presence of the actor argument as a subject noun later in the clause maintains clear reference to agency, although defocused. The youngest example of this type of construction comes from a Chilean child of 3;4.

(49a) *Al perro todas las ovejas [=abejas] lo[10] persiguen.*

to.the dog all the bees him chase (='All the bees chase the dog'; cf. *The dog is chased by all the bees.*) [*cS3h-3;4*]

As discussed in Chapter IVc, such inversions are functionally equivalent to English passives, which also occur in the preschool period (cf. *The dog's hiding so he doesn't get chased by that big deer* [*E3g-3;9*]). Such word-order variations are used freely by preschoolers to skillfully manipulate narrative perspective, allowing for topic maintenance and shift along with upgrading and downgrading of agency. The situation described in (49a) is especially prone to inversion, since the dog is generally more topic-worthy than the bees. Several variations are possible in Spanish, and all of them are attested at age 5 or younger in all three Spanish samples. In addition to the order in (49a) we find:

(49b) *Al perro le están persiguiendo las abejas.*

---

[9] Green (1990, pp. 256-257) notes that passives in Spanish, "though common in journalistic and technical writing, have been virtually ousted from speech and from literary styles to the advantage of the clitic forms, which may eventually generalise to all contexts."

[10] Most Latin American dialects preserve the distinction between *lo/la*:DIRECT OBJECT and *le*:INDIRECT OBJECT, generally neutralized in Madrid.

to.the dog him are chasing the bees [aS5-5;5]

(49c) *Le perseguía - [sic] al perro las avispas.*

him chased to.the dog the wasps [S5f-5;7]

Another story episode that calls for a choice in perspective is the fall from the cliff. The narrator has to make a topic choice between the under-goers (boy and dog) or the actor (deer) and, further, has to decide whether to maintain topic across the several phases of the episode. If the undergoers are selected as topic, canonical SVO word order is not available. The following example from a 3-year-old shows a successful struggle to introduce and main-tain the boy and dog as topic of successive clauses while defocusing the deer by means of postposing in the first clause and null reference in the second. The several pauses indicate the difficulty of formulating and reformulating this complex perspective.

(50) *El niño - le cogió un ciervo muy grande - y le llevó - con él ... luego al perro y al - y al niño les tiró.*

the boy - him picked.up a deer very big - and him carried - with him ... then to.the dog and to.the - and to.the boy them threw:3SG (='The boy - a very big deer picked him up - and carried him - with him ... then the dog and - and the boy, he threw them.') [S3j-3;11]

The word-order variations we have considered thus far adhere to various sorts of syntactic requirements. Preposed existentials are required by the lack of expletives, and preposed presentatives (and "negative presentatives") are required to establish the presentative interpretation of the predicate. Clitic object pronouns must precede the verb, thereby perhaps facilitating the post-posing of subject NPs. Other sorts of inversions are not syntactically required, but are options that are chosen on the basis of the narrator's organi-zation of information flow. In Spanish it is typical to postpose a subject that is a continuing discourse topic in order to foreground the predicate as new information. This sort of word-order flexibility is exploited by the youngest narrators. We have already seen an example of subject postposing in (47), with a transitive verb. In that sentence, the preposed clitic object pronoun is syntactically determined. In intransitive clauses, however, the speaker is completely free with regard to pre- or postposing of the single nominal argu-ment, following only pragmatic considerations, as shown in the following examples. Note that the postposed subject is always definite and is always a continuing topic. The examples in (51) foreground action verbs in the "vivid" progressive and those in (52) foreground states of desire/intention.

(51a) *Aquí está gritando el niño.*

'Here is shouting the boy.' [S3g-3;8]

(51b) *Y luego se va cayendo el niño.*

  'And then goes falling the boy.' *[S3a-3;6]*

(51c) *Estaba llamando a la rana éste.*

  was calling the frog this.one (='This one was calling the frog.') *[S3k-3;11]*

(52a) *Y ahora quiere esto el perro.*

  'And now wants this the dog.' *[S4b-4;1]*

(52b) *Quería subir el perro.*

  'Wanted to climb the dog.' *[S4e-4;6]*

(52c) *Quería alcanzar el perro a lo de las abejas.*

  'Wanted to reach the dog to the thing of the bees.' *[S5k-5;5]*

In sum, Spanish allows considerable manipulation of word order for discourse purposes, because extensive person/number marking on the verb often serves to identify the grammatical subject, and clitic pronouns along with oblique prepositional phrases allow for the tracking of topical nonsubject arguments. Preschool-age children make abundant and appropriate use of the resulting opportunities for flexibility in perspective-taking.

3.2. Valence

Another way to manipulate perspective is to alter the expression of verb-argument structure. The typical patterns in Spanish have been described by Talmy (1985). Consider a verb that figures in the frog story — *romper* 'break': (1) the basic form of the verb is transitive/causative: *El perro rompió el frasco* 'The dog **broke** the jar'; (2) the reflexive form is intransitive/inchoative: *El frasco se rompió* 'The jar broke'; (3) the participle is stative: *El frasco está roto* 'The jar **is broken**' (*roto* = *romper*+PAST.PART:MASC).

Narrators across the age groups take either a causative or inchoative perspective on this event, with 60-70% preferring the latter, using the reflexive *romper-se* 'break-REFL'. This form provides a mediopassive or middle-voice perspective that corresponds to agentless passives in English (*the jar got broken*) and Turkish (*kavanoz kırıldı* 'jar break:PASS:PAST). Again, Spanish provides an accessible alternative to the passive construction (as discussed further in Chapter IVc).

Spanish speakers do not take a stative perspective with regard to the broken glass, but elsewhere in the texts past participles play an important function to encode resultant states. It seems that they reinforce the perspective that is marked by the present perfect (which also uses the past participle) and the adverb *ya* 'already', as discussed above. In many instances, Spanish narrators use a stative description where English and German narrators tend to use active verbs. Compare, for example:

(53) **Picture 1:**

(a)   *Y éste está aquí, **sentado** en este sito.*

     'And this one is here, **seated** in this place.' [*S3c-3;7*]

(b)   *He sat down.* [*E4a-4;0*]

(c)   *Da sitzt der Junge.*

     'There sits the boy.' [*G3d-3;6*]

(54) **Picture 15:**

(a)   *El está **colgado** de la cabra [=ciervo].*

     'He is **hung** from the goat [=deer].' [*S4b-4;1*]

(b)   *And he slipped onto a deer.* [*E4b-4;4*]

(c)   *Da hält er den Hirsch fest.*

     'There he holds tight onto the deer.' [*G3b-3;11*]

Across construction types there seems to be a tendency towards stative descriptions in Spanish: present perfect + *ya*, extended locative state descriptions, and widespread use of participles.

4. CONNECTIVITY

Up to this point we have attended mainly to morphological forms and word-order patterns at the level of the verb and clause. In this section we turn our attention to the use of syntactic means to link clauses and relate information between clauses. Clauses can be joined by means of coordination (Section 4.1) and subordination (Section 4.2), and cross-clause information can be indexed by "null forms" (Section 4.3).

We had initially expected that the number and type of clauses would increase throughout the course of development. However, there is no significant increase in number of clauses per text across the four child age groups (Chapter IB, Table 3). In the case of the adults, we expected a greater diversity within the age group, following earlier discussions (Berman, 1988; Berman & Slobin, 1987) that adults can create extended narratives with a large number of clauses or can opt for a compact presentation of similar events, without presenting each of them in detail, as in (55):

(55) *Pero no obstante siguen buscando, a pesar de todas las persecuciones, a*
     pesar de los sustos y de las caídas, hasta que al fin, llamando a la rana,

el niño cae en los cuernos de un ciervo.

'But nevertheless they continue searching, in spite of all the chases, in spite of the fears and the falls, until at last, calling for the frog, the boy falls on the horns of a deer.' [*S20f*]

In fact, the adult texts range between 30 and 184 clauses in length (between 55 and 193 in the Latin American samples). It seems that length and complexity are interrelated factors in adult narratives.

4.1. Simple Clause Connection

As mentioned above, and in Chapter IIA, 3- and 4-year-olds often do not conceive of the story as a structural unity, but rather build their texts picture by picture rather than event by event. As a consequence, the means they use to connect their discourse are the deictic markers *aquí* 'here' and *ahora* 'now', both with the function of sequential **chaining**. The locative *aquí* is especially favored by some of the youngest narrators. Nevertheless, it is used together with temporal markers by some 3-year-olds and many 4-year-olds. (See Chapter IVA for crosslinguistic comparisons.)

In addition to locative and temporal deictics, the younger children also use person deictics such as *éste* 'this.one', frequently accompanied by *también* 'also', for indicating activities carried out jointly by two protagonists as well as the same activity carried out across more than one picture by a single protagonist. That is to say, the inability to grasp the narrative cohesion of the picture series can lead the child to think that various boys and dogs take part in the story and that all of them are involved in the same adventures. (See (33), above, for an example of adverbial marking of such recurrence.)

Many of the younger children do not seem to understand that an event that is extended in time can serve as the cause of a following event, and they do not take one event as the background for another. As a consequence, there are very few subordinate clauses — and only those of a particular type, as discussed below.

When children of about age 4 succeed in going beyond the here and now, there is often a resulting "fluidity" in the temporal organization of the text as they introduce elements marking temporal sequence, both with and without accompanying locative deixis. It is most characteristic of the 3-year-olds to use a single temporal marker repeatedly, whereas 4-year-olds begin to combine several such markers, even within a single clause, as, for example:

(56) *Y aquí luego después se escondió.*

'And here then afterwards he hid himself.' [*S4e-4;6*]

This sort of overmarking is reminiscent of redundant uses of aspectual and locative directional adverbs, as discussed above, reflecting the well-known phenomenon that the child often tends to overuse linguistic marking at points in development when form-function relations are being analyzed (Bowerman, 1982b; Karmiloff-Smith, 1979; Slobin, 1973). We find 4-year-old texts in which almost every clause has such excessive marking:

(57) *Y después el niño se cae y después el perro se escapa, después el buho se queda en un árbol y después el buho se va. El niño se ha ponido [=puesto] en un ciervo y después el perro se va corriendo, después los tira y el ciervo se para. Después se caen al agua, se ponen ahí y después se contentan y el otro se cae. Después suben por arriba, por el tronco, después bajan sin hacer ruido porque ahí dentro hay cosas.*

'And **afterwards** the boy falls and **afterwards** the dog runs away, **afterwards** the owl stays in a tree and **afterwards** the owl goes away. The boy has put himself on a deer and **afterwards** the dog runs away, **afterwards** (he) throws them and the deer stops. **Afterwards** they fall to the water, they end up there and **afterwards** they get happy and the other one falls. **Afterwards** they climb up, over the trunk, **afterwards** they go down without making noise because inside of there there are things.' [*S4c-4;4*]

The temporal markers that occur in the texts are *después* 'afterwards', *luego* 'after', and *entonces* 'then', with a similar distribution in texts with predominant present, past, or mixed tense. However, in the preschool period, these markers function to chain one event after the other, whereas they are used by 9-year-olds to establish temporal relations between larger events or episodes. Compare (57) with the following, from a 9-year-old narrative:

(58) *Entonces siguieron buscando en un sitio donde viven las ratas por el campo, y el perro buscaba por donde el panal, pero olía muy mal la rata. Entonces el niño dejó a la rata y se subió a un árbol y el panal se cayó. Después salió una lechuza y se asustó el niño y se cayó, y las abejas empezaron a perseguir al perro. Entonces la lechuza dejó al niño y se subió a una roca, el niño. Entonces se agarró a unos cuernos de un ciervo.*

'**Then** they continued searching in a place where rats live in the field, and the dog searched where there was the hive, but the rat smelled very bad. **Then** the boy left the rat and climbed a tree and the hive fell. **Afterwards** an owl came out and scared the boy and he fell, and the bees started to chase the dog. **Then** the owl left the boy and (he) climbed a rock, the boy. **Then** he held onto some horns of a deer.' [*S9b-9;2*]

The narrative immaturity of the youngest children is also reflected syntactically in the repeated use of the conjunction *y* 'and', to the exclusion of other possible adversative or disjunctive conjunctions to link successive clauses, as if the narration were the sum of a series of independent clauses to be interpreted contextually. This pattern disappears, of course, when narrators begin to make use of more types of conjunction — especially subordinate. As a result, the proportion of clauses linked by *y* 'and' drops with age, from about 55% at ages 4 and 5, to 41% at age 9, and only 24% in the adult texts.

4.2. Complex Clause Connection

The decline of coordination in favor of subordination beginning at age 9 should not be interpreted as a total absence of subordination in the three younger age groups. In fact, those children use various subordinate clauses, but with much less variability in type of subordination. The younger preschoolers are limited to the use of adverbial subordination, always placing the subordinate clause before the matrix clause. Beginning at age 5, children begin to show somewhat more flexibility in type and placement of subordinate clauses.

4.2.1. Temporal adverbial clauses

The temporal relation between a matrix and subordinate clause is basically expressed by the tenses of the verbs in the two clauses. However, there are instances in which the verb tenses are insufficient to establish the type of temporal relation, even in a language like Spanish with its abundance of tense/aspect marking on the verb. Accordingly, temporal connectives do not function simply as clause-linking devices, but also serve to indicate if the events expressed in the two clauses are to be interpreted as simultaneous or sequential in time.

The first temporal subordinate conjunction to appear is *cuando* 'when', already present in 3-year-old texts. This form in Spanish can indicate two kinds of temporal relations: **simultaneity** between the events in the two clauses (*cuando se estaba durmiendo la rana salió* 'when he was sleeping the frog escaped' [*S5e-5;4*]) or **immediate anteriority** of the event in the subordinate clause (*cuando se despertó el niño no se encontraba nada* 'when the boy woke up he didn't see anything' [*S4g-4;7*]).

This is the only temporal subordinator used by 3- and 4-year-olds, but it functions somewhat differently at the two ages. The first function of *cuando*, at age 3, is to chain clauses that don't necessarily require the establishment of a specific temporal relation between the two events. Three-year-olds use *cuando* as a means of advancing the narrative action, often as a sort of obligatory marker of the events in the next picture, as if they need a temporal conjunction simply to mark the fact of of spatio-temporal sequence — of moving on from the previous picture.

Beginning at age 4, subordinate clauses with *cuando* establish a temporal context, e.g.,:

(59) *Y luego, cuando era de noche, se metió en la cama.*

'And after, when it was night-time, he went to bed.' [*S4e-4;6*]

By age 5, children use subordinate clauses with *cuando* in a systematic fashion to mark narrative background, e.g.,:

(60) *Y cuando estaban durmiendo el niño y el perro, se escapó la rana.*

'And when they were sleeping, the boy and the dog, the frog escaped.' [*S5f-5;4*]

Until this age the subordinate clause is always in first position, but beginning with age 5, children begin to invert the order of mention of events, allowing the subordinate clause to occupy second position:

(61) *Y coge una bota cuando se levanta.*

'And (he) picks up a boot when (he) gets up.' [*S5c-5;4*]

The functions of this type of subordination are well established at this age, both for indicating immediate anteriority of one event to another and for backgrounding one of two events.

These two basic functions are maintained at age 9, but children of this age also make use of other temporal subordinate constructions. For example, if the narrator wants to mention two simultaneous events that have different protagonists, it is necessary to shift perspective from one protagonist to another. The first element used for this function is the subordinate conjunction *mientras* 'while':

(62) *Sale el buho y lo tira mientras las abejas le persiguen a su perro.*

'The owl comes out and throws him while the bees chase his dog.' [*S9a-9;1*]

4.2.2. Causal adverbial clauses

At age 5 we begin to find the use of other means of subordination, in addition to temporal subordination with *cuando*. Causal relations are interesting in this regard, since children possess a range of means for indicating such connections. A situation which lends itself to causal explanations is the boy's fall from the tree. As early as age 3;8, we find a causal role attributed to the owl, by means of a simple transitive clause:

(63a) *Aquí el buho le ha tirado del árbol al niño.*

'Here the owl has thrown him from the tree, the boy.' [*S3g-3;8*]

It is not until about a year later, however, that this event is analyzed into component phases:

(63b) *El niño se ha caído porque le ha tirado este buho.*

'The boy has fallen because him has thrown this owl' (=because this owl has thrown him). [*S4f-4;7*]

This sort of causal attribution, with a subordinate clause marked with *porque* 'because', requires an inverse order of mention of the two phases of the event — an ability which is generally considered to be beyond the skills of 5-year-olds (e.g., Clark, 1985). Some 4- and 5-year-olds apparently have difficulty with the inversion, and attempt other means to "package" together the phases of this causal event under one intonation contour. In the following example, a 5-year-old attempts to reverse order of mention with a causal connective, but has to backtrack and rephrase the account in iconic order:

(63c) *Se cayó porque salió ... esa era la casa de un buho, salió y le tiró.*

'(He) fell because (it) came out ... that was the house of an owl, (it) came out and threw him.' [*S5e-5;4*]

Another technique makes use of a relative clause, as discussed in the next section.

4.2.3. Relative clauses

In Chapter IVB there is a discussion of the greater frequency of use of relative clauses in Spanish and Hebrew in comparison with the other languages of this study (see Table 2, Chapter IVB). Slobin (1989) has suggested several factors that may play a role in this regard. The relativizer in Spanish (*que*) and Hebrew (*she*) is an invariant form, not marked for categories such as gender, number, or animacy. (In addition, the relativizer is obligatory in Spanish and Hebrew, while it can be omitted in some contexts in English.) Another contributing factor may be direction of information flow. Relative clauses, like other modifiers, follow the noun in Spanish and Hebrew. Compare, for example, the word-order patterns of the following 3-year-old relative clause (used to describe the log at the end of the story) and other sorts of noun modification in Spanish:

(64a) ...*un tubo que está roto* ... 'a tube that is broken' [*3a-3;6*]

(64b) *un tubo roto* 'a broken tube'

(64c) *un tubo de madera* 'a tube of wood' (=a wooden tube)

(64d) *la rana del niño* 'the frog of the boy' (=the boy's frog)

It is likely that the consistent postnominal placement of modifiers, along with morphological simplicity, contributes to the salience and accessibility of relative clauses. These issues are discussed in detail in Chapter IVB, and we will not summarize that discussion here. In general terms, we can speak of a "typology of use," in which relative clauses perform a range of frequent and significant functions in Spanish discourse.

There are no differences between the three preschool groups in the frequency of use of relative clauses. For each age group, less than 2% of the clauses are relatives, and a little more than half of the narrators use such clauses. All of the 9-year-olds and adults use relative clauses.

One explanation for the low rate of relative clause usage during the preschool period is the excessive use of *y* 'and', as discussed above. In many instances, *y* can perform the same clause-linking function as the relativizer *que*. Compare, for example, the two 5-year-old versions in (65), both referring to the same situation, using the same verbs:

(65a) *Salió un loro que le tiró al niño.*

    '(There) came out a parrot **that** threw the boy.' [*S5d-5;4*]

(65b) *Sale un cuco y le tira al niño.*

    '(There) comes out a cuckoo **and** throws the boy.' [*S5i-5;11*]

The difference here is not semantic, but rather, discursive. The version with *que* seems to "package" the two phases of the situation into a single event, while the version with *y* seems more like a description of two more separate events (as discussed further in Chapter IVC).

If we attend to the narrative functions of relative clauses, we find significant development with age. Consider first the function of relative clauses to **describe** a referent in some way.[11] Relative clauses are used by the youngest narrators for this function. We have seen one example, from our very youngest subject, the child of 3;6 quoted in (64a). Additional examples are:

---

[11] This function is differentiated further in Chapter IVB. Our general category here includes what Dasinger and Toupin call "General Discourse Functions" (naming, situating, reidentifying) and the Narrative Function of "presentation."

(66a) *Esto es una rana que coge el perro.*

'This is a frog that the dog takes.' [*S3c-3;7*]

(66b) *Y en el hoyo que había una ardilla se salía del agujero.*

'And in the hole that was there a squirrel came.out of the hole.' [*S4k-4;10*]

Although such uses of relative clauses are found in preschool texts, young children are apparently constrained by some limits of processing span that are no longer at play by age 9. An age difference we have noted is the ability of older children to chain two presentative relative clauses, as in (66c):

(66c)*Son un niño y un perro que están viendo una rana que tienen.*

'They are a boy and a dog that are looking at a frog that they have.' [*S9h-9;8*]

Another function of descriptive relative clauses is to provide the kind of static locative setting discussed in Section 2. (41a) and (41b) are examples of such relative clauses, using the locative relativizer *donde* 'where'. The need to provide such information in narrative is probably another factor leading to the frequency of relative clauses in Spanish.

A more mature narrative function of relative clauses is what Lambrecht (1988) has called the **continuative**. Such a relative clause, in the terms of Chapter IVB, "continues the narrative by depicting a subsequent or consequent event." This function appears at age 5 in Spanish (but is a late acquisition in the languages other than Hebrew). An early example was cited in (65a): *Salió un loro que le tiró al niño* '(There) came.out a parrot that threw the boy' [*S5d-5;4*]. As suggested in Section 4.2.2, this kind of relative clause provides another means of "packaging" together the two phases of a causal event in one continuous utterance. Most uses of continuative relative clauses by children are of this presentative type: The main clause puts a protagonist on the stage and the relative clause continues with an action of that protagonist. (Note that, contrary to some claims in the literature, the relative clause functions here to present foregrounded, plot-advancing material.) More mature uses present plot-advancing material in both clauses, e.g.,:

(67) *Y el niño cayó en la cabeza del alce, que aterrorizado, corrió.*

'And the boy fell on the head of the stag that, terrified, ran.' [*cS20c*]

Continuative relative clauses are used by significantly more adult narrators in Spanish than in the other four languages of the study (Chapter IVB, Table 3b).

Another function of relative clauses is that of **retrospection**.[12] Here the

---

[12] This is partly a subcategory of what Dasinger and Toupin (Chapter IVB) call the "motivating" function of a relative clause (the provision of information about a state of affairs

relative clause refers to a situation that is anterior to the event in the main clause. Such uses are very frequent in the 9-year-old and adult texts, e.g.,:

(68a) *Del agujero que había cavado el niño sale un animal.*

'From the hole that the boy had dug (there) came.out an animal.' [*S9e-9;6*]

(68b) *Estaba por la noche contemplando una ranita que habían cazado por la mañana.*

'At night he was looking at a froggie that they had caught in the morning.' [*S20c*]

In sum, relative clauses are remarkable in Spanish for their frequency of use, diversity of function, and precocity of acquisition. We refer the reader to Chapter IVB for an insightful discussion of factors that might account for the patterns of acquisition and use of this construction type.

4.3. Subject Ellipsis

Spanish differs from English and German (but not Turkish and Hebrew) with regard to the "pro-drop parameter" which has attracted much attention in formal syntax. It is not our intention to take up this literature here (for example, Hyams, 1987, 1989; Jaeggli, 1982; Rizzi, 1982, 1986; Suñer, 1990). Rather, our goal is to lay out some of the characteristics of subject ellipsis in Spanish in order to analyze the development of its narrative functions.

Sentences without overt subjects are normal in both written and spoken Spanish. Person/number marking on the verb allows for retrieval of the subject in most instances; contextual information is generally available for subject identification in those few cases of ambiguity (e.g., neutralization of 1SG and 3SG in the imperfective). This feature of Spanish will be evident to the reader from the many examples above where we have inserted subject pronouns in parentheses in the English glosses. (Here we represent a null pronoun with ∅.) In addition, Spanish has no expletive subjects (e.g., *hace calor* 'makes heat' [=it's hot]).

Null subjects occur in the youngest texts. The most obvious context is continuing reference to the same protagonist across clauses:

(69) *El perro estaba muy enfadado ... sube al árbol y no puede llegar y se cae lleno de moscas.*

---

that enables the event described in the main clause), but we include any case in which the event described in the relative clause precedes that described in the main clause (Sebastián, 1989).

'The dog was very angry ... Ø climbs on the tree and Ø can't reach and Ø falls full of flies.' [*S3b-3;6*]

By age 5, children are able to use null subjects across clauses with different subjects, keeping track of previous mention of protagonists and, where available, differences in number as well. In the following example, the narrator has already presented the protagonists; furthermore, the singular frog contrasts with the plural boy and dog.

(70) *Y cuando se estaban durmiendo la rana salió y luego se despertaron.* [*S5e-5;4*]

'And when Ø were:PL sleeping the frog left and afterwards Ø woke.up:PL.' [*S5e-5;4*]

Subject pronouns are exceptionally infrequent in the Spanish texts. There are only 14 instances in the entire corpus (*él* 'he' - 11, *ella* 'she' - 1, *ellos* 'they:MASC' - 2, *ellas* 'they:FEM' - 0). Of these, seven are used by 4-year-olds — five of them by the same child. There are no subject pronouns at all in the texts of 3- and 5-year-olds.

One reason for the rarity of subject pronouns in the frog story might be due to the genders of the participants. A main function of overt pronouns in Spanish is for contrastive reference. In this story, however, all of the major participants are masculine in gender, except for the frog, who is not present for most of the story (*el niño, el perro, el buho, el ciervo*; only the animal in the hole varies in gender: *la rata, el ratón, el topo, la ardilla*). There are therefore not many opportunities for contrastive use of pronouns (as in, for example, '**he** fell down and **she** ran away'). However, the one 4-year-old who makes frequent use of *él* does not use it consistently for shifting reference, but rather as a sort of deictic demonstrative, both for the same referent (71a) and for reference shift (71b):

(71a) *Y luego está de rodillas. Y él se sube y el perro también.*

'And afterwards Ø (=boy) is on his knees.' [Picture 20] 'And he (=boy) climbs and the dog too.' [*S4b-4;1*]

(71b) *Ahora el perro quiere comerse a las moscas y él quiere llamar a todos los animales.*

'Now the dog wants to eat up all the flies and he (=boy) wants to call all the animals.' [Picture 8] [*S4b-4;1*]

It strikes us as anglocentric to refer to a language like Spanish as "pro-**drop**." What the Spanish-speaking child has to learn is not when to drop a subject pronoun, but rather when to **add** one appropriately. Such an example is provided by (71b), but this one child's unsystematic use of subject pronouns suggests that he has not yet mastered the use of "pro-add." The few adult instances show appropriate contrastive use, as in (72a), or appropriate use for disambiguation, as in (72b) where there are two possible prior antecedents that are both plural.

(72a) *El buho siguió a Tomy, hasta que se refugió en lo alto de una piedra y ya lo dejó en paz, y él siguió buscando.*

'The owl followed Tomy, until Ø protected himself on the top of a rock and finally Ø[13] left him in peace, and **he** continued searching.' [S20d]

(72b) *Y acercan detrás de un tronco para ver si las ranas que ahí cerca son las que ellos andan buscando.*

'And Ø approach:PL (=boy and dog) behind a trunk to see if the frogs:FEM, that are nearby, are the ones that **they**:MASC are looking for.' [S20c]

Note that (72a) corresponds to a pronoun under contrastive stress in English, whereas (72b) does not. (Neither pronoun is stressed in the Spanish examples.) The acquisition tasks in Spanish and English are quite different. The English-speaking child has to learn that subject pronouns are almost always syntactically required, and, additionally, must sometimes be stressed as well. The Spanish-speaking child must learn that pronouns are required only in particular syntactic and discourse contexts — namely contexts in which agreement marking on the verb is insufficient to identify the subject referent. These contexts are defined pragmatically rather than syntactically, as is evident from the two null pronouns with different antecedents in (72a).

These typological differences also have consequences for event packaging. Consider, again, the event in which the owl throws the boy from the tree. We have noted that the use of *y* 'and' to link clauses with the verbs 'come.out' and 'throw' suggests a separation of the two phases of the event. Consider, now, the role of subject pronouns. The Spanish *y*-linked version in (73a) has a null subject in the second clause. We suggest that this level of packaging corresponds to an English *and*-linked version **with** a pronoun, as in (73b).

(73a) *Salió un buho y le tiró al niño.*

'(There) came.out an owl and Ø threw the boy.'

(73b) *An owl came out and he threw the boy.*

The two clauses can be more tightly packaged in Spanish, as noted above, by the use of a relative clause. This seems to correspond to *and*-linking in

---

[13] Note that the null pronoun here refers to the owl, and not the boy. This is evident from context and is not marked with an overt pronoun.

English with ellipsis in the second clause:

(74a) *Salió un buho que le tiró al niño.*

    '(There) came.out an owl that threw the boy.'

(74b) *An owl came out and Ø threw the boy.*

Note that the null pronoun is the default in Spanish, whereas it serves to link the two clauses more tightly in English. In both languages, a special construction type provides the means for what we have been calling event packaging.

To complete the picture, a stressed subject pronoun in English serves a contrastive function corresponding to an unstressed pronoun in Spanish. Imagine a scene in which a monkey is trying to throw the boy from the tree, and then an owl comes out and does the throwing instead:

(76a) *El mono se fue. Salió un buho y él tiró al niño.*

    'The monkey went away. (There) came.out an owl and he [unstressed] threw the boy.'

(76b) *The monkey went away. An owl came out and HE threw the boy.*

We would conclude, accordingly, that the Spanish-speaking child has to learn a "pro-add" language, whereas the English-speaking child has to learn when to stress or delete pronouns that are otherwise obligatory and unstressed.

5. SUMMARY

5.1. Tense/Aspect

Preschoolers make appropriate use of almost the full range of aspectual distinctions, using verbal morphology to distinguish between processes (PROG, IPFV), states (PRES, IPFV), and completed actions (PFV), and making aspectual distinctions in both past and present tenses at the youngest ages. Present participles are used for marking durativity and manner, and past participles are used to describe states. The present perfect is widely used by Madrid preschoolers, although it is absent in Chilean and Argentinian narrations at all ages. At first it is used for visible (depicted) endstates, but by age 5 it is also used to describe situations that can be inferred without immediate perceptual support; 9-year-olds also use it to reintroduce prior information that is relevant to the current situation in the narrative. The past perfect serves a retrospective function from age 4 onward. Aspect is also marked adverbially, and 3-year-olds make redundant use of *ya* 'already' with present perfect verbs. However, the rich system of inflectional marking of aspect seems to lessen reliance on the use of aspectual adverbs and verbs in preschool and school-age narratives.

5.2. Motion and Location

Consistent with the verb-framed typology of the language, speakers of all ages rely primarily on verbs of motion to encode trajectories, with limited encoding of source or goal, and very little attention to manner of movement. Some preschoolers add more detail by the use of directional locative adverbs, but this phase is short-lived, and school-age children and adults prefer to devote more narrative attention to stage-setting, thereby allowing locative trajectories to be inferred.

5.3. Perspective

Word order variation is flexibly and appropriately used by the youngest narrators, along with clitic object pronouns, for purposes of topic maintenance and shift, as well as introduction of new participants. These alternatives are supported by person/number marking on the verb, which is also mastered early on. (As a consequence, passive constructions are rare and mature forms in our texts.) Reflexive forms of transitive/causative verbs provide speakers with means of deriving intransitive/inchoative forms, providing a mediopassive or middle-voice perspective.

5.4. Connectivity

Preschoolers make abundant use of simple "chaining" connectives, equivalent to 'and', 'then'; older narrators tend to use such connectives only between larger narrative segments. Temporal subordination with *cuando* 'when' is present from age 3, indicating both simultaneity and immediate anteriority; causal subordination develops in the later preschool period. Relative clauses are used by the youngest children, but acquire an increasing range of functions with age. Presentative and continuative relative clauses are present at earlier ages than in most of the other languages of the study. The youngest children make appropriate use of null subjects. Subject pronouns are vanishingly rare — suggesting that the Spanish-speaking child is faced with the task of learning the appropriate contexts for the use of subject pronouns. Clitic object pronouns, by contrast, are appropriately used by the youngest narrators.

Chapter IIID

DEVELOPMENT OF LINGUISTIC FORMS: HEBREW

Ruth A. Berman & Yonni Neeman

0. INTRODUCTORY NOTE

The language of the Hebrew narratives is contemporary Israeli Hebrew, the standard version of which is exemplified by our adult subjects, who are native-Hebrew speakers from middle-class educated backgrounds, with high school or college-level education, like the parents of the children whose stories are described below. Descriptions of major features of the phonology, morphology, and syntax of current Hebrew are provided by Berman (1978, 1985, pp. 257-263, in press-e). Hebrew texts and examples are given here in a broad phonetic transcription, meant to represent the speech of the adults in our sample, rather than to capture morphophonological distinctions which may still be manifested in the consonantal orthography of Modern Hebrew, but have been neutralized in current pronunciation.

1. HEBREW TENSE/ASPECT

As noted in Chapter III0, Modern Hebrew has the least elaborated system of obligatory grammatical marking of tense/aspect distinctions by verb inflections of the five languages under study. Hebrew verbs have a rich array of agreement-marking inflections for grammatical number, gender, and person, but only five obligatory formal alternations marking grammatical mood and tense. These five categories are: infinitive, imperative, present, past, and future, described briefly below as they relate to our narratives.[1]

(1) **Infinitives**: These are the major nonfinite verb form in the language. They take a prefixal *l-*, and function primarily as complements of modal and aspectual verbs which carry tense-marking for present, past, or future, e.g. *roce li-nshox* 'wants to-bite' [*H3a-3;0*], *nisa la-alot* 'tried to-climb' [*H5b-5;1*], or *himshix le-tapes* 'continued to-climb = went-on climbing' [*H5c-5;2*]. They also occur in **purpose** adverbials, with or without an overt conjunction, e.g., *hu raca le-tapes **kdey limco** ota* 'he wanted to-climb **in.order to.find** it' [*H9b-9;2*].

(2) **Imperatives**: This category is marginal to the current study. Imperative forms occur only occasionally in direct speech address attributed to one of the protagonists, e.g., when the boy says to the frogs at the end of

---

[1] In this chapter, the term "verb" refers to a consonantal root as used in a particular *binyan* pattern or conjugation, e.g. the transitive verb *sagar* 'close, shut' and the intransitive change-of-state verb *nisgar* 'get/be shut' are formed from the same root s-g-r in two different conjugations, and the intransitive medio-passive verb *nistar* 'be-hidden/invisible', the reflexive-passive *histater* 'hide (oneself)', and causative *histir* 'hide (something or someone)' are all formed from the root s-t-r in different conjugations (Section 1.2.1). Examples of verbs in isolation are given in the morphologically simple form of past tense, 3rd person, masculine singular, even when translated by an English infinitive or present tense.

the story *"bo'u, bo'u"* 'come:PL, come:PL' [*H3j-3;9*], or the deer bids the boy *"bo ta'ale el-ay"* 'come climb.up to-me' [*H5i-5;6*].

(3) **Present Tense**: These forms are traditionally termed *benoni* 'intermediate' since they function both as present-tense finite verbs and as participles. They differ from past and future-tense verbs in not being inflected for person but, like nouns and adjectives, only for number and gender. Verbs in this category are used both for immediate present and for habitual and generic or extended present as well as for historic or narrative present. In copular sentences, there is no present tense form of the verb *haya* 'be'. This yields constructions termed "nominal sentences," which consist of a subject NP and a predicate complement without any overt verb form, e.g., *hem me'od acuv-im* '*they very sad-PL*' [*H5l-5;9*], *ulay ze lo hacfardea shelo* 'maybe it not his frog' [*H20c*].

(4) **Past Tense**: This is the form par excellence for describing events which took place prior to the time of speaking, irrespective of whether durative or telic in nature, and whether they were ongoing or completed at that time. There is no grammatical marking of aspect on past (or present) tense verbs. Past-tense forms are typically used for all kinds of narratives, including those in our sample. A stereotypic example of how each event in the sequence is presented in this simple past tense is provided by the following excerpt from a 5-year-old story:

(1)   *Ha-kelev **lakax** et ha-ke'ara shel ha-cfardea ve **sam** ota al ha-rosh shelo,*
      *az axarkax ha-yeled **patax** et ha-xalon ve hem **ra'u** ota, axarkax ha-kelev*
      ***nafal** ve ha-yeled **yarad** ve hu **xibek** oto.*

      'The-dog **took** the frog's basin and **put** it on his head, so afterwards the boy **opened** the-window and they **saw**:PL it, afterwards the dog **fell** and the boy **descended** and he **hugged** him' [*H5b-5;1*].[2]

These two forms, present and past, are thus used for the entire range of time-span from before and up to the time of speaking. As a result, relative tense in Hebrew is expressed by alternations between these two forms in matrix and complement verbs.[3] Past tense followed by present tense

---

[2] In translating motion verbs into English, we use the Latinate versions so as to retain their flavor as monolexemic compared with Germanic verb plus particle combinations like *go down*, *go up*, *go out*, etc. (see Chapter IIIo). In Hebrew these do not represent a higher register but are everyday colloquial verbs. This is also true of the verb *xipes*, which we translate as 'search', *barax* as 'flee', or *radaf* as 'pursue', rather than their everyday Germanic alternants 'look for', 'run away', 'run after'.

[3] There is one complex form: Habitual past is expressed by a past-tense form of *haya* 'be' followed by a present-tense *benoni* participle, e.g., *haya holex* literally 'was go(ing)' [=used to go]. This construction never once occurred in our Hebrew narratives.

represents the simultaneity of the two events, e.g., the boy's discovery of some frogs behind a log is described as: *ve axarey ze hu ra'a et ha-cfardea shelo ve od cfardea-ben kaxa **mitxab'im** ke'ilu beyaxad* 'and after that he **saw** his frog and another baby-frog sort of **hide**:PL together' [*H9e-9;6*]. Past tense followed by past tense specifies that the event described in the complement was anterior to the matrix-verb event (where the four other languages would use pluperfect forms), e.g., the scene where the boy discovers that his frog is gone is described as follows: *kshe hu **kam** hu ra'a she ha-cfardea ne'elma* 'when he **got.up**, he **saw** that the-frog *disappeared*' [*H9j-9;8*]. Where a narrative is set in present tense, sequence-of-tense requires that the complement remain in the present for simultaneous events, and switch to the past for anterior events, e.g., an adult describes the same scene thus: *mishe **mit'orerim** ha-kelev ve ha-yeled, hem **ro'im** she **eyn** cfardea, ve hem lo **yod'im** le'an hi ne'elma* 'Once they **awaken**:PL, the-dog and the-boy, they **see**:PL that **there** no frog, and they do not **know**:PL to-where it **disappeared**' [*H20c*]. In order to express relative tense between matrix and embedded clauses, Hebrew-acquiring children must thus learn how to alternate between the two forms of present and past — as well as future — tense.

(5) **Future**: Future-tense forms — the third finite-verb inflection in the language — are used for events located temporally subsequent to time of speaking, and in a variety of other contexts where other languages might use subjunctives, conditionals, and other irrealis forms. Like imperatives, future forms are relatively marginal in this set of narratives. They occur mainly in irrealis complements, e.g. *ha-cipor afa alav, ve az hu **poxed** she hi tered al ha-rosh shelo* 'the-bird flies over him, and then he **fears** that it **will.descend** on his head' [*H4g-4;6*].

By age 3, Hebrew-speaking children generally have command of these five forms of the verb, as part of the obligatory inflectional markers in the domain of the simple clause (Berman & Dromi, 1984). The texts of the youngest children in the Hebrew sample — aged 3;0 to 3;11 — all demonstrate command of a rich range of agreement markers, which include inflections for number and gender on verbs, nouns, and adjectives, as well as person marking for verbs.

1.1. Present and Past Tense

The verbs in the Hebrew frog stories rely heavily on two of the forms listed above: present and past tense. Here, we consider how these two sets of forms are used from three points of view: to encode sequence of tenses (Section 1.1.1), to mark a dominant tense (1.1.2), and in tense shifting (1.1.3).

1.1.1. Sequence of tenses

Children from the youngest age groups use complement clause constructions, mainly with the verbs of perception *ra'a* 'see' or *maca* 'find', with cognitive verbs like *xashav* 'think', *yada* 'know', and address verbs like *amar* 'tell'. No errors were found in sequence of tense use, although children quite often omitted the complementizer *she-* 'that', which is obligatory in these contexts (except in direct speech). Amount of complement clauses does, however, increase with age: Only four of the 3-year-olds and six of the 4-year-olds use such constructions, compared with all 12 of the 5- and 9-yearolds.

Choice of matrix-verb tense depends generally on the dominant tense favored for a particular narrative — either present or past. The single most common construction type has a matrix verb in the present or past tense, followed by a stative complement clause in the present tense "nominal sentence" form — with no overt verb-form, e.g. *hu ra'a she ha-kufsa reyka* 'he saw that the-jar **empty**' [*H3b-3;4*]. These account for well over half of all the complement clauses at ages 3 to 5. Only the 9-year-olds have more complements with lexical verbs than with zero-verb copulas. These manifest all possible combinations, from age 5 up, e.g.:

(2a) **Present + Present = Simultaneous:**

Hu ro'e she hu yored.

'He **sees** that he **descends**.' [=boy sees the dog falling out of the window]' [*H5k-5;9*]

(2b) **Past + Present = Simultaneous:**

Ha-kelev ra'a she ha-dvorim yoc'im.

'The-dog **saw** that the bees **exit**.' [*H4k-4;10*]

Ve raca lir'ot ma ha-cvi ose la-kelev.

'And (he) **wanted to.see** what the-deer **does** to the-dog.'

[*H5g-5;4*]

(2c) **Present + Past = Anterior:**

Ha-yeled ro'e she ha-cfardea barxa.

'The-boy **sees** that the frog **escaped**.' [*H4c-4;3*]

(2d) **Past + Past = Anterior:**

Hu xashav she hivriax oto.

'He **thought** that (he) **made.flee** him.' [=the boy thought that he had chased away the dog] [*H5c-5;3*]

(2e) **Present + Future = Modal-Irrealis**:

Lo roce she ha-kelev yir'e.

'not **wants** that the dog **will.see**' [*H5e-5;3*]

(2f) **Past + Future = Modal-Irrealis**:

ve amar she gam hem yavo'u

'and **said** that they also **will.come**' [=the other frogs should come along] [*H5a-5;0*]

These examples show that in order to define a temporal relationship of simultaneity, anteriority, or prospection to the complement, Hebrew speakers need to alternate between one of two tense forms for the matrix verb (either present or past, depending on the anchor-tense selected for narrative as a whole) and between one of three tense forms for the complement clause. Hebrew-speaking children from an early age learn to use the three tense forms to meet the functions of elaborated relative tense marked by distinct inflections in English or Spanish. But fully flexible use of a full range of alternations occurs mainly from age 5 years in our Hebrew narratives. Younger children tend to restrict complements to description of states with present-tense copula constructions without any overt verb form. Only the older children embed ongoing activities within more complex syntactic structures, e.g., the equivalent of 'He saw the frog disappeared' in preference to 'He saw the frog is not there' or 'the jar is empty'. Similarly, chains of complement clauses are found only from age 5 years up, e.g., *az yada ha-yeled she hu roce le-hagid lo she ha-cfardea kan* 'then the-boy **knew** that he [= the deer] **wants to-tell** him that the-frog (is) **here**' [*H5i-5;6*].

1.1.2. Dominant tense

We examined what tense is favored by Hebrew speakers for telling this story, and to what extent they are consistent in reliance on this form — either present or past — as an "anchor" for the narrative as a whole in a larger set of Hebrew narratives: 16 at each of seven age groups, preschoolers aged 3, 4, and 5 years, school-age children aged 7, 9, and 11 years, and a group of 16 college students as adults (Berman, 1988). Our concern was not with children's command of grammatical tense inflections, since this is found among the youngest age group we studied. Rather, each narrative was analyzed for a "dominant tense," defined as 75% or more of all clauses in the text being in either present or past tense, the other verbs being in one of the other three forms: infinitive, imperative, or future.

Findings are set out in Table 1, where the category of "mixed" applies to narratives which have a more or less equal number of clauses in both tense forms.

TABLE 1
Number of Hebrew Texts with Dominant Present or Past
Tense Forms in Seven Age Groups [N = 16 per group]

	3 yrs	4 yrs	5 yrs	7 yrs	9 yrs	11 yrs	Adult	Total
Past	5	9	10	14	15	12	8	73
Present	2	1	4	1	—	4	7	19
Mixed	9	6	2	1	1	—	1	20

Two-thirds of the subjects anchored their narratives clearly in the past tense, with only adults showing no clear preference in this respect. This favoring of the past is particularly clear among the school-age children, who rely predominantly on past-tense forms nearly 90% (41 out of 48) of the time. The rise in use of past tense from age 4 years up, and its stability across school age, confirms our prediction that school-age children would adhere quite strongly to the past tense, since this agrees with the narrative norms familiar to them from school readers and from other children's literature and storybooks. Reliance on past tense shows that these narratives were clearly in storytelling rather than in picture-description mode, where present tense is normative.

Yet contrary to what we had expected, the younger children do not rely largely on present tense. Only 15% of 48 preschoolers anchor their narratives consistently in the present, and only two out of the 16 children in the 3-year-old group do so. Instead, more than half the 3-year-old texts demonstrate "mixed" tense usage, creating texts which veer back and forth between present and past tense. This holds for nearly half of all the 3- and 4-year-old narratives (15 out of 32), but for very few of those from age 5 years and up. This indicates that the youngest children have not settled on a fixed temporal mode of predicating across the entire course of their narratives. Rather, they shift tense as they move spatially from one picture to the next and linguistically from one predicate to the next.

School-age Hebrew narratives adhere rigidly to pure past-tense forms — with the exception of occasional sequence-of-tense requirements — in contrast to the youngest children, who feel free to move back and forth across past and present tense as their narration proceeds. However, their shift in tense forms serves very different purposes compared with the more mature narratives.

1.1.3. Tense shifting

In considering grammatical sequence-of-tense, we noted that alternation between the three available forms of present, past, and future provides a means for specifying relative tense — to distinguish between simultaneity, anteriority, and prospection in relating the temporal locus of the matrix verb to the content of an associated complement clause. Here, we propose that switching back and forth between present and past tense forms provides Hebrew narration with a means for signaling aspectual distinctions of a more global, discourse-motivated nature. Speakers may choose to use the narrative past tense for the mainline, plot-advancing events associated with the notion of foreground, whereas background states describing scene-setting or associated circumstances will be presented in contrasting present tense.[4]

For example, a Hebrew adult story starts in present tense for setting the scene, and then proceeds to tell the story in the past, literally translated below:

(3) 'Well, first we **see** a boy and his puppy dog **look:PL** at a frog that he **keeps** in a jar. At night the frog **escaped** when he and the dog **slept**, the frog **removed.itself** from the jar and **fled**.' [H20a]

Another adult narrative starts out and proceeds in past tense consistently up until the beginning of the denouement, when the narrator switches to present tense right to the end, thus:

(4) 'And then it turns out that all he [=deer] **wanted to-do was** to get rid of this thing on his head, so when he **found** some kind of high place he **threw.down** the boy from there and the dog, that also **runs ˜ ran**[5] together with him also **flies** [=goes flying off]. And to their great good luck they **fall** into some kind of swamp and **are.saved**. And (they) **continue** to-search for the frog.' [H20b]

A different motivation for tense switching in adult narratives is illustrated by another narrator (H20c). Her long narrative is all in present tense, but she switches to past five times for a variety of purposes, including: to set off a background state from plot-advancing events, as in (5a), or to highlight an event treated as particularly important to the progress of the story, as in (5b). These points are indicated by the verbs in boldface in the literal translations of relevant excerpts in (5a) to (5e).

---

[4] This differs markedly from reliance on formal distinctions of grammatical aspect marked in Biblical Hebrew between sequentially ordered foreground events in the developing narrative compared with background states or simultaneous and anterior events marked by different verb-forms (Givón, 1977; Hatav, 1985, 1989; Longacre, 1981).

[5] The 3rd person singular Hebrew form *rac* of the verb *la-ruc* 'to-run' is ambiguous between present tense 'run(s)' and past tense 'ran'.

(5a) 'A moonlit night, a boy and a puppy play with a frog that (is) inside a jar. (They) **finished** to-play, the boy and the dog **went** to sleep. The frog plots an escape and runs away ...'

(5b) 'The dog continues to play with the bees and shakes the tree so that the hive will.fall. And indeed, the hive **fell**. Millions of bees threaten the dog ...'

(5c) 'And the bees pursue him, the owl threatens the boy, and the boy **climbed** onto a large rock, and looks for his frog, while the dog ...'

(5d) 'And here they run, run, run and **failed** to notice the abyss gaping before them ...'

(5e) 'And when they approach, they see that it concerns a whole family of frogs. So the boy **took** his frog into his hand, **says** goodbye ...'

This narrator seems to need to break out of the shackles of a monotonous one-tense, one-aspect discourse to highlight momentous change-of-state points in the plot. For her, past tense signifies perfective aspect — and, indeed, the past-tense verbs are all semantically punctual.

A similar use of tense switch is made by another adult whose narrative is in the past except for three present-tense clauses, all pronounced with a highly dramatic intonation: (1) Clauses 9-11: 'In the morning the boy and the dog awoke. What **see** they? No frog! The frog vanished ...'; (2) Clauses 24-25: 'They continued to search, wandered about near the house, and don't **find**'; and (3) Clauses 35-37: 'They asked animals they met on the way; (they) don't **find** the frog': [H20e].

Mature Hebrew narrators may thus choose to shift between present- and past-tense forms in different ways, and for different purposes. For them, tense shifting serves diverse discourse functions, all motivated by the overall thematic content of the narrative. In this the adult narratives contrast markedly with the children.

Among the Hebrew 3- and 4-year-olds, switching from present to past or from past to present is typically **item-based**. In some cases, a verb-form that is phonetically ambiguous between past and present tense (like English *cut* or *put*) may trigger a switch from one tense to another — specifically, the forms *rac* 'run/ran', *ba* 'come/came', and *sam* 'puts/has put', in the first conjugation, and the verbs *nixnas* 'come.in/came.in', *nitka* 'get.stuck/got.stuck', and *nishbar* 'breaks/broke' in the mainly intransitive second conjugation. There is also a **semantic** reason why young children switch tense in midgear. Certain verbs are construed as highly perfective or completive in nature, and so for some children they trigger a continuation in past tense even where formerly they had used present tense. This is particularly the case with the verb *nafal* 'fell' and its causative counterpart *hipil* 'make.fall' or 'drop' in our sample.

For example, following three clauses in present tense, a 3-year-old shifts to past tense for these two verbs, and then switches back to present, as in (6).

(6)   *Ve po hu ...* **holex** *ve hu* **mexapes,** *ve hu* **yashen.** *Ve po hu* **nafal** *ki ha-yanshuf* **hipil** *oto. Axarkax hu* **ose** *kaxa.*

'And here he ... **goes** and he **searches,** and he **sleeps.** And here he **fell** because the-owl **made.fall** him. Afterwards he **does** like this.' [H3c-3;5]

Conversely, a typically durative verb like 'want' may trigger a shift to present tense in the less well-formed narratives, as in the excerpt translated in (7).

(7)   'And the boy he **made** a hole, and the dog he **wants** to take it, and here the boy **dug** a hole, and then the frog **exited**.' [H4g-4;6]

Both directions occur in another 4-year-old's description of the boy's encounter with the deer in (8).

(8)   *Kan hu* **shaxav** *al ec, kan hu* **roce** *li-rkav al ha ... kivsa. Ve kan ha-ayil hu* **hipil** *et ha-kelev ve et ha-yeled.*

'Here he **lay** on a tree, here he **wants** to-ride on the ... sheep. And here the-deer he **made.fall** the-dog and the-boy'. [H4h-4;6]

Immature switches between past and present tense like these are strictly local, and unmotivated in more general, discourse-related terms.

Relatedly, certain temporal adverbs trigger present-tense verb forms in rather idiosyncratic ways among the younger narrators. For example, one 3-year-old starts in present tense, then switches to past tense to describe all the boy's falls and being made to fall, but towards the end gives one verb in present tense, thus: *Hem kol hazman mitgalgelim* 'they all the time roll.around' [H3k-3;11]. Another child starts in present tense, shifts to past when she uses the phonetically ambiguous verb *nitka* 'get/got stuck', then goes back to present tense four clauses later, to say: *Ve po hu benatayim holex ve hu mexapes* 'and here he meanwhile goes [=walks] and he searches' [H3c-3;5]. These durative or iterative adverbs seem to trigger present tense which younger children may construe (non-normatively) as aspectually durative, by contrast with the for them aspectually perfective past tense.[6]

---

[6] This suggests, in line with what has been proposed for early development of linguistic temporality, (Aksu-Koç, 1988; Weist, 1986), that these children do have some sense of aspect. Other usages in the 3- and 4-year-old Hebrew texts also indicate some aspectual differentiation. Tense-shifting of the same verb from one clause to the next may denote different phases of an event. For example, a 3-year-old describes the boy's being pushed into the water by the deer by switching from past to present, to false-start present repaired to past, back to present, and again to past tense: *Ve hi* **lakxa** *oto bakarnayim shela. Ve axarey ze hi* **yexola** *le-hapil oto. Mepi - hi* **hipila** *oto, mepila oto, kaxa haya.* 'And it **took** him in its horns, and after that it **can** [=is able to] **make.fall** him. **Makes** - it **made.fall** him, **makes.fall** him, that's how it **was**' [H3d-3;6]. Occasional use of lative is further evidence of aspectual

Lexically-motivated tense shifting is common in the 3- and 4-year-old Hebrew narratives which, as noted, tend toward "mixed" rather than "anchored" tense-usage. The 5-year-old narratives are more like those of the school-age children in this respect. They generally favor past tense, and tense is only occasionally switched in mid-course. In these cases, tense switching reflects a shift in discourse mode, rather than being simply lexically based. For instance, one child starts out in past tense, to tell a tale which opens with 'Once (upon a time) there was a boy ...', then later switches to present-tense in the picture-description mode, saying 'So now he looks for it and he calls to it' [H5j-5;7]. Avoidance of back-and-forth jerky swings from past to present and present to past noted for the 5-year-olds applies across the board among the school-age children with their strong reliance on past tense throughout their texts.

In sum, shifting between past and present tense in the Hebrew narratives closely mirrors the general developmental patterns outlined in Chapter IIA. Such shifts are common among the younger children, who fail to maintain a consistent storytelling mode — either deictically anchored present tense for picture description or temporally removed past tense for fictive narration — and they often lack any obvious motivation. The **item-based** nature of their shifts, triggered either by formal ambiguity or by aspectual features of inherent verb-semantics, accords well with Karmiloff-Smith's (1979, 1986b, 1987) "bottom-up" or databased accounts of immature narratives. The older children tend to less tense switching, generally sticking quite rigidly to a single tense. Where their narratives move between past and present, this tends to relate to **local reorganizations** in online text-production. Only the adults use tense shifting as a means of **global discourse organization**, to set off background settings or denouements from the central body of the plot, or to highlight events construed as critical to plot development.

Our findings thus far show that mature speakers of Hebrew, whose grammar confines them to only two tense forms for marking temporality in these narratives, can deploy these quite flexibly for multiple functions. We next consider whether they also use other, "compensatory" devices to express the aspectual distinctions marked inflectionally in the English, Spanish, and Turkish narratives.

---

distinctions, as in a 4-year-old's use indicating inception with the verb for 'go' in describing the same scene: *Ve axarey ze hu **dahar** al ha-ayil, ve hu **nafal** me ha-ayil, ve hu **halax lipol** me ha-ayil, basof hem **higiu** le-makom she yesh bo yerida ...* 'And after that he **galloped** on the-deer, and he **fell** from the-deer, and he **went to-fall** [=was about to fall] from the deer, in the end they **reached** a place which **has** a descent' [H4h-4;8].

1.2. Lexical Expression of Aspect

Hebrew has three lexical devices for expressing aspectual distinctions: derivational **verb morphology**, which differs from tense inflections in being nongrammaticized and so not fully productive across the lexicon — analogous to English prefixal *re-* to express iteration (Section 1.2.1); **verbs of aspect** that express inception — analogous to English *be about to, be going to* — and other phases in a process like *begin, go on, finish* (1.2.2); and **aspectual adverbs** like *already* for perfectness, or *meanwhile* for simultaneity (1.2.3).

1.2.1. Derivational morphology: binyan verb patterns

Modern Hebrew has a few restricted classes of aspectual marking by means of verb morphology. For example, motion verbs that are nondirectional in meaning may be changed from durative to iterative, as follows: Conjugation 1 *rac* 'run' compared with Conjugation 4 with prefixal *hit-* as in *hitrocec* 'run around', *af* 'fly' versus iterative *hit'ofef* 'fly around, hover'. Verbs in Conjugation 4 (*hitpa'el*) occur in our texts from the youngest age group — e.g., the verb *histakel* 'look (at)' is used without a related verb in another conjugation, and 3- and 4-year-olds also use this conjugation for derived, middle-voice or reflexive verbs that have transitive counterparts in other conjugations, e.g., *hitragez* 'get.angry' (cf. *merugaz* 'be.angry'), *hitxabe* 'hide:REFL' (cf. *hixbi* 'hide:TRANS'), *hit'orer* 'wake.up:INTRANS' (cf. *me'ir* 'wake.up:TRANS'). Yet there are only two instances of Conjugation 4 verbs with an iterative sense in the Hebrew sample: a 7-year-old describes the owl as *hit'ofef* 'flew.around' in the tree; and a 9-year-old describes the dog teetering on the windowsill as *hitno'anea* 'moved.about' (cf. the ordinary verb *na* 'move' from the same root).

Speakers use other devices for expressing iteration and repetition of activities. A favored means at all ages in Hebrew is through lexical **repetition**, with a single verb repeated several times to indicate protraction, as in the following examples.

(9a) *Ve hu **halax** le-tayel ... **halax ve halax**, ve kibel maka.*

'And he **went** for-a-walk ... **walked and walked**, and got hit.' [*H3h-3;8*]

(9b) *Az hem **hitgalgelu ve hitgalgelu ve hitgalgelu**.*

'So they **rolled and rolled and rolled**.' [*H3l-3;11*]

(9c) *Ve axarkax hem **halxu, halxu** ad she higiu ...*

'And afterwards they **walked, walked** until they came ...' [*H5d-5;3*]

(9d) *Ve ha-kelev **rac, rac, rac ve rac**.*

'And the dog **ran, ran, ran and ran.**' [*H5g-5;4*]

(9e) *Ve ha-yeled yashan ve yashan ve ha-kelev yashan leyad-o.*

'And the-boy **slept and slept** and the dog slept next.to-him.' [*H5h-5;7*]

Verb repetition occurs more sparingly in the older narratives, e.g., from one 9-year-old: *Ve hem xipsu, xipsu* 'And they searched, searched'; *Ve ha-kelev barax. Hu barax, barax, barax ve pit'om ra'a ...* 'And the-dog **fled. He fled, fled, fled** and suddenly saw ...'; or *Az ha-ayil saxav oto ve saxav oto* 'So the-deer **dragged him and dragged him**' [*H9c-9;4*]; and an adult also uses this device as follows: *Mexapsim, mexpasim, ha-kelev mexapes betox ha-cincenet, ha-yeled betox ha-magaf* '(They) **search, search**. The-dog **searches inside** the-jar, the-boy **inside** the-boot' [*H20C*]. Lexical repetition is a felicitous means of expressing aspectual iteration and protraction in current Hebrew. With the younger children, it sometimes indicates a disfluency, as a kind of hesitation phenomenon. Mature speakers use it more deliberately, often with a drawn out pronunciation of the stressed syllable of the repeated verbs expressive of intensely protracted activities.[7]

Another aspectual function of verb morphology is to express ingression or entering into a state. Conjugation 4 (*hitpa'el*) is used in this sense twice in the school-age Hebrew narratives, both with the verb for sitting. For example, after the boy climbed the tree: *hu **hityashev** shama* 'he **sat.down** there' [*H9a-9;0*] compared with simple Conjugation 1 *yashav* 'sat'. The other intransitive conjugation (*nif'al*) also occurs occasionally with an ingressive sense, e.g., in the verb *nishkav* 'lie down' compared with basic *shaxav* used by younger children to describe the boy's lying down in bed [*H3h-3;8*] and by older children for how the boy got settled onto the deer's head [*H9j-9;8*].

In general, use of verb morphology for such aspectual functions is rare in the Hebrew narratives, reflecting the generally nonproductive nature of this facet of the *binyan* system of verb-patterns in current Hebrew.[8]

---

[7] This should not be interpreted as an attempt to "compensate for" lack of grammatical aspect in Hebrew. The iteration or protraction expressed by repetition denotes the "extended" aspect relevant to different phases of a process, rather than the internal contour of a unified activity as is expressed by progressive inflections on English, Spanish, or Turkish verbs.

[8] This contrasts markedly with their very productive functioning for marking distinctions of transitivity and voice in current Hebrew (Chapter IVC) and in expressing resultativity and causativity. These properties of the *binyan* verb patterns are well known to, and widely exploited by, Hebrew 4-year-olds (Berman, 1985, in press-b).

1.2.2. Verbs of aspect

One class of aspect-verbs express lative aspect, in the sense of moving one's person or changing location in order to perform an activity. The relevant verbs in the Hebrew narrative are the general word for going — *halax*, and the directional verbs for exiting — *yaca*, descending — *yarad*, and ascending — *ala*. A superficially similar picture emerges from the distribution of these forms among the youngest children and the adults by contrast with the older children. There are only two such examples in the 3-year-old texts: *halax le-xapes* 'went to-search' referring to the dog wanting to find the frog [H3j-3;9] and *yarad la-asot dvash* 'went.down to-make honey' [sic] [H3d-3;6] talking about what the dog was doing with the jar. And among the adults, only the verb for 'go' is used in this way, by only two narrators, once to describe the frog as going outside to take a walk, and once to describe the protagonists' response to the frog's disappearance — in the phrase *holxim le-xapes* 'go:PL to-search'. In contrast, the inception of the search is marked by lative use of 'go' by four of the 5-year-olds, and by the combination *yaca le-xapes* 'exit [=go-out] to-search' by another three 5-year-olds — devices also used by eight of the 9-year-olds. Elsewhere, the basic motion verbs are hardly ever used in a lative sense across the Hebrew texts.

Older narrators make rather wider use of verbs of extended aspect to express different phases in an ongoing process. There are two such verbs: *hitxil* 'begin, start' and *himshix* 'go on, continue' — both followed by a verb in the infinitive.[9] There is a clear developmental trend in use of these forms. None of the 3-year-olds express the idea of inception or initiation of a process, through the verb *hitxil* 'begin, start'. The two children in the 4- and 5-year-old groups who do so, use the verb infelicitously, once as part of a false start at the beginning of a narrative ('The-boy **started**, the boy er ... at night he sat next to his bed and ...' [H4h-4;8]) and once as part of a process whose endstate is more relevant than its inception ('The boy slept, and the dog slept with him, and the frog **started** to go-out') [H5a-5;0]. This contrasts with the school-age children. Several 7-year-olds, 11 out of the 12 9-year-olds, and all the adults in the sample use this verb appropriately to mark inceptive aspect. This suggests that the Hebrew verb for 'begin' constitutes an important aspectual marker for mature renderings of the story. Examples are: 'The dog found a hive of bees and **began** to play with the hive' [H9a-9;0]; 'They didn't find the frog, so then they **began** to-search for it on all sides' [H9d-9;5]; or 'And just then came a swarm of bees that the dog made.fall, and **began** to-fly

---

[9] The verbs specifying termination of a process, *hifsik* 'stop, end' or *gamar* 'finish', do not occur across our database in this sense. This is true of the other languages, too, probably because the story does not include noteworthy instances of cessation or termination.

after the dog' [*H9k-9;8*]. Moreover, among the younger children, the verb 'begin' is confined to local activities, such as the dog's beginning to play with the bees. In more mature narratives, it primarily serves the function of episode instantiation (Chapter IVD).

The verb *himshix* 'continue, go on', also followed by a verb in the infinitive, indicates protraction or continuation of a process. It also is lacking in the youngest narratives, but occurs in two 5-year-old texts, e.g. 'And the dog continued to-scratch the tree and to-climb up it' [*H5h-5;5*]. Half the 9-year-olds and all the adults except one use this form at least once. The verb *himshix* thus shows a similar development to *hitxil*, although with lower frequency. The older children sometimes use it to express protraction in relation to events which are continuing concurrently with some other activity on the part of another protagonist, e.g., 'And suddenly there emerged from the burrow a mole, and the-dog **continued** to look up above, at the hive' [*H9f-9;6*]. A more childish use of this verb is: 'The dog searched inside the-hive and **continued** to search, and the-hive fell' [*H9i-9;7*]. Again, use of this aspectual marker, relating to the narrative plot as a whole rather than to an individual scene is confined to adults. For instance, one (*H20e*) repeats the same refrain *himshixu le-xapes* '(they) continued to-search' several times across her narrative, as each attempt gets thwarted.

In sum, Hebrew speakers use specific verbs for expressing the phasal aspects of inception and continuation from late preschool or school age. Earlier avoidance is not due to any structural difficulty, since 3-year-olds make free use of a finite verb plus infinitival complement in the construction traditionally defined as an extended predicate. However, they do so mainly with modal verbs like *raca* 'want', *yaxol* 'be able to', occasionally with verbs of lative aspect like *halax* 'go', *yarad* 'descend', but not with the verbs *hitxil* 'begin' or *himshix* 'continue'. Presenting events as having inceptive or continuative phases in this narrative context requires that children regard a series of events as interlinked and/or a given scene or event as constituting the starting-point or a continuation of a larger chunk out of the entire narrative. This is something which young children still need to learn, over and above the semantics of the verbs *hitxil* and *himshix* and the syntax of verb plus infinitive constructions, which are acquired well before 3 years of age.

1.2.3. Aspectual adverbs

Since the Hebrew verb-system lacks grammatical marking of aspectual distinctions, we might assume that the Hebrew narratives would rely heavily on aspectual adverbs as a periphrastic lexical device to express distinctions that are marked by verb inflections in languages like Spanish, English, or Turkish. In fact, this was not the case. Expressions like *kvar* 'already' for perfect aspect, *tamid* 'always' or *kol ha-zman* 'constantly, all the time' for durativity, and so on, are rare in the Hebrew texts. The few times they occur, it is in the narratives of the younger children, not of the mature speakers. Thus *kvar* 'already' is used five times in all, by preschool children, never by 9-year-olds or adults. One 3-year-old uses this word, in conjunction with another aspectual adverb *kim'at* 'almost, nearly' as shown in (10).

(10) *Az ha-yanshuf ra'a she hu **kim'at** hipil oto, ve po hu - **kim'at** hi - **kim'at** ... hu **ba-derex le-ze** ... po hu **kvar** hipil oto la-mayim.*

    'Then the-owl saw that he **almost** made.fall him, and here he - **almost** she - **almost** ... he (is) **on.the-way** to it ... here he **already** made.fall him into.the-water.' [*H31-3;11*]

The many hesitations and repairs and the unclear use of pronominal references make this extract hard to interpret even in context. Yet the child clearly means to specify incipient aspect by her use of the word for 'almost' and perfect aspect by use of *kvar* — particularly since the latter was pronounced with highly emphatic intonation. This is confirmed by a 4-year-old's use of *kim'at* to describe what happens to the boy after he climbs the rock.

(11) *Ve tipes al har exad, **kim'at** nafal. Ve hu nafal. Ve hu nafal la-mayim.*

    'And climbed up a mountain, **nearly** fell. And he fell. And he fell in the water.' [*H4c-4;2*]

The few instances of such forms among older narrators tend to have an explicitly contrastive function, e.g., a 9-year-old describes the dog playing with the beehive and goes on to say: 'And then the-hive **almost** fell, and the-mole came-out, and then the-hive fell **completely**', with *kim'at* 'almost' counterposed by *le-gamrey* 'completely, altogether'.

In sum, uses of adverbial expressions like those meaning 'already' (perfect), 'almost' (incipient), and 'all-the-time' (protraction) are occasional and idiosyncratic in the Hebrew texts, confined to the youngest children. Our findings suggest that any effort to "compensate" for lack of overt markers of such distinctions in the grammar is shortlived. More mature speakers evidently do not need to use periphrastic lexical means to make such distinctions explicit in the context of these narratives.

Two other adverbs which we had not predicted to play a role in these narratives demonstrate a very different picture: *pit'om* 'suddenly' and *benatayim* 'meanwhile, in the meantime'. The first shows an inverse U-shaped distribution, as shown in Table 2.

The word *pit'om* 'suddenly' is used by only a quarter of the youngest children, never more than once or twice per text, and equally sparingly by the

TABLE 2

Distribution of the Adverb *pit'om* 'suddenly' in the Hebrew Texts,
by Number of Narrators and Occurrences per Age Group

	3 yrs	4 yrs	5 yrs	7 yrs	9 yrs	Adult
No. of texts with *pit'om*	2	4	7	8	9	4
Total occurrences	3	8	22	32	25	9

adults. In contrast, two-thirds of the children in the middle age groups — 5, 7, and 9 years — use this form, on an average, three or four times per text. The pattern of usage is also developmentally determined. The youngest children use the form in idiosyncratic, unconventional ways. For example, one 3-year-old uses it to mark change, not of event, but of participants: 'And the-bird [=owl] pushed him down. And the dog he ran ... And **suddenly** there is a tortoise here. And here there is also a tortoise' [*H3k-3;10*]. From age 5, the word marks noteworthy new occurrences, as a means of dividing up the narrative into its component parts (see Chapter IVD). Typical is the 5-year-old who uses *pit'om* no fewer than nine times, e.g., Clause 14 — 'Suddenly the dog fell with the jar', Clause 22 — 'And ... the-dog suddenly saw a nest [=hive]', Clause 33 — 'Suddenly Uri [=boy] had the idea to climb the tree ...', Clause 40 — 'And suddenly he saw a tree' ... Clause 43 — 'Then suddenly came an owl' [*H5h-5;5*]. Another 5-year-old uses the word at the beginning of six clauses, e.g., 'And suddenly the boy woke up', 'And suddenly he saw a little hole', 'Then suddenly fell the bees' house' [*H5c-5;6*]. But, as is evident from the English translations, these are not fully felicitous even in the non-canonical function of marking new or noteworthy events in the ongoing narrative. For instance, the content of the story shown in the pictures in no way suggests that the child's waking up was an unexpected or abrupt change of state — as required by the normative referential sense of the word 'sudden'.

Nine-year-olds use *pit'om* more selectively. It is a high-frequency item in their texts, too, but they use it less mechanically than the 5-year-olds. It is not necessarily combined with the coordinator *ve* 'and' as a stereotypic introducer of each successive clause, and may occur in clause-medial or final position, e.g., 'They searched so much in all kinds of holes, that [=till] there jumped out at them **suddenly** a mouselike thing' [*H9b-9;2*], or 'So he swam with the-dog and arrived **suddenly** at a certain place' [*H9d-9;4*]. One 9-year-old always uses the form together with the verb *ra'a* 'see', to signal each encounter with a new and unexpected creature. But even these usages are juvenile, or non-normative, when compared with the adult narratives. Only four adults use this word (often its more literary counterpart *lefeta pit'om* 'all of a sudden'), and they do so sparingly. The one adult who has the expression several times across her narrative (*H20c*) adopts it as one of several devices to create a self-conscious style suited to more traditional children's literature in Hebrew — including high-register vocabulary and subject-verb inversion (Section 3.1).

A similar developmental pattern emerges for the temporal adverbial *benatayim* 'meanwhile'. It is used by only **one** of the children aged 3 and 4 years, by four 5-year-olds, by half the 9-year-olds, and again by only about a quarter of the adults. In the one 3-year-old text, it seems to function as a semantically unmotivated discourse filler, thus: 'And here the dog gets stuck **meanwhile**', 'And when he once gets stuck **meanwhile**', 'And here he **meanwhile** walks' [*H3c-3;5*].[10]

The 5-year-olds use the word for 'meanwhile' in a mixed fashion. One child, who also uses *pit'om* conventionally, says: 'And he [=boy] and then he went to the tree instead of calling to-it, and afterwards he went **meanwhile** to see who was there' [*H5g-5;9*]. Only from school age is the term used with a well-defined temporal function of indicating **simultaneity** in the sense of one event being background to another co-occurrent event (Chapter IVA), e.g., 'And afterwards the boy went to sleep and the dog climbed up on top of him to sleep together (with him) and **meanwhile** the frog got out of the jar' [*H9d-9;5*]; or 'And the boy continued to search, and the hive fell. And the the boy **meanwhile** searched inside the hollow trunk of a tree' [*H9h-9;7*]. Adults use the word less often, always with the sense of co-occurrence, e.g., 'And from excess of fright, he fell from the-tree. **Meanwhile** the dog searched in another region' [*H20b*]; or 'And out of the tree emerged an owl, and threw him down to the ground. **Meanwhile** the-bees chased after Yoye [=dog]' [*H20g*].

Certain more general observations emerge from the way these two temporal adverbs are used in the Hebrew narratives. First, as relatively high-register items, they are rare in the youngest children's texts. Where the 3- and 4-year olds do use them, they lack any clear referential content. Five-year-olds use them more, with a function which, while semantically unconventional, is discourse-motivated. By age 9 years, usage is closer to the adults, but the terms have a stereotypic, mechanical quality. Adults alone use them sparingly, reflecting individual choice of expressive options. In the present context, *pit'om* 'suddenly' suggests adherence to a style evocative of children's storybooks, while *benatayim* 'meanwhile' stresses co-occurrence of foreground and background events. Second, it is not a priori obvious from the

---

[10] This child's text in general is sprinkled with temporal adverbs, like those meaning 'once', 'again', and 'over again', used without any clearly conventional referential content.

literal semantic or referential content of such terms what their function is in extended discourse. Thus *pit'om* serves to mark new or noteworthy events in a dramatic presentation of juvenile style narratives; and *benatayim* serves to link two or more events which are concurrently ongoing at a local level for some but not all the older Hebrew narrators. Third, in crosslinguistic terms, seemingly parallel forms may function differently in different languages. Thus *pit'om* appears to behave similarly to its counterpart in German, but not in English; and the word *benatayim* occurs over 20 times across the Hebrew narratives, but its literal counterpart, *meanwhile* is used only once in the entire English corpus.

2. EVENT CONFLATION

We have characterized Hebrew as a **verb-framed language** (Chapter IIIo), since the core information concerning locative trajectories is contained in the verb.[11] We start with a brief description of the motion verbs and prepositions relevant to expression of locative trajectories in the Hebrew database.

2.1. Verbs of Movement

Hebrew verbs of motion typically encode both direction and causation, as illustrated below:

(12)	**Root**	**Gloss**	**Basic Verb Pattern**	**Causative Pattern**
	k-n-s	enter	*nixnas* [P2-*nif'al*]	*hixnis* [P5-*hif'il*]
	y-c-?	exit	*yaca* [P1-*pa'al*]	*hoci* [P5-*hif'il*]
	y-r-d	descend	*yarad* [P1-*pa'al*]	*horid* [P5-*hif'il*]
	'-l-y	ascend	*ala* [P1-*pa'al*]	*he'ela* [P5-*hif'il*]
	n-p-l	fall	*nafal* [P1-*pa'al*]	*hipil* [P5-*hif'il*]

The unmarked, general-purpose motion verb *halax* 'go' (and also 'walk') is widespread in the narratives of the younger children, who also use other, more specific motion verbs. For instance, in describing the "ascent" scenes — climbing onto the bed, the tree, the rock, the deer, and the log in the water —

---

[11] Recall that for a Semitic language like Hebrew, the term "verb" refers to the combination of a consonantal root and an associated morphological verb-pattern (Section 1.2.1). For instance, the four semantically related verbs *nixnas* 'enter, go in', *hixnis* 'insert, put in', *hitkanes* 'assemble:INTRANS, come in together', and *kines* 'assemble:TRANS, bring in together' all derive from the same root *k-n-s* signifying movement towards the inside of a place, used with four different *binyan* conjugation patterns, termed *nif'al*, *hif'il*, *hitpa'el*, and *pi'el*, respectively.

half of the 3-year-olds use the verb *ala* 'ascend, go.up', and another three use the verb *tipes* 'climb'. Their causative counterparts, too, are found in the youngest narratives, e.g., *ha-kelev* **maxnis** *et harosh letox ha-kufsa* 'the-dog **inserts** his head into the-jar' [*H3e-3;7*]; *ve kan hu* **hoci** *oto* 'and here he **extracted** him (from the water)' [*H4f-4;3*].

These direction-of-motion verbs function much like constructions with the verb for 'go' plus a locative particle in English and German, e.g., *hu* **ala** *al ha-ec* 'he **ascended** [=went-up] on the-tree' [*H3d-3;6*]; *ve az* **yaca** *ha-cfardea* 'and then **exited** [=went-out] the-frog' [*H4i-4;6*]. Like their Germanic bilexemic counterparts, Hebrew direction-of-motion verbs may occur alone, or governing a preposition before the noun phrase specifying the source or goal of motion, e.g., *ha-dvorim* **yac'u** *ve xazru le-...* 'the-bees **exited** and returned to ...' [*H9j-9;8*], and also *me ha-xor* **yaca** *eyze axbar* '**from** the-hole **exited** some mouse' [=a mouselike creature came out of the hole] [*H9j- 9;8*]. The Hebrew narratives make use of both options — bare verb or verb with prepositional phrase — across the age groups, although the younger children use the bare verb far oftener. In describing the dog and/or boy falling from the window, the tree, and the cliff, preschoolers aged 3 and 5 years use a bare verb 70% of the time, compared with 45% of the 9-year olds, and only 8% of the adults. The 9-year-olds add prepositional phrases, while the adults add prepositional phrases and/or locative adverbials meaning 'outside' and 'down(wards)'. Younger children also occasionally use an incorrect preposition, e.g , *nixnas be-* 'enter in' for required *nixnas le-* 'enter to'.

Motion verbs which encode **manner** in our sample include *rac* 'run', *af* 'fly', *kafac* 'jump', used from the youngest age groups. These verbs also have causative counterparts in the *hif il* conjugation, e.g., *ha-cvi* **he'if** *otam* 'the-deer **made.fly** them' [*H5c-5;3*]. The verbs *barax* 'flee' and *radaf* 'pursue' are used from school age to describe, for instance, the dog running away from the bees, and the bees running after the dog. Again, these can be used alone, as bare predicates, or with a prepositional phrase — *barax mi* 'flee [=run-away] from', *radaf axarey* 'pursue [=run after']. But these are not structurally parallel to Germanic verb plus particle constructions since the verb itself encodes the direction and/or manner of activity. Nor do Hebrew motion verbs — whether or not they are marked for manner — have the equivalent of motion verbs like idiomatic 'run into','run around', 'run up'. The Hebrew counterparts of such expressions have no etymological relation to the verb *rac* 'run' or to each other.

In principle, Hebrew-speaking children might use directional adverbs as a redundant compensatory device for marking directionality. Yet this turns out not to be the case. For instance, the adverb *haxuca* '(to the) outside' occurs in only one-quarter of the children's narratives — at most once or twice per text — and it is used with the semantically related verb *yaca* 'exit' only around half the time. The only difference between young children and adults in this respect is that the older narrators make more use of this adverb, with a wider range of verbs. This is true of other adverbs of direction as well. For example, the verb *ala* 'ascend' is followed by *lemala* 'up(wards)' only once across the texts, as is *yarad* 'descend' with *lemata* 'down(wards)', while *nixnas* 'enter' is never once used with the adverb *pnima* 'to.inside'. These adverbs are used more — and with nonsynonymous verbs — by the adults than by any of the children, e.g., *boraxat haxuca* 'flees to.outside' [H20j], *afim lemata* 'fly:PL downwards (into the water)' [H20l], and *mecic lemala* 'peeps upwards' [H20c]. But this merely expresses the lexical specificity and richness typical of the adult narratives. Hebrew narrators in no way make a consistent effort to specify over and beyond what is encoded within the verbs of movement as independent lexical isolates.

2.2. Falling and Throwing in Hebrew

The same trend emerges in the way Hebrew narrators describe the various instances in which the boy and/or dog fall or are thrown — from the window, out of the tree, and into the water. Children rely almost exclusively on the verbs for falling — intransitive *nafal* and its morphologically related causative counterpart *hipil* 'make.fall', equivalent to English *drop* and also *push down* or *throw down*. All of the Hebrew 3- and 4-year-olds use the verb *nafal* on an average three times per story, and over half of them use its causative counterpart. But the children at all ages use *nafal* with some kind of locative prepositional phrase to indicate directionality only around half the time, and they hardly **ever** use expressions of directionality with the causative verb *hipil*.

Where 3-year-olds use a prepositional locative, it will be to express **goal**, e.g. *al ha-rosh* 'on his-head' [H3a-3;0], *la brexa* '**to**.the pool' [H3c-3;5]. Four- and 5-year-olds occasionally express **source**, e.g., *me ha-ec* '**from** the-tree' [H4d-4;2], but only two preschoolers conflate both into a single clause. One child does so after some backtracking and self-repair to produce the sequence *me ha-ayil **letox** ha-mayim* '**from** the-deer into the-water' [H4h-4;8], and another uses a complex prepositional in the form *me al ha-giv'a* '**from on** the-hill' [=from on top of the cliff] [H5g-5;4]. Among the preschoolers particularly, the bare verb for falling or causing to fall suffices to express these downward trajectories most of the time.

School-age children, too, often state quite barely that 'he fell', or 'X made.fall him', with a sentence-final intonation indicating that no further specification is deemed necessary. They differ from the younger children in their occasional use of different verbs and/or adverbs, e.g. *ha-yeled af axora* 'the boy flew backwards' [*H9a-9;0*], *ha-cvi zarak oto la-yam* 'the-deer threw him to.the-sea' [*H9l-9;8*], and they occasionally express more elaborate trajectories, e.g., *nafal pnima im ha-rosh* 'fell inwards with his-head' [*H9j-9;8*]. Adults make use of both these devices far more liberally than any of the children. They use the verb *nafal* much less frequently; they occasionally replace it by a more specific manner verb — e.g., *conxim letox* ... 'parachute:PL [=plunge] into ...' [*H20l*]; and they use causative verbs like *he'if* 'make.fly' or *zarak* 'push' in addition to the ubiquitous *hipil*. Moreover, they alone provide relatively elaborate descriptions of locative trajectories, by one of two means. Adults may use prepositional phrases to conflate several facets of a complex event into a single clause, *hu' af al-ydey ha-cvi **el me'ever la** giv'a **el** ha-nahar* 'was.made.fly by the-deer **over to beyond**.the hill **to** the-river' [*H20i*], *hipil **me'ever la** tehom **letox** ha-bica* 'made.fall **ifrom beyond**.the cliff **into** the-marsh' [*H20k*]. But they are more likely to separate out different facets of the event by means of several distinct predicates, e.g. *Hu **me'if** oto mi ha-macok lema'ala. Ha-kelev **af**, hem **noflim** ltox ha-nahar* 'He **makes.fly** him from the-cliff on.top. The-dog **flies**, they **fall**:PL into the-river' [*H20b*].

2.3. Summary: Locative Trajectories

Hebrew lacks grammatical particles to specify direction of movement in combination with a nondirectional verb. However, motion-of-direction verbs may combine with prepositional phrases to further specify the source, goal, or path of movement. In our Hebrew narratives, the preschool texts generally contain no more than six or seven prepositions. These are basic, they tend to be monomorphemic and polysemous, and they serve both locative and other functions — e.g., to mark verb-argument case-relations or as lexically governed by verbs which take oblique rather than accusative objects. On the whole, the preschool narratives provide minimal locative information by means of prepositional phrases. In addition to stative *be-* 'in, at', younger narrators use *le-* 'to', *al* 'on (top of)', and ablative *mi-* '(away) from', and the all-purpose comitative preposition *im*, as in *nafal im ha-kad al ha-rosh* 'fell with the-jar on his head'. They also use two lexically complex prepositions *be-tox* 'in-within [=inside]' and *le-tox* 'to-within [=into]'. School-age children add several other locative prepositions, reaching an average of 10 per story. These include *mi-tox* 'from-inside [=off, out of]', *ad* 'up to, until', *leyad* 'next-to', *mi-taxat* 'under(neath), below' and *me-axorey* 'from-behind'. Adults average as many as 13 different locative prepositions per narrative, with not one adult using fewer than 10 such expressions.

This use of a wider range of locative prepositions can be attributed mainly to increased lexical diversity and use of a more formal register from school age on. On the whole, however, Hebrew speakers fail to elaborate locative trajectories with much specific detail. This impression is confirmed by the paucity of prepositional phrases and other adverbials used to describe the upward (climbing) as well as the downward (falling) paths motivated by the search story. And it is supported by Hebrew descriptions of the location of the calling and searching activities of the boy and his dog. The lexically specific verb *xipes* 'search, look for' occurs in the text of only two children at age 3 and another two at age 4, in each instance with a direct object NP (grammatically appropriate) and no specification of locational goal. Of the five 5-year-olds who use this verb, two mention location, both with the preposition *betox* 'in(side)' referring to the boy's looking in his boots. In marked contrast, **all** the 9-year-olds specify location of the searching activity at least once, as in the following examples from four different texts: *xipes betox xor* 'searched inside a hole', *xipes mitaxat la-avanim* 'searched under to-stones [=underneath rocks]', *xipes leyad ha-kaveret* 'searched next-to [=beside] the hive', *xipes axarey geza-ec* 'searched behind a log of wood'. But this does not mean that these more mature Hebrew narrators are elaborating on locative trajectories in any **linguistically** significant fashion. Rather, consistently detailed specification of the location of the search by the 9-year-olds, in contrast to the younger children, demonstrates increased descriptive expressiveness, on the one hand, and greater reference to overall plot-structure and the search motif as an organizing element, on the other. Over half the Hebrew 9-year-olds use this verb with a locative expression giving a sense of the search as iterative and protracted, by means of the quantifier *kol* 'all, every' to express the equivalent of English *in all kinds of places, in every nook and cranny, throughout the forest.*

In sum, the Hebrew narratives — including those of the older school-age children — lack complex elaboration of locative paths, goals, or sources. At most, speakers mention either the goal or the source, typically in relation to verbs which lack inherent directionality — like looking or searching. The greater reliance on more — and more elaborate — locative and other prepositional phrases among preschoolers compared with older children, and children compared with adults, is attributable to a combination of Hebrew-particular and more general factors. Hebrew-educated schoolgoers and adults have access to a higher-register lexicon and the impact of literacy — in a language which manifests considerable diglossia between everyday spoken and more formal usage (Berman, 1987b; Ravid, in press). They also demonstrate greater attention to thematic coherence and a more general cognitive capacity for expressing richer descriptive detail typical of a more mature narrative style across the languages in our sample (Chapter IIA)

3. PERSPECTIVE

Here, "perspective" refers to the point of view narrators select in presenting the contents of a particular scene (Chapter IVC). This is expressed through the three interrelated factors of: (1) argument array — which referents are selected as syntactic subject or direct and/or oblique objects; (2) transitivity — does someone perform or undergo an activity, and is that activity self-contained or perpetrated upon some other entity; and (3) grammatical voice — active, passive, or middle. Perspective can be either local or global, depending on whether the scene is treated as an isolated situation or as part of a larger narrative context.

Different such options are analyzed for the Hebrew narratives through two scenes which represent complex interactions between a protagonist and an object (the dog getting its head stuck in the jar — Picture 4) and between protagonists (the boy getting carried away by the deer — Picture 16). Table 3 sums up how Hebrew narrators describe the latter scene. The categories encoded are: **No mention** — only one or neither of the protagonists is mentioned; **Boy as agent** — e.g., *hu ra'a cvi ve halax alav* 'he saw (a) deer and went on.him' [*H3l-3;11*]; **Deer as agent** — e.g., *cvi kaze lokeax et ha-yeled* '(a) deer like.that takes the-boy' [*H5;l-5;9*]; **Boy as patient** — e.g. *hu nitla al ha-karnayim shela* 'he got.hung on its-horns' [*H9f-9;6*]; and **Deer and boy have equal weight** — e.g., *ha-cvi gam asa lo, lakax oto + ve hu haya mamash al ha-cvi* 'the-deer also did to.him, took him + and he was right on the deer' [*H5g-5;4*]; *ha-cvi hitxil li-dhor im ha-yeled + kshe ha-yeled al ha-karnayim shelo* 'the-deer began to-gallop with the-boy + while the-boy (is) on its-horns [*H20k*].

The general development from an agent to a patient perspective, with a concomitant downgrading of the boy as active initiator of all that happens to him, is consistent with what has been noted for the development of narrative abilities in other contexts (e.g., Karmiloff-Smith, 1981, 1983) as well as in these narratives in Hebrew (Berman, 1988) and in other languages (Berman & Slobin, 1987; Slobin, 1990). The global perspective which treats this scene as merely one instance of a more general cluster of events was noted in Chapter IIA. It is confined to the more mature narratives, as in the following translation from Hebrew: 'In the course of their pursuit, they saw different animals, experienced different adventures, an elk and an owl' [*H20f*]. The development of a plot-motivated perspective is also evident from children's descriptions of the dog's entry-into-jar scene. Over half the Hebrew 9-year-olds refer to the jar as where 'the frog was' [=had been] or 'escaped from', but only two 5-year-olds and not a single 3-year-old describe it as 'the frog's jar'.

TABLE 3

Hebrew Perspectives on Boy's Getting Caught by Deer (Picture 16)
in Four Different Age Groups [N = 12 per group]

	3 yrs	5 yrs	9 yrs	Adult
No mention	6	0	0	0
Boy = agent	4	2	1	0
Deer = agent	2	7	6	3
Boy = patient	0	2	4	7
Both weighted	0	1	1	1
Generalized mention	0	0	0	0[a]

a. The adult column adds up to 11, since one adult did not mention this scene at all.

Several linguistic devices are available for differentiating perspectives in Hebrew (Berman, 1993). One means of distinguishing between arguments is by prepositional and inflectional casemarking. This is shown in the examples preceding Table 3, e.g., *Hu halax alav* 'He went on.him'; *Hu lakax oto* 'He took him', *ha-cvi asa lo* 'The-deer did (something) to.him'. Also, dative *le-* can be used to signal an "affectee" or "malefactee" perspective — e.g. *Hu yashan, ve ha-cfardea yac'a ve barxa lo* 'He slept, and the-frog exited and fled to.him [=away from him]' [*H5g-5;4*]. Even the youngest children in our sample have command of these common casemarking prepositions, either as free forms preceding nominals or as prefixes fused to a pronominal stem (Berman, 1985). In their narrations, they use them in the standard form of an unmarked subject NP followed by a direct-object NP with the accusative marker *et* and an adverbial prepositional phrase, e.g., *Hu sam et ha-kad al ha-rosh shel-o* 'He put ACC the-jar on the-head of-him [=his head]' [*H3d-3;6*]; *Ha-kelev hixnis et ha-rosh letox kufsa* 'the-dog inserted ACC the [=his] head into (a) can' [*H3f-3;7*]. Within these favored sentence schemata, two devices emerge as central to alternating perspective in Hebrew: (1) Speakers may adhere to the canonical SVO order of Modern Hebrew (Berman, 1980; Givón, 1977) and change the verb-argument array by focusing on patient rather than actor as surface subject (Section 3.1); or (2) they may change the basic SVO word order in order to focus on nonsubject elements, and so topicalize predicates, arguments, and/or adverbials by preposing them to pre-subject position (3.2).

3.1. Transitivity and Voice

We noted the *binyan* systems of verb conjugations as having little productivity for expressing aspectual distinctions in current Hebrew (Section
1.2.1). However, it is largely obligatory, and highly productive, for expressing changes in transitivity and voice. There are two major types of transitivity
alternations — between intransitive activities (usually in *pa'al* forms) and
their causative *hif'il* counterparts, and between intransitive, middle-voice
events ("achievement" type predicates) in *nif'al* or *hitpa'el* and their transitive
activity alternants. (Compare, for instance, the intransitive and causative
verbs in (12) of Section 2.1.) These are generally mastered soon after
inflections for grammatical tense and agreement, between ages 3 and 4 (Berman, in press-b). Full syntactic passives, in contrast, occur mainly from quite
advanced school age. Use of the intransitive *nif'al* conjugation, which can
function both as a middle-voice intransitive and as a full passive form, was
analyzed for our narratives as expressing a patient rather than an actor-
oriented perspective.[12] Verbs in this pattern are intransitive. They never
govern the accusative casemarker *et*, so that they do not take direct objects
and cannot be passivized, nor can they ever take the agentive casemarker *al
ydey* 'by'. Verbs in the *nif'al* conjugation include (1) a basic direction-of-
motion verb — *nixnas* 'enter' (Section 2.1); (2) other change-of-state or
achievement verbs of the type termed "unaccusative" (Borer & Grodzinksy,
1986; Grimshaw, 1987), generally with causative counterparts in the *hif'il*
conjugation, e.g., *ne'alam* 'disappear' (cf. causative *he'elim*), *nish'ar* 'stay,
remain' (causative *hish'ir*); and (3) verbs which may function either as unaccusatives (hence always agentless) verbs or as the passive counterparts of
pa'al verbs, e.g., *nishbar* 'break [=get-broken]', *nishpax* 'spill [=get spilt]',
and also *nitpas* 'be caught, get caught', *nitka* 'be stuck, get stuck'.

Among 3-year-olds, this pattern was used mainly with the motion verb
nixnas 'enter' (Section 2.1), occasionally for other change-of-state intransitives, e.g., *ve hem **nish'aru** kan* 'and they **remained**:PL here' [*H3c-3;5*]; *hi
ne'elma haxuca* 'she [=frog] **disappeared** outside' [*H3l-3;11*]. There are
only three instances of medio-passives in the 3-year-old narratives: one child
refers to the jar as *nishbar* 'broke [=got-broken]', another refers twice to the
dog as *nitka* 'stuck [=got-stuck]'. The 5- and 9-year-olds use far more
change-of-state verbs in general, and over half of them use medio-passives to

---

[12] There are two other verb-patterns besides *nif'al* which function as passive voice forms,
pu'al and *hof'al*. However, even 7-year-olds have been shown to avoid these forms in structured elicitation tasks, by contrast with their occasional use of *nif'al* to mark either "true" passives or middle-voice "medio-passives" (Berman, in press-b). Besides, *nif'al* is the only one
of these three patterns which figures in our Hebrew children's narratives.

talk about the jar being broken or the beehive having spilt, while a third also talk about the boy and/or the dog as being *nitpas* 'caught', *nitla* 'hung', *nisrat* 'scratched', etc.[13] For instance, in describing the scene of the boy getting caught on the deer, patient-oriented verbs in the *nif'al* form are used by no 3-year-olds, by two children aged 5, by four aged 9, and by five adults. Also, two adults, but none of the children, use a reflexive-type intransitive *hitpa'el* conjugation verb to present the boy as undergoer — *hitlabesh* literally 'get (oneself) dressed, get wrapped around', and *hityashev* 'sit (oneself) down'. In a more extensive data-set analyzed for the dog's entry into the jar scene (Berman, 1993), the patient-perspective predicates *nitpas*, *nitka*, *nilkad* 'caught, stuck, trapped' were used by only 2 out of 28 preschool children, by one-quarter of those aged 7, 9, and 11 years, and by half of the adults. That is, with age, Hebrew speakers make increased use of a productive system of verb morphology to present a non-agentive perspective on events as befalling the boy-protagonist, rather than as prime activator of whatever happens. The means they prefer for doing so is with single-argument intransitive verbs rather than by full or syntactic passives which allow an oblique agent argument.[14]

3.2. Word Order

Modern Hebrew has canonical SVO order, favored at all levels of usage, especially conversational and colloquial narrative style. Departures from SV order are caused mainly by subjectless constructions, which occur in different syntactic contexts at all levels of usage (Berman, 1980, 1990). Our narratives show that subject ellipsis is an important device for achieving text cohesiveness in current Hebrew (Section 4.5). On the other hand, everyday Hebrew shows few traces of the predominantly VS order of Biblical narrative (Givón 1977; Hatav, 1985, 1989). Such predicate-initial constructions occur mainly in existential and possessive contexts with the verb *haya* 'be' or the present-tense existential particle *yesh* '(there) be'. These are common from the youngest narrations — e.g., *yesh yeled ve yareax ve kelev* 'be (a) boy and (a) moon and (a) dog' [H3f-3;7]; *pa'am axat haya yeled ve haya lo kelev* 'one time was (a) boy and was to.him dog [=Once there was a boy and he had a

---

[13] 9-year-olds and adults also make quite wide use of the "unaccusative" verb of inner-state *nivhal* 'be.scared, get a fright', although only the adults use its causative counterpart *hivhil* 'make.scared, frighten'.

[14] These occur in only **one** Hebrew text, as a device used three times in a short narrative for each instance where the boy is described as being harmed by animals, e.g., **hutkaf** *al-ydey shney-hem* '**was.attacked by both.of-them**, *hu'af al-ydey ha-cvi* '**was.plunged** by the-deer' [H20i].

dog]' [*H5d-5;3*]. In the adult texts, such constructions are confined mainly to the initial **scene-setting** part of the story.

Another common, though non-obligatory context for VS constructions is with "presentatives," i.e., predicates which describe appearance on (or disappearance from) the scene (Givón, 1976; Ziv, 1988). Typical contexts in our narratives are scenes where new characters emerge — the mole out of a hole in the ground, the owl out of the hole in the tree, and the bees out of the hive. Examples are given in (13).

(13a) *Ve me ha-xor* **yaca** *axbar*

    'And from the-hole **exited** (a) mouse.' [*H5g-5;4*]

(13b) *Ve pit'om* **hecic** *me ha-xor axbarosh.*

    'And suddenly **peeped** from the-hole (a) rat.' [*H7d-7;5*]

(13c) *Ve bediyuk* **ba** *nexil ha-dvorim.*

    'And just (then) **came** the swarm of bees. [*H9j-9;8*]

(13d) *Le-feta pit'om* **megiax** *xoled mitox xor.*

    'All-of a sudden **pops** (a) mole from-inside (a) hole.' [*H20c*]

These are contexts where the grammatical subject is not a possible (or at least a good) candidate for topichood. VS order assigns the subject nominal a dominant status, serving to introduce new information into the text — in our narratives, to present a new participant in the story — and at the same time focuses on the predicate as clause-initial (Giora, 1981, 1985a, 1985b).[15]

Inversions of the normal SV order are rare in spoken Hebrew, and they are grammatically prohibited if the subject is a personal pronoun (and hence represents topical old information).[16] Nonetheless, we expected the VS option to be quite common in our sample, since this order — which was basic to the narrative discourse mode of classical Hebrew and is still favored by

---

[15] VS constructions sound distinctly odd with nonpresentative predicates or verbs of durative activity predicates and/or with definite NP subjects, e.g., the second of these two clauses: *Hu yaca haxuca ve* **nafal** *ha-kelev* 'He exited outside and **fell** the-dog' [*H5i-5;6*]. Similarly, the first of the following two clauses is well-formed, with a VS presentative predicate, but the one which follows it is anomalous: *Ve* **yaca** *mi-shama cipor ve* **barax** *ha-kelev* 'And **exited** from-there (a) bird and **fled** the dog' [*H5i-5;6*]. Even in English, a presentative predicate allows such inversion, particularly if preceded by a locative expression, e.g., *Out of the reeds come some baby frogs* [*E-20j*].

[16] A cross-sectional survey revealed fewer than 10% VS clauses in preschool children's conversational usage, nearly all of them existentials and possessives with initial *be* (Dromi & Berman, 1986). Longitudinal data also reveal very low occurrence of VS constructions in the speech of Hebrew-speaking children aged 1;6 to 3 years as well as in their parental input (Berman & Weissenborn, 1991).

some contemporary Hebrew novelists — is widespread in the archaic-sounding texts of much current Hebrew children's literature (Ziv, 1988). And we expected VS order to be favored for scenes where a new participant enters the stage — as in the examples in (13). Our findings only partially confirm these predictions. VS constructions are rare among the younger children — used by three 3-year-olds and seven of the 4-year-olds, in only 2.5% of their clauses altogether. Three-year-old usage is occasionally anomalous, but 4-year-olds use VS appropriately, with an existential or possessive 'be', or with a change-of-state verb like *nishbar* 'break, get-broken', *nirdam* 'fall.asleep', *nafal* 'fall', and an occasional presentative *ba* 'come', *yaca* 'exit [=come-out, emerge]'. Older children use VS with lexically specific verbs rather more, in nearly 5% of all clauses in the texts of the 5-, 7-, and 9-year-olds. The bulk of 5-year-old VS clauses are used by only two children, but they are more evenly distributed across the 12 9-year-olds. The 5-year-olds also use VS with a variety of predicates, whereas most such clauses among the school-age children have presentative predicates — *ba* 'come', *yaca* 'exit' *higia* 'arrive'.

We conclude that children know the grammar of VS constructions by as young as age 3 or 4. Later on, they may extend it to inappropriate contexts, to give their texts a deliberately "literary" or storylike flavor. In contrast to 5- and 7-year-olds, the 9-year-olds tend to adhere conservatively to SV order, most of them using it with an occasional presentative or else not at all. Adults, in contrast, show several different patterns of VS usage. Most use it sparingly, like the 9-year-olds, with a varied range of more lexically specific presentative verbs; one avoids it altogether (H20a); and some use VS in one-quarter to a third all their clauses (H20c, H20d, H20k). For them, it constitutes an expressive option suited to a deliberately narrative style of presentation.

In sum, Hebrew narrators learn to use VS constructions as part of an emerging narrative stance. At one level, they use this device in a plot-motivated way, in describing the entry onto the scene of a new protagonist — in this story, another creature that suddenly attacks the boy — an owl, a gopher, or a deer. Some form of the verb *yaca* 'exit, come-out, emerge' is so common as to seem almost formulaic. Yet narrators are free to select other options for introducing a new topic with ordinary SV order, whether with a presentative verb or not. Examples, in translation, include: 'He sees the owl exit(ing)' [H5l-5;9], 'And suddenly the boy saw that a mole comes out' [H7g-7;6], as well as 'And the boy searched near where a mole digs, and the mole exited' [H9g-9;6] or 'They looked in the hole of (a) mole. Suddenly the mole exited' [H9l-9;8]. Speakers have various options for specifying **topic perspective**, an ability which is well-established in the 9-year-old narratives. They may use VS to introduce new participants, but they can also alternate between nondefinite clause-final **object** nominals in one clause and definite clause-initial subject nominals in the next. On the whole, Hebrew speakers very much adhere to canonical SV(O) order wherever a surface subject is required. Two 5-year-olds (*H5g-5;6* and *H5h-5;6*) and three 7-year-olds in the early phases of literacy acquisition show a stylistic preference for VS — evidently aiming to confer a literary or archaic flavor to their narratives; in contrast, it is avoided by 9-year-olds, and is selected as a self-conscious rhetorical option by an occasional adult.

This finding is confirmed by analysis of SV constructions which are not clause-initial. Modern Hebrew allows a wide range of dislocated constructions, in which a nonsubject argument or an adverbial adjunct is preposed to the subject NP for purposes of focus and topicalization. These include the left-dislocation traditionally termed *yixud* 'particularization' in literary Hebrew, in which the clause retains a pronominal copy of the fronted NP, e.g. *Ha-cfardea, hem xipsu ota be-xol makom* 'The-frog, they sought **her** in-every place', *Cfardeo, ha-yeled kara la shuv va shuv* 'His.frog, the-boy called **for.her** again and again'. Only one such construction was found in our narratives, which are typical of spoken usage rather than of more formal written style. Hebrew also allows simple fronting of postverbal nonsubject arguments, e.g. *Haya lo cfardea she ota hu sam betox cincenet* 'He had (a) frog that **her** he put inside (a) jar' [*H20e*]; *Ax et ha-cfardea lo mac'u* 'Yet **ACC the-frog** (they) not found' [=but the frog they did not find] [*H20f*]; *Ve **mi** mishpaxat ha-cfarde'im hu'elu hem lakxu cfardea* 'And **from the family of those frogs** they took (a) frog' [*H20h*]. Such constructions are also very rare, and occur mainly in the adult narratives. Again, our Hebrew narrators fail to avail themselves of a rich apparatus for fronting of object arguments as sentence topics.

The commonest type of dislocation we found are preposed adverbials, e.g., *Hem ra'u ec. Al ha-ec hem ra'u kadur hoki* 'They saw (a) tree. **On the-tree** they saw (a) hockey-ball' [sic] [*H5a-5;0*]; *Az **ba-xor shel ha-ec** haya yanshuf* 'So **in.the-hole of the-tree** was (an) owl' [*H9e-9;6*]; *Sham leyad ha-nahar shama eyze kol mukar* '**There by the-river** (he) heard a familiar voice' [*H20i*]. Preschoolers only rarely prepose locative adverbials, whereas over half the 9-year-olds, and nearly all the adults do so once or twice across their narratives. These serve to break up the monotonous SVO order of stringing one simple clause after another, by focusing on the locative site or source of an event which is presented as new information.

Some narrators also use right-dislocation, e.g., *Aval hu ka'as, ha-yeled* 'But he was.angry, the-boy' [*H3a-3;0*]; *Hu ala al ha-ec, ha-yeled* 'He ascended on the-tree, the-boy' [*H3d-3;6*]; *Hem yashvu, ha-kelev ve hu* 'They sat, the dog and he' [*H9k-9;8*]. These, too, occur occasionally, although they are a well-established device in colloquial Hebrew. With the younger children, they are indicative of disfluency, or of a need to clarify the identity of a referent, rather than a deliberately focused perspective.

In sum, Hebrew speakers avail themselves primarily of verb morphology, less of subject-verb inversion or adverbial preposing, to depart from the neutral, unmarked perspective of SV(O). Across their narratives, these constructions are typically identified with Actor-Activity with or without specification of Undergoer and/or Location or Source — in that canonical order. With age, the narratives show more departures from this standard presentation of events, through increased reliance on an SV Patient-Event orientation, on the one hand, or through clause-initial lexical, presentative predicate or locatives which focus on the site of the event, on the other.

4. CONNECTIVITY

Narrators' choice of means for marking the temporal and logical relationship between events is affected by a combination of factors: (1) The range of devices available in the grammar and lexicon of a given language — their **structural** options — and the preferences they have for expressing certain kinds of relationships — the **rhetorical** options favored by their native language; (2) the overall organizational schema they adopt for presenting their narrative — at both the local and global level; and (3) stylistic preferences and inclinations of individual narrators. This section aims to show how these factors interact in the Hebrew texts to yield the following developmental and rhetorical patterns: The youngest children rely on deictic means of marking the discourse as ongoing (Section 4.1); children in the middle age ranges organize their narratives by means of temporal chaining (4.2); use of the coordinating conjunction *ve* 'and' decreases with age, serving quite different functions at the different stages; subordination increases as a means of event packaging with age (Section 4.3); and topic ellipsis is available to children on a local syntactic level and is used by adults as a means of organizing longer stretches of text (4.4).

4.1. Deictic Utterance Chaining

Various forms demonstrate that the Hebrew 3-year-olds are chaining their narratives from one point in the here-and-now (hence deictically anchored) situation of the ongoing discourse, rather than in terms of an overall plot schema. These include: reliance on deictics like 'now' or 'here' rather than markers of temporal sequence like 'then' or 'afterwards'; repetition of the same lexical items, phrases, and/or clauses coupled with the word *gam* 'also, as well'; and lengthy sequences of clauses all introduced by the single conjunction *ve* 'and'. The texts of the 3-year-olds average around five instances per text of the deictic items *po* 'here', *hine* 'here's' (like French *voici*), and *axshav* 'now' — significantly more than any other age group (Berman, 1988). Deictics are used slightly less by 4- and 5-year-olds, around four times per text, as against once or twice per text among schoolchildren (7, 9, and 11 years of age), and hardly at all among adults.

Deictic anchoring is illustrated by the excerpt in (14) from the first part of a 3-year-old Hebrew text (set out with one clause above the next).

(14) *Po ha-yeled yoshev*   **Here** the-boy sits

      ve ha-cfardea ... yoshevet,   **and** the-frog ... er sits:FEM

      ve ... az ha-cfardea yocet.   **and** ... then the-frog exits:FEM.

      Ve po ha-kelev nitka benatayim,   **And here** the-dog is.stuck meanwhile,

      ve hu merim et ha-magaf gavoa.   **and** he raises ACC the-boot high.

      Ve hu mexabek oto   **And** he hugs him

      *Merov she hu lo mitnaheg yafe **kan**,*   From that he not behaves well **here**,

      ve she hu pa'am nitka benatayim.   **and** that he once is.stuck meanwhile.

      Ve od pa'am hem halxu   **And** another time [=again] they went

      ve hem nish'aru kan.   **and** they stayed here.

      Po hu gam od pa'am raca la'usot kaxa **Here** he once more wanted to do like that.

      Ve po hu benatayim holex.   **And here** he meanwhile goes. [*H3c-3;5*]

The text in (14) manifests considerable connectivity, since each segment echoes an earlier one or is marked as the next step in the narrative. This is achieved by deictic chaining — overt marking of each clause as being added on to what has just been said — by the clause-initiating *po* 'here' and *ve* 'and', alone or in combination. 24 of the 29 clauses of this child's text are initiated by one or both of these markers. Nor is this an exception for the younger children, as shown in (15), a literal English translation of a full 3-year-old Hebrew text.

(15) 'A frog went into the jar, and then the ... the boy fell, and the frog went out. And the dog put its head inside the jar. The boy took the dog in his arms. And the boy calls for the frog. And the dog wants to climb up [=the tree]. And ... and **here** a mouse goes inside the hole. **Here** the dog fell. And the dog ran [=away from the bees]. And then the bird came. And the boy went up the mountain [=the rock]. And the deer up ... and the deer went up the mountain. And **here** the deer **also** went up the

mountain. And the boy went to the sky. And the boy went into the sea with his shoes (on). And **here's** the boy. **Here** the dog goes into the sea. **Here** are frogs. **Here's** the dog and frogs.' *[H3g-3;8]*

Examples (14) and (15) are typical 3-year-old narrations, where the spatial term 'here' anchors the ongoing discourse in deictic picture description. Repeated use of 'and' to introduce each new utterance communicates that more is to come, the main function of children's early use of this marker in interactive conversational discourse; in these texts, it also provides a means of successive chaining of each new predication to the preceding ones (Berman, in press-c).

Children use two other means for cementing the discourse into a unit which is cumulatively rather than hierarchically organized. First, the word *gam* 'also, too, as well' is widely used by the younger children — at least once by nine of the 3-year-olds, eight of the 4-year-olds, and only six of the 5-year-olds. As shown in (15), this word reveals an immature reliance on repetition of the same content to describe distinct events. Another example is when a child says 'And the boy goes up on the deer, and also the boy sits on the deer' *[H3e-3;7]*. From age 5 on, the word is used more felicitously, with the semantically appropriate function of specifying the same situation as applying to two different participants — e.g., 'And the dog wanted to jump from the window, and and ... he jumped, and the boy watched, and after that the boy **also** jumped' *[H5e-5;3]*. In the 9-year-old narratives, the form is used with a combination of semantic felicity, syntactic complexity, and discourse-based motivation, e.g. *Ha'ayil hipil **gam** et ha-yeled ve **gam** et ha-kelev* 'The-deer threw.down **also** ACC the-boy and **also** ACC the-dog [= both the boy and the dog]' *[H9k-9;8]*. In the adult narratives, *gam* provides a **stylistic** option for marking thematic reiteration, or else it has a distinct discourse motivation. Narrator H20b, for instance, uses *gam* only to describe the **dog's** activities. She refers first to the boy as main protagonist, then to the dog as of secondary importance, in such terms as: 'And the dog also slept', 'And the dog also ran with him', 'And the dog also flew (off the cliff)'.

These different uses of the Hebrew form *gam* illustrate points which recur throughout this chapter (and the book, in fact). In terms of form-function relations, occurrence of *gam* as a means of marking narrative connectivity shows that it is not always possible to establish a priori what range of forms will prove relevant to any particular range of functions in extended discourse. In crosslinguistic terms, the literal counterpart to this term need not have the same function in discourse produced by children speaking languages other than Modern Hebrew.[17]

---

[17] The form *auch* seems to perform a similar function in the German children's frog

From a developmental point of view, we see the following progression. (1) The younger children make non-normative use of the form, giving it the unconventional discourse function of an immature device for marking connectivity, where this is defined as some ill-defined connection between what has just been said and what is currently being talked about. This form thus functions as a **precursor** to more mature, normative marking of connectivity in Hebrew narrative discourse. (2) From around age 5 years, *gam* is used with conventional semantic content. (3) Among older children, it may be combined with complex syntactic constructions to present different facets of a particular event, as a means of **event conflation**. (4) Lastly, some adults will choose to use the term with overarching discourse-based motivation — as a matter of personal rhetorical choice though not of grammatical necessity. Use of the form *gam* in these texts illustrates another developmental theme, linking the narrations of the youngest subjects with those of the adults. The 3- and 4-year-olds' often infelicitous use of the term is sometimes quite idiosyncratic. Because they do not fully master the conventional meaning or the syntactic constraints relevant to its discourse-appropriate usage, different children tend to use the term in rather different ways. The children from age 5 up use it conventionally, without much individual variation. The adults, again, are free to use it in individual ways suited to each narrator's selection of a particular narrative style and his or her own range of expressive options.

4.2. Temporal Chaining

Temporal chaining characterizes the texts of children who have a sense that events are organized sequentially, following one another in time within narrative mode (Berman, in press-c). The Hebrew forms which demonstrate this are the expressions *az* 'then', *axarey ze* 'after that', and *axar kax* 'afterwards' — often used with the coordinator *ve* 'and'. Children from age 4 to 9 years use these forms significantly more than either 3-year-olds or adults (Berman, 1988). They occur an average of around 10 times per text in these "middle" age groups, but only around four times per text in the two extreme groups. Example (16) is a typical example from a Hebrew 4-year-old who fails to organize his story in a plot-motivated way around the theme of the search.

(16) 1 'So he saw

    2 And afterwards the frog went out.

    3 Afterwards the dog went inside the frog's jar.

---

stories (see Chapters IIIB, IVA).

4 And he was mad at him.

5 He fell, the dog.

6 Afterwards, he called for the frog,

7 And - and the dog also. [= And the dog did so, too]

8 Afterwards he ... afterwards - afterwards he went out.

9 And he - and he climbed the tree.

10 And afterwards he fell from the tree.

11 And afterwards the dog ran away.

12 And afterwards he sat on those things.

13 And afterwards he went up on stones.

14 Afterwards he - he - he went with him [=deer].

15 Afterwards he, he falls, with the dog. ...

22 And afterwards they took the little frog,

23 And they said goodbye to the big frog.' [*H4d-4;2*]

Children's overuse of these temporal markers shows they have entered the narrative mode. These forms provide a mechanical means for temporal chaining, to announce each successive step in an unfolding discourse. With age, children learn to use these markers more selectively, and more appropriately. Mature narrators will introduce these overt markers of temporal sequentiality only occasionally, to emphasize a discourse-motivated shift from one stage in the plot to another (Chapter IVD).

4.3. Coordination

Hebrew coordination is structured much like in English, by means of the basic conjunction *ve* 'and'. Use of this form for connecting events in Hebrew shows the following development. Initially, children use *ve* as a merely "utterance-chaining" device, to introduce any new clause — as in the 3-year-old texts (14) and (15). There is no necessary semantic or discourse-motivated relation between the clauses introduced by *ve* — e.g., 'The frog er ... it was here, **and** - he also looked at it, **and** it was night' [*H4b-4;2*]. Most of the 3- and 4-year-olds use *ve* in this way, as a "next-utterance introducer," whereas 5- and 9- year-olds use it to chain **clauses**, so marking events in sequence. Around half of all clauses of the 5- and 9-year-old Hebrew texts are introduced by *ve*, compared with only one-third of the adults. (A detailed analysis of this phenomenon is provided in Berman, in press-c, comparing early conversational with narrative data.) This is exactly in line with our finding for the limited adult use of sequential connectives like 'then' or 'afterwards'. The conclusion is that the older children in our sample have mastered the grammar of coordination, both its syntax and semantics, and they know, moreover, that in narratives, events follow one another in temporal sequence. Consequently, they use *ve* together with other forms that mark the unfolding or chaining of events in sequence. Adults in contrast know that these markers are unnecessary, since having one event follow another constitutes the **default** case in narrative. They use *ve* mainly as a syntactic (primarily same-subject) coordinator; they rarely use *ve* or any other means for explicit marking of narrative sequence; and they rely on other devices for embedding, as noted next.

4.4. Subordination

Subordinate clauses are constructed in much the same way in Hebrew as in English, with the following differences. A single subordinator marker *she-* 'that' serves current spoken Hebrew in all three types of subordination.

(1) It is the only complementizer occurring with non-question complement clauses — e.g., *Hu xashav **she** hu hivriax oto* 'He thought **that** he chased.away him' [*H5c-5;3*]; *Hu me'od da'ag la, ki ra'a **she** hi ne'elma* 'He was.worried about.it, **because** (he) saw that it disappeared' [*H9c-9;4*]. The complementizer is obligatory, and cannot be elided like English *that*. Children from age 3 years use these constructions in the context of verbs for seeing and thinking and, among the older children, of being afraid (that something will happen).

(2) The subordinator *she-* is also the main relative clause marker in spoken Hebrew, and is found occasionally in our 3-year-old narratives. The form *she-* is not a relative pronoun, since it merely subordinates the relative clause, and occurs either alone, or with a resumptive pronoun copy of the head NP, as follows. Clauses which relativize subject NPs need no such copy, e.g., *Hu lakax cfardea axat **she** hayta shayexet lo* 'He took one frog that used.to belong to.him' [*H5a-5;0*]. Clauses which relativize direct-object NPs may but need not have a pronoun copy. The following are both well-formed, (a) without a resumptive pronoun — *Hem xipsu betox geza ha-ec **she** hem mac'u* 'They searched inside the tree-trunk **that** they found' [*H7k-7;9*]; and (b), with a resumptive pronoun — *Hayta sham kaveret shel dvorim **she** ha-kelev nora raca litfos otam* 'Was there a hive of bees **that** the-dog terribly wanted to-catch **them**' [*H9j-9;7*]. A resumptive pronoun is obligatory where the relativized NP is oblique, i.e., marked by any preposition other than the accusative direct-object marker *et* — e.g., *ha-kli **she** ha-cfardea hayta **bo*** 'the-jar **that** the-frog was **in.it** [= that the frog had been inside]' [*H9i-9;6*] (see Chapter IVB).

The number of speakers using a relative clause one or more times increases exponentially in the Hebrew texts: from two at age 3 years to five at age 4 and eight at age 5; and 11 of the 9-year-olds and adults use them.

Nearly all the 3- and 4-year-old relative clauses, and over half those of the 5-year-olds, contain relativized **subjects** rather than objects, e.g., the equivalent of 'a boy that threw the frog' [*H3e-3;7*], 'the cube that hangs on the tree' [*H4g-4;3*]. In contrast, around two-thirds of the 9-year-old relative clauses relativize object or locational NPs — e.g., with a direct object, the equivalent of 'the toad that they found' [*H9i-9;7*]; with an oblique object — 'the owl that he called to' [*H9f-9;6*]; and, predominantly, with a locative phrase such as '(a) burrow that above it [=above which] was (a) beehive' [*H9e-9;6*].

Surprisingly, many of the relative clauses used by children are structurally ill-formed, even by standards of everyday colloquial usage. This is most notable among the 9-year olds, possibly because they construct more complex relatives than the younger children. Nearly all errors are in use of the resumptive pronouns. Younger children tend to insert redundant subject pronouns — e.g., the equivalent of 3-year-old 'a boy that **he** was very cute', or 5-year-old 'a boy that **he** caught a frog'; older children either omit the oblique pronoun, or else they repeat the full noun phrase or produce some incorrect version of the required pronominal form. The example in (17) is with a repeated NP and in (18) with omission of the obligatory resumptive pronoun, both from 9-year-olds.

(17) *Az ha'ayil saxav oto ve saxav oto, ve hu nafal im ha-kelev shelo letox ha-nahar. Em ... hu nafal letox ha-nahar **she ba-nahar betox** yesh cfarde'im*. (cf. **she betoxo** *yesh cfarde'im*)

'So the deer dragged him and dragged him, and he fell with his dog into the-river. Er ... he fell into the-river **that in-the river inside** are frogs.' (cf. **that inside-it** are frogs) [*H9d-9;4*]

(18) *Hu higia le-macok **she mitaxat** haya bica*. (cf. **she mitaxat-av** hayta bica)

'He reached to a-cliff **that under** was (a) swamp.' (cf. **that under-it** was:FEM (a) swamp) [*H9i-9;7*]

These errors seem due to difficulty in processing of the internal structure of relative clause constructions rather than to lack of grammatical mastery of the syntax of relative clause formation at the level of the isolated sentence. They suggest that in ongoing discourse, given the pressures of online processing and organization of information, speakers will opt for descriptive expressivity — which may sometimes be at the expense of structural accuracy.[18]

---

[18] This seems to be the case in relative clause construction in general. Listening to native adult speakers of English, even in relatively structured situations of lecturing or formal addresses, one is struck by the number of breakdowns in grammaticality in the relative clauses which they produce.

(3) The subordinator *she-* also serves in a third type of dependent clause construction — adverbials. These are typically introduced by prepositions which combine with *she-* to form subordinating conjunctions, e.g. *axarey she hem halxu lishon* '**after that** they went to-sleep' [*H9f-9;6*]; *hem himshixu lexapes ad she ha-kelev nafal* 'they continued to-search **until that** the dog fell' [*H9g-9;6*]; *bimkom she ha-kelev yihye acuv, hu likek oto* '**instead that** the-dog will.be sad, he licked him [=instead of the dog being sad, he (=dog) licked him (=boy)]' [*H9k-9;8*].

The Hebrew narratives show a clear age-related development in amount and variety of adverbial subordination. Only two 3-year-olds use these constructions, but seven 4-year-olds, nine 5-year-olds, and all the 9-year-olds. The 3- and 4-year-olds use no more than one or two subordinators per text, limited to the monolexemic items *ki* 'because' and *she-* 'that' used as a truncated form of *kshe-* 'when, while, as', which they use to express cause and temporal contiguity. The 9-year-olds average around four such constructions per text, with as many as nine different subordinators. These include the more normative *kshe* 'when, while' (as common as the general subordinator *she-* in this temporal sense); several other temporal conjunctions — *ad she-* 'until', *me'az she* 'since', and *axarey she* 'after'; and other logical connectives — causative *mipney she-* 'because' (a higher-register variant of *ki*), purposive *kdey she* 'in order that' and *bishvil she* 'so that', and concessive *bimkom she-* 'instead that' and *afilu she* 'even that = even though'. The adult texts average five or six subordinators each, with a much wider range of lexical items — on a higher register of usage and denoting more specific semantic relations — e.g., *mi-she mit'orerim* '**from-that** (they) wake.up [=upon their waking up]', *be-od she ha-kelev xozer ...* '**in-another that** [=whereas] the-dog returns ...' [*H20c*]; *bi-zman she hem yeshenim* '**in-time that** they sleep [=while they are sleeping]' [*H20h*], *lifney she hem holxim lishon* '**before (that)** they go to-sleep' [*H20l*], and *kax she ha-cincenet nish'ara tfusa* '**such** [=so] **that** the-jar remained stuck' [*H20k*].

Hebrew has two other structural options for clause-subordination, infinitivals and nominalizations. The first express purpose, and are typically used alone by preschoolers, without an overt purpose marker like *kdey, al mnat* 'for, in order that' — e.g., *raca lavo la-cfarde'im shelo lexapes oto* 'wanted to.come to.his-frogs **to.search** (for) him' [*H4i-4;9*]; *raca lehikanes letox ze, lir'ot ma yesh po* 'wanted to go inside it, **to.see** what is there' [*H4l-4;11*]. The most complex subordinating constructions are nominalizations, in the form known as *shem ha-pe'ula* 'action noun' in Hebrew grammars. These are characteristic of a more formal register, and are mastered only at late school age by Hebrew-speaking children (Mayroz, 1988). They are translatable by both gerundive *-ing* forms and abstract nominals in English — e.g., *mi-bli* **yexolet** *shel ha-yeled la-redet* 'without **ability** of the-boy to.go.down' [*H20c*] translates as both 'without the boy being able to-go.down' and 'without the boy's ability to go down', and it has a more transparent finite clause equivalent *mi-bli* **she** *ha-yeled yaxol la-redet* 'without **that** the boy is.able to-go.down'. This nonfinite nominalized construction is syntactically very different from simple clause structure, since it contains no surface subject or else has the subject follow the nominalized verb. Such a nominalization is used once by only one child across the Hebrew children's texts: *Ha-yeled haya ąsuk benatayim* **be-xipus** *axarey ha-cfardea* 'The boy was busy meanwhile **in-search** for the-frog' [=searching for the frog] [*H9h-9;7*]. In contrast, eight out of the 12 adult narrators use such constructions at least once, and some of them do so several times, e.g., *Hem mamshixim bi-* **merucat-am** 'They continue in-flight-their [=they continue with their flight, they continue to flee'] [*H20d*], *Ha-kelev merim et ha-ozen shelo le-shema ha-kirkurim* 'The dog raises its ear **at-hearance** the-croakings' [=to hear, upon hearing] [*H20k*]. In structural terms, this is a fully productive option for syntactic subordination. The fact that it fails to occur in the children's narratives confirms that Hebrew nominalizations constitute a higher-level stylistic device, not nearly so typical of everyday colloquial (and hence children's) usage as either gerunds in English or the corresponding subordinating nominalizations in Turkish (see Chapters IIIA, IIIE).

In sum, the Hebrew narrators rely increasingly with age on subordination as a means of syntactic connectivity, whereas they make only occasional use of the more complex, and higher-register option of nominalization as a means of conflating separate predicates within a single surface clause.

4.5. Subject Pro-Drop = Topic Ellipsis

Languages characterized as "pro-drop" from the perspective of parametric syntax typically license the omission of surface subject pronouns in all types of clauses (Borer, 1984; Hyams, 1989; Weissenborn 1991). Yet Hebrew is not uniform in this respect (Berman, 1990). In simple clauses, verbs can occur without a surface subject pronoun in past and future, but not present tense, and in first and second person, but not in third person. We might therefore expect subject elision in the Hebrew frog stories mainly in coordination with same-subject predicates (Section 4.3), e.g., *Hem kar'u lo ve Ø lo mac'u oto* 'They called to.it and Ø not found it [=did not find it]' [*H5f-5;4*], *Ha-yeled kafac min ha-xalon ve Ø herim et ha-kelev* 'The-boy jumped from the-window and Ø lifted the-dog' [*H9e-9;5*]. But subjects may be elided in other, noncoordinating contexts in the Hebrew narratives, as a discourse-motivated device for establishing connectivity by means of **topic elision**. The surface subject is often omitted when there is no change of referent, even where single-sentence syntax requires a grammatical subject. The extended adult excerpt in (19) illustrates topic elision.

(19) *Ba-boker **ha-yeled ve ha-kelev** hit'oreru. Ma **hem** ro'im? Eyn cfardea, ha-cfardea ne'elma!* Ø *hitxilu le-xapes ba-xeder,* Ø *herimu et ha-mita,* Ø *herimu et ha-mnora,* Ø *hezizu et ha-xalon,* Ø *xipsu mitaxat ha-na'alayim, betox ha-garbayim,* Ø *lo mac'u shum davar.* Ø *patxu et ha-xalon,* Ø *ca'aku baxuc, **ha-kelev** navax ...*

In.the-morning **the-boy and the-dog** awoke. What (do) **they** see? (There's) no frog, the-frog disappeared! Ø began:PL to-search in-the-room, Ø lifted:PL the-bed, Ø lifted:PL the-lamp, Ø moved:PL the-window, Ø searched:PL under the-shoes, inside the-socks, Ø not found:PL a thing. Ø opened:PL the-window, Ø shouted:PL outside, **the-dog** barked ... [*H20c*]

Third-person pronoun elision of the kind indicated by a zero in (19) is not syntactically licensed in Hebrew. Yet the need to use the overt pronoun *hem* 'they' for each clause referring to the boy and dog — established as the topic at the outset of this segment — is obviated by the discourse factor of **topic maintenance** across a stretch of text. The Hebrew children's narratives (as noted, largely in SVO order), reveal a marked rise in overall occurrence of null subject clauses with age: only 9% of clauses in the texts of the 3- and 4-year-olds, 16% in the 5- and 9-year-olds, and as high as 34% of the adults' clauses. With age, subject elision also occurs in different contexts. Among the 3-year-olds, the occasional null subjects occur in coordinated clauses or else they are referentially opaque. The 5- and 9-year-olds all use syntactically well-formed null subjects in coordinated clauses, and occasionally in subordinate clauses — e.g. *Hem halx-u ve halx-u, ad she* Ø *higi-u le-makom ...* 'They walked:PL and walked:PL until (that) Ø came:PL to (a) place ...' [*H5g-5;3*]; *Ba-boker hu kam ve me'od da'ag la, ki* Ø *ra'a she hi ne'elma* 'In.the-morning he got.up and was very worried about.it, because Ø saw that it disappeared' [*H9c-9;4*]. The older children also sometimes use topic elision as a device for connectivity, in grammatically separate but sequentially congruent clauses with a shared discourse topic, as in (20).

(20) *Ve ha-yeled yashan ve ha-kelev yashan al yado.* Ø *hit'oreru, ve lo* Ø *ra'u et ha-cfardea.*

And the-boy slept and the-dog slept next to-him. Ø awoke:PL, and not Ø saw ACC the-frog. [*H5h-5;5*]

This shared-topic application of subject elision is rare in the 3- and 4-year-old narratives (1.3% of their clauses) and is relatively infrequent among the 5- and 9-year-olds (15% of their subjectless constructions, compared with nearly half the subjectless clauses among adults). And even the older children, the 9-year-olds, use subject elision for topic-maintenance in connecting single pairs of adjacent clauses as in (20), rather than across entire segments of narrative as in the adult text in (19). Among adults, thematic organization is commonly achieved by elision of a shared subject-topic, although not all of them rely equally on this device for achieving text connectivity. Four of the 12 adults produce texts 25% or more of whose clauses have thematically-determined null subjects, compared with an average of under one-tenth of the clauses in the other adult narratives. For some but not all mature narrators, so-called "pro-drop" is a favored expressive option which serves to create tightly-packed texts consisting of large chunks of verb-initial clauses with no surface subject.

5. NARRATIVE STYLE

Hebrew-acquiring children face the same task as children acquiring other languages from the point of view of narrative style. They need to recognize the linguistic conventions appropriate to this particular discourse mode in their culture. In Hebrew, this entails a rather extreme diglossia between normative, more classical forms of expression typical of literary style and the everyday conversational usage that underlies children's early language acquisition. Hebrew children's literature, including prose and verse works meant for toddlers and children of nursery-school and kindergarten age, to this day manifests peculiarly "literary" usages. We noted subject-verb inversion as an example of such a device, which is used quite widely by only a few preliterate children and self-consciously literary adult narrators in our sample (Section 3.2). A second indicator of higher, more literary style is use of bound morphology where spoken Hebrew prefers analytical expression — particularly in possessives and other genitive constructions. Although the preschoolers all show good command of tense and agreement inflections, they never use bound forms of possessive pronouns in these texts. They occur occasionally in school-age texts, e.g. *xadro* 'room.his' rather than colloquial *ha-xeder shelo* 'the-room of.him' both meaning simply 'his room' [H7e-7;5], *kalb-o* rather than *ha-kelev shelo* 'his dog' [H9b-9;2], *rosho* rather than *ha-rosh shelo* 'his head' [H9d-9;5], *beyt-am* 'house-their' for *ha-bayit shelahem* 'the-house of-them' = 'their house' [H9k-9;8]. They are commoner in the adult Hebrew texts, again used mainly by those who in general adopt a higher-level, self-consciously literary narrative style.

A third means of "raising" the narrative to a literary register is by higher-level vocabulary. In Hebrew, this is readily available for numerous vocabulary items, where a more formal term exists alongside of a relatively synonymous colloquial counterpart, often one deriving from the earlier Biblical stage and the other from the later Mishnaic stage, or vice versa. The more formal alternatives are, again, a school-age development, not found in the preschool texts. For example, preschoolers use colloquial *hitxabe* for the verb 'hide (oneself)', but a few school-age children and adults use the higher register item *histater* 'hide [=secrete] oneself'. This is also true of certain closed class items, e.g. *le-axar mi-ken* 'thereafter' for everyday *axarkax* 'afterwards' [*H9f-9;6*] and *le-feta* 'of-a-sudden' in place of casual *pit'om* 'suddenly'. Use of the higher-level alternants indicates recognition that a more official or "bookish" narrative style is called for. This knowledge typically emerges with acquisition of literacy and the formal study of language at school, and is applied selectively by educated adult speakers of the standard dialect.[19]

6. SUMMARY

The Hebrew database reported on in this chapter in part relates to texts elicited from 7-year-olds and 11-year-olds (2nd and 6th graders) in addition to the age groups dealt with in the other chapters in this part of the book. Findings for these two groups confirm the two major breakoff points noted for the development of narrative abilities across the book: preschoolers compared with school-age children as against adults — where the 11- to 12-year-olds are in most respects more like their 9-year-old counterparts than like fully mature narrators (Berman, 1988) The following summary of the main findings reported in this study thus treats all the school-age children as a homogeneous group.

6.1. Tense/Aspect

Since Hebrew lacks grammatical marking of aspect, relative tense is expressed through alternation of the three simple tenses, present, past, and future. Five-year-olds already are able to vary tenses appropriately between matrix and complement clauses for this purpose. Moreover, unlike 3- and 4-year-olds, from age 5 years, children typically anchor their narrations in one dominant tense, whereas the 3-year-olds, and to a lesser degree the 4-year-olds, tend to move back and forth unsystematically between present- and

---

[19] A further source of evidence for a more formal, self-consciously "correct" style of usage is phonological — whether speakers observe classical alternations in certain morpho-phonological environments, which are typically violated in colloquial everyday usage of even standard speakers. Examples include substitution of the back vowel *u* for consonantal *v* (historically *w*) in pronouncing the coordinator meaning 'and' before bilabial consonants or a syllable with a schwa and spirantization of the stops *p*, *b*, and *k* in the appropriate environments. For example, speakers typically say *ve-be-kol a-...* 'and-in-all-the ...' instead of normative *u-ve-xol ha- ....* Again, some of the older, school-age children occasionally, and sporadically, as well as several adults, more consistently, observe these alternations — providing a more formal, higher-register delivery to their oral narratives.

past-tense forms of verbs. All the school-age children, and most of the 5-year-olds anchor their texts in the past tense, in a markedly similar fashion, with only the adults in several instances preferring present tense as the temporal anchor for their narratives.

There is a marked change in the function served by tense shifting between present and past across the age groups. As noted, the younger children do this unsystematically, motivated by local considerations of the form or content of the particular verb they have just uttered in the preceding clause; from age 5 years, tense shifting in Hebrew serves a normative grammatical function of sequence of tenses to mark relative tense in complex clause constructions; among adults, tense shifting is also used for its traditional literary purpose of creating contrasts between foreground and background material in extended discourse.

There is little use of other, "compensatory" means for expressing aspectual distinctions which are grammaticized in other languages in this sample. Verb-pattern *binyan* morphology is rarely exploited for this purpose across the Hebrew frog stories. The two aspectual verbs meaning 'start' for inception and 'go on' for protraction are quite common, but only from age 5 years on, increasing as a function of age from schoolchildren to adults. The other single favored means for lexical expression of aspect is through two adverbs: the first, meaning 'suddenly', is a favored marker of inception or abrupt change of state among children aged 5, 7, and 9 years old, in contrast to its low use among younger preschoolers and adults; the second, meaning 'meanwhile', is a preferred means of expressing simultaneity of two events, starting from age 5 years, with a clearly defined temporal function from age 9.

6.2. Event Conflation

In Hebrew, as a verb-framed language, children use verbs encoding direction of motion from age 3 years on, but there is little elaboration of locative trajectories across the sample, even though 9-year-olds and adults do occasionally mention both source and goal in a single clause (typically through prepositional phrases), and with age there is an increased variety in the range of prepositions used to express locative relations. Speakers also avail themselves of *binyan* verb morphology to encode causativity within the verb rather than across clauses.

6.3. Perspective

The devices used by Hebrew narrators to vary perspectives on a scene include changing verb-argument relations within the simple active clause by alternating nominatives, accusatives, and datives. This children can do from age 3 years on, although they vary these options less flexibly and skillfully than older children and adults. Adopting a patient perspective through use of intransitive, inchoative-type verb-morphology occurs from age 3, but is found increasingly both in quantity and variety of predicates so alternated from school age on.[20] Use of VS rather than standard SV order to vary perspective by highlighting a presentative predicate (e.g., 'and suddenly jumps out a strange animal') becomes established only at school-age, with adults making selective use of this option in some but by no means all of their narrations. Younger children again, vary word order in a less well-motivated fashion, with schoolchildren adhering more typically to standard, quite stereotypical SVO canonical order.

6.4. Connectivity

Three-year-olds chain one utterance after another in their ongoing discourse, typically by means of spatial deictics meaning 'here' and/or by reiteration of utterance-initial 'and'. A precursor of more normative connectivity marking is an additive element meaning 'also, too' to indicate that the same thing is happening again, or the same character is appearing again. In contrast, 5-year-olds and school-age children typically link up each ensuing clause to the one just preceding in a mechanical overmarking of temporal sequentiality or successiveness, by expressions meaning 'and then, afterwards', with older children making increasingly felicitous use of syntactic coordination with same-subject deletion. Two more mature devices to achieve textual cohesiveness in Hebrew are by subordination, which shows a clear linear progression across the different age groups, and subject elision, which serves in grammatical coordination and subordination increasingly from age 5 years up, and for maintained topic elision among some 9-year-olds but more extensively among the adults alone. Another means of packaging clauses within more tightly bound syntactic bundles is through use of nominalizations, again a device confined to the older Hebrew texts.

---

[20] Flexible deployment of the same verb-root in different *binyan* affixal patterns is probably a major means for selecting, maintaining, or alternating perspectives in Hebrew discourse.

Chapter IIIE

DEVELOPMENT OF LINGUISTIC FORMS: TURKISH

Ayhan A. Aksu-Koç

0. INTRODUCTION

This chapter tells the story of the Turkish frog stories, with particular focus on the expressive means used in their telling. The Turkish frog stories come from child and adult native speakers of standard Turkish from urban middle-class backgrounds in Istanbul. The majority of the 3- and 5-year-olds were seen individually in their preschools, and a few in their homes. The 9-year-olds were all seen at home. The adult group consists of 20-24 year-olds, all students at Boğaziçi University. There were 10 subjects in each group. Although some of the adult narratives reflect a playful attitude and an intentional choice of more "literate" syntactic forms, all the narratives represent colloquial Istanbul Turkish.

An evaluation of the Turkish preschool narratives in terms of the criteria of general narrative ability formulated in Chapter IIA yields the following picture. The 3-year-olds, like their peers in other languages, describe independent picture frames rather than recounting events organized around a plotline. A few narrators point to the escape of the frog as the event marking the beginning of a sequence of events, one refers to the search, and two note the termination of the search with the finding of a frog. As a result, the texts of the 3-year-olds do not meet the standards of a narrative, and lack coherence and cohesion (Halliday & Hasan, 1976). While there are no apparent grammatical errors in the use of the highly regular verb morphology, a few errors are observed in the use of more complex subordinate clauses.

About half of the 5-year-olds follow this same pattern, while the other half produce narratives which display a more sophisticated narrative structure, with reference to the inception, the continuation, and the termination of the plotline. Their texts provide evidence for the differentiation of a narrative time distinct from speech time (see Chapter IVA), displaying linguistic means such as sequentiality markers and an anchor tense. These texts contain more grammatical errors since they contain many more complex syntactic constructions.

The 9-year-old narratives present a very stable picture: All refer roughly to the three major components of the plot; all maintain an anchor tense and use temporal markers with a global, theme-related motivation. The two temporal axes are differentiated in the sense that children can go back and forth between sequencing events in narrative time and making evaluations about them in discourse, but they do not exploit this possibility much, preferring to stick to the linear progression of events.

Additions in the adult narratives involve the use of a formally rich language to express a tightly cohesive and coherent story. Most of these texts suggest that our adult narrators interpreted their task within a "children's storytelling frame" and produced detailed descriptions and elaborations as they probably would if they were really telling the story to a child.

This chapter summarizes developments in the formal means of expression in the Turkish narratives: After a sketch of the tense-aspect-modality system (Section 1), we examine the development of means for describing the component parts of a situation (Section 2), means for encoding different perspectives (Section 3), and means for achieving textual cohesion (Section 4).

Descriptions of major features of the phonology, morphology, and syntax of Turkish are available in various grammars of Turkish (Banguoğlu, 1974; Gencan, 1975; Kononov, 1956; Lewis, 1967; Underhill, 1976, to cite a few) and major trends in the acquisition of Turkish as a native language can be found in Aksu-Koç and Slobin (1985). Analyses relating to linguistic and structural aspects of adult narratives based on film retellings are found in Erguvanlı-Taylan (1987) and Aksu-Koç (1992a, 1992b). Other treatments of specific aspects of Turkish grammar will be referred to in the relevant sections.

1. TURKISH TENSE/ASPECT/MODALITY

Turkish, which has an agglutinative morphology, expresses the categories of tense, aspect, and modality: (1) morphologically by a set of affixes appended after the invariant verb root, and (2) lexically, with verbs and adverbs. A brief summary of the most basic affixes is sufficient in the present context.

The essential pattern is a root followed by a series of affixes, adjusted by vowel harmony and voicing assimilation to fit the root and each other, proceeding from left to right.[1] The verb complex itself can be quite long, consisting of a string of affixes between the root and the final tense-aspect and person-number affixes. The intervening affixes indicate valency and voice

---

[1] Vowel harmony operates throughout all words of native origin and for all grammatical suffixes, which harmonize with the last vowel of the lexical root. There are two main sets of vowel allomorphs in grammatical morphemes: a two-way alternation, e/a, for the plural, most oblique cases, and several verb affixes; and a four-way alternation, i/ı/ü/u, for accusative, genitive, possessive, and most verbal and deverbal affixes. The two-way contrast is a front-back alternation of unrounded low vowels, as in the plural suffix -ler/-lar, e.g., büyük-ler 'parents' and çocuk-lar 'children'. The four-way contrast is a front-back, rounded-unrounded alternation of high vowels, as in the present progressive suffix -iyor/-ıyor/-üyor/-uyor, e.g., gel-iyor 'coming', al-ıyor 'taking', düş-üyor 'falling', and koş-uyor 'running'. For the sake of simplicity, all examples of grammatical morphemes in this volume are given in the front unrounded form (e.g. -ler PLURAL and -iyor PRESENT/PROGRESSIVE). An additional morphophonemic change affects stop consonants, which undergo voicing assimilation. As a consequence, the past-tense suffix, represented here as -di, has a d/t alternation along with the four-way vowel contrast, resulting in forms such as gel-di 'came', git-ti 'went', bul-du 'found,' düş-tü 'fell', and so forth. In addition to verb and noun inflections, the yes/no question particle mi and the topic/focus particle de undergo the alternations described above. As reported by Aksu-Koç and Slobin (1985), vowel harmony is mastered early and without error by Turkish children, and all of these variants are equally accessible and productive.

(causative, reciprocal, reflexive, passive), negation, modality (ability, necessity, probability, optativity), and illocutionary force. For example, consider the following verb from the frog story, which conveys negative ability in the past tense and was predicated of the boy and dog: *bul-a-ma-dı-lar* 'find-ABILITY-NEG-PAST-PLURAL' (=were not able to find). In addition, there are various nonfinite and deverbal forms. (Most important for our texts are the various "converbs" that function for temporal coordination and subordination, discussed in Section 2.)

The Turkish tense-aspect-modality system can be characterized in terms of two main dimensions, one temporal, PAST-NONPAST, and one modal, DIRECT EXPERIENCE - INDIRECT EXPERIENCE. The indirect experience modality includes both **inference** and **hearsay**. A choice of one of the two modal forms is obligatory when reporting past events. The suffix indicating direct experience is *-di*, and this form is glossed as D.PAST, which can be read as either "direct experience past" or "*di*-past." The indirect experience (or "nonwitnessed") form is *-miş*, glossed here as M.PAST, which can be read as "*miş*-past," summarizing over its several functions as described below. The past-tense distinction can be illustrated by the following example. If I have seen the boy fall from the tree, I must say *Çocuk düş-tü* 'boy fall-D.PAST; if I infer that he fell from the evidence of seeing him on the ground, or if I have been told that he fell, I must say *Çocuk düş-müş* 'boy fall-M.PAST. Because the inferential use of the M.PAST reports a completed past process on the basis of its result, it is often translated by a present perfect ("The boy has fallen"); however this form is not, in itself, a perfect, and in most instances it can also be translated by a simple past ("The boy fell").[2] In its hearsay use, however, it is a simple past tense ("The boy (evidently) fell"). The M.PAST is also the modality of folktales and traditional stories, and some of our narrators use this "narrative modality" to convey the entire frog story. In such narrations the D.PAST is absent and the M.PAST serves as the sole past tense.

Within the domain of aspect, the morpheme *-iyor*, which is traditionally glossed as PROGRESSIVE, is more of an imperfective and serves as present tense for both states and processes, contrasting with the habitual/generic *-er*. In this study we gloss V + *-iyor* simply as PRESENT (abbreviated as PRES). In the past tense, however, *-iyor* combines with both D.PAST and M.PAST to produce past progressives: *düş-üyor-du* 'fall-PROG-D.PAST (=was falling) and *düş-üyor-muş* 'fall-PROG-M.PAST' (=was (apparently) falling). There is no grammaticized marking of perfectivity (i.e., completion or boundedness) as in

---

[2] For a discussion of the relations between perfects and evidentials, see Anderson (1982, 1986).

languages like Spanish or Russian.[3]

In the domain of tense, the affix -ecek indicates future tense (and has modal uses that need not concern us here). Turkish has recourse to compound tense/aspect constructions in both the past and future. Of relevance to the frog story is the past perfect, which is formed in both modal versions of the past. The D.PAST suffix is affixed to -miş, historically a participle, to produce a **direct experience** past perfect: *düş-müş-tü* 'fall-PERFECT-D.PAST' (=had fallen). Within a narrative text anchored in the M.PAST, the past perfect is formed by combining the participial use of -miş and its modal-temporal use: *düş-müş-müş* 'fall-PERFECT-M.PAST (=had apparently fallen).[4]

1.1. Tense

1.1.1. Anchoring tense/modality

One of the criteria for the well-formedness of a narrative is the choice of a consistently favored tense. In the present context this was defined as the tense of at least 75% of the clauses in a given text. In Turkish narratives, either the PRESENT, the D.PAST, or the M.PAST can be the dominant or anchor form. Between 2 to 3 years of age, Turkish children learn to use all three inflections quite flexibly and without any error of form. Around age 3 they begin to oppose the two past-tense forms to distinguish the two evidential modes.

---

[3] The morpheme -iyor, historically the progressive marker, is better characterized as an imperfective aspect marker today, as recent analyses suggest (Aksu-Koç, in preparation; Dahl, 1985; Erguvanlı-Taylan, 1992). In the narrative context investigated here, its use in reference to past situations serves to present temporally-bounded situations in their ongoingness and as such makes the gloss of PAST PROGRESSIVE, in keeping with the traditional use, more appropriate.

[4] There are many other complex combinations, but this sketch should be sufficient to orient the reader to the distinctions that play a role in the frog story texts. Analyses of both acquisition and adult data suggest that modal and aspectual distinctions are more basic than tense distinctions in Turkish. For example, Yavaş (1980) proposes that in Turkish, the present tense receives zero marking and that the only true tense marker is -di for past tense. Slobin and Aksu (1982) analyze the semantics of -miş, with discussion of its aspectual and modal as well as temporal functions. Aksu-Koç (1978, 1988a) reviews the developmental progression of the aspectual, temporal, and modal functions of -iyor, -di, and -miş in acquisition. Savaşır (1986) describes the modal as well as aspectual character of -er and traces the development of future reference in children's language (1983). Tura (1986) shows that dir is a modal operator that assumes different values on a scale of factivity. Work by Johanson (1971), Dilaçar (1974), Slobin (1993a), Aksu-Koç (1988b, 1992), and Erguvanlı-Taylan (1988, 1993) suggests the dominance of aspectual or modal meanings carried by various subordinating structures.

.At age 3, all three forms can be observed in the children's narrations, but they are not used with clear discourse organizational functions. This is evident from the children's inability to maintain an anchor tense across a piece of narrative discourse. By age 5, more than half of the children can adhere to a dominant tense and make discourse-appropriate use of tense/aspect shifts; and by age 9 and beyond, all speakers manipulate tense/aspect in accordance with the demands of a thematically organized and cohesive narrative. The distribution by age of Turkish texts anchored in the present, the D.PAST, and the M.PAST is presented in Table 1.

TABLE 1
Frequency Distribution of Turkish Texts Anchored in
PRESENT, D.PAST, and M.PAST, by Age

Age Group	Mean Age	Mean No. Clauses	Dominant Tense			
			PRES	D.PAST	M.PAST	MIXED
3 yrs	3;11	35	3	—	1	6
5 yrs	5;5	52	4	—	3	3
9 yrs	9;7	39	7	1	2	—
Adult		82	6	2	2	—

The ability to follow the plot structure goes together with the tendency to maintain a dominant tense. Those narrators who incorporate the major plot components into their stories are also the ones who use an anchor tense. More than half the 3-year-olds do not keep to an anchor form but shift between the three tense forms, as motivated by the inherent aspectual properties of the verbs evoked by the pictures. The remaining children prefer the PRESENT, as a tense anchored in the deictic present, or use the M.PAST, which can indicate either state or narrative modality. The number of 5-year-olds maintaining an anchor tense increases, and only three show mixed use. Examples (1) and (2) illustrate mixed tense/aspect use.[5]

(1) *Bir de kozalak düş-müş. Arılar çık-mış, dala çık-mış deliğe bak-ıyor çocuk.*

'And a pine cone fell-M.PAST. The bees exited-M.PAST, the boy climbed-M.PAST the branch, and is.looking-PRES at the hole.' [*T3b-4;0*]

---

[5] Verbs in subordinate clauses in (2) and (3) are nonfinite converbs, with no tense marking, as described in Section 2.

(2) *Çocuk elbisesini ters giy-iyor. Camdan bakarken çocuk başına giy-di o kurbağanın olduğu şeyi.*

'The boy is.wearing-PRES his clothes backwards. While the boy was looking [while.looking:CONVERB] out of the window (the dog) wore-D.PAST the thing the frog was in on its head.' [*T5e-6;0*]

At age 9, all the narrators maintain an anchor tense, favoring either the PRESENT or the M.PAST, with only one text in the D.PAST. The 10-clause text below exemplifies this 9-year-old strategy very well, with all main-clause verbs marked with the PRESENT (-/fIiyor).

(3) *Çocuk bir kurbağa yakal-ıyor. Akşamleyin çocuk uyurken kurbağa kaçıyor. Çocuk sabah kalkınca kurbağayı arıyor, bulam-ıyor. Çesitli hayvanları kurbağa zanned-iyor, en sonunda bir geyiğin sırtına düş-üyor. Geyik onu suya atıyor. Suda kurbağayı bul-uyor.*

'The boy catches:PRES a frog. In the evening while the boy is sleeping [while.sleeping:CONVERB] the frog escapes:PRES. When he wakes up [when.wake.up:CONVERB] in the morning the boy searches:PRES for the frog, he cannot.find:PRES it. He mistakes:PRES various animals for the frog, finally he falls:PRES on the back of a deer. The deer throws:PRES him into water. He finds:PRES the frog in the water.' [*T9h-9;11*]

The majority of the adults similarly prefer to anchor their narratives in the present, though two use the D.PAST and two use the M.PAST. It could be argued that a preference for the present is a function of the task, which involves looking at the pictures while telling the story. However, a tendency to use the present as a narrative form was also observed in a study in which adults had to retell a segment of a Turkish movie immediately after viewing it. In this task, 70% of the narrators used the present -*iyor* as the anchor tense, 10% used the habitual present -*er*, and 20% chose the past of direct experience -*di* (Erguvanlı-Taylan, 1987). In other words, these findings suggest that the present is the appropriate tense for a vivid narration in Turkish. The present may be preferred for recounting events viewed from inside, i.e., regarded as psychologically relevant to the self, and the narrative -*miş* may be preferred if a psychologically distant perspective is chosen.

Since the frog stories were elicited with the use of a picturebook, our texts contain many static descriptions. These are nominal predications with a demonstrative plus noun, or predications with the existential forms *var/yok* 'exist/not exist', either unmarked or marked with -*miş*. These constitute 23% of the total number of clauses of the 3-year-olds, and are deictically anchored to the moment of speech and perception, as in the following example:

(4) *Bu da kurbağa anne bu da bebek.*

'And this (is the) frog mother and this (is the) baby' [T3d-3;7]

In adult texts, on the other hand, only about 9% of clauses use nominals to predicate locative or experiential states.

Stative predications can be either juvenile, perceptually-motivated, or mature, thematically-motivated, as shown in the following two examples, both from 5-year-olds.

(5) *Burda bir köpek var, kurbağa var, çocuk var. Burda da bir çocuk var. Uyuyor yatağında. Burda kurbağa var.*

'Here there is a dog, there is a frog, there is a boy. And here there is a boy. He's sleeping in his bed. Here there is a frog.' [T5b-5;0]

(6) *Sonra bakıyor çocuk uyandığında, kurbağa yok. Çizmesinin içine bakıyor, yok orda da.*

'Then, at.his.waking the boy looks, the frog is not there. He looks inside his boot, it is not there either.' [T5a-5;4]

More mature functions of such predications are found in older texts. Example (7), from a 9-year-old, shows the use of an existential predication for the purely discourse purpose of backgrounding, and example (8), from an adult, describes the psychological state of a protagonist.

(7) *Daha sonra geyik tam uçurumun kenarına geliyor, orada da bir göl var, onu - onları oraya atıyorlar.*

'Later on they come just to the side of the cliff, and there, there is a lake, they throw him - them there.' [T9a-9;3]

(8) *Çocuk- şey- korkulu ama hiç urkutucu, panik bir hava yok, resimlerde hiç bir şekilde.*

'The boy is in fear but there isn't a scary, panicky atmosphere, in the pictures in any way.' [T20f]

In sum, the static descriptions are triggered by the perceptually available pictures at all ages but the function of such predications in narrative discourse changes with development.

1.1.2. Tense shifting

The major functions of tense shifting in narrative are to indicate changes in temporal perspective and to speak in "different voices." Tense shifting allows the speaker to make grounding distinctions between events, and to move between narrative and discourse time for digressions, asides, and evaluations. For example, in (9) the narrator shifts out of narrative time (marked with D.PAST) to the PRESENT HABITUAL to make a statement of opinion:

(9) *Ama büyük bir şanssızlık topraktan kurbağa — tabii kurbağa ne arar toprağın içinde — kokarca çıktı.*

'But with real bad luck, out of the hole, the frog — of course what does a frog do-PRES.HAB in the ground — a skunk came.out-D.PAST.' [*T20c*]

Another function of tense shifting is to mark retrospection to a past time relative to the anchoring point. Example (10) illustrates a shift from the PRESENT to PAST PERFECT to refer to a past event, then to -*miş* to refer to its present result, then back to the PRESENT:

(10) *Sonra dışarı pencereden bağır-ıyorlar, ha, ha, ha, köpek de kafayı sok-muş-tu ya kurbağanın [=kavanozun] içine orada kal-mış kafası. O da onunla birlikte otur-uyor pencerenin pervazına.*

'Then they call-PRES out the window, ha, ha, ha, you know the dog had.inserted-PAST.PERF its head into the frog [=frog's jar], there remained-M.PAST its head. It is sitting-PRES together with him on the windowsill.' [*T20f*]

Shifts from the PRESENT to the M.PAST also serve to retrospectively express the coda at the end of the story. Example (11) shows such a switch for presenting an evaluative statement arrived at by inference from evidence.

(11) *Ve kurbağayı gör-üyorlar, yanında eşi de var hatta. Demek kurbağa eşine ve çocuklarına kavuşmak için herhalde özgürlüğü seç-miş kavanozdan kaç-mış.*

'And they see-PRES the frog, he even has his wife beside him. It turns out that the frog probably has.chosen-M.PAST freedom and escaped-M.PAST from the jar in order to be together with his wife and children.' [*T20d*]

The 9-year-old sample reveals a different picture. Six of the ten narrators display no tense switching. They maintain an anchor tense and use adverbial, complement, and relative clauses as well as aspectual shifts to present events from different perspectives. They keep to the forward moving tempo of the story, relating events sequentially or simultaneously, without diverging from the timeline of events for elaborations. The few instances of tense shifting mark retrospection. Example (12) illustrates an interesting shift from the M.PAST to the D.PAST for referring to a prior event:

(12) *Çocuk da atla-mış ve köpeğine çok kız-mış kavanoza gir-di diye başı.*

'The boy jumped-M.PAST as well and really got.mad-M.PAST at his dog because its head got.into-D.PAST the jar.' [*T9c-9;1*]

A 9-year-old whose story is anchored in the present switches to the M.PAST for expressing the resolution of the story with an inferential statement.

(13) *Yani böyle birsürü macera geç-iyor başlarından. Ondan sonra bir ağacın şeyinde kurbağa, çocukları var, bir de eşi var. Yani evine git-miş kurbağa.*

'They go.through-PRES a lot of adventures. After that at a thing of a tree [=hive] there's the frog, there are its children and there is its wife. That is, the frog went-M.PAST home.' [*T9b-9;5*]

The 5-year-old stories present frequent alternations between tense/aspect forms but these are aspectual rather than systematic tense shifts, in line with this age group's tendency to move between the narrative and the picture description modes. Children who display tense switching are those whose texts show some level of plot organization. Example (14) comes from a text in which the preferred tense is the PRESENT but there are frequent shifts to the D.PAST. The motivation for type of shift is not so clear, but it allows the child to juxtapose an ongoing activity with a concurrent event:

(14) *Arılar da köpeğe saldır-ıyorlar. Çocuk düş-tü.*

'The bees are.attacking-PRES the boy. The boy fell-D.PAST.' [*T5e-6;0*]

Some 5-year-olds also display the use of the M.PAST to express inferred information, if not exactly for retrospection, as illustrated in (15):

(15) *Sonra bak-ıyor, bak-ıyor, kurbağa yok. Kurbağa yok ol- kurbağa kaybol-muş.*

'Then he looks-PRES, he looks, the frog is not there, the frog be.NONEXIS is- the frog got.lost-M.PAST.' [*T5c-5;1*]

The majority of the 3-year-olds use mixed tense aspect. Their shifts are motivated by the nature of the activities in the pictures, and are, therefore, aspectual in character, as discussed in the next section.

1.2. Aspect

Turkish speakers have several means to express aspect: (1) grammatically, in the verb inflectional system; (2) with a few serial-verb constructions composed of a main verb plus an aspectual verb, functioning like a grammatical morpheme (such as *bak-a-kal-mak* 'stay-looking', *koş-u-ver-mek* 'give-running' (=run in haste)); (3) with verbs of aspect that express inception, cessation, protraction, and the like; (4) aspectual adverbs such as *hala* 'still', *zaten* 'already', *heryerde* 'at all places', *hertaraf* 'all over'; and (5) nonfinite verb forms such as converbs and nominalizations used in subordination. The devices in the last category are discussed in Section 2 (event conflation), in Section 4.2 (grammaticized connectivity), as well as in Chapters IVA on the expression of simultaneity and IVC on event packaging; therefore they are not examined here.

1.2.1. Grammatical aspect

In this section we examine how shifts between present (-*iyor*), stative, and habitual forms are used in texts anchored in the present and the two modal forms of the past tense.

TABLE 2
Proportion of Simple and Aspectually Marked Clauses
over Total Number of Clauses,
by Age and Tense[a]

Verb Form	3 yrs	5 yrs	9 yrs	Adult
		Age		
Present Tense				
EXIS (substantives)	22.8	10.0	8.5	8.9
PRES (-*iyor*)	26.6	39.6	44.9	32.4
HAB (-*er*)	0.3	-	-	1.2
D.Past Tense				
D.PAST (-*di*)	5.6	9.5	7.5	7.5
D.PAST.PROG (-*iyor-di*)	0.8	1.2	0.5	1.6
D.PAST.PERF (-*miş-di*)	0.3	-	-	1.0
D.PAST.HAB (-*er-di*)	-	-	-	-
M.Past Tense				
M.PAST (-*miş*)	35.9	26.7	18.3	15.7
M.PAST.PROG (-*iyor-miş*)	2.6	4.1	1.3	1.2
M.PAST.PERF (-*miş-miş*)	0.3	-	0.3	0.6
M.PAST.HAB (-*er-miş*)	-	0.2	-	-

a. The proportions do not add up to 100 because subordinate clauses with nonfinite verb forms are not included.

In the present tense, existentials (*var/yok*) and predicate nominals serve to present states of existence. Verbal predicates take either the PRESENT -*iyor* for ongoing/durative activities/states or the HABITUAL -*er* for generic statements about states of affairs viewed from outside the narrative line (background information). If the story is told in the witnessed modality, anchored in the D.PAST, background information can be provided in the PAST PERFECT -*miş-di*, the PAST PROGRESSIVE -*iyor-di*, and the PAST HABITUAL -*er-di*. If the story is told in the nonwitnessed or narrative modality, anchored in the M.PAST, *-miş* is interpreted as anchored at a past temporal point. Aspectual distinctions in M.PAST narratives parallel those described above for D.PAST: the PAST PROGRESSIVE *-iyor-miş*, the PAST PERFECT *-miş-miş*, and the PAST HABITUAL *-er-miş*.

Table 2 presents the proportion of simple versus aspectually marked clauses with the three anchor tense/modality bases. The PRESENT *-iyor* occurs with high frequency at all ages. The proportion of clauses in the D.PAST PROGRESSIVE and the M.PAST PROGRESSIVE is much lower. In fact, these decrease in the 9-year-old and adult texts together with the shift away from the use of the M.PAST as the preferred anchor form.

In the adult texts anchored in the present, stative information about the setting or characters is typically introduced at the beginning with substantive predicates, while the dynamic events of the story are presented with *-iyor*. In texts anchored in the past, shifts from the D.PAST to the D.PAST PROGRESSIVE *-iyor-du*, or from the M.PAST to the M.PAST PROGRESSIVE *-iyor-muş*, serve to make grounding distinctions, to present two or more events as simultaneous, or to introduce narrator's comments or evaluations. The nature of these relations may be further specified with aspectual or temporal adverbs. In (16) a switch from the anchoring M.PAST to the M.PAST PROGRESSIVE functions to present the dog's activities as an ongoing background event, further emphasized with the imperfective adverb *hala* 'still'. In (17) the alternation between the D.PAST and the PAST PROGRESSIVE similarly relates the two events as cotemporal, but the adverb of simultaneity assigns equal value to both.

(16) *Derken o yuvanın içerisinden sıncap çıkınca, şey, çok şaşır-mış ve kork-muş çocuk. Köpek de **hala** arı kovanına bak-ıyor-muş.*

'When a squirrel came out of that nest, the child really got.surprised-M.PAST and got.scared-M.PAST. And the dog **still** was.looking-M.PAST.PROG at the beehive.' [*T20a*]

(17) *Osman olanca gücüyle bağır-dı. **Bu sırada** Bobi de kafasındaki kavanozdan kurtulmaya çalış-ıyor-du.*

'Osman called-D.PAST with all his might. **Meanwhile** Bobi was.trying-D.PAST.PROG to get rid of the jar on his head.' [*T20e*]

These same functions are observed in the texts of the 9-year-olds. In the following example, the setting is described with the M.PAST in its inferential/perfect functions, introducing already achieved states. Then the PRESENT *-iyor* is used as the dominant tense for the foreground events of the story:

(18) *Şimdi bir çocuk bir kurbağa bul-muş. Bunu bir kavanozun içine koy-muş. Ondan sonra çocuk uyurken kurbağa kaç-ıyor.*

'Now, a boy found-M.PAST [=it seems] a frog. This he put-M.PAST [=it seems] in a jar. And then, while the boy (is) sleeping [while.sleeping:CONVERB], the frog escapes-PRES'. *[T9e-10;0]*

Shifts in the 5-year-old texts are typically for local contrasts between events/states and ongoing activities. However, there are also sporadic examples of more mature uses. One child who uses the M.PAST for recounting the main story events sets the scene with M.PAST.PROGRESSIVE as in (19), and comments on the typical characteristic of a protagonist with the M.PAST.HABITUAL as in (20).

(19) *Bir varmış bir yokmuş. Burada çocuk yatağının başında otur-uyormuş. Sonra köpek de kaplumbağaya bak-ıyormuş. Sonra çizmelerinin arasında otur-uyormuş çocuk. Bir gün yatağına gir-miş horl-uyormuş. Sonra köpek gel-miş, üstüne atla-mış.*

'Once there was once there wasn't [=once upon a time]. Here the boy was.sitting-M.PAST.PROG on his bed. Then, and the dog was.looking-M.PAST.PROG at the tortoise. Then (he) was.sitting-M.PAST.PROG between his boots, the boy. One day he got.into-M.PAST his bed and was.sleeping.deeply-M.PAST.PROG. Then the dog came-M.PAST and jumped-M.PAST on him.' *[T5g-5;2]*

(20) *Çocuk cok kız-mış çünkü kargayı görünce, hiç sev-mezmiş kargayı.*

'The boy really got.angry-M.PAST on seeing the crow because he didn't.like-M.PAST.HAB the crow at all.' *[T5g-5;2]*

For some of the younger children, shifts between aspectual forms seem to be motivated by a need to contrast dynamic events with states from the perspective of an anchoring point which coincides with the moment of perception (see Chapter IVA). This perspective seems to be true of all of the 3-year-olds, and it occurs in portions of 5-year-old narrations when they move into picture description. This kind of aspectual contrast is particularly evident in cases where PRESENT *-iyor* alternates with *-miş*, as in (21) and (22):

(21) *Burada gid-iyorlar. Bir ağaç bul-muş-lar. Kurbağa, arılar gid-iyor şu resimde. Kork-muş bu da.*

'Here they are.going-PRES. They found-M.PAST a tree. The frog, the bees are.going-PRES in that picture. And that one got.scared-M.PAST.' *[T5h-5;0]*

(22) *Köpekle çocuk ormana çık-ıyor. Kozalak, bir de köpek, bir de çocuk, bir de delik ... bir de kozalak düş-müş. Arılar çık-mış, dala çık-mış, deliğe bak-ıyor çocuk.*

'The dog and the boy are.going.out-PRES to the woods. A pine cone, and a dog, and a boy, and a hole ... and a cone fell-M.PAST. Bees came.out-M.PAST, the boy climbed-M.PAST the branch (and) is.looking-PRES in the hole.' [*T3b-4;0*]

Sometimes a shift between -*iyor* and -*miş*, contrasting activities with states, may be a function of the half-narrative half-descriptive strategy of the narrator. Even adults move between the two modes, but their aspectual alternations function to describe the physical setting or the emotional state of a protagonist inferred from the pictures.

1.2.2. Lexical aspect

The proportion of utterances with lexical specification of aspect increases with age: 3% and 4% of the clauses in the data of 3- and 5-year-olds contain some lexical specification of aspect, rising to 8% for 9-year-olds and 12% for adults. These relatively low proportions are not surprising, since aspect is grammaticized in the verb inflectional system. Table 3 presents the distribution of aspectual verbs and adverbs in aspectually specified clauses by age.

TABLE 3
Proportion of Aspectual Verbs and Aspectual Adverbs in Clauses
with Lexical Specification of Aspect, by Age

	3 yrs	5 yrs	9 yrs	Adult
Aspectual Verbs	20.0	41.0	34.2	50.8
Aspectual Adverbs	50.0	51.0	64.1	41.4
Repetition of Main Verb	30.0	10.0	—	3.6
Serial Verb	—	—	—	1.8

First, it is observed that the rhetorical strategy of repeating the main verb for expressing protracted aspect is favored by younger narrators, as in *Ağaç düşüyor, düşüyor, düşüyor, düşüyor* 'The tree is falling, falling, falling, falling' [*T3e-4;0*] or, *Koşmuş koşmuş geyik* 'Ran, ran the deer' [*T5j-5;3*]. The few instances of repetition in the adult data mark iterative aspect: *Arılara havlamış, havlamış, havlamış.* 'He barked, barked, barked at the bees' [*T20i*].

Second, only the adults use certain aspectual verbs conjoined in serial-verb-like constructions. These are locative verbs with stative meaning such as *kal* 'stay, remain', *koy* 'put', *dur* 'stop, remain', and the verb *ver* 'give'. There are several examples of this category in the data, signifying protracted or inceptive aspect, as in the following example, with *ver*:

(23) *Bu arada ilerideki bir ağaçta asılmakta olan arı kovanı gözlerine ilişi-ver-di*

'In the meantime a beehive hanging on a tree ahead attracted their attention [lit. 'gave-touch to their eyes'].' [*T20e*]

Table 3 shows that the children tend to favor aspectual adverbs over verbs, while adults prefer aspectual verbs. Two possible explanations come to mind: First, younger narrators may prefer adverbs because these can be used for modifying one or two constituents within the clause, while verbs have the whole clause under scope of modification. A second explanation rests on the discourse functions that are typically served by these forms in our stories: aspectual adverbs have a **local**, and aspectual verbs a **thematic** function

1.2.2.1. Aspectual verbs. Aspectual verbs occur as the main verbs of infinitival complements of the form V+INF(+CASE). This complement type is already observable in the 3-year-old narratives, although almost exclusively with the modal verb *iste* 'want'. Aspectual verbs in such constructions start to be used at age 5, becoming more frequent in the data of older children and adults. Adult narratives show that complement clauses with verbs such as *başla* 'start', *çık* 'set.out', and *devam et* 'continue' function to express the instantiation, reinstantiation, and continuation of the search, the general theme of the story. It is, therefore, not surprising that younger children, whose narrations proceed picture by picture, do not use these linguistic means.

Adults express twice as many different categories of aspect with verbs as compared to children, who mark only **inceptive, protracted**, and **lative** aspect. The first two categories can also be adverbially marked, whereas lative aspect, denoting an agent's movement to perform an action, can only be expressed with verbs (e.g., *çık* 'exit', *koyul* 'set.out'). Only three of the 5-year-olds specify lative aspect, two locally, as in (24) and one thematically, foreshadowing the mature uses to mark the beginning of the search as in example (25) from a 9-year old:

(24) *Köpek de arıların yuvasındaki şeyi rahatsız ediyor, onlar da sokmağa geliyor.*

'And the dog bothers the thing in the bee hive, and they **come to.sting**.' [*T5e-6;0*]

(25) *Sonra köpeğiyle beraber kurbağayı aramağa çıkıyorlar.*

'Then together with his dog they **set.out to.search**.' [*T9e-10;0*]

Inceptive aspect is the most frequently marked category across the different ages. The verb *başla* 'start' is similarly used to mark the beginning of a locally specific activity by 5-year-olds, as in (26).

(26) *Arı eviymiş dediler, vurmağa başladılar.*

'They said "it's a bee house," they **started to.hit**.' *[T5a-5;4]*

'Start' is also used to indicate the beginning and the reinstantiation of the search, as in *aramağa başlıyorlar* 'they start to.search' *[T20b]* or *seslenmeğe başlıyor* 'he starts to.call.out' *[T20a]*, as well as in relation to a local activity by some 9-year-olds and almost all adults.

Verbs of protracted aspect such as *devam et* 'keep.on' and *kal* 'remain' are rarely used by 5-year-olds, and not at all by 9-year-olds. Adults use these verbs to carry on the search theme as in (27) and less often, to refer to a locally specific situation as in (28):

(27) *Daha sonra arayış ormanda sürmeğe başladı.*

'Later on the search **started to.proceed** in the woods.' *[T20e]*

(28) *Baykuş çocuğu korkutmağa devam ediyor.*

'The owl **continues to.scare** the child.' *[T20b]*

Perfective and cessive aspects are rarely expressed verbally.

In sum, the use of aspectual verbs for thematic purposes develops with age. Younger children use these verbs infrequently and only in reference to local activities, whereas older narrators use them for episode instantiation (see Chapter IVD). As noted, aspectual verbs occur in infinitival complements, which are already acquired by 3-4 years. Therefore, their infrequency in the children's narratives cannot be explained on syntactic grounds. Rather, younger children still lack the ability to conceive of a complex process in its totality while relating different subprocesses or events to it.

1.2.2.2. Aspectual adverbs. Aspectual adverbs increase in both variety and frequency with age. The most frequent aspectual adverbs in the data are those of **iterative** and **recurrent** aspect, two categories which are not marked with verbs. Recurrence adverbs are used rather infelicitously (e.g., in reference to an activity that occurs once) and locally by the younger children, and serve to indicate the continuation of the search theme only in the 9-year-old and adult stories, as in (29):

(29) *Kurbağalarını aramağa başlıyorlar tekrar.*

'They start to.seek their frog **again**.' *[T20b]*

Iterative aspect is expressed by 5-year-old and older narrators with locative terms functioning adverbially, such as *heryer* 'everywhere'. These always occur in the contexts of calling or searching for the frog and assume a thematic role:

(30) *Kurbağayı orada göremedikleri zaman heryere bakıyorlar.*

'When not seeing the frog there they look **everywhere**.' [*T5d-5;3*]

Adverbs of **protracted, perfect, immediate**, and **inceptive** aspect are used for modification at the local level only. Protracted aspect is rarely marked in the children's data: *çünkü devamlı havlıyordu* 'because it [=dog] was constantly barking' [*T9j-9;1*], and is not very frequent in the adult texts.

Adverbs of imperfect aspect, *hala* 'still', are used by 5- and 9-year-olds and adults to indicate the relevance of a given state to the moment of speech or to a designated reference time, as in the following examples.

(31) *Sonra çocuk ona kızdı, köpek **hala** seviyor.*

'Then the child got mad at him, the dog **still** loves (him).' [*T5e-6;0*]

(32) *Köpek **hala** o arı kovanını almağa çalışırken...*

'While the dog was **still trying to get that beehive**...' [*T9d-9;11*]

Immediate aspect is marked by both children and adults for stylistic purposes as in (33):

(33) *Hemen giyinerek hemen onu aramağa koyuldu.*

'**Immediately** getting dressed, he **immediately** set out to search for it.' [*T9j-9;1*]

Finally, adverbs of inceptive aspect such as *birdenbire* 'all of a sudden', which increase with age, are used to mark new events in the story.

In summary, verbal and adverbial marking of aspect serve several purposes in the frog stories. Adults mark the instantiation of the plot with verbs of inceptive aspect and iterative adverbs imposing a focus on the repeated nature of the search, and foreshadowing its continuity. Nine-year-olds also use verbs or adverbs of inceptive aspect thematically, to mark the beginning of the search, though to a much lesser extent than adults. Five-year-olds are not systematic in the way they use the different kinds of aspectual devices they control. Three-year-olds mark aspect only by verb inflection.

2. EVENT CONFLATION

Event conflation involves the distribution of information across the verb and its associated elements within the clause, as discussed in Chapter III0. Given its agglutinative morphology, Turkish is a language which has various means for event conflation. Information can be so tightly packaged that it is expressed in a single verb, modified, for instance, with particles which indicate agentive causation (*-dir*) or reciprocal action (*-iş*),[6] or it can be integrated

---

[6] Turkish has productive grammatical rules for transitivizing intransitive verbs with the causative particle and intransitivizing transitive verbs with the passive particle, or changing the verb stem into a reflexive or reciprocal one. These are discussed further in Section 3.1.

in a slightly looser fashion and expressed, for instance, in another clause with converbs compressing two situations as aspects of one, or in a close temporal connection. Events may also be related sequentially, respecting their boundaries, and expressed in independent or subordinated clauses.

At this point it will be useful to introduce some of these structures. **Converbs** are nonfinite verb forms which function as adverbials and take their temporal specification from the tense of the main clause. They have the following meanings, where X and Y represent clauses, with the converb suffixed to the verb of the X-clause:

X-*ince* Y   'when X, Y' / 'as soon as X, Y'

X-*ken* Y   'while X-ing, Y'

X-*ip* Y   'X and (then) Y'

X-*erek* Y   '(in,by) X-ing, Y'

These converbs are illustrated below from the Turkish frog story texts, labeled as follows: V+*ince* 'when', V+*ken* 'while', V+*ip* 'and (then)', and V+*erek* 'by V-ing'.

V+*ince*:
Çocuk kalk-ınca kurbağayı arıyor.
boy get.up-INCE frog:ACC search:PRES
'When the boy gets up he searches for the frog.'

V+*ken*:
Çocuk uyur-ken kurbağa kaçmış.
boy sleep:HAB-KEN frog escape:M.PAST
'While the boy was sleeping the frog escaped.'

V+*ip*:
Çocuk camdan atlay-ıp onu alıyor.
boy window:ABL jump-IP 3SG.PRO:ACC take:PRES
'The boy jumps from the window and picks him [=dog] up.'

V+*erek*:
Köpek pencereden aşağı düş-erek kavanozu kırıyor.
dog window:ABL downwards fall-EREK jar:ACC break:PRES
'The dog, in/by falling down from the window, breaks the jar.'

Both V+*ince* 'when' and V+*ken* 'while' clauses designate the time of the event they refer to as a reference time with respect to which the event encoded in the main clause is anterior, posterior, or cotemporal (Aksu-Koç, 1988a). Thus they set up a close temporal relation between events expressed in

adjacent clauses. Syntactically, the subjects of clauses joined by these converbs can be the same or different. V+*ince* indicates immediate succession or
partial overlap, and thus may imply a simultaneous or causal meaning as well
as sequence. V+*ken* is a pure marker of simultaneity, and presents the event
in the conjunct clause in its temporal extension, from an imperfective perspective.

V+*ip* 'and (then)' and V+*erek* 'by V-ing', allow for a variety of temporal
and circumstantial relations between the two events, and require the same
subject in the conjunct and main clause. In the frog stories, V+*ip* functions to
link clauses together in narrative units, packaging constituents of an event into
a larger event (Slobin, 1993a; Chapter IVC). And, given its nontemporal
character, V+*erek* can assume various meanings in context, such as simultaneity, succession, instrumentality, reason, or manner of action.

Since this is the story of a search for a lost frog, it provides ample opportunity for narrators to talk about causation and path of movement, which may
or may not be elaborately specified. There are three scenes in the frog story
conducive to descriptions of caused movement and locative trajectories: (1)
the fall of the dog from the window; (2) the fall of the beehive from the tree
shaken by the dog, and the fall of the boy, scared by the owl, from the tree;
and (3) the fall of the boy and the dog, thrown by the deer, from the cliff into
the water. Section 2.1 presents data on causation of movement, and Section
2.2 on path of movement in these scenes. Finally, Section 2.3 deals briefly
with manner of movement.

2.1. Causation of Movement

Turkish codes notions of agency and caused action through its productive verb morphology. Intransitive verbs are transitivized by adding a causative particle — e.g., *düş* 'fall' (intransitive) → *düş-ür* 'drop' (transitive), and
transitive verbs are causativized with the same particle — e.g., *kır* 'break'
(transitive) → *kır-dır* 'cause to break' (causative). There are exceptions to the
rule and some verbs have lexical causative counterparts as in *gir* 'enter'
versus *sok* 'insert', *gel* 'come' versus *getir* 'bring'.

Across the three main scenes of falling, the most frequently used verb is
düş 'fall' for change of locative state. Its use shows extremely stable proportions across the age groups (70% for 3-year-olds and 66% for 5- and 9-year-
olds and adults). Conversely, the proportion of verbs expressing caused movement (*düşür* 'make.fall', *at* 'throw', *it* 'push') increases from 20% at age 3 to
27% at age 5 and remains stable for the older groups. These findings point to
some change in preference for verbs expressing causation of movement
around the age of 5-6. Further developments relevant to event conflation
involve the use of devices other than lexical verbs incorporating causation and

movement in their meaning. Various ways of expressing causation of movement are illustrated in descriptions of the fall of the beehive by the adult narrators:

(34) *Neyse köpek havlıyor mavlıyor **sonra** kuut, arı kovanı yere düşüyor.*

    'Anyway the dog barks-shmarks **then** bam, the beehive falls to the
ground.' [*T20f*]

(35) *Öte yandan Karabaş ağacı sallamış, havlay-**ınca** arılardan tepki
gelmediği için fazla sallamış ve kovan yere düşmüş.*

    'On the other side, Karabash [=dog] shook the tree, (and) because
when.barking [V+*ince*] didn't get a reaction from the bees, he shook too
much **and** the hive fell to the ground.' [*T20i*]

(36) *Ağacı sallay-**ınca** arı kovanı yere düştü **ve** köpeğin peşine takıldı bütün
arılar.*

    '**Upon.shaking** [V+*ince*] the tree, the hive fell to the ground **and** all of
the bees set off after the dog.' [*T20c*]

(37) *Daha sonra ağacı sallar-**ken** ağaçtaki oğulu düş-**ür**-üyor ve arılar
kızgınlıkla yuvalarından fırlıyor.*

    'Later on, **while.shaking** [V+*ken*] the tree, (he) **knocks down**
[=cause.fall] the hive on the tree and the bees furiously swarm out of
their nest.' [*T20b*]

The relation in (34) is not causal but an antecedent-consequent relation
encoded in two independent clauses with finite verbs and conjoined with
sonra 'then,' implying a temporal lag. In (35) the dog's act of shaking is
recognized as causal but the two events are again presented as successive.
Although the causal link is not explicitly expressed, the two situations are
connected with *ve* 'and', which implies immediate succession and therefore a
more integrated relation. Example (36), on the other hand, connects the two
situations more tightly with the converb *-ince*, expressing sequential
overlap/causal connection, while still using the nonagentive *düş* 'fall'. Finally
(37) presents the two events in a highly conflated fashion: The close temporal
relation between the two events is specified with the converb *-ken* expressing
simultaneity and the agentive role of the dog is explicitly specified with the
transitivized form of the main verb *düş-ür* 'cause.fall'.[7]

---

[7] It is interesting to note that in this context the converb *-ken* always occurs with the transitive form of the verb and the converb *-ince* with the intransitive form. Simultaneity in time
strongly suggests physical/spatial contact, which strongly suggests direct causation.

Nine-year-olds exhibit similar strategies. Some simply refer to the two events successively, as in (38), leaving the causal relation to be inferred from context. Others make the causal relation explicit with a causative verb and a causal adverb as in (39):

(38) *Daha sonra arı yuvasını sallıyorlar, içinden arılar çıkıyor.*

'Then they shake the beehive, bees exit from inside.' [*T9a-9;3*]

(39) *Köpek sonunda arı kovanını ağaçtan düşürüyor, bir sürü arı böylece çıkıyor kovandan.*

'The dog finally **causes.fall** the beehive from the tree, a mass of bees **consequently** exit from the hive.' [*T9d-9;11*]

The preschool children tend to keep the events discrete as in (40) or even unrelated as in (41):

(40) *Köpek sonra bu şeyi yakalamış, bütün arılar üşüşmüş köpeğe.*

'Then the dog caught something, all the bees swarmed around the dog.' [*T5j-5;3*]

(41) *Bir de kozalak düşmüş, arılar düşmüs, arılar çıkmış.*

'And the hive fell, the bees fell, the bees exited.' [*T3b-4;0*]

In the boy-and-owl scene, where the boy's fall is more likely to be interpreted as a consequence of the fear instigated by the appearance of the owl, the causal relation is even less explicitly specified, possibly because psychological rather than physical causation is involved. Only two adults describe this scene in a relatively conflated manner, using the causative *düş-ür* 'make-fall' which incorporates both causation and direction of movement, and *kork-ut* 'make-scared' which incorporates causation in its meaning:

(42) *Ve bu arada bir baykuş da o kovuktan çık-ıp çocuğu kork-ut-uyor ve ağaçtan düş-ür-üyor.*

'And in the meantime an owl, **exiting** [V+*ip*] from that hole, **scares** the boy and **makes** him **fall** from the tree.' [*T20d*]

Five adults establish a less direct causal relation between the different phases of the whole event, as illustrated in the following example, which is almost exactly the same as (42) except that the verbs 'scare' and 'fall' are not causative:

(43) *Tam o sırada ağaç kovuğunun içersinden bir baykuş çıkmış. Çocuk kork-up içeri, aşağı düşer-ken köpek de hızla yanından koş-arak geçmiş.*

'Just then an owl exited from inside of the hole in the tree. The boy **got.scared** [V+*ip*] (and) **while.falling** [V+*ken*], the dog passed by running [V+*erek*] quickly.' [*T20a*]

The following nonconflated version is also interesting in formulating the indirect causation explicitly:

(44) *Bu arada ağaçtaki kovukları yoklayan Tim baykuşu* **rahatsız ed-ip** *baykuşun dışarı çıkmasına* **neden oldu.**

'Meanwhile Tim, who was going up to the holes in the tree, **disturbed** [V+*ip*] the owl (and) **was the cause** of the bees' exiting outwards.' [*T20c*]

Three adults, similar to half the 5- and half the 3-year-olds, simply note the appearance of the owl and imply no causal relation to any other event. Of the children, only one 9-, one 5-, and one 3-year-old present an integrated account of this scene, using an agentive or causative verb as in (45) and (46).

(45) *Oradan bir baykuş çıkıyor, çocuğu yere* **atıyor.**

'An owl comes out of there, **throws** the boy to the ground.' [*T9a-9;3*]

(46) *Çocuk da ağaca çıkıyor, sonra baykuş* **düşürüyor** *onu.*

'The boy climbs the tree, then the owl **makes** him **fall**.' [*T5f-6;1*]

In the descriptions of the remaining narrators, the causal connection is implied by the sequential relation between the events. Some of these involve a tight packaging of events with the converb -*ince* and with the specification of the causal source although a causative verb is not used:

(47) *Baykuşu* **gör-ünce korkudan** *düşüyor.*

'U**pon.seeing** [V+*ince*] the owl he falls **from.fright**.' [*T9e-10;0*]

These examples from the beehive and the owl scenes illustrate that between 5 and 9 years of age, further developments take place in the use of clause-linking devices, integrating their aspectual, modal, temporal, or causal meanings with meanings inherent in the main verb. Furthermore, these examples show a sensitivity to the tightness of the semantic link between two situations, reserving the use of causative verbs for situations of direct, successful manipulation, and using other types of linkage for more loosely integrated situations.

2.2. Locative Trajectories

As noted in Chapter III0, Turkish can be characterized as a verb-framed language, where the verb carries information concerning locative trajectories (source, goal, and direction) while details of path and manner may be elaborated in associated adverbs, locative phrases, and converbs. Turkish verbs of motion typically encode direction. As in Spanish and Hebrew, there are verbs which specify movement into/out of — *gir* 'enter' and *çık* 'exit', and verbs which specify movement up/down — *in* 'descend' and *çık* 'ascend', or movement away from — *kaç* 'escape'. (Note that *çık* means both 'exit' and 'descend'. As indicated in the chart, below, this verb is often accompanied by disambiguating adverbs: *dışarı* 'outwards' and *yukarı* 'upwards'.) It is also possible to express the same notions with a general verb of movement and a directional adverb, such as *içeri gel* 'come towards.inside'.

Verbs of motion most frequently encountered in the Turkish frog stories are the following:

Gloss	Transitive	Intransitive	Causative	Passive
enter	*sok*	*gir*	*sok-tur*	*gir-il**/*sok-ul*
exit	*çık-art*	*çık (dışarı)*	*çık-art-tır*	*çık-ıl**/*çık-art-ıl*
ascend	*çık-art*	*çık (yukarı)*	*çık-art-tır*	*çık-ıl**/*çık-art-ıl*
descend	*in-dir*	*in*	*in-dirt-tir*	*in-il**/*in-dir-il*
fall	*düş-ür*	*düş*	*düşürt-tür*	*düş-ül**/*düş-ür-ül*
come/bring	*getir*	*gel*	*getirt-tir*	*gel-in**/*getir-il*
go/take	*götür*	*git*	*götür-t-tür*	*gid-il**/*götür-ül*

> * The passives of these verbs are grammatical only when used in impersonal constructions.

The data present both all-purpose motion verbs such as *git* 'go' and *gel* 'come' and directional motion verbs such as *çık* 'exit' versus *gir* 'enter', *çık* 'ascend' versus *in* 'descend', from the youngest age onwards.[8]

Contrary to what might be expected, directional verbs of motion occur not only with their associated arguments specifying the source or goal or both, but also quite often with a locative adverb or a locative postposition in the dative, further specifying direction. The following examples illustrate this in the various uses of the verb *çık* exit/ascend'. The verb may be used alone as in (48), with the source argument specified with a locative demonstrative as in (49), with a directional adverb only (50), or with the source NP plus a postposition (51):

---

[8] While the transitivized counterparts of intransitive verbs of motion are used correctly in general, younger children sometimes have problems with verbs with lexical counterparts. Contrast the correct use of the transitive *sok* 'insert' in *Sonra kafasını da soktu* 'Then it [=dog] inserted its head as well' [*T3i-3;11*] with the intransitive *gir* 'enter' infelicitously used with an object in the accusative in **Sonra köpek kavanoza girmiş, kafasın-ı yani.* 'Then the dog entered the jar, I mean its head-ACC' [*T3c-4;3*].

(48) *Arılar küçük köpeği kovuyor, baykuşlar çıkıyor, akşam olmağa başlıyor.*
'The bees follow the little dog, owls **exit**, evening is coming along.'
[*T20j*]

(49) **Oradan arılar çıkıyor, buradan da köstebek çıkıyor.**
'Bees **exit from.there**, and a gopher **exits from.here**.' [*T5d-5;3*]

(50) *Daha sonra arı yuvasını sallıyorlar. İçinden arılar çıkıyor.*
'Later on they shake the beehive. **From.inside.it exit** the bees. [*T9a-9;3*]

(51) *Tam o sırada ağaç kovuğunun içersinden bir baykuş çıkmış.*
'Just at that moment an owl **exited from (the) tree trunk's interior**.'
[*T20a*]

During the preschool years, the proportion of clauses using *çık* with locative adverbs or postpositions increases, although always remaining below the use of the verb alone. This is not surprising since *çık* in itself indicates directionality. In fact what needs to be explained is why such locative modifications are used at all. A closer look at the data suggests that such use is motivated by discourse-related factors. As the examples above illustrate, direction of motion verbs occur in the following ways: (1) verb alone, if the source or goal can be presupposed from the nonlinguistic context or real world knowledge as in (48), (2) VERB+NP/PRO+DAT/ABL to indicate goal/source as in (49), (3) VERB+LOC.MOD if the source or goal is given in the previous linguistic context as in (50), and (4) VERB+NP+LOC.MOD for an additional, more detailed specification of the goal or the source as in (51). Furthermore, this is more or less the developmental sequence observed. (In addition, as noted above, *çık* is ambiguous, meaning both 'exit' and 'ascend'. This factor necessitates adverbial specification of direction in some discourse contexts.)

Such developmental change can be explained by two closely related factors. First, young children do not use locative modification to elaborate on locative trajectories because they are not yet concerned with establishing discourse internal relations. Some 3- and 5-year-olds who operate in the picture description mode tend to regard events as unrelated, and talk about them as discrete situations. Second, young children tend to describe what is most salient as new information in the pictures, which is typically the movement itself, while the source is given and the goal needs to be inferred. Thus, they use just the verb, or a deictic, or at best an associated casemarked NP to indicate source or goal. Older children, just like adults, use locative modification in a discourse motivated way, referring back to something already established in the previous context. It is these mature speakers who engage in elaborate specifications of source, goal, direction of movement, and manner of movement. A 9-year-old example is given in (52).

(52) *Arılar* **yuvalarından** *çıkarak çocuğun köpeğinin* **üstüne** *doğru yürümüşler.*

'The bees, exiting [V+*erek*] **from their hive**, went straight for the boy's dog.' [*T9c-9;1*]

What has been discussed above with regard to the verb *çık* applies equally to other verbs of motion used with and without locative modification for elaborating locative trajectories, as summarized in Table 4, below.

TABLE 4
Distribution of Motion Verbs (MV) Used with and without Locative
Modification (LM) for Direction of Movement, by Age

	3 yrs	5 yrs	9 yrs	Adult
Number of types of LM[a]	5	9	13	16
Total MV+LM	23	32	34	77
No. LM for GOAL	17	25	22	64
No. LM for SOURCE	6	7	12	13

a. LM includes locative adverbials and locative postpositions; each form is counted only once, regardless of the different case inflections it occurs with (locative, dative, ablative).

As can be observed, the variety of locative adverbials and postpositions specifying the trajectory of motion increase, from five at age 3 (such as *içine* 'to.inside', *dışarıya* 'to.outside', *üstüne* 'to.top', *aşağı* 'downwards') to 16 for adults (to include items such as *kenarına* 'to.edge', *dibine* 'to.bottom'). Also, the ratio of clauses with motion verb plus locative modification to motion verbs used alone is 1:4 in the preschool data, whereas it is about 1:2 in the data of the two older groups. This suggests that with age, the tendency to elaborate on locative trajectories increases in our sample.

Three-year-olds and adults have a greater tendency to add locative modification to stative predicates. The 3-year-old locative state expressions are existential or substantive predications put together in a nonrelational descriptive way as in (53).

(53) *Köpek de kafası* **aşağıda**, *bacakları denizin, suyun* **içinde**.

'And the dog, his head **below**, his legs **inside** the sea, the water.' [*T3j-4;2*]

The locative expressions of adults, on the other hand, include stative verbs used in elaborate descriptions of locative states as in example (54).

(54) *Çocuk da geyiğin kafasının üstünde olmuş oluyor. Geyik bunu boynuzlarının üstünde, kafasının üstünde götürüyor.*
'The boy **comes to be on top of** the deer's head. The deer takes him **on top of its antlers, on his head.**' [*T20d*]

Table 4 also presents information about how direction of movement is elaborated in the frog story. Narrators of all ages, and particularly adults, tend to specify the **goal** of movement much more than the **source**. This should not be surprising since in the present story concerning a search, the goal of movement is more informative than its source. Children typically specify either the source or the goal, and conflation of the two is more characteristic of adults. Example (55) illustrates the adult strategy of talking about the different phases of the event by means of several predicates and elaborating on the source and the goal of the movement.

(55) *Geyik bir tane uçurumun kenarına geliyor ve uçurumun ucunda çocuğu başından aşağı atıyor. Köpeği de düşüyor bu arada, ikisi, hep beraber, bir suyun içine düşüyorlar, bir nehrin içine düşüyorlar.*
'The deer **comes** to the side of a cliff and at the edge of the cliff **throws** the boy from its head downwards. In the meantime his dog also **falls**, the two of them together **fall to.inside the water, they fall to.inside a river.**' [*T20h*]

It is proposed in Chapter IA that speakers of verb-framed languages tend to use more elaborated descriptions of locations of protagonists or objects and of end states of motion, while speakers of satellite-framed languages tend to use more detailed descriptions of path and manner of motion. Although Turkish has a number of verbs which incorporate direction of motion in their meaning, this does not preclude the use of postpositions and locative adverbials that further specify the source and goal of movement. While example (55) above suggests that in Turkish narratives we can find path elaborations that are typical of satellite-framed languages, example (56) below shows the sort of static locative elaboration typical of verb-framed languages such as Spanish.

(56) *Geyik tam uçurumun kenarına geliyor. Orada da bir göl var. Onu - onları oraya atıyor.*
'The deer brings them right to the edge of the cliff. And there is a lake there. He throws him - them to there.' [*T9a-9;3*]

2.3. Manner of Movement

Verbs of motion which encode manner of movement frequently observed in the frog stories are *koş* 'run', *üç* 'fly', *yüz* 'swim', and *atla* 'jump'. The converb *-erek* functioning adverbially as in *koşarak çıktı* '(he) exited running' or adverbs such as *yavaşça* 'slowly' or *yavaş yavaş* 'slowly slowly' are also used frequently. Only *yüz* 'swim', *kaç* 'escape', and *atla* 'jump' are used by 3-year-olds. Five-year-olds add other verbs such as *kovala* 'chase', *yuvarla* 'roll', *üşüş* 'collect around'; and older narrators use *devir* 'make fall on its side', *dolaş* 'wander around', *fırlat* 'hurl', *izle* 'follow', as well as those which occur with adverbial extensions such as *peşine takıl/düş* 'follow go after' [lit. set/fall on the trail of], *üstüne uç* 'fly up.onto'.

A scene appropriate for the use of manner of movement verbs in the frog story is shown in Pictures 2 and 3, in which the frog leaves the jar and runs away. This event is mentioned by four of the 3-year-olds, seven of the 5-year-olds, and all 9-year-olds and adults, using almost exclusively two directional motion verbs, *çık* 'exit' and *kaç* 'escape'. Although it does not specify the exact nature of the movement, *kaç* implies manner of motion in its meaning. The absence of manner adverbs in clauses containing this verb, in contrast to the presence of such modification in clauses with *çık*, supports this view. Moreover, *kaç* has the aspectual connotation of achievement of an end point. *Kaç*, then, is more suitable than *çık* for the presentation of the event in a conflated form.

The younger children typically use *çık*, mentioning either the source or the goal of motion. Source is mentioned more often, possibly because it is clearly represented in the pictures of this scene, as suggested by the use of the demonstrative in example (57).

(57) *Kurbağa bunun içinden çıkıyor.*

'The frog exits from.inside of.this.' [T3j-4;2]

Only two 5-year-olds use *kaç*, one as a motion verb, the other as an aspectual verb indicating the achievement of a goal as shown below.

(58) *Kurbağa dışarı çıkmış, kaçmış.*

'The frog exited outwards, (and) escaped.' [T5i-6;0]

Two narrators in this group also specify manner of movement with the adverb *yavaş yavaş* 'slowly slowly'. Nine-year-olds use *kaç* more often (eight narrators) than *çık*, and only two narrators use both verbs, elaborating on different phases of the event as in (59) or integrating them more closely with the converb *-erek* as in (60):

(59) *Kurbağa kavanozun içinden çıkıyor ve kaçıyor.*

'The frog **exits** from.inside of the jar and **escapes.**' [*T9a-9;3*]

(60) *Kurbağa kavanozdan çık-arak kaçtı.*

'**Exiting** [V+*erek*] from the jar the frog **escaped.**' [*T9j-9;1*]

Finally, seven adults use *çık* and six use *kaç* and several other manner of movement verbs such as *kaybol* 'get.lost', *sıyrıl* 'slip.out', *adım at* 'take a step'. In five instances, *kaç* occurs with another verb suggesting that it functions more like an aspectual than a motion verb for adults. These narrators also use adverbs of manner of motion or attitude in their descriptions. The majority of adults also mention source of movement more often than its goal. While some adults give conflated descriptions like in (60) above, most adult descriptions are elaborated as in (61).

(61) *Kurbağa kavanozdan emin adımlarla sıyrıldı ve dışarıya doğru ilk adımını attı. Evet, kurbağa kaçıyordu.*

'The frog **slipped.out** of the jar with sure steps and **took his first step towards.outside.** Yes the frog **was escaping.**' [*T20e*]

To sum up, these observations suggest that Turkish narrators make use of a limited lexical repertoire of verbs in describing manner of movement, but prefer clausal or phrasal descriptions of manner, particularly at older ages. To impose an elaborated versus a conflated perspective on events, the Turkish speaker can rely heavily on the verb, given the possibility of modification of both its finite and nonfinite forms. In a way, Turkish compensates for the lack of lexical richness characteristic of English and German verbs of manner by the use of productive verb morphology that allows for packaging of events in a variety of ways. The frog's escape is a significant point in the story, where the force motivating the search is introduced. It would therefore seem that proficient narrators would choose to elaborate the events of this scene in separate clauses or phrases, as both the Turkish- and the English-speaking adults seem to do, even if they have the means for a conflated presentation.

3. PERSPECTIVE

Perspective refers to the point of view which narrators adopt in presenting a given situation. In the case of the frog story, narrators can talk about a given scene either from a local perspective, as a self-contained totality, or from a global perspective, regarding it in the context of the larger story. Narrators can also take the perspective of different protagonists as they appear in the series of events, or maintain the perspective of the main protagonist(s) all the time, or do both by embedding the former in the latter.

Turkish uses several devices for the manipulation of perspective (see Chapter IIIo). These are (1) the syntactic role assigned to different arguments in the clause, (2) flexible word order which can be varied for pragmatic purposes, and (3) the use of the topic/focus particle *de* 'too, also, and'. The first two mechanisms are made possible by the consistent casemarking on NP arguments and subject agreement marking on the verb. (1) and (2) are discussed in the next two sections. The use of the particle *de* is dealt with in the context of these discussions rather than in a separate section; it also figures in the section on connectivity (4.1).

3.1. Transitivity and Voice

The arrangement of the verb-argument arrays is closely tied to transitivity and voice in Turkish. As noted earlier, Turkish verbs can be classified as intransitive or transitive. The causative particle *-(d)ir* converts an intransitive verb root into a transitive one, as in *geç-* 'get.on' (intransitive) versus *geç-ir* 'put.on' (transitive). Arguments are distinguished by a very transparent and regular case inflectional system: The subject is always in the unmarked nominative case and the direct object (DO) takes the accusative if [+definite], but if [-definite] it remains unmarked or takes the indefinite article *bir* 'one'.[9]

Indirect objects (IO) are marked with the dative, and oblique objects are marked with the ablative, genitive, or comitative suffixes. The following examples illustrate changes in transitivity and casemarking. Example (62) shows an intransitive verb with its arguments and (63) presents its transitivized agentive counterpart.

(62) *Kavanoz-Ø köpeğ-in baş-ın-a geç-miş-ti.*

jar-NOM dog-GEN head-POSS-DAT get.on-PERF- D.PAST

'The jar had gotten on the dog's head.'

(63) *Köpek-Ø kavanoz-u baş-ın-a geç-ir-miş-ti.*

dog-NOM jar-ACC head-POSS-DAT get.on-CAUS-PERF-D.PAST

'The dog had put the jar on its head.'

In (62) the dog [=dog's head] is the IO / locative undergoer, and the action is conceived of as spontaneous and non-agentive, whereas in (63) the dog is the subject / agent of action.

Transitive verbs are passivized with the suffixes *-il/-in*. The passivized version of (63) where the dog is the IO/locative undergoer, is given below.

(64) *Kavanoz-Ø köpeğ-in baş-ın-a geç-ir-il-miş-ti.*

jar-NOM dog-GEN head-POSS-DAT get.on-CAUS-PASS-PERF-D.PAST

---

[9] Indefinite and nonreferential/nonspecific objects get neither the accusative nor the indefinite article.

'The jar had been put on the dog's head.'

Two other morphologically marked categories that effect differences in transitivity are the reflexive and the reciprocal. Verbs in the reflexive (derived with the addition of *-in* to the verb root, as in *yıka-n-dı* 'washed.oneself') and in the reciprocal (derived with the addition of the suffix *-(i)ş* as in *karşıla-ş-tı* 'came.face.to.face') present the situation from a perspective where the entity is simultaneously an actor and an undergoer and thus correspond to "middle voice." The reflexive and the reciprocal forms thus signal reduced transitivity.

To see the extent to which Turkish narrators manipulate perspective, consider the following two scenes: Picture 4, where the dog's manipulations of the jar result in his getting his head stuck in it, and Picture 16, where the interactions of two protagonists, the boy and the deer, result in the boy and dog's fall into the water.

An examination of both scenes shows that there is a developmental shift from an agent to an undergoer/patient focus. Only three of the 3-year-olds mention the scene of the dog with the jar, two from an agentive and one from a patient focus. The majority of the 5-year-olds, three of the 9-year-olds and three adults similarly adopt a transitive perspective and present the dog as an agent. The preschool child's agentive focus may be a function of the tendency to treat each picture as a self-contained frame and to assign the agent role to the most prominent figure in it, as suggested by (65).

(65) *Sonra camdan bakarken bir kavanozu alıp da köpek başına geçirmiş.*

'Then, while looking out the window, taking a jar the dog put (it) on his head.' [*T5g-5;2*]

The adults' choice of an agentive perspective, on the other hand, might be a function of stylistic concerns: The characterization of the dog as a mischievous agent allows for the use of this scene as a humorous point in the story. A patient focus becomes dominant in the stories of the 9-year-olds and adults who present the dog as an undergoer, referring either to the final state of the jar on its head or to the accidental nature of the event with an intransitive verb. These strategies are summarized in the first part of Table 5, which presents the distribution of narrators in terms of the different perspectives adopted in (1) the dog and the jar, and (2) the boy and deer scenes, by age.

In the case of the deer scene, again there is a developmental shift from an agentive to a patient focus between ages 5 and 9. Younger children talk about one or both of the protagonists as the agent, as in:

(66) *Onu taşırken geyik köpek kaçıyor.*

'While **the deer** is.carrying him, **the dog** runs away.' [*T3i-3;11*]

TABLE 5
Frequency of Different Perspectives on the Dog and Jar Scene (Picture 4)
and the Boy and Deer Scene (Picture 16), by Age

	3 yrs	5 yrs	9 yrs	Adult
Dog and Jar:				
No Mention	7	1	1	1
Dog Agent	2	7	3	3
Dog Patient	1	1	6	4
Stative Foci	—	1	—	2
Boy and Deer:				
No Mention	7	1	1	1
Boy Agent	—	4	1	—
Deer Agent	2	3	2	3
Boy Patient	1	1	6	4
Two Foci	—	1	—	2

About half of the 5-year-olds behave like the 3-year-olds, shifting from one agent to the next across successive clauses. Those 5-year-olds who have adopted a narrative stance appear to maintain a subject/agent focus on the boy as if to hold onto the thread of the plot by holding onto a topic, as suggested by *Sonra, sonra hayvanın üstüne bindi.* 'Then, then (he) got.on top of the animal' [*T5a-5;4*]. In fact, all four narrators who chose the boy and one who chose the deer as agent maintain the subject as the topic across the utterances describing this scene, as below.

(67) *Boynuzlarına almış onu götürmüş. Koşmuş, koşmuş geyik bir uçuruma getirmiş onları, uçuruma, sonra denize atmış sonra geyik.*

'It [=deer] took him on its antlers and carried him off. Ran and ran the deer, brought them to a cliff, to a cliff, then threw them to the sea, then, the deer. [*T5j-5;3*]

Older children and most adults, on the other hand, maintain the boy as the topic in the subject position, but in the role of undergoer. This is illustrated in the following examples of reduced transitivity with an intransitive verb in (68), a passive in (69), and a reflexive in (70). Thus, they prefer to keep the perspective of the boy as the main protagonist but while doing so, can present him in a variety of roles besides that of agent.

(68) *Bu sırada işte geyiğin başına düşüyor.*

'In the meantime he just **falls** on the deer's head.' [*T20h*]

(69) *Daha sonra çocuk yine kurbağasını aramaya başlamış, o zaman bir geyiğe takılmış.*

'Later on the boy started to search for his frog again, at that point he **got.caught** on a deer.' [*T9c-9;1*]

(70) *Kendini birden kayalıktan geyiğin boynuzlarında buluverdi.*

'He suddenly **found.himself** off of the rocks (and) on the antlers of the deer.' [*T20c*]

Two adults present the situation from a stative perspective of low transitivity, focusing equally on the boy and the deer:

(71) *Geyik kafasını kaldırdığında çocuk da geyiğin kafasının üstünde olmuş oluyor.*

'When the deer lifts up its head the boy **comes to be** on top of its head.' [*T20d*]

This view of the boy and the dog as undergoers in a series of events in search for the frog is expressed succinctly by a 9-year-old (who summarizes the whole story in 16 clauses) in the following way.

(72) *Bir sürü macera geçiyor başlarından*

'A lot of adventures befall them.' [*T9b-9;5*]

Some adults, on the other hand, shift the topic to the deer, picking it as the subject/agent and the boy as the object/patient, as in the following example:

(73) *Çocuğu alıyor, boynuzlarının arasına kaldırıyor.*

'It takes the boy and lifts (him) up to between its antlers.' [*T20f*]

Shifting perspective to a new protagonist with clauses high in transitivity has the effect of maintaining an active narrative tempo and breaking the monotony of a single perspective in adult narratives.

In summary, we see the following developmental progression: For the younger children, who proceed picture by picture, the subject is an agent but changes from one protagonist to the other (the boy, the deer, or the dog) in successive clauses describing the same scene, without any regard for topic maintenance. The older children, who are telling the story as a narrative, on the other hand, tend to maintain the topic by choosing one of the protagonists (the boy or the deer) as the subject who is consistently assigned the agent role. It is as if for them this parallelism between subject position and agentive role is necessary for topic maintenance in narrative. Finally, the mature narrators prefer to maintain the same protagonist as the topic, telling the tale as his story, but playing around with semantic roles and transitivity in order to present events from different perspectives. For them it is not necessary for the subject position to be occupied by an agent for topic maintenance.

Parallel to the change from agent to patient focus in these scenes, with age there is an increased tendency to use verbs of reduced transitivity. The 3- and 5-year-olds describe the deer scene with simple active sentences using a transitive or an intransitive verb without any voice modifications (e.g., age 3: *git* 'go', *düş* 'fall', *düş-ür* 'drop', *taşı* 'carry'; age 5: *bin* 'get on', *götür* 'take along', *al* 'take', *çık* 'appear', *kovala* 'chase'). Their occasional use of the passive is limited to transitive change-of-state verbs such as *kır* 'break' and *dök* 'spill', and of the causative to change-of-state verbs such as *düş* 'fall' and *geç* 'go.in'. The 9-year-olds and adults, on the other hand, use voice alterna- tions flexibly, for transitivizing or intransitivizing verbs of motion, cognition, and emotional experience as well as change of state. In addition, they reflexivize motion, activity, and change-of-state verbs to refer to entities which are simultaneously the actor and the undergoer as in *sık-ış* 'get.stuck', *kendini bul* 'find oneself', or they passivize verbs not common in the children's descriptions, such as *tak-ıl* 'get caught', or use a reciprocal verb such as *karşı karşıya kal* 'come face to face' as in the following example.

(74) *Ali de bir baykuşun haşin kanat çırpınışıyla karşı karşıya kalmış.*

'And Ali came face to face with the fierce wing flappings of an owl.' [*T20i*]

The proportions in Table 6 show that with age there is a decrease in the use of the causative but an increase in the use of the passive, reflexive, and reciprocal forms, with the net effect being one of reduced transitivity.

TABLE 6
Proportion of Clauses with Valence Modifications, by Age

	3 yrs	5 yrs	9 yrs	Adult
Causative	21	18	12	11
Passive	12	10	26	19
Reflexive	3	2	15	11
Reciprocal	—	2	3	6

Turkish children control the morphological system of voice quite early. Their occasional errors are either in the direction of over- or under-productivity (Aksu-Koç & Slobin, 1985). Therefore the low frequency of voice modifications in the data of the younger narrators is more a result of constraints on shifting perspectives in narrative discourse than constraints related to knowledge of syntax.

3.2. Word Order

The second device Turkish syntax offers for manipulating perspectives is its flexible word order. The canonical SOV order can be varied for the pragmatic purposes of indicating contrastive focus, topicalization, and backgrounding. In her analysis of the pragmatics of word order in Turkish, Erguvanlı (1984) observes that deviations from the canonical order are subject to certain syntactic and semantic restrictions under particular discourse conditions. Three syntactic positions in the sentence are associated with three pragmatic functions: (1) the sentence-initial position marks topic, (2) the immediately preverbal position marks focus, and (3) the postpredicate position marks background information.

First, semantic-syntactic restrictions on the sentence-initial topic position require that the subject NP occupying it be [+definite] and/or [+animate]; indefinite subject NPs occur immediately before the verb. Object NPs in topic position must be either [+definite] or [-definite, +specific]; otherwise they are fixed to the preverbal position. An NP other than the subject which has been fronted is a marked topic. Topics which carry contrastive overtones are marked by the postposed particles *de* or *ise*. (See Erguvanlı, 1984, for a detailed analysis of word order in Turkish.) Second, under normal conditions of SOV, the preverbal focus position is the slot for any [-definite, -animate] NP which provides the least "given" information. In any marked order where definite NPs can move around, the NP just before the verb is in "contrastive" focus, i.e., is regarded as the most information-bearing element in that context. Third, in a marked-order sentence, the postpredicate position is used to background or defocus a [+definite] NP, an adverb, or a subordinate clause. This is also the position for afterthoughts.

For adverbials of time and place, the unmarked word order is as follows: S (Time/Place Adv) OV. In the absence of a subject NP, the time/place adverb occupies the sentence-initial topic position, setting the scene within which the predication is to hold. These adverbs may occur in topic, focus or background position in a sentence without any restrictions, but the result is marked word order sentences that differ pragmatically (Erguvanlı, 1984).

In summary, with transitive verbs, SOV and OV constitute unmarked orders, and with intransitive verbs, SV is the normal order. Pragmatically

marked orders occur when the NPs in the sentence are all [+definite] but their
positioning deviates from the normal SOV order. Marked orders are: (O)VS,
OSV, (S)VO, VSO, VOS. Table 7 presents a summary of canonical versus
the most frequent nonstandard word orders observed in the data.

TABLE 7
Distribution of Clauses According to Word-Order Type, by Age

	3 yrs	5 yrs	9 yrs	Adult
Total No. of Clauses with Finite Verb	246	415	344	671
Unmarked Orders:				
SOV/SV	95	154	161	308
OV/V	128	210	164	321
Total	223	364	325	629
Percentage	91	87	94	94
Marked Orders:				
(O)VS	18	18	5	15
(S)VO	3	27	8	23
Other	1	6	6	4
Total	23	51	19	42

The proportion of clauses with canonical, unmarked SOV word order is
very high across all age groups. Furthermore, the proportion of subjectless
(OV, VO, and V only) constructions is around 50% at each age level, with
noncanonical VO sentences constituting a very low proportion of these. A
high proportion of subjectless clauses is to be expected since subject-verb
agreement allows for subject ellipsis, which is, furthermore, required for text
cohesion.

The most frequent nonstandard orders observed in our narratives are the
verb-medial ones, where S or the O is moved to postverbal position for de-
emphasis. The element remaining in preverbal position is then under focus.
It may or may not be the topic as well, depending on whether or not an adverbial occupies sentence-initial position.

(O)VS constructions are used occasionally by about half of the narrators
in each age group. Movement of the subject to postverbal position occurs
typically in contexts where the subject of the preceding clause becomes the

patient/undergoer, but is still maintained as the topic, as in (75) and (76). Thus, one factor motivating subject postposing is topic maintenance. (Note, in the following examples, that Turkish does not have a definite article, but that the accusative indicates a definite direct object.)

(75) *Köpek düşmüş. Köpeğini almış kucağına çocuk.*

'(The) dog fell. Took his dog in his arms, **(the) boy**.' [*T3c-4;3*]

(76) *Ağacı sallayınca arı kovanı yere düştü ve köpeğin peşine takıldı bütün arılar.*

'When (the dog) shook the tree, (the) beehive fell down and followed the dog **all (the) bees**.' [*T20c*]

(S)VO order, on the other hand, is rarely used by 3-year-olds; much more frequently by the 5-year-olds; again by a few 9-year-olds, and by six adults. The following example illustrates how postposing the object has the effect of defocusing given information and underscoring the action.

(77) *Sonra bir babasının çizmesine bakıp orada buldu kurbağayı.*

'Then looking into (his) father's boot, there (he) found **the frog**.' [*T5a-5;4*]

Example (78) shows a postverbal subordinate clause encoding given information.

(78) *Çocuk da atlamış ve köpeğine çok kızmış, kavanoza girdi diye başı.*

'And (the) boy jumped and got real mad at his dog, **because its head got into (the) jar**.' [*T9c-9;1*]

Topic changes constitute possible contexts for perspective shifts and in the frog story these arise where a new character emerges (e.g., a gopher out of the ground, bees from the hive, an owl from the tree). The new character, which constitutes new information, will be encoded with a [-definite, +animate] NP, and can therefore occur in the preverbal focus or the sentence-initial topic position if it is the grammatical subject. In these contexts the most commonly used verb is the intransitive *çık* 'exit', which takes a locative phrase as an oblique object. Typically, narrators first introduce the location of the new character with a [-definite] NP in the preverbal position of an unmarked (S)OV sentence, then encode it with a [+definite] NP and front it to the topic position, introducing the new character in the preverbal focus slot. Finally, the latter may be referred to with a [+definite] NP and assigned to the topic position now that it is given information. In this context, younger children typically use demonstratives with or without an NP, or an infelicitous [+definite] NP in the topic position, given the contextual support of the pictures:

(79) *Sonra çocuk daldan düşüyor. Kuş da ... kuş çıkıyor yuvadan.*

'Then (the) boy falls from (the) branch. And (the) bird ... (the) bird comes out of (the) nest.' *[T3b-4;0]*

Older children and adults use [-definite] NPs. Mature narrators also use relative clauses to introduce the location and the character in a compact manner. In (80) the new character is introduced in a relative clause in the object role, without any change in topic or perspective.

(80) *Sonra bir arı kovan-ı bulmuş, eşek arılarının bulunduğu bir kovanı. Kovandaki arılara havlamış. Arılar uçmağa devam ediyorlar.*

'Then (dog) found a beehive [-def DO], a hive in which there (were) bumblebees [REL.CLAUSE]. (It) barked at the bees [+def IO] in (the) hive. (The) bees [+def SUBJ] continue to fly. *[T20i]*

In (81) the first clause gives relevant preparatory information which renders the [-def] NP in the subject slot of the second clause less than new information, and appropriate for the topic position.

(81) *Köpek sonunda arı kovanını ağaçtan düşürüyor. Bir sürü arı böylece çıkıyor kovandan.*

'(The) dog finally makes the.beehive [+def DO] fall from (the) tree. A mass of bees [-def SUBJ] come out of (the) hive in this way.' *[T9d-9;11]*

The new character may also be introduced in preverbal position, as [-definite] IO of a reciprocal verb of reduced transitivity, as discussed in the preceding section, and exemplified in (82).

(82) *Karabaşı arılar kovalarken, Ali de bir baykuşun haşin kanat çırpınışıyla karşı karşıya kalmış.*

'While (the) bees were following Karabash [=dog], Ali came face to face with the fierce wing flappings of an owl.' *[T20i]*

The above examples also show that locative and temporal adverbs occur frequently in the topic or the postpredicate position in these scenes, where a new protagonist appears. A temporal or locative adverb in sentence-initial position signals topic shift (Chafe, 1987) and sets the scene for the new event as in (83).

(83) *Tam o sırada, ağaç kovuğunun içerisinden bir baykuş çıkmış.*

'Right at that moment out of the tree hole exited an owl.' *[T20a]*

By postposing the temporal or locative adverbial the narrator can de-emphasize the time and place and thereby the event itself, as in the following example:

(84) *Köpek de arı oğuluyla ilgileniyor bu arada arkada.*

'And the dog is attending to the beehive in the meantime at the back.' [*T20b*]

Left-dislocation in active verb clauses can be used for re-topicalization of old information, as shown below.

(85) *Köpeği de arılar kovalıyormuş.*

'As for the dog, the bees were chasing him.' [*T9j-9;1*]

This example also uses the topic/focus particle *de* to bring the item of old information under contrastive focus. Another example of left-dislocation is:

(86) *Bu sefer dışarıya bakmaya başlamışlar. Köpek, kafasında hala kavanoz varmış.*

'This time they started looking outside. The dog, it still had the jar on its head.' [*T20a*]

If the narrator had used a relative clause instead, the effect achieved would have been to background this old information rather than assigning it a value equivalent to the other forward moving events of the story.

In summary, with development narrators become more sophisticated in presenting background information for recasting [-definite NP] to [+definite NP]. While 3-year-olds present such information with existential clauses, if at all, adults do so with elaborate relative clauses. Shifts in word order do not seem to pose any problems for young children in Turkish. However, the low proportion of noncanonical orders in the sample suggests that this is not a strategy much resorted to in narrative discourse. A comparison of the proportion of standard versus deviant word order clauses in the frog stories with proportions from conversational data of Turkish children and adults (Slobin, 1982, p. 191) reveals that the proportion of standard SOV clauses is much higher in narrative as compared to conversational data. The verb-medial orders are also the most frequently preferred orders in conversational speech, suggesting that both in conversational and in narrative discourse the nonstandard orders preferred for perspective shifting are the same, though the frequencies of their use are different. This difference probably has to do with the different demands of dialogic versus monologic discourse for organizing information in terms of emphasis, focus, and topic maintenance.

4. CONNECTIVITY

The syntactic complexity of our narratives increases with age: while the texts of younger narrators are composed of simple independent clauses, those of 9-year-olds and adults have complex sentences with more than one subordinate clause dependent on or embedded in a main clause. Table 8 presents the distribution of simple and complex clauses in the Turkish narratives by age.

TABLE 8
Percentage of Simple (Main Clause Only) and Complex
(Main and Subordinate) Clauses, by Age

Clause Types	3 yrs	5 yrs	9 yrs	Adult
		Age		
Simple Clauses	90.1	73.8	64.7	55.0
Complex Clauses	9.9	26.1	35.2	45.0
Complex Clauses				
Main	4.5	12.2	13.8	17.1
Subordinate	5.4	13.9	21.4	27.9

Age-related changes in syntactic complexity even after the preschool years are not surprising, since an important feature of mature narrative discourse is the connectivity of its different parts through temporal, causal, or logical relations. The narrator composes a story in accordance with such relations at the conceptual level and deploys the structural options of the language (e.g., syntactic coordination or subordination and lexical devices such as pronouns, nominals) in accordance with personal stylistic preferences. Such connections can be at the local level, between adjacent clauses constituting a unit, as in example (87), or at the global level, between a larger unit of text and the whole through a thematic relation, as in (88).

(87) *Sonra bakıyor çocuk uyandığında, kurbağa yok.*

'Then the boy looks upon waking, the frog is not there.' [*T5a-5;4*]

(88) *Daha sonra arıları çağırarak kurbağasını bulmak için onlardan yardım istedi.*

'Later on, calling the bees he asked their help in order to find his frog.' [*T9j-9;1*]

In this section, we examine the syntax of clause combining as a means of effecting discourse connectivity. For clause combining, Turkish relies on (1) **conjunctions** joining two independent clauses: *ve, ama/fakat, ancak, buna rağmen* 'and, but, however, despite this'; (2) **converbs**, i.e., nonfinite verb forms which yield dependent but nonembedded adverbial clauses: *V+ince, V+ken, V+ip,* and *V+erek*; (3) **nominalized verb plus postposition** also functioning as adverbial clauses: *V+me+*POST, *V+mek+*POST, *V+dik+*POST;

(4) **complement constructions** with nominalized verb forms, involving both dependency and embedding relations: *-dik, -ecek, -me*; and (5) **relative clauses**, which may or may not involve embedding. The grammar of **subject marking** also plays a natural role in connectivity, since Turkish, a "pro-drop" language with systematic person and number marking, makes extensive use of subject (as well as object) ellipsis, and uses pronouns for contrastive reference, topic shifts, and the like.

The following sections consider the first four types of clause-linking mechanisms used to effect connectivity in narrative discourse. Relative clauses and subject marking are not treated here since these are discussed in Chapters IVB and IVC.

Different types of connectivity are characteristic of the different age levels. For the youngest children, the pictures of the storybook provide the scaffold that ensures continuity, and the use of deictic terminology with regard to the pictures provides a sort of connectivity (Section 4.1). Five-year-olds replace spatial deictics with temporal adverbials and work on establishing grammaticized connectivity with coordinate and subordinate structures at the clause level (Section 4.2). Nine-year-olds, whose stories are tightly organized around a plotline, perfect the use of these formal means and add a few new ones. They achieve some level of thematic integration by chunking several events together. Finally, adults add the use of specific lexical items, increased layers of embedding, and specific discourse strategies such as flashbacks and foreshadowing, which all contribute to creating thematic connectivity rhetorically (Section 4.3).

4.1. Deictic Chaining of Utterances and Coordination

In coordination, constituent clauses in the joined sentences are not grammatically dependent, but are added together in sequence, with or without conjunctions. We can therefore expect coordination to be the earliest syntactic mechanism of connectivity in discourse. Turkish uses a variety of devices for this purpose such as the topic/focus particle *de* 'and, too, also', the coordinating conjunction *ve* 'and', the adversative conjunctions *ama/fakat* 'but', *ancak* 'however', *buna rağmen* 'despite this', as well as unmarked chaining. Temporal adverbs *ondan sonra* 'then, after that', and *o sırada,* 'meanwhile' function anaphorically for intersentential connectivity. However, these formal means do not appear all at once in our texts, but follow a developmental progression partially determined by the changes in capacity for narrative organization.

The texts of the 3-year-olds present no evidence for a conceptualization of events as temporally related (see Chapter IVA). Instead, two entities or situations are spatially related by virtue of their being in the same picture frame, available to a single act of perception. This is evidenced by the use of the deictic locative adverbs *burada/orada* 'here/there' before almost every utterance, anchoring the discourse in the axis of perception. Connectivity between situations is implied by the particle *de*, which connects the word it modifies to another word of the same class, either already mentioned or presupposable in terms of a relation of likeness, equality or participation (Gencan, 1975, p. 411). The main function of *de* is pragmatic: It serves to present the two entities or situations referred to as **contrastive topics** or brings them under **contrastive focus**. For example, after an NP in topic position, *de* functions to bring old information into the forefront of consciousness as contrastive topic.

In deictic chaining, *burda/orada* 'here/there' occur frame-initially and mark progress from one picture to the next. Eighty percent of the 3-year-olds use these forms with high frequency. Two narrators use *sonra* 'then', for the same function of sequencing utterances in discourse rather than events on the temporal plane. The following example illustrates such deictic chaining with *burada* 'here', *orada* 'there', *şimdi* 'now', and the particle *de* (translated as 'and' or 'too' in the gloss).

(89) *Çocukla köpek oturuyorlar.* **Burda** *kurbağa, çocuk yatıyor. Bir tanesi* **de** *oturuyor.* **Orda da** *o çocuk* **da orda** *uyuyor.* **Burdaki** *çocuklar napıyor yaa? O zaman bu* **da** *evin içindeler.* **Burda,** *köpek düşmüş aşağıya camdan bakarken.* **Burda** *camdan o* **da** *bakıyor.* **Şimdi burdaki** *köpeği almış eline ama camdan aşağı düşmüşler.*

'The boy and the dog are sitting. **Here** the frog, the boy he's lying. **And** one of them is sitting. **And there** and that boy **too** is sleeping **there**. What are the children that are **here** doing? Then they **too** are inside the house. **Here** the dog fell down while looking out the window. **Here** he is looking out the window **too**. **Now** he took the dog that is **here** in his hand but they fell down from the window.' [*T3a-3;6*]

An explicit indicator of the low degree of connectivity characteristic of the 3-year-old stories is the use of the demonstrative *bu* 'this' in reference to the boy or dog as in *bu çocuk* 'this boy' or *bu köpek* 'this dog' in each picture, as if this were a new character different from the boy in the previous picture.

All 3-year-olds except one use *de* extensively (in 26% of total clauses) as if marking successive acts of perception and thereby connecting predications about entities successively focused. *De* functions as an additive "tag" for successive utterances, particularly when it follows *burda* 'here'. When it follows an NP in the second of two clauses with the same verb and tense, it functions to specify a given situation as applying to two different participants as in the following example.[10]

(90) *Çocuk uyuyor, köpek de uyuyor*

'The boy is sleeping, the dog is sleeping **too**.' [*T3f-4;0*]

In the absence of any further temporal specification such constructions with different participants imply a relation of simultaneity between two situations, as discussed in Chapter IVA.

Five-year-olds use this particle more or less like the threes but less frequently (in 16% of total clauses). They use it after spatial or temporal deictics for discourse continuity, to shift focus to a different participant engaged in the same situation, and to emphasize the recurrence of a given situation, as in (91) (glossing *de* as 'either' in these negative clauses).

(91) *Çocuk uyandığında kurbağa yok, çizmesinin içine bakıyor, yok orda da, ondan sonra terliklerine bakıyor, elbiselerine bakıyor, orda da yok.*

'At the boy's waking the frog is not there, he looks inside his boot, it is not there **either**, and then he looks in his slippers, his clothes, it is not there **either**.' [*T5a-5;4*]

In the 9-year-old texts the proportion of *de* decreases (to 13% of the clauses) but its use becomes more discriminative. In addition to marking shift of focus to a different participant, *de* is used to shift focus to a different event/process going on at the same time. It may occur either after temporals *o sırada/bu sırada* 'in the meantime' to anaphorically designate a previous discourse unit as reference time as in (92) or after a temporal adverbial clause as in (93).

(92) *Bir baykuş çıkıyor oradan, fakat o sırada da köpeğin arkasında bir arı sürüsü var.*

'An owl comes out of there, but **at the same time** *de* there is a mass of bees after the dog.' [*T9d-9;11*]

(93) *Çıkarmak için pencereden atladı. Vazo kırıl-dığı zaman da kendini kurtarabildi.*

'In order to get it off, he jumped off the window. **And when the vase broke** *de* he could save himself.' [*T9j-9;1*]

In other words, 9-year-olds insert syntactically larger units under the scope of *de* and thus topicalize a clause or chunks of clauses.

A further use appears at the discourse level: that of packaging several related events together into a single chunk. In the example below, three

---

[10] *De* in these contexts functions like the Hebrew particle *gam* 'also' in one of its uses (Chapter IIID).

events are enumerated and tied together, with emphatic focus on the last item or participant.

(94) *Oradan bir baykuş çıkıyor, çocuğu yere atıyor, köpek **de** bu sırada kaçıyor.*

'An owl comes out of there, throws the boy to the ground, and in the meantime the dog *de* escapes.' [*T9a-9;3*]

In adult texts the use of the particle shows variation across narrators: some never use it, some use it over 25 times (in 12% of the clauses). A new function is its rhetorical use, coupled with the indefinite article *bir* for introducing new information, as in (95):

(95) *Bir de ne görsünler, **bir de** bakmışlar ki orda bir kadın bir erkek, bir dişi bir erkek kurbağa başbaşa oturuyorlar.*

'And what should they see, once [***bir de***] they look and there are a man and a woman, a male and a female frog sitting tête-à-tête.' [*T20a*]

Developmental progress in the positioning of *de* can be summarized as follows: *burda da* 'and here' > *sonra da* 'and then' > *o sırada da* 'and in the meantime' > *kavanoz kırıldığında da* 'and at the breaking of the jar'. That is, *de* starts off as a multifunctional particle which takes its meaning from context, and as other explicit devices for marking semantic relations such as simultaneity or sequence emerge, it becomes more and more of a discourse operator, to mark contrastive topic/focus, and to effect event packaging.

Other forms observed in the texts of the youngest children are the conjunction *ama* 'but' and the adverb *o zaman* 'at that time', both used rather infelicitously:

(96) *Burda camdan o da bakıyor. Şimdi buradaki köpeği almış eline. **Ama** camdan aşağı düşmüşler.*

'Here he is also looking out the window. Now he took the dog here in his hands. **But** they fell out of the window.' [*T3a-3;6*]

Both 3- and 5-year-olds use the coordinate *ama* 'but' as if it were the negation of *de*, and relate two situations engaged in by two protagonists through simple contrast, as in (97).

(97) *Sonra köpek çıkmış, sonra **ama** çocuk çıkmamış*

'Then the dog went out, **but** then the boy didn't go out.' [*T5b-5;0*]

Although these early uses express the basic function of *ama* to indicate what is contrary to expectation, they sound juvenile because the implied expectation is based on what is apparent in the pictures, not on a temporal or causal relation between events. In 9-year-old and adults narratives, on the other hand, *ama* expresses the narrator's stance by properly negating the implication of the first clause:

(98) *Epeyce ıslanmışlardı ama olsun önemli değildi bu.*
     'They were quite wet **but** this wasn't important.' [*T20c*]

    In summary, the texts of all 3- and some 5-year-olds display deictic discourse connectivity between utterances. Clause-initial *burda* 'here' or *sonra* 'then' serve to inform the listener that more is to come — either a picture or an utterance. The topic/focus particle *de* plays an important role in establishing connectivity between successive clauses. While there are examples of concessive conjunctions, Turkish children do not use the coordinating conjunction *ve* 'and', which appears with high frequency only in the adult narratives, presumably because it does not function for simple coordination but for packaging chunks of events into larger units (Slobin, 1989, 1993a; Chapter IVc).

4.2. Temporal Chaining and Grammaticized Connectivity

    Texts of children who can impose a linear organization on events on the time axis display temporal chaining and grammaticized connectivity. Use of sequence or simultaneity markers such as *sonra* 'then', *ondan sonra* 'after that/and then', *o zaman* 'at that time, then, when' results in temporal chaining of events. Grammaticized connectivity is realized with the converbs *V+ince*, *V+ip*, *V+erek*, and *V+ken*; or with nominalized verbs in casemarked form as in *V+diğinde* 'at his V-ing'; or followed by postpositions such as *V+dikten sonra/önce, V+meden sonra/önce*, 'after/before V-ing', or by the noun *zaman* 'time' as in *V+diği zaman* 'at the time of his V-ing'. Such subordinating constructions appear in the texts of the 5-year-olds and increase in frequency with age. The temporal adverbs *daha sonra* 'afterwards/later on' and *bu arada/o sırada* 'meanwhile' appear in the 9-year-old and adult texts only and are functional in thematic connectivity as discussed in the next section. Table 9 presents the proportion of clauses with different types of temporality markers and grammaticized forms across all ages.

    As can be observed, sequence markers such as *sonra, ondan sonra* 'then, and then' increase noticeably at age 5, with one-fourth of the clauses so marked, and remain frequent at 9 years. The lower proportions in the 3-year-old and adult texts, on the other hand, are not surprising since (1) 3-year-olds, who cannot organize narrative events temporally, do not need such markers, and (2) sequential relation between events is the default case in narrative and therefore does not need to be marked, as adults are well aware.

TABLE 9
Percentage of Clauses with Different Types of Temporal Markers, by Age

Temporal Marker	Age			
	3 yrs	5 yrs	9 yrs	Adult
No Temp. Marker	78.3	68.5	63.3	72.6
Deictic Temp. Adv.	2.8	0.8	3.4	2.2
Sequence Marker	15.5	24.4	19.6	10.5
Temporal Adv.	0.0	0.0	1.0	1.9
V+*ince*	1.4	1.4	1.3	1.9
V+*ken*	1.1	1.2	2.9	3.3
V+*ip*	0.6	1.9	2.1	3.8
V+*erek*	0.0	0.2	4.1	1.2
V+*dik/me*+POST	0.3	0.4	1.5	1.0
V+*diğinde*	0.0	1.2	0.8	1.6

The overuse of sequence markers by 5-year-olds suggests that these children have entered the narrative mode. However, this in fact applies only to about half of the narrators. The remaining children are in transition from description to narration. For example, all the clauses marked for sequence with *ondan sonra* 'and then' in (99) refer to the same picture apprehended in a single moment of perception, whereas those in (100) refer to successive events in time, not utterances in discourse.

(99) *Şimdi o oturuyor. Ondan sonra o kurbağaya bakıyor. O köpek ondan sonra o köpek de gülüyor. Ondan sonra köpek onun içine girmek istiyor. Sonra çocuk orda oturup bakıyor girecek mi girmeyecek mi diye.*

'Now he is sitting. And then he's looking at that frog. That dog, and then that dog is laughing too. And then the dog wants to enter inside that [=jar]. Then the boy is sitting there looking to see if it will enter or not.' [*T5a-5;4*]

(100) *Ondan sonra bu kavanoz kırılıyor, çok kızıyor çocuk. O da, köpek de onu yalıyor. Ondan sonra "kurbağa, kurbağa" diye bağırıyor. Orda ağaçlar gözüküyor. Ondan sonra bir de bakıyor belki buradadır diye köpek. Buraya [=kovana] bakıyor.*

'And then this jar breaks, the boy gets very angry. And it, and the dog licks him. And then he calls "frog, frog." There the trees are seen. And then the dog looks saying maybe it's here. It looks here [=hive].' [*T5d-5;3*]

Texts with a temporal organization are not restricted to forms like *sonra* 'then' used to introduce successive frames, but have explicit marking of temporal/aspectual relations with the converbs *V+ken* 'while V', *V+ince* 'when V', *V+ip* 'and (then) V', *V+erek* 'in doing V', and with nominalized verb forms *V+diğinde* 'at time of V-ing' and *V+dik+*ABL *önce/sonra* 'before/after V-ing'. Of these forms, *V+ince*, *V+ken*, and *V+ip* appear as early as age 3, and increase in frequency around age 5. *V+erek* shows a late development and is felicitously used by most 9-year-olds and all adults.

The conjunct clause marked with *-ince* 'when/as soon as' sets up a condition — temporal or causal — in which the main clause can be realized. Given its narrowly temporal meaning, this converb allows for a minimal set of inferences about the speaker's communicative purpose in syntactically linking the two clauses (Slobin, 1993a). There are very few examples of *V+ince* in the 3-year-old data, but from age 5 onwards it is used variously to mark simultaneity/causality between perceptual and affective states as in (101), or sequence as in (102):

(101) *Köpek de şaşırmış onu gör-ünce.*

'And the dog was surprised upon.seeing [*V+ince*] it.' [*T5h-5;0*]

(102) *Çocuk sabah kalk-ınca kurbağayı arıyor.*

'Getting.up [*V+ince*] in the morning the boy searches for the frog.' [*T9h-9;11*]

Although *-ince* presents the first event as in some way subsidiary to the second, it is not necessarily a narrative backgrounding device since the events in both clauses can advance the plot.

V+ken 'while', which carries the same meaning for younger and mature speakers, presents an event as an extended state or ongoing process simultaneous with the event referred to in the main clause. It thus serves a backgrounding function, as illustrated in the following examples.

(103) *Onlar uyur-ken çocuğu ile köpeği kurbağa kaçıyor.*

'While they are sleeping [*V+ken*] — the boy and his dog — the frog escapes.' [*T5e-6;0*]

(104) *Sonra çocuk yukarıya dogru çıkar-ken geyiğin boynuzlarına takılıyor.*

'Then when the boy is going.up [*V+ken*] he gets caught on the antlers of the deer.' [*T9a-9;3*]

-Ip corresponds to a general conjunction such as the English *and/and then*. The nature of the relation expressed is to some extent constrained by the coreference requirement on the subjects of the joined clauses. Typically this is a relation of close succession, since two events for which a single actor is responsible will be interpreted as sequential in time unless the meanings of

the verbs allow for a simultaneity interpretation. The following examples illustrate how the -*ip* clause presents one event as, in some sense, subsidiary (Slobin, 1993a) but an integral part of another, while the -*ken* clause specifies a backgrounded event as reference time for their occurrence:

(105) *Sonra camdan bakar-ken, bir kavanozu al-ıp da köpek başına geçirmiş.*
'Then while looking [*V+ken*] out the window, taking [*V+ip*] the jar the dog put it on his head.' [*T5g-5;2*]

(106) *Onlar uyur-ken kurbağacık usulca kavanozdan çık-ıp usulca ortadan kayboldu.*
'While they were sleeping [*V+ken*] the little frog, silently coming.out [*V+ip*] of the jar, silently got lost.' [*T20c*]

Finally, the converb -*erek* 'in/by doing' contributes to discourse connectivity by presenting two situations in a highly integrated fashion, as aspects of one event. It carries aspectual meaning: while -*ip* can be characterized as perfective in meaning parallel to D.PAST -*di*, -*erek* can be characterized as imperfective parallel to PRESENT -*iyor*. Noting that -*erek* gets its meaning from the types of situations it frames and the inferences thereby licensed, Slobin (1993a) suggests that this form has several semantic functions. Briefly, the V+*erek* clause presents a situation which is either a preparatory phase, or a goal-oriented instrumental phase, or a simultaneous/accompanying phase for the situation mentioned in the main clause. Thus, conjoining with -*erek* requires taking into account the aspectual character of the subordinate and the main verbs and the possible ways they could be related. -*Erek* is used only once in the entire sample of preschoolers, in a construction which is almost a frozen form. Mature uses appear only in the 9-year-old narratives, but even then not without errors. Some of these involve the violation of the coreferentiality requirement as in (107), and some the violation of the ordering requirement between events, presenting the action instead of the motivation for action as the background preparatory event, as in (108):

(107) *O da [=çocuk] ağaca tırmandığında bir delik gör-erek bir baykuş çıkıyor oradan.*
'At his [=boy] climbing the tree, (boy) seeing [*V+erek*] a hole an owl comes.out from.there.' [*T9d-9;11*]

(108) *Çocuk ağaca çık-arak kurbağanın bir deliğe saklanmış olduğunu sandı.*
'The boy climbing [*V+erek*] the tree thought that the frog had hidden in a hole.' [*T9j-9;1*]

In sum, as Slobin (1993a) puts it, this converb is, essentially, a narrative form and its proper use requires an ability to manage attention flow in narrative in addition to the cognitive ability to mark two actions as constituent parts of a superordinate event, without actually naming the event. (See, further, Chapter IVC, Section 2.3.3.)

Adverbial clauses with the nominalized verb plus a postposition, such as V+*dik*+POSS+LOC 'at time of V-ing', V+*dik*+POSS+ABL *önce/sonra* 'before/after V-ing', and V+*me*+POSS+ABL *önce/sonra* 'before/after V-ing' are almost totally absent from the 3-year-old and rare in the 5-year-old data. They show a fourfold increase in the 9-year-old and adult texts (see Table 9). V+*dik*+POSS+LOC, typically appended to change-of-state verbs, presents a situation as a background state for a plot-advancing event and is the most frequently used subordinating construction at age 5. Most narrators use it in the context of the frog's escape as illustrated in the following example:

(109) *Çocuk uyan-dığ-ında kavanozu boş görünce çok korkmuş.*

'Upon.waking [V+*dik*], the boy was very scared when he saw the jar was empty.' [*T9c-9;1*]

There are also a few instances of V+*dik*+ABL followed by the noun *zaman* 'time' as postposition, meaning 'when', similarly used as a backgrounding device. It appears that the 5-year-olds are discovering how to make grounding distinctions and trying out differential marking to this end. They use temporal adverbs for sequencing equally weighted foreground events and grammaticized subordinators for introducing background states. Nine-year-olds prefer the V+*dik*+POSS *zaman* construction to V+*dik*+POSS+LOC, which is more perfective than stative in meaning. They also use V+*dik*+ABL *sonra* 'after having/being V-ed' for integrating successive events in a close sequential relation. These are exemplified below:

(110) *Seslen-diğ-i zaman da köpek aşağı atlayıp onu bulmağa çalışıyor.*

'And at the **time** of his calling [=when he calls], jumping down the dog tries to find it.' [T9g-9;9]

(111) *Ondan sonra, çocuk yat-tık-tan sonra kurbağa bu cam kavanozun içinden kaçıyor.*

'And then, **after** the boy's going to bed, the frog escapes from inside the glass jar.' [*T9d-9;11*]

The proportion of adverbial clauses expressing causal relations with V+*dik*+POSS *için* 'for/because of V-ing' also increases at this age. Finally, the adult texts display these forms with much higher frequency and contain subordinators that mark relations of cause, purpose, intention, consequence, and concession as well as temporality, as the following examples demonstrate. Grammaticized connectivity is in fact a defining feature of mature narratives.

(112) *Ertesi sabah çocuk kurbağasını kavanozun içinde bulama-dığ-ı için çok üzüldü.*

'The next morning the boy got very sad because of not finding his frog in the jar.' [*T9j-9;1*]

(113) *Geceleri yat-madan önce kurbağasına iyi geceler diliyormuş Ali.*

'In the evenings, Ali used to say goodnight to his frog **before** going to bed.' [*T20i*]

In summary, in this middle phase of connectivity we see sequential chaining with temporal terms such as 'then', 'and then', 'later', and grammaticized connectivity mainly with converbs and other subordinators. These all involve local rather than thematic relations between situations.

4.3. Mature Thematic Chunking

The ability to use the time concept as a basis for hierarchical organization of discourse appears in the narratives of school children and adults. Pairs of clauses joined by different types of subordinators are embedded within bigger chunks which are in turn presented as simultaneous or sequential with the use of adverbs. Overt markers of discourse connectivity which rely on intersentential relations typically occur clause initially and refer back anaphorically to an already established state of affairs, while those grammaticized into a nonfinite verb form establish interclausal relations.

Narrators differ in their choice of connective. Some use adverbs of sequence such as *ondan sonra* 'and then' or *daha sonra* 'later on' to preface a set of clauses that refer to a series of events which together constitute a single episode, while others use adverbs of simultaneity such as *bu sırada/o sırada* 'meanwhile' to similarly package events into larger units. In the following example, *daha sonra* 'later on/afterwards', which first appears in the 9-year-old stories, marks the boundary between the dog's fall from the window, the encounter with the gopher, and the disturbing of the bees.

(114) *Daha sonra köpek camdan düşüyor. Çocuk da camdan atlayıp onu alıyor. Daha sonra orman gidiyorlar, ormanda arıyorlar. Sonra bir arı yuvası buluyorlar. Yerde bir sincap yuvası buluyorlar. Oraya bakıyorlar. Oradan bir sincap çıkıyor. Burnunu ısırıyor çocuğun. Daha sonra arı yuvasını sallıyorlar.*

'**Afterwards** the dog falls from the window. The boy, jumping from the window picks it up. **Afterwards** they go to the woods, they search in the woods. **Then** they find a beehive. They find a gopher's hole in the ground. They look there. A gopher comes out of there. It bites the boy's nose. **Afterwards** they shake the bee hive.' [*T9a-9;3*]

Furthermore, these narrators reinstantiate the search theme at the beginning of a new episode and preface such utterances with their preferred adverb. This 9-year-old systematically pairs the sequential adverb *daha sonra* 'afterwards' with the discursive strategy of explicitly stating the search theme as in *Daha sonra çocuk yine kurbağasını aramağa başlamış* 'Afterwards the boy started searching for his frog again', while reserving *sonra* 'then' for sequencing events within an episode, as above. *Bu sırada/o sırada* 'meanwhile/in the meantime', much more frequent in the adult texts, are used for chunking sequences of events engaged in simultaneously by the different protagonists, and thus signal topic shifts. In short, temporal adverbs are used for thematic purposes to mark movement through different phases or episodes of the search. Peterson and McCabe (1991) have similarly observed the use of connectives as markers of macrostructure in narratives of 9-year-old children.

Not surprisingly, there are differences between the 9-year-olds and adults in the degree of text cohesion. Devices such as *V+ince, V+ken, V+diğinde, V+diği zaman* are used by adults not only to relate adjacent utterances but also to pick up information introduced a number of utterances earlier and re-present it as background for a new situation. There is, thus, a continuous process of tying up of nodes of information into a single thread of discourse:

(115) *Kovandaki arılara **havlamış havlamış**, arılar uçmaya devam ediyorlar. Henüz bir tepki gelmemiş arılardan. Öte yandan Alinin burnunu soktuğu kovuktan bir kokarca çıkmış. Alinin burnuna pis kokular gelmiş. Öte yandan Karabaş ağacı sallamış. **Havlayınca** arılardan bir tepki gelmediği için fazla sallamış.*

'He **barked and barked** at the bees in the hive, the bees continue to fly. There's yet no reaction from the bees. On the other hand a skunk came out of the hole Ali put his nose in. Bad odors came to Ali's nose. On the other hand Karabash shook the tree. He shook hard because there was no reaction from the bees **when he barked** [*V+ince*].' [*T20i*]

Temporal terms such as *gece, geceleyin, sabah* 'night, at night, in the morning' are used by school children and adults. Temporal adverbs such as *bir gece* 'one night', *bir gün* 'one day' become functional in establishing purely discourse internal reference points in these stories.

(116) ***Geceleyin** köpekle çocuk uyuduktan sonra kurbağa kavanozun içinden çıkarak kaçmış. **Sabahleyin** uyandıklarında köpekle çocuk kurbağanın kaçtığını görmüşler.*

'**At night,** after the dog and the frog slept the frog coming out of the jar escaped. **In the morning,** at their waking the dog and the boy saw that the frog escaped.' [*T20a*]

Modal verbs and adverbs qualify descriptive statements that introduce the narrator's perspective. Adults use these in complement clauses to describe an event and a related attitude or mental state simultaneously.

(117) *Fakat Frog bir kavanozun içinde.* **Mutlu olmasına rağmen kendini hapsedilmiş gibi hissediyor.** *Küçük köpeği onu inceliyor. Gece küçük çocuk ve köpeği uyurken Frog kaçmağa kalkıyor.*

'But Frog is in a jar. **Although he is happy he feels as if imprisoned.** His little dog is inspecting him. At night while the little boy and his little dog are sleeping, Frog attempts to escape.' [*T20j*]

Complement clauses, other than infinitival complements, are late to appear in our narratives. Turkish makes extensive use of nominalized forms such as VERB + INFINITIVE -*mek*, the nominal particle -*me*, the past participle -*dik*, and the future participle -*ecek*. *V+dik*, *V+ecek*, and *V+me* complements take casemarking and person/number marking for agreement with the subject which surfaces in the genitive (e.g.*V+dik*+POSS+CASE). *V+mek* complements take only casemarking since the subject of the complement verb is coreferential with the subject of the main verb, and can therefore be said to be syntactically simpler. The -*mek* complementizer occurs with modal or aspectual verbs and forms a very tightly linked unit, almost a single clause, expressing a relation not between discrete situations but rather a focus on a phase of a single situation. The -*dik*, -*ecek*, and -*me* complements, on the other hand, are more sententialized and form looser linkage between situations (Lehmann, 1988). Table 10 presents the distribution of different types of complementizers by age.

TABLE 10
Frequency of Different Types of Complementizers, by Age

Type of Complementizer	Age			
	3 yrs	5 yrs	9 yrs	Adult
-*mek*	10	18	20	52
-*dik*	—	5	3	10
-*me*	—	—	1	4
-*ecek*	—	—	—	3

Nominal constructions with -*mek* are quite frequent in the data and start at the youngest age with modal verbs such as *iste* 'want' and *çalış* 'try', as in *yakala-**mak** istiyor* 'wants to catch' at age 3, and aspectual verbs such as *başla, devam et* 'start, continue' as in *ara-mağa başlıyor* 'starts to search', at age 5, serving local functions. These constructions increase, particularly in the adult texts, where they assume the discourse organizational function of marking episodic boundaries (Aksu-Koç, 1993), as already noted in Section 1.2.2.1.

-Dik complements, where the main verb is typically a cognitive/perceptual verb such as *bil* 'know', *anla* 'understand', *gör* 'see', *farkında ol-* 'be aware', occur occasionally in the preschool texts (Aksu-Koç, 1992b). These constructions appear to pose problems, particularly when the complement verb is the irregular verb *ol* 'be' with its existential forms *var/yok* 'exist/not.exist'. In the following, an initial attempt at a complement results in a finite clause:

(118) *Kurbağa yok.* **Kurbağa yok ol-** *kurbağa kaybolmuş görüyor.*

'The frog isn't there. **The frog isn't there** [*yok ol-*] he sees the frog has gotten lost.' [*T5c-5;1*]

The single instance of a *-me* complement in the children's data is found in a 9-year-old text with a verb of saying: *Çocuk köpeğe sus-ma-sını söyledi* 'The boy told the dog to be quiet'. The complement clause in such a construction is compacted into a single deverbal noun — something like 'the-dog's-being-quiet — which also indicates a nonfactive reading. What is difficult for children is probably this sort of conceptual abstraction and condensation, rather than syntactic complexity per se, since there is evidence from non-narrative data for the use of *-me* complements earlier than this age (Aksu-Koç, 1992b).

The adult narratives show higher frequencies of different types of complements, though with the same relative proportions observed in the children's texts. *-Mek* complements mark the beginning of new episodes, *-dik* complements refer to mental states of the protagonists with cognitive verbs, as in (119), and *-me* complements are used both with utterance and manipulative verbs, as in (120):

(119) *Kavanozun saydam birşey ol-duğ-unu kestiremiyordu.*

'(The dog) couldn't figure.out that the jar is [*V-dik*] something transparent.' [*T20e*]

(120) *Onun kendisini yala-ma-sına izin verdi.*

'He permitted it [=dog] to.lick [*V-me*] him.' [*T20e*]

The scarcity of complement constructions in the frog story is hardly surprising, given that these have a rather specialized discourse function. Complement constructions serve to present a situation either (1) in terms of the emotional, cognitive, perceptual, or communicative activity of a narrator (with verbs of thinking or saying, such as 'know', 'think', 'say'); or (2) as a function of the manipulative activity of a subject (with verbs such as 'make', 'tell', 'order', 'ask'); or (3) in terms of a subject's binding relation or perspective towards a situation (with modality and aspectual verbs such as 'want', 'begin', 'finish', 'try', etc.) (see Givón, 1990). As such, these constructions do not play an essential role in the formation of a linear relation between events, but function in the construction of more complex abstract relations. In other words, complement constructions do not encode a relation between two discrete situations, but present a situation as the object of the cognition, perception, intention, communication, or manipulation of an experiencer or agent. Studies of children's understanding of mental verbs in English show that the presuppositional and implicational properties of such verbs are learned around 4-5 years of age — based not only on learning the semantics of the verbs or their use in different types of complement constructions (e.g., Abbeduto & Rosenberg, 1985; Moore & Davidge, 1989), but also on the development of an understanding of the representational nature of mind (Astington, 1990). It is therefore not surprising that these types of constructions are only used by mature narrators, who relate events hierarchically, manipulate perspectives, introduce narrator's comments, or speculate about cognitive or emotional states of protagonists.

To sum up, the kind of cohesion realized by adults is more advanced on the functional plane, reflecting the kinds of relations that mature narrators weave between events, states, actions, and intentions. Mature elaboration of discourse structure with regard to issues of grounding and introduction of a narrator perspective requires a number of devices not to be found in the children's stories.

5. CONCLUDING OBSERVATIONS

This survey of the development of grammatical and lexical forms in Turkish narratives has shown that the major change that occurs with age is in form-function relationships. That is, linguistic devices assume different functions at different ages and are effective in creating different levels of textual cohesion.

Our youngest narrators are 3- to 4-year-olds who have acquired the basic syntactic devices of their language. Although further developments take place in the various aspects of their grammar, the more significant changes occur in their skills related to narrative construction. In our sample, the ability to organize narrative events on a temporal axis starts around age 5 as evidenced by the use of (1) temporal adverbs relating successive utterances that refer to a sequence of events, and (2) grammaticized means such as V+ince, V+ken and V+dik+POST that contract clause internal relations. By using these devices children start establishing one event as a reference point for another in narrative time. Furthermore, the narrative ability that involves attending to two or more components of an event also emerges, in Turkish, as in other languages, at about age 5. This was observed, for example, in the description of the frog's escape in two distinct, though successive, phases. The more mature narrators, on the other hand, integrate event components from a specific perspective, using various linguistic means such as the converbs -ip or -erek or the conjunction ve.

The next level of development observed in narrative structuration involves the organization of sequentially related events in terms of a higher level goal of the story. The 3- and 5-year-olds provide little or no evidence for a distinction between linear and thematic organization of events. Most 9-year-olds and all adults on the other hand, produce stories structured in accordance with a guiding theme as well as a temporal sequence, but they differ in the extent to which they mark these different levels of organization linguistically. Adult narrators differentiate between episode boundaries and within-episode event transitions, marking the former with aspectual verbs and adverbs, and the latter with temporal adverbs of sequence. Nine-year-olds do not use differentiated linguistic forms although they have the same conceptual organization as the adults. Their use of sequential adverbs just at the beginning of new episodes, but rarely within an episode, suggests that they feel the need to indicate the relation of successive events to the guiding theme, but can only use temporal sequence markers as a readily available means to do so. Establishing such form-function relations at the hierarchical level, then, is the last step in this development.

As for the particulars of the developing form-function relationships, it was observed that the functions of linguistic forms change with development. For example, temporal adverbs first function as discourse fillers and then as connectives: sonra 'then/after', a term expressing temporal sequence, is first used as a discourse sequencer, then to introduce independent clauses referring to successive events, and last as a subordinator following a dependent clause. Similarly, adverbs that are based on discourse-internal deixis appear at different stages of narrative development, depending on their functions in the text. Sequential adverbs appear early to relate successive events, while adverbs expressing simultaneity between sequences or chunks of events are used later. Another example for a change in form-function relations is observed in the domain of locative modification. Turkish children have a very early command of casemarking (Aksu-Koç & Slobin, 1985) and correctly use locative postpositions such as içinde 'in', üstünde 'on' by age 3 (Johnston & Slobin, 1979). However, they come to use these devices for modification of locative trajectories in a narrative context only gradually. Similarly, the linguistic forms used in the elaboration of causation and manner of movement are available to children from quite a young age, but they occur with a narrative function only in the texts of the older speakers in our sample. Other examples of the same phenomenon are the -*mek* and -*dik* nominals that first appear in subordinating constructions, and later in complement clauses.

It was also found that a given function is realized by different forms for establishing levels of connectivity at different ages. For example, with age, existential predications are largely replaced by relative clauses in the introduction of background information. Similarly, adversative relations are expressed by younger children with the coordinating conjunction *ama* 'but' joining two independent clauses. In the texts of the older narrators the same relation is also expressed with *rağmen* 'despite' functioning either as a subordinator after a nominalized verb or as a text-level coordinating conjunction between sentences.

In conclusion, we have seen that children's skill in narrative construction involves changes both in conceptual organization and in the ability to manipulate form-function relationships. Underlying both however, may be a deeper level cognitive change. Investigations of narrative abilities within the framework of children's theory of mind suggest that there is "a general change that underlies children's cognitive abilities at about the age of four years [that allows them] to comprehend representations as representations, and that this ability enables the child to appreciate the dual landscape of a story" (Astington, 1990, p. 157). That is, children start to regard the events and actions of the story from the perspective of its protagonists, understanding their beliefs, fears, mental states and intentions around this age. Thus, 4-year-olds, but not 2-year-olds, "are able to see that another's belief is in fact his or her representation of reality. It therefore represents the realworld for the other person, and is the world in which that person will act..." (Astington, 1990, p. 158). In the present data, this ability manifests itself relatively later, with occasional examples in the texts of the 5-year-olds, to be observed fully only in the stories of the older children. This should not be surprising, since in a complex narrative task such as the telling of the frog story, the child is expected to construct a coherent text relating a long sequence of events, and make it meaningful from the point of view of the protagonists experiencing those events. The interweaving of these two levels or landscapes takes place between age 5, when we see the beginnings of it, and 9, when we observe it in almost a mature form. One might say that while the 5-year-old is working on the construction of an objective series of events, the older child has accomplished the higher level task of attributing them as subjective experiences to the person of a protagonist, presenting them from his point of view, that is, the task of subjectification (Bruner, 1986).

6. SUMMARY

6.1. Tense-Aspect-Modality

There is a developmental change from use of mixed tense to a preference for the present and, somewhat less, to one of the two past tenses as an anchor form. Static descriptions, available to Turkish speakers at an early age, are used for the function of discourse backgrounding only by older children and adults.

Tense shifts are unsystematic in the younger age group, but function for backgrounding at older ages. For example, a shift from -di past to the present habitual serves for general informational backgrounding in evaluations, and a shift from the present -iyor to the past perfect serves for temporal backgrounding in retrospection.

Aspectual shifts between stative, habitual, and progressive within a given tense/modality anchor in the preschool texts are also more random, and at best they involve local contrasts between different types of events. In the adult narratives, such shifts function at a more global level, for example for framing the story events recounted in the present or in the past by describing the setting with the use of stative aspectual forms.

In the lexical expression of aspectual distinctions, children prefer the use of adverbs over aspectual verbs. Aspectual modification is made adverbially at the clause level, and so is restricted locally to a single event in the children's texts. Aspectual verbs, marking inceptive, protracted, and lative aspect, increase in the adult texts, and are used for demarcating episode boundaries, so that a series of events falls under the scope of the perspective set by aspectual marking. Adverbial marking is particularly common for categories such as recurrent and iterative aspect, which are not marked morphologically. Adults express twice as many different types of aspect as do children.

6.2. Event Conflation

Different syntactic mechanisms play a role in event conflation in Turkish. These include: sequencing of independent clauses, subordination with adverbials or converbs, tightly embedded complements, and lexicalization. As compared to schoolchildren and adults, who may or may not use a conflating form to present two or more events as closely integrated, the preschool children fail to mark events as related. The proportion of verbs expressing **caused** movement increases slightly from around age 5 years. Also, causative verbs are used to express direct manipulative causation, while other, more syntactic devices, are used for linking less closely integrated situations.

In describing locative trajectories, all-purpose motion verbs and directional motion verbs are both used at all ages. However, with age, there is an increase in the variety and use of locative adverbs and postpositions to the verb, to specify the goal and/or source of an action. Relatedly, with age there is a greater variety of verbs used to encode manner of movement as well as manner adverbs. Adults use the productive verb morphology (particularly the converbs -ip and -erek) for presenting an elaborated view of closely related events.

6.3. Perspective

Younger children prefer an agent focus, while older children and adults can flexibly adopt an undergoer/patient orientation. The strategy of making valency changes on the verb (for example, by passivizing or reflexivizing) and thus presenting events from a perspective of reduced transitivity while maintaining topic, increases with age.

Both younger children and adults prefer the canonical SOV word order. There appears to be no developmental change in the frequency of more marked orders. Although infrequent, subject postposing for topic maintenance appears in the texts of both younger and older narrators. Shifting word order for topic change and defocusing does not seem to present a problem for children.

6.4. Connectivity

The use of different devices for clause linkage in the interests of textual connectivity increases with age. This is reflected in the higher proportion of complex clauses in the texts of the older narrators. The very young children's texts contain only perceptual-spatial connectivity, realized by the use of deictics and the topic/focus particle de 'also' as well as some connectives such as ama 'but'. Starting around age 5, connectivity is indicated by temporal adverbials like sonra, ondan sonra 'then, and then' and by coordinate and subordinate clause-linking devices. Among these devices are the different-subject converbs -ince and -ken and later, the same-subject converbs -ip and -erek. Temporal adverbial clauses with nominalized verb forms and postpositions also increase in frequency during this period. As the proportion of such devices for tighter linkage increases between ages 5 and 9, the proportion of sequential adverbs decreases. Finally, some older children and adults present events in more integrated syntactic packages. For this purpose, speakers make use of adverbs of simultaneity which allow for the temporal aligning of a sequence of events, as well as complement clauses which present one situation as a component of another. Chunks of events linked to one another by converbs and adverbials occur commonly in more mature narratives.

Part IV

DEVELOPMENT OF
FORM-FUNCTION RELATIONS

Chapter IV0

FORM-FUNCTION RELATIONS
IN THE DEVELOPMENT OF NARRATIVE

The four chapters in this part of the book integrate themes which have been introduced from different points of view in the three preceding sections. They combine concern for developing skills in narrative construction (Part II) and for crosslinguistic comparisons in the development of linguistic forms (Part III) with a focus on the interaction between form and function that is a central theme of the book as a whole (Part I). This theme is analyzed for four domains: (1) temporality, (2) backgrounding, (3) perspective taking, and (4) episodic plot structure.

Chapter IVA concerns the evolution of forms and functions for expressing **temporal** relations in the five languages, with a focus on German and Turkish. It follows on from research by Aksu-Koç (1988b) on the development of tense/aspect/modality systems in early child language, with particular attention to Turkish, and von Stutterheim's (1986) work on spatial and temporal organization in narrative compared with descriptive and expository discourse, with particular attention to the acquisition of German by Turkish speakers. Their analysis shows how the same forms become differentially deployed as narrative discourse abilities evolve from spatial to temporal principles of organization, and from local to more global frames of reference. Three relations of sequentiality apply within a narrative text — (1) the default case of sequentially ordered events, referring forward to each new event in time (e.g., 'the boy found a frog and it ran away'); and the more marked cases of (2) retrospection, or referring back to prior events (e.g., 'the boy found the frog **that he had lost**'), and (3) simultaneity, or referring to situations as concurrent or overlapping in time (e.g., 'the boy found the frog when he looked behind the log'). This analysis focuses on the third type of relation — one which has not received detailed attention in studies of tense/aspect systems. This chapter provides insights into the syntactic and lexical mechanisms available to speakers for the expression of simultaneity, showing that these differ in nonobvious ways from one language to the next. The authors make a contribution to narrative discourse theory by showing how the linguistic forms which narrators deploy in the expression of simultaneity interact with foreground/background distinctions in differentiating between various phases of an event or event-complex in the ongoing flow of discourse.

Chapter IVB deals with relative clauses, and as such starts from an opposite point of departure to IVA: Rather than taking a particular "function" (such as simultaneity) and examining forms used in its expression, the authors of this chapter took as their starting point a particular construction type, of the class traditionally analyzed under the heading of "relative-clause structures" in formal terms, and as performing the role of noun modification or object specification in semantic terms. The aim here was to examine the nature and development of complex syntax in narrative discourse across five languages which all have some kinds of relative clause construction. This investigation underlines certain important themes of the larger study. First, development of complex syntax plays an important role in the development of narrative abilities for purposes of packaging information, organizing the ongoing flow of discourse, and interrelating earlier and later parts of the narrative (e.g., in talking about 'the frog **that he had lost**'). Second, while linguists have provided us with a rich literature on the forms and structures of relative clauses within and across languages, few have attended to the functions of these forms in extended discourse. A contribution of this chapter, then, is to articulate a taxonomy of discourse functions, and to separate out those which are peculiar to the narrative mode of discourse. The authors also consider in detail the interrelation between morphosyntactic complexity of forms and their use across different phases of development in the five languages which they compare. And they address the challenging question of how different forms interact within the range of expressive options available for a certain purpose in a language (e.g., for specifying participant identity), and how these in turn meet the rhetorical preferences of speakers in a particular language or register. Finally, their analysis of relative clause usage reiterates themes which recur from different perspectives in the other chapters of this section. For instance, they show that the use of relative clauses for "presentative" purposes changes with age. That is, not only is the same form recruited for different purposes across development, but this particular function also changes with time, as children acquire overall narrative competence and are able to relate the introduction of new participants or identification of previously mentioned participants in the story to their role in the global plotline.

In Chapter IVC, we return to the two themes of "filtering" of experience for purposes of speaking, and the "packaging" of event descriptions into larger units, introduced at the beginning of the book (Chapter IA). This is done crosslinguistically, taking into account all five languages, and developmentally, considering how young children differ from older speakers in the relevant respects. For example, in order to examine how events depicted in the frog story are "filtered" in producing these narratives, forms of passive and mediopassive and word-order alternations are compared in the different languages, as means for downgrading agency and presenting an undergoer perspective on events. Given the complexity of comparing different age ranges in different languages across entire texts, in dealing with the question of how speakers select and encode a particular **perspective** on events, a methodology is adopted which has been the source of considerable insights since the inception of the frog story project. Particular "scenes" or segments of the story are analyzed in detail to examine how speakers attend to different facets of a given event, in this case, in talking about events with more than one protagonist. One conclusion which emerges is that certain linguistic forms may be mastered structurally, and applied in other discourse contexts, well before they are recruited for narrative functions.

The second part of Chapter IVC considers how speakers "package" events syntactically, by combining two or more clauses within a single structural unit. In crosslinguistic terms, different languages turn out to have preferred means for achieving the packaging effects of narrative syntax. Developmentally, this chapter provides further, typologically motivated support for the findings reported in the sections on "connectivity" in the language-specific chapters in Part III: There is a long developmental history of the ability to package events into complex and tightly-woven, globally motivated narrative units by means of available syntactic as well as lexical devices for connectivity.

Chapter IVD, which ends this part of the book, follows on from research conducted by its two authors in analyzing the development of narrative abilities in establishing reference and temporal organization of the story in German (Bamberg, 1987) and in evaluating importance ratings for plot components of the frog story in English (Marchman, 1989). The procedure adopted in this chapter is to identify critical points in the story, then to establish what linguistic forms speakers use at these points. The points analyzed in the unfolding plot are: instantiation of the search, reinstantiations of different points in the search, generalizations across different phases of the search, and plot completion with the ending of the search. The authors first examine how adult speakers of German and English use aspectual markers and other linguistic forms of expression at these story points, as a basis for comparison with 9- and 5-year old children speaking these two languages. (Three-year-olds in their sample did not appear to perform the relevant functions of "foreshadowing" and "wrapping up.") The study points to the important role of aspectual markers in moving from a sequentially ordered description of events to a globally organized hierarchical construal of these events. It shows how the same forms are differentially deployed at more local levels of event description, which is all that the younger children are capable of doing, compared with the larger discourse frame within which mature speakers refer to such notions as inception, reiteration, and prospection.

The four chapters which make up this part of the book, then, although conceived by several authors who proceed from different points of departure and focus on distinct areas for analysis, combine to underline themes reiterated across our study. There is a complex interaction between form and function across development; language-specific factors and language typology impinge on the particular forms favored for expressing certain functions; and these diverse factors in turn are affected by the development of general discourse abilities, on the one hand, and specifically narrative competence, on the other, and by the gradual emergence of the ability to integrate the telling of the frog story, like other types of connected discourse, from a narrowly local level to a hierarchically motivated global level of organization.

Chapter IVA

TEMPORAL RELATIONS IN NARRATIVE: SIMULTANEITY

Ayhan Aksu-Koç
Christiane von Stutterheim

1. AIMS OF THE STUDY

The general research question of this project, of which the following chapter is a part, can be described as follows: "How does the ability develop to conceptualize, organize, and express complex temporal structures in discourse?" This involves questions of general cognitive development and of linguistic development, as well as the interrelation of these two domains. In order to tackle these questions, a crosslinguistic perspective was chosen, because "only through the study of discourse across various languages, and across the entire developmental periods, can we sort out the role of various types of linguistic devices in the development of temporal cognition and its expression" (Slobin, 1985b, p. 14). To present the problem in these terms calls for an analytical frame which takes a concept (notions such as "simultaneity" or functions such as "background/foreground") as the starting point for the analyses. On this basis, different language systems can be made comparable.

In selecting a concept or function, the following aspects must be taken into account:

- The concept must be **basic** in the sense that it represents a core notion of a conceptual domain. It should not be compound in nature, because complex conceptual clusters could already be language specific.

- The concept should also be basic in another sense: It should be accessible and manageable for children at a fairly young age.

Both conditions are met by the concept analyzed in this chapter. **Simultaneity** is a basic element in our concept of time. It is one of the three "basic relations," or *Grundrelationen* (*Grundzüge einer deutschen Grammatik*, 1981), the other two being the temporal relations of 'before' and 'after'. Simultaneity of events is also perceptually accessible to children from very early on.

In pursuing the general aims of the project in one specific domain, we will be concerned with the following questions:

- How do children at different ages, and also adults, express the temporal relation of simultaneity across languages?

- What are the functions of the expression of simultaneity within the complex temporal structure of narrative discourse?

- How does the ability to conceptualize and express simultaneous relations of different types develop?

We start by discussing theoretical aspects of the temporal concept of simultaneity and its multilayered function in discourse.

2. THE TEMPORAL RELATION OF "SIMULTANEITY"

2.1. Theoretical Background

Although there is a vast literature in linguistics on the expression of temporal categories, there is, to the best of our knowledge, not a single study devoted specifically to the concept of simultaneity.[1] There is thus no prior

---

[1] One exception is an unpublished article by Hicks (1986).

investigation which could provide an immediate basis for our study. Much of the previous work on temporal concepts is, however, indirectly relevant. First, the domain of theoretical linguistics provides analyses of the semantics of expressive devices for time reference — mainly tense/aspect systems and lexical items like adverbials, conjunctions, and particles — which include reference to simultaneity (e.g., Kamp & Rohrer, 1982; Löbner, 1989; Partee, 1984; Smith, 1983).

Research on discourse structure, in particular narrative discourse, also provides relevant insights (e.g., Givón, 1982; Hopper, 1982; Klein, 1981; Labov, 1972). In these studies, simultaneity is analyzed as a temporal relation which signals a particular function within the overall discourse structure. The dominant temporal relation between utterances in narrative discourse is defined by the *after*-relation which constitutes the chain of foregrounded events. In contrast, the relation of simultaneity (henceforth *sim*) can be taken as an indicator for all kinds of supplementary background material. These distinctions will be critical for our analysis.

Language acquisition is, of course, another branch of linguistic research relevant for our study. The development of temporal concepts has been a major topic in the study of semantics in child language. Much of this work has focused on the two concepts of 'before' and 'after' (e.g., Clark, 1971; Cromer, 1968; Flores d'Arcais, 1978). This is probably because these relations are expressed at a stage where children do not as yet produce coherently organized pieces of text, when temporal relations are deictically anchored. Simultaneity, on the other hand, is usually not expressed overtly when deictically anchored. Explicit reference to the *sim*-relation is, rather, typical of complex temporal structure in discourse. And although there has been an upsurge in interest in children's discourse in recent years, little of this work has been undertaken from a temporal perspective.

Language acquisition studies have shown that the first marking of temporal notions in children's speech is typically through the verb inflectional system. Children in different languages have been shown to first acquire inflections used for marking the present (and/or progressive) and the past in the adult language (Aksu-Koç, 1988; Antinucci & Miller, 1976; Berman & Dromi, 1984; Bloom, Lifter, & Hafitz, 1980; Brown, 1973; Clark, 1985; de Lemos, 1981; Fletcher, 1979; Jacobsen, 1981; Sachs, 1983; Stephany, 1986; Szagun, 1977; Weist, 1986). The commonly noted observation is that these inflections occur only with certain types of verbs in restricted environments where scope of reference is limited to the present moment. This has led to the interpretation of their function as aspectual rather than temporal. During this period there is also some marking of modal notions such as willingness or ability, with auxiliaries or inflections, depending on the language. The next development, around age 2;6, is characterized by an increase in the number of auxiliaries and/or inflections, which come to be used in in more varied contexts, and by the emergence of temporal adverbials. Deictic adverbs such as 'yesterday', 'tomorrow', and 'when'-constructions are typically reported to precede the use of the nondeictic terms 'before' and 'after' used prepositionally or as subordinating conjunctions (Aksu, 1978; Clancy, Jacobsen, & Silva, 1976; Clark, 1985; Fletcher, 1979; Weist, Wysocka, Witkowska-Stadnik, Buczowska, & Konieczna, 1984). The aspectual and tense functions of the inflections are now differentiated in utterances which refer to past or future. That is, children can order events on a time line that has the moment of speech as the anchoring point. Finally, children start expressing the more complex relations of "anterior," "posterior," or "simultaneous" between events, an achievement which requires the coordination of different temporal points such as event time, reference time, and speech time. To this end, they use complex tense-aspect marking and temporal adverbs (Amidon & Carey, 1972; Barrie-Blackley, 1973; Berman & Dromi, 1984; Clark, 1970, 1985; Cromer, 1974; Ferreiro & Sinclair, 1971; Fletcher, 1981; Stephany, 1981; Szagun, 1976, 1979). These studies have suggested that in constructing the nondeictic relations of temporal reference, children progress from juxtaposing two independent clauses which express events in their order of occurrence, to sequentially relating two clauses with adverbials that preserve order of occurrence to, finally, free use of conjunctions or adverbials without attention to correspondence between order of occurrence and of mention. These developments eventually lead to the coordination of the deictic temporal axis of events with the nondeictic time axis of discourse, around the age of 3;0-3;6 — the age of the youngest children in our sample.

2.2. The Concept of Simultaneity

So far we have talked about simultaneity as if it were a clear-cut concept, but this is not in fact the case. Let us first consider a narrow definition of this temporal relation:

Two events, processes, or states are simultaneous if they have identical values on the time axis. This means that their respective right and left temporal boundaries must coincide.

If we were to adopt this definition, then we would find hardly any cases of simultaneity in our data, first, because simultaneity in this narrow sense very rarely holds between two situations in reality[2] and second, because we often

---

[2] Following Comrie (1976), we use the term "situation" as a temporally neutral expression that can refer to activities, states, or events.

cannot tell whether two situations referred to in discourse were actually simultaneous. Information given linguistically usually does not have this level of precision.

Therefore, we will take a somewhat looser definition of simultaneity as our starting point:

> Two events, processes, or states are simultaneous if they share a value on the time axis. Temporal boundaries need not coincide.

This definition extends the concept of simultaneity to all kinds of temporal overlap and inclusion. These include, for example, where **e** stands for events and **s** for states and the numerals **1** and **2** indicate two distinct events or states, situations such as the following: (a) **e1** and **e2** have identical values on the time axis; (b) **e1** and **s2** share a value on the time axis, but the left and right temporal boundaries of **s2** extend beyond **e1**, that is, **s2** begins prior to **e1** and continues after it; (c) **s1** and **s2** share a value on the time axis, but the temporal boundaries of **s1** extend beyond those of **s2** to both left and right; (d) **s1** and **s2** have identical values on the time axis; (e) **e1** and **s2** share a value on the time axis, but **s2** extends beyond **e1** to the right, that is, it continues after it; etc. Language in general does not provide specific means to distinguish these and other conceivable subcategories of simultaneity explicitly; and only a handful of these options are reflected in the linguistic systems of the five languages of this study.

2.3. Simultaneity as Part of a General Concept of Time

If two situations are conceptualized and verbally presented as being simultaneous, then more is involved than the perception of the mere facts in the referential world. The speaker has to have an abstract concept of a time-line, to which both situations can be related.[3] That is, in order to refer to two situations as being simultaneous, a concept of time is required which includes a number of basic notions:[4]

- the deictically given speech-time (S)

---

[3] This may sound trivial, but it is not, if we look at how children talk about temporal relations. Precisely this general concept of a time continuum seems not to exist for 3-year-olds (see Piaget, 1960, pp. 99ff, where he discusses the specific difficulties children have with the concept of simultaneity).

[4] The categories are taken from Reichenbach's (1947a, 1947b) work on tense logic. Although many suggestions have been made for modifying Reichenbach's system, his basic categories — S, R, E — can still be taken as common ground for those working on problems of temporal reference.

- a reference time (R)
- the event time (E)

These notions are crucial for distinguishing different "levels" of simultaneity which can be found in discourse. They complicate the picture and add another dimension of diversity to the different types of simultaneity which can be identified.

Three levels of simultaneity are pertinent to our database: the time axes of (1) events, (2) discourse, and (3) perception.

(1) The standard case is simultaneity of two or more "event-times." The situations are located on the time axis by means of the same S and R parameters and the time intervals referred to are either identical or overlap. An example would be a sequence of two clauses such as in example (1).

(1)   The frog was in the jar

and the boy was looking at him.

Here the time intervals overlap (from the point of view of the pictures, in reality the boy's looking is contained within the longer stretch of time).

(2) The "time axis of discourse" is another level on which simultaneity might occur. This is the line which speakers take for the presentation of the events. It may follow the actual temporal location of the events, in which case it is identical with the time axis in (1). But it may also deviate from the real time structure by introducing a subjective perspective on the events. In that case, a particular relation between the Es no longer implies the same relation between the Rs. Thus, a constellation becomes possible in which the Rs of two situations fall temporally together — and can thus be regarded as simultaneous — whereas the Es are sequential in time, as in the example in (2).

(2)   e1 *Er wacht auf.* 'He wakes up.'

e2 *Inzwischen hat sie das Zimmer betreten.* 'In the meantime she has come into the room.'

Here, the second event e2 is related to the temporal reference of the first event, in that the result of e2 is presented as being simultaneous with e1. The present perfect is the typical device for introducing this type of temporal relationship in German (as well as English and Spanish). The temporal structure in this case is complex since on the axis of **events**, we get a relation of **retrospection** implying a sequential relation such that e2 precedes e1, while on the axis of **discourse** we get a relation of **simultaneity** between the two reference points involved, that is, R1=R2.

(3) A third, distinct level on which simultaneity can occur is the "time axis of perception." This concept is relevant to the particular discourse type

dealt with in our database. A description of a picture-story differs greatly from, for example, a real-world story, a fantasy, or recounting of a film, in that a story must be developed on the basis of a series of static scenes in which different activities are presented as simultaneous. The more closely a speaker follows the pictures, the more descriptive the task becomes. As a result, the co-presence of situations in one picture, which implies simultaneity of perception, will be a structuring factor in the temporal organization of the text. We will see that this is the "temporal approach" taken by the 3-year-old children, and that it can also play a role in adult narrations, where we find sentences such as example (3).

(3)   *Man sieht den Jungen lachen und den Hund in Witterungshaltung.*

'One sees the boy laugh and the dog standing in sniffing position.' [*G20b*]

In sum, several levels of temporal structure are involved in considering temporally related situations. The most important for our study is the **time axis of events**, but we also need to take account of the **time axis of discourse**, which results from a particular perspective taken on events, and the **time axis of perception**, which is relevant to the picture-description nature of our task. Most importantly from our point of view, the *sim*-relation can be established on all three levels.

2.4. Simultaneity in Discourse

The contribution that an utterance of the *sim*-type can make to the informational structure of a text is by no means uniform. It depends on the type of discourse, on the one hand, and on the particular function of the utterance within that discourse, on the other. Both factors have an impact on whether, and how, the temporal relation will be expressed. Below we consider the status of utterances expressing the *sim*-relation in the two types of text elicited by our study: narrative and description.

2.4.1. Narrative discourse

Temporality is a critically important factor, some would say the most basic element, in the organization of narrative structure. Following from this, the central distinction between **foreground** and **background** in much contemporary research has been based on temporal categories (e.g., Hatav, 1985; Hopper, 1979; Reinhart, 1984). According to these definitions, foregrounded utterances can be characterized as (a) referring to an event (with the crucial property being temporal boundedness), and (b) standing in a shift-in-time-relation. A principle of chronological order applies as the "default case" for foregrounded clauses, which constitute the temporal skeleton of the narrative.

Background material, in contrast, is not part of the advancing plotline; one main way in which it can be related to foregrounded utterances is by the temporal relation of simultaneity.

But simultaneity is not necessarily always an indicator of backgrounding. Rather, we need to distinguish between two types of simultaneity in narratives: (a) simultaneity of events in the foreground, and (b) simultaneity of events and states within the background, or across foreground and background. A typical context for (a) arises when several participants are involved in a story, acting simultaneously at different places, as is clearly true of the frog story. Such contexts often demand explicit marking of the temporal relations between events. Otherwise the events would be interpreted as sequential, according to the default case for structuring a narrative.

With regard to (b), utterances which refer to temporally unbounded states cannot be part of the storyline. If they do not leave the temporal frame of the story — as in the case of personal comments by the speaker which shift time reference to the deictically given speech-time — the states will temporally overlap with one or more events in the foreground. Utterances of this kind are typical instances of background material. They may contain information about situational circumstances (temporal and spatial); or they may provide explanations or comments from the point of view of the speaker or the protagonist. Thus, the basic type of discourse relief shows the following pattern:

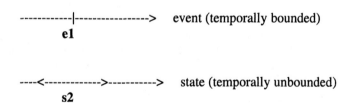

These basic patterns will not suffice to account for all the cases of simultaneity in our database. Complications result from the fact that (a) simultaneity of reference can hold between utterances which are not adjacent, and (b) simultaneity can be established between chunks of events which are internally sequentially ordered. The following examples illustrate some possible patterns of this kind (bg = background, fg = foreground, seq = sequential).

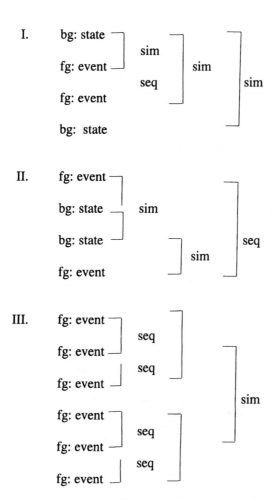

The different configurations in I to III above show that simultaneity in narrative discourse needs to be analyzed beyond adjacent pairs of utterances, taking into account a wider discourse context.

2.4.2. Descriptive discourse[5]

---

[5] Descriptions do not form a homogeneous class. In terms of temporal organization, there are two basic types: "dynamic descriptions," such as processes, which follow the same temporal pattern as narratives, and "static descriptions," such as picture-descriptions. Only the latter category is relevant to our particular database. (A detailed discussion of these text types is provided in von Stutterheim & Klein, 1989.)

In picture descriptions, the function of utterances expressing simultaneity can be characterized as the reverse of what we have said about narratives. Those utterances which form the backbone of the text, and as such constitute the foreground in a description, stand in the relation of simultaneity. All the information given in one picture is frozen into a static simultaneity of events, processes, and states. Verbalization of such a situation must somehow convey that all the information given in the sequential utterances remains within the same temporal frame.

Background material can also be inserted in a descriptive text, but then it has a different character and function (Giora, 1990). Narrative discourse, of the kind which concerns us here, has two main kinds of background material. (1) Comments by the speaker — personal opinion, evaluation, etc. — are temporally anchored in speech time, and so depart from the temporal frame of the foregrounded utterances. (2) Utterances providing information not given in the pictures need to have some temporal reference of their own, in order to be integrated into the temporal structure of the text. They may be linked to the temporal frame in a shift-in-time relation, or they may introduce their own independent temporal reference. It follows that in **descriptive** texts, a temporal relation which is **not** simultaneous is an indicator of background material.

Crucial to the context of our particular database is the fact that the task of narrating a picturebook is essentially ambiguous. The text types elicited by this procedure yield a hybrid of description and narration. Speakers can either choose to produce a number of descriptions following the picture frames, or they can transform the static pictures into a continuous story, in which the pictures are no more than clues to an advancing plotline. A third possibility is a mixture of these two text types — which turns out to be quite common in our sample, and not easily given to analysis.

3. THE EXPRESSION OF SIMULTANEITY IN GERMAN AND TURKISH

The bulk of this chapter presents a systematic comparison of German and Turkish, followed by brief comparisons with developments in Spanish, Hebrew, and English (Section 5.2). Below is an overview of how the *sim*-relation is expressed in German (Section 3.1) and Turkish (3.2).

3.1. German

The means available in German for reference to simultaneity are — compared to other languages — rather poor. In most cases, the *sim*-relation is not overtly expressed at all, particularly in the case of the relation between a backgrounded state and a foregrounded event. Most of the *sim*-utterances in the adult German frog stories are not overtly marked for their temporal relation. Instead, the relevant meaning is conveyed by the inherent temporal properties of the situations referred to — most crucially information concerning temporal boundedness and unboundedness.[6]

German has no morphological means, and uses two types of lexical items for expressing simultaneity: (1) sentence-modifying adverbs and adverbial phrases such as *währenddessen* 'meanwhile', *gleichzeitig* 'at the same time', *mittlerweile* 'in the meanwhile' and *in der Zwischenzeit* 'in the meantime', *in dem Moment* 'at the moment', *zur gleichen Zeit* 'at the same time'; and (2) subordinating conjunctions such as *als* 'when', *wenn* 'as, when', *während* 'while', *wie* 'how'. Nominalization provides a further, syntactic means for integrating two simultaneous situations within one utterance, where a nominalized verb is combined with a preposition which indicates simultaneity, e.g., *bei* 'at, with' + NOMINALIZED INF; *während* 'during' + NOMINALIZED INF.

The lexical inventory of German reflects the following conceptual subcategories of the notion of simultaneity:

- Devices for referring to an **event-event** relation — e.g., *in dem Moment, als* 'at the moment, when' — in contrast to a **state-event** or **state-state** relation — e.g., *währenddessen, während* 'meanwhile, while'.

- Devices for expressing simultaneity between an episode (more than one event) and an event/state or another episode — e.g. *in der Zwischenzeit* 'in the meantime' in contrast to the *sim*-relation between two single situations — e.g., *gleichzeitig* 'at the same time'.

- Different means for expressing the *sim*-relation between two foregrounded situations — e.g. *dabei* 'in doing this' — compared with the relation between a foregrounded and a backgrounded situation — e.g., *als* 'when'.

- The device of clause ordering can be used to mark the distinction between topic and focus — particularly in subordinating constructions, where the order of two clauses will reflect topic-focus structure.

- Other distinctions which can in theory be made with respect to simultaneity are not overtly marked, and need to be inferred from the semantics of the specific utterances.

---

[6] Inferences about temporal relations can be derived from other sources than the temporal properties of a situation — including reference to other conceptual domains, such as space or person.

Other means contribute to the interpretation of two situations as simultaneous without marking them explicitly as such. For example, expressions which have a durative, imperfective meaning make an utterance temporally unbounded. If such an utterance is preceded or followed by one with no specific temporal reference, then the two utterances will be interpreted as simultaneous. Devices of this sort are: *immer* 'always', *gerade* 'just (now)', *immer noch* 'still', *am* + NOMINALIZED INF 'in the process of V-ing', etc. In addition, complement and adverbial clauses of reason are also consistent with an interpretation of simultaneity in the absence of any other explicitly marked temporal relation marked explicitly (e.g., by tense shifting), as in (4) and (5).

(4) *Er sieht, daß der Hund schläft.*

     'He sees that the dog sleeps.'

(5) *Er läuft, weil die Bienen ihn verfolgen.*

     'He runs because the bees follow him.'

Finally, a form that figures as a compensatory device in young children's usage is the adverb *auch* 'also', which can also imply simultaneity in certain contexts.

3.2. Turkish

The relation of simultaneity between two single situations (event-event, ongoing process-event, and state-event) is expressed by means of verbal morphology in Turkish. The morphological devices are adverbial clauses formed by converbs (also called gerunds) and nominalized forms of the verb.

The **converbs** are nonfinite verb forms which form adverbial clauses that take their tense specification from the clause-final main verb. The following sections consider the properties of converbs relevant to simultaneity and grounding. (See Chapter IIIE, Section 2, for definitions and a more comprehensive treatment.)

V+*ince* 'when' and V+*ken* 'while' function within the temporal paradigm and present the time of the event referred to in the adverbial clause as reference time (R) for the event referred to in the main clause. V+*ken* presents an event in its extension, i.e., as an ongoing process, and expresses simultaneity alone, whereas V+*ince* denotes point or partial overlap between bounded events and may carry a causal or temporal meaning. These converbs add an aspectual coloring to the verbs they are attached to: Inherent to the meaning of -*ken* are notions of duration and progression, and inherent to the meaning of -*ince* is the notion of completion. V+*ip* 'and (then)' and V+*erek* 'in/by V-ing', on the other hand, are discourse-level operators, subject to coreferentiality constraints. They lie outside of the temporal paradigm and serve to closely integrate two situations, as immediately successive or as simultaneous, depending on context.

The **nominalized verb**, which is marked for person and number, either takes a postposition or is inflected with a case marker, to form a unit that functions as an adverbial clause. Such clauses can set R and mark simultaneity between a state and an event when the postposition is the noun *zaman* 'time', or the case marker is the locative inflection *-de*. The morphemes are arrayed as follows, where *dik* represents a deverbal nominalizer: V+*dik*+PERSON/NUMBER *zaman*; V+*dik*+PERSON/NUMBER+*de* (*-dik* appears as *-diğ* if a vowel follows, as in the examples below). An adverbial clause which is formed in this way with a past participle presents the situation as a bounded state. The construction V+*diği zaman* 'at the time of V-ing' implies perfectivity and at times causality or condition; V+*diğinde* 'at V-ing' presents the situation from a stative perspective. In sum, between two situations, event-event relations are typically referred to by V+*ince* and V+*ip*, ongoing process-event relations by V+*ken* and V+*erek*, and state-event relations by V+*diğinde* and V+*diği zaman*.

Turkish uses **adverbial phrases** for expressing the simultaneity between an episode (more than one event) and an event/state or a second episode — *bu/o arada* 'meanwhile', *bu/o sırada* 'in the meantime', *öte yandan/öbur tarafta* 'on the other side/hand', as against phrases used to express a simultaneous relation between two isolated situations — *tam o sırada* 'right at that moment', *o zaman* 'at that time', *aynı anda* 'at the same time'. The first type indicate full or partial overlap of event/state sequences over a time interval: *bu arada* 'meanwhile' presents the event or sequence of events from an imperfective perspective implying their progress or duration during the interval; *bu sırada* 'in the meantime' localizes the subsequent event at some temporal value within the interval; *öte yandan* 'on the other side', implies simultaneity by analogy through spatial opposition. The second group of adverbials imply a full overlap between bounded situations. The adverbial *o zaman* 'at that time, then' expresses either simultaneity or more so, logical consequence. Such expressions function in switching perspective to simultaneous but independent activities of different actors, while the bound forms serve to connect situations that are causally or temporally contingent on one another.

Furthermore, different options will be used to express *sim*-relations between two foregrounded situations as compared to the *sim*-relations between a foregrounded and a backgrounded situation. The converbs V+*ip* and V+*erek* can mark simultaneity between two foregrounded or a background and a foreground event, while V+*ken* and the subordinating constructions V+*diğinde* and V+*diği zaman* present the situation they refer to as backgrounded. These morphological devices connecting adjacent utterances function to make grounding distinctions at the **local** level. Adverbial phrases, on the other hand, effect grounding distinctions at a more **global** level: They typically mark a topic shift and present the situation they introduce as foregrounded.

The distinction between topic and focus is signaled by the order of the clauses in complex sentences. In Turkish, the subordinate clause preceding the main clause — in line with the canonical SOV order — reflects topic-focus structure. This means that V+*ince* and V+*ken* clauses typically introduce information that is already given or is easily inferrable, i.e., the topic, which is backgrounded relative to the information in the main clause. However, it is also possible for these converbs to present new information, in which case they serve to establish a temporal relation between two foreground events.[7]

Turkish thus has a far richer set of devices than German. The pervasiveness of these devices in the verb morphology as well as the availability of adverbial phrases allows for the expression of different types of *sim*-relations (event-event, state-event, process-event), and for finer foreground/background distinctions between pairs or chunks of situations. However, as in German, the kind of *sim*-relation that is typically left unmarked in Turkish or expressed implicitly (e.g., by nominal constructions or by tense-aspect alternations), will be between background states and foreground events, where temporal boundedness/unboundedness plays a role in the inferencing of the nature of the temporal relation. Since tense-aspect shifts play a role in the expression of simultaneity, the relevant distinctions in the inflectional system of Turkish are briefly noted here. (See, further, Chapter IIIE, Section 1.)

Turkish makes a temporal distinction between the past and the nonpast, and a modal distinction between direct experience and inference/hearsay. The inflection *-iyor* is a present tense form contrasting with *-er*, which is used for habitual or generic statements. In the past tense, however, *-iyor* combines with a past-tense suffix to indicate past progressive. There are two such past-tense markers: the direct experience form *-di*, contrasting with *-miş* for various kinds of nondirect experience, as described in Chapter IIIE. Aspectual distinctions in the past are made by appending *-iyor* or *-er* to the verb, before *-di* or *miş*.

Various forms of expression which are not explicit markers of simultaneity but whose meaning contributes to the interpretation of two situations

---

[7] If the order of clauses is reversed, then the subordinate clause occupies the postverbal position, where it carries reduced informational value, and is therefore further backgrounded. The preverbal position in Turkish is the focus position; whatever occurs in the postverbal position functions like an afterthought.

as simultaneous are similar to those in German. Thus, utterances which contain expressions with a durative, imperfective meaning will, if preceded or followed by an utterance which does not contain a specific temporal reference, yield the interpretation of simultaneity. Devices of this sort are: *hala* 'still', *hemen* 'immediately', *tam* 'just', NOMINALIZED INF+LOC (V+*mekte*) 'in the process of V-ing', locative phrases, etc. Also, as in German, complement and causal clauses yield an interpretation of simultaneity if there is no other temporal relation marked explicitly, as in (6) and (7).

(6) *Köpeğin uyuduğunu görüyor.*
     'He sees that the dog is sleeping.'

(7) *Arılar onu kovaladığı için kaçıyor.*
     'He's running away because the bees are chasing him.'

Finally, the particle *de*, which means 'and' or 'also/too', depending on context, and which has the pragmatic force of focusing the element which it follows, implies simultaneity. It functions as a compensatory device in the children's speech, similar to the German *auch* 'also', as in the following 5-year-old example:

(8) *Çocuk da sesleniyor köpek de arıların yuvasındaki şeyi rahatsız ediyor*
     'The boy *de* calls the dog *de* disturbs the thing in the bee's nest.' [T5e-6;0]

The explicit devices for expressing simultaneity in the two languages thus differ significantly, since German relies only on lexical means, whereas Turkish can make quite extensive use of morphological means as well. The range of devices in these two languages can be summed up as follows:

Adverbs:
  German: *währenddessen, gleichzeitig, mittlerweile...*
  'meanwhile, at the same time, in the meantime'

Adverbial Phrases:
  German: *in der Zwischenzeit, in dem Moment, zur gleichen Zeit...*
  'in the meantime, at the moment, at the same time'
  Turkish: *bu/o sırada, bu/o arada, öbur tarafta, o zaman...*
  'in the meantime, on the other side, at that time'

Connectives:
  German: *als, wenn, während, wie...* 'when, while'
  Turkish: converbs: V+*ince*, V+*ken*, V+*ip*, V+*erek*
  'when, while, and (then), by doing'

Adverbial Clauses with Nominalized Verbs:
German: *bei*+NOMINALIZED INF, *während*+NOMINALIZED INF
Turkish: V+*diğinde*, V+*diği zaman*

4. DEVELOPMENTAL HYPOTHESES

Two developmental domains can be studied in interrelation through the concept of simultaneity: (1) development of discourse competence and narrative structure, and (2) development and use of expressive devices.

With regard to discourse competence, although even the younger speakers produce sustained pieces of discourse, they still have a long way to go before they reach the narrative proficiency of the adults. Prior research, coupled with findings from the present study, suggest the following developments along different but interrelated dimensions (see Chapters IIA and IIB).

- The type of discourse will change from picture-to-picture description to narration.

- This implies a change in the type of cohesion established in the texts from local (utterance by utterance, pairs of utterances) to global, text-level organization.

- This in turn implies development of the ability to conceptualize a number of single states and events as parts of one complex overall event on the basis of their temporal relations

- Once children are able to organize their speech output along a narrative thread, they are ready to move from mere juxtaposition of equally weighted pieces of information to hierarchical structures in discourse.

- Between the 5-year-old age group and the adults there is an elaboration of hierarchical structures in discourse (grounding, chunking, giving perspective, referring backwards and forwards, etc.).

These general observations about developing discourse abilities yield the following predictions for how the functions of simultaneity in narration can be expected to change. Initially, at the early phases of development, verbalization will be governed by simultaneity of perception (for each picture frame) and deictic orientation will provide the anchor for the different pieces of information. As children move on to developing a temporal structure in discourse, they learn to distinguish the different functions of simultaneity with respect to foregrounding and backgrounding. The first steps in this direction are characterized by a struggle for expressive devices making these distinctions. The course and speed of development in this as in other areas will by influenced by the verbal means available in the native language. The more elaborate the narrations become, the more *sim*-utterances of all different types they will contain in quantitative terms, serving the narration function of adding background information to the events given in the pictures.

With respect to the linguistic devices available for expressing the concept of simultaneity, three different, but interrelated types of developmental changes can be predicted:

- New forms will be acquired and added to the available repertoire.
- The functions of available forms will change across time.
- Certain juvenile forms will be abandoned.

For the concept of simultaneity specifically, there will be a stepwise development of forms reflecting the complexity of types and functions of simultaneity (Section 2). The structural properties of the devices available in a language (morphological marking, lexical expressions, forms used in coordinate or subordinate constructions as outlined in Section 2) will also affect the developmental process. Yet it is not *a priori* obvious how the two factors of conceptual complexity and structural complexity interact to determine the developmental sequence of simultaneity marking in narrative discourse. To this end, we turn to an analysis of the form and function of simultaneity in our frog story sample.

5. DATA ANALYSIS

This analysis focuses on the data from German and Turkish (5.1) followed by a brief overview of findings for Spanish, Hebrew, and English (5.2).

5.1. The German and the Turkish Data

This section provides a quantitative overview of the linguistic devices used for the expression of simultaneity in German and Turkish followed by a discussion of each age group in turn under the three headings of: (A) discourse structure, (B) function and level of simultaneity in discourse, and (C) expression of simultaneity. [8]

5.1.1. Means for expressing simultaneity

Table 1 presents the quantitative breakdown for the German, and Table 2 for the Turkish data. The first part of each table lists all lexical items (Ia — conjunctions, Ib — adverbs) used for referring to simultaneity; part II lists the devices which, in the given context, imply the simultaneity of two situations;

---

[8] The first heading, "discourse structure," summarizes patterns for each age group, as presented in Chapter IIᴀ, Section 4, where developmental profiles are given for the entire language sample, with examples from English and Hebrew.

part III lists "compensatory" devices, found mainly in the data of younger children. The first figure gives the absolute number of occurrences of a given form in a given age group, the second — following the slash — the number of speakers who use the form — e.g., 10/5 means the form was used 10 times, and occurred in 5 texts.

TABLE 1
Distribution of Expressions of Simultaneity in German, by Age

	3 yrs	5 yrs	9 yrs	Adult
Ia)				
CONJUNCTIONS:				
als		2/2	10/5	13/8
wenn			1/1	
während			1/1	18/6
wie	1/1		2/2	6/4
Ib)				
ADVERBS:				
inzwischen			2/1	9/6
in der Zwischenzeit			3/1	1/1
mittlerweile				3/1
währenddessen				3/1
derweil				1/1
dabei				8/6
gleichzeitig				1/1
II)				
da	1/1	5/3	14/7	13/7
denn/weil	3/2	2/1	9/5	12/6
ob	2/2	3/3	5/3	2/2
gerade	3/2		6/2	
plötzlich		1/1	8/5	6/6
auf einmal		1/1	4/2	4/2
bei + INF			1/1	
III)				
auch	2/2	11/7	20/7	4/3

TABLE 2
Distribution of Expressions of Simultaneity in Turkish, by Age[a]

	3 yrs	5 yrs	9 yrs	Adult
Ia)				
CONVERBS:				
V+*ince*	2/1	6/3	4/3	13/6
V+*erken*	3/2	5/3	11/8	28/10
V+*ip*		5/6	1/1	11/7
V+*erek*		1/1	12/3	10/5
ADVERBIAL CLAUSES:				
V+*dik*+*de*		7/2	3/3	13/8
V+*diği zaman*		2/2	9/4	
Ib)				
ADVERBIALS:				
o zaman	6/3		3/2	
bu/o sırada		1/1	8/3[b]	18/5[c]
bu/o arada			2/3[b]	27/7[c]
öte yandan				6/3
tam o sırada				4/3
II)				
COMPLEMENT CLAUSES:				
V+*dik* V		2/2	1/1	14/9
V+*me* V				2/2
V *ki*		3/3	3/2	1/1
ADVERBIAL CLAUSES:				
V+*dik için*	1/1	4/2		6/5
çünkü		2/1	1/1	2/2
III)				
de[d]	16/7	28/9	24/7	31/9

a. All occurrences in contexts where simultaneity is implicitly or explicitly expressed.
b. Same 3 children.
c. Total of 9 adults.
d. All occurrences in contexts where simultaneity is implicitly or explicitly expressed.

5.1.2. 3-year-olds

A. Discourse structure: 3-year-olds

The 3-year-old children produce descriptions based on the picture frames.[9] The following are indicators of a descriptive text-type. First, most of the utterances are introduced by, or contain a deictic adverb referring to the spatial arrangements in the pictures (*da/hier, burda/orda* 'here, there'). That is, the children describe what they see in the picture without relating the different situations to each other — either across pictures or within one picture. This results in a discourse structure in which the utterances are added to each other as "equal" pieces of information. There is no differentiation between foregrounded and backgrounded clauses. Second, no distinction is made between situations of different types (events, states). The children take the spatio-temporal frame of a picture as given (both for the interlocutor and the speaker), and this allows them to present the information piece by piece, without marking internal relations explicitly.[10] A third kind of evidence for this strictly descriptive mode derives from the fact that the children "count" the events or states if they occur in subsequent pictures (*nochmal, wieder* 'once more, again', *burda da* 'and here, here again'). This shows that they do not conceive of the pictures as part of one overall story, but as separate items.

Although none of the 3-year-olds constructs a coherent story based on a temporally advancing plotline, the first steps towards a temporal structure appear in groups of utterances referring to one picture, as reflected in the type of connector used in utterance-initial position. The German children vary between a deictic pointer (*da, hier* 'there, here'), *und* 'and' as a connector, and zero. Although the use of the different forms is not totally systematic, a clear tendency can be observed. If two or more pieces of information are conceptualized as belonging together — either as simultaneous activities or as temporally sequential actions of one or more protagonists — then the utterances will be connected by *und* without an additional deictic adverb. The Turkish children also use the spatials *burda/orda* 'here/there' or sometimes the temporals *şimdi/sonra* 'now/then' as deictic pointers. If two or more situations are conceptualized as simultaneous, this is indicated by the absence

---

[9] G3k, T3b, and T3i are exceptions in that they partly conceptualize an underlying temporal structure.

[10] Pronoun usage supports this interpretation. The children do not use pronouns anaphorically, but deictically, pointing to the pictures. What seems to be a wrong use of a pronoun under discourse perspective is perfectly acceptable if interpreted as deictic reference, e.g. *und da kuckt der Junge und da leckt der* 'and there the boy looks and there he [=dog] licks' [*G3f-3;3*]. This is also characteristic of Turkish 3-year-olds.

of deictics and by the use of the focus particle *de* 'and/too/also' in the second clause. Use of a DEICTIC POINTER + *de* simply indicates movement to the next frame and, occasionally, sequence.

As summarized in Chapter IIA, at this age children "produce deictically related descriptions in which spatial co-presence, and not temporal sequence, is the major structuring factor."

B. Simultaneity in discourse: 3-year-olds

If it is the case, as we assume, that children at this age do not yet have a concept of a timeline which allows the integration of separate events or states into one overall conceptual representation, then their concept of simultaneity must differ essentially from a fully developed concept. The concept of an abstract time axis would be a precondition for relating situations internally to each other. Therefore, the children do not conceive of two situations as being simultaneous (or sequential) in the fictive temporal frame of the story. Simultaneity on the "time axis of events" does not exist for them.

This claim is well supported by the German data, where there is not a single occurrence of an expression referring to the relation of simultaneity in the 3-year-old texts. The Turkish data, on the other hand, present a few exceptions. Some of the children try to use an explicit marker, although few of these attempts are successful. Beyond these exceptions, what we find in the texts of both groups of 3-year-olds is simultaneity of a different type. The children follow what we have called "simultaneity of perception" in the organization of their discourse. All the information given in one picture frame is embedded into one temporal frame which is defined by the act of perception. In the examples which follow, German precedes Turkish. Examples are presented clause-by-clause, as in the transcripts, in order to highlight relations between events encoded in each clause.

(9) *und da hat der Angst*
    'and here he is afraid'
    da fliegen die ganzen Fliegen
    'there fly all the flies'
    und da ruft der nach
    'and there he calls after them' [G3g-3;8]

(10) *köpek ağlıyor*
    '(the) dog is crying'
    kaçıyor
    '(he)'s running away'

bu da onu yakalamak istiyor

'and this one wants to catch him' [*T3h-3;11*]

All utterances are independently anchored at the deictic center.

One could argue that this type of presentation does not involve any temporal concept at all. There is, however, clear evidence that these children have developed some concept of time, compared to the state of a 2-year-old pointing at a picturebook and saying something like, *Da ist die Kuh* 'there is the cow', *Da ist das Auto* 'there is the car'. This is shown by a string of clauses as in (11).

(11) *und daraus kommt gleich die Ente*

'and the duck comes out of there right away'

und da das Bienenhaus runtergefallen

'and there the beehive fallen down'

und da erschreckt sich der Hund

'and there the dog is scared' [*G3c-3;11*]

The use of the present perfect in the second clause, referring to a state which is the result of a temporally preceding event, shows that 3-year-olds may take the deictic center as a **reference point** which they maintain for all utterances related to one picture. For the German child, the shift from present to present perfect might be a trigger for conceptually separating the three time axes involved in discourse (event, reference point, and time of perception). At this point they cannot be handled separately. In presenting the information, reference point and time of perception always coincide. But this step seems to provide the basis for the formation of a temporal structure in discourse later on.

Turkish children also show alternations between tenses which are deictically anchored: the present *-iyor* for ongoing activities and the perfect *-miş* for resultant states.[11]

(12) *arılar çıkmış*

'the bees (have) exited' [V+*miş*]

---

[11] The *-miş* form has several related functions, as discussed in Chapter IIIE. Here, in alternation with the present, it serves as a sort of resultative, stative, or present perfect. In contrast, as the dominant tense of a story, *-miş* serves as the narrative tense. As a modality marker, it indicates indirect or non-witnessed source of information (inference, hearsay).

dala çıkmış
'(has) climbed the branch' [V+*miş*]
deliğe bakıyor çocuk
'and is looking into the hole, the boy' [V+*iyor*] [*T3b-4;0*]

Additionally, in the texts of three children we find occasional attempts to switch to a past anchoring point by more complex tense shifting, as in the excerpt from a 3-year-old text in (13), switching in the past from *-miş* to the past progressive V + *iyor+di*.

(13) *öyle çocuk da domuzun üstüne düşmüş*
   'and the boy also fell on top of the pig like that' [V+*miş*]
   sonra, sonra, şey yapmış
   'then, then, he did something' [V+*miş*]
   çocuk düşüyordu, düşüyordu düşüyordu
   'the boy was falling, was falling was falling' [V+*iyor+di*]
   az kalsın düşmüş
   'he almost fell' [V+*miş*]
   bak düsmüş yaa!
   'look he fell!' [V+*miş*]
   sonra, sonra şey yapmış
   'then, then he did something' [V+*miş*]
   böyle denizden çıkıyordu
   'he was coming out of the sea like this' [V+*iyor+di*] [*T3c-4;3*]

It is evident from these examples, however, that the shifts are mainly aspectual and determined by how events are depicted in the pictures — as bounded events that can be viewed perfectively or as unbounded states/processes that can be viewed imperfectively. An utterance in the past progressive, for example, remains as much deictically anchored as one in the present since there is as yet no discourse-internal timeline that can provide an anchoring point. Nevertheless, such sporadic shifts of tense suggest that these children are at the beginning of the process of differentiating the temporal axis of events from that of perception. The fact that some of the 3-year-olds use explicit markers also supports this view.

The tense forms are not the only area in which the first signs of a time concept are manifested. Further contexts which seem to be especially important for the development of the concept of simultaneity are created by **combinations** of specific situations, as in the following three sets of different temporal relations between the protagonists.

(14) **Protagonist 1 + verb of perception / Protagonist 2 + verb of action/state:**

(14a) *und kucken sie hinter*
'and they look behind'
und da sitzen zwei Frösche
'and there sit two frogs' [*G3d-3;6*]

(14b) *köpek de başına kavanozu geçiriyor*
'and the dog puts the jar on his head'
çocuk da bakıyor
'and the boy looks' [*T3b-4;0*]

(15) **Protagonist 1 + verb of mental/affective state / Protagonist 1 or 2 + verb of action/state:**

(15a) *der meint*
'he believes'
da is immer noch gerade
'that it is still flat there' [*G3c-3;11*]

(15b) *sonra ağacın üstüne konunca*
'then when it lands on the tree'
onlar korkuyorlar
'they are afraid' [*T3i-3;11*]

(16) **Protagonist 1 + verb of position / Protagonist 2 + verb of action/state:**

(16a) *der Hund, der sitzt da*
'the dog, he sits there'
und der hat die Augen zu
'and he [=boy] has his eyes closed' [*G3k-3;7*]

(16b) *bir tane baykuş çıkıyor*
'an owl comes out'
çocuk yere yatmış
'the boy is on the ground' [*T3g-4;1*]

Pairs of clauses like these provide the contexts in which early forms of *sim*-marking occur, as in the following use of *-ken* by a child of age 3;11.[12]

---

[12] These are also the contexts in which the first forms of subordination occur (complement

(16c) *uyurken de*

'and while.sleeping' [=boy and dog] [V+*ken*]

ordan çıkıyor uslu uslu

'it [=frog] comes out of there slowly slowly' [*T3i-3;11*]

In sum, these 3-year-olds have developed only part of the concept of simultaneity. **Simultaneity of perception** is the basis for their discourse organization. This implies that the temporal relation of simultaneity does not have a specific discourse function in opposition to other temporal relations. The first movement towards a conceptualization of temporal relations is made locally between adjacent clauses, and depends on the **content** of the specific clauses.

C. Expression of simultaneity: 3-year-olds
GERMAN

Explicit devices for expression of time relations are not used by German children of this age, in line with what has been said about conceptual development in this domain. Certain verbal patterns can be interpreted as incipient markings of simultaneity, all on the level of two adjacent utterances, thus:

- Use of deictic adverbs could be the basis for a rule which says that those clauses which do **not** contain a deictic adverb are to be interpreted as simultaneous with the one preceding.

- Elliptical clauses (subject or verb ellipsis) indicate a closer relation to the preceding utterance and often imply simultaneity.

- Parallel constructions and wording are used to refer to simultaneous activities of two or more protagonists — sometimes supported by the adverb *auch* 'also', as in *Der Junge kuckt und der Hund auch* 'the boy looks and the dog also' — two occurrences at age 3 (G3d-3;6, G3g-3;8).

- A few instances can be found of devices which imply simultaneity because of their lexical semantics — e.g., complement clauses with *daß* 'that' and causally connected clauses with words like *weil, ob* 'because, whether'; and also verbs like *zugucken* 'watch' or *hinterherlaufen* 'run.after' which presuppose two simultaneous situations.

None of these devices explicitly express simultaneity. Understanding of the temporal relation is always based on inference. Therefore we cannot be sure whether the child actually intends to establish a temporal relation or whether this is just the interpretation of an adult drawing upon a fully developed time concept.

---

clauses, adverbials of reason, and relative clauses).

TURKISH

In contrast to the total absence of explicit markers in the German data, half of the Turkish children use an explicit form to indicate simultaneity. Although this seems to make them ahead of their German peers, their narratives show a similar lack of abstract temporal organization. For most of the 3-year-old Turkish texts, like those in German, simultaneity must be inferred from typical verbal patterns and some compensatory devices that operate on the level of two adjacent clauses:

- The reference of those clauses which do **not** contain a spatial or temporal deictic adverb is to be interpreted as simultaneous with that of the preceding one, frequently supported with the particle *da* 'and/also'.

- Elliptical clauses typically imply simultaneity.

- Use of parallel constructions and wording to refer to simultaneous activities of two or more protagonists, frequently supported with the particle *de* 'also/too', as in *Çocuk uyuyor; hav hav da uyuyor* 'The boy is sleeping; the dog is sleeping too' [*T3f-4;0*].

- Devices which imply simultaneity because of their lexical semantics include verbs like *bakmak, seyretmek* 'watch' and *yakalamak istemek* 'want to catch', which presuppose two simultaneous situations.

Explicit markers of simultaneity found in the Turkish 3-year-old texts are adverbial clauses with the converbs V+*ince* 'when', and V+*ken* 'while', and the adverbial *o zaman* 'at that time/then'. About half of these occurrences (5/11) are infelicitous, however, because they are redundant, involve a grammatical error, or occur in fictive statements with confused content. The few meaningful examples are successful in setting up the time of event 1 as reference time for event 2, but refer to situations that are part of the same picture frame, described in deictically anchored clauses, as in the Turkish 3-year-old examples in (17) and (18).

(17) *burda köpek düşmüş aşağıya*
      'here the dog has fallen down'
      camdan bakarken
      'while.looking out the window' [V+*ken*] [*T3a-3;6*]

(18) *arılar çıkıyor*
      'the bees come out'
      o zaman birşey görüyor
      'at that time he sees something' [*o zaman*]

onun içinde arı varmış
'there are/were bees in it' [*T3i-3;11*]

In sum, most of the Turkish 3-year-olds make use of devices which imply simultaneity, while a few try out explicit forms — but half of the clauses so paired cannot really be interpreted as making reference to simultaneity. In other words, the presence of a surface form does not necessarily indicate that a meaningful temporal relation has been established. Thus, in both German and Turkish, 3-year-old narrations seem to rely largely on context for the inference of a temporal relation.

5.1.3. 5-year-olds

A. Discourse structure: 5-year-olds

The 5-year-old children do not form a homogeneous group in either German or Turkish. Rather, they are at an intermediate stage between description and narration. Some of their texts still look very much like the descriptions given by the 3-year-old children (G5d, G5g, G5j, G5k; T5b, T5c, T5g, T5j), though with a difference, in that they make more reference to the events or processes that protagonists are engaged in. And the majority of their texts show clear signs of temporal organization. These children use a number of different temporal expressions (German: *erstmal, am nächsten Morgen, schon, noch, jetzt, zuerst, und dann*, etc. 'first of all, the next morning, already, still, now, at first, and then'; Turkish: *şimdi, sonra, birgün, V+ken, V+ip, V+diğinde, V+diği zaman*, etc. 'now, then, one day, while, and (then), when'). Most of these serve to establish temporal relations between adjacent clauses. Interestingly, some of the German and most of the Turkish 5-year-old texts forego spatial deictic adverbs (*hier/da, burda/orda* 'here/there') in favor of temporal adverbs (*jetzt, şimdi* 'now', or *dann, sonra* 'then') which fulfill the same function: anchoring separate situations or introducing new frames. Compared to the younger children, the underlying principle structuring their texts has progressed from spatial to temporal (or combined) organization, implying the development of different temporal categories, such as sequence and simultaneity.

In terms of discourse organization, the 5-year-olds are to some extent similar to the 3-year-olds. They construct their texts utterance by utterance, without indicating any functional differences between them. The beginning of their narrations provide good evidence for this strategy, since they fail to make a functional distinction between scene-setting and the beginning of the actual story (event-line).[13] And there are hardly any indications signaling

---

[13] Exceptions are G5a and G5j, where the onset of the plotline is indicated by *auf einmal*

larger units of discourse beyond the two-clause level, such as narrative chunks based on specific types of referential continuity. The most important step which has been taken by the 5-year-olds is the development of a time concept. But this is not yet used as a basis for a hierarchical organization of discourse, with a few isolated exceptions. Thus, a few of their texts show initial, still rather chaotic, signs of functional differentiation by means of tense shifting. And two Turkish 5-year-olds show the beginnings of chunking through use of converbs, resulting in discourse units of three clauses long.

B. Simultaneity in discourse: 5-year-olds

In developing an abstract concept of time, a new dimension emerges: In our terms, simultaneity between situations in the story on the axis of events. The 5-year-olds make a distinction between a **sequence** of events and **simultaneous** events or states, reflected in German by the motivated use of *dann* 'then' in contrast to other nontemporal connectors and the pattern of tense shifting, and in Turkish by the use of *sonra* 'then', by morphological markers of simultaneity (V+*ince*, V+*ken*, V+*diği zaman*, V+*diğinde*) and by tense-aspect alternations.

It thus appears that the 5-year-olds have conceptually mastered all three types of simultaneity. But these are not yet integrated into one overall temporal structure. Just as the texts of these children alternate between descriptive and narrative modes, they may also vary types and functions of simultaneity within a single text. Some segments follow the pattern observed for the 3-year-olds, with simultaneity of perception supplying the structuring principle, whereas others show a narrative pattern with temporally sequential events as the backbone of the discourse. In the latter case, simultaneity is established between an unbounded state and an event, as in (19) and (20).

(19) *und der Hund steht da*
    'and the dog stands there'
    das Bienenhaus fällt runter
    'the beehive falls down' [*G5f-5;10*]

(20) *burda da bu çocuk uyuyor*
    'and here this boy is sleeping'
    köpek de yanında uyuyor

'all at once' in G5a, and a change from the spatial adverb *da* 'there/here' to the temporal adverb *dann* 'then' in G5j. Exceptions in the Turkish group are T5a and T5g. Both children make use of different temporal adverbs (*şimdi-sonra* 'now-then') and tense shifting for this type of demarcation.

'and the dog is sleeping next to him'

kurbağa çıkıyor şeyin içinden

'the frog is coming out of the thing' [*T5b-5;0*]

We also find two events related to different protagonists, as in the following example.

(21) *da rennt der Hund vor weg*

'there the dog runs away'

und der Junge fällt vom Baum runter

'and the boy falls down from the tree' [*G5c-5;11*]

(22) *baykuş geldi*

'the owl came'

çıkarken

'while.climbing' [=boy] [V+*ken*] [*T5e-6;0*]

These first steps towards grounding do not as yet result in a consistent temporal organization that would link the events/states to a continuous time axis (axis of discourse). The relations established are always local. As a result, simultaneity remains ambiguous with respect to its discourse function within the text as a whole.

C. Expression of simultaneity: 5-year-olds

The means used for referring to this temporal relation reflect the fact that the 5-year-olds are in the middle of a developmental process, with the Turkish group apparently ahead of the German.

GERMAN

On the one hand, all the forms that the youngest children use are present among the 5-year-olds as well: deictic and anaphoric connectors for expressing the difference between shift and maintenance of temporal reference, elliptical clauses, and parallel wording and constructions. The reinforcing *auch* 'also' is used more frequently by the 5-year-olds, as shown in examples (23) and (24).[14]

(23) *da lief der Hund*

'here the dog ran'

---

[14] Sometimes *auch* 'also' is used inappropriately with different verbs, suggesting that it carries a mainly temporal meaning.

und da lief das Reh auch

'and here the deer ran too' [G5a-5;7]

(24) *der rennt ganz, der rennt weg*

'he runs far, he runs away'

und der Junge ist auch vom Baum runtergefallen

'and the boy has also fallen down from the tree' [G5d-5;3]

The German 5-year-olds also use a few more subordinating constructions — complement clauses with *daß* 'that', and adverbials with *weil* 'because'. These occur in the same types of situations as those signifying the first conceptualizations of simultaneity in the 3-year-olds' texts, that is, co-occurrences of a state (affective, cognitive, or perceptual) with an event or state, as in (25) and (26).

(25) *und dann ist der Hund froh und der Junge*

'and then the dog is happy and the boy'

daß er jetzt ein [sic] *Frosch hat, ein* [sic] *kleinen*

'that he has a frog now, a little one' [G5e-5;0]

(26) *und jetzt sehen die da*

'and now they see there'

daß er raus ist

'that he is gone' [G5g-5;3]

Five-year-olds use a few new forms, especially the conjunction *als* 'when' to express simultaneity of an event and another situation (only two instances). There is also a change in tense usage. The incipient temporality signified by present/present-perfect alternations among 3-year-olds is restricted mainly to those 5-year-olds who still favor the descriptive mode of narration, as illustrated in (27) for German.

(27) *und die Bienen fliegen daher*

'and the bees fly from there'

und der Junge ist umgekippt

'and the boy has fallen over'

und da sind Steine...

'and there are rocks there...' [G5j-5;3]

Moreover, an age-related change in tense usage is the use of the simple past and sometimes even the pluperfect in addition to the present perfect and the present. Some 5-year-old texts even show an apparently unsystematic shifting of tenses across the board (e.g., G5a, G5e, G5h).[15] The different tenses do not appear to have a clear functional import — for either time reference or discourse organization, so that these 5-year-olds can best be regarded as being at an "experimental" stage. There is, however, a tendency for the simple past to occur in the context of what would be backgrounded material in an adult narrative — mainly states, as in (28) and (29).[16]

(28) *und dann ruft er ganz laut*

'and then he calls really loudly'

aber er kam nicht, der Frosch

'but he didn't come, the frog' [*G5e-5;0*]

(29) *der ist runtergefallen*

'he has fallen down'

weil die Eule da war

'because the owl was there'

die beißt ja

'it bites, you know'

und die Eule fliegt weg

'and the owl flies away' [*G5d-5;3*]

These findings suggest that shifting of tenses between simple present, simple past, and present perfect constitutes an early device for expressing simultaneity as a temporal relation and also serves as an indicator of the discourse function of backgrounding. Note, finally, that even in clearly narrative passages, the temporal relation of simultaneity is never explicitly marked by adverbials in the German 5-year-old texts. Rather, it needs to be inferred from the inherent temporal properties of the situations or from world knowledge about situations with this property, as in (30).

(30) *schlafen die jetzt*

---

[15] The 5-year-old German texts characterized by extensive shifting between tenses are also those which use a wider range of temporal forms, suggesting that these children rely particularly on temporal notions as a means for organizing their narrations.

[16] The negative clause in (28) could be interpreted as a possible "event," although negatives are typically analyzed as background material in adult texts.

'they sleep now' [**temporally unbounded state**]

der Frosch geht aus das Wasser raus

'the frog goes out of the water' [**event**] [*G5e-5;0*]

TURKISH

The Turkish 5-year-olds use all the forms found in the 3-year-old texts, such as deictic and anaphoric connectives and elliptical clauses, together with increased use of *de* 'and/too' and of the converbs V+*ince* 'when' and V+*ken* 'while', the latter occurring with a wider variety of verbs rather than just statives of perception and cognition. Moreover, these forms appear to have a new discourse function: V+*ince*, to introduce new information and so relate two foreground events and V+*ken*, to present a background event, as in (31) and (32).

(31) *sonra cam kırılınca*

'then when the glass breaks' [V+*ince*]

köpek de içinden çıkıyor

'the dog comes out of it' [*T5h-5;0*]

(32) *sonra camdan bakarken*

'then while.looking out the window' [=boy or dog] [V+*ken*]

bir kavanozu alıp da

'and taking a jar' [V+*ip*]

köpek başına geçirmiş

'the dog put (it) on his head' [*T5g-5;2*]

The Turkish 5-year-olds also use a number of new devices to mark simultaneity, in contrast to their German peers. First, they use the converb V+*ip* 'and (then)', a connective which presents two events by the same protagonist as closely related either in immediate succession or simultaneity — equally for both meanings at this age. In the last example above, two closely connected events are integrated with V+*ip* and juxtaposed as simultaneous against a third situation presented with V+*ken*. This example of a three-clause chunking of events illustrates how converbs provide the early means for integrating events in discourse. Other forms which occur for the first time in our 5-year-old Turkish sample are subordinating constructions V+*diğinde* 'at doing' and V+*diği zaman* 'at time of doing', which set reference time — mainly with perception/mental state verbs, as in the examples (33) and (34).

(33) *sonra bakıyor çocuk,*

'then the boy looks,'

uyandığında

'at.his.waking.up' [V+*diğinde*]

kurbağa yok

'the frog isn't there' [*T5a-5;4*]

(34) *kurbağayı orda göremedikleri zaman*

'at.the.time they.cannot.see the frog there' [V+*diği zaman*]

her yere bakıyorlar

'they look everywhere' [*T5b-5;0*]

These constructions typically serve to stativize an event and introduce it as background — at this age, only at the local level. A third device which comes in occasionally (only three instances) is use of complement clauses for implying the *sim*-relation — again in the same contexts, as in (35) and (36).

(35) *bir hayvanın birşeyini gördüler*

'they saw some thing of an animal'

ne olduğunu bilmiyorlardı

'they didn't know what it was' [*T5a-5;4*]

(36) *sonra çocuk "sus" diyor*

'then the boy says "quiet"'

köpek ne olduğunun farkında yok

'the dog isn't aware of what's happening' [*T5e-6;0*]

There are also a few instances of the causal conjunction *çünkü* 'because' or V+*diği için* 'because of its V-ing' introducing a cotemporal state as a reason for another state or event, as in (37).

(37) *sonra köpek de şeyin içine baktı*

'then the dog looked into (that) thing'

çünkü köpek pek göremiyordu

'because the dog couldn't see much' [*T5a-5;4*]

Use of tense markers shows a varied development: alternation of tense-aspect forms differentiates between events and unbounded situations, yielding the interpretation that they are simultaneous, as in (38) and (39).

(38) *çocuk düştü*

'the boy fell' [V+*di*]

arılar da köpeği yakalıyorlar

'and the bees are catching the dog' [V+*iyor*]

baykuş da seyerediyor

'and the owl is watching' [V+*iyor*] [*T5e-6;0*]

(39) *sonra da çocuk ona kızdı*

'and then the boy got mad at it' [V+*di*]

köpek hala seviyor

'the dog still loves (him)' [V+*iyor*] [*T5e-6;0*]

A more significant change, observed in a few 5-year-old texts (and hinted at in a few by age 3), is marking of progressive aspect in past tense, contrasting it either with the past of direct experience (*-di* versus *-iyor+di*) or with the narrative past (*-miş* versus *-iyor+miş*). This yields a clear marking of unbounded situations as backgrounds relative to plot-advancing events, as in (40).

(40) *sonra bir ara geyiğin üstünde çocuk*

'then for a while the boy is on the deer' [V+$\emptyset$]

bir küçük kurbağa yakalamak istiyorlardı

'they were wanting to catch a little frog' [V+*iyor+di*]

burda çocuk ve köpeği düşüyor

'here the boy and his dog fall' [V+*iyor*] [*T5e-6;0*]

Now, tense switches are motivated by factors internal to discourse (such as the tense of the previous clause) rather than by event properties depicted in pictures. A shift from past to past progressive may serve to present background information through a retrospective switch as in the example from T5e above, or through establishing a new spatio-temporal framework for subsequent events, as in the rather unusual example excerpted in (41).

(41) *kurbağa daha uzaklaştığında*

'at the frog's being.further.away' [V+*diğinde*]

kurbağa diye bağırıyorlar

'they call "frog"' [V+*iyor*]

ormanlara girdiğinde

'at.its.entering [=frog's] the woods' [V+*diğinde*]

yine kurbağa diye bağırıyordu

'again he was calling "frog"' [V+*iyor+di*]

ondan sonra bir delik buldular

'then they found a hole' [V+*di*] [*T5a-5;4*]

In contrast to the 3-year-olds' deictically anchored alternations between -*iyor* and -*miş*, 5-year-olds' use of such shifts within the past or nonpresent/irrealis, combined with temporal connectives, show that children are no longer tied to the temporal axis of perception, but are trying to differentiate between the time axis of events and the time axis of discourse. This points to a noticeable move away from the descriptive towards the narrative mode in certain segments of the 5-year-old Turkish texts.

These observations, together with the finding that most Turkish 5-year-olds use at least some explicit marker of simultaneity, indicate that, at this age, the Turkish children display a richer repertoire than their German counterparts. They are thus in a more advantageous position for discovering the various semantic and discourse functions of these devices. This, we suggest, may in turn lead to earlier achievements in the differentiation and integration of temporal relations at a local level.

5.1.4. 9-year-olds
A. Discourse structure: 9-year-olds

The 9-year-old texts reflect a narrative pattern in their basic structure, adopting the time axis of events as the organizing factor. The sequence of pictures has been transformed into an abstract representation of a temporally sequential chain of events, embedded in particular situational contexts. This means that the children conceptualize a twofold temporal structure, consisting of the time axis of events, on the one hand, and the time axis of discourse on the other. These two coincide most of the time, with the reference time moving along with the sequence of events.

An important progression in this age group is that the temporal thread of discourse has become independent from the time axis of perception. This is manifested in the frequent use of *dann* or *sonra* 'then' and other temporal connectives and adverbials within and across pictures. Temporal expressions now frame short episodes moving across three to four pictures within which events are related to one another as sequential or as simultaneous. This is particularly evident in some of the Turkish texts (T9a, T9c, T9d, T9g, T9i, T9j) where, typically, new episodes are marked with adverbs such as *daha sonra* 'later on', *şimdi* 'now', *birgün* 'one.day', and episode-internal events are related temporally by converbs and subordinating constructions. Nonetheless, there are still switches into the descriptive mode, such as the examples in (42) and (43) from German and Turkish 9-year-olds.

(42) *da ruft der*
    'here he calls'

> *und da ist ein Geweih von dem Hirsch*
> 'and here are the deer's antlers'
> *da ist der Hund*
> 'here is the dog'
> *und da rennt der Hirsch so los*
> 'and here the deer is running away' [G9g-9;10]

(43) *tosbağa ordan çıkıyor*
'the frog comes out of there'
çocuk da orda bir delik görmüş
'and the boy saw a hole there'
orda ağaca çıkmış
'there he climbed a tree' [T9f-10;1]

None of the 9-year-old texts, however, rely on this as the only way of presenting information. They all contain narrative passages, and most are predominantly narrative in content and organization.

Does this mean that by this age, children have achieved adult-like discourse competence? Even a superficial glance at the adult texts shows that this is not the case. Constructing a text along a temporal thread is not the whole story. Nine-year-olds do not integrate the individual events into a temporal and thematic whole; rather, they present event after event, often separated by the temporal shifter *dann/sonra* 'then' without attributing different informational weight to the various parts. This implies that temporal organization in terms of foregrounding/backgrounding or chunking into episodes cannot be found on a global discourse level. This clearly does not mean that the overall discourse structure of the 9-year-olds is the same as that of the younger groups. As noted in Chapter IIA, 9-year-olds refer to the global search theme, particularly in contexts where the boy and the dog are depicted as calling out to the frog. But such reinstatements do not serve as a thematic background, since the subsequent events are presented as if they were independent happenings, as in example (44) from a Turkish 9-year-old.

(44) *sonra köpeğiyle beraber aramaya çıkıyor*
'then he goes out to search with his dog'
ondan sonra üstünü giyiyor,
'then he puts on his clothes'
sonra köpek burdan aşağı düşüyor
'then the dog falls down from here' [T9c-9;1]

A few 9-year-old texts (e.g., T9i, T9j) do, however, illustrate the beginnings of a more adult-like thematic integration. Compare, for instance, example (45) from T9i, who relates the dog's fall explicitly to searching for the frog, to the example (44).

(45) *dışarda seslenmişler kurbağaya*

     'outside, they called out to the frog'

     o zaman da bulamamışlar

     'at that time they couldn't find it either'

     köpek de bağırırken

     'the dog, while calling'

     düşmüş

     'fell' [*T9i-9;5*]

Nonetheless, for most of the 9-year-olds, the first elements of discourse-level organization are confined to the **local** level, usually in connection with a single picture frame — in the form of elaborations on the situation or the mental states of the protagonists, comments on the story, etc. In such contexts, we can expect changes in the function of simultaneity.

B. *Simultaneity in discourse: 9-year-olds*

The narratives of the 9-year-olds contain all the levels of simultaneity found in the texts of the 5-year-old children, but with a change in frequency. Simultaneity on the axis of perception is now rare. Another difference concerns the types and functions of simultaneity which are expressed: Besides the basic concept of simultaneity as a relation between an unbounded state/ongoing process and an event, some 9-year-olds express the specific concept of two event-chains encoded by a number of clauses (*in der Zwischenzeit* 'in the meantime', *inzwischen* 'meanwhile'; *bu/o sırada* 'meanwhile', *bu/o arada* 'in the meantime'). This shows that they are able to make a distinction between simultaneous **chunks** of events, as foregrounded parallel activities of two or more protagonists, and **pairs** of simultaneous situations. They differ from adults in this respect, however, in generally being unable to chunk more than two events at a time.

The function of simultaneity as a relation shaping foreground and background in discourse finds expression in most of the 9-year-old texts. However, these children do not as yet control a full range of linguistic options with respect to this function. For example, the distinction between simultaneous states versus simultaneous events, is not linguistically reflected by the 9-year-old German children. For them, the two types seem to form a single category, expressed by the temporal conjunction *als*.[17] The Turkish children, on the

---

[17] It is interesting that the first *als* clauses occur in the same scene (Picture 3) in most of the texts. The formulation sounds almost stereotypical: *als der Junge aufwacht...* 'when the

other hand, express this distinction as early as age age 5, by use of *V+diğinde* compared with V+*ince*.

C. Expression of simultaneity: 9-year-olds

GERMAN

As shown in Table 1, the 9-year-olds do not add many devices to the repertoire of the younger groups. Very few adverbials (group Ib) are used for referring explicitly to the relation of simultaneity (*inzwischen* 'meanwhile', *in der Zwischenzeit* 'in the meantime' in G9a and G9f are the only items). In most cases, the temporal relation needs to be inferred, either from the inherent temporal properties of the situations, or from the absence of a temporal shifter such as *dann* 'then'. Yet the same expressive devices as occur among the younger children here show a change in function based on the the change in discourse structure. For example, the adverb *gerade* 'just, exactly', used as a deictic temporal expression by some of the 3-year-olds, is now used as a temporal adverb, relating two situations on the time axis of discourse, for example:

(46) *da kommt **grad** 'n Maulwurf aus dem Loch raus*

'here a gopher comes **just** out of the hole'

wo der Junge reingekuckt hat

'where the boy has looked in' [G9i-9;11]

The same change is found in the tense shift between present and present perfect. The reference point no longer relates to the time of perception, but to the internal timeline of the discourse, as in (47).

(47) *und morgens ist der Junge aufgestanden*

'and in the morning the boy has gotten up'

und dann sieht er

'and then he sees'

daß der Frosch verschwunden ist

'that the frog has disappeared' [G9b-9;0]

An expansion of meaning is also evident with respect to the adverbial *da* 'there'. For the 3- and 5-year-olds, the word has a deictic spatial meaning, whereas the 9-year-olds use it as a temporal anaphor indicating simultaneity, as in (48).

(48) *und der Hund war auf der Bettdecke*

---

boy wakes up...' and is closely parallel to the Hebrew 9-year-olds' description of this scene.

'and the dog was on the bedspread'

da schlüpfte der Frosch aus dem Glase heraus

'**there** [=then] the frog sneaked out of the glass' [G9l-9;5]

Another detail to note is the frequent use of *auch* 'also' to refer to simultaneous events or states. This increase could be due to the fact that these older children have become sensitive to temporal relations of different types, and therefore feel the need to express not only sequentiality by *dann* 'then', but also simultaneity, as in (49).

(49) *und **dann** rufen sie den Frosch hier*

'and **then** they call for the frog here'

und der Hund der bellt auch

'and the dog he barks too' [G9f-9;9]

Overall, then, development of temporality in German between ages 5 and 9 is manifested not so much by an increase in the lexical inventory as in a change in the functions of the same expressive devices — a change based on the development of discourse organization.

TURKISH

As in German, few devices have been added to the repertoire of the Turkish 9-year-olds: the adverbials *bu/o sırada* and *bu/o arada* 'meanwhile, in the meantime' (in only three texts) and the converb V+*erek* 'by doing' (see Table 2). However, both the frequency of existing forms and the number of children using them show an increase in this age group. Thus, most 9-year-old narratives mark simultaneity explicitly, by converbs, subordinating constructions, or adverbials, or else indicate it implicitly by tense-aspect shifts. There is no change in the use of complement or relative clauses for the expression of simultaneity.

The adverbials *bu sırada/o sırada* 'in the meantime', *bu/o arada* 'meanwhile', which indicate simultaneity between **chunks** of events in the adult texts, are used for interweaving **individual** parallel activities of two protagonists within a sequence of plot-advancing events. Thus they connect a pair of simultaneous situations rather than a chunk, as in (50).

(50) *çocuk hemen üstünü giyiyor*

'the boy immediately puts on his clothes'

bu arada köpek de kafasını kavanoza sokuyor

'**meanwhile** the dog inserts its head in the jar' [T9f-10;1]

The foregrounding function of *bu arada* 'meanwhile' derives from its clause-initial position.[18] When coupled with other devices that function for local

---

[18] When the adverb is non-initial, it tends to mark background information or to assign secondary status to the activity of the other protagonist.

backgrounding (such as converbs or other subordinating constructions), adverbs meaning 'meanwhile, in the meantime' may serve the more global function of signaling topic shift. Such interplay between grounding distinctions at the global versus the local levels is observed in the text of one 9-year-old, as illustrated by (51).

(51) *her yeri arıyorlar*
'they search everywhere'
bu sırada köpek ararken
'**meanwhile** while the dog is searching' [*bu sırada* = topic shift; V+*ken* = local backgrounding]
cam kavanoz köpeğin başına geçiyor
'the glass jar gets on the dog's head'
köpekle çocuk camdan beraber bakınıyorlar
'the dog and the boy are looking out of the window together'
o sırada köpek yere düşüyor
'**at that moment/meanwhile** the dog falls down' [*o sırada* = local foregrounding] [*T9d-9;11*]

The other new form is the converb V+*erek* 'by V+ing', used by only three narrators, in some cases erroneously. V+*erek* implies simultaneity by virtue of presenting two situations involving a single actor as very closely related, almost a single situation (Slobin, 1993a; Chapter IVc). This is illustrated in (52) and (53).

(52) *göle düşmüşler*
'they fell into the lake'
bir ağaç kovununa tutunarak
'holding on to a tree trunk' [V+*erek*]
çıkmışlar
'they came out' [*T9c-9;1*]

(53) *ve ondan sonra bu hayvan da kızarak*
'and after that, this animal [=deer], getting-angry' [V+*erek*]
çocukla köpeği beraber
'the boy and the dog together'
sonu boşluk olan biryere getirerek
'bringing to a place which is empty at the end' [V+*erek*]

ordan göl, yani su birikintisine atıyor

'throws from there to the lake - that is, to the water pool'

[= And after that, this animal, getting angry, bringing the boy and the dog to a place where it's empty at the end, throws them from there to the water pool.]   [*T9d-9;11*]

With the entry of V+*erek*, a corresponding change occurs in the semantic function of V+*ip* 'and (then)': It becomes restricted to indicating sequence, while V+*erek* takes over the function of implying simultaneity.[19]

The other developments involve changes in the discourse-structuring functions of already existing forms. The subordinating constructions V+*diğinde* and V+*diği zaman* are now used to present a situation as a background for a subsequent pair of sequential or simultaneous events marked with converbs or with the conjunction *ve* 'and', as in (54).

(54) *daha sonra bunlar gece uyuduğu zaman*

'later on at the time they sleep at night' [V+*diği zaman*]

kurbağa kavanozun içinden çıkıyor

'the frog goes out of the jar'

ve kaçıyor

'**and** escapes' [*T9a-9;3*]

Again, similar to German, spatial deictics assume a discourse-internal function and are used as means of indicating simultaneity, as in example (55).

(55) *ormanda arıyorlar*

'they search in the woods'

orda bir arı yuvası buluyorlar

'there they find a beehive' [*T9a-9;3*]

In contrast, there is a decrease in use of *de* 'also' as a simultaneity marker and it is used more as a focus particle. Given the availability of numerous explicit markers of simultaneity to the Turkish 9-year-old or adult, *de* is liberated for its normal pragmatic function, and can cooccur with explicit temporal adverbials.

Another difference from the younger age groups is a decrease in tense-aspect shifting. While an anchor tense is not clearly discernible for the 3-

---

[19] This is suggested by the 9-year-olds' use of V+*erek* in certain contexts where 5-year-olds use V+*ip* as a sequence marker: *Onlara güle güle deyip uzaklamış* 'Saying [V+*ip*] bye he went off' [*T5i-5;0*] as against *Ve el sallayarak gidiyor* 'And waving [V+*erek*] his hand, he goes'.

year-olds and for a third of the 5-year-olds, all of the 9-year-olds stabilize to a single anchor tense: 70% with *-iyor*, 20% with *-miş*, and 10% with *-di*. Where the anchor tense is *-iyor*, shifts to the unmarked present and to *-miş* indicate simultaneity between background states and foreground events. If the anchor tense is *-di* or *-miş*, shifts to unmarked present indicate simultaneity of background states, and shifts to past or narrative progressive *-iyor+di*, *-iyor+miş* serve to background the simultaneous activity of the nonfocused protagonist of secondary importance to the storyline. Such clauses are inserted in a sequence of foreground clauses and result in local backgrounding.

Only one 9-year-old uses this type of aspectual shift for global backgrounding, contrasting clauses which serve to reintroduce the overall search theme with ones which describe specific events in the plot, as in example (56).

(56) *heryerde kurbağalarını aramışlar*

'they searched for their frog everywhere' [V+*miş*]

ve arı kovanı görmüşler

'and they saw a beehive' [V+*miş*]

bir sincap yuvası görmüşler

'they saw a squirrel nest' [V+*miş*]

ismini bağırıyorlarmış kurbağanın

'they were calling the frog's name' [V+*iyor* ı *miş*]

fakat ne yazık ki bulamıyorlarmış

'but unfortunately they were not finding (it)' [V+*iyor+miş*] [T9c-9;1]

Such shifts between *di*-past and *miş*-past demonstrate that the reference point is internal to discourse. The small amount of tense-aspect shifting among 9-year-olds can be explained by the increase in the type and frequency of explicit markers of simultaneity, since these can now effect the grounding distinctions signaled by tense-aspect shifts. There is also an increase in the use of relative and complement clauses for introducing background information, particularly from a retrospective perspective. Although they cannot exploit each device for all of its functions, 9-year-old children will try to use these complex constructions in constructing a cohesive text.

5.1.5. Adults

The German adults differ from the 9-year-olds in that they all use the present as the basic tense for their narratives. The Turkish adults are more mixed in their choice of anchor tense: 60% use the present *-iyor*, 20% the past of direct experience *-di*, and 20% the narrative *-miş*. There is, moreover, great variety between the adult Turkish texts in the elaborateness and lexical richness of their narrations.

A. Discourse structure: Adults

The adult texts are organized on the basis of an overall thematic and temporal structure. They all follow a narrative pattern as the dominant form of presenting the information. Switches to a descriptive mode occur in some of their narrations, but then they are explicitly introduced by expressions such as *auf dem nächsten Bild, bir sonraki resimde de* 'in the next picture'; *man sieht* 'one sees', *biz görmüyoruz, çeviriyoruz biz de görüyoruz* 'we don't see, we turn the page, we see'; or *im Hintergrund* 'in the background'. In these cases the temporal organization of discourse is only locally replaced by a spatial frame.

The major difference between adults and 9-year-olds lies in (a) the degree of **cohesiveness** between specific events or states and (b) the degree of **elaborateness** at particular points in the chain of events. Thematic, temporal, and causal cohesion is expressed by grammatical means — subordination, ellipsis, anaphora, complementization, nominalization, relativization; by a wide variety of lexical devices — modal adverbs and particles, temporal adverbials, prefixed verbs, locative phrases; and by rhetorical strategies — questions, repetitions. There is a remarkable increase in the linguistic inventory and particularly in the flexibility of its deployment — evidently a precondition for achieving mature discourse competence.

Elaboration with regard to content continues along the lines already described for the 9-year-olds: background information about the situation is introduced; many utterances relate to internal states, intentions, and emotional reactions of the protagonists; and there are retrospective and prospective contractions of events which serve a structuring function in discourse, as in (57) and (58), from a German and a Turkish adult.

(57) *Das nächste Unheil zieht schon heran in Form eines Bienenschwarms.*

'The next disaster already approaches in the shape of a beehive.' [G20c]

(58) *Baykuş rahatsız olmuş bir tavırla Osmanın üzerinde kanat çırpmaya başladı. Gerek köstebek, gerek baykuş, gerekse arılar rahatsız edilmekten pek hoşnut değil gibi gözüküyorlardı.*

'The owl started flapping its wings over Osman in a disturbed manner. The gopher, and the owl, and the bees seemed not very happy about having been disturbed.' [T20e]

While the first example is an instance of **prospection** — looking ahead to forthcoming events — the second is a **retrospective** summary of a prior situation, colorfully formulated in terms of the emotional reactions of the protagonists involved. This example is also a good illustration of how Turkish adults make abundant use of modal constructions in introducing the narrator's perspective.

Development in both the domains of cohesiveness and elaboration entails a change in the contribution of backgrounded as against foregrounded material. Compared with the 9-year-olds, development has taken place in both the quantity and textual integration of background information. The creation of thematic integration at the global level, then, constitutes a crucial difference between the older children and adults. These developments converge with changes in type and function of the temporal relation of simultaneity.

B. Simultaneity in discourse: Adults

From the point of view of the three levels of simultaneity distinguished in Section 2, the adult narratives yield much the same picture as the 9-year-olds. The only difference is that where adults shift to the axis of perception, they do not simply use a deictic adverb like one meaning 'here', but an explicit formulation such as *man sieht* 'one sees'.

The adult texts demonstrate changes in the types of simultaneity expressed, and use of a full range of possible distinctions. German adults differentiate between states and events in *sim*-relations (*als* 'when' versus *während* 'while'); they use different adverbs to refer to simultaneity of pairs of events/states compared with simultaneity of chunks of events/states (*gleichzeitig, mittlerweile* 'at the same time, in the meantime'); and they give expression to a concept which combines simultaneity and a causal relation, by means of *dabei* 'in so doing, thereby', as in (59).

(59) *und stürzt zu Boden;*

'and crashes to the ground;'

dabei zerbricht das Glas

'in doing this the jar breaks' [*G20a*]

Most of these developments in the adult German data are ones we noted in Turkish as well: the distinction between V+*ince* / V+*ken*, V+*diğinde* 'when / while' is found in 5-year-old texts, with V+*erek* 'by V-ing' for combining simultaneity with causality being used by some 9-year-olds, although with errors. The only corresponding advance in the Turkish adults is the differentiation between simultaneity of **pairs** of events/states (by means of V+*diğinde*, V+*diği zaman*, V+*ken* 'at V-ing' 'at time of V-ing', 'while') and simultaneity of **chunks** of events/states (by means of *bu/o sırada, bu/o arada, öte yandan* 'meanwhile', 'in the meantime', 'on the other side').

Within the hierarchical structure of discourse, two basic functions of simultaneity emerge as distinguished in the adult texts. One is the relation of simultaneity between one or more events in the foreground. As claimed in Section 2.4.1, parallel activities of two or more protagonists must be marked explicitly for their temporal relation in narrative discourse. The actions performed by the boy and the dog in the pictures are presented as simultaneous chunks of foregrounded events by speakers. This is in fact the context in which most of the adverbial expressions for simultaneity occur, as in the Turkish example in (60).

(60) *köpek de hala arı kovanına bakıyormuş*

'and the dog was still looking at the beehive'

ve arı kovanını düşürmüş

'and made the beehive fall'

bu sırada çocuk da ağacların kovuklarına bakıyormus

'meanwhile the boy was looking into the holes of the trees'

tam o sırada ağaç kovuğunun içinden bir baykuş çıkmış

'right at that moment an owl came out of the hole'

çocuk korkup aşağı düşürken

'the boy (was.)scared [V+*ip*] (and) while.falling [V+*ken*]'

köpek de hızla yanından geçmiş

the dog went by him fast' [*T20a*]

Adverbials such as *bu sırada* 'in the meantime' in clause-initial position signal a topic-shift to another protagonist, and introduce a foreground event/event sequence as simultaneous with a previous sequence of events. This results in what can be called a "stepwise" creation of text, since the adverbial which refers to a time interval presents the two situations as partially overlapping and therefore as moving forward. Thus the type of simultaneity expressed by these forms serves the double function of creating temporal unity between events while ensuring sequential progress on the timeline.

Most of the typical background material (unbounded states) is not explicitly temporally related to the foregrounded event-line. Although the adults produce more of these kind of background clauses, there is no change in the form of how they present these structures, as shown in the two extended examples, in German in (61) and in Turkish in (62).

(61) *dort sitzen nun beide in dem seichten Wasser*

'there they both sit in the shallow water'

beide brauchen nicht zu schwimmen

'both don't have to [=neither must] swim'

das Wasser ist nicht sehr tief
'the water is not very deep'
und der Hund sitzt auf'm Kopf von Tom
'and the dog sits on Tom's head'
und beide gucken immer noch nach dem Frosch
'and both still look for the frog'
und versuchen ihn verzweifelt zu finden
'and desperately try to find him' [G20f]

(62) *Ali'yle Karabaş cumburlop kendilerini suyun içinde bulmuşlar*
'Ali and Karabas, splash, found themselves in the water'
bereket versin, su derin değilmiş
'fortunately, the water wasn't deep'
çünkü Ali yüzme de bilmiyormuş
'because Ali didn't know how to swim'
Ali suyun içinde oturmuş
'Ali sat in the water'
su ancak beline kadar geliyormuş
'the water came up only to his waist'
oturduğunda
'when (he).sat' [V+diğinde] [T20i]

Adults exhibit a more sophisticated pattern with respect to background **events** than 9-year-olds. They provide discourse relief by means of subordination, and so attribute different "weight" to simultaneously ongoing activities. This is a form of presenting the events from a specific perspective not found in the texts of the German children, although already observed in simpler forms in those of the Turkish 9-year-olds. (63) and (64) give examples from an adult German and a Turkish text.

(63) *in Windeseile zieht sich Tom an*
'Tom dresses in a flash'
während der Hund nochmal in dem Glas schnuppert
'while the dog sniffs again in the jar' [G20f]

(64) *bu sırada Bobi de kafasındaki kavanozdan kurtulmaya çalışıyordu*
'meanwhile Bobi was trying to get rid of the jar on his head'
çocuk bağırmaya devam ederken

'while the boy (was).continuing [V+*ken*] to call'

birden kafasındaki kavanozla birlikte Bobinin düştüğünü gördü

suddenly he saw that Bobi fell with the jar on its head' [*T20e*]

Mature use of the *sim*-relation in the elaboration of discourse structure thus requires a variety of devices not to be found in the children's stories. Yet once again, the main difference between the Turkish 9-year-olds and adults relates to degree of text cohesion. Devices such as V+*ince*, V+*ken*, V+*diğinde*, V+*diği zaman* are used by adults not only to relate adjacent utterances but also to pick up information introduced several clauses earlier and re-present it as background for a new situation. This gives rise to a continuous process of tying up nodes of information into a single thread of discourse.

C. Expression of simultaneity: Adults

GERMAN

The German adults all use adverbs or prepositional phrases as summarized in Table 1 (Group Ib) for explicit indication of simultaneity relations. This group reveals the most marked change compared to the younger speakers. They show an increase in both types and tokens of conjunctions, and simultaneity is also expressed by lexically specific terms such as *er nutzt die Gelegenheit* 'he uses the opportunity', *zugucken* 'to watch', or *nebenherlaufen* 'to run beside'.

The adults do not use the temporal connector *und dann* 'and then' as frequently as the 9-year-olds, and where they do, it is mostly in clause-internal position. That is, the 9-year-olds' strategy of marking the distinction between simultaneity and sequentiality by the systematic use of 'and then' is abandoned by the adults. They leave the temporal relation implicit where it can be inferred and use the explicit devices for cases which are ambiguous, as well as for purposes of grounding and introducing subjective perspectives.

TURKISH

All of the Turkish adults make use of the various explicit markers of simultaneity discussed so far. Their repertoire is enriched by specific indicators of the *sim*-relation, including lexical items (adverbs and verbs) as well as casemarking on nominalized sentences for aspectual distinctions that play a role in grounding, as in (65).

(65) *çocuk odasında kavanoz içine koyduğu kurbağasıyla ilgilenmektedir*

'the boy is.in.the.course.of.attending [V+*mektedir*] to his frog which he put in a jar'

köpeği de yine kurbağaya bakmaktadır

'his dog too is.in.the.course.of.looking [V+*mektedir*] at the frog' [*T20b*]

Adults use locative phrases for tight packaging of simultaneous events or states, as in (66) for example.

(66) *çocuk geyiğin kafasında, köpek de onların yanı koşmaya başlamışlar*

'the boy on the deer's head and the dog by their side, they started running' [*T20a*]

As with the German adults, there is a decrease in the use of the sequential connector *sonra* 'then' in clause-initial position. Instead, as already noted, there is an increase in use of adverbs of simultaneity which allow for stepwise connections, and of more specific adverbs which set R, such as *birgün* 'one day', *geceleyin* 'at night'. Adverbial clauses formed by *-diği zaman* 'at the time of V-ing' drop out entirely; instead there is an increase in the use of adverbial clauses formed by V+*diği için* 'because of V-ing' which overtly mark causality but imply simultaneity in the given context.

In sum, adults in both German and Turkish achieve relative gradations in grounding distinctions by manipulating a variety of subordinate constructions, adverbials, and tense-aspect shifts.

5.2. Data Analysis for the Other Languages

This section briefly reviews developments in the expression of simultaneity and its role in narrative organization in the Spanish, Hebrew, and English data.

5.2.1. Spanish

A. Discourse structure: Spanish

In terms of discourse structure, a similar pattern of development is observable from a descriptive, piece-by-piece presentation of information by the 3-, 4-, and 5-year-olds, to a cohesively connected piece of text by the 9-year-olds and adults. The preschool children make heavy use of coordination with *y* 'and'. Three-year-olds use the spatial deictic locative marker *aquí* 'here' as a means of indicating sequential points of attention in the pictures. At age 4, this tends to be accompanied by a temporal marker of sequentiality which suggests that "the child is anchoring to locative deixis while trying out other markers of sequentiality" (Sebastián, 1989), as in example (67).

(67) *Y aquí luego después se escondió debajo de aquí.*

'And here then afterwards he hid himself under here.' [*S4e-4;6*]

The sequentiality markers *luego* 'then, later', *entonces* 'then', and *después* 'after(wards)' are overused by 3- and 4-year-olds, sometimes marking each sequential clause, similar to the overuse of *und dann* 'and then' in

German and *ondan sonra* 'after that, then' in Turkish. Coordination and sequential markers decrease with age while subordinate markers rise. Temporal expressions such as *por la noche* 'at night', *por la mañana* 'in the morning', which serve to establish R on the temporal axis of discourse, are not used by preschoolers, but they are systematically used by 9-year-olds and adults.

B. Simultaneity in discourse: Spanish

The use of the first explicit marker of simultaneity for backgrounding, *cuando* 'when', appears at age 4 and becomes widespread at age 5, as in (68).

(68) *Y cuando estaban en el tronco encontraron a los dos ranas.*

'And when they were on the trunk they found the two frogs.' [*S4g-4;7*]

The first instances of inversion of order of mention of events for foregrounding two events in immediate succession appear in the 5-year-olds, as in (69).

(69) *Y coge una bota cuando se levanta.*

'And he picks up a boot when he gets up.' [*S5c-5;4*]

Clauses with *mientras* 'while', the explicit marker of simultaneity relating two clauses with different protagonists, appear at age 9 but again, this never serves to incorporate more than two events in broader episodes. Adults, who provide more elaborate chains of interlocked events by different participants, mark these adverbially by *mientras tanto* 'meanwhile' or *entre tanto* 'in the meantime' rather than by subordination with *mientras*, as in (70).

(70) *Mientras tanto el niño se ha metido dentro de un árbol grande, que tiene un agujero, del que sale un buho.*

'Meanwhile the boy has gotten into a big tree, that has a hole, from which an owl comes out' [*S20j*]

In other words, adults use the connectives *mientras tanto* and *entre tanto* to combine clauses that correspond to episodes where "the temporal nexus...would be the beginning of each of these conjoined superordinate events, allowing us to consider this a mechanism for marking episode boundaries which is not used by any of the children" (Sebastián, 1989).

Particularly noteworthy developments in how simultaneity is expressed and deployed in narrative organization are realized through the tense-aspect system of Spanish, as discussed below.

C. Expression of simultaneity: Spanish

The earliest explicit devices used to mark simultaneity in Spanish are adverbial clauses. The temporal *cuando* 'when', the only connective used by 3- and 4-year-olds, indicates the superposition of the beginning of the second event with the end of the first, and denotes (1) simultaneity between the verbs of matrix and subordinate clauses, or (2) immediate anteriority, as in (71).

(71) *Y cuando se tirado al agua encontró una rana.*

'And when (he was) thrown to the water he found a frog.' [*S3c-3;7*]

Interestingly, the semantics of this form corresponds exactly to that of the Turkish converb V+*ince*, one of the two explicit devices used by 3-year-olds.

Another construction that has the same temporal value as *cuando* and marks simultaneity is the preposition *al* + INF. It first appears in 5-year-old texts, as shown in (72).

(72) *Al subirse cayó el mieleno.*

'On climbing.up [= dog] the beehive fell.' [*S5b-5;2*]

Mientras 'while', used to narrate two clauses with different protagonists, appears in 9-year-old texts, as in example (73).

(73) *Sale el buho y lo tira mientras las abejas le persiguen a su perro.*

'The owl comes out and throws him while the bees chase his dog.' [*S9a-9;1*]

Causal adverbial and complement clauses appear late. Relative clauses appear earlier but also show a sharp increase at 9 years. Those which can imply simultaneity are continuative relative clauses that function to advance the narrative action and which tend to have verbs of appearance in the main clause (see Chapter IVB). These begin to be used at age 5, as in (74).

(74) *Salió un loro que le tiró al niño.*

'(There) came out a parrot that threw the boy.' [*S5a-5;1*]

As discussed in Chapter IIIC, Spanish is very rich in tense-aspect distinctions, and young children learn early on to exploit these possibilities in their narratives. Although 3- and 4-year-olds have difficulty in adhering to an anchor tense, certain patterns can be detected. The 3-year-olds prefer the present — functioning as a form for picture description; the 4-year-olds and the 5-year-olds — the past; and the 9-year-olds again favor the present — this time functioning as a genuinely narrative tense. No children use the imperfective as an anchor, apparently appreciating its role for introducing secondary events. The 3- and 4-year-olds show unsystematic contrasts of present, past, past imperfect, and present perfect, with no clear narrative, grammatical, or semantic motivation.

The commonest shift from present tense is to the present perfect. For the 3- and 4-year-olds, the present perfect functions to indicate a visible action or endstate depicted in the pictures, e.g.:

(75) *Aquí se ha subido*

'Here he has climbed' [S3a-3;6]

This use of the present perfect to mark resultant state or perfective aspect makes it functional in the context of simultaneity of perception, and is in line with what was observed for Turkish and German. No 3-year-old texts contain the past perfect.

Another type of aspectual shift, one frequently observed in the 3-year-old data, is to the progressive, which encompasses the notions of 'duration' and 'progress' in Spanish. It is in fact the earliest means to mark simultaneity, used in the context of describing pictures with two participants, as done in (76).

(76) *Y luego ve a una rana y el niño está llorando.*

'And then (the dog) sees a frog and the boy is crying.' [S3a-3;6]

Although the past imperfective and past progressive appear interchangeable in many instances in Spanish usage, 3-year olds make a motivated contrast between them when they juxtapose two simultaneous events that are both durative, as in the following.

(77) *El niño miraba en la bota y el perro estaba comiendo los zapatos.*

'The boy looked:IPFV in the boot and the dog was eating:PROG the shoes.' [S3l-3;8]

Young children's use of imperfective — with or without progressive — indicates durative events or states, or expresses attributions of desire or intention to a participant. They do **not** use them to background a secondary event. Contrasts of progressive and nonprogressive are commonest among the 4-year-olds, where the progressive marks the duration of a process, as in (78).

(78) *Aquí se sentó en el agua y el perro subiéndose en su cabeza.*

'And here he sat.down:PFV in the water and the dog climbing on his head.' [S4a-4;7]

At age 5 years, the present perfect is additionally used in a retrospective sense, expressing information inferred from a previous situation, as below.

(79) *Y cuando se despierta el niño se encuentra que se ha ido.*

'And when the boy wakes up he finds that it [=frog] has gone.' [S5c-5;4]

The contrastive use of the imperfective and perfective is notably coherent from the beginning. The perfective is used for completed actions and the imperfective to indicate states (existence, location, desire) or durative events that are presented as secondary, background situations.

Children of all ages contrast past imperfective and past progressive when juxtaposing a state of existence with an activity in progress, for example as in (80).

(80) *El bichejo estaba ahí y el niño estaba buscando en ese árbol.*

'The rat was:IPFV there and the boy was searching:PROG in that tree.' [S5g-5;8]

The 4- and 5-year-olds abandon the 3-year-old strategy of contrasting these forms to indicate simultaneity of two durative activities. Instead, they use the past progressive for both situations, as in the next example.

(81) *El niño estaba gritando y el perro estaba intentando coger una piña.*

'The boy was shouting and the dog was trying to catch a pine cone.' [S5a-5;1]

The 9-year-olds use the aspectual and temporal distinctions of their language totally systematically. They use the present perfect for indicating past action, the results of which are relevant to the present moment, as in (82).

(82) *Pero el perro está haciendo ruido y el niño le ha dicho que se calle.*

'But the dog is making noise and the boy has told him to be quiet.' [S9c-9;3]

The 9-year-old Spanish narrators also shift to the past perfect from the present for marking current relevance, an alternation which is never made by the younger children. They use the progressive only occasionally, like the adults, only for stage setting at the beginning, or for denoting an durative activity maintained throughout the story (such as 'search', 'call', 'look'). All 9-year-olds who use the past as anchor tense, use the perfective to present successive foreground events. To mark simultaneity between a background and a foreground event, they use the imperfective together with *mientras* 'while' in the background clause.

In sum, Spanish children from age 3 years use all the tense-aspect forms in their narrations, except for past perfect and past perfective progressive. By age 5 years, tense oscillation ends, and there is an increase in perfective past narratives. Sebastián (1989) takes this to be the developmental point at which the perfective comes to be used systematically for presentation of foreground events, and "the age at which narrative capacity begins, as based on a use of aspectual forms in the past that have different discursive functions." As noted in Chapter IIIC, the complexity of the Spanish verbal system does not impede but rather seems to stimulate the child to acquire aspectual and temporal markers.

Aspectual verbs, in contrast, first appear only at 5 years. This supports our initial hypothesis that markers of aspect outside of verbal morphology will be late to develop, given the richness of the inflectional system. The majority of the aspectual verbs observed are inchoatives such as *empezar* 'start' and verbs denoting temporal extent such as *seguir* 'continue'.

5.2.2. Hebrew

A. Discourse structure: Hebrew

Hebrew-speaking children also proceed from a descriptive to a narrative organization. Three-year-olds cannot sustain talk about several events and their narrative attempts typically give way to picture descriptions or to digressions. Just as in the other languages, 3-year-old Hebrew speakers demonstrate overuse of *ve* 'and' and the spatial deictics *po*, *kan* 'here'. Some also use *ve (az)* 'and (then)' as the required way of marking the next picture, fact, or object, so that its absence implies either a simultaneous or causal relation. Nine-year-olds, on the other hand, use adverbials as explicit markers of simultaneity. Only adults exploit the full potential of their language and their discourse organizational skills in creating their narrative texts.

B. Simultaneity in discourse: Hebrew

Similar changes in the discourse organizational role of the notion of simultaneity are observed in the Hebrew texts. Three-year-olds, not making a distinction between simultaneity and sequence, or between co-occurrence and recurrence (Berman, 1986b), relate situations on the basis of "simultaneity of perception." They juxtapose two events with only a participant switch but no other change, or repeat the same verb with a modal such as 'want' or 'try'. A pair of utterances so juxtaposed may express simultaneity between a state and an event, where the state is usually one of existence, as in example (83).

(83) *Ve cfardea po lemata, ve cfarde'im po lema'ala, ve cfarde'im she lema'ala hem holxim al shluliyot.*

'And (there's) a frog here on top, and (there are) frogs here below, and the frogs that are below they walk on puddles.' [H3e-3;7]

This juxtaposition may also be of two events which are unrelated in any other way than being simultaneously available to perception, as in (84).

(84) *Ve hakelev nixnas letox hacincenet ve hayeled sam et hana'al shelo al harosh.*

'And the dog goes inside the jar and the boy puts his boot on his head.' [H3a-3;0]

In these examples, there is no sense that one situation is more important or salient than the other. Thus, simultaneity has, as yet, no grounding function in discourse.

Older children also do no more than juxtapose simultaneous situations, but with an increase in syntactic interrelating of subordinate versus main clauses to effect some kind of grounding. Adults use paired utterances expressing simultaneity of the closely related activities of a single participant (i.e., conjoining predicates with the same subject — marked on Hebrew verbs by number and gender inflections) as in (85).

(85) *Ve hayeled mamshix baxipusim axarey hacfardea kshe hu moce et acmo na'uc al hakarnayim shel ayil.*

'And the boy continues with his search for the frog when he finds himself impaled on the antlers of a deer.' [*H20l*]

Hebrew school-age children also use parallelism to achieve stylistic ends as in (86).

(86) *Dani xipes betox hamagaf, Yoye xipes betox hadli shel hazxuxit.*

'Danny searched inside the boot, Yoye [=dog] searched inside the glass jar.' [*20g*]

Finally, adults embed chunks of simultaneous events within sequential chains, or intersperse two or three clause chains of sequential events in between long units related as simultaneous. The major functions served by simultaneity in adult narratives are discourse-motivated, such as elaborating on events, presenting and switching perspective, or summarizing.

Tense shifting is used both for narrative chunking and for more local switch of perspective across simultaneous situations. Switches from past to present, in adults, signify punctual events in opposition to ongoing durative activities, as in example (87).

(87) *Eyze yanshuf yaca lo mehaxor ba'ec ve hipil oto ve hakelov - bedlyuk hadvorim rodfot axarav. Shneyhem borxim gam mehayanshuf ve gam mehadvorim.*

'Some owl came out at him from the hole in the tree and made him fall and the dog - just at that moment the bees chase after him. The two of them flee both from the owl and also from the bees.' [*H20a*]

C. *Expression of simultaneity: Hebrew*

The means of expressing simultaneity in Hebrew are (a) overt lexical forms and (b) syntactic devices which imply simultaneity in context. The first set consists of sentence-modifying adverbials — mainly *benatayim* 'meanwhile'; conjunctions like *kshe* 'when' used in subordination or with verbless (copula) clauses — e.g., *kshe ha-dvorim axarav* 'when the-bees (are) after him'; and explicit simultaneity markers combined with a nominalized verb, e.g., *tox kedey haxipusim* 'in the course of the searches', *bish'at hashena* 'at the hour of sleep'. The developmental path, well observed by now, is from nonmarking, to use of basic marking devices, to varied marking — only by adults.

The texts of 3- and 4-year-olds have very few explicit markers of simultaneity: one instance of *benatayim* 'meanwhile' used (infelicitously or at least vaguely) by a 3-year-old and two instances of *kshe* 'when' used by 4-year-olds, as in (88).

(88) *Hu benatayim holex ve hu mexapes.*

'He [=dog] meanwhile walks and he [=boy] looks.' [*H3c-3;5*]

The use of verbless clauses without an overt marker of simultaneity is relatively early, and is observed in 4- and 5-year-olds, as in (89).

(89) *Hayeled hithapex lashlulit ve hakelev al harosh shelo.*

'The boy fell upside down in the puddle and the dog (is) on his head.' [*H5a-5;0*]

The 3- and 4-year-old children use these devices for expressing state-event and event-event relations in an unsystematic fashion, while starting with the 5-year-olds, the devices are linked more systematically with situation types.

At age 5, there is an increase in the use of *benatayim* 'meanwhile' (four instances) while *kshe* 'when' is still rather rare (two instances). While closely related state-event relations are described by *kshe*, event-event relations involving two participants are introduced by *benatayim*, a pattern which becomes particularly apparent in the 7- and 9-year-old texts. The preschool group occasionally use complement and relative clauses to juxtapose events and states.

A significant increase in the use of varied markers of simultaneity is observed at 7 years. Both the frequency of the devices increase (*kshe* = 13; *benatayim* = 5), and new means begin to be used, including nominalizations and verbless clauses with an explicit marker of simultaneity. Nine-year-olds begin to use adverbs such as *be'oto yom* 'on that same day' in addition to 'when' and 'meanwhile' (*kshe* = 13; *benatayim* = 10). In sum, both 7- and 9-year-old children use subordination and adverbials, and show full command of sequence of tenses with simultaneous pairing of two clauses. Only the adults use lexical elements other than the standard *benatayim* and *kshe* and display use of more explicit, higher register terms for 'while', such as *ba-besha'a-she* 'at the very time that', *agav* 'in the course of'. In Hebrew adult texts, adverbial clauses like these function mainly in "chunking," while complement and relative clauses are preferred for pairing of simultaneous events. In fact, relative clauses change function by age; while children use them for event-state relations, adults use them for event-event relations, as in (90).

(90) *Ve az yoce xoled she kcat mavhil oto.*

'And then comes.out a beaver that startles him somewhat.' [*H20d*]

Adult narrations show full use of both explicit and implicit devices for the expression of simultaneity, as in the following example of a high-register simultaneity preposition combined with an abstract verb-derived nominal.

(91) *Bish'at hashena hacfardea hexlita lacet lesiyur.*

'At the hour of sleep(ing) the frog decided to go out on an expedition.'
[*H20j*]

Hebrew has no aspect marking of perfectivity or of durative/progressive, and is therefore more similar to German than to Turkish, Spanish, or English. Only older speakers use tense shifting or other devices, such as nominalizations, for background attendant circumstances and descriptive states.[20]

In sum, in Hebrew, as in the other languages we have surveyed, only adult usage deploys the full range of devices — many of which 9-year-olds certainly "have" in the sense of knowing what their referential content is, more or less. And with adults, this deployment shows a flexibility within and across narrators not to be found among even the 9-year-old children.

5.2.3. English

A. Discourse structure: English

The narrations of the English-speaking subjects are very similar to those of the other languages in terms of discourse structure. Children of 3 and 4 years proceed in a descriptive and conversational style, producing deictically anchored utterances prefaced by spatial deictics *here, there* to refer to events/entities perceived in the pictures, or they use *and then* with a discourse function. Around the age of 5, children start maintaining an anchor tense, either the past or the present and there is an increase in sequentiality markers (Renner, 1989) — both suggesting that a temporal organization is replacing the earlier perceptual one. English 9-year-olds narrate more like adults than the preschoolers, but just like the 9-year-olds in the other languages, they do not show the same kind of elaboration of style, variety of linguistic devices, or flexibility in their use as fully mature speakers.

B. Simultaneity in discourse: English

An early means for indicating simultaneity in English is the progressive aspect marker *-ing*, occurring with physical event and perception verbs in the 3-, 4-, and 5-year-old texts. In some of the 9-year-old and most adult narratives, *-ing* occurs with mental state verbs such as *think* and *wonder*, reflecting the same types of changes in discourse abilities observed in the other

---

[20] Berman (1986b) suggests that there are contexts in the 3-year-old texts where modal verbs like 'want' are used as precursors of aspect (similar to the use of 'try' in English to indicate action in progress), as in: 'Here he wants to go out and here he goes out' [*H3c-3;5*], or 'The dog wanted to go to the tree and he went' [*H3j-3;9*]. Similarly, 'also' appears to function as a precursor of endstate devices, similarly to what was noted for German *auch*. (See Chapter IIID).

languages. This way of indicating simultaneity by aspect marking does not as yet reflect any grounding distinctions in most of the 3- and 4-year-old texts; these make wide use of the spatial terms *here* and *there*, suggesting that the *-ing* form needs to be interpreted as deictically anchored for the younger children.

Inflectional marking of perfect aspect for expressing simultaneity between an earlier but currently relevant situation with a present one, is not exploited by (American) English-speaking children before about age 5.[21] However, younger subjects do occasionally use lexical aspect markers (e.g. *still*). A few of the younger children also mark simultaneity between pairs of clauses by means of the subordinating conjunctions *when* and *because*, resulting in local interclause relations. Using aspect marking for discourse organizational purposes appears to decline at age 9 years, while other strategies for indicating grounding distinctions take over in the older children's texts, as well as those of the adults.

C. Expression of simultaneity: English

The first explicit markers of simultaneity in English, observed at age 3 years, are the subordinating conjunctions *when* (used by two children) and *while* (used by one child). Frequency of occurrence, as well as number of children using these forms, increase at age 4, as in examples (92) and (93).

(92) *Look - when he's sleeping, and his frog getting out.* [E3a-3;1]

The boy and the dog slept while the frog quietly got out of the jar. [E4b-4;0]

The subordinator *when* is very common in the 5-year-old texts (used 14 times by 7 children), leveling off in the 9-year-old and adult texts (10 times by six speakers in each group). The 9-year-old example below illustrates the use of *when*, and the adult example shows the use of a complement clause for the same scene.

(93) *Then, when the boy wakes up, he finds that the frog is gone.* [E9b-9;3]

In the morning the boy and the dog awake to find that the frog is gone. [E20f]

In contrast, *while* is used less by the 5- and 9-year-olds but increasingly by the adults (24 occurrences in seven adult texts). The conjunction *as* occurs only in the adult data, while PREPOSITION *V-ing* is rare across the sample.

---

[21] The present perfect is more frequent, and is acquired earlier, in British English. Slobin's (p.c.) preliminary examination of frog stories gathered in England by Elena Lieven suggests that the development of narrative uses of this form is earlier, and quite different, in British English. See, further, Chapter IIIA.

Interestingly, the adverb *meanwhile* occurs only once in one adult text, contrary to what has been observed in the other languages.

As for morphological devices, the earliest — used by nearly all 3-year-olds (46/10) and 4-year-olds, although with lower frequency (24/9) — is the progressive aspect marker *-ing*. This appears to be a strong and predominant strategy for indicating simultaneity, since it continues with high frequency in the texts of the 5-year-olds, 9-year-olds, and adults, even though the latter also use a variety of other devices. Adverbial participles with *-ing*, on the other hand, are mainly used by adults, with only a few instances at age 9, and one instance in a 3-year-old text. Compare the 5-year-old and adult examples in (94) and (95).

(94) *And the boy's looking down the hole and calling in the frog and the dog is looking at the bees.* [E5k-5;11]

(95) *So, as the boy is looking in the hole for his frog, the dog seems interested in this beehive with all the bees flying out.* [E20e]

It could be that in English, it is the opposition between progressive and simple present which triggers the distinction between event time/reference time and time of perception as the necessary basis for developing a hierarchical narrative structure.

Other means used for implying simultaneity in English are the adverb *too* — used rather less than the words for 'also' in German, Turkish, or Hebrew — and lexical aspect markers such as *still*, becoming common in the 9-year-old and adult texts and, occasionally, the aspectual verb *keep on*.

As in the case of German and Turkish, there are certain contexts where simultaneity is implied although not marked, as in pairs of clauses with a verb of perception, in parallel constructions, or in clauses with a durative meaning followed by the adverb *suddenly*. Not surprisingly, all these different means are used in combination mainly by adults, in constructing texts full of elaborations, retrospective or prospective summaries, evaluations, and digressions.

American English speakers thus appear to rely heavily on the use of subordination and inflectional aspect, particularly the progressive and less so the perfect, for the expression of simultaneity in discourse. In contrast to what we observed in the other languages, there is almost no use of adverbs such as *meanwhile, in the meantime* connecting independent clauses and functional in weaving chunks of sequential events taking place concurrently.

6. CONCLUSION

Taking the perspective of the development of language forms and language functions, this chapter has considered two developmental domains as interrelated through the concept of simultaneity: the development of discourse competence, and of expressive devices and their use. We have observed that the five language groups are very similar in the development of discourse structure and the changing role of simultaneity in discourse. Although even the youngest children at times produce coherent pieces of discourse, they still have a long way to go before reaching adultlike proficiency in producing what can truly be called a "narrative."[22]

The general developmental trend from 3-year-olds to adults involves a change in the type of discourse, from picture-to-picture description to narration. This is correlated with a change in the type of cohesion established in the texts from local (clause-per-clause, pairs of clauses) to global organization. This in turn implies the development of the ability to conceptualize a number of single states and events as parts of one complex overall event on the basis of their temporal relations. The 3- and 4-year-olds' use of spatial deictics ('here/there') together with markers of sequentiality ('and then') strongly suggests that the shift is from a spatio-perceptually based to an abstract-representational conceptualization of time. We have seen that as soon as children are able to organize their speech along a narrative thread, they can move from a mere juxtaposition of equally weighted pieces of information to hierarchical structures in discourse. The age at which this is evidenced in our study is 5 years, when children gradually start moving towards the adult norm of elaborating hierarchical structures in discourse by grounding, chunking, giving perspective, and referring backwards or forwards.

During this process, the function of simultaneity changes as well. At the early stage, simultaneity of perception (for each picture frame) governs the verbalization, and a deictic orientation provides the anchor for the different pieces of information. As the children move on to developing a temporal structure in discourse, they learn to distinguish the different functions of simultaneity with respect to foregrounding and backgrounding. The first steps in this direction are characterized by a struggle for, or a submission to, the expressive devices making these distinctions. That is, the course and speed of development in this area depend on the verbal means available in the language. The more elaborate the narrations become, the more *sim*-clauses of all different types they will include, adding background information to the events presented in the pictures. Thus, gradually, simultaneity is used to

---

[22] It is interesting to compare the picture-description data to story-telling data from the same age groups (see Chapter IIA). It turns out that 3- and 4-year-olds cannot produce longer pieces of discourse without the help of scaffolding questions from the interviewer. Children at this age are not able to construct or sustain an overall conceptual representation of a story. In a way, the pictures seem to have the same supporting function for the child as do the questions of the interlocutor (see Hoppe-Graff, Scholer, & Schell, 1981).

effect the building up of complexly integrated scenes.

As for expressive devices, we find a stepwise development of forms reflecting the complexity of types and functions of simultaneity. In this process, new forms are acquired, the functions of existing forms change, and some forms lose their earlier functions altogether. For instance, subordinating devices that connect adjacent clauses and express simultaneity between contingent situations (temporal/causal) are acquired earlier than adverbs that connect independent clauses and relate independent sequences of cotemporal events. Or, while young children use subordinate constructions for describing pictures, from age 5 on, they use them as a mechanism for prospection and retrospection, showing that the function of a given form is dependent on the speaker's narrative capacity. And, across time, certain devices cease to serve a particular purpose, as was noted for the marking of simultaneity in our texts for such expressions as *o zaman* 'at that time' and *de* 'also' in Turkish, *auch* 'also' and *gerade* 'just' in German, verbless copula clauses with no explicit *sim*-marking in Hebrew, and certain aspectual contrasts in Spanish.

From a crosslinguistic perspective, the array of structural properties and the particular devices available in a given language — morphological markings and lexical expressions used in coordinate or subordinate constructions — emerge as another determining factor for acquisition. Our detailed analysis of the expression of simultaneity in German and Turkish has revealed that the temporal course of development is quite divergent for these two languages, and while development in Spanish and English is more similar to Turkish, that in Hebrew is more like German.

Spanish-, Turkish-, and English-speaking children differ from the German and Hebrew speakers mainly in the use of the tense/aspect/modality systems of their languages. Spanish is clearly very rich in the aspectual notions marked in its morphology, Turkish provides a different set of aspectual-modal distinctions, and English is closer to these two compared with German and Hebrew, which are relatively impoverished from this point of view. These differences in linguistic structure are reflected in the children's early use of tense switching. The switches found in the 3-year-old stories are aspectual rather than temporal in nature, and there are clear differences between the different language groups in the extent to which such shifts occur.

The major contrast is between Spanish-, Turkish-, and English-speaking preschoolers who have difficulty in adhering to an anchor tense, and German- and Hebrew-speaking children who show the tendency to stick to one tense from early on (from age 3 in German, from age 4 or 5 in Hebrew). This is not surprising, since German marks only the perfect, and Hebrew marks no other tense than simple present and past (and future) in the grammar. German children, therefore, appear to have a more precocious narrative style with regard to temporal switches (see also Bamberg, 1987). In contrast, Spanish- and Turkish-speaking children face a variety of alternatives for marking distinctions of both tense and aspect, as well as modality, and this leads them into varied and rather unsystematic alternations in the early phases of their text construction. Sebastián (1989) has interpreted these as "try outs to discover the various available possibilities for indicating different functions in the complex verbal system of their languages." That is, if the language provides the options, children try to use them. Again, this need not be to their disadvantage, because it is quite likely that in the process of deciphering a complex set of verbal distinctions, they will concurrently be making some relevant conceptual distinctions. This is what is suggested by our findings for the use of more explicit devices marking simultaneity.

The first overt temporal marker relevant to simultaneity that occurs in the youngest children's texts in three of our languages corresponds to the notion 'when'. Interestingly, the German and Hebrew 3- to 4-year-olds do not use it at all. Typically a subordinating construction, 'when' is more frequent in the narratives of the Spanish (*cuando*), English (*when*) and Turkish (V+*ince*) children — even at age 5, when it is first used in Hebrew ((*k*)*she*) and German (*als*).

Subordinators that denote pure simultaneity, corresponding to 'while', are present at age 3 in English (*while*) and Turkish (V+*ken*), but not the other languages. The two forms both present a relation of simultaneity between an ongoing process and an event (with a strong indication of progress/durativity'), suggesting that young children are sensitive to this distinction if the language marks it. Spanish does not observe this distinction, with *cuando* subsuming notions of both 'when' and 'while', like Hebrew *kshe*. German and Hebrew, which are alike in their low marking of verbal aspect, are thus different in this respect. In German, unlike Hebrew, the conceptual distinction between simultaneity of 'event and x' and 'state and x' is marked by different conjunctions (*als/während*). While in German only *als* appears at age 5, and *während* is not used until age 9, in Hebrew both *kshe* and the adverbial *benatayim* 'meanwhile' occur at age 5. However, we cannot attribute the late use of *während* by German children to the additional complexity posed by a finer conceptual distinction, since both Spanish and Turkish children start using subordinating devices which establish simultaneity of 'state and x' at age 5 (*al*+INF and V+*diğinde*). The delay in the use of German *während* may be due to the fact that this form is also used as a preposition with the genitive case (meaning 'during'), and therefore poses further complexity. Although German children do not appear to "compensate" with other linguistic means to express the simultaneity of 'state and x', the only aspectual distinction available in the language (perfect/nonperfect) does serve this purpose. What is more surprising is the use of *benatayim* in Hebrew, because corresponding adverbs do not appear in the other languages before 9 years. The early appearance of this adverb in Hebrew might be explained by the fact that Hebrew has neither a conjunction corresponding to 'while' to mark simultaneity nor morphological aspect as a means of indicating 'stativity'.

It appears, then, that the marking of verbal aspect in Spanish, English, and Turkish "draws attention" to internal temporal relations, and therefore other means of expressing temporal relations, where they exist, are also deployed earlier. In German, where aspect marking is limited to the perfect, its role is compensatory rather than facilitative; and in Hebrew, total lack of verbal aspect leads to earlier use of a given lexical form from the right semantic domain but with much simpler functions. These observations suggest that explicit marking of aspectual distinctions in the morphology of a language contributes positively to or facilitates the child's differentiation of similar temporal notions embodied in the lexical forms of the language. In the absence of such a system, however, children still find means of communicating the kinds of semantic distinctions when they have discovered them conceptually.

Adverbials meaning 'meanwhile', 'in the meantime', on the other hand, are much more specific to adult use in all languages, with occasional instances observed at 9 years in Turkish (*bulo sırada*), Spanish (*mientras*), and German (*inzwischen*). It is interesting that *meanwhile* is used only once in English, in the adult data. Hebrew *benatayim*, as noted above, constitutes an exception to this pattern. It is not surprising that these adverbs, which function to connect independent sequences of events as simultaneous, are late to emerge, because their function is discourse-organizational as well as temporal. They are used to introduce foreground events and to mark beginnings of new episodes, in addition to designating reference time. As such, using them depends on the ability to manipulate pieces of discourse for hierarchical structuring of a narrative, an ability which appears around the age of 9. And recall that, across the languages, we found expression of simultaneity to be restricted to adjacent utterances even among most 9-year-olds.

Another interesting point is that forms which are explicitly temporal (i.e., function for setting reference time) are used earlier than forms that have purely discourse cohesive functions with their exact meanings dependent on inferences from context (e.g., V+*erek* in Turkish and *dabei* in German). It should, therefore, not be surprising that adverbs such as *meanwhile*, which have both functions, are acquired late.

Our five languages also differ with respect to the use of implicit devices for the expression of simultaneity. For instance, the use of nominalized forms is much more frequent in Hebrew than in German, where, although they are possible, they are hardly ever used. Verbless copula clauses are quite frequent in young children's usage in Hebrew, whereas they appear late in Turkish, together with nominalizations. Causal and complement clauses appear late in Turkish, Spanish, and Hebrew, and do not function in the expression of simultaneity as they do for young German children, possibly because tense-aspect shifts serve this function in the first two of these languages, and relative clauses in the third.

In all five languages, aspectual verbs acquire a discourse function by age 5. Starting with age 9, inchoatives tend to mark the beginning of an episode rather than a single event and thus to introduce a situation as a global background. Continuatives, on the other hand, mark the extension of an activity that continues throughout a long stretch of the story and establish simultaneity at the thematic level (see Chapter IVD).

In summary, in all our languages, the first organization of situations according to the time axis of events and the beginnings of the development of narrative capacity are observed around the age of 5. The capacity to coordinate this axis with the temporal axis of discourse is found in the 9-year-olds. Data from 7-year-olds in all the languages would help us to better understand the nature of the changes that take place between 5 and 9 years of age. Nonetheless, clear differences emerge between our age groups, which we attributed to the structure of the language being acquired, and which appear at the earlier, preschool ages we investigated (age 3 to 5 years). We concluded that the lexical as well as the morphological options available in a given language appear to have a close bearing on the ability to attend to and conceptualize different types of temporal relations, in this case simultaneity. The effects of such an advantage on the overall ability to structure narratives, however, is not so clear. It is possible to note immediate effects at the local or linear level of narrative organization (e.g., grounding distinctions between paired clauses easily marked with subordinating devices), and to suggest increased flexibility or precocity at this level. The ability to simultaneously integrate such local units around an overall guiding theme, resulting in a hierarchically structured text, on the other hand, does not appear to benefit much from the availability of a rich set of devices in the language, as it emerges several years after such devices are already functional. In other words, one cannot say that the early acquisition of linguistic devices leads to a relatively earlier development of temporal structuring of discourse at the higher, global level.

Chapter IVB

THE DEVELOPMENT OF RELATIVE CLAUSE FUNCTIONS IN NARRATIVE

Lisa Dasinger and Cecile Toupin[1]

[1] In this, as in other co-authored chapters of the project group, order of authorship is alphabetical. We would like to thank Ruth Berman and Dan Slobin, who encouraged us throughout this project, and provided useful comments and suggestions for revision. We would also like to specially thank Aylin Küntay for her comments and insights with regard to the Turkish data.

This chapter deals with the uses in narrative of a particular grammatical construction — the relative clause — by children and adults speaking disparate languages which exhibit versions of this one linguistic structure. The narrow focus of our study is motivated by the fact that relative clauses are both flexible in form and variable in function. Moreover, rather than viewing this particular construction as a separate, isolated grammatical object in its own right, we wished to understand its role in each of the languages we analyzed and how it is used in narratives produced by speakers of these languages. The crosslinguistic comparative method afforded by the overall project provided us with an unusual opportunity to pursue these goals, since the grammar of each of the five languages has constructions which are characterizable as relative clauses, and yet which differ in formal structure and in range of functions. These differences as well as similarities between the languages play a role in adult uses as well as in children's developing mastery of relative clause uses in narrative. We begin with a brief overview of properties characterizing relative clauses in the languages of the world in general (Section 1).[1] We then delineate a taxonomy of relative clause functions which we established as the basis for comparison of our sample across languages and age groups (Section 2); this is followed by analysis of morphosyntactic factors in the distribution of relative clauses across the age groups (Section 3) and comparison of the functions served by relatives in adult narratives in all five languages (Section 4), as a basis for discussion of the development of relative clause usage by children (Section 5).

1. THE RELATIVE CLAUSE CONSTRUCTION

Relative clauses have many variants both within and across languages. These may differ in structural composition and surface morphology, as well as in semantics and range of pragmatic functions.[2] In this section, we briefly

---

[1] Not all languages have relative clauses. The Australian aboriginal language, Warlpiri, which has exceedingly free word order, is one example (Comrie, 1981).

[2] Linguistic definitions of the relative clause construction tend to vary both in the inclusiveness and degree of formality of their formulation, depending on the researcher's aims and general orientation. For example, Keenan (1985b) and Comrie (1981) give a functional

address what is common to relative clauses in general, and then consider particular properties based on the English sample.

The relative clause is part of a larger construction consisting of a main clause and a relative clause. Typically, the relative clause is considered to be a type of noun modification structure which constitutes part of a complex NP constituent. However, various types of relative clauses are treated as differentially linked to the NP or head element of the main clause, with affinities to more "loosely-linked" types of subordination. Thus, the relative clause is also treated as a kind of subordinate clause that may be of varying types.[3] On the whole, relative clauses are construed as expressing some information about a "head" referent, or nominal category in the main clause. This head referent is co-construed with a "relativized" element in the relative clause, which is commonly, though not necessarily, expressed by a relative pronoun.

Relative clauses thus include a variety of structural and functional subtypes. The English examples in (1a) to (1d) illustrate some of these, which are common to the languages in our sample. (Details relevant to each of the five languages are given in Section 3).

(1a) **headless, restrictive**: *[He] holds onto what looks like a branch...* *[E20j]*

(1b) **infinitival, restrictive**: *[The dog] has found something new to look at...* *[E20f]*

(1c) **nonrestrictive**: *The boy, who had climbed the tree, looked in it.* *[E9i-9;10]*

(1d) **participial, nonrestrictive**: *There's a deer hiding up there.* *[E4f-4;7]*

The examples in (1a) to (1d) illustrate three structural properties of relative clauses relevant to our sample: (1) the grammatical realization of the head referent, (2) the characteristics of the verb in the adjoining clause, and (3) the presence or absence of a relative pronoun. In relative clauses like (1a),

---

definition of the restrictive relative clause for crosslinguistic comparative purposes. Syntacticians, on the other hand, have tended to focus on the variable syntactic composition of a wider range of relative clause types from different perspectives (e.g., Fillmore, 1987; Lambrecht, 1988; McCawley, 1988). We have tried to capture general structural and functional features common to the types of relative clauses relevant to our study while not espousing any particular formal analysis.

[3] Fillmore (1987) notes that "not every use of a relative clause is modificational" (p. 2), while McCawley (1988) offers a more structuralist description of the subordinated relative clause as a "truncated S, i.e., something having the general form of an S except for lacking a constituent corresponding to the relative expression" (p. 417). The "continuative" and "presentational" type relative clauses discussed in this chapter are examples of this latter type (see Lambrecht, 1988).

the head referent of the relative expression (*what looks like a branch*) is not lexically specified — hence the name "headless" or "free" relative; the relative pronoun *what* in (1a) can be roughly taken to mean 'the thing (things or stuff) which', and thus refers to some kind of entity (Fillmore, 1987). Relative clauses also need not contain a finite verb form (particularly in a language like Turkish), or any verb at all (as is often the case in Hebrew — see Section 3). This is shown by the infinitive *to look* in (1b) and the participle *hiding* in (1d).[4] Relative clauses like those in (1b) and (1d) also illustrate the fact that relative pronouns can be omitted under certain conditions (Keenan, 1985a; McCawley, 1988).

A major distinction is made in linguistic analyses between restrictive and nonrestrictive relatives. In semantic terms, a restrictive relative is one that functions to further specify the category designated by the head referent, and so "provides essential information in the identification of the object being referred to" (Fillmore, 1987, p. 2). Examples (1a, 1b) are restrictive relatives clauses, in which the categories represented by *what* and *something new* are further specified in the relative clause. Nonrestrictive relative clauses, in contrast, may serve to further comment on, or predicate something about, a fully-identified referent. Thus in examples (1c, 1d) above, the head referents *the boy* and *a deer* independently specify the entity referred to. This semantic distinction between the two types of relative clauses typically has associated prosodic and grammatical reflexes in different languages (Lambrecht, 1988; McCawley, 1981).

Our sample thus includes both restrictive and nonrestrictive relatives. Yet the distinction as such does not figure in our analysis, since our taxonomy of the discourse functions of relative clauses cuts across the two categories. On the other hand, this distinction is, in principle, important, since it underscores a major feature of the relative clause construction: its potential plurifunctionality in fulfilling two distinct purposes in discourse, namely, reference and predication.

2. GENERAL DISCOURSE AND NARRATIVE FUNCTIONS: A TAXONOMY

Two major concerns guided us in developing a a taxonomy of the functions of relative clauses in narrative discourse: (1) to capture similarities and

---

[4] Noun-modification expressions involving participial forms not readily distinguishable from their use as derived adjectives were excluded from our analysis. Thus the following example from a Spanish text was not taken into account as in our analysis of relative clauses: *Oyen un ruido detrás de un tronco tirado.* 'They hear a sound behind a **thrown** log' [= log thrown down] [*S9a-9;1*].

differences in the range of relative clause uses across our five languages; and (2) to define descriptive categories capable of accounting for developmental trends. A third aim evolved out of these two in the interest of relating our findings to previous research: to distinguish between certain **general discourse** uses of relative clauses and more specialized **narrative** uses.

2.1. General Discourse Functions

One of the basic requirements of intelligible discourse is that speakers provide enough information about the entities referred to — individuals, objects, concepts, etc. — so that listeners know who or what is being talked about. This requirement applies to single utterances produced in isolation as well as to extended discourse in which listeners (or readers) must be able to identify and track both new and previously mentioned referents over time. We reserve the term **general discourse** functions for those uses of relative clauses that serve this basic discourse need.

Languages provide a variety of devices which speakers can use, in varying combinations, in order to successfully identify who or what is being talked about. These may include proper names (*Socrates*), simple nouns (*man*), pronouns (*he*), definite and indefinite articles (*a man/the man*), adjectives (*a bald man*), and prepositional phrases (*a man with a bald head*). Relative clauses, as another device for noun modification, are also used in identifying referents (*the man who knew Plato*). How speakers refer to an entity will naturally depend on the available means in their language. Choice of referring expression will also depend on both the assumed needs of the listener and the particular information goals of the speaker in a given discourse context.

Speakers' assumptions about what information is **given** (or **old**) and what is considered **new** to the listener play an important role in their choice of referring expression (see Prince, 1981). Given information is roughly that which "the speaker assumes the hearer knows, assumes or can infer about a particular thing." New information is accordingly that which "the speaker assumes the hearer does not yet know" or could not infer" (Prince, 1981, p. 230). Thus, for example, we normally use proper names, without further identifying information, when we assume that the referent is familiar or known to the listener, and we use simple pronouns when we assume that the listener can infer the referent from the extralinguistic situation or from the preceding linguistic context.

Interestingly, relative clauses allow for various combinations of given and new information when referring to an entity: Both the head referent and the information contained in the relative clause may convey either given or new information. These variable combinations of old and new information can have differing pragmatic functions. For example, a speaker may use an existential main clause to introduce a new referent into discourse, and then immediately provide additional identifying information about the referent in a relative clause, as in, "There was this guy who only wore polka-dots." In this use, both the head referent (*this guy*) and the relative clause (*who only wore polka-dots*) are new information. This relative clause construction and its corresponding discourse function have been widely noted in the linguistic literature (Fox, 1987; Fox & Thompson, in press; Lambrecht, 1988; Prince, 1981). Other combinations of new and old information and their concomitant discourse functions have received less notice. For instance, relative clauses may also be used to provide old information about an old, or previously mentioned referent. Continuing our example of the "polka-dot man," one might further add, "That guy who wore only polka-dots called himself The Polka-Dot Man." In this use, the relative clause serves to reidentify or remind the listener (or reader) of the "sameness" of the earlier mentioned referent with the one now spoken about. Naturally, relative clauses can also be used to provide new information about an old referent, as in "The Polka-Dot Man, who was also on the tall side, used to hang out in Sproul Plaza."[5] As discussed below, these basic combinations of new and old information can be used to delineate three general types of referring functions that relative clauses serve in discourse. An additional type of referring function, which we call "naming," is independently motivated, and so is not defined on the basis of any one combination of given and new information.

Against this background, we arrived at a set of nine classes of relative clause functions, as follows: four general discourse functions — (1) naming referents (**NAME**), (2) situating new referents (**SIT-NEW**), (3) situating old referents (**SIT-OLD**), (4) reidentifying old referents (**REID**); and five specifically narrative functions — (5) presenting main characters (**PRES**), (6) motivating or enabling narrative actions (**MOT**), (7) continuing the narrative (**CONT**), (8) setting up expectations about narrative entities and events (**EXP**), and (9) summing up over past or upcoming events (**SUM**). These are described and illustrated below.

---

[5] The fourth possible combination — providing old information about a new referent — does not make pragmatic sense according to this scheme. One cannot remind the listener of what he or she already knows about a particular referent, and have it be the case that the listener also doesn't know the referent which he/she knows something about. However, Prince (1981) has noted that when new referents are first introduced into discourse, some **part** of the information contained in the relative may be given information. Prince terms these "brand-new anchored" discourse entities. These uses are included within the broader category of what we call "situating" new referents (see Section 2.1.2: SIT-NEW).

(1) Naming referents (NAME)

The simplest way to refer to something is by denomination, that is, by using a word which refers to that particular entity. However, a language may not have a lexical item for a particular referent, or the identity of the referent may be indeterminate or ambiguous, or the speaker simply may not know, or be unable to access, the required lexical item. In such circumstances, speakers may resort to alternative means of reference. Relative clauses are one device which can serve this function, where the head noun together with the relative clause constitute a name, or category label, for a particular referent. This naming or categorizing function is akin to standard definitions of a restrictive relative clause, where the head noun represents a general category, typically expressed by means of an indefinite pronoun (*someone, something*) or a superordinate lexical category, which is further specified by the relative clause (Keenan, 1985b).

This "naming" function of a relative clause is often used by our younger narrators to identify a referent where more mature speakers used a single lexical item. These uses thus appear to be motivated either by lack of knowledge of the appropriate lexical item or failure to access it when needed, as in the examples in (2a) and (2b).

(2a) *Und der Hund versuchte an **de Dings da** ranzukommen **wo die Bienen immer rausfliegen.***

'And the dog tried to get onto **the thing there where the bees always fly out.**' [referring to the beehive] [*G5a-5;7*]

(2b) *Esto es **un tubo que está roto.***

'This is **a tube that is broken.**' [referring to the log] [*S3a-3;6*]

In contrast, adults exhibit naming uses that appear to be motivated by uncertainty about the appropriate way to identify a particular entity. For example, the small creature that was variously identified as a *gopher, groundhog, mole*, etc., was also referred to less specifically using a relative clause, as in the adult examples in (2c) and (2d).

(2c) *Aber stattdessen kommt ein Maulwurf oder ein Biber, jedenfalls **ein Tier was unter der Erde lebt.***

'But instead a mole or a beaver comes, in any case **an animal that lives under ground.**' [*G20b*]

(2d) *The boy gets his nose either bitten or sniffed at by **some little animal living in the hole.** [E20b]*

Other naming uses served to identify something for which the language apparently does not have a noun, as in the German and Turkish examples in (2e) and (2f).

(2e) *Der Junge findet was zum rausklettern.*
'The boy finds **something to climb out with**.' [*G3k-3;7*]
(2f) *Önce odanın içindeki eşyaları araştırıyor.*
'First they search **the things that are inside the room**.' [*T20d*]

(2) Situating new referents (SIT-NEW)

Previous research has revealed a number of crosslinguistic regularities in the way that new referents are introduced into discourse (Hickmann, Liang, & van Crevel, 1989; Lambrecht 1987, 1988; Prince, 1981). In general, new referents tend to take full lexical (i.e., nonpronominal) NPs which are also linguistically marked in ways that distinguish them from established or given topic/subject NPs. Existential *there* constructions, *it*-clefts, and left dislocations out of subject position are examples of syntactic devices used to introduce new referents in nonsubject/nontopic position. It has also been noted that the clauses in which new discourse referents are first introduced tend to share certain characteristics. New referents are first often "neutrally" depicted in clauses that are "intransitive, containing verbs indicating existence or coming into existence of some referent or appearance of a referent at the scene of the discourse" (Kuno, cited in Lambrecht, 1987, p. 370).

Relative clauses constitute another device which can fulfill an introducing function. Several discourse-based analyses of relative clauses have focused on their use in introducing new and important referents into discourse (Bates & Devescovi, 1989; Lambrecht, 1987; Prince, 1981). However, as our narratives show, relative clauses are commonly used to introduce new, but less major referents as well. In this section we discuss the introductory function of relative clauses only in relation to such subsidiary or relatively minor story characters or entities. Introduction of major protagonists is treated separately as a special case and is discussed under the heading of PRES (in subsection 2.2.(5) below).

The general function of these SIT-NEW relative clauses, in relation to a minor story character or entity, is to situate a new referent in the current "scene of the discourse." The new referent is first mentioned in a main clause, in nonsubject/nontopic position, and the relative clause serves to provide some further information about its existence or appearance on the scene. This use of a relative clause commonly has the effect of depicting a new referent as if in snapshot view, capturing some salient aspect of what it looks like, or what it is doing, or where it is located in the current scene, as in the excerpts from three children's narratives in (3a) through (3c).

(3a) *Köpek de ağaçta asılan arı kovanına bakıyor.*

'The dog is looking at **the beehive hanging from the tree.**' [*T5f-6;1*]

(3b) *They see there is lots of frogs playing.* [*E4b-4;4*]

(3c) *Le estuvieron buscando por **un tronco que había.***

'They were searching for him at **a trunk that was there.**' [*S9g-9;6*]

In other uses of this function, a new entity can be situated or "anchored" in the narrative (Prince, 1981) by relating its existence to an already established or known discourse entity, as in example (3d).[6]

(3d) *Out of the reeds come **some baby frogs that obviously are the little baby frogs of his frog.*** [*E20j*]

A related, yet more sophisticated use of this function is to provide background information, off the main storyline, that in effect explains the appearance or existence of a new entity in the current situation.

(3e) *Estaba por la noche contemplando **una rana que habían cazado durante el día y a la que habían puesto en un recipiente de cristal...***

'At night he was gazing at **a frog that they had caught during the day and that they had put in a glass container.**' [*S20c*]

(3f) *Das is jetzt **ein Froschparchen und es ist 'ne Froschmann und 'ne Froschfrau vermutlich die irgendwo ein Parchen geworden sind.***

'This is now **a frog couple and it is a frog husband and a frog wife presumably that have become a couple somewhere.**' [*G20b*]

(3) Situating old referents (SIT-OLD)

Relative clauses may also be used to situate or resituate old, or previously mentioned referents, in the ongoing scene of the discourse.[7] This function is typically applied when new information about a previously mentioned referent becomes relevant as it appears or reappears in later scenes. These relative clauses serve in effect to update the listener about the referent's current status in the narrative, as in (4a) through (4c).

---

[6] Prince (1981) has shown that in informal conversation a new entity is commonly introduced by immediately linking it to a more familiar discourse entity via a relative clause, as in, *A rich guy I know bought a Cadillac.* In this example, the already known or familiar identity of the speaker serves to "anchor" the new referent in the discourse.

[7] Thus we distinguish two types of "situating" functions in discourse: The previous one concerns situating new referents, that is, introducing them for the **first** time in a given discourse. Here, we are concerned with referents that have already been introduced into the discourse at least once before.

(4a) *El perro está encontrando al niño, que estaba en las piedras encima.* [*S3d-3;8*]

'The dog is meeting **the boy, who was up on top of the rocks.**'

(4b) *Y luego el buho que estaba aquí estaba en la piedra.*

'And later **the owl, who was here,** was on the rock.' [*S5e-5;4*]

(4c) *Ve levasof hakelev nafal beyaxad im hacincenet she berosho.*

'And eventually the dog fell down together with **the jar that (was) on its head.**' [*H9d-9;5*]

This "situating of old referents" function of relative clauses also includes instances of **contrastive** reference, where one of a set of previously mentioned referents is singled out by means of a distinctive or salient attribute, as in (4d) and (4e).

(4d) *Hay una que salta.*

'There is **one that jumps.** [=one of many frogs] [*S9k-9;11*]

(4e) *Aralarında sevinçle zıplayan kendi kurbağalarını hemen tanıdılar.*

'**The one that joyfully jumped out from among their midst** they immediately recognized as their own frog.' [*T20c*]

(4) Reidentifying old referents (REID)

In coherent discourse, the listener must also be able to keep track of referents over time, identifying them as the same referents that have been mentioned earlier. Relative clauses can meet this discourse function by providing old information about an old referent. This need commonly arises when the speaker believes a particular discourse entity has become "inactive" for the listener (Chafe, 1976) — a state of affairs that typically arises following at least one topic shift. Thus, a discourse entity may be "reactivated" via a relative clause in order to remind the listener of who or what is being referred to, or to reidentify a known referent by previously given information (McCawley, 1981).[8] Examples of this "reidentifying" function are given in

---

[8] McCawley has noted that nonrestrictive relative clauses can have a "reminding" function as an independent speech act in the way that restrictive relatives clauses do not. Thus, the nonrestrictive relative clause in *Has John, **who was here a minute ago,** left?* has a reminding function in a way that the restrictive relative clause in *Have you seen **the strange man who was here a minute ago**?* does not. In our coding scheme, both types are included in this same category. Note that it is intuitively clear in McCawley's examples that both the head referent and the information provided in the relative clause are treated as given or recoverable information for the listener. We suggest that the restrictive relative clause in his second example illustrates the identifying or "reidentifying" function that relative clauses can be used for.

different languages, from a child and two adults, in (5a) through (5c).

(5a) *This is it* [pointing] ***the frog they had.*** *[E4e-4;7]*

(5b) *El perro tiene que salir corriendo porque las abejas lo persiguen, **las que cayeron del panal.***

'The dog has to run away because the bees are chasing him, **the ones that fell from the hive.**' [cS20][9]

(5c) *Bu sırada köpek de kovanı görmüs, **ağaca asılı olan**, ve bununla oyalanıyor.*

'At this point the dog has seen **the hive, that was hanging from the tree**, and gets interested in it.' [T20h][10]

2.2. Narrative Functions

In addition to the general discourse requirement for introducing and identifying new and old referents, the creation of a narrative involves a number of other special concerns and goals. Storybook narratives of the type studied here, like narratives in general, consist of a sequence of events experienced by a set of characters located in time and space. Consequently, to construct a narrative entails describing a series of events as related both temporally and causally. Typically, a story also revolves around "complicating actions" or problems (Labov, 1972) which need to be resolved. This imposes an additional responsibility on the narrator: that of omniscient status, in which the narrator's foreknowledge of events to come must be deliberately concealed or adeptly revealed at appropriate moments.

In our frog-story narratives, relative clauses often serve to achieve these specialized narrative goals. Although relative clauses, like subordinate clauses in general, have often been treated as a kind of "backgrounding" device (Labov, 1972), we have found that they are skillfully used by our mature narrators in presenting foregrounded events and other information which is crucial to the unfolding of the story. Narrators can also use relative clauses in ways that recruit their referential functions for more specialized narrative purposes. The use of relative clauses to meet these specialized goals is what we

---

[9] The letters "cS" stand for Chilean Spanish. At the time the analyses for this chapter were being conducted, there were only six adult texts available in the European Spanish sample (Chapter IIIC), to which we added six texts gathered in Chile by Aura Bocaz.

[10] This Turkish example is noteworthy in that the relative clause is in postnominal position (follows the noun it modifies) and is postposed (follows the main clause) — see Section 4.1. We suggest, however, that its postpositional use here is pragmatically motivated by the reminding function it serves. It has the flavor both of an independent speech act and an afterthought.

have called their **narrative** functions.

(5) Presenting main characters (PRES)

Story beginnings typically call for a kind of scene setting or "orientation," in which the narrator "identifies in some way the time, place, persons and their activity or the situation" (Labov, 1972, p. 364). The archetypal fairytale beginning — *Once upon a time there was an X who...* — is one of the most familiar and stylized ways of setting the scene (see Chapter IIA). It also provides a favored context for the "presentational" relative construction (Lambrecht, 1988; Prince, 1981).

Several features of this use of a MAIN CLAUSE — RELATIVE CLAUSE construction make it especially suitable for introducing new and important referents, such as the main protagonists of a narrative. In this type of construction, it is the main clause that typically has the semantically neutral characteristics of an introductory clause. It may take the form of an existential or copula construction (*There/here/it is an X, This is a story about an X...*), or contain a verb indicating the knowledge or perception of the coming into existence or appearance of a referent at the scene (*We have/know/got/saw an X...*).[11] Syntactically, these presentatives allow the new referent to be introduced in nonsubject/nontopic position. The relative clause, on the other hand, is used to assert relevant new information about the new referent, thereby establishing it as a topic of importance. Typically, this new NP is the subject head of the relative clause.[12]

---

[11] These constructions contrast with the situating function of relative clauses (SIT-NEW in subsection (2) above), in which the existence or appearance of a new referent is usually expressed in the relative clause, rather than the main clause.

[12] Two "substandard" features of presentational relative clauses have been noted in the literature: One is the tendency in English for speakers to drop the obligatory subject relative pronoun in this construction, as in the children's song *There was a farmer had a dog*, cited by Lambrecht (1987). The other is the tendency in German presentational relatives for the relative clause to exhibit verb-medial order, rather than the verb-final order normally required of subordinate clauses. Schuetze-Coburn (1984) cites the following example from an original Grimm's fairy tale: *Es war einmal ein Mann der verstand allerlei Künste* 'There once was a man who knew all kinds of tricks'. Both usages are explained in discourse-pragmatic terms: The relative clause in presentational relatives has the pragmatic status of an asserted independent clause, and so retains the grammatical characteristics of one. Examples (6b) and (6c) are instances of this type in our narratives. Recently, Fox and Thompson (in press) have noted that the grammatical role of a "head" referent tends to correlate with its degree of animacy: Human agents are more likely than animals or things to be subject rather than object or direct object heads (see also Fox, 1987).

Use of a relative clause to introduce one or more of the three main protagonists of the frog story (the boy, the dog, or the frog) was categorized as having a "presentational-narrative" function.[13] These uses included both highly stylized and more informal versions of the presentational relative construction, as shown in (6a) through (6d).

(6a) *Pa'am haya yeled she hu haya im kelev.*

'Once there was **a boy that he was with a frog**.' [*H5h-5;5*]

(6b) *Da ist ein Junge*...und ein... *der hat ein Frosch.*

'There is **a boy**...and a... **who has a frog**.' [*G9c-9;6*]

(6c) *There's this little boy sitting in his room, has a pet frog in a jar.* [*E20h*]

(6d) *Erase una vez - un niño que tenía en un frasco una ranita.*

'There was a time - **a boy who had in a jar a little frog**.' [*S20e*]

(6) Motivating or enabling narrative actions (MOT)

Two independently expressed propositions can express an implicit relationship between them, in the form of "relational propositions" which provide an inferential basis for discourse cohesion (Mann & Thompson, 1986). Interpropositional relations such as causation, enablement, or temporal sequence are often overtly signaled in syntactically-linked clauses by terms such as *because, in order to*, and *and then*. They may also be less explicitly signaled by the syntactically linked propositions expressed in a main clause and a relative clause.

One such relation is where a relative clause serves to depict an event that is antecedent to the event expressed in the main clause. This use of a relative clause can provide the "enablement" condition for a main clause event (Zorriqueta, 1988) or it may contain information about the physical possibility of the action expressed in the main clause, as in these two 9-year-old examples:

(7a) **The boy, who had climbed the tree,** *looked in it.* [*E9i-9;10*]

(7b) *Ve hakelev xipes ota bacincenet she hu nixnas eleha im harosh.*

---

[13] This was the only criterion for inclusion in this functional category. The fact that these uses invariably exhibited the syntactic and semantic characteristics of presentational relatives can be taken as independent support for the discourse-motivated features of this construction. However, it is important to note that presentational-type relatives can and do serve to introduce secondary characters or other referents that narrators treat as worthy of further comment. These were included in the SIT-NEW category (subsection (2) above) or, where a presentational main clause was used in combination with a continuative relative, in the CONT category (see subsection 7, below).

'And the dog searched for it in **the jar that he went into with his head.**'
[*H9c-9;4*][14]

The antecedent event in the relative clause can also provide information about the motivation for a volitional action expressed in the main clause, as in (7c):

(7c) *Und **der Hund, der vorher die Wespen geärgert hatte,** der wird jetzt von den Wespen verfolgt [...]*

'And **the dog, who had angered the wasps before,** is now chased by the wasps [...]' [*G20h*]

In other uses of this function, the relative clause conveys a transient psychological state or an enduring character trait of the head referent, thereby providing the rationale for a character's actions, as in (7d) and (7e):

(7d) ***Baykuştan korkan Tim** bir kayanın tepesine çıktı.*

'**Tim, who was afraid of the owl,** climbed up onto a rock.' [*T20c*]

(7e) *El sapito, **que era muy diablo y muy ágil,** empezó a treparse.*

'**The little frog, who was very devilish, and very agile,** began to climb out.' [*cS20f*]

(7) Continuing the narrative (CONT)

A causal relation can also be expressed where the relative clause provides the **consequent** event of the event expressed in the main clause.[15] This

---

[14] In this Hebrew example, it is not entirely clear whether the dog's searching in the jar precedes or follows the event of his putting his head into the jar. Since Hebrew does not mark aspect on the verb (Chapter IIIo, IIID), the verb *nixnas* in the relative clause is ambiguous as between a simultaneous reading of 'was inserting' or an anterior 'had inserted'. Since the story (as well as real-life pragmatics) makes it more likely that first he put his head into the jar and only then searched in it, we have coded this relative clause as motivational rather than continuative (see subsection (7)). This interpretation is supported by detailed analysis of Hebrew descriptions of this scene (Berman, 1993). In this, as in other cases of possible ambiguity in interpreting sequence of events relations in Hebrew relative clauses, we have based our interpretation on the most plausible order of events in the frog story, and have coded the functions accordingly. We encountered a related example from a Spanish narrator, in which the event in the relative clause was linguistically marked as anterior to the main clause event, although logically it must follow the first in time (*Del agujero que había cavado el niño sale un animal que le había pegado en la nariz.* 'From the hole that the boy had dug comes out an animal who had hit him on the nose.' [*S9e-9;6*]) Again, our interpretation of this event sequence was based on realworld plausibility, and so this relative clause was coded as continuative (CONT) rather than motivational (MOT).

[15] Note that the continuative (CONT) and the motivational (MOT) functions of relative clauses differ in that the causal or temporal relation of events expressed in the main clause and the relative clause are in inverse order in the two cases.

use of relative clauses has traditionally been characterized as "continuative" (Jespersen, cited in Lambrecht, 1988) or as "narrative advancing" (Fillmore, 1987), since the information in the relative clause has the effect of continuing or advancing the narrative plotline.

Not uncommonly, the head referent of a continuative relative plays a dual semantic or thematic role: It is an affected patient in the main clause and an active (or reactive) agent in the relative clause:

(8a) *And then all the bees start chasing **the dog, who runs away**. [E20a]*

(8b) *El niño cayó en la cabeza **del alce, que, aterrorizado, corrió**.*

    'The boy fell on the head of **a deer, that, terrified, ran**.' [S20c]

Note that in using a relative clause to relate two events, the head referent of the relative clause (and antecedent of the relative pronoun can refer to the **entire event** expressed by the main clause:

(8c) *The boy and the dog wake up to find that the frog is gone, **about which they are very concerned**. [E20a]*

(8d) *And the deer stops abruptly, **which causes the boy to lose his balance**. [E20f]*

This category also includes temporally sequenced events in which the relative clause simply depicts an action or event that closely follows upon the main clause event:

(8e) *Sie kommen an **einen Abhang wo dann der Hirsch plötzlich stehen- bleibt***

    ***und den kleinen Jungen abwirft** und Junge und Dackel fallen dann in einen*

    Teich rein.

    'They come to **a cliff, where the deer then suddenly stops and throws off the**

    little boy, and boy and dog then fall into a pond.' [G20a]

Finally, this category also includes presentational relative constructions where the narrator introduces a new character on the scene via an existential main clause and then uses a relative clause to continue the narrative by immediately making the character a part of the action. In these cases, the relative clause, in contrast to the main clause, depicts a foregrounded event:

(8f) *Now the frog isn't there either, but there's **an owl in there, who bumps him down to the ground**. [E20j]*

(8g) *Salió **un loro que tiró al niño**.*

    'There came out **a parrot that threw the boy**.' [S5d-5;4]

(8) Setting up expectations about narrative entities and events (EXP)

In normal discourse, speakers are expected to identify referents in accordance with the assumed needs of the listener. For example, whether a speaker chooses to say that *Fred, someone I know,* or *some guy* is in the next room will depend on certain assumptions about the listener's degree of familiarity with the referent (and the speaker). In general, cooperative speakers will attempt to tailor their identifying descriptions to the most familiar level possible (Prince, 1981). Indeed, the failure to do so, as Prince notes, is likely to be perceived as "deviant" in some way: either "evasive, childish, or building suspense as in a mystery novel" (p. 245). Thus, for example, if the speaker reports that *Some guy is in the next room* and it is in fact a mutual friend, the listener can accuse the speaker of withholding information. On the other hand, the remark that **Someone you know is in the next room** is suspense-building, and sets up an expectation in the listener that the true (more familiar) identity of the referent will be revealed.

The practice of withholding information is in the realm of a narrator's creative license. Narrators may choose to conceal or delay revealing the identity of an entity that is known to the listener and/or a character in the story for suspenseful effect. The same devices that speakers use to name an entity in lieu of an existing word (see section 2.1.(1): NAME) may also be intentionally deployed to conceal the identity of a familiar referent. In our narratives, headless and participial relative clauses are commonly used for this function, as in the examples in (9a) and (9b).

(9a) *Resulta que en la madriguera lo que había era una topilla.*

'It turns out that in the burrow **what there was** was a mole.' [*S9l-9;11*]

(9b) *It seems like they both hear **something coming from behind the log**... and they find on the other side of the log two happy frogs, one of which was the frog in the jar.* [E20b]

The narrator may also set up an expectation about the identity of an object using modal and other predicates that suggest subjective uncertainty (e.g., *looked like, thought, appeared to be*). This uncertainty can be conveyed from the perspective of the omniscient status of the narrator as in (9c), or by taking the perspective of a character in the story as in (9d):

(9c) *Und das **was zuerst wie Zweige aussahen** entpuppt sich auf einmal als Hirsch...*

'And that **what at first looked like branches** turned out to be a deer...' [*G20i*]

(9d) *Gördüğünü ağaç zannetmiş.*

'**What he saw** he thought was a tree.' [*T20i*]

Finally, there are a few instances included in this category where the narrator uses a relative clause to build suspense about a particular moment, place, or event in the narrative:

(9e) *Und beide klettern jetzt über diesen Baumstumpf, hinter dem sich wahrscheinlich des Rätsels Lösung verbergen wird.*

'And both now climb over **the log, behind which is probably hidden the solution to the puzzle.**' [*G20b*]

(9) Summing over past or upcoming events (SUM)

Telling a story involves more than recounting a series of sequentially ordered events. Narrative events on the whole have a theme or point to them which warrants their recounting (Chapters IIA and IIB). There are two points in a story where narrators typically provide an encapsulation or summary of events. One is prior to a recounting of the particulars, in what Labov (1972) calls an "abstract." Another is following a series of recounted events, where the narrator seeks to close off a sequence of complicating actions and relate their significance to the point of the story, what Labov calls a "coda." Both of these encapsulating functions may be served by relative clauses.

In the former instance, the narrator may forecast the nature of the events to be recounted by collectively referring to new entities and events to come, as in (10a) and (10b).

(10a) *Hu menase lexapes bexol tlulit ve bekol xor she hu pogesh.*

'He tries to search in **every hillock and every hole that he meets.**' [*H20d*]

(10b) *En el bosque había un panal de abejas, había una madriguera, había muchas cosas donde la rana podía estar.*

'In the forest there was beehive, there was a burrow, there were **many things where the frog could be.**' [*cS20c*]

In the latter instance, the narrator may refer collectively to **previously** identified entities and events to highlight their shared significance in the story, as in (10c) and (10d).

(10c) *And oddly enough, after looking in all these strange places where other animals have their homes and obviously not finding their frog, these animals chase them into water, which happens to be the home of the frog.* [*E20e*]

(10d)*A pesar de **todo lo que he la pasado**, sigue buscando a su ranita.*

    'In spite of **everything that has happened to him**, he keeps looking for his froggie.' [*S20d*]

Perhaps not surprisingly, all four examples in this section are from adult narratives, suggestive of the high level of thematic organization required by the encapsulating function of relative clause constructions, irrespective of a particular native tongue.

2.3. Coding Procedures and Summary of Functions

    We identified 516 relative clauses in our sample of narratives across the five languages.[16] Each relative clause was coded as to whether the head referent (HR) and the information expressed in the relative clause (RC) represented new or old information. The criterion we used in coding this distinction was adapted for fictional narratives, where all the events and entities referred to need to be verbally created by the narrator "from scratch." (In other forms of discourse some degree of prior familiarity with the entities and events referred to can often be assumed.) Accordingly, HR or RC information was coded as new if it was mentioned for the first time and old if it had been previously mentioned by the narrator.[17] Linguistic indicators of old and new information such as definite and indefinite articles were **not** criterial in coding this distinction. The linguistic encoding of the old-new distinction varied somewhat depending on the narrator's assumptions about the investigator-hearer's prior familiarity with the story and/or knowledge of, or access to, the story pictures, which could serve as a shared nonlinguistic referential context. This was particularly true of our younger narrators, who tended to rely more heavily on assumptions of shared knowledge in general. Thus in coding this distinction, the mentioned/not mentioned criterion took precedence over linguistic markers. This coding criterion also provided us with a useful independent measure of the narrator's assumptions about, and linguistic marking of, the old-new distinction.[18]

---

[16] Of this total, 512 were included in the functional analysis. The few excluded relative clauses were either incomplete or could not be classified according to our functional scheme. The total number of relative clauses produced by subjects in each age by language group is indicated in Table 2.

[17] In a few instances, entities were coded as old if they had a set-member or part-whole relationship to a previously mentioned referent. For example, the relative clause 'the tree on which a beehive hangs' [*G20f*] was coded as old information, since it had been previously mentioned that *a beehive hangs at the edge of the wood*.

[18] In coding the data the authors worked from the original English and German texts and from translations of the Hebrew, Spanish, and Turkish texts, which consisted of glosses of the relative clauses and pertinent surrounding text. In the latter case, the coding of old versus new information for the head referent and relative clause was provided by native or near-

Two major considerations constrained our application of the functional coding categories described in Section 2 to the relative clauses in our database. First, the new versus old status of the HR and RC was criterial in determining the four functions of situating new or old referents, of reidentifying an old referent, and of introducing a major protagonist (the SIT-NEW, SIT-OLD, REID, and PRES functions); but this distinction was not critical for the remaining functions — naming a referent, motivating an event, continuing the narrative, setting up expectations or summarizing over events (NAME, MOT, CONT, EXP, SUM). In the case of the continuation category (CONT), however, the invariably new information provided in the relative clause followed from its function. Second, a narrative function would quite often incorporate a more general discourse function, in which case the relative clause would be double-coded for both. For example, a referent might be reidentified (and so coded for REID) with the added purpose of motivating a main-clause event (and so coded for MOT) as in *the dog is limping... it looks like it got bit by a couple of the bees that were chasing him* [E20c]. Similarly, old referents might be reidentified (REID) for the purpose of summarizing their role in the story (SUM), or a referent might be named (NAME) with the aim of concealing its true identity (EXP) as in *They both hear something coming from behind the log* [E20b]. In every such case, the narrative function of the relative clause superseded its coding as a general discourse function. This coding decision was motivated by the principle that general discourse functions can be recruited to serve more specialized narrative purposes.[19]

Table 1 summarizes the taxonomy of functions used to code the relative clauses in our sample.

3. DISTRIBUTION OF RELATIVE CLAUSE USAGE ACROSS THE DATABASE: MORPHOSYNTACTIC FACTORS

This section describes the use of relative clauses across the age groups and languages in our sample. As shown in Table 2, there are significant

---

native speakers, since this part of the analysis required a review of the entire text.

[19] The authors initially coded the relative clauses for function for different languages independently, and then cross-checked each other's work in order to obtain an estimate of coding reliability and clarity of the functional coding categories. Problematic cases and discrepancies in coding were discussed and jointly resolved. The authors then independently coded all of the relative clauses from each language. Reliability of coding for the functional categories was determined for the entire data set by calculating the percentage of perfect agreement between the authors. For all languages, percent agreement fell within the 93% to 100% range.

TABLE 1
Summary of Relative Clause Functions[a]

HR	RC		General Discourse Functions
n/o	n/o	NAME	Names/identifies referent in lieu of available lexical item
n	w	SIT-NEW	Situates new referent in ongoing discourse scene
o	w	SIT-OLD	Situates old referent in ongoing discourse scene
o	o	REID	Reidentifies old referent
HR	**RC**		**Narrative Functions**
n	n	PRES	Introduces and presents a main story character
n/o	n/o	MOT	Motivates/enables a narrative event
n/o	n	CONT	Continues narrative with subsequent/consequent event
n/o	n/o	EXP	Sets up expectation about identity of upcoming object/event
n/o	n/o	SUM	Summarizes over old or upcoming objects/events

a. HR = head referent, RC = relative clause information, n = new information, o = old information

differences in the prevalence of relative clause use across the five languages, as indicated by two measures: the percentage of subjects in each age group who use a relative clause at least once, and the mean number of relative clauses produced by subjects who do use relative clauses. Most notably, Spanish and Hebrew speakers are more likely to use relative clauses and to use them more frequently at earlier ages than their counterparts in the other three languages.

TABLE 2
Relative Clause Use by Age and Language[a]

	3 yrs			5 yrs			9 yrs			Adult		
	%Ss	M	n	%Ss	M	n	%Ss	M	n	%Ss	M	n
En	17	1.5	3	25	1.5	4	50	2.0	13	100	6.5	64
Ge	8	2.0	2	17	1.0	2	67	1.5	11	92	4.5	48
Sp	50	1.5	10	55	2.0	12	100	3.0	36	100	11.5	139
He	17	2.5	5	67	1.5	13	92	3.5	37	100	4.5	51
Tu	10	1.0	1	50	1.0	6	40	2.0	8	90	5.5	51

a. Means are to the nearest 0.5, indicated by M. The total number of relative clauses produced in each age by language group is indicated by n. Ss = subjects (narrators).

Two of our findings for relative clause usage are to be expected. One is the fact that at least one 3-year-old from each language group spontaneously produced a relative clause. This finding accords with previous studies indicating that relative clauses are within range of the child's productive competence by at least this age, if not earlier (see Berman, 1985, for Hebrew; Ferreiro, Othénin-Girard, Chipman, & Sinclair, 1976, for Spanish; Slobin, 1986, for English and Turkish). Secondly, both indices show an expected developmental trend of increasing relative clause use with age across all languages.[20] However, the finding that relative clauses are not used with comparable frequency across the languages[21] is unexpected; one assumes that relative clauses constitute a comparable linguistic device across adult language use or in language development.

The notion that the morphosyntactic properties of a linguistic construction contribute to the relative ease or difficulty with which it is acquired is a cornerstone of acquisition research (Slobin, 1973, 1985a). These considerations are also commonly appealed to in accounting for differences in the relative ease with which a construction can be accessed or produced in online speech processing — both within and across languages (Bates & Devescovi, 1989). In this section, we consider crosslinguistic variations in the morphology and syntax of relative clauses which might account for developmental differences in the productive use of relative clauses across these languages.

The morphosyntax of relative clauses in the five languages in our sample can be compared along the following dimensions: (1) number of relative pronouns in the language (one versus many), (2) constraints on relative-pronoun agreement (none versus many), (3) relative clause word orders (canonical versus noncanonical), and (4) the position of the relative clause with respect to the head noun (postnominal or prenominal).

Spanish and Hebrew are similar in that both make use of a general relativizer, *que* and *she*, which does not require agreement with the head noun.[22] In addition to this all-purpose relativizer, Spanish speakers alternatively make use of a locative relative pronoun *donde* 'where' and, less frequently, *quien*

---

[20] An analysis of variance conducted on the mean number of relative clauses used by age and language shows a significant main effect for age (F (3,209) = 62.63, p < .001).

[21] An analysis of variance shows a significant main effect for language (F (4,209) = 8.03, p < .001), and a significant language by age interaction (F (12,209) = 3.62 p < .001).

[22] These all-purpose relativizers are morphologically related to complementizers which, like English *that*, may mark other types of subordinate clauses as well. The term "relative pronoun" is normally reserved for pronominal forms, typically morphologically related to interrogative and demonstrative pronouns, which have specialized uses in forming relative clauses (Keenan, 1985b).

'who' and *lo que* 'what'. Hebrew differs from Spanish in the additional use of a resumptive pronoun copy of the head NP, which is obligatory when the relativized element is an oblique object, optional when it is a direct object (in accusative case), and generally disallowed when it is a sentence subject (see Chapter IIID, Section 4.4 for details). Word order in both Spanish and Hebrew relative clauses is the same as in simple clauses.

English and German, by contrast, make use of a wider variety of relative pronouns. In addition to the general relativizer *that*, English speakers commonly use animate *who*, as well as *which*, *what*, and *where*. In German, unlike English, relative pronouns require agreement in gender, number, and case with the head noun, except for *wo* 'where' and *was* 'what', which are undeclined. In both German and English, prepositions are commonly used in combination with a relative pronoun in nonsubject relatives (e.g., *in which*, *about which*). The word orders of relative clauses in these two languages do not mirror the canonical order of main clauses. English nonsubject relatives have an OSV order which deviates from canonical SVO word order (*they had a frog/the frog they had*). In German, relative clauses, like other subordinate clauses, require verb-final word order, which differs from the SVO word order of main clauses.

Turkish relative clauses present a somewhat different set of morphosyntactic features (see Slobin, 1986; Chapter IIIE). There are three basic relative clause types. One is a locative construction, in which a locative inflection (LOC) and a relativizer particle (REL) are suffixed to the noun designating the location of the head noun, as shown in (11a).

(11a) **Locative Relative:**

masa-da-ki baklava

table-LOC-**REL** baklava

'the baklava that is/was on the table'

The other two types differentiate between subject (SR) and nonsubject relatives (NSR). Each makes use of special nominalizing particles and, like other subordinate clauses in Turkish, they require nonfinite verb forms. Nonsubject relatives additionally require that the subject of the embedded clause appear in the genitive as the possessor of the nominalized verb. Both types deviate from canonical SOV word order: Subject relatives have OVS order and nonsubject relatives have SVO order, as shown in (11b) and (11c).

(11b) **Subject Relative:**

şüt-ü iç-en kedi

milk-ACC drink-SR cat

'the cat that drinks/drank the milk'

(11c) **Nonsubject Relative:**

kedi-nin iç-tiğ-i süt

cat-GEN drink-NSR-POSS milk

'the milk that the cat drinks/drank'

With the exception of Turkish, the relative clauses in our language sample are positioned after the head noun, i.e., they are postnominal, as is typical for verb-medial languages. Turkish relative clauses are prenominal, occurring before the head noun, as is more common in verb-final languages (Keenan, 1985b). German also allows limited use of prenominal relative clauses for main clause subjects (although none were produced by the German narrators in this study).

These contrasts suggest varying degrees of processing complexity in the number and type of constraints involved in online production of a well-formed relative clause. Relative clauses which entail fewer constraints on well-formedness are presumably not only easier to produce but also involve fewer advance commitments in sentence planning and lower risk of error — factors which Bates and Devescovi (1989) propose enhance the attractiveness of a grammatical construction as an expressive option.

The relative complexity of relative clause formation in these languages correlates with differences in their frequency of use by the children in our study. Relative clauses occur earlier, and more often, in Spanish and Hebrew, which have the fewest constraints on relative pronoun choice, word order, and agreement, than in the texts of the English-, German-, and Turkish-speaking children. German relative clauses, which involve the most agreement requirements in our sample, occur less frequently at age 5 years than in either English or Turkish, and they are used more sparingly by the 9-year-olds.

Additional support for the importance of morphosyntactic factors is provided by the types of relative clauses that are most commonly used by younger children. In contrast to the adults, the 3- to 5-year-olds show a preference for relative clauses that involve the fewest processing constraints in their language. English 3-year-olds, for example, are more likely to produce subject relatives which have canonical word order and can occur without a relative pronoun (e.g., *There's **a mouse coming** [E3f-3;9]*). Young German narrators, on the other hand, are more likely to use relative clauses with an undeclined relative pronoun: mostly *wo* 'where' but also *was* 'what' (e.g., *Die* *haben noch **ein Fluß** gefunden **wo die rauskönnen** 'They found **a river where they could get out**' [G5e-5;0]).* In Turkish, the locative relative is more commonly used at earlier ages than the more complex subject and non-subject relatives (***Elindekini** atıyor [T3a-3;6]* 'He throws **the thing that is in his hand**'). This preference accords with Slobin's (1986) finding that the Turkish locative relative is the first type to be acquired by children.

It is not until 5 years in English, and 9 years in German and Turkish, that these early preferences decline to under half the relative clause types used. Even then, undeclined *wo* relatives still account for 45% of German children's relative clauses at 9 years of age. Moreover, nonsubject relatives involving use of prepositions together with relative pronouns (e.g., *a deer **on which he gets caught***), which are arguably the most complex relative clause constructions in English and German, are used only by adults in these two languages (with the exception of one German 9-year-old occurrence).

Spanish and Hebrew children, like their counterparts in the other three languages, also show increasing differentiation in the range of relative clause types used with age, particularly in the increasing use of nonsubject relatives. Spanish narrators begin to make use of the relative pronouns *lo que* 'what' and *donde* 'where' only at age 9 (with one occurring at age 4), as alternatives to the general relativizer *que*. Interestingly, in Hebrew, errors in use of the resumptive pronoun required by relativized oblique objects and locative objects are still considerable at 9 years, but nevertheless children do produce these more complex constructions quite widely at that age (Chapter IIID, Section 4.4). This suggests that the availability of a general relativizer (*she*) and lack of word-order constraints combine to make relative clauses an accessible expressive option for Hebrew-speaking children. In principle, high rates of error, or violations of the required constraints, might just as well be risked in English, German, or Turkish, in a similar effort to make wider use of this construction. However, the absence of a general relative marker together with constraints on relative clause word order in these languages appear to lead instead to more conservative uses of this construction overall with few errors.

Morphosyntactic complexity is thus one factor which contributes to the productive accessibility of relative clauses in development. Whether, and to what extent, it plays a role in adult use is still to be considered. But it is clear that morphosyntactic variations alone do not account for crosslinguistic differences in the frequency of relative clause use. While Spanish adults use relative clauses at roughly twice the rate of the other adults (with a mean of 11.5), Hebrew adult use is among the lowest in our sample (4.5). Moreover, while Hebrew use is comparable among adults and 9-year-olds, the mean number of relative clauses used in the other four languages more than doubles between these two age groups. These disparities in overall frequency demand further investigation of the **functions** which these constructions perform within and across the different languages.

4. ADULT RELATIVE CLAUSE USAGE IN FIVE LANGUAGES: A FUNCTIONAL ANALYSIS

The taxonomy of relative-clause functions presented in Section 2, like other crosslinguistic taxonomies of its kind, demonstrates that relationships between linguistic form and function are not merely arbitrary, nor are they wholly determined by language-particular variations in grammatical form. However, while a comparable linguistic device can serve similar functions across languages, the range and distribution of these functions may differ from one language to the next. In this section, accordingly, we address sources of variability and constancy in **adults'** deployment of these functions across the languages in our sample — as a basis for crosslinguistic comparison of endstate usage and for analysis of developmental trends from one age group to the next.

The uses of relative clauses in our adult narratives are shown by language in Tables 3a and 3b, divided according to general discourse functions and narrative functions, measured (1) by the percentage of narrators who use a relative clause at least once for each type of function (%Ss), and (2) by the total mean number of relative clauses used for each function (M).

The percentage of adults shown in Tables 3a and 3b as having encoded a given function shows that some relative clause functions occur more frequently than others in the adult narratives. By this measure, three general crosslinguistic patterns can be discerned: (1) uncommon functions used by one-fifth or fewer of the adults in all languages: NAME and SUM; (2) common functions used by more than a third of the adults in all languages: SIT-NEW and REID; and (3) language-dependent functions that show differential patterns of use across languages: SIT-OLD, PRES, MOT, CONT, and EXP. Each of these three general crosslinguistic findings will be discussed in turn.

The infrequent adult use of the naming function (NAME) follows from the fact that, for mature speakers, this usage is typically prompted by the uncertain or ambiguous identity of a referent (e.g., as in *Where did you get that thing you're wearing?*), by failure to access an appropriate lexical item, or by a language's lack of a word for a particular referent (e.g., *things that go bump in the night*). Since the entities in this story are fairly commonplace, and their referents commonly lexicalized in these languages, one would expect low rates of naming uses among adult speakers across the languages.[23] The

---

[23] By the same token, one might predict higher rates of naming uses in specialized technical domains where few referents are lexicalized in the language and must therefore be con-

TABLE 3a

Adult Uses of General Discourse Functions by Language

	NAME		SIT-NEW		SIT-OLD		REID	
	%Ss	M	%Ss	M	%Ss	M	%Ss	M
English	20	.20	60	1.10	30	.30	70	.80
German	8	.16	41	.66	16	.16	58	.75
Spanish	16	.16	66	1.60	58	.91	50	1.25
Hebrew	0	0	41	.41	16	.16	58	.75
Turkish	10	.10	60	1.90	40	.50	40	.90

TABLE 3b

Adult Uses of Narrative Functions by Language

	PRES		MOT		CONT		EXP		SUM	
	%Ss	M	%Ss	M	%Ss	M	%Ss	M	%Ss	M
English	50	.50	50	1.20	50	1.00	60	.90	20	.30
German	16	.16	25	.50	58	1.08	25	.25	8	.16
Spanish	66	1.08	66	1.25	75	2.30	58	2.30	16	.25
Hebrew	75	.83	41	.58	41	.83	25	.33	16	.25
Turkish	20	.20	80	1.10	0	0	20	.30	0	0

equally infrequent uses of relative clauses for summing over prior and prospective upcoming entities or events in the story (SUM) rests, in part, on similar grounds. These referents are typically unique to this particular story, (e.g., *animals that they met on the way, obstacles that he had behind him*), and thus must be constructed in lieu of an existing lexical term. In addition, the SUM function of relative clauses fulfills a highly conventionalized narrative purpose. As such, it is not only an optional component of narratives, but one that is infrequently called for (at the outset or end of a story). It may also be readily fulfilled by other linguistic means (e.g., 'In the forest all kinds of strange adventures befell him' [*H20i*]).

The need to provide contextually relevant information about new referents (SIT-NEW) and to reidentify previously mentioned referents (REID) is, on the other hand, frequently called for in extended discourse of all kinds.

structed. This appears to be the case, for example, in Prince's (1981) analysis of written academic prose compared to informal conversation among friends. One would also expect higher rates of naming uses of relative clauses in memory-impaired adults, such as anomic aphasics, who frequently fail to access common lexical items and must resort to identifying common referents via a more complex construction. Examples of naming responses for common objects from an anomic aphasic, cited by Gardner (1974, p. 76), are suggestive: "this is a kind of bag you use to hold something" for *wallet*, and "the part of my body where my hands and shoulders ... no, that's not it" for *elbow*.

Both functions, it will be recalled, serve the listener's basic need to know who or what is being talked about. Accordingly, one would expect these functions to be commonly used by mature speakers, especially in discourse contexts which involve reference to a number of different entities, as does this story.

The mixed patterns of relative clause use for certain functions (SIT-OLD, PRES, MOT, CONT, and EXP) have several different sources. In what follows we discuss typological, language-particular, and speaker-based sources of variability in the use of these functions across these languages.

4.1. Absence of Continuative Relatives (CONT) and Prevalence of Motivating Relatives (MOT) in Turkish

The absence of continuative relatives (CONT) in Turkish stands in striking contrast to the prevalence of this category in the other four languages. This finding can be attributed to three typological features of Turkish: (1) the prenominal placement of relative clauses, (2) the nonfiniteness of relative clause predicates, and (3) SOV word order.

Recall that a continuative relative clause serves to relate an event that **follows upon** the occurrence of an event related in the main clause — in a temporal, causal, or some other logical sense (e.g., *The bees start chasing the dog, who ran away* [E20a]). This interpretation is implicitly signaled by, and dependent on, the relative ordering of the two clauses and the tense/aspect of the predicates in the two clauses (*start chasing, ran away*). Notice, for example, that reversing the order of the two propositions in this example as two juxtaposed independent clauses reverses the temporal order of events, and hence, the causal nature of the original event (compare *The bees start chasing the dog. The dog ran away* — to: *The dog ran away. The bees start chasing the dog*). Additionally, an alteration of the tense/aspect of the relative clause predicate to a temporally unbounded event (*The bees start chasing the dog, who is running away*) signals temporal simultaneity rather than temporal or causal sequentiality (Chapter IVA). The construction also requires that the relative clause modify the **object** or other clause-final argument of the main clause, which then plays the role of **subject** in the relative clause. The relative clause is therefore postposed to the end of the main clause, a feature which Lambrecht (1988, p. 328) argues is necessary for a continuative reading.

Given these features of the continuative type of relative clause, it is clear that Turkish does not have such a construction at its disposal. The prenominal position of relative clauses and the SOV word order of Turkish prevent clause-final relative clauses, while the nonfinite status of the relative clause predicate in subject and nonsubject relatives prevents event sequencing (e.g., 'The bees **the running-away dog** start-to-chase'). These typological constraints often permit no more than an interpretation of temporal **simultaneity** between two events, as in (12a).

(12a) *Köstebek de bir ağaç kovuğunu inceleyen Osman'a doğru bakıyordu.*

    mole TOPIC a tree hole investigate:SUBJ.REL Osman.at directly was.looking

    'The mole was looking straight at **Osman, who was investigating a hole in the tree.**' [*T20e*]

Interestingly, the typological features which preclude continuative relatives in Turkish seem to favor motivating relatives (MOT). As shown in Table 3b, MOT relative clauses are the commonest of all the relative clause functions for Turkish adults (80%), and they are more commonly used in Turkish than in any of the other languages.

Recall that in motivational relative clauses, the information in the relative clause provides the cause or enablement condition for the event in the main clause — in effect, a continuative relative in reverse. Unlike continuatives, however, the motivating relative clause is not restricted to any one argument in the main clause: It can express information about any clause argument, and its interpretation depends more on an inference drawn between the main clause and relative clause propositions than on their relative ordering. In the Turkish examples of a nonsubject and a subject relative in (12b) and (12c), the relative clause depicts an event that **precedes** the main clause event. Although both relative clauses precede the main clause verb, this interpretation is based on inference rather than on the relative ordering of the two clauses:

(12b) *Daha sonra çocuk yerde gördüğü bir deliğe eğiliyor.*

    then boy ground.in see:NONSUBJ.REL a hole.DAT leans

    'Then the boy leans over **a hole that he sees/saw in the ground.**' [*T20b*]

(12c) *Kovanın içinden çıkan arılar bunlara saldırıyor.*

    hive's interior.from emerge:SUBJ.REL bees them attack

    '**The bees that come out of the hive** attack them.' [*T20g*]

Relative clauses which modify the subject of the main clause can also depict a character trait or temporary state of the subject referent, which motivates or enables the action in the main clause. The Turkish examples in (12d) and (12e) illustrate this:

(12d) *Daha sonra uyuya kalan Osman olacaklardan habersizdi.*

    later sleep.to remain:SUBJ.REL Osman what.will.become.of ignorant.was

'Later **Osman, who was fast asleep,** had no knowledge of what was to come.' [*T20e*]

(12e) *Baykuştan korkan Tim bir kayanın tepesine çıktı.*

owl.from fear:SUBJ.REL Tim a rock's top.to ascended

'**Tim, who was afraid of the owl,** climbed up onto a rock.' [*T20c*]

Note that the nonfinite status of the verb in Turkish relative clauses does not pose the problem for MOT relatives that it does for CONT relatives. Rather, it is particularly well-suited to motivational uses of relative clauses since they typically involve events which are durative or temporally unspecified in nature, as in examples (12b) through (12e) above.

4.2. Use of Presentational Relatives (PRES) Across Languages

The use of presentational relatives across languages is widely claimed to be motivated by a general pragmatic principle, defined by Lambrecht as "a universal constraint on the introduction of pragmatically nonrecoverable discourse referents in sentence-initial subject (or topic) position" (Lambrecht, 1988, p. 322). Lambrecht argues that the presentational relative functions to "introduce a new referent in non-initial sentence position and to express a pro-position about this new referent in the same minimal sentential processing unit" (*op cit*). For example, in such classical fairytale openers as *Once upon a time there was a little boy who had a frog and a dog* [*E20i*], the relative clause allows the speaker to assert some further information about a newly introduced topic.

This "universal" motivation for this use of a relative clause finds support in our crosslinguistic data. As shown in Table 3b, presentational relatives are used in all five languages to introduce one or more of the major story characters. However, we also find striking differences across these languages in the degree to which speakers make use of this device. Whereas this function is one of the most commonly used by Hebrew (75%) and Spanish (66%) narra-tors, it is one of the least commonly used by German (16%) and Turkish (20%) narrators, with English (50%) somewhere in between. These crosslinguistic differences remain unilluminated by a general appeal to what universally motivates their use.

Crosslinguistic differences in the use of presentational relatives were also found by Bates and MacWhinney in a 1978 study comparing Italian and English (discussed in Bates & Devescovi, 1989). In a simple picture descrip-tion task, Italian speakers were more likely to use a presentational relative clause, such as 'There's a monkey that's eating a banana', compared to English speakers. While English speakers also used this type of construction (e.g., *There's a monkey eating a banana*), they more commonly used simple declarative sentences with indefinite sentence subjects, such as *A monkey is eating a banana.*

Bates and Devescovi (1989) point to an important typological difference between these two languages in interpreting these findings. They base their proposal on crosslinguistic work by Li and Thompson (1976), which shows that languages can be typologically classified along a continuum with respect to their encoding of discourse topic and sentence subject. From this perspective, Italian is a relatively "topic-dominant" language, as it exhibits a greater tendency to reserve grammatical subject for established or given discourse topics.[24] English, on the other hand, is a more "subject-dominant" language in that it tends to assign the subject role to the highest or most agentlike semantic argument of the verb whether or not it is the discourse topic. Bates and Devescovi propose that Italian speakers are more likely to favor using devices such as presentational relatives, as they allow speakers to introduce new and important referents in nonsubject position. By the same token, presentational relatives would be less strongly favored in English, as new indefinite subjects are more acceptable, though somewhat less common than definite subjects "due to a universal albeit imperfect correlation between subjecthood and topicality in all natural languages" (Bates & Devescovi, 1989, p. 238).

These typological considerations can be brought to bear on our findings in a number of ways. First, one would expect that Spanish, which is typologically akin to Italian, would similarly make more frequent use of presentational relatives.[25] The comparatively frequent use of presentational relatives in Hebrew would follow from its typological similarities to Spanish (and Italian): Like these languages, word order can be varied for discourse-pragmatic (topic-focus) purposes. Moreover, the general relativizer *she*, like Spanish *que* and Italian *che*, provides a highly accessible way of topicalizing new referents via a relative clause — i.e., immediately making a main clause argument the topic of a relative clause predication.

The languages in our sample which, in contrast to Spanish and Hebrew, lack an all-purpose relativizing particle — English, German, and Turkish — tend to prefer alternative presentational constructions, as shown in examples

---

[24] At the extreme end of this continuum, new indefinite subjects are ungrammatical, as in Tagalog.

[25] A closely related finding is reported by Kail and Hickmann (1992) in analyzing how children speaking French, another Romance language, introduce referents in the frog story. They note that "some of the 9- and 11-year-olds' uses of indefinite determiners occurred in presentative utterances of the type *C'est un X (qui ...)* 'it's an X (who) ...'," and they point out that "such utterances are commonly used in French to introduce referents within narrative discourse and they clearly differ from the youngest children's labeling" (p. 86).

(13a) through (13f).

(13a) *There's a boy and a dog in a room and they're both looking at a frog....* [E20c]

(13b) *It's late at night, and a boy has a frog in a jar in his bedroom.* [E20g]

(13c) *Es geht hier um 'nen Frosch 'nen Jungen und 'nen Hund zunächst und der Junge hat 'nen Frosch in 'nem Glas...*

'It's about a frog, a boy, and a dog to begin with, and the boy has a frog in a jar.' [G20b]

(13d) *Also ich möcht jetzt die Geschichte erzählen von dem kleinen Hund, der Frau Frosch, und dem Jungen. Die beiden, die wohnten in trautem Heim zusammen.*

'Okay, I would like now to tell the story about the little dog, Mrs. Frog, and the boy. The both of them, they lived in a cozy home together.' [G20c]

(13e) *Küçük bur çocuk köpeğiyle birlikte, ıı, bir kurbağası varmış.*

'A little boy together with his dog, um, his frog existed [=there were].' [T20a]

(13f) *Bir odada bir oğlan çocuğu, sevimli bir oğlan çocuğu köpeği ve kurbağasıyla beraber bir hayat sürüyor.*

'In a room a boy, a cute boy, together with his dog and his frog, lead a life.' [T20g]

As one would expect, the bulk of these constructions avoid introducing these new, major-protagonist characters in sentence-initial position; and they make liberal use of presentational verbs (e.g., 'exist', 'have'). However, none exploit the option of topicalizing these new referents via a relative clause. Instead, prepositional phrases such as *boy with a dog*, *frog in a jar* are the preferred noun-modificational device as opposed to relative clauses such as *boy who had a dog* and *frog that was in a jar*. Furthermore, clause connectors such as *and they're* and *und der* 'and he' in examples (13a) and (13c) and left-dislocation like *die beiden, die wohnten...* 'the both of them, they live...' in example (13d), provide alternative ways of immediately topicalizing the newly introduced referents via pronominal forms and asserting a relevant new proposition about them; in short, they function very much like a (simple) subject relative pronoun in a presentational relative. These commonly used functional equivalents of presentational relative constructions suggest that it is the greater overall accessibility of relative clause constructions in Spanish and Hebrew that facilitates their more frequent use as presentational devices.

However, none of the above typological considerations explains why Turkish and German uses of presentational relatives are comparatively rare —

in contrast to, say, English. Indeed, the explanation for this infrequent use is, we think, quite different for these two languages. In the case of Turkish, typological factors play an important role in the infrequency of presentational relatives and in accounting for what might appear to be a counterintuitive finding: More relative clauses are devoted to introducing (or "situating") new discourse referents in Turkish than in any other language in our sample. Consider, next, Turkish adults' use of situating new, and often minor, characters in discourse (the SIT-NEW function) compared with use of the presentational relatives (PRES) discussed so far in this section. It turns out that we need to explain this in quite different terms than will be seen to account for the infrequent use of presentational relatives by German adults under the heading of "rhetorical" factors.

We have seen that postposed-postnominal relative clauses allow for continuative relatives in SVO languages, contrasting with their absence in Turkish (Section 4.1). The postnominal position of relative clauses in these other languages also plays an important role in the discourse-pragmatic function of presentational relatives, because the sequence MAIN CLAUSE — RELATIVE CLAUSE allows the speaker to **first** introduce a new referent in nonsubject position and **then** to assert a proposition about it. The "naturalness" of this order of information has two sources: (1) it exploits the topic-comment order characteristic of an asserted main clause proposition; and (2) it respects the tendency that given information — or that which the listener already knows or can assume — generally precedes new information. This information structure is schematically represented in (14a).

(14a)	This story is about		a frog		that was kept in a jar.	
[	MAIN CLAUSE	[	head	]	RELATIVE CLAUSE	]
[	TOPIC		FOCUS-TOPIC		COMMENT	]
[	GIVEN		NEW-GIVEN		NEW	]

The corresponding presentational construction in **Turkish,** with a preposed, prenominal relative clause, presents this information in reverse order — or what amounts to a mirror image of this construction in an SVO language. The following is an example of a presentational relative used by one of our Turkish narrators:

(14b)   'It [story] deals with **a frog that (someone) put in a jar.**'
               Kavanoz içine koyduğu kurbağasıyla ilgilenmektedir.

     jar into put:NONSUBJ.REL   frog.with   is.interested

[	RELATIVE CLAUSE	[	head	]	MAIN CLAUSE	]
[	COMMENT		TOPIC-FOCUS		TOPIC	]
[	NEW		NEW-GIVEN		GIVEN	]

The preposed-prenominal relative clause in (14b) appears to present an "unnatural" order of information flow: The prenominal relative clause requires that the proposition or comment about the new referent precedes its being introduced as a new topic, and its preposed placement presents the most newsworthy information — a frog that was kept in a jar — before what is presumably given information for the listener, that this is a story about something. We suggest that this infelicitous order of information conveyed by the structure of a Turkish presentational relative accounts for its infrequent use as device for introducing the main characters of a narrative.

Along the same lines, one might predict that Turkish relative clauses would in general prove fairly infelicitous for introducing new referents into discourse. Indeed, one might venture an even more specific prediction: that relative clauses introducing new referents would more commonly occur in **non-sentence-initial** position and **following** an established subject-topic argument, as opposed to the order exemplified in (14b). This alternative type of construction in Turkish is illustrated in (14c) below, where Osman is an established topic-subject, and the rock is being introduced for the first time (from the SIT-NEW category):

(14c) *Osman **orada bulunan kayalığ**-ın üzerine çıktı.*

Osman there.at be.found:SUBJ.REL rock's top.to ascended

'Osman climbed up **a rock that was located there.**' [*T20e*]

However, neither of these predictions is borne out by our findings. As shown in Table 3a for the SIT-NEW category, more relative clauses are used on average to introduce new referents in Turkish than in any other language in our sample. Moreover, both construction types, exemplified in (14b) and (14c), are commonly used in introducing new referents: in fact, sentence-initial relative clauses are somewhat more common.

These findings, however, follow from a more considered analysis of Turkish in discourse-pragmatic terms. First of all, Turkish differs from the other languages in our sample in that it is an SOV (rather than an SVO) language. Thus, what has been hitherto referred to as the focus, non-sentence-initial, and nonsubject position is the **preverbal** slot in Turkish — or the argument that occurs just before the main verb. As one would predict, the newly introduced referent in both types of relative clause constructions —

frog in (14b) and *rock* in (14c) — occur in preverbal, or focus position. Second, while the topic/subject argument commonly occupies sentence-initial position in Turkish, subject arguments can also be omitted, since they are obligatorily marked on the verb. The absence of a topic argument — or zero-topic marking — occurs when the topic is most predictable or readily recoverable from the immediate discourse context (i.e., can be treated as a given).[26] This is shown in (14b) where the given topic information — that this is a story about something — is not realized by a topic/subject argument, but is marked on the verb. Thus, this example actually has the structure: [relative clause-[O] V]. Finally, the preposed-prenominal relative clause in this presentational construction effectively prevents a brand-new indefinite referent (a frog) from being introduced in sentence-initial/subject position. The one other presentational relative used by a Turkish adult, shown in (14d), also has this structure.

(14d) ***Kovuğun içindeki kurbağasına baktı.***

    jar's interior.at:LOC.REL his.frog.at looked

    'He looked at **his frog that was inside (a) jar**.' [*T20e*]

This brings us to the question of why relative clauses are more frequently used in Turkish for introducing all but the main characters of the narrative. The question also remains of why sentence-initial relative clauses are as common as, possibly slightly commoner than, sentence medial relative clauses. These two phenomena are, we think, pragmatically related: Sentence-initial relative clauses are principally used in Turkish to **shift** the topic of discourse from an already established and maintained topic — or what is referred to as a "continuous" topic — to a new, pragmatically salient topic (Herring, 1990)[27]. Examples (14d) and (14c) are contrastive in this respect. The sentence-initial relative clause in (14d) shifts the listeners' focus to the new and major referent, the frog, and relegates the already given and continuous topic of the boy to zero-marked status. In (14c) the boy, Osman, is

---

[26] Omission of subject arguments for zero-topic marking occurs in Hebrew and Spanish as well, and Turkish is even more flexible than these two languages in its use of word-order variation for discourse-pragmatic purposes (see Chapter IIIo, Table 1, and further discussion in Chapter IVc, Section 2).

[27] Herring distinguishes between "continuous" topics, which encode given information, and "shifted" topics which may encode either new or given (reactivated) information. She also distinguishes the use of focus position for "contrastive" focus, which encodes given or implied information, versus "presentational focus," which encodes only new information, and she queries claims for "natural" principles of information flow, given the important role of basic word-order type in predicting the strategies which languages use to encode these different types of information.

maintained as continuous, active topic/subject of the narrative, and the new, minor (inert) referent, the rock, is introduced in nonsubject/focus position. This pragmatic word-order strategy for contrastively marking a continuous, established topic and a shifted new topic further helps to explain why presentational relatives like (14b) are so rare at the outset of the story: because the most active and important referents of the narrative have not yet been established. Indeed, this is the principal function of constructions that begin with a semantically empty introductory phrase such as 'There existed an X that...'. This subtle but important distinction between syntactic devices which are used solely for presentational focus and those that serve a topic-shifting function, both of which can introduce new referents in discourse, accounts for an otherwise puzzling finding: While relative clauses are rarely used at the beginning of a story to introduce the main characters, they are used with great frequency for introducing secondary story characters and other new referents with low pragmatic salience.

We are now in a position to compare Turkish and Spanish in this respect. Both these languages use relative clauses that modify an argument in focus position for both presentational focus and for topic-shifting. But Spanish uses a post-verbal placement strategy whereas Turkish uses preverbal placement. This dual function is illustrated by Bates and Devescovi, who point out that the English sentence *Here is the monkey that is eating a banana*, with a **definite** head noun in focus position, can only be interpreted as having a contrastive focus; that is, the monkey eating a banana is being distinguished from some other monkey who is not. However, the same sentence in Italian which, like Spanish, uses a postverbal strategy (*Qui c'e` la scimmia che mangia una banana*), can also be used simply to "place [an] established (definite) referent into discourse focus" — that is, it has "a more general topic-marking function" (p. 239). We would make the more specific claim that this argument is being marked as a shifted topic (in contrast to an already established but continuous one). This brings us to another possible affinity between Spanish and Turkish: Both show a somewhat higher tendency to use relative clauses to situate or resituate old, or previously established referents (SIT-OLD). We suggest that this trend may reflect the "retopicalizing" function that relative clauses can serve in these languages.

We return now to the question of why our German adult narrators rely so little on a construction that is, after all, readily available in German storytelling. We suggest that this traditional fairytale opener — made classical by the Brothers Grimm — is part of the solution, rather than the puzzle. The circumstances in which our German narratives were collected involved extended and personal contact between the investigator-hearer and the adult respondents. This more familiar and casual context seems to have engendered the use of less formal, more colloquial German in "getting started" on the narrative task. These story beginnings are frequently marked by conversational fillers like *ja* 'yeah', *also* 'okay', *also jetzt* 'okay now', and *gut* 'fine', as well as informal warm-ups like 'Good, okay we're now in a room, a boy is sitting on a chair' [*G20e*], and 'Okay, it is evening and we see here the little Moritz — I'm calling him now the little Moritz' [*G20d*]. We think this is why German adults are the only ones who show a considerable **decrease** in the use of presentational relatives compared with the 9-year-olds (half as many), whereas there is no corresponding disparity between English and German 9-year-old use (33% in both languages) of presentational relatives. [28]

4.3. Rhetorical Patterns of Relative Clause Use

In Section 4.2 we briefly addressed the issue of alternative constructions in accounting for why English, German, and Turkish speakers show lower use of presentational relatives, and suggested that the greater constraints imposed by relative clauses in these languages, combined with the existence of alternative constructions, in part explains the differences we found between these three languages compared with Spanish and Hebrew. This kind of analysis raises the broader question of why languages might differ in their preferences for using alternative, although functionally equivalent structures in expressing a given function.

As we have seen, factors other than what a linguistic construction **can** be used for in a language will affect how often it is used and, indeed, whether it will be used at all in a given discourse context. The relative formality or informality of the speech context is one such factor, as we have suggested in the case of German adult presentational uses. Other factors which may play a role in language use — particularly in the use of syntactically complex, enriched or elaborated speech — are individual and cultural differences in rhetorical style. Labov (1972), for example, found more frequent uses of what he termed "evaluative syntax" in the oral narratives of Black adolescents from Harlem than among White adolescents from a working-class control group in Inwood. This measure was quantitatively defined in terms of an array of syntactic devices which "have the effect of suspending the action of the narrative...indicat[ing] to the listener that this has some connection with the evaluative point [of the story]" (p. 374).

---

[28] This account raises the more general problem of findings which might be artifacts of differences in methods of data collection. As noted in Chapter IB, the procedures were by and large similar across the sample, but there are clearly differences in style on the part both of narrators and of investigators in different countries and languages.

Labov's finding is interesting in light of our data on the EXP function of relative clauses — the use of relative clauses to set up an expectation in their listener for suspenseful effect. In contrast to the other relative clause functions, EXP uses show striking individual differences, as well as a possible cultural effect of rhetorical style. As shown in Table 3b above, this function was used by more narrators in English (60%) and Spanish (58%) than in the other three languages, where it was used by no more than 20-25% of the narrators. Moreover, Spanish speakers seem to make greater use of the EXP function than any other language group, with a group mean frequency of 2.3 — more than twice that of English (.90).

Closer inspection of these data reveals that the bulk of Spanish adult EXP uses are accounted for by only a few individuals. Four of the 12 Spanish adults provide 82% (23/28) of the total EXP uses, at a rate of about six EXP relative clauses per narrative, whereas the mean number among other subjects who use this function is about 1.5. Moreover, three of these four narrators come from the Chilean subgroup and only one from the European half of our Spanish-speaking adult subjects.

We do not find comparable individual differences in any other language. In English, per subject EXP uses are uniformly low, as in the remaining three languages — though they are used by rather more of the subjects. In fact, EXP uses across these languages tend to show up at the same key points in the story, where a suspenseful turn of events reveals the true identity of an object. This occurs when what appear to be the branches of a tree turn out to be the antlers of a deer, and when the familiar sound heard from afar turns out to be the long lost frog (see the EXP examples in Section 2.2.(8)). However, this same device can be used in artful ways throughout the narrative for suspenseful effect. For example, one Spanish narrator uses multiply-embedded relative clauses to build suspense about the dog's first encounter with the beehive:

(15a) *Su perro empezó a jugar con **una cosa que no había visto nunca y que le parecía muy bonita: una especie de balón que estaba colgado de un árbol y que el perro pensaba que era un balón.***

'His dog began to play with **a thing that he had never seen before and that seemed very pretty to him; a kind of balloon that was hung from a tree and which the dog thought was a balloon.**' [*S20a*]

Another type of EXP function, also common in our Spanish narratives, is used in Labov's "evaluative" sense: The narrative is momentarily suspended, and the narrator heightens the suspense of the story by parenthetically commenting on what might have been or could be coming, as in (15b) and (15c).

(15b) *Incluso llegan a tener **una aventura que podía haber acabado muy mal** porque las abejas persiguen al perro*

'They even go so far as to have **an adventure that could have ended very badly** because the bees chase the dog.' [*S20e*]

(15c) *Ya parece que está cerca el momento en que él cree encontrar a su ranita...*

'Already it seems that it is near **the moment in which he thinks to find his frog...**' [*cS20d*]

The high rate of EXP uses by our Spanish subjects cannot be attributed to aspects of the formal or structural characteristics of relative clauses or to the general typological features of Spanish. If this were true, one would not expect to find differential rates of use of the EXP function between the two Spanish subgroups. Rather, we suggest that the divergence may stem from differences in narrative style, much like those operating in the use of the PRES function in Hebrew adult narratives. The highly rhetorical nature of some of the adult Chilean narratives extends beyond the more frequent use of EXP relative clauses, and may reflect a more elaborated narrative style — due to either individual preferences or differences in the elicitation setting. In English, as well, individual differences may be at play. Those English subjects who produced EXP relative clauses also produced more embellished narratives in general. Thus, the effects of rhetorical style appear to operate throughout a narrative — whether they are due to cultural or individual predilections — and are not limited to the use of any one structure or form. This generalization is confirmed by the exercises in "contrastive rhetoric" emerging out of examination of different ways speakers of different languages perform the frog-story task (see Chapter VB, Section 3).

Bates and Devescovi (1989) raise just this concern about their crosslinguistic findings as well. They query whether the more frequent use of presentational and continuative relatives by their Italian compared with their (American) English-speaking subjects could be due to a "cultural" difference. In order to rule out this possibility, they compared results from their original English-speaking undergraduate subjects to a more highly-educated group of graduate students and postdoctoral fellows. Finding no appreciable difference from their previous results, they concluded that the crosslinguistic differences they found were indeed "based on linguistic/psycholinguistic differences between the two languages, and not on differences in culture or educational level" (p. 252). That is, they conclude that their findings are best accounted for by differences in the type of functions served by relative clauses **within** each language. Where they found no comparable evidence for crosslinguistic differences, as in the case of continuative relative clauses, they have recourse to processing factors such as "accessibility" and "commitment." More specifically, they propose that "if a surface form serves a wider range of functions in one language (or one individual), then it will be called into service

more often. The more often it is used, the lower its threshold of activation"
(p. 252). In other words, the greater frequency of occurrence of presentational
relatives in Italian might simply enhance the availability of this construction
for other functions, such as the continuative.

This line of argument is, however, less compelling with respect to our
comparative findings on Spanish and Hebrew. We have no clear grounds for
believing that relative clauses are more productively accessible in Spanish
than in Hebrew, or that these two languages differ in the range of functions
that relative clauses can serve. Yet these two languages represent the highest
(11.5) and the lowest (4.5) adult mean uses of relative clauses, respectively
(see Table 2). And there is another, no less striking divergence between them:
While both languages show similar use of presentational relatives, they differ
markedly in their use of continuative relatives. As shown in Table 3b, in
Spanish, the **continuative** function has highest frequency of use (along with
EXP), with a mean frequency of 2.3 — more than twice that of any other
language; Hebrew, in contrast, uses continuative relatives far less, with a
mean frequency of only 0.83, more like that of English (1.0) and German
(1.08). This divergence is remarkable when one considers that both presentative and continuative relative clause uses deploy similar syntactic forms in
both Spanish and Hebrew, in contrast to the other three languages. This
makes it difficult to argue that one is more accessible than the other on morphosyntactic grounds. As Lambrecht (1988) points out, both types are unique
in that the sequence MAIN CLAUSE — RELATIVE CLAUSE can readily be
replaced by the same sequence expressed as two independent clauses. The
difference is that continuative relatives are akin to two **coordinated** clauses
connected by *and, and so,* or *and then,* whereas presentative relatives are akin
to two merely **juxtaposed** clauses, as can be seen by comparing (16a) and
(16b).

(16a) CONT Relative versus Coordination:

And then all the bees start chasing the dog, who runs away.

[And all the bees start chasing the dog, **and (so, then) he runs away**].
[E20a]

(16b) PRES Relative versus Juxtaposition:

Once upon a time, there was a little boy who had a frog and a dog.

[Once upon a time, there was a little boy; **he had a frog and a dog.**]
[E20i][29]

---

[29] In fact, in German, these alternative constructions in (b) are often morphologically and
syntactically indistinguishable: The subject relative pronoun *der* 'who' and verb-medial order
of the presentational relative clause mimics the colloquial use of the demonstrative pronoun

This analysis suggests a somewhat different question: Why might languages differ in their preference for using one or the other type of relative clause construction, or both, over these alternative options? Here one cannot readily claim, as Bates and Devescovi do for Italian versus English, that a well-motivated, and thus frequently used function enhances the use of this device for other functions, where no such special motivation is clear. We are still left with the question of why the frequent use of presentational relatives in Hebrew does not enhance its "availability" for the continuative function.

One highly suggestive answer to this question is that languages, on the whole, exhibit different "rhetorical norms" in their preferred patterns of clause-linkage (Bar-Lev, 1986; and see, too, the concluding section to Chapter VB). Bar-Lev's study of this crosslinguistic issue combines with Lambrecht's insights into the PRES and CONT constructions to explain why Hebrew might differ from Spanish, and appear more like German in its use of continuative relatives clauses. Bar-Lev argues that the discourse structures produced by speakers of varying languages exhibit different rhetorical norms in their preferred patterns of clause-linkage: Specifically, in their preference for coordination versus subordination versus "parallelism" (or Lambrecht's juxtaposition). Of particular interest, for our purposes, is his finding that in the retellings of the same original narrative, Spanish, Arabic (a Semitic language, as is Hebrew), and American-English speakers showed strikingly different clause-connecting patterns: 48% of the Spanish clauses were linked by subordinating conjunctions, as compared to only 8% in English and 5% in Arabic. By contrast, 49% of the English and 46% of the Arabic clauses were linked by coordinating conjunctions, as compared to only 22% of the Spanish. Bar-Lev's comments on these findings are particularly suggestive. Whereas the Spanish preference for subordinating conjunctions revealed a "heavy use of *that* and *because*," Arabic and English discourse structures showed a consistent "preference for flat, serial clause-connection, symbolized by connectors of continuation such as *so* or *and*" (p. 237). This latter preference, Bar-Lev argues, is characteristic of Semitic rhetorical structure in Biblical as well as Modern Hebrew. These findings might lead one to predict that where a coordinated and subordinated construction present a comparable expressive option, as Lambrecht has shown for the CONT relative, the former may be the preferred clause-linking device in Hebrew and English.[30]

---

der 'he/this one' in the juxtaposed independent clause. Thus these pragmatically equivalent structures are formally ambiguous with respect to these two interpretations. Schuetze-Coburn (1984) attempts to resolve this by proposing that the relative clause in these presentational uses nevertheless retains the "linking intonation" of a subordinated rather than an independent demonstrative clause.

[30] Besides, Hebrew-speaking adults may have been affected by the normative, schoolbook

The existence of rhetorical norms is nevertheless not easy to explain. These linguistic practices cannot be attributed to "cultural" factors in any simple sense. After all, as Bar-Lev points out, the discourse structure of American English turns out to be more similar to Arabic than to Irish (which showed a stronger preference for subordination). At the same time, typological affinities do not play an obvious role either; otherwise one might expect Hebrew and Spanish to be more similar than either is to English. Nor do levels of usage, or of education, appear to play a straightforward role in determining such preferences. The proposal of Bates and Devescovi would thus seem the most plausible, namely, that the use of certain types of constructions may have the force (and underlying mechanisms of) a linguistic "habit."

We have nonetheless suggested two caveats to this claim. In some cases, cultural differences in rhetorical conventions may be operating in the more frequent use of a particular linguistic device, as could be true for the EXP uses of some of the Spanish narrators. However, in line with Labov's research, one might expect this type of finding in situations where there are considerable cultural or subcultural differences in the functions and practice of **oral narrative** per se. In particular, one might expect subcultural differences in the use of (oral) narrative devices whose function, as with EXP uses, is arguably more rhetorical than purely referential in nature — or devices that are used to further heighten and engage a listener's attention. By the same token, one might expect a **reduced** effect of "culture" in the case, say, of undergraduate compared with more advanced university students, all of whom have alike been inducted into the linguistic practices of academic discourse.

Secondly, while one linguistic habit may well simply generalize to another, one is hard-pressed to account for why this sometimes happens, but not always. In the case of Hebrew, it appears that the frequent use of a highly accessible construction, and a functionally well-motivated one, does not generalize to other functions. Rather, Modern Hebrew appears to be a language which is divided in its choice of constructions for introducing new referents, on the one hand, and for linking together related events in narrative, on the other. And this might possibly relate to a situation of conflict between colloquial usage and more classical norms in the language (Berman, 1987b; Ravid, in press), confounded by the difference between storytelling and expository forms of discourse (Chapter IIID). At the same time, and in marked contrast

---

interdiction against the use of continuative clauses. This might have led them to prefer, in the storytelling context of our narrative data-base, the more classical, Biblical device of paratactic clause-linkage, compared with the subordinate constructions which Modern Hebrew speakers (or writers) favor more in expository than in literary style — and see, further, Chapter IIID, Section 4, and Chapter VB, Section 3.4 in this connection.

to this state of affairs, it may be that the ubiquitous use of relative clauses in Spanish is partially driven by a more general "taste for" subordination as a favored rhetorical device across different discourse functions in the language.

We have speculated at some length on the question of what might be involved in being a proficient user of a particular grammatical construction (relative clauses) as part of the repertoire of the rhetorical norms and preferences of the different languages in our sample. These are both themes which are taken up in the conclusions to the book (Chapters VA and VB). We return now to the question of **becoming** a proficient user of the particular form/function relations involved in the use of relative clauses in a narrative discourse setting.

5. CHILDREN'S USE OF RELATIVE CLAUSES: DEVELOPMENTAL TRENDS

The use of these various relative clause functions by children reveals a strikingly similar order of emergence across languages. Tables 4a and 4b give the percentages of narrators who encoded a given function at least once, at each age level (collapsing across languages). Table 4a summarizes the development of general discourse functions and Table 4b summarizes narrative functions. The functions presented from left to right — across both parts of Table 4 — can be seen to reflect two developmental dimensions: the relative order in which the functions emerge, and the relative pace at which they develop.

As shown in Table 4, the general discourse functions of relative clauses generally precede the more specialized narrative functions in development. Moreover, within and across these two general categories, particular functions emerge at different points in time, and develop at different rates. These findings are not simply reducible to relative degrees of difficulty in the **grammatical** encoding of these functions. Rather, on the whole, they reflect increasing levels of discourse competence and narrative organization required for the use of these functions.

In what follows, we discuss these cognitive-pragmatic developments for the general discourse (Section 5.1) and narrative functions (Section 5.2), with special attention to the development of the continuative and motivating functions of relative clauses in narrative (Section 5.3).

TABLE 4a
Percentage of Narrators Using a Function At Least Once by Age:
General Discourse Functions

	NAME	SIT-NEW	REID	SIT-OLD
3 yrs	8	6	5	3
5 yrs	8	15	8	1
9 yrs	12	36	27	8
Adult	10	53	55	32

TABLE 4b
Percentage of Narrators Using a Function At Least Once by Age:
Narrative Functions

	PRES	MOT	CONT	EXP	SUM
3 yrs	5	1	0	0	0
5 yrs	8	1	7	0	0
9 yrs	36	15	6	6	3
Adult	46	51	46	37	12

5.1. Development of General Discourse Functions

Early uses of all the general discourse functions suggest that these **referential** functions are potentially accessible as early as 3 years. Nevertheless, some functions appear to be more accessible earlier and/or progress more rapidly towards adult rates of use in the order: NAME < SIT-NEW < REID, SIT-OLD.

Of these relative clause functions, the NAME function is arguably the least discourse-sensitive, as it is motivated by a speaker-based need to merely identify a referent. One would expect it to be the most accessible to children, as it is comparable in function to the naming uses of a simple lexical item. The fact that it is the earliest and most frequently used function in the frog story as told in five different languages underscores its relative cognitive and pragmatic simplicity. The finding that the NAME function shows virtually no development reflects the early consolidation of the function of denomination (Section 2.1.(1) above). Yet there are subtle cognitive differences between children and adults in what typically motivates use of a relative clause for this purpose (compare the examples in (2a) and (2b) with those in (2c) and (2d) above). Whereas children will use this more complex construction in lieu of knowing, or being able to readily access, a lexical item (e.g., beehive, log), adult uses are more often motivated by uncertainty about what the best or most appropriate lexical label might be for a certain referent.

In contrast to the naming function, the three other referential functions provide, in addition, contextually relevant information about an identifiable referent. In so doing, they require that the speaker be sensitive to the listener's need to know something more about who or what is being referred to. However, the different rates at which these functions develop underscores differences between the cognitive-pragmatic abilities that underlie their use.

Recall that the SIT-NEW function serves to anchor or situate a brand-new discourse referent in the immediate discourse context. As such, it requires only that the speaker provide new contextual information of immediate or present relevance. The progressive use of this function between 3 and 5 years shows children's emerging ability to coordinate speech acts that merely identify and introduce novel referents in a scene (e.g., *Bees. Here there's bees.* [*E3c-3;4*]), with the need to say something of contextual relevance about them (*The bees are going to sting them* [*E3j-3;10*]) and to do so within the same minimal processing unit (*Now there's **bees going around** [E4l-4;11]*); *He's looking at all **the bees flying out of the honey**.* [*E3g-3;9*]).

The REID function is both cognitively more demanding and pragmatically more sophisticated. This reminding function requires that the speaker recall information of past relevance about a referent, typically following at least once topic shift. It also requires an awareness of what is nonrecoverable information for the listener and therefore in need of reactivation. These added dimensions — of memory for things said or given, and attendant awareness of what bears repeating for the listener — account for the progressive development of this function between age 5 and 9. Indeed, it is not until 9 years that REID uses are deployed **throughout** the narrative, motivated by a need to reidentify earlier mentioned referents which reappear after a complete topic shift. Prior to this age, the REID function is used primarily for reidentifying the lost frog found at the end of the story — a use that is highly motivated by this particular story. In the following exception, produced by a Hebrew 5-year-old, we see an attempt at an adult use of this function, following a "near" topic shift (from the frogs to the boy and dog):

(17) *Ve hacfarde'im histaklu aleyhem milemala, ve - ve hacfardea haktana xikta lahem al haxol, ve hem halxu. Ve **hacfarde'im she alu**, hem histaklu ve hem samxu.*

'And the frogs looked at them from up top, and - and the little frog waited for them on the sand, and they [=boy and dog] went. And **the frogs that went up**, they looked and they were pleased.' [*H5k-5;9*][31]

The finding that the SIT-OLD function is the latest to develop does not reflect a higher cognitive/pragmatic demand so much as the relative marginality of its discourse function. SIT-OLD uses, like REID uses, provide background information about an already established discourse referent, and typically have the quality of an afterthought. The difference is that the information provided in SIT-OLD relative clauses is new or unfamiliar, and serves to update the listener about the current status or situation of a referent. What makes these uses sophisticated is their parenthetical quality: Either the speaker forgot to introduce or situate a referent on first mention and/or s/he now wishes to update the listener about its current status as a reinstated topic. In either case, its use indicates the speaker's continual awareness of the need to provide contextually relevant information about a referent, an awareness which the younger children may reserve only for first mention. The earliest uses of this function are, in these respects, immature. In the following two examples from 3-year-olds, the relative clause contains information of current relevance about a reinstated topic, the dog. However in the first instance, the narrator seems to have failed to connect the dog mentioned earlier with the presently seen one; and in the second, the relative clause functions alone as a simple picture description device.

(18a) *Ve yesh **kelev she noveax ve holex**.*

'And there's **a dog who barks and goes**.' [*H3e-3;7*]

(18b) *El perro **que le está mirando al lado**.*

'**The dog who is looking at him on the side**.' [*S3h-3;10*]

These contrast with a mature SIT-OLD use by a 9-year-old narrator, where the jar left empty by the frog in an earlier scene is among the things searched in a later scene:

(18c) *Ve az hem hitxilu lexapes oto mikol hacdadim, betox kutonet, betox náalayim, betox **hacincenet she haya sham**.*

'And so they began to search for it on all sides, inside a shirt, inside shoes, inside **the jar, that (it) was there**.' [*H9d-9;5*]

---

[31] That this is still an incipient and quite immature use of this function is shown by the unnecessary, and even ill-formed repetition of the subject pronouns *hem* 'they' following this center-embedded clause, as well as the fact that the main clause of the sentence with the relative clause repeats the same verb *histaklu* 'looked' as the preceding sentence.

5.2. Development of Narrative Functions

The narrative functions of relative clauses also reveal an emergent order of development: PRES > MOT , CONT > EXP , SUM. This order clearly reflects increasing levels of narrative organization: from the need to introduce important referents, to expressly linking together successive events, to relating events as episodes of significance to the unfolding of the narrative as a whole.

5.2.1. Development of the PRES function

Like early uses of the SIT-NEW function, early PRES uses also indicate an ability to go beyond speech acts that "merely" identify a salient new referent (*There's a frog* [*E3g-3;9*]) by expressing something more about it (*A frog...A frog jumping out* [*E4h-4;8*]), and to do so, increasingly, in the same syntactic package, or single processing unit (*Esto es **una rana que coge el perro** 'This is **a frog that the dog takes**'* [*S3j-3;11*]).

The main difference between the two functions, SIT-NEW and PRES, which our coding distinction was meant to capture, is that PRES uses have the more specialized function of establishing the most important referents of an ensuing discourse, such as the main protagonist(s) of a narrative. As such, developments in the PRES function need to be evaluated in terms of the child's overall developing ability to use mature linguistic means to **establish and maintain** reference to the major participants in a discourse. This not only calls for an ability to linguistically signal new versus established topics at the clause level — by means like indefinite versus definite articles with full nouns (*a boy* versus *the boy*), pronominal forms (*he*), and omitted subject/topics — it also entails an ability to linguistically structure the flow of a narrative with respect to an established topic once introduced, for example, by keeping an established referent as the subject of subsequent predications.

A few instances of relatively mature use of the PRES function appear around 5 years of age, along with the relevant aspects of pragmatic-narrative discourse organization. Prior to this age, PRES uses, like early SIT-NEW uses, function primarily to identify and describe salient new referents in isolated speech acts — a use more akin to simple picture description. It is not until age 9 that PRES uses function as an integral part of a linguistically mature system for establishing and maintaining reference to the major characters in the narrative. By this age, presentational relatives are not only consistently used to introduce important new referents in nonsubject/focus position via indefinite full nouns, but they are also used to set up and maintain an already introduced referent as an established topic/subject of subsequent predications.

These concurrent developments in narrative structure and in use of relative clause constructions are exemplified in the linguistic means used to establish the three most important referents of the narrative (boy, dog, frog) in the story beginnings of narrators aged 3 to 9. In the examples in (19) below, the linguistic forms used to encode the first mention of each of these topical main characters are highlighted in boldface.

3 Years

(19a) *Look at **this frog**. When **he's** [=boy] sleeping and his frog getting out. Look what happened to the guy [=?]. **He** [=dog] licked on his face...* [E3a-3;1]

(19b) *There's **a dog**. There's **a frog**. And there's boots. **He** [=boy] wake up!* [E3e-3;1]

(19c) *Esto es **una rana** - que coge **el perro**. Y éste está aquí, sentado - en este sitio. Éste está durmiendo. Éste está aquí en esta jaula, y ésta - y éste está durmiendo con su perro.*

'This one is **a frog** that **the dog** catches. And this one [=boy] is here seated. This one [=boy?] is sleeping. This one [=frog] is here in this cage and this one [=frog] and this one [=boy] is sleeping with his dog.' [S3c-3;7]

5 Years

(19d) ***The dog's** looking at **the boy**. **The frog** - and he's looking - at the frog too. They're in bed.* [E5g-5;9]

(19e) ***The frog** and **the boy** have **a pet dog**. And they like the pet dog. When the boy and the dog fell asleep the frog crawled out.* [E5c-5;3]

(19f) *Well it's about **a little boy** that has **a pet frog** and **a dog**. And then the dog puts um his nose in the frog's jar. And then when the boy's sleeping...* [E5h-5;10]

9 Years

(19g) *Well there was **a boy**. And he had **a frog** and **a dog**. He loved his frog very much, and maybe his dog did too.* [E9c-9;6]

(19h) *Also **ein Junge** hat **einen Frosch** gefangen ... und am Abend nee ... der ist im Glas eingesperrt. Und am Abend bekucken die den noch und **der Hund**, der beschnuppert den.*

'Okay, **a boy** caught **a frog** ... and at night, no ... who/this one is kept in a jar. And at night they/those ones look at him/this one and **the dog**, he/this one sniffs at him/this one. [G9e-9;11]

(19i) *There's **a boy who has a pet frog** and **a pet dog**. And one night, after he goes to bed, the frog sneaks out and he wakes up and it's gone.* [E9k-9;11]

Examples (19c), (19f), and (19i) show the use of a PRES relative at each of these ages. However, these uses differ in a number of subtle but relevant ways. All of these story beginnings illustrate an important development in the child's linguistic encoding of the major referents of the narrative: The referent most often introduced and established by mature speakers as most important to the narrative — the boy — is the one most likely to be encoded as an already established, or familiar referent by the youngest narrators. Note that in the examples at 3 years, the boy is introduced via pronominal forms (*he, this one*), whereas at 5 years, a noun with a definite or indefinite article is more firmly established as the topic of a subsequent predication (*the dog...and he*; *the frog and the boy...and they*). However, although the boy is introduced by means of a presentational relative clause in (19f), the narrator does not maintain him as a topical referent in the following sentence, but switches to the dog as topic instead. It is not until 9 years of age that the boy is consistently introduced as a new, and major, character, and is also subsequently maintained as the central figure in the narrative.

These findings reflect something other than a general insensitivity at earlier ages to what is shared and unshared knowledge between listener and speaker. Although the younger children often fail to appropriately mark the major characters in the story as new when they first mention them, they do encode their **relative status** by different linguistic means. They typically focus on the most active and/or visually salient character(s) in the opening scenes — the frog and the dog — as the major new referents, while treating the main protagonist of the story — the boy, and to some extent his dog — as established or given. This relative weighting typical of the younger children gives way in the older groups of children to a more equal treatment of all three characters as new and important, with mature narrators giving more weight to establishing the main protagonist — the boy — as the major referent of the ensuing narrative. These findings suggest a progressive reorganization in terms of the relative weight accorded to which referents are construed as new and central to the plot, as well as a developing ability to structure the discourse in advance in terms of these characters. Thus, while PRES relative clauses are used to introduce important referents throughout this period (19c, 19f, 19i), their presentational function undergoes a significant development: from being used in isolated utterances as a simple picture-description device, to serving for introducing new referents, to an integrated use as a mature linguistic means for establishing and maintaining the most major, most consistently active participants in the narrative.

5.2.2. Development of the MOT and CONT functions

Age-related advances in use of motivating and continuative relative clauses — the MOT and CONT functions — reveal rather different developmental patternings. In contrast to the PRES and general discourse functions, the MOT and CONT functions of relative clauses encode a temporal or causal relation between two events which could be construed as conceptually independent. As such, they require the ability to expressly relate the events and states encoded in the main and relative clauses. As shown in Table 4, above, early uses of these functions emerge between ages 5 and 9, with considerable increases occurring between 9-year-olds and adults.

There are a number of qualitative differences between the emerging uses of these functions, and their use by adults. MOT relative clauses are noteworthy in that they may precede or follow the main clause, as in the following examples:

(20a) Postposed MOT Relative Clause:

Cogieron una ranita que les dió la rana.

'They took **a little frog that the frog gave them.**' [*S9b-9;2*]

(20b) Preposed MOT Relative Clause:

The boy, who had climbed a tree, searched in it. [*E9i-9;10*]

The earliest uses of MOT relative clauses are invariably postposed, that is, they **follow** the main clause. The linearly additive nature of this construction presumably facilitates the early use of relative clauses for this function since, unlike the preposed MOT relative clause, a MOT which follows the main clause requires no advanced sentence-planning commitments. Such postposed MOT uses are also akin semantically, and in clause ordering, to the subordinating conjunction ([event 1] *because* [event 2]), which is already in use by 3 years. Indeed, the earliest use of a MOT relative clause by an English 3-year-old, in (20c), occurs within a postposed because-clause. Moreover, the relative clause in this early instance reidentifies an event previously mentioned by the narrator. As such, it illustrates the recruitment of a referential function for a narrative purpose.

(20c) *Now they're mad and they might sting him because I think he's **the one who knocked all the bees down.*** [*E3g-3;9*]

A few uses of preposed MOT relative clauses first appear at 9 years, along with purposive motivations ([event 1] *in order that* [event 2]), as in example (20b) above. However, only adult narrators refer to psychological states as motivating causes. Not only do adults make frequent use of MOT clauses in general, but they deploy postposed clauses in order to motivate events in subsequent conjoined clauses, thereby depicting a chain of related events. These adult MOT uses are illustrated below:

(20d) *...while the dog is running away from all the bees, who seem to be quite angry*, because the dog broke their beehive. [*E20c*]

(20e) *...und gleichzeitig jagen die empörten Bienen dem Hund hinterher, der jetzt plötzlich nicht mehr so mutig ist sondern zusieht daß er wegkommt.*

   ' *...and at the same time the enraged bees chase after **the dog, who is suddenly now not so brave**, but rather sees to it that he gets away.*' [*G20b*]

The use of CONT relatives also develops between 9 years and adulthood. They first occur as a variant of PRES relatives: In these uses, the main clause introduces an important new referent's appearance on the scene, and the post-posed relative clause which follows it continues or advances the narrative by immediately making it part of the story action, as in the examples in (21).

(21a) *Salió **un loro que le tiró al niño**.*

   'There came out a parrot **who threw the boy**.' [*S5d-5;4*]

(21b) *Ve hayta sham kaveret **dvorim she hakelev nora raca litfos otam**.*

   'And there was a hive of bees that **the dog terribly wanted to catch them**.' [*H9h-9;7*]

There are a few instances at 9 years where the CONT relative begins to be used to express an action-result sequence, but these remain somewhat ambiguous as to their antecedent-consequent interpretation:

(21c) *Ve hakelev xipes ota **bacincenet she hu nixnas eleha im harosh**.*

   'And the dog searched for it in **the jar that he went into.it with his head**.' [*H9c-94*]

(21d)*Ve hakelev hivriax **dvorim she yacu ve xazru lanexil dvorim shelahem**.*

   'And the dog frightened away **bees that came out and went back to their hive**.' [*H9j-9;8*]

In (21c) the dog's searching in the jar is ambiguous as to whether it pre-cedes or follows the event of his putting his head into the jar — inter alia, because, as noted earlier, Hebrew has no means of marking the grammatical aspect of anteriority on its verb forms. Similarly in (21d), the bees' coming out of the hive can be interpreted as an event that preceded or resulted from the dog's frightening them. Again, as noted in Section 2, (21c) was coded as motivating and (21d) was coded as continuative, since that is the order of events suggested by the storybook. But in fact, the adult narrators are alone in using CONT relatives that have an unambiguous antecedent-consequent interpretation of the kind considered to be prototypical of this function, as in (21e) and (21f):

(21e) *...and the deer stops abruptly,* **which causes the boy to lose his balance.** [E20f]

(21f) *...y ellos, agradecidos, le regalan uno de sus sapitos a* ***Juanito, que se va muy contento...***

'...and they, pleased, give one of their little frogs to **Juanito, who goes off very content...**' [cS20d]

5.2.3. Development of the EXP and SUM functions

In contrast to the MOT and CONT functions, the EXP and SUM functions require something other than an ability to relate two consecutive events temporally or logically. Rather, these narrative devices require that narrators take an omniscient or atemporal perspective on events and that they use this perspective in revealing or concealing at appropriate moments their knowledge of events and the significance of these events to the story. From a purely formal standpoint, these devices are often of the same type that are used by 3-year-olds to simply name a referent. Thus, the late development of these narrative functions of relative clauses, which emerge at only 9 years of age, cannot be attributed merely to inadequate mastery of the construction as such.

Support for the claim that an advanced kind of cognitive ability underlies these uses can be found in earlier occurrences of relative clauses that are noticeably immature in these respects. The following example from a Spanish 3-year-old has some components of an EXP function in that the identity of a referent to be revealed is described from the point of view of the boy in the story as he peers over a log:

(22a) *...para ver si hay* **alguien que tenga un cuchillo y le mate.**

'...to see if there is **anyone who might have a knife and would kill him.**' [S3h-3;10]

Although this sequence is suspenseful in its effect, the narrator has failed to make use here of her knowledge of the plot; the expectation raised is never resolved, but remains as a curious non sequitur. In contrast, this same point in the story is skillfully handled by a 9-year-old by means of an EXP relative clause:

(22b) He heard **something coming from behind the log** [singsong]. *And he looked over the log and um his frog was with a female frog.* [E9f-9;8]

Similarly, an element of the SUM function can be seen in the following example produced by a Hebrew 5-year-old who is introducing the main protagonist, the boy, at the outset of the story (in its PRES function):

(23a) *She ha -* **hayeled she yaca** *ve haya lo kelev ve hem ra'u bacincenet ve hayta sham cincenet ve hem ra'u ba cfardea.*

'That [=when] the - **the boy that** [=when?] **went out**, and he had a dog and they saw in the jar, and there was a jar there, and they saw a frog in it.' [*H5k-5;9*]³²

The relative clause in this example makes use of the narrator's foreknowledge of the event that the boy goes out in search of his lost frog. However, this subsequent plot development is inappropriately revealed at this point, again, leading to a non sequitur as the narrator backtracks to set the opening scene in the same utterance. In spite of these apparent counterexamples, it is thus not until 9 years of age that the SUM function is used at appropriate points in the story for its canonical purpose in narrative discourse, as in the following two examples.

(23b) *Ve hem xipsu bekol xor, bekol makom she efshar limco...*

'And they searched in **every hole, in every place that it is possible to find...**' [*H9h-9;7*]

(23c) *Baktıkları her yerden çeşitli hayvanlar çıkıyor.*

'**From every place they look,** various animals come out.' [*T9g-9;9*]

5.3. Language-Dependent Factors in Development

In the foregoing discussion, we have suggested that discourse-pragmatic factors, independent of particular native language, play a major role in determining the order of emergence of the nine relative-clause functions we identified. The robustness of this claim is underscored by the fairly stable order of emergence of these functions in the productive use of relative clauses by children of comparable ages, as discussed in Sections 5.1 and 5.2. However, as with adult uses of relative clauses (Sections 4.1 to 4.3), one would expect that children's emerging usage, too, would be affected by language-particular factors relating to the relative accessibility of relative clause constructions and other typological considerations. Below we consider how the development of relative-clause functions interacts with and is affected by processing, rhetorical, and other crosslinguistic factors.

Table 5 summarizes our findings on the use of relative clauses by age, function, and language. The most striking finding reflected in Table 5 is that Spanish- and Hebrew-speaking children seem, overall, to recruit relative clauses for a range of functions earlier, and with greater frequency, than their counterparts in the other three languages.³³ More specifically, the general

---

³² This use of the subordinator *she* 'that' is ambiguous between its function as a relative-clause marker and as a truncated version of the temporal conjunction *kshe* 'when' (see Berman, 1985).

³³ One notable exception is the use of the NAME function which, for reasons discussed in

discourse functions are expressed as early as age 3 years by Spanish and Hebrew children (the SIT-NEW, SIT-OLD, and REID functions occur in the youngest texts in both languages), and these continue to develop between 5 and 9 years, generally in advance of their use by English-, German-, and Turkish-speaking children at these ages. Except for an isolated use of the SIT-NEW function by two English-speaking 3-year-olds, children in these three languages show no instances of the general discourse functions until age 5 (and even then only one Turkish child with a single use for each of SIT-NEW, SIT-OLD, and REID). In other words, the general discourse functions of relative clauses are used only sporadically in English, German, and Turkish until age 9 years, whereas they show a steady and continuous development from age 3 up in Spanish and Hebrew.

We suggest that the differential rate and frequency of relative clauses for the general discourse functions derives from three interrelated factors: (1) the morphosyntactic complexity of relative clauses in each language, (2) the existence of alternative forms for expressing the same functions, and (3) the means of event conflation in each language. Below, we address each of these in turn.

Spanish and Hebrew, as noted in Section 3, pose the fewest constraints on accessibility: Both languages have a nondeclinable relativizing particle and relative clauses show the same (flexible) word order as do simple clauses, so demanding few additional processing constraints in their production. We suggest that use of a relative clause for the discourse functions discussed here provides an added benefit that alternative constructions in these languages do not — the opportunity to delay long range commitment in the expression of meaning, an option which we believe children, as well as adults, are likely to take advantage of.

Speakers of Spanish and Hebrew, like speakers of any language, have a number of **noun-modification** devices to choose from in formulating reference, including: prepositional phrases, adjectives, and genitives, as well as relative clauses. What is important in Hebrew and Spanish is that all these noun-modification devices occur postnominally (Slobin, 1989). Relative clauses are therefore consistent with the placement of noun-modification devices in these languages in general, and this may enhance their attractiveness. Besides, comparatively speaking, they also "buy the speaker time" in

---

Section 5.1, shows no development across ages and languages in our sample. This function is therefore excluded from the present analysis.

TABLE 5a
Percentage of Child Narrators Using a Relative Clause Function
at Least Once, by Language and Age:
General Discourse Functions

	NAME	SIT-NEW	SIT-OLD	REID
3 yrs				
English	0	16	0	0
German	8	0	0	0
Spanish	16	8	8	16
Hebrew	0	8	8	8
Turkish	10	0	0	0
5 yrs				
English	8	0	0	0
German	8	0	0	0
Spanish	0	36	0	18
Hebrew	8	33	0	16
Turkish	20	10	10	10
9 yrs				
English	0	25	0	16
German	8	8	0	25
Spanish	16	58	16	25
Hebrew	25	50	25	66
Turkish	10	30	0	0

online formulation of meaning, a strategy which Bates and Devescovi (1989) claim that speakers tend to maximize in their production of speech. As soon as Spanish- and Hebrew-speaking children are able to produce relative clauses, it is to their advantage to use them over other devices for noun modification. When commitment to the expression of meaning is at stake, an unvarying relativizer allows for a delay in this commitment, since it leaves the speaker with numerous options as to what can follow, while preserving the "speed, coherence, and well-formedness" of the utterance (p. 230). Speakers of English, German, and Turkish do not have this option, owing to the additional constraints on the production of relative clauses in their language (relative pronoun choice, word order changes, and so on). In fact, in these languages relative clauses may impose more processing difficulties than their functional equivalents (adpositional phrases, genitives, and adjectives), and so the latter may be more viable options for speakers in expressing certain discourse functions.

The finding that the general discourse functions emerge early in the narratives of Hebrew- and Spanish-speaking children shows that the functions

TABLE 5b
Percentage of Child Narrators Using a Relative Clause Function
at Least Once, by Language and Age:
Narrative Functions

	PRES	MOT	CONT	EXP	SUM
3 yrs					
English	0	8	0	0	0
German	0	0	0	0	0
Spanish	16	0	0	8	0
Hebrew	8	0	8	0	0
Turkish	0	0	0	0	0
5 yrs					
English	16	8	0	0	0
German	0	0	8	0	0
Spanish	0	0	18	0	0
Hebrew	25	0	8	0	0
Turkish	0	0	0	0	0
9 yrs					
English	33	8	0	8	0
German	33	8	0	0	0
Spanish	75	25	8	25	0
Hebrew	25	33	25	0	8
Turkish	10	0	0	0	10

themselves are indeed accessible, where the morphosyntactic complexity of relative clauses may be prohibitive for child speakers in languages like English, German, and Turkish. One would therefore expect to find that these children use alternative linguistic means, such as the noun-modification devices noted above, to encode the same information. The following analysis of how the situating function of relative clauses (SIT-NEW) is variously expressed by our young narrators is illustrative.

In the frog story, the appearance of a tree with a hole in it represents one component of a sequence of events in the evolving plot. It is one of the many places that the boy looks in search of his missing frog, and the place from which an owl flies out, thereby causing the boy to fall to the ground, and on to the next adventure. There is thus good reason to mention this particular location. In our texts, this simple locative proposition — that there is a hole in a tree, that the tree has a hole in it — is commonly expressed by a SIT-NEW relative clause (e.g., *Hayeled xipes betox xor she haya ba'ec* 'The boy searched inside a hole that was in the tree' [*H9b-9;2*]). Between ages 5 and 9, there are seven instances of SIT-NEW relative clauses which express this particular proposition: three at age 5 years (two in Hebrew and one in Turkish) and four at 9 years (two in Hebrew and two in Spanish). However, there are no such instances found at this point in the English and German child texts. Rather, these speakers encode this proposition by means of alternative noun modificational devices: (1) prepositional phrases (*a hole in the tree, in a tree, a hole*), (2) compounding (*in a treehole*), and (3) adjectival modifiers (*in a hollowed tree*). Alternatively, some speakers choose to express the appearance of the tree and the hole in two separate clauses (*the little boy climbs up a tree and looks into a hole [E9k-9;11]*). These same preferences hold true for the adult descriptions as well. Of the seven relative clause encodings of this situation in our adult sample, six are from Hebrew, Spanish, and Turkish adults (two per language), one from German (*...und kommen denn an einen Baum wo ein Loch drin ist [G20h]* 'and come then to a tree where a hole inside is'), and none in English.

This type of analysis highlights an important aspect of the interaction between productive accessibility and function not emphasized in the discussion of structural factors in Section 3. The relative accessibility of a form depends not only on its morphosyntactic complexity, or the relative ease with which it can be produced or acquired, but is also affected by the number and type of alternative forms available in the language that can readily perform the same function. In this particular case, the prepositional phrase, *a hole in a tree*, is a preferred choice among English child speakers, whereas their German counterparts make use of all the above-mentioned alternatives, with a marked preference for compounding at 9 years. Systemic factors of this kind may be contributing to the comparatively low rate of relative clause use in German at all ages. They may also be important in explaining distributional differences, within and across languages, in the types of information relative clauses are used to encode.

Another systemic influence we believe to be operating in the use of the general discourse functions of relative clauses is the means of event conflation in a language. This idea, proposed by Talmy (1985, 1991; see Chapter III0), proposes that languages can be classified as verb-framed or satellite-framed, based on the way in which information is distributed between a main verb and its supporting elements, or satellites. Verb-framed languages like Hebrew, Spanish, and Turkish, conflate movement and direction in the verb, with manner expressed by an optional satellite, whereas satellite-framed languages like English and German conflate movement and manner in the verb and express direction in verb satellites. In narrating a story which involves frequent change of location, as does our frog story, satellite-framed languages can easily express this in verb satellites, while verb-framed languages are more limited in their choices for elaborating direction of motion. As Slobin has suggested (1991, in press-a, in press-b; also see Chapter VB), speakers of verb-framed languages may devote more attention to setting up the static locations of objects and events than will speakers of satellite-framed languages. This is of direct consequence for two of the general discourse functions of relative clauses, SIT-NEW and SIT-OLD, which are often used in describing the locations of objects in a scene. The early emergence of these functions in Hebrew and Spanish is therefore not surprising in this regard. Turkish, also a verb-framed language, shows more consistent use of these functions earlier than we find in English and German, starting at 5 years, and reaching greater overall frequency at age 9. We suggest that the morphosyntactic complexity of relative clauses in Turkish is responsible for the relative delay in their use of the SIT-NEW and SIT-OLD functions compared with Hebrew and Spanish speakers.

The narrative functions in Table 5 also show comparatively earlier and more frequent expression in Spanish and Hebrew. Although there are occasional uses of the MOT function at 3 and 5 years in other languages, 9-year-old Spanish and Hebrew speakers use this function far more than the English and German speakers, while no Turkish 9-year-olds do so at all. Additionally, the CONT function appears to emerge earlier among Spanish-speaking children (several 5-year-olds use it), and occurs with equal frequency among Hebrew- and Spanish-speaking children by age 9 years. Finally, Spanish-speaking children stand out with respect to their use of the PRES and EXP functions at age 9 years, where all the other languages show either a much lower frequency of use, as in the PRES function, or virtually no use at all, as in the EXP function.

We attribute the apparent advantage of Hebrew and Spanish speakers with regard to these functions to two factors: morphosyntactic and rhetorical. On the one hand, relative clauses are simply easier to construct in these two languages than in the other three. Speakers of Hebrew and Spanish may therefore take advantage earlier of the additional flexibility which this device affords as a means of relating what would otherwise be treated as independent events: hence the relatively early and frequent use of the MOT and CONT functions in these two languages.[34] Indeed, one might further surmise that the accessibility of the relative construction in Hebrew and Spanish actually facilitates the development of the functions themselves.

In contrast to this finding, note that Turkish 9-year-olds do not take advantage of the MOT function, even though it is the one commonest among Turkish adults (80%), and is particularly well-suited to the morphosyntax of relative clauses in the language. It is surprising, then, that neither the

---

[34] This flexibility is not available in Turkish which, for reasons noted in Section 4.1, disallows the CONT construction on morphosyntactic and typological grounds.

felicitous information structure of this device, nor its frequency in adult usage, shows a developmental influence. However, this finding is consistent with the determining role played by cognitive-pragmatic developments: As discussed in Section 5.2.2, preposed MOT relatives are just beginning to emerge at 9 years, across the languages in our sample, evidently because they require more sophisticated sentence-planning commitments in ongoing discourse production and narrative organization. Therefore, just as the "naturalness" of information flow in the ordering of relative clauses can promote relatively more advanced functions earlier in some languages (MOT and CONT in Spanish and Hebrew), it can also delay the use of a function, even if it is one favored by adult speakers of the language (MOT in Turkish).

Moreover, our findings with respect to earlier emerging use of the CONT and EXP functions in Spanish point to a significant influence of language-specific rhetorical norms in development. Languages appear to have preferences for the ways in which clauses are linked together (Section 4.3). In adult Spanish, this is expressed by a relatively broad reliance on subordination which, in turn, has consequences for the relatively high use of the CONT and PRES functions of relative clauses in Spanish. As noted, the Spanish-speaking children make earlier, and more frequent, use of PRES relatives than do speakers of the other languages, and in this they presage the striking preference for this clause-linking device shown by Spanish adults, who use twice as many of each type of relative clauses as the other adults in our sample. Similarly, use of EXP relatives by the older Spanish-speaking children, coupled with their relatively broad reliance on PRES relatives for establishing and maintaining reference to the major characters in the narrative, suggests an influence of preferred rhetorical norms of usage in their language (Section 4.3). Indeed, we were struck by the singular, repeated efforts on the part of one 3-year-old Spanish narrator to make some use of this device, at the risk of veering off a coherent plotline (see example 22a).

Taken together, these crosslinguistic findings on the developing functions of relative clauses in narrative show that if a grammatical construction is made more accessible in a language through a variety of factors (morphosyntactic complexity, fewer competing expressive options, language typology, and rhetorical norms), children may begin to make use of it, and to deploy its different functions, more frequently, and earlier, than children who speak languages in which this is not the case. The interactions of these various factors in language development and in adult language use are demonstrably complex, and reinforce our conviction that an investigation of how one piece of a language is mastered calls for an understanding of the functions it performs, and of how that piece fits into the language of which it forms a part.

Chapter IVC

FILTERING AND PACKAGING IN NARRATIVE[1]

In Chapter IA we proposed that experience is **filtered** through language for purposes of speaking and that event descriptions are **packaged** into larger units for purposes of narrating. The preceding chapters have offered many examples of these processes and their development. On the level of narrative structure, narrators come to organize their stories in terms of problem, goal-oriented behavior, and solution, with increasing attention to motivation and evaluation. On the level of text structure, narrators come to segment the text into episodes, using a variety of means to mark episode boundaries. On the level of morphosyntax, narrators come to use devices such as relative clauses and temporal connectives to mark the status of information — old or new, situating or motivating, foreground or background — and the temporal and causal relations between events.

---

[1] This chapter is based, in part, on two earlier papers. The section on filtering draws from Slobin (1993b) and the section on packaging draws from Slobin (1993a).

In this chapter we take a finegrained approach at the **event** level, exploring two ways in which a speaker can choose a perspective: **event construal** and **event analysis and packaging**. For our purposes, the level of "event" is smaller than the episode and often larger than an individual act. This level is difficult to define precisely. In our analysis, events are changes of state or location with a clear beginning or end, relevant to the plot, carried out within a delimited space-time frame. Perhaps the best definition is by example. In the first part of the chapter we will be especially concerned with the following "events":

- **The Bee Event.** Picture 12: dog runs away from bees. (It is evident from the outset — in these descriptions of events — that it is impossible to verbalize an event without taking a perspective. For example, is this the "proper" definition of the event shown in Picture 12, or is it, perhaps: "bees chase dog"? As we have argued in Chapter IA, there is no single, objective event definition; rather, every verbalization constitutes a choice of event construal.)

- **The Deer Event.** Pictures 15-18: deer picks up and carries boy; boy and dog fall.

- **The Entry-into-Jar Event.** Picture 4: dog sticks head in jar.

- **The Broken Jar Event.** Pictures 6-7: dog falls from window; jar breaks.

Because language always provides for more than one way to encode an event, the speaker has a choice of **perspective** — that is, an event can be construed from a particular point of view and it can be analyzed into particular constituent segments. For example, consider the Broken Jar Event. In terms of construal, English syntax allows for an active, agent-oriented perspective (*The dog broke the jar*), a passive, patient-oriented perspective (*The jar was broken (by the dog)*, *The jar got broken*), and a middle-voice, patient-oriented perspective (*The jar broke*). In terms of analysis, various components can be isolated and packaged (e.g., *The dog fell and broke the jar; The jar broke when the dog fell; In falling to the ground, the dog broke the jar*). The speaker also has a choice with regard to the "granularity" of analysis — that is, the degree of detail of event description (e.g., *the jar broke into pieces when the dog's head hit the ground*). One of the major tasks of childhood is to master and flexibly use the range of perspective-taking devices in the language.

1. FILTERING: EVENT CONSTRUAL

Before one can say anything, one must decide what one wants to say. As Levelt has put it: "The construction of a preverbal message is a first step in the generation of speech" (1989, p. 107). We propose that, in constructing a preverbal message, the speaker must make decisions on at least four **dimensions of event construal**:

- selection of **topic**
- selection of **loci of control and effect**
- selection of **event view** (Cause, Become, State)
- selection of **degree of agency**

These decisions are not serial choices, but rather reflect dimensions of the overall conceptualization of an event that a speaker chooses to communicate linguistically. Together, they determine the form and content of a particular verbal message: number of participants mentioned, syntactic and thematic roles of participants (in one or more clauses), word order and construction type (voice, valence), and lexical choices. Any particular event, therefore, is amenable to a range of expressive options, depending on the event construal that results from these four types of choices.[2]

As noted in Chapter IIA, the youngest narrators are most likely to construe events from the perspectives of the main protagonists, the boy and dog. As a consequence, the most neutral event descriptions will be in the active voice, with actor as subject. A major problem in the development of narrative syntax arises when it would be more appropriate — for reasons of discourse organization — to bring a patient or undergoer argument into focus and to downgrade the expression of agency. This can happen, for example, when a major protagonist becomes an undergoer, as when the dog *is chased by* the bees. Or it can happen when the focus is on an inanimate object, as when the glass *is broken*. Or it can happen when agency is not clear, as when the boy *gets caught* on the deer or the dog *gets stuck* in the jar. In all such instances, children must learn how to manipulate the expression of events in order to present noncanonical construals.

We explore these issues with regard to the four Events listed above, looking particularly for the various devices for focusing on the undergoer of an event and defocusing the role of agency. In Sections 1.1 to 1.4 each of the

---

[2] This list is not exhaustive. Other issues are also involved in event construal, especially those concerned with affect and evaluation (e.g., modality, register). The four dimensions explored here contribute particularly to choices of voice, valence, construction type, and word order.

Events is examined in some detail, in order to lay out the range of options of event construal and linguistic expression in each of the languages. (In order to cover four dimensions of event construal with regard to four Events, the presentation is necessarily rather dense.) In Section 1.5 these options are summarized developmentally, showing that preschoolers command most of the basic devices for patient topicalization and downgrading of agency that are provided by the target language.

Our case study thus focuses on passive constructions and their alternatives in the five languages. We suggest that, in order to understand the development of any particular construction type (e.g., the English passive, the Spanish or Hebrew mediopassive), it must be considered as a member of a set of options within the target language. Thus, for example, the English passive represents one of a set of event construal options available in English, and it can only be fully understood within this set. German and Spanish passives, although formally equivalent, play roles within different sets of options.

1.1. Construals of the Bee Event

Consider, to begin with, various construals of the Bee Event. This event is the culmination of a series of preceding events with the dog as protagonist. The actions of the dog in Pictures 9-11 result in the fall of the beehive from the tree; thus, in Picture 12, both dog and bees have been "on the set" for some time.

1.1.1. Selection of topic

Both participants in the event — dog and bees — are animate and highly active in this event, and neither is new; therefore both are available as potential topics. In each of the five language groups, over half (55-65%) of the narrators who describe this event select the bees as topic and, accordingly, as subjects of a transitive verb (variants of 'chase') in the active voice. But let us follow those who, for various reasons of empathy and plot continuity, have selected the dog as topic, choosing to defocus the bees — because this choice yields an interesting range of passive-like construals with regard to the remaining three dimensions.

1.1.2. Selection of loci of control and effect

Choice of topic does not necessarily commit the speaker to the identification of actor and undergoer. One could, for example, say, "The dog has gotten the bees to fly out of the hive." However, almost all narrators who pick the dog as topic — across age and language — construe this event as one in which he is the victim. Having made this choice — dog as topic and undergoer — there is a variety of possible event views.

1.1.3. Selection of event view

The three event views — CAUSE, BECOME, and STATE — reflect the primitives of lexical analysis of verbs. However, here we intend these terms to apply to cognitive perspectives on events, rather than to verbs. That is to say, an event view is part of the preverbal message that determines the choice of constructions. A **Cause-View** represents an event as having an actor that, in some way, causes a change of state in an undergoer; a **Become-View** orients to a change of state without attribution of external causality; and a **State-View** simply orients to a state in itself.[3] With the dog as topic, this scene can be construed in terms of two possible event views. The most common is a Cause-View, in which the bees play a controlling role in the dog's actions (e.g., *The dog was being chased by the bees* [E5f-5;8]). Some narrators, however, take a Become-View, selecting the dog as actor, but with no mention of controller (e.g., *Now the dog's running* [E5j-5;10]). And there is no obvious State-View, because the dog and the bees are all active in this event. (One English-speaking adult gave a stative kind of summary of the activities of the boy and dog: *So both of them are in kinda chase scenes* [laughs] *running away from the other animals* [E20c].)

1.1.4. Selection of degree of agency

Having chosen the dog as **topic** and **locus of effect**, bees as **controller**, and a **Cause-View**, the narrator still has a range of options open. "Degree of agency" refers to a construal of the **entire** event: its dynamic and motivational loading, the extent of its consequences, etc. Compare, for example, *The dog runs away as bees follow him* [E20h] and *The dog runs howling by with this swarm of bees chasing him* [E20f]. Agency can be heightened or diminished by lexical choice of verbs and associated adverbs, and it can be downgraded by placement of the controller in a peripheral phrase, as in these two examples. Information placed in a coordinate or subordinate clause can modify the degree of agency in the main clause.[4]

---

[3] This framework has obvious parallels to semantic classifications of verbs in linguistics and philosophy, such as Croft (1990, 1993), Foley and Van Valin (1984), and numerous others with roots in Dowty (1979) and Vendler (1967). When event views are encoded in single verbs, **Cause-View** typically results in Accomplishments, **Become-View** in Achievements and Activities, and **State-View** in States. In our treatment, however, these "views" have encoding consequences beyond the choice of verb class, and even beyond the scope of a single clause. For example, the following German narration takes a Cause-View with the dog as topic and the bees as controllers, relating the dog's activity in the first clause to the role of the bees in the second: *Und der Hund, der rennt auch ganz schnell weg weil die Bienen hinter ihm her sind* 'And the dog, he runs away really quickly because the bees are after him' [G9f-9;9].

[4] The analysis in this chapter is limited to event construals that are expressed in one or two

This dimension of degree of agency increases the set of options with regard to voice, topicalization, and lexicon. The notion of "degree" suggests a cline. However, since we have no obvious cognitive metric of this dimension, we simply categorize expression types on three levels, **high**, **mid**, and **minimal** degrees of agency.[5]

High degree of agency. Active verb forms can be considered to represent a higher degree of agency than passives. All five languages provide means for topicalizing the patient while maintaining active verbs. Thus we find various types of active sentences, in each language, serving to encode this event as one in which the role of the bees is salient.

English. Although English allows for topicalization and fronting, such forms do not occur in our texts. However, high agency can be expressed in an explanatory subordinate clause with a verb in active voice: *The dog raced away because the bees were chasing him [E5b-5;2].*[6]

German. There are no instances of OVS order, although they are possible in German; however, the action of the bees occurs in coordinate or subordinate clauses with active verbs, as in English. Such an example was given in footnote 3: *Und der Hund, der rennt auch ganz schnell weg, weil die Bienen hinter ihm her sind* 'And the dog, he runs away really quickly because the bees are after him' *[G9f-9;9].* This kind of topic introduction followed by a pronoun is also frequent in the texts.

Spanish. Active verbs occur in sentences with object fronting. Although it has frequently been proposed that object fronting in a language like Spanish plays the same role as passive constructions, we suggest that this construction represents a higher degree of agency, since passives also occur in the Spanish data.[7] Two orders of left dislocation

---

clauses. Obviously, all of these dimensions can be manipulated in longer stretches of discourse, as occurs in some adult narrations. For example: *Pero de repente (el niño) se dió cuenta que su perro salía corriendo a toda prisa y que detrás de él venían muchas abejas que querían castigarle por haber roto su casa* 'But suddenly the boy realized that his dog went running by at full speed and that behind him came many bees that wanted to punish him for having broken their house' *[S20a].* Consideration of such elaborated descriptions would carry us into more extended narrative analysis than we are able to undertake here, and would be more relevant to issues of adult stylistic variation than to the 3-9 year age range of our developmental study.

[5] The dimension of "degree of agency" seems to have the same cognitive basis as Van Valin's (1990) "agentiveness," used to account for split intransitivity in Acehnese and Tsova-Tush. He proposes "non-agentive/agentive" as a "primary semantic parameter."

[6] Examples are offered here from various ages, in order to lay out the dimensions of analysis. Developmental considerations are taken up in Section 1.5.

occur with reference to the Bee Event: *Al perrito le persiguen todas las avispas* 'OBJ+DEF dog:DIM CL.PRO chase:PL all the wasps' (=To the doggie, him chase all the wasps) *[S5j-5;11]*. *Le perseguían al perro las avispas* 'CL.PRO chased:PL OBJ+DEF dog the wasps' (=Him chased, to the dog, all the wasps) *[S5f-5;7]*.

Hebrew. The Hebrew texts have explanatory subordinate clauses with active verbs, as in English: *Ve ha-kelev barax ki ha-dvorim racu la-akoc oto* 'And the-dog fled because the-bees wanted to-sting him' *[H4k-4;1]*. Hebrew allows for both simple fronting of a nonsubject NP (*Axarey ha-kelev radfu milyon dvorim* 'After the-dog chased:PL a.million bees' *[H9l-9;8]*) and left dislocation with a pronominal copy (*Ve ha-kelev bediyuk ha-dvorim rodfot axar-av* 'And the-dog just.then the-bees chase after-him' *[H20a]*).

Turkish. OSV orders occur, sometimes with a topic particle (*de*) following the first noun: *Köpeği de arılar kovalıyormuş* 'dog:ACC TOPIC bees were.chasing' *[T9i-9;5]*.

Mid degree of agency. This is the realm of the passive construction. Full passives are available in English, German, Spanish, and Hebrew and occur in the texts: *The dog was being chased by the bees [E5f-5;8]*. *Inzwischen wird der Hund von einem Wespenschwarm verfolgt* 'Meanwhile the dog is followed by a swarm of wasps' *[G20l]*. *El perro es perseguido por las abejas* 'The dog is chased by the bees' *[S20l]*. (Full passives are rare in Spanish and Hebrew; the only full passives in Hebrew occur with regard to other events than this one.) Turkish has only agentless passives, and in none of the five languages were agentless passives used for this event (probably because this construction does not present a resultant state; see below). We suggest that such forms encode a lower level of agency than full passives, in that the agent is not mentioned at áll.

English also provides the option of the *get*-passive: *The dog's getting chased by the bees [E4k-4;10]*. This form differs from the other constructions considered here in that it suggests that the **patient** has a degree of agency or responsibility, as well as the agent. Budwig (1990) reviews numerous proposals that the *get*-passive deviates from prototypical agency in that the patient "shares responsibility," "plays a causal role," or "catalyzes" the action in which it is involved, and that the action is often to the detriment of the patient. She presents evidence that preschool-age children use both *get-* and *be-*

---

[7] However, as noted in Chapter IIIc, there is also a register difference between the two constructions; this perhaps is why only adults use passives, while preschoolers use object fronting in their stories.

passives, preferring the former for comments about animate patients that are negatively affected. Both forms occur in our stories, beginning at age 4. There is no independent evidence that individual narrators distinguish between the two forms, but it is clear that this event is partially caused by the dog, who suffers the consequences, thus creating a favorable context for a *get*-passive. In other languages, a degree of agency is attributed to the dog by various sorts of extended commentary, as in the elaborate Spanish example in footnote 4, where the narrator suggests that the bees wanted to punish him for having broken their hive. Such examples support the suggestion that **degree** of agency is relevant when an animate patient is topicalized.

Low degree of agency. There are two levels of low degree of agency with regard to this event. In both, a Become-View is taken, but there is also an indication that the activity is telic. In some descriptions, the bees are mentioned in an oblique phrase or adjoined clause, suggesting that they contribute some degree of agency to the event, e.g., *The dog was running away from the bees [E5e-5;8]. El perro vino corriendo y las abejas detrás* 'The dog came running and the bees behind' *[S5d-5;4]*. At a lower level, the bees are not mentioned at all, but the meaning of the verb implies that the dog's action is caused, or at least has a source; e.g., *Der Hund läuft weg* 'The dog runs away' (i.e., from something) *[G5i-5;2]*; *O da kaçmış* 'He TOPIC escaped/ran.away' *[T3i-3;11]*. Conceptually, these descriptions seem to lie at the border between a Cause-View and a Become-View, due to lexical indication of a minimal degree of agency. The preceding two sentences represent the lowest degree of agency possible (with respect to the bees). Below this level, one takes a pure Become-View, with no hint of source or goal. If one simply says something equivalent to 'the dog was running', as some young narrators do, the dog is no longer the locus of effect, and one ends up with a one-participant event. Note, however, that intransitive syntax in itself does not always encode a totally non-causal event view. In versions of 'the dog runs away/escapes' there is still a hint that locus of control lies outside the dog. Thus, syntax and lexical semantics **jointly** reflect event construal.

Examination of the remaining three events reveals a wide range of possible event construals. After we have laid out these possibilities, we will then be in a position to turn to developmental considerations.

1.2. Construals of the Deer Event

This is a more complex event, allowing for varying interpretations of locus of control and responsibility. The central feature is that the outcome of the event is accidental and surprising, to both the boy and the deer. It thus invites interpretations of varying degrees of agency.

1.2.1. Selection of topic and control locus

Our narrators choose either the boy or the deer as topic, with no clear pattern by age or language. When the deer is chosen, it is also construed as actor; the boy as topic, however, is construed as either actor or undergoer.

1.2.2. Selection of event view

With the deer as topic, narrators take a Cause-View: 'the deer lifts/carries/takes... the boy'. The grammatical form adheres to canonical word order in the active voice but, as we shall see, lexical choices reflect varying degrees of agency. With the boy as topic, narrators use a greater range of options. In Cause-Views with the deer as actor, we find object fronting and passive constructions; in Become-Views there are verbs of motion and inchoative/middles; and in State-Views, locative and participial constructions. As shown below, degree of agency interacts with topic and event view selection.

1.2.3. Selection of degree of agency: Cause-view with deer as topic

The diminished agency of the deer in this event is often marked by lexical choice, using a fairly neutral verb such as *get* in English (e.g., *A deer got the boy* [E5j-5;10]), or equivalents of 'take' in all five languages (e.g., *Ha-cvi gam lakax oto* 'The-deer also took him' [H5g-5;4]). There are frequent attempts to introduce the horns as "quasi-instrument," as if indicating the involuntary action of the deer (e.g., *It got him by his horns* [E9a-9;1]; *A deer caught him between his horns* [E9c-9;6]). And there are adverbial additions that underline diminished agency, such as: *The deer pops out of the rock and, after being disturbed, starts giving him a ride, **unintentionally** [E20e].*

1.2.4. Selection of degree of agency: Cause-view with boy as topic

As in the Bee Event, high agency is encoded in Spanish and Turkish (but not in Hebrew) by means of object fronting in clauses with active verbs: *Le cogió un ciervo* 'CL.PRO picked.up a deer' [=him a deer picked up] [S3j-3;11]. *Çocuğu boynuzlarının arasına alıyor* 'boy:ACC its.horns between takes' [=(the deer) takes the boy between its horns] [T20g]. Again, as in the Bee Event, passive clauses express a lower degree of agency than active clauses. Full passives occur in English and German: *The boy has been picked up by some antlered beast* [E20a]. *He got picked up by a reindeer* [E5f-5;8]. *Dann wird er vom Hirsch aufgegabelt* 'Then he is forked up by the deer' [G20j]. In Spanish, Hebrew, and Turkish, by contrast, the availability of mediopassive constructions seems to favor a Become-View, as does the English *get* + PARTICIPLE construction. These options are discussed below.

1.2.5. Selection of degree of agency: Become-view with boy as topic

These event construals attribute no agency to the deer. Rather, they present the boy as coming into a locative relation with the deer or its antlers.

Active voice. The event can be seen from the perspective of the boy as subject of a verb of motion. For some of the youngest narrators, equivalents of 'climb onto' are used in all five languages, suggesting high agency — probably due to difficulty in comprehending the involuntary, indirect nature of causality in this event. For example *He climbed on him* [E3d-3;5]; *Se subió encima de un ciervo* 'He climbed on top of a deer [S5a-5;1]. But most narrators who treat the boy as topic and actor, use inchoative verbs of lessened agency, marking the boy's lack of volitionality: 'fall on' (*En, Sp, Ge, Tu*), 'slip on' (*En, Sp*), 'run into' (*En, Sp*), and English *hop on, land on,* and, most frequently, the neutral change-of-state verb, *get on.* Agency can also be adverbially decreased, e.g., *Und jetzt ist der Junge aus Versehen auf den Hörner raufgefallen* 'And now the boy has **accidentally** fallen onto the horns' [G9k-9;0]. Only Hebrew speakers do not make use of such marking of lessened agency, probably because of the extensive use of the morphologically available mediopassive.

Mediopassive and equivalents. In English, Spanish, Hebrew, and Turkish there are verbal forms that are specialized for this sort of event construal, and they are widely used from the youngest ages. English speakers have recourse to inchoative/middle *get* + PARTICIPLE constructions: *He got caught by a deer* [E5b-5;2]; *He got caught* [E9j-9;11]. The equivalent Spanish construction is a reflexive mediopassive, also with inchoative meaning when used with a verb in the past perfective: *Se colgó de una cabra* 'REFL hang:PFV from a goat' [S5d-5;4]. Hebrew provides the mediopassive conjugation (*nif'al*), which is realized in this event in the verb forms *nitpas* 'got.caught' and *nitla* 'got.hung.(onto)' — e.g., *Ve pit'om hu nitla al cvi* 'And suddenly he got.hung on (a) deer' [H5d-5;3]. The Turkish agentless passive performs the same function: *Geyiğin boynuzlarına takılıyor* 'deer's antlers:POSS+DAT attaches:PASS' [=(he) is attached to the deer's antlers] [T9a-9;3]. Only in German do we find no equivalent forms. Here narrators have recourse to other means of marking inchoativity. One option is to modify a stative view with 'suddenly': *Plötzlich ist er auf dem Kopf eines Hirsches* 'Suddenly he is on the head of a deer' [G9e-9;11]. This option is also used in Turkish, using the adverb *birden* 'suddenly', sometimes along with a verb form with the affixed auxiliary *ver* 'give', indicating something like speed, immediacy, unhindered change of state (Kononov, 1956, p. 209): *Kendini birden kayalıktan geyiğin boynuzlarında bulu-ver-di* 'self:ACC suddenly rock:ABL deer's antlers:LOC find-IMMED-PAST' [=suddenly he came to find himself off of the rock (and) on the deer's antlers] [T20c]. What all of these examples have in common — along with the Spanish perfective, English *get*, and Hebrew *pit'om* 'suddenly', exemplified above — is clear attention to the **onset phase** of the event. Depending on the language, this feature is marked inflectionally or lexically — but, in all cases, it is present.

1.2.6. Selection of degree of agency: State view with boy as topic

Finally, the event can be construed as one in which the boy is simply located on the deer or its antlers, with no indication of how he came to be there. These construals thus attribute no degree of agency to either the boy or the deer, and have no indication of inchoativity. There are three semantic types in the data:

Active verb. In English and German, simple verbs of posture in the active voice are used, e.g.: *He held onto a deer's horns [E9f-9;8]; Und dann haltet er sich an der Reh fest* 'And then he holds himself tight on the deer' *[G5h-5;1]*. The corresponding Spanish and Turkish forms are reflexive verbs in the active voice, where the reflexive functions as a kind of intensifier ('to take a firm hold of'): *Se agarró a unos cuernos de un ciervo* 'REFL held to some horns of a deer' *[S9b-9;2]; Bir dala tutunuyor* 'a branch:DAT holds:REFL' *[T20d]*. There are no equivalent Hebrew forms in our texts.

Past participle. This option is frequent in English and Spanish: *Now he's stuck on a deer [E4l-4;11]; Está colgado de la cabra* '(He) is hung from the goat' *[S4b-4;1]* (also *apoyado* 'supported', *agarrado* 'held', *sujetado* 'stuck, fastened'). The corresponding Turkish construction is a locative with the past participle of *ol* 'be': *Çocuk da geyiğin kafasının üstünde olmuş oluyor* 'Boy TOPIC deer's head on:LOC be:PARTICIPLE is' [=as for the boy, he's located on the deer's head] *[T20d]*. In Hebrew there are only a few adult uses of stative locatives, e.g.: *Hu moce et acmo na'uc al karnayim shel ayil* 'He finds himself nailed to the horns of (a) deer' *[H20l]*. Comparable constructions are not found in the German data. An equivalent perspective is given by the verb *hängen* 'hang': *Da hängt der Junge* 'There hangs the boy' *[G3a-3;11]*.

Locative. The most neutral State-View occurs in all five languages as versions of a simple locative, such as *The boy is on the deer [E3i-3;9]; Geyiğin üstünde çocuk* 'deer's top:LOC boy' [=the boy is on the deer] *[5f-6;1]*.

1.2.7. Summary: Deer event

This is a complex event, allowing many types of construal. As discussed below, children often have difficulty establishing a perspective on this event. In addition, narrative options seem to be influenced by the ready availability of particular morphosyntactic constructions in the narrator's language. It appears that the accessibility of some sort of mediopassive or inchoative/middle form encourages narrators to take a Become-View with boy as topic in the four languages (except for German) that provide accessible versions of such linguistic devices. Past participles in Spanish and English facilitate a State-View. At the same time, all languages provide speakers with lexical means to reinforce particular event construals. (This seems to be the most accessible option in German.)

1.3. Construals of the Entry-into-Jar Event

The remaining two events to be analyzed have a single animate participant, the dog. In the Entry-into-Jar Event, he puts his head into the empty frog receptacle, which remains stuck on his head. The dog is almost always chosen as topic and, since the jar is inanimate, there is no issue of locus of control. That is, choice of event construal is also limited by the objective circumstances of the event. The major option is whether to take a Cause-View or a State-View. In Cause-Views, the dog as agent either puts his head in the jar, or, less frequently, puts the jar on his head. In State-Views, his head is simply described as located in the jar. We will return to these options after considering an additional major option provided by English alone, of the five languages in our sample.

In English, 36% of the narrators take a Become-View, using the inchoative/middle construction, *get* + PARTICIPLE. The varieties are:

> *The dog got stuck/caught.*
> *He got his head stuck/caught (in the jar).*
> *The dog got the jar stuck on his head.*

This construction neatly solves the problem of describing an event with the features: (1) enter state, (2) with unexpected consequences, (3) which endure. The inchoative/middle, along with the lexical semantics of *stuck* or *caught*, conveys the modal coloring of diminished agency and the aspectual coloring of enduring result. Lacking these means, speakers in the other languages make use of negative potentials ('he couldn't get out') and aspectual verbs ('remain/stay'). (There are also some uses of middle voice in Hebrew for this event [Berman, 1993], but less frequently than the English construction. As suggested below, the multi-purpose English verb, *get*, may facilitate acquisition of both inchoative/middle and passive voices in English.)

Given these differing sets of options, descriptions of the Entry-into-Jar Event represent a different set of constructions than the events with two animate participants discussed above. Taking a Cause-View, we find many two-clause descriptions: an affirmative clause of entry followed by a negative clause of potential exit. The following are representative examples: *He sticks his head in there and then he can't get it out [E4d-4;6]. Der Hund klettert in den* [sic] *Glas, und hier hat - kann der Hund das nicht mehr rauskriegen* 'The dog climbs in the glass, and here the dog has - can't get it out any more' *[G5l-5;0]. El perro se metió en la botella y no se la podía sacar* 'The dog put himself in the bottle and couldn't get it off' *[S9b-9;2]. Ha-kelev xipes ota bacincenet she hu nixnas im harosh ve lo yaxal lehoci oto* 'The-dog searched for her [=frog] in the jar that he entered with his head and couldn't get it out' *[H9c-9;4]. Köpek de kavanozun içine kafasını soktu, bir türlü çıkaramadı* 'The dog stuck his head in the jar, couldn't get it out at all' *[T9j-9;1]*.

Interestingly, German speakers take this option about twice as often as speakers in the other four languages. The following are percentages of narrators mentioning negative consequences: English — 11%, German — 26%, Spanish — 17%, Hebrew — 13%, Turkish — 12%. These differences are probably attributable to differing linguistic resources and to characteristics of narrative style, which arise partly in response to the availability of particular sorts of linguistic devices. Overall, it is our impression that the German narrators use more analytical and lexical devices for accumulating or adding on aspects of this (and other) events — entering and then not getting out, being inside and unable to get free — and adding locative directional detail. In the German versions the activities of 'looking', 'smelling', 'sniffing' are frequently accompanied by statives of 'being' or 'having' with locative particles like *in, drin, auf* 'in, inside, on' and an additional comment on the dog remaining in that state or being unable to get out of that state, for example: *Der Hund schnüffelt immer noch in das Glas. Das Glas kriegt der nicht mehr runter von Kopf* 'The dog keeps on sniffing in the glass. He doesn't get the glass off of his head anymore' *[G9g-9;10]*.

Taking a State-View, narrators use locatives and participles. The English *stuck* seems to convey durativity in itself (e.g., *He had a jar stuck on his head [E5d-5;6]*). In the other languages there are occasional uses of an aspectual verb: *Er bleibt mit seinem Hals im Glas stecken* 'He remains with his neck sticking in the glass' *[G20c]. Se le queda la cabeza atascada en la jarra* 'His head remains stuck in the jar' *[S9j-9;11]. Hacincenet nish'ara la-kelev tfusa al harosh* 'The jar remained stuck on the dog's head' *[H20k]. Kafası kavanozun içine sıkışıp kalmıştı* 'His head remained stuck in the jar' *[T20c]*.

1.4. Construals of the Broken Jar Event

The predominant construal of this event focuses on the jar. With the jar as topic, all five languages provide a Become-View, using differing syntactic means. In each language, at least half of the narrators who mention this Event take a Become-View: English — 50%, Spanish — 65%, German — 100%,

Hebrew — 69%, Turkish — 80%. For encoding change of state, English and German provide intransitive verbs with inchoative/middle semantics; Spanish and Hebrew have mediopassives; and Turkish has an agentless passive. For example: *The jar broke* [*E3i-3;9*]. *Dann ist das Glas kaputt gegangen* 'Then the glass has gone kaputt' [*G3l-3;3*]. *Da zerbricht das Glas* 'There the glass breaks' [*G9a-9;3*]. *Se rompe el tarro* 'REFL breaks the jar' [*S9l-9;11*]. *Hakufsa nishbera* 'The-jar broke' [*H5j-5;7*]. *Kavanoz kırılıyor.* 'Jar breaks:PASS' [*T9g-9;9*].

Note that there are no passives in English for this event. The *get*-passive is probably not appropriate, since the jar cannot be construed as a "responsible victim." The *be*-passive also seems inappropriate, because it is indistinguishable from a State-View (*the glass is/was broken*), and this is a dynamic scene. (The State-View is rare across all five languages.) The communicative demands posed by this event, therefore, appear to exclude the English passive, though the passive is used with great frequency by English speakers for describing the first three events (exceeding its use in the other languages).

English speakers take a Cause-View on this scene more frequently than do speakers of the other four languages, especially at early ages. German speakers never do so, and only three Turkish adults present the dog as agent of a transitive verb. It is not clear why this should be so.

1.5. Developmental Patterns

Table 1 presents the set of options that emerge from this examination of various means for patient-upgrading and agent-downgrading, along with their first ages of appearance in narrating the four Events. The upper section of the table presents constructions that are traditionally examined in studies of voice and topicalization. The lower parts present additional means for encoding degrees of agency and inchoativity that appear in the data. Each column represents a set of options available in the particular language; the entire table represents part of the overall collection of constructions that must be considered crosslinguistically for purposes of typological analysis of devices for undergoer focus and diminution of agency.

The four Events thus provide a sampling of basic event construal devices for each language. First consider the languages overall, ignoring age differences: They represent different types with regard to the array of constructions covering the same set of semantic/discourse functions. When both actor and undergoer are encoded, Spanish, Hebrew, and Turkish tend to use object fronting in active clauses, whereas English and German use full passives. When undergoer is topic, similar functions are performed by English *get* + PARTICIPLE constructions, Turkish agentless passives, Spanish and Hebrew

TABLE 1
Devices for Undergoer Focus and Diminution of Agency,
by Language and Age[a]

CONSTRUCTIONS	LANGUAGES				
	English	German	Spanish	Hebrew	Turkish
Full passive	P (4)[b]	A	A	A	(n.a.)
Object fronting, active	-	-	P (3)	P (4)	P (5)[c]
Agentless passive (En: *get*+PART, Tu: inflectional)	P (3)	-	-	(n.a.)	P (3)
Morphological mediopassive	(n.a.)	-	P (3)	P (3)	P (3)
Inchoative/middle intransitive	P (3)	P (3)[d]	(n.a.)	(n.a.)	(n.a.)
Lower agency in adjoining phrase or clause	P (3)	P (3)	P (3)	P (3)	P (5)
Lower agency in lexical choice	P (4)	P (5)	P (5)	-	S
Lower agency adverbial marking	S	S	S	S	S
'Find-self' inchoative	-	-	-	A	A
Enter jar - negative result	P (4)	P (3)	P (4)	P (3)	P (5)
"Quasi-instrumental" antlers	S	S	S	S	S

a. Entries in the table represent the first age at which a construction appears in the data. P = preschool (with age in parentheses); S = school age (9); A = adult; - = not attested; n.a. = not applicable.

b. Full passives with both *be* and *get* are present at age 4.

c. Object fronting is present at age 3 elsewhere in the Turkish texts.

d. The only form at age 3 is *ist kaputtgegangen* 'has gone kaputt'; *zerbricht/zerbrach* 'breaks/broke' appears at age 9.

mediopassives, and, in some instances, English and German inchoative/middle intransitive verbs. The 'find-self' inchoatives in Hebrew and Turkish perform functions similar to *get* + PARTICIPLE in English and reflexive in Spanish. Beyond these typological differences, speakers of all five languages have recourse to similar lexical and periphrastic means for manipulating the expression of degree of agency: selection of particular verbs and adverbs and more elaborate constructions (such as the "quasi-instrumental" references to antlers in the Deer Event, and clauses of negative potential in the Entry-into-Jar Event).

The entries labeled "P" (preschool-age) in Table 1 indicate the core of constructions that are available early on in each language. Setting aside German for the moment, the other four languages present a consistent picture. Preschoolers make use of the basic devices for topicalization and de-emphasis of agency provided by their language, generally before age 5.[8] Beyond this

---

[8] Due to small numbers, our developmental criterion is the occurrence of at least one construction type for a given age and language, with regard to one of the four Events.

core, school-age children in all five languages use devices that show a more mature understanding of narrative discourse and plot structure, using adverbs and phrases indicating suddenness or involuntary action. Preschoolers show some ability to mark diminished agency by lexical verb choice and adjoined constructions. The patterns for each language show children to be mastering different means to carry out the discourse functions under consideration.

English. The passive is the primary means of topicalizing non-agents, and it is an early acquisition in all of its forms. Inchoative *get* + PARTICIPLE constructions appear by age 3, and full *get-* and *be*-passives by age 4 in our data. Three- and 4-year-olds also select verbs of diminished agency (*slip, hop, land,* etc.) in describing the Deer Event and make reference to lower agency in the Bee Event by the use of adjoined phrases (*from the bees*) and clauses (*cause the bees were trying to get it*). One 4-year-old gave evidence that the morphology of the full *be*-passive is still being worked out at this age, saying: *The dog was be chasing by the bees* [sic] [*E4b-4;4*]. The many functions of *get* in English, along with the paucity of topicalization devices, probably make the passive salient to English-speaking children.[9] It is striking that *get* occurs in a wide range of functions in preschool English. In its agentless form it serves as a kind of inchoative/resultative by age 3 (*got caught*), and in the full passive by 4. (Actually, by 3 in another scene in the frog story: *The dog's hiding so he doesn't get chased by that big deer* [*E3g-3;9*].) It is also a general verb for encoding changes of state for which the child may not have a specific lexical item, or to which s/he may wish to attribute diminished agency, e.g., *The dog gets into there* [*E4f-4;7*]; *He got on a deer* [*E4a-4;0*]; and even, *And then a deer gots him* [*E5g-5;9*]. Such uses of *get* may help draw the child's attention to the prototypical agent defocusing function of the passive.[10]

---

[9] This claim may seem paradoxical in light of the ample literature that the passive is a late and difficult acquisition in English. This literature sees the passive as emerging in the second half of the fourth year, following the acquisition of many other constructions over the preceding two years or so, but see the discussion of Bowerman's data in Section 1.6, below. In any event, most of our children are older than 3;6, and many of them are adept at using the English passive to serve discourse functions such as those examined here (see Chapter IIIA).

[10] These uses of *get* are also consistent with the satellite-framed typology of English. As Talmy (1991) has pointed out, such languages make use of "generic" or "dummy" verbs, such as *get, go, put,* and *do.* Verbs of this sort "can act, in effect, as syntactic 'place holders' while conveying a relatively generic or neutral semantic content and thus permit the sentence to proceed to the satellite, whose semantic content is the relevant factor" (p. 186). Thus, in stating *The dog gets into there,* the core message is that the dog has (somehow) moved **into** (something).

As noted above, Budwig (1990) has shown that children in the age range 3;6-5 distinguish between *get-* and *be*-passives, tending to use full passives with *get* to express "speaker attitude about the consequences (usually negative) of the action described," and agentless passives with *be* "in talk about an agent who was generic, unknown, or irrelevant to the discourse." In naturalistic data, she found use of both *get-* and *be*-passives "to talk about actions without taking an agentive perspective." This perspective is clearly available to English-speaking children in our narrative data as well.

German. The paucity of topicalizing and de-agentivizing devices in our data is surprising. As noted in previous chapters, we have found complex syntax to be mastered later in German. Unless this reflects an unknown difference in our sample or in the conditions of story elicitation, it seems plausible to suggest that German grammar poses particular acquisitional problems. With regard to the issues considered here, it may be of importance that variation of verb position in subordinate clauses is syntactically determined and serves no obvious pragmatic functions, and that object-fronting in simple sentences is only transparent if the object is masculine singular (otherwise nominative and accusative forms are identical). Word order is also sensitive to a verb-second rule, which moves the subject around the verb, again for no pragmatic purpose. (Compare: *Da lief der Hund* 'there ran the dog' with *Der Hund lief* 'the dog ran'.) In addition to this array of formal problems, only accusative NPs can be promoted to subject in passives (excluding, for example, the equivalent of *I was given a book*). Accordingly, passives probably occur less frequently in the language modeled to children. What we find, then, is a far more "active-oriented" narrative strategy in the German children's stories, stringing events one after another with less "syntactic packaging" than in the other languages. It is only with regard to the Broken Jar Event that German children produce many undergoer-oriented descriptions — primarily of the same sort (e.g., *Da ist es kaputtgegangen* 'There it has gone.kaputt' [*G3i-3;11*]). In German, then, the relative inaccessibility of various morphosyntactic devices seems to have a clear effect upon the development of event construal and narrative style. That is, the requisite linguistic forms seem to be both morphosyntactically complex and relatively infrequent, in comparison with the other languages (see Chapter IIIB).

Spanish. The full passive is used by only one adult narrator, suggesting that it is a rare (and probably literary) form (see Chapter IIIC, footnote 8). However, left-dislocated OVS orders are readily used by the youngest narrators. Object-fronting also automatically occurs when a clitic pronoun encodes a continuing topic; compare *le ha cogido* 'CL.PRO has picked up' and *le ha cogido el ciervo* 'CL.PRO has picked up the deer', both meaning that the boy, as topic, has been picked up by the deer. This parallel probably facilitates the acquisition of object fronting with full NPs (e.g., *al perrito le persiguen todas las avispas* 'OBJ+DEF doggie CL.PRO chase all the bees' [*S5j-5;11*]). Because these constructions have verbs in active, rather than passive voice, they are morphologically more accessible — and perhaps expressive of a higher degree of agency than English passives (though such crosslinguistic comparisons cannot be clearly substantiated). As for the mediopassive, it simply requires the reflexive particle along with a normally conjugated active verb. The reflexive serves a range of functions in Spanish, and is a frequent and morphologically regular form. Its early mediopassive use with regard to the Broken Jar Event is not surprising, as this function is expressed by age 3 in all five languages.

Hebrew. Patient orientation is primarily expressed — from age 3 onwards — by the use of a productive verb pattern (*nif'al*). As discussed in Chapter IIID, this pattern produces intransitive verbs which function as the passive counterparts of transitive activity verbs (e.g. *nitpas* 'be/get caught', *nitka* 'be/get stuck', *nishbar* 'break/get broken'). Hebrew narrators of all ages prefer to use such single-argument intransitives rather than full passives with an oblique agent argument. They also make relatively little use of object fronting, although this option is available for topicalizing non-agent arguments. The accessibility of alternating verb-pattern morphology, which is deeply ingrained in the entire system of the language, seems to provide the favored option for varying construals of the Events under consideration.

Turkish. Become-Views are expressed from age 3 by agentless passives, on a par with Spanish and Hebrew mediopassives, and a few object-fronting constructions also occur at age 3. Our preschool sample is much smaller in Turkish (10 3-year-olds versus 24 3-4-year-olds in English, Spanish, and Hebrew). The more recent Turkish sample collected by Aylin Küntay (see Chapter IB) provides another 20 texts in this age range, providing many examples of such constructions, parallel to Spanish and Hebrew. Küntay's texts include both OVS orders (e.g., *Fareyi alıyor çocuk* 'mouse:ACC takes boy' [=the boy picks up the mouse] [*nT3a-3;10*]) and OSV (e.g., *Köpeği geyik almış* 'dog:ACC deer took' [=the deer picked up the dog] [*nT4p-4;7*]).[11] However, these early constructions are often not discursively tied to preceding or following clauses. Thus, at first, they may not reflect discourse-organized information flow but rather shifts in attention. This is especially clear if we examine the broader context for the 3-year-old example cited from Küntay's data. Looking at the preceding and following clauses, it seems that the first noun in each clause simply foregrounds the next

---

[11] Küntay's data are coded as "*nT*" (new Turkish).

participant in a chain of clauses.

(1) *Köpek de şöyle yapıyor. Fareyi alıyor çocuk. Köpek düşürmüş onu.*
'(The) dog TOPIC/FOCUS is doing like this. The.mouse:ACC picks.up the boy. (The) dog knocked.down it [=beehive].' *[nT3a-3;7]*

In other preschool contexts, however, word-order patterns are used with a degree of narrative felicity. In the second example noted above, the dog has first been introduced as subject (along with boy) in a subordinate temporal clause and is then continued as object in the following clause, which has OSV word order. ¨As discussed in Chapter IIIE, the preverbal position is used for focus in Turkish. Therefore, in this instance, the deer remains a focused agent although the patient is in first position:

(2) *Sonra köpek - köpek-le çocuk kaçmaya başlarken köpeği geyik almış.*

then dog - dog-with boy run:NOML+DAT start:CONVERB dog:ACC deer took

'Then while the dog with the boy were starting to run away, the deer took the dog.' *[nT4p-4;7]*

We also find OVS orders, which allow for patient-fronting while maintaining a defocused topical agent NP in postverbal position. In the following example, the beehive has attracted the dog's attention, then the narrator's attention shifts to the boy and returns to the beehive in (3).

(3) *Arı kovanını hala oynuyor köpek.*

bee hive:ACC still plays dog

'The dog is still playing with the beehive.' *[nT5b-5;9]*

1.6. Precursors and Prerequisites

The ability to flexibly construe events in narrative requires that children have some linguistic control of the necessary morphological and syntactic devices and that they have the cognitive ability to take more than one perspective on an event. There is evidence that such abilities begin to appear in the third year of life, that is, at considerably younger ages than our youngest subjects. Here we briefly review some of the evidence in the domains of both language and cognition for precursors and prerequisites for the patterns displayed in Table 1.

1.6.1. Linguistic precursors

Many of the specific linguistic forms required for flexible event construal are available from early on. For example, studies of children's spontaneous speech in Turkish (Aksu-Koç & Slobin, 1985; Ekmekçi, 1986b; Slobin & Talay, 1986) indicate mastery of pragmatic word-order variation well before age 3 (as has been shown in studies of other "flexible word-order languages" as well). In Ekmekçi's study, a child of 1;11 placed new information in sentence-initial position, using post-verbal and sentence-final positions to "provide background information which is already predictable from context or previous discourse" (p. 270). In English, Bowerman (1990) has documented agentless passives as early as age 1;11 and passives with agent phrases beginning at about 2;6.

As noted in Chapter IB, such early control of pragmatic word order is shown in interactive **dialogue**, rather than monologic narrative, which is a later development (Ervin-Tripp, 1989). The situations in which children manipulate perspective in conversation are those in which actions, consequences, and responsibility are at issue. When there is topic continuity, it is in the context of action, as the following example from Slobin's unpublished Turkish data. A child of 2;8 is playing with a toy boat and announces:

(4) *Bir tane daha vapur var, onu da getireceğim ben.*

one item more boat exists, PRO+ACC FOCUS will.bring I

'There's one more boat, IT I'll bring.' [age 2;8]

The first clause introduces the topic — another boat — which becomes the fronted patient in the second clause, marked by a pronoun casemarked in the accusative along with the topic/focus particle *de*. The first-person subject is postposed, producing a grammatically and pragmatically appropriate OVS clause. This example is parallel to the frog-story example provided by a 5-year-old in (3). In Bowerman's data, the first full passives are in contexts of action and consequences as well, such as:

(5a) *If Christy don't be careful she might get runned over from a car.* [age 2;7]

(5b) *Do you think that flower's supposed to be picked by somebody?* [age 2;10]

Early practice in the manipulation of perspective in dialogue undoubtedly prepares the child for the narrative uses of varying the sentence positions of nominal arguments. Such practice, in all five languages, gives the child experience in using various linguistic means of focusing on selected parts of messages.

Agentless passives also occur by 2;0-2;6 in samples of spontaneous speech from younger Turkish children, as do the various mediopassive and middle-voice forms in Hebrew, Spanish, and English. The earliest forms of such passives in Turkish express two types of non-agentive perspective: (1) resultant states of verbs of object destruction, as in the Broken Jar Event, using past-tense forms (e.g., *kırıldı* '(it) broke:WITNESSED.PAST', *yırtılmış* '(it) tore:NONWITNESSED.PAST' [=must have gotten torn]); (2) potential change of state, using present-tense (progressive and generic) forms (e.g., *takılmıyor* '(it) isn't being attached' [=it doesn't stay on], *açılır* 'it opens' [=can be opened]). Bowerman reports various types of early agentless passives, often with the child as patient. For example, at 2;1 Christy objects to having her hair brushed, saying, *I don't like be brushed.* Non-animates are also treated as patients in such constructions; at 1;11 Eva commented, *My pillow get washed,* when her mother took her pillow case to put it in the laundry.

The use of such forms of patient focus — with and without encoding of agent, and in a variety of tense/aspect, person, and affirmative/negative patterns — indicates that these types of non-agentive perspective are cognitively available to children long before they are used in narrative. The challenge of narrative syntax lies in the flexible use of a range of construction types in order to maintain and shift reference, upgrade and downgrade agency, focus and defocus participants — without the scaffolding of dialogue and the support of ongoing nonlinguistic interactions, such as those involved in manipulative and instrumental behaviors. It is evident that the separate linguistic devices needed for building well-structured narratives are available long before these more advanced discourse challenges are fully met. Thus, to repeat one of the basic themes of this book, the development of linguistic forms involves an expanding and interconnected set of discourse functions that those forms come to serve.

1.6.2. Cognitive flexibility

In order to select one of a set of linguistic options such as those reviewed here, children must also have a degree of **cognitive flexibility** in taking various perspectives on events. Bowerman (1990) has examined the emergence of passives in English at about age 2, noting that several other construction patterns emerge at the same time. The collection of constructions indicates the child's ability to attend to agent and change-of-state as separate components of an event, thus laying the groundwork for selection of event perspective. She notes:

> The emergence of passive constructions was not an isolated phenomenon in my data, but rather coincided with the emergence of a variety of related construction patterns. Taken together, these developments suggest the onset of **a new cognitive flexibility in construing events as taking place spontaneously or as initiated by external agents or causes.** (p. 4; emphasis added)

That is to say, 2-year-olds can already distinguish between Cause-Views and Become-Views. The following examples are indicative of this emerging flexibility:

(6a) **Agent + change of state (Cause-View):** *I can't get door open.* [age 2;1]

(6b) **Novel transitive (Cause-View):** *I came this off* (=made this come off). [age 2;0]

(6c) **Novel intransitive (Become-View):** *Can I plant them? Will they plant?* [dried beans] [age 2;0]

(6d) **Spontaneous event (Become-View):** *It's getting dry for me to play.* [after a rainstorm] [age 2;1]

Such early cognitive flexibility in choice of construction type has the support of interactive dialogue and nonlinguistic context, as does early flexibility in choice of word and verb form discussed above. These precursors and prerequisites to event construal in narrative must later be accessed in situations where the child's ongoing text construction itself provides the support for the selection of event construals and their linguistic expression. Monologic text construction is more demanding than dialogue — as indicated most clearly in children's attempted reformulations in telling the frog story.

1.7. Children's Problems in Finding an Event Perspective

Self-repairs in the narrative transcripts indicate that children often find difficulty in arriving at selection of perspectives on event construal dimensions. There are a few self-repairs at age 4, and many from ages 5 and 9, in all of the languages. Indeed, these Events seem to engender more backtracking and self-repair than many other parts of the story. Such attempts show children at work on all four dimensions.

In narrating the Bee Event, children hesitate in topic selection, as shown in the following examples, where a hyphen indicates a short pause and three dots a longer pause.

(7a) *He's - the bees are chasing the - dog.* [E4l-4;11]

(7b) *And - they - the dog is getting chased by the bees.* [E9d-9;6]

(7c) *Y al perro emm las avispas le - le iban a por él.*

'And OBJ+DEF dog um the wasps CL.PRO - CL.PRO went at for he.' [The end result is an ungrammatical sequence of two prepositions, *a por*.] [S9i-9;10]

(7d) *Und der Hund - und die Bienen verfolgen jetzt den Hund.*

'And the dog - and the bees chase now the dog.' [G9b-9;0]

In the Deer Event, all four dimensions are at issue:

(8a) *And - a moose ... the boy got caught on the moose's - antlers.* [Switch from moose (=deer) to boy as topic, and locus of effect, taking Cause-View with minimal agency.] [E5l-5;11]

(8b) *Then it turns out they're antler - a deer's antlers. So - and he gets - he lands on his head.* [Switch from Cause-View of *get*-passive to Become-View with verb of diminished agency.] [*E9k-9;11*]

In the Entry-into-Jar Event speakers hesitate in making a figure-ground choice: head-in-jar or jar-on-head. (For more detailed analysis, see Berman, 1993.)

(9a) *Und der Hund der hat das Glas - der da der Kopf ist im Glas.*

'And the dog he has the glass - the there the head is in the glass.' [*G5g-5;3*]

(9b) *Pero como tiene el tarro en eh - come tiene la cabeza metida en el tarro, se rompe el tarro y no y no se rompe la cabeza.*

'But since he has the jar on um - since he has the head placed in the jar, the jar breaks and not and not the head breaks.' [*S9l-9;11*]

Another perspective choice is between the dog placing himself or just his head into the jar. A Turkish preschooler shifted perspective from dog to head, beginning with an intransitive verb of motion and ending up with an accusative marking on head, but no corresponding transitive verb:

(9c) *Köpek kavanoza girmiş. Kafasını yani.*

dog:NOM jar:DAT entered. head:POSS+ACC that.is

'The dog went into the jar — his head, that is.' [*T3c-4;3*]

Spanish preschoolers sometimes have difficulty with the distinction between use of the reflexive for self-movement versus the simple transitive of the same verb for movement of a body-part as object, as shown in the following ungrammatical uses of the reflexive with body-part insertion:

(9d) *El perro se metió la cabeza en el bote.*

'The dog put:REFL the head in the jar.' [*S3j-3;11*]

(9e) *Se mete el perro el morro.*

'Puts:REFL the dog the snout.' [*S4d-4;5*]

Hebrew preschoolers sometimes have difficulty in choosing between a Cause-View and a Become-View, as shown in the following mixed construction:

(9f) *Ha-kelev nitka ha-kufsa im ha-rosh.*

'The-dog got.stuck:MASC the-can:FEM with the-head.' [*H5l-5;9*]

The fact that many repairs occur in 9-year-old stories shows that narrative organization remains a problem long after the acquisition of complex syntax and basic narrative capacity, as pointed out repeatedly throughout our study. Even after constructions have been acquired, they must be accessed and integrated online.[12] Even some adults have difficulty finding a perspective on a complex situation such as the misperceptions leading up to the Deer Event.

In all of the cases of filtering examined here, the speaker is involved in constructing a preverbal message that embodies a particular event construal. Similar issues arise when we examine the development of means for packaging such construals into integrated sequences of clauses in the flow of narrative.

2. PACKAGING: CLAUSE COMBINING

We use the term "packaging" as a kind of visual metaphor for the various ways in which situations can be analyzed into components and encoded in multiclausal constructions. As an idealization, imagine the contrast between a series of free clauses and a single, complex sentence:

(10a)It was morning. The boy woke up. He looked at the jar. It was empty.

(10b)When the boy woke up in the morning he saw that the jar was empty.

The second version is more economical, of course — but this is not the most important thing about it. In the first version, each of the clauses seem to carry equal weight. But in the second everything is subordinated to a focal point: the boy's discovery. The first clause gives the background to this highpoint and the following two clauses package it into one event, in which the act of seeing (*he saw*) and the mental result of that act (*that the jar was empty*) are conflated into a verb-complement construction. Thus we see two rhetorical effects of packaging here: (1) the subordination of event components to a highpoint, and (2) the conflation of different phases of the event into a single event-complex.

Packaging can also serve a third function, as shown in the following narration of the same episode:

(10c)When the boy woke up in the morning he saw that the frog had run away.

Here, some components are missing and have to be inferred by the listener. The boy cannot, literally, see that the frog "**had** run away," because the temporal frame of this clause is retrospective with regard to the act of seeing, as indicated by the use of the past perfect. Relative tense here signals that the event components packaged in (10c) have some missing elements. Packaging allows the narrator to avoid the full sequence represented in (10d):

---

[12] In this regard, it would be worthwhile to compare oral with written narrative, where the pressures of online production are lifted.

(10d)When the boy woke in the morning he saw that the jar was empty and
realized that the frog had run away.

The third rhetorical function of packaging, then, is to allow for the omission
of some event components.

We identify a fourth function of packaging — one that is more elusive.
By shifting the density of packaging across a narration, the speaker has control over the **rhythm** and **tempo** of presentation of the narrative, allowing for
the creation of suspense and surprise. For example, shifting into a series of
free clauses can slow down the action and highlight attention to key events,
while a densely packaged account of attendant circumstances can forestall
presentation of a dramatic moment. Packaging of subevents into subordinate
clauses can, by contrast, speed them up. And so on. (All of these effects are,
of course, created by acoustic means, along with syntactic devices of the sort
indicated in (10). Rate of speech, intonation contours, pitch, stress, and pause
all play central roles in rhythm and tempo of presentation. Unfortunately, we
have not been able to undertake acoustic analyses in the framework of this
study. The following discussion, therefore, relates only to syntactic means of
varying the density and prominence of information in narrative.)

On the syntactic plane, consider the following segment of an adult
English narration. We have tried to suggest "syntactic rhythm and tempo" by
typographical means, using larger typeface to suggest the narrative prominence of main clauses and simple sentences. This is, of course, a subjective
portrayal, reflecting our feeling that various sorts of subordinate clauses
present background and supporting information that is presented in more
compact form than the main clauses that propel the narrative forward.

(11) While running away from the owl who he bothered while he was sleeping in his
hole in the tree he crawls up on a rock to call for his frog some more and
holds on to what looks like a branch. But it's not really a
branch. It's the antlers of a deer. The deer picks him up.
[E20j]

Labov (1972) has proposed that syntactic complexity of the sort we term
"packaging" often serves to provide the **evaluative component** of the narrative: "the means used by the narrator to indicate the point of the narrative, its
raison d'être: why it was told, and what the narrator is getting at" (p. 366). He
notes that many features of syntactic complexity serve this function:

they intensify certain narrative events that are most relevant to the
main point; they compare the events that did occur to those which
might have but did not occur; they correlate the linear dimension of

the narration by superimposing one event upon another; and they explicate the point of the narrative in so many words (p. 392).

He further notes that these features have a long developmental history. In his research, teenagers (aged 13-16) had still not fully mastered the evaluative uses of narrative syntax. In our study, as well, school-age children show considerably less control of packaging than adults, and preschoolers are only beginning to exploit the possibilities of narrative syntax.

2.1. Crosslinguistic Patterns

In order to explore these issues further, we segmented the texts into "packages" defined in syntactic terms, regardless of the narrative functions of the various means of clause combining. The following types of packages are represented in the quantitative summary presented below:

- **Coordination with null subject**: same-subject clauses joined by 'and' with null subject in second clause, such as: *The owl popped out and knocked him down.*[13]

- **Verb gapping**: clause-linking in which the predicate and/or a tense-bearing auxiliary is absent for a second subject, such as: *The boy was happy and the dog was too. / Der Junge fällt runter und der Hund auch* 'The boy falls down and the dog too.'

- **Finite linking**: clauses linked by a subordinating or nonsubordinating conjunction with a finite verb in the conjunct clause, such as: *The dog raced away because the bees were chasing him. / Hakelev likek et hayeled, aval hayeled lo haya sameax* 'The dog licked the boy, but the boy was not happy'. This category includes adverbial clauses marked by temporal, causal, or logical connectives such as *because, when, while, so that, but, before, after, as, now that,* and equivalents in the other languages.

---

[13] We did not use this category in Spanish because, as discussed in Chapter IIIc, subject pronouns are almost nonexistent in the Spanish texts, where null subject is the norm for successive same-subject clauses. (There are only 14 subject pronouns in the entire Spanish corpus, five of them used by one 4-year-old.) Null subjects are more optional in Hebrew, as indicated by the fact that narrators of all ages use subject pronouns in one-third to one-half of all clauses (age 3 — 43%, age 4 — 51%, age 5 — 37%, age 9 — 40%, adult — 32%). Therefore we did use this category in Hebrew. (For more on Hebrew as a limited sort of "pro-drop" language see Chapter IIID and Berman, 1990.) We also used this category in Turkish, because, as discussed below, coordination with *ve* 'and' is a rare and mature form of packaging. (Nonfinite linking is favored by Turkish typology.)

- **Nonfinite linking:** gerundive and infinitival constructions, such as: *He looked under the bed, messing up his room.* / *He climbed on some rocks to look.* / *Al caerse se rompe* 'PREP+DEF.ART fall:INF REFL breaks' (=on falling, it breaks). Turkish converbs are also included in this category, such as: *düş-erek kırıyor* 'fall-CONVERB breaks' (=in falling, it breaks) (see Chapter IIIE).

- **Relative clauses:** all types of relative clauses, including restrictive and nonrestrictive as well as headless relatives (e.g., *He looked where the frog had been*).

Table 2 presents the mean percentages of clauses occurring in these five types of packages combined, by age and language. (The figures represent the means of the percentages calculated for each individual child in each group.)[14]

TABLE 2
Mean Percentage of Clauses in Packages,
by Age and Language

| Language | Age | | | | |
	3 yrs	4 yrs	5 yrs	9 yrs	Adult
English	13	19	29	38	60
German	9	-	13	35	60
Spanish	19	20	17	32	47
Hebrew	15	23	32	42	66
Turkish	6	-	16	39	49

It is evident that syntactic packaging increases across the entire age span — from preschool to school age, and beyond. Consider, first, the 9-year-olds and adults: In all five languages there is a considerable increase after age 9. In addition, it is noteworthy that the rate of use by 9-year-olds is quite similar, across languages, in spite of the fact that the constructions involved differ. It is also evident from Table 2 that there is considerable growth between ages 5 and 9. The preschool patterns, however, are not as uniform. Whereas we see clear growth between ages 3 and 5 in English, Hebrew, and Turkish, there is only a slight increase in German, and none at all in Spanish. We return to this issue below.

---

[14] Thanks to Lisa Dasinger and Cecile Toupin for carrying out the calculations and preliminary analyses of these data.

TABLE 3
Mean Number of Clauses per Package,
by Age and Language[a]

Language	Age				
	3 yrs	4 yrs	5 yrs	9 yrs	Adult
English	2.1 (7)	2.0 (11)	2.1	2.2	2.6
German	2.0	-	2.1	2.1	2.6
Spanish	2.0	2.1	2.1 (11)	2.1	2.5
Hebrew	2.2 (8)	2.1	2.3	2.2	2.5
Turkish	2.0 (4)	-	2.1 (9)	2.1	2.4

a. The number of narrators is 12 for the first four languages and 10 for Turkish, unless otherwise indicated by a number in parentheses, giving the number of narrators for this analysis. Those numbers show that some children in the age sample used no packages at all (e.g., five English 3-year-olds, etc.).

Another way to examine the growth in syntactic packaging is to compare packages in terms of the number of clauses that are syntactically linked. In this regard, we see very little development, as shown in Table 3. Across the entire preschool and school-age period, narrators tend almost always to link only two clauses in one syntactic unit, and hardly ever more than three.[15] In addition, some preschoolers used no packages at all, as indicated by numbers in parentheses in the table.

Development up to age 9 is seen in the frequency and diversity of such linking rather than in the **size** of units. Syntactic rhythm and tempo are thus primarily built by means of two-clause packages interspersed with free clauses. Only at the adult level do we find a considerable increase, averaging about 2.5 clauses per package and ranging as high as 8 in dense packages as in (11), broken down into clauses in (12):

---

[15] For purposes of this analysis, a complement-taking verb and its associated clause were treated as a single clause, because of the obligatory nature of such linking. For example, the following was counted as a package of two clauses: [*when the boy and dog wake up*] [*they realize that the frog was gone*]. That is, the narrator did not have the choice of either stopping with *realize* or adding another clause. Such obligatory linkings, counted as one clause here, include verbs such as 'see', 'know', 'search', 'tell' and their complement clauses.

[16] The next clause, *It's the antlers of a deer*, is nonsyntactically linked in a sort of "colon construction" to the last clause in (12). We did not attempt to count instances of this type of packaging. It is our impression, though, that narrators of all ages link clauses in terms of possible inferential relations between events, generally marked by prosody. The development of means of prosodic and inferential clause-linking is in need of detailed future analysis.

(12) *while running away from the owl* [nonfinite linking]
   who he bothered [relative clause]
   while he was sleeping in his hole in the tree [finite linking]
   he crawls up on a rock [main clause]
   to call for his frog some more [nonfinite linking]
   and holds on to [coordination with null subject]
   what looks like a branch [relative clause]
   but it's not really a branch [finite linking][16]

Detailed summaries of the development of connectivity in each of the five languages, taken separately, are presented in the chapters in Section III; Chapter IVA compares the languages in terms of marking of temporal relations between clauses; and Chapter IVB traces the development of relative clause functions. Clearly, the patterns represented in Tables 2 and 3 reflect a complex interaction of form and function, with a number of language-specific variants. Here we limit ourselves to a brief summary of the various types of constructions involved in packaging, in the form of a narrative overview of relative frequencies of use of the various types by age and language. Each of the languages shows a characteristic pattern, based on the range and complexity of construction types.

2.1.1. Development of clause-linking types

Relative clauses. The major overall development in clause-linking after age 9 is an increase in relative clause use in English, German, and Turkish. In Spanish and Hebrew, as discussed in Chapter IVB, this construction has an earlier development. In Hebrew the proportion of relative clauses increases from ages 4 to 5 and remains close to the adult level thereafter, whereas in Spanish the adult rate is approximated by age 9. In English and German, relative clause use increases gradually from age 5 onwards. This is a rare option in Turkish, increasing only after age 9.

Nonfinite linking. Between the ages of 5 and 9, Spanish and Turkish children are especially involved in the elaboration of nonfinite constructions. In Turkish, this is the major means of packaging, as discussed in more detail below. In the other three languages, nonfinite linking is a minor option.

Finite linking. This large and diverse category is a major option for all of the languages except Turkish, where typological factors favor nonfinite linking. The developmental patterns, however, differ by language. In English, the period from 3 to 5 shows the greatest increase in relative frequency, with the marking of temporal (*when, while*), causal (*because*), and adversative (*but*) relations between clauses. In German, comparable growth takes place later, between ages 5 and 9. In Spanish and Hebrew, finite linking shows a fairly steady relative frequency across the ages, on a par with other means of packaging.

Verb gapping. This type of linking is predominant only in the preschool period, and primarily in German. Older narrators have more sophisticated ways of indicating the parallel or related activities of two protagonists, as discussed in Chapter IVA. The greater relative frequency of verb-gapping in German may be due to the fact that it is syntactically simple, requiring no auxiliary choice, by contrast with English. Compare, for example, *Da kuckt der hinter und der Hund auch* 'There he looks behind and the dog too' [*G3d-3;6*] with English equivalents such as: *There he is looking behind and so is the dog* or *There he is looking behind and the dog is too*. Verb gapping is syntactically simple in Spanish and Hebrew as well, but it shares the field in the preschool period with a broader range of clause-linking constructions than in German. (Verb gapping is not an option in Turkish.)

Coordination with null subject. As noted above, this is a major developmental option in English, Hebrew, and German. It increases in relative frequency in the preschool period in the first two languages, and between the ages of 5 and 9 in German.

2.1.2. Language-specific patterns

During the preschool period of ages 3 to 5, each language shows a characteristic pattern of use and development of the various clause-linking devices:

- **English**: frequent finite linking and sharp increase in coordination with null subject
- **German**: frequent verb-gapping and coordination, with some increase in finite linking
- **Spanish**: fairly balanced use of relative clauses, finite linking, and verb gapping
- **Hebrew**: predominant and increasing use of coordination, with some increase in relative clauses
- **Turkish**: rapid increase in nonfinite linking, with little use of other devices

These patterns suggest that the languages differ in terms of the most "accessible" devices for packaging. All of the available devices in each language are used by some preschoolers, but the devices differ in relative frequency of use (as well as functions, discussed below).

The Spanish children are well on their way towards mastering a number of construction types in this early period. They make active use of finite and nonfinite linking, relative clauses, and verb gapping. Paradoxically, this "embarrassment of riches" may account for their lack of increase in mean percentage of clauses in packages, as shown in Table 2. Perhaps, in the presence of several strong options, no single one can take easy precedence, and as a consequence it may sometimes occur that none is chosen. In German, by contrast, some of the options seem to be less accessible to preschoolers, perhaps due to factors of morphosyntactic complexity and associated processing load. As noted in earlier chapters, the syntax of subordination is complex in German, apparently delaying mastery of relative clauses and various means of finite linking considered here. German children may be more involved in mastering basic constructions after age 5, while the children in the other languages are refining more advanced constructions. In the remaining three languages, preschoolers are consolidating their command of basic clause-linking devices.

The school-age period also shows different types of developmental patterns for the five languages (though we only have the comparison points of ages 5 and 9). The German children drop the use of verb-gapping and work primarily on various types of subordination. Relative clause use increases for all of the languages except Turkish, with Spanish and Hebrew children elaborating mature functions for relative clauses during this age period. Coordination takes on more specialized functions, sharing the field with other types of packaging (Berman, in press-c). And in Spanish and Turkish there is a great increase in the use of nonfinite linking, as discussed in more detail below.

2.2. Analysis and Synthesis of Events

In order to create a packaged event description, it is first necessary to have analyzed the event into two or more components. Or, alternatively, it is necessary to see that two "situations" can be construed as part of an "event." In either case, clause-linking requires hierarchical organization, because the individual clauses are treated as part of a larger unit. We refer to these interdependent processes of analysis and synthesis simply as "event packaging." Our data suggest that there are four developmental levels of increasing complexity of event packaging in narrative: (1) temporal, (2) causal, (3) constituent, and (4) event-complex.

2.2.1. Level 1: Temporal packaging

Three-year-olds in all of the languages use two-clause combinations that relate two situations as simultaneous or sequential in time, as discussed in Chapter IVA. This sort of packaging places limited conceptual demands on relating events described in the two clauses. For the youngest children, each event can be seen as independent and foregrounded, with the linking provided

by perceptual contiguity in the pictures. Within the domain of temporal packaging there is further development on the basis of narrative ability, resulting
in various kinds of foreground/background relations between the events
encoded in a package. The basic lexical and syntactic devices for this kind of
packaging, however, are acquired during the preschool period. For example,
3- and 4-year-olds link finite clauses into packages of sequence and simultaneity:

(13) *Y cuando se tirado al agua encontró una rana.*

'And when (he was) thrown to the water he found a frog.' [*S3c-3;7*]

(14) *The boy and the dog slept while the frog quietly got out of the jar.*
[E4b-4;0]

2.2.2. Level 2: Causal packaging

Three-year-olds also link clauses by causal connectors such as *because*.
The youngest example occurs in the text of a Hebrew child of 3;5:

(14) *Ve po hu nafal ki hayanshuf hipil oto.*

'And here he fell because the owl threw him.' [*H3c-3;5*]

However, analysis and synthesis of components of cause, motive, and purpose
continue through the school years, requiring advances in both syntactic and
conceptual abilities (see Chapter IIB). Preschool causal packaging deals
almost entirely with physical causality, as in (14). As discussed in Chapter
IIA, it is not until age 9 that narrators pay much attention to the inner states of
protagonists as motivating their behaviors. Attention to such factors has
consequences for various types of packaging.

Clause-linking that encodes physical causality follows the order of
CONSEQUENCE-CAUSE shown in (14). Inner states, however, can be treated as
either causes or consequences of situations. The following examples follow
CONSEQUENCE-CAUSE order: in (15) the boy's emotional state is attributed to
the behavior of the dog, whereas in (16) a physical event is attributed to the
boy's emotional state.

(15) *Und der Junge ist wütend weil er [=Hund] das kaputt gemacht hat.*

'And the boy is furious because he [=dog] has broken that.' [*G9c-9;6*]

(16) *El niño se cayó porque una lechuza le asustó.*

'The boy fell because an owl scared him.' [*S9i-9;1*]

Nine-year-olds can also link clauses in the CAUSE-CONSEQUENCE order, both
for emotional consequences, as in (17) and physical consequences as in (18):

(17) *The owl came out of its tree and scared the little boy.* [*E9c-9;6*]

(18) *Del agujero sale un buho que hace que el niño se caiga.*
    'From the hole comes out an owl that makes the boy fall.' *[S9c-9;3]*

This last example also shows the use of a relative clause for what Dasinger and Toupin define as the MOT function, that is, the function of "motivating or enabling a narrative event" (Chapter IVB). This is a function that
flowers at age 9 in Spanish and Hebrew, developing only later in the other
languages. As discussed in Section 5.2.2 of Chapter IVB, it is only adults who
are able to flexibly use both pre- and postposed relative clauses to refer to
psychological states as motivating causes. And it is only adults who present a
clear CAUSE-CONSEQUENCE relation in the use of another relative clause function, CONT, used to "continue the narrative by depicting a subsequent or consequent event," as in:

(19) *And the deer stops abruptly, which causes the boy to lose his balance
    and fall with the dog down into the stream. [E20f]*

Beginning at age 9, however, narrators are able to make use of the syntactic means at their disposal to present more complex causal relations in a
single event package. In (20) the narrator presents a chain of causal circumstances, seen from a retrospective point of view:

(20) *And then the boy was mad, cause he knew that the frog went away cause
    he was playing with him. [E9e-9;7]*

In (21) the syntax is not complex — two clauses are joined by *porque*
'because' — but the causal relation itself requires a degree of inferencing not
encountered in younger texts:

(21) *El niño hace callar al perro, porque veía una rana detrás de un tronco
    seco.*

    'The boy makes the dog be quiet, because (he) saw a frog behind a dry
    trunk.' *[S9j-9;11]*

In sum, although temporal and causal packaging both have their roots in
early childhood, the frog story calls for considerable development of means of
packaging of causal relations through the school years and beyond. In the
temporal domain, syntactic means for combining clauses to encode temporal
sequence and simultaneity seem to be more easily mastered, and elaboration
of temporal relations is carried further by verbal aspect, aspectual verbs and
adverbs, and other lexical means.

2.2.3. Level 3: Constituent packaging

So far we have treated the contents of two linked clauses as roughly
equal "situations" of independent status that are narratively joined because of
their temporal or causal relation. A more complex type of packaging involves

the analysis of an event into **constituents** which, taken together, make up a single event. Consider the following two clauses as constituents of one event:

(22) *He started calling for the frog, thinking that he'd probably come* [...]
    [*E9f-9;8*]

The focus here is neither on temporal nor causal relation per se, though both are present. Example (22) does not mean 'he started calling for the frog **because** he thought he'd probably come'; nor does it mean 'he started calling for the frog **while** he was thinking that he'd probably come'. The calling and the thinking are two components of the same event, one focusing on the external behavior and the other focusing on the inner state. Nonfinite forms are centrally involved in this kind of packaging. In Spanish we have 9-year-old uses of present participles like *pensando* 'thinking' and *creyendo* 'believing', as well as PREPOSITION+INFINITIVE constructions such as:

(23) *Al subirse a una roca, se chocó con un animal de esos que tienen cuernos.*

    'On climbing [PREP+INF] a rock, he collided with one of those animals that has horns.' [*S9g-9;6*]

The packaging in (23) does not express simple sequence — it does not mean 'he climbed and then collided'; nor does it mean simultaneity — 'while he climbed he collided'. Rather, the climbing and the collision are two constituent phases of the same event, separated out into two clauses, but expressing a unitary event of 'climbing and colliding'.

As mentioned above, nonfinite linking increases in importance in Spanish in the school years, and in Turkish it is the major means of packaging across the age span. Turkish provides an exceptionally useful case study of the development of constituent packaging, since a single syntactic construction, the **converb** construction, is used to express a range of types of packaging (see Chapter IIIE, Sections 2 and 4.2, and Slobin, 1993a). The basic construction, consistent with the verb-final typology of Turkish, consists of a nonfinite verb form in the first clause followed by a finite verb form in the second. There are four converbs used in the frog stories, schematized below with English glosses and using X and Y to represent clauses, with the converb suffixed to the verb of the X-clause. The first two are used for temporal packaging, the third is used for various kinds of coordination, and the fourth is used for constituent packaging:

(24) **Converb constructions**:

(a)   *X-ince Y* 'when X, Y' / 'as soon as X, Y'

(b)   *X-ken Y* 'while X-ing, Y'

(c)   *X-ip Y* 'X and (then) Y'

(d)   *X-erek Y* '(in,by) X-ing, Y'

All four constructions are highly frequent in the speech that children hear and all are identically transparent and accessible morphologically. The first three are used from the youngest ages, yet the fourth, the "phasal" converb *-erek* (Slobin, 1993a), is not used until after age 5. Table 4 shows the percentage of narrators appropriately using each converb type at least once, combining Aksu-Koç's and Küntay's data to provide a large sample, including 7-year-olds.

TABLE 4

Percentage of Narrators Appropriately Using Each Converb
at Least Once (Turkish Data of Aksu-Koç and Küntay Combined)

Converb	Age					
	3 yrs (N=15)	4 yrs (N=13)	5 yrs (N=27)	7 yrs (N=16)	9 yrs (N=22)	Adult (N=12)
-ince	7	23	33	31	50	42
-ken	20	46	44	69	68	92
-ip	13	54	59	56	55	92
-erek	0	0	0	25	32	58

The late emergence of *-erek* at school age must be due the conceptual complexity of constituent packaging, as reflected also in the emergence of nonfinite forms in the other languages during this age period. Five-year-olds are able to analyze an event into phases, and, in Turkish, even package them together with a coordinating converb, as in (25a); but only older children can use *-erek* to tightly package two constituents into a single event representation, as in (25b):

(25a) *Yavruyu al-ıp ona bakıyorlar.*

  baby.[frog]:ACC take-*ip* it:DAT they.look

  'They take a baby frog and look at it.' [*T5e-6;0*]

(25b) *Bir tanesini eline al-arak onu sevdi.*

  one item:POSS:ACC hand:POSS:DAT take-*erek* it:ACC (he) loved

  'Taking one of them [=baby frog] in his hand, he loved it.' [*T9j-9;1*]

It is characteristic of phasal linking devices, such as *-erek*, that they treat two situations as constituent parts of a superordinate event, without explicitly naming or categorizing that event.[17] These constructions thus create a kind of

---

[17] Slobin (1993a) suggests that such constructions are like the serial verb constructions of languages like Mandarin, as described by Li and Thompson (1981, p. 594): "...the verb

implicit composite event category, such as 'think-call', 'climb-collide', and 'hold-love'.

TABLE 5

Functions of *erek*-Packages in Frog Stories

CONSECUTIVE:

Preparatory Act/Movement

'He shut-*erek* his eyes slept.' [age 9]

'The boy climb-*erek* tree was.looking in hole.' [age 9]

Motivating State

'The boy get.angry-*erek* picks.up dog.' [age 7]

'The deer get.nervous-*erek* started to.run wildly.' [age 9]

Cause

'The owl chase-*erek* the boy frightened him.' [age 9]

'The dog fall-*erek* from the window broke the jar.' [adult]

PURPOSE:

'The boy bring-*erek* his hands to his mouth was.trying to.silence the dog.' [age 7]

'The frog leave-*erek* the jar ran.away.' [age 9]

CIRCUMSTANCE:

'The boy approach *erek* a log says "sh" to the dog.' [age 9]

'Wave-*erek* his hand he goes.' [age 9]

MANNER:

'Swim-*erek* they went back.' [age 7]

'The dog quickly run-*erek* alongside passed.' [adult]

The types of packages linked by -*erek* represent a mature kind of perspective-taking, dealing with interlaced dimensions of events. There are several subtypes, as presented in Table 5, using English glosses of examples from Turkish texts. **Consecutive** uses present a slightly retrospective view of a preliminary event phase that enables the subsequent phase. Similar functions are performed by motivational and continuative relative clauses, which are also late developments. **Purpose** uses define an act in the *erek*-clause and give its goal in the main clause. Although the events occur in sequence, it is

---

phrases in the serial verb construction always refer to events or states of affairs which are understood to be related as **parts** of **one** overall event or state of affairs. The exact way in which they are related varies according to the meanings of the verbs in these verb phrases."

the global event that is focused on. **Circumstance** uses present event constituents as an amalgam, the *erek*-clause providing the circumstances under which the event takes place, similar to uses of present participles in English, German, and Spanish. **Manner** uses describe manner of movement, as is typical of verb-framed languages (cf. the parallel use of present participles in Spanish). This is the earliest developmental function of *-erek* (and is also an early function of the corresponding forms in Spanish).

   Similar uses of nonfinite forms and relative clauses for some of these purposes are found in English, Spanish, and Hebrew. (In German, however, syntactic event packaging is much less frequent.) The following constructions, for example, perform functions parallel to *erek*-packages, along with the sort of consecutive packaging represented by relative clauses such as shown in (18), above.

(26a)*The dog stuck his head in the jar, looking for him.* [gerund: purpose] [*E9i-9;10*]

(26b)*Y el perro, al buscar-lo, se metió en la botella.*

   'And the dog, PREP.ART look:INF-CLITIC.PRO, put himself in the bottle' (=And the dog, in looking for it...) [infinitive: purpose] [*S9b-9;2*]

(26c)*Ve hakelev xipes ota bacincenet she hu nixnas [eleha] im harosh.*

   'And the dog looked for it in the jar that he went into with his head.' [relative clause: circumstance] [*H9c-9;4*]

   Precursors and prerequisites. In Section 1.6.2 we reviewed evidence offered by Melissa Bowerman that 2-year-olds can attend to agent and change-of-state as separate event components. She has also discussed the development of "event compression" during the preschool period (Bowerman, 1984; see also 1977, 1982b). A prerequisite is the ability to make reference to an event as an entity. Two-year-olds can use the deictic *this* or *that* to refer to an event, such as:

(27) [patting hand over mouth in "Indian war-whoop"] ***This*** *what Marc do-s sometimes when I be-s there.* [age 2;5]

Sometime after age 3, children can use the same construction to refer back to an event that has been verbally introduced:

(28) *I probably got some snow on my hands and **that** made my whole body be cold.* [age 3;6]

Soon after the establishment of this type of discourse anaphora to events, Bowerman finds nominalizations which refer to an event within the context of a larger event, as in (29), along with other devices for referring to complex causal sequences as if they were simple events, as in (30) and (31).

(29) [stepping off plywood slab on which her mattress usually rests; mother had told her earlier not to bounce on bed springs under another mattress] *Stepping down from it won't break it; of course not.* [age 3;10]

(30) [after pulling apart a stapled book] *I pulled it unstapled.* [3;8]

(31) [after mother puts desired object out of reach] *You made me cry with putting that up there.* [age 3;6]

Bowerman notes that these various "devices for expressing complex causal events all emerged **more-or-less simultaneously**... Their common denominator is conceptual, not linguistic: they all require the speaker to be able to hold two complete propositions in mind simultaneously (causing event and resulting event) and **merge** them to form a new, higher-order event" (1984, p. 4). This is a definition of the conceptual ability underlying constituent packaging, and, like the other sorts of perspective considered in this chapter, the conceptual ability presents itself long before all of its linguistic consequences have been worked out. Level 3 syntactic packaging introduces compressed events into the structure of narrative — many years after the emergence of the abilities summarized by Bowerman. Finally, at the adult level, we find syntactically packaged events with multiple components.

2.2.4. Level 4: Event complexes

The three levels considered thus far deal almost entirely with two-clause packages. As shown in Table 3, there is a major developmental increase between age 9 and adulthood in the number of clauses per package — about 2.5 in adult texts, and ranging to as high as 8, as shown in example (12). On the level of what we call "event complexes," the narrator does more than analyze one event in detail and package the details together into one "syntactic envelope." An event complex is a higher level of organization, syntactically combining several subunits into an overarching macroevent or even mini-episode. The event complex in (12) follows the boy from his escape from the owl just up to his involvement with the deer. It has several layers: (a) action sequence: *while running away from the owl ... he crawls up on a rock ... and holds onto (something)*; (b) retrospective causal circumstance: *(the owl) who he bothered while he was sleeping in his hole in the tree*; (c) continuing purpose: *to call for his frog some more*; (d) suspense (from the viewpoint of the omniscient narrator): *what looks like a branch but it's not really a branch.*

No children produce this degree of elaboration, although some 9-year-olds, in each language, begin to show the ability to produce event complexes which package several clauses. One scene that seems to elicit such productions occurs near the beginning of the story, where there is a temporal overlap between the frog's escape and the sleeping/waking of the boy. The relations are entirely temporal, which might facilitate such packaging. For example, an English 9-year-old begins the story, *Once there was a boy who had a pet frog and a dog. And that night he was watching it* .... The story continues with the following event complex:

(32) *and ... when he went to sleep, the frog - got out of his jar - and got away.*
    [E9a-9;1]

By our criteria, there is a package of three clauses here: an event segmented into two phases — *the frog* [*got out of his jar*] [*and got away*] — placed in a temporal frame — [*when he went to sleep*]. The same scene is packaged into two small event complexes by a Turkish 9-year-old, one of four clauses (33a) and one of three (33b).

(33a) *Gece olduğu için çocuk köpeğiyle birlikte yatağına uzan-ıp hemen gözlerini kapay-arak uyudu.*

'Because it was night, the boy together with his dog stretch.out-*ip* in bed, immediately shut-*erek* their eyes, slept.' [*T9j-9;1*]

(33b) *Sessizce patırdı yapmadan kurbağa kavanozundan çık-arak kaçtı.*

'Silently, without making a sound, the frog exit-*erek* from his jar escaped.' [*T9j-9;1*]

In (33a) there is an initial causal clause, which also establishes a temporal frame ('because it was night'), followed by two kinds of converb clauses: The *ip*-clause sets up the temporal antecedent to the *erek*-clause, which packages a preparatory act and its consequence ('shut eyes — sleep'). This sort of multiple layering of clause types within one syntactic unit is characteristic of more mature speakers. There is also an *erek*-clause in (33b), serving to package the two phases — 'exit-escape' — that are more loosely packaged in the English coordinate construction with null subject in (32).

By contrast to the two packages of (33a-b), adults are able to package all of the relevant components of this event complex into a single syntactic construction, such as the following Spanish example:

(34) *Durante la noche, mientras Federico y Can su perro están dormidos en la cama, Ran la rana sale de la pecera, y desaparece.*

'During the night, while Federico and Can his dog are asleep in the bed, Ran the frog exits from the jar, and disappears.' [*S20l*]

As a final observation about Level 4, consider adult use of the Turkish coordinate conjunction *ve* 'and'. As noted in footnote 13, this is a rare and mature form in Turkish, because the verb-final typology favors the use of converbs for clause linking. The conjunction is a borrowed form from Arabic and is used by adults to build a special sort of event complex in which converbs are used to set up preparatory phases which are then linked to a consequence by means of *ve*. (35) is an example of the complexity that can be achieved by this composite use of several kinds of clause-linking devices:

(35) *Camın açık bırakıldığını farked-ip camdan bakarlar-ken köpek aşağıya düşüyor, kavanoz başında ve kavanoz kırılıyor.*

window open having.been.left notice-*ip* window.from look:PL-*ken* dog downwards falls, jar on.his.head *ve* jar breaks

'Having noticed that the window was left open, while they are looking out of the window, the dog falls down, jar on his head, **and** the jar breaks.' [*T20d*]

It is evident from this example that the use of a "simple" coordinating conjunction is not so simple in Turkish, where its usual functions are carried out by converbs. To reiterate one of the themes of the first section of this chapter, one cannot understand the development and use of a type of linguistic form without placing it in the context of the array of forms that carry out related functions within the language — in this instance, a consideration of a coordinating conjunction in the context of converb constructions.

Level 4 is the culmination of all of the means of event packaging that we have considered. The use of various types of clause-combining to create event complexes requires a hierarchical organization of the narrative into events and subevents, embracing temporal and causal relations, and often evaluated from the narrator's viewpoint.

In sum, narrative demands to **filter** and to **package** grow throughout the developmental span — and probably well into adulthood. These demands motivate the discovery and exploitation of a wide range of syntactic and lexical means of expression, always within the typological constraints of the particular language. The analyses presented in this chapter fill in some of the details of both the developmental and typological themes that run throughout our study. It is clear, from our brief examination of precursors and prerequisites, that much of the conceptual ability to select perspectives and analyze events is available well in advance of the full use of these skills for the construction of narrative. The demands of narrative — along with all other temporally extended and hierarchically organized verbal activities — require the child to create and integrate linguistic structures that will make a chosen event construal clear to the listener. Eventually, all of the many tools of the native language are brought to bear on this task — lexical choice, voice and word-order alternation, and complex syntax. The endstate is a "proficient speaker," as discussed in Chapter VA. Further, as a final developmental consequence, each language represents a unique choice of options, resulting in a characteristic rhetorical style, as discussed further in Chapter VB.

Chapter IVᴅ

FORESHADOWING AND WRAPPING UP
IN NARRATIVE

Michael Bamberg and Virginia Marchman

0. INTRODUCTION

Regardless of whether text production is viewed as movement from parts to the whole or from a pre-existing whole to its parts, each individual move of putting parts together involves joining individual pieces in a way that is both dependent on previous moves and establishes the presuppositions for subsequent moves. In previous work, we have compared this process with that involved in constructing a building (Bamberg & Marchman, 1990, 1991). In the actual process of constructing a building, parts are prerequisites for assembly, so that a whole can emerge out of the parts. However, it should be clear that these parts are selected out of the universe of possible parts for some particular job and for that job alone. That is, not only are parts fitted functionally together on the basis of an underlying concept, but at the same time, the object in question needs to be considered in terms of its form, in order to determine its function.[1] Thus, the individual parts and the whole only gain their separate existences in light of and in close connection with each other (see also Bamberg, 1993, for elaborations of this argument).

In this chapter we focus on one particular aspect of the organization of part-whole relationships in text construction. In contrast to two previous articles (Bamberg, 1992; Bamberg & Marchman, 1991), where we focused on this relationship in terms of a simultaneous "binding" and "unfolding" relationship, here we suggest a slightly different metaphor. While the notions of a simultaneous binding and unfolding (see also Coste, 1989) more closely resemble the opposite movements of putting something together and simultaneously pulling something apart (so revealing what holds parts and whole together), the metaphor adopted in this chapter seeks to highlight the spatial arrangement of the part-whole relationship and the narrative activity of moving through this space. The notion of **foreshadowing** is meant to capture that aspect of the narrative activity that sets up the hearer with regard to what is coming next. That is, the narrator points forward, orienting to parts that are about to come. **Wrapping up** is meant to capture the backward orientation that narrators take with regard to the previously established discourse. In this case, the narrator is pointing back, revealing the relevance of what is said here to what has been said before, often in the form of tying things together or "wrapping them up."[2]

"Foreshadowing" and "wrapping up" thus form part of the creation of a relevancy system, and they are not employed at random in text constructions. In terms of their interactive function, they are used at strategically relevant points in the narrative activity, i.e., at points where it is more likely the listener may get lost, for instance in sudden (= unexpected) changes of spatial scenes, in complete changes of interaction constellations, and/or in transitions from one episode to another. In traditional theater and stage theory, these points are clearly marked by curtain drops, or by breaks and intermissions, which together enable the audience to wrap up previous information and set

---

[1] The position taken here may sound counterintuitive to the commonly shared folk belief that **form** is primary to **function**. However, constructing the relationship between form and function in dialectic terms (see Bamberg, 1993a) seems far preferable to any unidimensional view of this relationship.

[2] The metaphor of "wrapping" is very similar to that of "binding," though the particle *up* gives this process a telic and completive orientation, signaling a more retrospective vantage point.

the mind for a new unit.

The present chapter sets out to investigate how such changes are linguistically signaled in the frog-story narratives. For this purpose, we start by identifying segments of the picturebook, which we call "story points," that lend themselves to contrastive comparisons (Section 1). We then establish an inventory of the linguistic devices used by adult narrators for identifying these points in the frog book (Sections 2.1, 2.5, 3.1.1). This serves as the background to our analysis of linguistic forms used by the 9-year-olds (Sections 2.2, 2.6, 3.1.2) and subsequently by the 5-year-olds compared with the adults (Sections 2.3, 2.6, 3.1.3).[3]

Our analysis is based on the English and German sample only. Our goal is to evaluate whether the availability of particular linguistic devices in the two languages affects the way the part-whole relationship is construed. At the same time, we aim to document changes in form-function relationships across the different age groups, to see how these changes reflect different strategies in the constitution of part-whole relationships.

Our strategy for comparing and contrasting linguistic devices that serve foreshadowing and wrapping up functions required two major decisions. First, we needed to define what points in the narrative constitute "good" points for comparisons. In order to ensure that our choices of "story points" were not influenced by our preconceptions of the pictures or how the stories were told by our subjects (and ourselves), we chose a more objective way of demarcating the scenes and actions depicted in the picture story to determine which story points would be included in our analysis (see Section 1, and see also Bamberg & Marchman, 1991; Marchman, 1989).

Second, it was necessary, especially for the children's narratives, to determine what would count as a "good" match between form and function, and what would count as a "bad" match or even as a no-match. We did this, as noted, by first establishing an inventory based on the adult narratives, and then determining the significance of these forms for our analysis. While other analyses, including several of those in this book, start with the identification of linguistic forms and move from there to examining where in the narrative these forms are employed and for what purpose, we start from strategic points in the story and move from there to examining the linguistic forms that speakers employ at these story points. Once recurring markers for these story

---

[3] Analysis of the texts of the 3-year-old children did not produce any positive results, suggesting that "foreshadowing" and "wrapping up" are narrative activities which — at least for the frog-book story, and for those segments of the story that we submitted to analysis — emerge after the age of 4.

points have been identified in the adult narratives, we examine whether the same forms are employed by the adults and particularly by the children at other points in the narrative for potentially different purposes.

1. THE IDENTIFICATION OF PICTURE POINTS

From a global perspective, the frog-story pictures can be clustered together into a skeleton of a plot, using categories similar to those adopted in story-grammar analyses (relevant references are given in Chapter IIA). The pictures clearly delineate a **setting** (frog leaving) and an **episode** (search for the frog); and the episode can be further differentiated into a **beginning constituent** (frog jumping out), a **development** (complex reaction resulting in a goal path, constituting a number of attempts with subsequent outcomes), and an **ending constituent** (reaction of the protagonists to finding a frog). It is this common structure which makes each individual's narrative a "frog story" (as opposed to a story about something else), and so identifies his or her verbalizations with the contents of the pictures.

One way to capture the interaction of story pictures and narrator interpretations is to analyze how narrators establish causal chains and individual goal paths for each protagonist (see Chapter IIB). By isolating out how each picture contributes individually to the body of information about a protagonist, we come to understand how the individual goal-paths of the protagonists are interwoven into the story as a whole. The frog story becomes differentiated in terms of the motives and goals of the frog (at the beginning of the story), of the gopher, the bees, the owl, the deer and the other frogs (towards the end of the story), and of the motives and goals of the boy and the dog (throughout the story). Such structural differentiations between the main and sub-protagonists (and antagonists) are necessary in order to capture the interaction of global story structure and how its is organized at the local level. Here, analysis is confined to the episodic structure in terms of the "story" of the boy alone, i.e., the search for the frog constitutes the main storyline, and the information included in any given narration is interpreted in relation to that storyline. The story of the dog will be considered only when it impinges on the boy's motives or plans for further actions.

Table 1 outlines the subcategorization of the 24 pictures into five episodes. We first intuitively judged each picture's role in terms of its individual contribution to the search theme, i.e., to the overall, most global theme of this story. According to recurrences of such roles, we then delineated the episodic structure of the story (E1-E5). For example, in any given episode, a picture, or a set of pictures, can (a) **instantiate**, (b) **reinstantiate**, or (c) **continue** the activities and goals of the protagonist.

TABLE 1
The Episodic Structure and Roles of the 24 Pictures

Picture #	Episodic Role	Episode
1-3	Prelude	
4	INSTANTIATION	E1: Initiating event
5-7	CONTINUATION	E1: Consequences
8	REINSTANTIATION	E2: Initiating event
9	CONTINUATION	
10	goal-blocking	E2: Consequences
11	REINSTANTIATION	E3: Initiating event
12	goal-blocking	
13	CONTINUATION	E3: Consequence
14	REINSTANTIATION	E4: Initiating event
15	goal-blocking	
16-18	CONTINUATION	E4: Consequences
19	REINSTANTIATION	E5: Initiating event
20	CONTINUATION	E5: Consequences
21-23	COMPLETION	E5: Consequences
24	final response	

As shown in Table 1, episodes E1-E5 are ordered sequentially and they do not overlap or weave back and forth within the story. The first episode (E1) begins with an initiating event (the frog running away) and motivates the remaining episodes (the search for the runaway frog). The last episode (E5) leads to the completion, when the search ends after the boy finds a frog (his own or another). Episode E1 (Pictures 4-7) can be seen as the most complex, in that the boy's activities are most intricately involved with those of the sub-protagonist, the dog. This episode begins with the dog sticking his head in the jar where the frog had been kept. The resulting consequences of that activity, in Pictures 5-7 (the dog cannot get his head out of the jar, he falls or jumps out of the window, and the jar breaks) temporarily serve to distract the boy from his goal of finding the frog. In contrast, in E2, E3, E4, and E5, the boy's activities are separate from the dog's, though contemporaneous in some cases. These episodes are strikingly similar in structure and content, and are in fact interchangeable. In each, the consequence of the initiating event is an immediate blocking of the goal due to the appearance of an unexpected agent, i.e., an antagonist.[4] These unexpected consequences lead to a temporary

---

[4] The sub-protagonist, the dog, also has a series of encounters with antagonists across the story. These involve an additional set of antagonists and create a temporal structure different from the one contained within the "story" of the boy. An episodic analysis of the "dog's story" would, therefore, result in a similar but not identical clustering of the pictures into units,

deviation from the boy's goal path, yet the boy soon finds his way back on track, and the search for the frog is "reinstated" at the beginning of the subsequent episode. Lastly, the overarching goal of the story is accomplished in the concluding episode, E5, where the boy and his dog find a/the frog.

Taken together, episodes E1-E4 comprise the plot of the story. These episodes move the story spatially and temporally along by linking each reinstantiation of the storyline to its unsuccessful consequences. Aesthetically speaking, the adventures (or mishaps) presented in these episodes are what make the "story" of the boy interesting. Including only the instantiation of the storyline, its recurrent reinstantiations, and the completion — that is, Pictures 4, 8 (possibly 9), 11, 14, 19, and 22/23 — or narrating the story only in terms of the actual search and the final solution, would fail to capture the complexity of the episodic structure of this picturebook.[5]

This first, somewhat intuitive, episodic structuring was compared with results from a Picture Judgment Task, an experimental procedure testing adults' impressions of the "importance" of each picture to the overall plot of the story (Marchman, 1989). Results of this experiment provided information about which events are considered most central or crucially plot-defining, and served to identify "importance units" within the story. Series of pictures that together are important for "understanding what is going on in the story" warranted similar ratings, while pictures that do not help in discerning the overall plot structure were rated of lower importance. Shifts in the patterns of importance values across the series of pictures identify units of information which reflect how the pictures are utilized in understanding the story as a whole.

College students were asked to make a decision about the importance of each picture "in its own right." For each picture, subjects were told to ask themselves "whether the story could be understood without this picture." They were not given the idea that their task involved **grouping** the pictures in any way, making our procedure crucially different from one which explicitly requires subjects to cluster the pictures into "episodes," "groups," or even "meaningful units."[6] The notion of importance as a defining criterion for

---

so that a plot structure taken from the point of view of the dog would require an analysis of the functions of linguistic forms in light of a different episodic clustering.

[5] These episodic factors may also relate to how people determine the goodness of "storyhood," that is, what makes a good vs. a bad story (Stein, 1983; Stein & Policastro, 1984).

[6] This was to avoid any cues which could have led subjects to organize the narrative in terms of higher-level guiding constructs in ways that might be a product of the experimental design. Our procedure aimed to determine to what degree the pictures would be clustered together as a function of importance (i.e., how much information they provide for understanding the overall plot), as opposed to explicitly requiring subjects to access the exact abstract categorization or clustering that the task was meant to define (i.e., the episode).

narrative structuring is not without controversy, since it may not be fully consistent with the basis for establishing episodes in story-grammar analyses. Nonetheless, the results from this task nicely mirrored our qualitative clustering of the pictures, and so provided support for our intuitive *a priori* episodic analysis. Table 2 presents the mean importance ratings for the 24 pictures clustered into groups on the basis of similarity in importance rating.

TABLE 2

Mean Group Judgments of "Importance for Understanding
What Is Going on in the story" for Each of 24 Pictures on a Scale from 1-5[a]

Picture #	MEAN	
1	3.37	
2	4.16	**Prelude** (mean = 3.6)
3	3.26	
4	2.56	
5	2.20	**Episode E1** (mean = 1.89)
6	1.42	
7	1.41	
8	2.86	
9	2.41	**Episode E2** (mean = 2.39)
10	1.91	
11	2.44	
12	2.33	**Episode E3** (mean = 2.34)
13	2.33	
14	2.97	
15	3.39	
16	3.37	**Episode E4** (mean = 3.14)
17	3.48	
18	2.67	
19	3.25	
20	3.14	**Episode E5** (mean = 3.15)
21	3.06	
22	4.16	
23	4.53	**Completion** (mean = 4.24)
24	4.06	

a. Judgments were done using a scale of 1 (very unimportant — the story would make perfect sense without this picture) to 5 (very important — story could not be understood without this picture). [N=64]

Several parallels emerge from the picture clusterings in Tables 1 and 2. First, the importance ratings (Table 2) generally reflected the overall plot structure represented by our qualitative analysis (Table 1). That is, Picture 2 (frog leaving, rating = 4.16), and Pictures 22-24 (the completion and final response, mean rating = 4.24) were judged to be the most important for understanding the overall story. These pictures provide the starting and end points of the skeletal structure of the story, depicting the establishment and resolution of the major goal of the story.

Second, the importance scores reflect the sequential and temporally organized nature of the 24 pictures in three ways: (a) The mean importance of the episodes increases as one proceeds across the story, with Episode E1 rated as the least important (mean rating = 1.89), and Episodes E4 and E5 rated as "somewhat important" to "very important" (mean ratings = 3.14 and 3.15, respectively); (b) the first episode, E1, was seen as the least crucial to the story, possibly because it is first in the series (and thus farthest from achieving the goal), or because the boy has been temporarily distracted from his search for the frog, as discussed above; and the fact that Episodes E2 & E3 and E4 & E5 were seen to be virtually identical in importance value reflects the interchangeable nature of these episodes.

Third, even though the importance ratings tended to over-differentiate the pictures, since each picture had to be distinguished from all 23 others, patterns of importance values were identified which paralleled the episodic roles defined in the qualitative analysis. For example, again, the INSTANTIATION + COMPLETION of the search was ranked highest overall. Further, subsequent pictures that CONTINUE the activity in an episode generally received similar importance ratings, especially in episodes E1, E3, E4, and E5. Lastly, as one proceeds through the story, each REINSTANTIATION of the boy's search was rated higher than the preceding picture, and often higher than the entire preceding episode. Using within-subject nonparametric analysis of variance procedures, significant differences were found between the ratings of Pictures 7, 10, 13, and 18 (which all present the consequence of searching/looking for the lost frog at a particular location) and the corresponding subsequent REINSTANTIATION of the search depicted by Pictures 8, 11, 14, and 19 (which all present the consequence of not having been successful in finding the frog at the previous location).

These two analyses provide a substantive basis for outlining the structure of the frog story as presented in the 24 pictures. Taken together, they enable us to identify two contrastive pairs of story points, one that contrasts the beginning and the end of the plot in terms of the INSTANTIATION + COMPLETION of the search theme, and the other that contrasts the boy's various search activities in terms of REINSTANTIATION + CONTINUATION. These comparisons provide a structured way to analyze what linguistic devices are used as a function of the episodic structure of the story.

The two contrastive pairs of story points so identified can be summed up as follows:

1. *The beginning and end of the plot:* Picture 4, the INSTANTIATION of the story, and Pictures 22/23, the COMPLETION, together constitute the frame which holds together the sequence of search episodes. These are the natural story points for the narrator to foreshadow and wrap up by overtly commenting on the establishment and completion of the boy's goal path in the story, i.e., where the plot is heading — as a form of instantiating the search theme, and where it is coming from — as a form of completing the search theme.

2. *Reinstantiations and continuations of the plot:* Six pictures (apart from Picture 4 which instantiates the search for the lost frog) depict actions which fall within the range of the boy's search activities. Four of them, Pictures 8, 11, 14, and 19, depict the REINSTANTIATION of the search and two, Pictures 5 and 9, represent CONTINUATIONS of the search. Reinstantiations represent new attempts to reestablish the goal path of searching for the frog, and so they must occur after the search has encountered difficulties and is in danger of being suspended. Continuations, in contrast, appear less relevant for the plot structure, since they can be inferred from previous information. They function to provide specific information regarding the whereabouts of the search activity and also, apparently, to orient the listener with regard to the whereabouts of goal blockings. (For example, Pictures 8 to 9 lead to the gopher's appearance in the hole in Picture 10, which blocks the boy's goal of finding the frog, and forces him to reinstantiate the search elsewhere — in Picture 11 — so starting a new episode).

2. THE LINGUISTIC DIFFERENTIATION BETWEEN INSTANTIATIONS AND COMPLETIONS

2.1. Instantiation in Adult Narratives

2.1.1. The use of inceptive aspect[7]

Three of the 12 adult English speakers and six of the German adults use explicit aspectual markings in encoding the initiation of the protagonist's search activity in Picture 4. The following two examples illustrate this for the two languages.[8]

---

[7] This notion is defined in Chapter IIIo, Table 3, as referring to the initiation of an event or state, or to the start of a change of state.

[8] Examples are given clause-by-clause, with no capitalization (except for German nouns), as in the original transcripts (see Appendix II).

(1) *they start looking for the frog*
     the little boy looks into his boots [*E20h*]

(2) *sie fangen an zu suchen*
     'they begin to search'
     der Junge guckt im Stiefel nach
     'the boy looks (=searches) in thc boot' [*G20e*]

The English forms used for marking inceptive aspect are the verbs *start/begin*
+ *looking* and *going to go look for*, the German forms are *fangen an/beginnen*
+ *zu suchen* 'begin + to search', *sich auf die Suche machen/begeben* 'start up
the search/go in search'.

Compare these encodings of inceptive aspect at the instantiation of the
search with how it is expressed elsewhere in the story. In the German adult
texts, there is only one other occasion where inceptive aspect is overtly
marked by the verb *beginnt* + V 'begins + V' — at the point when the frog
leaves home in Picture 2. There are nine instances where inceptive aspect is
expressed by verb-satellite constructions (Chapter III0) with the satellites *los-*,
ab-, *weg-*, and *davon-* attaching to the verb stems *laufen/hauen* 'run/dash' in
the sense of 'run off', 'dash away'. These occur in descriptions of the deer's
carrying the boy to the cliff (three instances), of the boy and dog leaving the
happy-ending scene and heading home (two instances — as in example (3)
below), the frog leaving the jar (two instances), and the boy leaving home
wíth thé dóg to embark on the search in the forest — as depicted in Picture 8
(two instances). That is, only two of these nine occur at what were defined as
"episode beginnings."

Thus, in the adult German narratives, inceptive aspect — whatever surface form it takes — functions to signal the "opening" of a narrative sequence
of events which requires a subsequent "closure." This closure can be provided in the same clause, as shown in example (3), but it may also be held off
for most of the text, culminating in the finding of the frog towards the end of
the story, as in example (4).

(3) *und gehen zu dritt fort nach Hause*
     'and go off as a threesome towards home' [*G20h*]

(4) *jetzt beginnen Max und sein Hund den Frosch überall zu suchen in den
     Stiefeln im Glas überall* [...]
     'now Max and his dog begin to search for the frog everywhere in the
     boots in the glass everywhere [...]'

und zur ganz großen Überraschung findet der Junge auch seinen kleinen Frosch wieder [G20k]

'and to (his) great surprise the boy also finds his little frog again'

Examples (3) and (4) also contrast at the level of discourse organization. (4) illustrates use of inceptive aspect and the associated achievement in the verb *wiederfinden* 'find again/regain' as a signal to open and close the global discourse unit "search." In (3), the opening 'go off' and closure 'towards home' function at a local level, that is, they are not relevant for the representation of discourse units which convey the episodic structuring of the story. These examples illustrate the use of aspectual markers at both ends of the global-local continuum of discourse organization. (Discourse units intermediate between these two extremes are discussed below.)

In support of these claims, consider two German adults who use inceptive aspect to mark the boy leaving the house (Picture 8). This is perfectly plausible at this point in the narrative, since the search outside the house reaches closure in Pictures 22/23. However, it is unlikely for a narrator to establish the opening of the search more than once. So these two narrators seem to convey a particular message by using inceptive aspect for the event depicted in Picture 8, which others simply treat as the continuation or transition of the search from inside the house to the forest. These same two narrators also describe the boy's looking into his boot (in Picture 4) as 'getting dressed', and so they defer marking the instantiation of the search to a later point — to the boy leaving the house (Picture 8), which for the other adult narrators forms the reinstantiation to the second search episode.

To summarize, four German-speaking adult narrators conform to the results from our pictorial rankings, with overt linguistic marking of the beginning of the search, while two others deviate from this pattern to create their own structuring. But these two also use inceptive aspect marking for the same function, to signal "search instantiation." Thus, German speakers use an inceptive marker to demarcate and instantiate the narrative theme that leads to a closure later on, in giving linguistic expression to finding the runaway frog near the end of the story (Pictures 22/23).

2.1.2. Forestalling and nesting

The narratives of the English-speaking adults yield a somewhat less consistent picture. As mentioned, only three out of the 12 explicitly encode Picture 4 by use of inceptive aspect *begin/start* + V. Two questions arise: First, since inceptive aspect marking is rarely used by English-speaking narrators for the particular purpose of instantiating the search part of the story, is some other linguistic device used in English to signal this function? Second, is there potentially another function that inceptive aspect marking serves in these narratives?

A closer look reveals that the English adults do not simply describe the actions of the boy in the picture (e.g., *hold up a boot and look into it*). Three state that the boy looked into his boots, using a plural referent not actually shown in the picture. They evidently have inferred that if the boy looked into one of the boots to find his frog, he must have looked into the other one as well. The remaining nine narrators gave a whole range of verbal information which is likewise not reflected in the pictorial information of Picture 4, most commonly of the following two types:

(5) *and then he looks everywhere*

   looks in his boots [E20a]

(6) *well the boy and the dog - they look all over for - for the frog*

   they look off in the rooms

   and they can't seem to find the frog [E20c]

These kinds of devices operate on the assumption of a cooperative recipient. The narrators generalize over a singular activity of the protagonist as depicted in the picture, leaving it to the listener to infer appropriate reasons for doing so. The same is true of the German-speaking adults, too. Those who did not use an overt inceptive marker to signal the search as on its way opted for a similar strategy as most of the English adults, as in the following German example.

(7) *sie suchen ihn überall*

   'they search for him everywhere'

   der Junge sucht den Frosch im Stiefel

   'the boy searches for the frog in the boot' [G20i]

Both this device and overt marking of inception allow the narrator to forestall what will be the theme not only for the immediately next event mentioned in the next line, but rather for the next few episodes in the narrative. Whether it is mentioned that this is the opening of the search, or that the protagonist is going to look 'everywhere'/'all-over-the-place', the function of this global level discourse information is the same: The listener is informed about what to expect next, and moreover, that there will be a "closure" to the protagonist's search activities in subsequent discourse. Consequently, subsequent mentions of specific search activities do not, strictly speaking, refer to events that are subsequent to the first mentioned search activity. In this sense, the event mentioned in the second line of example (7) is not subsequent to the event referred to in the previous line. Rather, those events subsequently referred to are all parts (better, elaborations) of the previously introduced (nonspecific) search activity. Thus, the marking of nonspecificity signals the overall theme, and as such carries the same force as explicit inceptive marking. Further specific elaborations of the search activity will be interpreted as "nesting" in what has been forestalled (cf. examples 1, 2, 4, 5, and 7). And at the same time, both linguistic devices direct speaker and story recipient towards a closure of the mentioned activity as a whole in the form of making explicit the success of the search activity.

2.1.3. Summary of adult narratives

Two ways of indicating instantiations have been specified. The first involves overtly inceptive markings and occurs in most of the German narratives and in a few of the English ones. A second device involves the use of forestalling and nesting. This strategy dominates the English narratives, and is also found in those German narratives which do not have overt inceptive aspect markings. It is not clear to us why fewer of the English narrators use inceptive markings than the Germans. Yet, disregarding unclear cases such as locally semantic inchoatives like *getting mad, getting tired, getting late* or lative expressions like *they go call in the woods*, or *he went and looked in a hole*, there were no more than 15 cases of inceptive markings in the English adult narratives. Three signal the instantiation of the search. Another four mark the beginning of the bees' chase (Picture 12), while three narrators spread inceptive markings across their texts (once when the dog "starts" barking, once when the dog "starts" running, and once when the deer "starts" carrying the boy on its back). These inceptive aspectualizations, using the present participle as complement, protract an activity which other narrators view as contained or bounded.

Only one English adult (E20c) disperses aspectual marking throughout her narrative, in contrast to the others, not in the instantiation scene depicted in Picture 4, but on five subsequent occasions. Surprisingly, in all five instances, the pictures represent scenes in which the boy (or dog) is depicted as performing a search activity, that is, calling for the frog, as shown in (8).

(8) *um - they - both the dog and the boy - they - stick their head out the window -*

*and they **start** yelling for the dog*

well the boy and the dog they go wandering out in the woods

*and the boy **starts** yelling for his frog*

the bee - the dog um - discovers the beehive

*and **starts** yelling at it*

while the boy wan- climbs on top of the tree

and starts yelling in a hole for the frog

and he leans onto some branches and starts yelling for ... his frog
[E20c]

These uses of inceptive marking sound rather odd at first. They do not seem to conform to the general discourse function performed by inceptives in either German or English, to foreshadow a narrative frame at the global level of discourse organization which later on is wrapped up when the frog is found. Instead, this narrator opens the search frame by means of the simple lexical device *look for*, as shown in example (6). All four activities that are subsequently described as "calling" (invariably by the verb *yelling*) are marked inceptively. Note also that the calling activity is always the second of a sequence of clauses, following the schema:

he does X   and (he) starts yelling for the frog
they do X   and (he) starts yelling for the frog

Thus, this use of inceptive aspect marking seems to signal particular discourse segments which coincide with episodic blocks in the overall search theme. In other words, the use of inceptive aspect by this particular narrator can be interpreted as signaling the "re-opening" of the search frame at the level of her discourse organization. However, only in the context of one genuine opening (=the instantiation) and four "re-openings" does the search follow through to being wrapped up with Picture 22 of the story. But note that use of this particular formal device in such a regular fashion is not required. That is, nothing in the pictures themselves necessitates their being encoded as "inceptive." This narrator's usage implies a series of inferences based on a higher level of discourse organization which give the events an overall structuring.

2.2. Instantiation in the 9-Year-Old Children

Of the 12 German-speaking 9-year-old narrators, nine lexically encode Picture 4 as searching (*suchen*). Six of the nine explicitly use the forestalling device *überall* 'everywhere' and one makes use of the inceptive *sofort auf die Suche gehen* 'immediately go on the search'. Two German 9-year-olds do not use any particular marking or mention of the search, they simply "label" the activity of the boy in the picture looking into his boot and getting dressed. The remaining subject (as shown in example 9), may have hinted at the instantiation of the search by encoding the previous picture in terms of a complex reaction on the protagonist's part (first line), followed by the description of his activity (second line), so hinting at the beginning search by use of indirect means: "complex reaction" → "goal path" (looking into shoe =

"attempt" in the frame of the overarching goal path of the search).

(9)   *ooh wo ist denn der Frosch geblieben?*
    'ooh where is the frog gone to?'
    na und da guckt der in'n Schuh
    'well and there he looks into a shoe'
    der Hund guckt da nach
    'the dog looks over there'
    und stellen sie alles auf'm Kopf
    'and they turn everything upside down' [G9j-9;11]

Note, however, that this narrator turns to a level of description in the last line which corresponds to what was labeled "forestalling" in discussing the adult narratives. In the narrative of this 9-year-old, if this statement had been made before the last line of this excerpt, it would have counted as a forestalling device and would have provided a nesting for the information given in the subsequent lines. Placed here, though, it seems that the narrator became aware of the overall motif of the search only retrospectively, after having specified the boy's action.

Nine-year-old German children almost never use an explicit inceptive marking. There is only one such occurrence, in encoding Picture 8: *losgehen, um den Frosch zu suchen* 'to set off in order to search for the frog'. However, one narrator (G9e) makes recurrent use of the forestalling device *überall suchen* 'search everywhere', prior to giving a specific event description of the boy looking into the boot. He uses this device in the same fashion as the English-speaking adult narrator discussed above (E20h), for signaling the discourse blocks which coincide with the reinstantiation of the search after it has turned out to be unsuccessful at the four previous locations.

The 12 English-speaking 9-year-olds present a somewhat different picture in the use of linguistic devices. Half of them describe Picture 4 as the dressing scene (*putting on clothes*) and so do not mark it as the beginning of the search. Yet all of them use inceptive markings on subsequent occasions. Only three subjects clearly mark the beginning of the search where we predicted, two by use of a forestalling device, *looking all over the place*, and one by inceptive aspect, *started + looking*. Two others simply summarize by *they are looking for him*.

Six English 9-year-olds, three of whom treat Picture 4 as the dressing scene, use a particular linguistic form *going to look/search for* to encode Picture 8, the scene where the boy and the dog have left their home and are outside near the forest calling their pet frog. Though this formal device by itself does not necessarily encode the beginning of the search, it nevertheless signals a focus on the change in location intended by the boy, and as such potentially functions to mark the beginning of a new activity such as the search. Thus, for those three subjects who have not mentioned the search for the frog up to this scene, the use of *going to look/search for the frog* may function to mark the instantiation of the search. For the other three subjects, the search already had been mentioned, so that we have no grounds for assuming that this form *per se* encodes the instantiation of the search.

As for explicit aspectual marking of the beginning of the search, 9-year-old English speakers, like adults, rarely use aspectual marking for this purpose. However, when it comes to the overall use of inceptive aspectual markers, the 9-year-olds employ this device approximately twice as often as adult English speakers. Of the seven subjects who use inceptives, six use them for describing the bees leaving the beehive after their beehive has fallen down (Picture 11). The frequency and pattern of usage of inceptive markings by the 9-year-olds suggests that these narrators are striving to use this particular formal device at the micro-level of discourse organization, i.e., at a level where information units smaller than the search (Pictures 4-22) are viewed as having a beginning and an ending (including a possible continuation and high point in the middle), such as the bees' pursuit of the dog (Pictures 11-14) or the deer's reaction to the boy's intrusion (Pictures 15-17/18).

2.3. Instantiation in the 5-Year-Old Children

Although 5-year-old children are generally very adept at understanding stories and referring to past events, they have difficulty when it comes to integrating the hierarchical and sequential ordering of events in these narratives. There is quite a bit of variation among the 5-year olds in structuring the story and in the different kinds of linguistic devices they use to mark story cohesion and coherence, as discussed in Chapter IIA.

Four English-speaking and three German-speaking 5-year-olds show no overt marking at all of either the instantiation, the completion, or any instance of the continuation of the search, even though they comment substantially on the actions depicted in the pictures in question. While we have no independent grounds for assuming that these narrators do not know what the story is "about," we can only conclude that they do not pay special "linguistic" attention to these particular story points. They may assume that these story points do not need to be acknowledged in terms of "foreshadowing" or "wrapping up," because they are clear to the story recipient, or for other reasons. But the narratives of these seven subjects are quite unlike the others; they lack internal organization and give the impression of being unstructured or, at times, aimless. In contrast, two English-speaking and five German-speaking 5-year-olds clearly mention where the search begins, where it is reinstantiated, and where and how it ends. In sum, there are 10 subjects (out of the total 24 English and German 5-year-olds) who mark these story components some of the time, but not consistently throughout their narratives. These variations make the group of 5-year-olds of particular interest to our analysis. Our concern is not so much with what these children "cannot" yet do compared with adults on the same story-telling task but, rather, with the questions: What **do** they do? How do they make use of linguistic devices that serve cohesive and coherence functions? Where do they use them? And how does this use reflect their understanding of the relevant form-function relationships?

Collapsing the English- and German-speaking 5-year-olds who encode the instantiation scene, a forestalling device, such as *überall, all over the place* is used only three times, while the lexical item *suchen* 'search, seek' occurs three times in the German texts. There is no use of overt inceptive marking for this scene, and two subjects simply refer to the boy's activity as *calling for the frog*. But we do find two other forms of inceptive markings at other points in the narrative: one is use of an aspectual verb-satellite construction in German — *losreiten* 'start riding', 'ride off'; the other takes the form of a forestalling device of two kinds.

One English-speaking 5-year-old (*E5d-5;6*) uses inceptive aspect inappropriately to encode Picture 14, where the boy is standing on top of a rock, calling for his frog. Inceptive aspect is inappropriate here, since the narrator has already mentioned the calling activity earlier in the story. The narrator could either have marked the activity of calling as continuous, that is, as reinstantiated at this point in the narrative (e.g., "they are **still** calling"), or as recurrent, so conveying that the activity started anew (e.g., "and they **started** calling again"). Instead, child E5d opted for the inappropriate *and they start calling*.

The second use of overt inceptive aspect signals that the bees are beginning their pursuit (Picture 12), as in (10).

(10) *and the bees **started** running after the dog* [*E5i-5;10*]

However, in contrast to its common use by the adults, and particularly in the 9-year-old English narratives, this 5-year-old's use of inceptive aspect does not serve to encode the previous picture (Picture 11), where the bees come out of their hive, "beginning" their pursuit of the dog). More important, it is not followed by a marking of the "closure" of that scene later in the narrative, for example, that the bees subsequently pursue the dog and punish him for destroying their hive. In both examples, the use of inceptive aspect as a formal device does not fulfill a discursive function of segmenting the text, since it neither opens up a scene nor is it followed by an appropriate discursive sequential closure, as in adult usage .

The same point can be made with regard to the use of the forestalling device by subjects E5b and E5h. After having instantiated the search by use of the forestalling device in the first line of the following excerpt, subject E5h later elaborates with the same device:

(11) *and then he looks all over the place for his frog ...*

and then he calls frog

*he's calling frog **all over the place** [E5h-5;10]*

Though it could be argued that the activity encoded in the last line, *calling*, is different from the earlier *looks for*, the use of *all over the place* gives it a different force. Another child (E5b) uses this same device (*all over the place*) for encoding Picture 12, for the dog's actions in the bees' pursuit:

(12) *he was running **all over the place** [E5b-5;2]*

This example demonstrates that the forestalling device is not used for the same purpose by 5-year-olds as in the narratives of either adults or 9-year-olds. It functions for the younger children to locally **intensify** the action, but not to foreshadow, that is, to mark a starting point from which the events can later be elaborated.

2.4. Summary of Instantiation

In sum, 5-year-old children only rarely use linguistic devices to mark the instantiation of the search, unlike older and more sophisticated narrators. However, when 5-year-olds do use the linguistic devices of inceptive aspect and/or forestalling, they mark a particular subjective stance. Specifically, these markers serve to intensify particular actions or activities at a more local level of picture descriptions. This contrasts with the English 9-year-olds, who increasingly use inceptive aspect to identify the beginnings of smaller-than-search-sized information chunks. These narrators appear to operate predominantly with "middle-level units" — small blocks of discourse which represent information units relevant to the construction of hierarchies, even though the top-level components of the hierarchy are not discursively realized. Adult narrators in both languages, in contrast to both groups of children, clearly set up and discursively demarcate the instantiation of the search.

One difference between the two languages is that half the 9-year-old English-speaking children encode Picture 4 as a dressing scene, compared with only one German 9-year-old. Although this could be a random effect, the manner in which the two languages encode the relevant concepts may account for this disparity. English conflates the two types of activity in a predicate with the same verb, *look around* vs. *look for* whereas German has two distinct verbs, *kucken* 'to look' and *suchen* 'to search'. A 9-year-old English-speaking child might not consider the distinction between a purely descriptive statement like *the boy looked into the boot* and a more elaborate specification of the search activity such as *the boy looked everywhere* or *the boy looked for the frog* to be relevant. Confusion about the distinction between these two uses of *look* in English may lead speakers to avoid the problem by describing the scene as the dressing scene, rather than using the verb *to look*.

Another crosslinguistic difference is that English-speaking 5- and 9-year-olds use inceptive aspect constructions more frequently than German children. This may be due to complexities in German word order, particularly the clause-final position of the nonfinite verb. Use of a verb for inceptive aspect in English does not require any deviation from standard SVO word order, whereas in German, speakers using the finite aspectual verb *beginnt/fängt an* 'begins/starts' must then wait to use the nonfinite verb-form *suchen* until the object or location and possibly also a temporal adverb has been mentioned (see example 4, above, literally: 'now begin Max and his dog the frog everywhere to search...'). Many German 9-year-olds have difficulty with this kind of construction, which may be why we find the German children avoiding them. This is supported by the two adult groups: In German, the frequency of these constructions increases with age and linguistic sophistication; in English, these simple and early occurring constructions decrease in frequency as their function shifts from marking locally defined units to identifying the global structure of the story.

2.5. Completion in Adult Narratives

After the narrator has instantiated a search, it is necessary at some point to signal the achievement of the goal, that is, that the frog has been found and so the search has been successfully completed. For our analyses, the narrator may choose one of the two adult frogs (Picture 22) or one of the nine baby frogs (Picture 23) as the frog that originally ran away from them, or else not view any of these frogs as identical with the boy's original pet frog. In all cases, the narrator must mark the completion of the search at this point in the narrative (Picture 22/23), since some frog has been found (the third major plot component in the analysis of Chapter IIA). In fact, the last option (a nonidentical frog), which is rarely taken, requires an even more overt statement about the finalization of the search. If the search is instantiated based on the identity of the "frog lost" and the "frog searched for," but then turns en route into a search for any frog (or even any pet animal), these changes in plans make communicative clarification absolutely necessary (see "the principle of analogy," Brown & Yule, 1983, pp. 64ff).

Consider, next, how English-speaking narrators linguistically signal the completion of the search. The examples in (13) and (14) illustrate the perspectives that can be taken at this point in the story: The discovery or rediscovery can be viewed from the perspective of the protagonist (example 13) or of the frog (example 14). In the former, the narrator simply notes the achievement of the protagonist's search efforts, whereas in the latter, the narrator provides a more "descriptive" account of the location and activity of the frog(s). The protagonist perspective encodes the achievement of the goal and the resolution of the problem. This perspective lessens the inferential load placed on the interlocutor in figuring out who the frogs are and what they are doing here. The narrator in example (14) may be aware of the inferential weight of his choice of perspective, which may be why he elaborates the whereabouts of the newly introduced referents by explicitly noting the frog's identity.

(13) *and they find on the other side of the log two happy frogs*

   one of which was the frog in the jar [E20b]

(14) *and they're looking over on the other side*

   on the other side are two frogs

   um - one - possibly the frog

   that escaped from his front room [E20h]

One German-speaking adult opts not to identify any of the newly discovered frogs as the boy's runaway frog who caused the search in the first place. This narrator takes elaborate pains, as shown in (15), in order to convey the underlying motives for the search (in particular the switch to the simple past at two points, so as to express retrospection).

(15) *und beide klettern jetzt über diesen Baumstumpf*

   'and both of them climb now over this tree stump'

   hinter dem sich wahrscheinlich das Rätsel - des Rätsels Lösung verbergen wird

   'behind which most likely the puzzle - the solution of the puzzle will be hidden'

   und tatsächlich da ist ein Froschpaar zu sehen

   'and indeed there is a pair of frogs to be seen'

   und es war ja das Ziel des Jungen gewesen die ganze Zeit

   'and it had been the aim of the boy for the whole time'

   mit vielen Hindernissen

   'with many obstacles'

   die er hinter sich hatte

'which he had behind himself'

wo er auch die Natur kennengelernt hat und auch Geschöpfe der Natur

'where he has gotten to know nature and also nature's creatures'

und eben daß er ein bißchen vorsichtig sein muß in unbekanntem Gelände

'and also that he has to be a little careful in unknown territory'

da ist jetzt ein Froschpärchen

'there is now a little pair of frogs' [G20a]

In spite of these different options that narrators can take in perspectivizing the events, nearly all the adult narrators in both languages view the event from the perspective of the protagonist(s): 11 of the 12 English adults and 11 of the 12 German adults. And most of them do so by using the verb *find*, 8 in English and 5 in German (with the verb *finden*). One other German speaker uses the verb *wiederentdecken* 'rediscover', which implies an earlier discovery, and — though rather less than *find* — some efforts in the journey that led to the fulfillment of the "rediscovery." Thus, 14 narrators (of 24) use lexical aspect by means of English *find* and its German counterpart *finden* or *wiederentdecken*. The 10 other adults do not explicitly mark the completion of the search theme by use of lexical aspect, but nearly all of them encode the frogs' location and/or their activities from the perspective of the story's main protagonist, the boy.

2.6. Completion in the 9-Year-Old and 5-Year-Old Children

In contrast to the adults, very few children clearly identify any of the frogs in the discovery scene (Pictures 22/23) as the same runaway frog established in the story's setting (Pictures 1/2). Table 3 shows how often children use possessive pronouns, and indefinite and definite articles to clarify the frog's identity. Use of the possessive pronoun (e.g., *his frog*) can be taken as a clear indicator of the frog's thematic identity, but use of the definite or even the indefinite article does not provide conclusive evidence that these children did **not** know the frog's identity.

Establishing the identity of the frog by mentioning that the protagonist(s) completed the search, alluding to a rediscovery, or any other type of recognition of the frog as the runaway pet, is not common in the 9-year-old and 5-year-old narrations in either language. Only three 9-year-olds and two 5-year-olds use verbs like *find/finden/wiedersehen* to indicate the termination of the search. One German-speaking 5-year-old uses *finden* for this function, but this is a verb that occurs at four other points in his narrative. Each of these is

TABLE 3
Use of Identifying Expressions for 'Frog' in "Endings"

	9-year-olds			
	possessive pronoun	definite article	indefinite article	zero pronoun
English	7	2	3	0
German	2	6	4	0
Sum	9	8	7	0

	5-year-olds			
	possessive pronoun	definite article	indefinite article	zero pronoun
English	0	3	8	1
German	2	4	6	0
Sum	2	7	14	1

associated with the failure of the protagonist's search at the different locations, and so demarcates the endpoints of episodic segments within the narrative at a more intermediate level of discourse organization. In addition, only those children who clearly mark the instantiation of the search with inceptive aspectual devices also use verb forms which overtly signal the end of the search. In general, however, the youngest children are more likely to describe the completion from the perspective of the frog, taking a more descriptive stance on the scene (19 out of 24).[9] In contrast, the majority of the 9-year-olds (18 out of 24) adopt the boy's perspective of "seeing," "discovering," or "finding" the frog(s). Again, this shift in perspective does not necessarily indicate lack of knowledge of the story script, that is, about the identity of the runaway frog in Picture 2 and the found frog in Picture 22; rather, it represents a decision made by the narrators regarding what they consider communicatively necessary and what should be left unsaid.

---

[9] Additional remarks about the notion of "description," and "describing" as a narrative activity, are given below; see Section 3.3.

3. THE LINGUISTIC DIFFERENTIATION BETWEEN REINSTANTIATIONS AND CONTINUATIONS

3.1. Reinstantiating the Search

If a narrator has foreshadowed the overall goal of the story in terms of the search for the runaway frog, we would expect him/her to signal when that overall goal is reactivated or "reinstantiated" after it has been suspended. For example, after Picture 5 where the boy is calling the frog from the window, the search is temporarily suspended in Pictures 6 and 7, when the dog falls out of the window and breaks the jar. In Picture 8, the dog rejoins the boy and the search for the frog is reinstantiated, marking the beginning of the next scene. At three other points in the story (Pictures 10, 12, and 15), the goal of finding the frog is blocked by the appearance of an antagonist, and the search is temporarily suspended to be reinstantiated later in subsequent pictures. At these four points in the story (Pictures 8, 11, 14, and 19), then, the overall goal of the story is reestablished and each reinstantiation directs the plot into the next episode.

3.1.1. Adults' reinstantiation

Starting with the 12 German adults, recall that only ten of them begin the search theme where anticipated, with the encoding of Picture 4. (Two subjects instantiate the search using inceptive marking at the point which would normally be considered a reinstantiation of the search, namely at Picture 8.) Of these 10 narrators, seven use a continuity marker to describe the activities identified to reinstantiate the search, most typically the particle *weiter* 'further', a satellite to the infinitives *suchen* 'search' and *gehen* 'go', placed after the verb in (16), due to German word-order constraints.

(16) *aber dann vertragen sie sich doch wieder*

  'but then they make up with each other again'

  *und suchen **weiter** nach dem Frosch*

  'and search **further** for the frog'

  *und so gehen sie jetzt noch **weiter** nach draußen in den Wald*

  'and so they move ever **further** outside into the forest'

  *und **rufen und rufen und suchen***

  'and **call and call and search**' [*G20h*]

In this excerpt, the narrator clearly marks the end of the side sequence presented in Pictures 6 and 7 and reestablishes the overall goal that she stated previously. The search is reintroduced with the second line of this excerpt as she was turning the page, and the boy and the dog are described as moving *further* in space in the next line, encoded by the same particle: *gehen weiter*. Finally, in the last line, the narrator makes use of another kind of continuity marker, protracting the act of calling (and searching). Though this last kind of device does not overtly make the point that there has been a previous event of the same goal orientation, it closely resembles the "forestalling and nesting" function of the foreshadowing device used by the German-speaking narrators for Picture 4 (see above).

For Picture 11, only half (six out of twelve) of the German-speaking narrators marked the reinstantiation of the search, usually with German *weiter*. Another, perhaps more explicit means to express that the reinstantiation of the search is shown in (17).

(17) *der Junge hat immer noch das Problem*
'the boy still has the problem'
den Frosch wiederzufinden
'to find the frog back/again'
und guckt in einem Baumloch nach
'and looks into a tree hole' [*G20b*]

In Picture 14, the boy reinstantiates the search after the owl-adventure by standing on top of a rock, holding on to a deer's antlers which look like branches, and calling for the frog. Here narrators use the particle *weiter* less frequently than in Picture 8 or 11, choosing instead to signal the reinstantiation of the search by taking a **protracted** aspectual perspective. At this point in the story, the search has been clearly identified as an ongoing, not yet completed event sequence. Mentioning the search by taking a protracted event perspective immediately evokes the concept of a process that is linked to an earlier point in time.[10]

The English-speaking narrators provide fewer explicit markings of the reinstantiation scenes. Combined across all three scenes, they show 10 such clear cases, that is, under half the number used by the Germans. However, there is a greater variety of different markers than in the German sample, with no clear best candidate for marking reinstantiation scenes. The devices range over *continue + V, keep + V, going on, some more, again, not give up the search, go back looking for,* and two uses of *still*. While English *still* functions to hook up the event referred to with a previous event, so calling up the

---

[10] This observation nicely demonstrates that the same aspectual markers can provide different discursive orientations as a function of where they occur: The protracted perspective in the first search scene (Picture 4) invites foreshadowing orientation, while the same device calls up more of the past when used midstream (Picture 14).

overarching frame of the search, a narrator's description of the event as *still looking for the frog* (E20j) or *still calling* (E20l) does not reflect the fact that the search has been intermittently suspended.

Why do so few of the English-speaking adult narrators (28%) explicitly mark the three scenes as reinstantiations of the search in contrast to a majority of the German speakers (60%)? Recall that one particular device is used by almost all of the German narrators, whereas in English, several different devices are used. This suggests that the availability of this particular form may contribute to the difference. The German verb particle (or satellite) *weiter* (the comparative of spatial *weit* 'wide, broad') is used productively with activity verbs to signal spatial contiguity or continuity of the activity in question, and can be easily extended metaphorically to express temporal contiguity. German-speaking narrators may have access to a more readily available means to signal reinstantiation and thus do so more frequently than English speakers, who in contrast have to choose among many competing options, and linguistically more complex devices.

3.1.2. 9-year-olds' reinstantiations

On the basis of the above, we would expect those German-speaking 9-year-olds who make reference to the instantiation of the search to also make use of *weiter + suchen* (or *rufen* 'call') to signal a return to the ongoing search after an interruption. We would further expect them to signal the reinstantiation more frequently than their English-speaking peers for two reasons: because adult Germans prove more likely to do so than English adults, and because German-speaking are more likely than English-speaking 9-year-olds to mark the instantiation of the search in the first place.

There are only four instances of German-speaking 9-year-olds marking the reinstantiation, twice by use of *weiter*, and only one English 9-year-old does so. Recall that six of these subjects did not refer to the instantiation of the search earlier in their narrative (Picture 4), and so they would have had less motivation to view the search as in progress, or even to mark the boy as returning to the search theme in Pictures 8, 11, and 14.

One German 9-year-old clearly attempts to mark the boy's activities in these pictures as part of an overarching goal by use of what we referred to earlier as "forestalling." This child (G9e) "nests" the events in the narrative by relating each specific search event in Pictures 4, 5, 8/9, 11, and 13/14 to an explicit searching everywhere, *überall*. Thus, while not explicitly relating those events where the search is set off temporarily with reinstantiation events, this child appears to nevertheless be trying to account for how the different episodic blocks (search out of window, in the ground, in the tree, and on top of rock) are grounded in an overall motive.

3.1.3. 5-year-olds' reinstantiations

Clear markings for reinstantiations are very rare in the narratives of the 5-year-olds. One German-speaking child clearly encodes the reinstantiation of the search at a different story location, namely in her encoding of Picture 20, after the boy has come out of the water and signaled the dog to be quiet:

(18) *und da suchen se immer noch den Frosch*

    'and there they still search for the frog' *[G5k-5;4]*

For three different pictures which are clearer candidates for marking reinstantiations, the form *weiter* is used, but only in its spatial sense: *weiter-gehen* 'further-move' and *weiter-klettern* 'further-climb'. At a few other reinstantiation points, the German 5-year-olds use protracted aspectual perspectives in order to nest the subsequent individual events.

The English-speaking 5-year-old narratives are also lacking in marking reinstantiations of the search. One child uses *again* (e.g., *call again*), while another uses *still, kept on* + V, and the forestalling/nesting device *all over the place*, in order to show that the event to be reported is linked with previous events in an overarching manner.

These few cases can at best be taken as evidence that some 5-year-olds have the ability to linguistically signal connection of individual events into an episodic structure. Although 5-year-olds sometimes make use of *still, again, all over the place*, and in German *weiter*, their usage differs in function from the discursive purposes for which these devices are used by adult narrators. For instance, *again*, as used by subject E5b in example (19), is discursively misplaced, since the dog's activity (playing) should have been perspectivized as a continuous event, i.e., there is no reason to believe that the event was recurrent. The use of *again* in this example, as well as elsewhere in this text, demonstrates that the child has not drawn a clear distinction between continuous and recurrent events: Both seem to be fused into one temporal/aspectual notion.[11]

(19) *he (=dog) was playing with the bees*

    *he was playing with the bees **again***

    and the dog was still playing with the bees [E5b-5;2]

---

[11] The notion of "fused" is not meant to imply that the two concepts of "recurrence" and "continuity" first exist independently and then are fused into one. Developmentally, it is more conceivable that the two notions first appear in the form of one "fused" aspectual concept before they are differentiated and hierarchically integrated (Bamberg, Budwig, & Kaplan, 1991; Werner, 1957; Werner & Kaplan, 1963/1984).

3.2. Continuing the Search

In Pictures 5 (calling out of the window) and 9 (calling into a hole in the ground), an event is pictorially represented that is immediately linked to the activity represented in the previous pictures, Pictures 4 (looking for frog in a boot) and 8 (calling for frog outside in the forest), respectively. All events in these two pictures are most likely to be encoded as search activities. Of course, each speaker's decision about which aspect of the scene he/she will focus on is reflected in particular lexical choices (*searching, seeking, looking for, calling* + quoted speech, *calling for*, etc.). However, English- and German-speaking narrators do not seem to favor any particular linguistic device to encode the fact that the search activity **continues** in these scenes. Having instantiated the search with the encoding of Picture 4, and reinstantiated with Picture 8, there is no need to signal the next event as following the same plan, especially when this event is more specific than the previous one, as in the following two examples:

(20) *und dann machen sich die beiden auf*

'and then the two of them get going'

und suchen den Frosch weiter

'and search further for the frog'

und rufen

'and call'

und ziehen durch den Wald

'and go through the forest'

der Junge sucht im Maulwurfloch

'the boy searches in the mole-hole' [*G20a*]

(21) *after a while - the boy and his dog went out into the forest*

in search for their frog

they looked everywhere - in the woods - and - um - even in the gopher holes [*E20d*]

English *even* (or German *sogar*) can serve to signal that an event is added to a series of previously mentioned events. However, this device is used only once, most likely signifying that an orderly presentation of the event sequence from a more general towards a more specific event has the same effect. In general, then, **shifts** in the thematic structure require overt discursive marking, and as such lend themselves to foreshadowing and wrapping up, whereas the immediate continuation of the main activity or topic event is what is expected and thus does not require explicit marking. In these narratives, once the search has been established or re-established, the fact that the search activity is continuing is the norm and therefore the aspectual character of the event needs not be made explicit by a particular linguistic marking.

In the two groups of children, very few instances could be reliably interpreted as "continuations." While the adult narrators in both languages nearly always refer to these picture sequences (Pictures 4-5 and 8-9) as instances of searching, many of the 9-year-olds and most of the 5-year-olds fail to do so. Table 4 presents the frequency of narrative sequences (per age group/per language) which could be taken as legitimate candidates for a (Re-)Instantiation + Continuation sequence for the child narrators.[12]

TABLE 4
Number of Candidates for
(Re-)Instantiation-Continuation Sequences

		Pictures 4-5	Pictures 8-9
5-year-olds	English	3	8
	German	3	6
9-year-olds	English	4	11
	German	10	12

Given that continuations are rarely marked by adults and that 9-year-olds typically do not mark instantiations of the search, it is not surprising that explicit marking of continuation is nonexistent in the 9-year-old group. Perhaps the same communicative principle holds here as with the adult narrators: If the search is on, any subsequent activity which can be interpreted as a subcategory of search-activity (e.g., *calling, looking for, trying to find*, etc.) need not be marked as a continuation of this activity.

Interestingly, however, two of the German and one of the English 9-year-olds use subtle devices that hint at the recurrent theme of the search in these kinds of continuous/repetitious activities (cf. examples 22-24). Just as the German speakers in these examples use *auch* 'also' and *wieder* 'again', the English-speaking narrator in example (24) ties the ongoing search to the discovery/finding of a gopher hole.

---

[12] The "poor" performance of the English-speaking 9-year-olds relates to the fact that 6 (out of 12) subjects interpret Picture 4 as representing the boy's dressing scene (see discussion above).

(22) *"hey Frosch wo bist du?"*

'"hey frog where are you?"'

ruft er

'calls he'

da schreit der Frosch in den Loch "Hey Frosch wo bist du?" **wieder**

'there the frog (=boy!) calls into the hole "Hey frog where are you?" **again**' [G9j-9;11]

(23) *und dann suchten sie*

'and then they searched'

der Hund und der Junge suchten den Frosch

'the dog and the boy searched for the frog'

und dann gucken sie aus dem Fenster

'and then they look out of the window'

und suchten **auch** *da*

'and searched **also** there' [G9k-9;0]

(24) *the boy and the dog went looking for the frog*

they yelled for the frog

they **found** *a beehive and a gopher hole* [E9c-9;6]

These devices are not necessarily inappropriate for signaling that the action/activity in Pictures 5 and 9 continues the search that was previously (re)instantiated at the discourse level. However, what distinguishes this use of linguistic devices from those of the adults is that mature narrators plan over a larger stretch of the discourse, while children's planning is restricted to briefer units. Forestalling and nesting are rarely used. Instead, 9-year-olds orient the discourse forward, breaking down the sequence of events into sequentially distributed "action centers."

The tendency to distribute activities sequentially is even more conspicuous among the 5-year-old narrators.

(25) *and he's calling frog all over the place*

and he's **still** *calling frog* [E5h-5;10]

(26) *"frog! frog! are you in here?"*

but there was no ribbit ribbit sound

so they **went on** *to look* [E5i-5;10]

(27) *und da hat er in 'nen Stiefel geguckt*

'and there he has looked into a/the boot'

*war **auch** nix drin*

'was **also** nothing in there'

und da hat der Junge nach draußen geguckt

'and there the boy has looked outside'

*und da war er **auch nicht***

'and there he wasn't **either**' [*G5j-5;3*]

These three examples illustrate the ways in which the 5-year-old narrators tend to contextualize each local characterization of the events. As they encode each frame, they signal its connection to the overall theme of the search for the runaway frog. This is especially clear in the last example, where in an otherwise present-tense narrative, the subject introduces two searching attempts in the German present perfect, and then finalizes the negative outcome of each attempt in the simple past (*war* + negation). This represents a sophisticated parallelization within two-line frames, each consisting of a comment about attempt and outcome. But here, as typical for this age group, the overarching theme is constituted retrospectively, instead of prospectively as in the narratives of the adults, who mark the beginning of the search in Picture 4 and nest the subsequent events into the overarching theme.

3.3. Summary of Reinstantiations and Continuations

While adult narrators generally give linguistic expression to the three cases of reinstantiation by use of a continuity marker, 9-year-old narrators rarely, and 5-year-olds almost never do so. These linguistic markings play two discursive roles. First, they serve to connect each event to one at an earlier reference time, providing continuity of the search theme throughout the narrative. Thus, they can be seen as thematic "continuity markers." Second, through the marking of thematic continuity, the narrator is able to "nest" each relevant activity in the context of the ongoing search. The marking of the reinstantiations in this way, in conjunction with linguistically instantiating the search at its origins, serves to contextualize the establishment of what we called a "forestalling center." We found that in German, the verbal satellite *weiter-* (as in *weiter-suchen, weiter-rufen*, etc., 'search further, call further') is the prototypical candidate for performing this discourse function. In English, in contrast, no one particular device is favored. The availability of one form which clearly serves these discursive roles may motivate the more frequent marking of reinstantiations in German narratives compared to the American English counterparts.

We found no linguistic marking of continuative "non-boundaries" of the search — that is, where two **consecutive** activities of the protagonist are described as being search activities — in the adult narratives in either English or German, but we did find an increase in linguistic marking for iterative aspect at these story points in the younger groups. These results can be interpreted in the light of Gricean conversational postulates: If a topic or theme (the search) is clearly established or reestablished, topic continuity is what is to be expected. If the narrator wants to signal topic discontinuity, then s/he has to provide special linguistic marking, since discontinuity violates the norm. Thus, in these narratives, perhaps counter-intuitively, continuity markers are **not** used to mark "genuine" continuity. Rather, they mark reinstantiations of the search theme after it has been temporarily suspended. Genuine continuity does not get marked at all.

An even more interesting finding concerns the interrelation between marking reinstantiation and continuation. For both English and German, marking of the genuine continuation points in the story is more frequent among the younger narrators. This is quite possibly a result of two different discourse-planning strategies in the different age groups. The "forestalling and nesting" of the adult narratives requires overt marking of the forestalling center and no marking of the nested event. Such an organization reflects a discourse activity that organizes thematic progression in a top-down fashion. In contrast, younger children make their choices of discourse contextualizations "online," that is, at the same time that the coherence of the overall theme is realized in the actual ongoing speech event. In other words, young children do not signal the directionality of event sequences from the start, but rather retrospectively from their end. This difference in planning strategy contributes to the impression that younger children seem to more often simply "describe" what they see in the pictures. One must remember, however, that this task is at its core a descriptive task for all subjects, in all languages and age groups. All narrators must "describe" the events in order to establish the theme of the story. The important difference between the different age groups is not their different "descriptive abilities," but rather the different planning strategies by which they accomplish the task of transforming the picturebook into a narrative.

4. SUMMARY AND CONCLUSION

In moving through a text, speakers refer to events and present them in a linear order. In addition — though not unrelatedly — speakers, at times, point backward or forward, relating where the events "come from" and where they are "leading to." As argued in the introductory section to this chapter, such moves seem to be grounded in narrators' attempts to provide motives for actions which in turn bring thematic coherence and life to a story. It has been our goal in this chapter to more clearly delineate points in the frog story for contrastive comparisons in order to identify linguistic forms that perform this kind of job. To this end, we have focused on four types of narrative scenes: (a) the instantiation of the search theme, where we hoped we would find clear foreshadowing of what is happening later; (b) the completion of the search theme, where we hoped to find clear wrap-ups. With regard to the remaining two scenes, (c) reinstantiations of the theme after it had been out of focus, and (d) continuations of the theme, that is, references to the same activity as in the previous picture, we originally had no clear prediction as to whether narrators would point in any direction of the narrative activity.

In considering how adult narrators performed on this task in English and German, we found considerable variation in their reliance on specific formal devices, both among speakers of the same language, and between the two languages. Yet our comparisons also revealed several trends which suggest certain generalizations about the development of discourse skills.

Adult narrators overwhelmingly choose to signal the instantiation of the search at a common location in the picture sequence (Picture 4). Two linguistic options were identified, inceptive aspect and a forestalling device, but these were differentially preferred in the two languages: English speakers prefer the forestalling device over inceptive aspect, while German narrators make use of both means equally often. The adults consistently mark the ending of the search sequence by using the lexical items *finden/find*, by a definite article/possessive pronoun (*they see the/their frog*), or by explicit reference to the thematic identity of the frog. Further, adult narrators in both languages generally retain the perspective of the protagonist(s) up until the final scene — that is, the boy *finds, rediscovers* or *sees* his lost frog — as against the frog just sitting there, waiting *to be found, seen*, or *rediscovered*. As such, our expectation that instantiation and completion points of the story are good predictors for foreshadowings and wrapping ups, was confirmed — at least for the adult English- and German-speaking narrators.

In contrast to the relatively consistent marking of these components of the thematic frame, the reinstantiations of the search were differentially marked in the two languages. German adults do so about three times more often than English adults, perhaps due to the accessibility of the satellite *weiter-* (a particle that can be used productively with any action verb, expressing prolonging/continuing of an activity). Further, the intermittent signaling of reinstantiations implies that these story points play a different role in the composition of the narrative than the instantiation and/or conclusion of the search. Instantiation and ending are excellent candidates for overt appeals to the hierarchical, "eventful" structure of the narrative whole, and as such to foreshadowings and wrapping ups, while reinstantiations do not as clearly lend themselves to this function. Considering that their organizational function ranks lower in the hierarchy when compared with instantiations and ending, this difference in discursive organization of the narrative becomes more understandable.

In addition, adult narrators consistently avoid specifying that the protagonist's activities continue. Rather, when the search theme is in play, each subsequent action of the protagonist is simply described as a search activity at a particular location. This finding is consistent with a hierarchical positioning of a continuing activity within the narrative whole. It is thus not surprising that narrators "fail" to mark their organizational perspectives at these points in their narratives. The sequential arrangement of the events "carries" the plot, and the location of continuing activities at the lowest level of the hierarchy simply provides no motivation for an overt appeal to what will happen later in the story or what has happened before.

However, this finding suggests another point: If we were to take a strictly referential or ideational view of language and language function, we would expect that continuing activities, if referred to in subsequent, linearly ordered speech, would coincide with overt reference to their continuity. However, the linguistic continuity marker is reserved for instances of reinstantiations, and is never applied by adult narrators to continuous acts or activities. This suggests that narrative texture consists of both kinds of organizational orientations, the horizontal concatenation of references to events in light of the implicitly vertical and hierarchical axis of narrative organization.

Concerning the children's performance on the narrative task, our analyses not only focused on those linguistic markings that were used to establish the hierarchical organization, but also how those markers were used at other points in the children's narratives. Beginning with the most complex finding, we found that the frequency with which the beginning of the search is signaled increases with age in both language groups. However, a more detailed analysis revealed interesting developmental differences. First, the forestalling strategy used by adult narrators as a foreshadowing device is used by the 5-year olds to intensify the description of a particular activity at a local level (e.g., the dog being followed by a swarm of bees). These activities are not relevant to the goal path of the story, yet they are apparently seen as more salient or interesting by children. Second, an inceptive aspect marker is rarely used to mark the instantiation of the search theme by children in either language. Inceptive aspect is used with higher frequency by the English 9-year-olds, but at points in the narrative other than instantiation points. We conclude from this that these same grammatical devices serve different functional purposes for adults and children. Inceptive aspect is employed, especially by the 9-year-olds, in order to package small discourse units, that is, "middle-level episodes," such as the bees' pursuits of the dog or the deer's throwing the boy off his antlers (see Chapter IVC). A few 5-year-olds also appear to use inceptive aspect for a similar purpose, providing some evidence for this kind of discursive packaging. However, 5-year-old children are more likely to use inceptive aspect or the forestalling device to shift perspective from a seemingly purely descriptive level to a more involved and intensifying subjective stance.

In sum, the discursive devices which serve to foreshadow and wrap up, and so to signal the hierarchical, top-down structure of a story in the adult narratives, appear to emerge earlier in development at the local level of narrative organization. Children's early utilization of these devices serves primarily to intensify isolated referential events in the narrative; later, they serve to linguistically identify and so to foreshadow small "middle-level" packages within which local level themes are bounded and discursively organized. Eventually, linguistic attention is oriented to the top nodes of the hierarchy, and to the overall theme within which local-level events are organized and integrated.

The ways in which children differentiate reinstantiations from continuations revealed two opposing trends: The younger children do not use forms expressing continuous aspect (*weiter* + V, *continue* + V, etc.) to mark reinstantiations at specific story points. Instead, they use these devices to mark "activity continuations." In other words, young children appear to employ continuous aspect markers to refer to aspects of the theme that "go without saying" for the 9-year-olds and adults. Again, these patterns of results suggest that young children work their way into appropriate discourse marking from local to global levels. They begin by adding information to the linearly ordered sequences of events, which from an adult perspective is an "overmarking." However, for the child, this usage may represent an initial phase in which the device is "freed" from the referential level of language use, allowing it to take on a nonreferential, subjective perspective, and discursively to organize larger and larger discourse units. Finally, this nonreferential organization will be integrated in a hierarchical form of organization along a vertical axis, thus differentiating the two kinds of organizational orientations along the horizontal **and** vertical axes.

This investigation has certain limitations. First, it examines one particular discourse genre, telling a story from pictured material. Second, the crosslinguistic comparisons involve two languages that are closely related to one another. Third, it relies primarily on descriptive or qualitative rather than statistical analyses. Nonetheless, several insights have emerged. The first concerns the nature of the relationship between grammatical devices, in particular, aspectual markings, and discourse functions. In both languages we examined, inceptive and continuous aspect were not used exclusively to characterize the contours of activities. Rather than supporting a referential or ideational perspective on the function of grammatical devices in language use, our analysis reveals that aspectual markings function to construct the linear ordering of events within the framework of a nonlinear, hierarchical discourse structure.

Second, we found crosslinguistic differences in the relationship between complexity of form and frequency of usage. Such differences suggest that the coordination of horizontal and vertical axes of narrative organization may be related to language-specific properties of the structure of the linguistic system. The ready availability of small sets of grammaticized forms, as discussed in Chapter VB, might facilitate expression of higher-order, global discourse boundaries in the case of aspectual notions such as those considered here: inception, reiteration, and prospection.

Third, our developmental comparisons revealed that children at all ages are able to sequence the story in terms of linear events. However, young children do poorly with respect to foreshadowing what is about to come, and wrapping up what has been said thus far. Further, the forms used by adults for such global discourse functions are used by children mainly to mark local highlightings and subjective stances. This does **not** imply, however, that children's acquisition of aspectual expressions begins at the referential, ideational level of language use. The early, local-level use of aspectual distinctions to highlight and intensify particular information reflects, rather, a detachment from a purely ideational and referential perspective on events (see Labov, 1984). At the same time, it represents the initial stages of viewing the discourse unit from a subjective point of view. Viewing the acquisition of linguistic forms in this way is compatible with the assumption that children take into account what particular grammatical devices **do** in discourse (apart from their referential functions) from very early on.

Our most important contribution lies in a clearer identification and differentiation of the two organizational orientations that operate in holding a narrative together. In telling a story, language is used on the one hand in an ideational or referential function to delineate and sequentially order events. On the other, it also serves a textual and interpersonal function, providing "eventfulness" and meaning to a linear sequence of events from within a hierarchical and global perspective. Both orientations are instrumental in the constitution of the narrative as a whole as well as in the constitution of its parts. Our analysis showed that aspectual markers, i.e., viewing events from a particular perspective (internally as well as externally), are prime candidates for signaling changes in narrative orientation. (The same shifts can also be expressed by use of other linguistic devices as well, such as emotionals, negatives, or voice shifts; see Bamberg, 1991b.) More specifically, the use of aspectual markings in a narrative must be viewed beyond the semantic delineation of the event contour. Discursively, aspectual markings function as "contextualization cues" to the kind of narrative orientation which the narrator is in the process of adopting (Gumperz, 1982). As such, they enable the narrator to relate events to what has been said previously and what will be said subsequently, i.e., they point to the level of discourse organization. Consequently, the use of formal devices such as aspectual markings not only indicates the quality or contour of an event, but at the same time the motivational force from which the event has been given this contour. The motivational forces for taking such vantage points, at least as far as we can uncover them from discourse data, are ultimately the organizational factors in the constitution of what are to be considered the narrative whole and the parts.

For the language learner, then, we can identify two forces that motivate the child in identifying and using such formal means. On the one hand, there is the identification of events as semantic entities. This enables the child to differentiate between different event contours, and to refer to such contours as parts of the part-whole relationship. However, the ability to decontextualize and characterize events in and of themselves does not enable the learner to master the appropriate uses of markers such as inceptive or continuous aspect. Rather, each event is viewed and gains its contour in the context of the narrative whole. In this sense, the ability to step back and to take a subjective stance at events, as documented for the 5-year-old children in our two language samples, constitutes the mediating force for the learning of putting together a whole out of the parts and concurrently creating the parts in light of the textual whole. Adopting this perspective, learning to tell a story, and probably learning to participate in other modes of discourse as well, involves the gradual association of particular linguistic devices with the discourse-based functions which they express. Consequently, these form/function relationships can have a different character in different languages, and may influence the surface shape of a narrative in complex and interesting ways.

Part V

CONCLUSIONS

Chapter V0

IMPLICATIONS

In the concluding chapters we return to the three guiding themes set forth in Chapter IA: the filtering and packaging of experience through the linguistic forms and rhetorical options available in a particular language, and the child's developing proficiency in making use of the expressive options offered by the native language. The following two chapters also return to the guiding assumptions and predictions of *IB-3*.[1] Chapter VA focuses on issues relating to the development of language structure and language use in general (as suggested in Predictions 5 to 7) and Chapter VB situates development in the typological framework of the individual native languages of the study (as suggested in Predictions 8 to 10). (Issues of narrative development, relating to Predictions 1 to 4, are dealt with primarily in *IIA*.)

The general perspective on the acquisition and development of language underlying these conclusions integrates the findings that have emerged from the present study with the prior developmental and crosslinguistic work of the two authors. Throughout this work, it has been evident to us that the mastery of language structure and language use cannot be explained in monolithic terms, by any single type of mechanism or within the framework of any single linguistic, psycholinguistic, or sociolinguistic theory. Rather, the child relies on multiple sources of information — perceptual, processing, conceptual, grammatical, social-interactional, and others — to bootstrap into knowledge of linguistic forms. The child relies on a similar "confluence of cues" not only for initial entry into the system, but also across the course of development, in adding to, integrating, and reintegrating different levels and types of linguistic knowledge.

The present study begins in the mid-preschool period, and therefore does not address issues of primary acquisition. Our youngest children have mastered the essentials of the "core grammar" of their native language: They use coordinate and subordinate syntactic constructions, voice alternations, pro-forms, and almost all of the tense/aspect forms provided by their grammars. However, they are far from the "endstate" of a proficient speaker or proficient narrator. Indeed, our 9-year-old subjects have still not arrived at that endstate, as indicated by comparison with the adult narrators. A major

---

[1] We refer back to other sections of the book by the convention of indicating the chapter in Roman numerals and capital letters, followed by the section or subsection in that chapter. Thus, reference here is to Section 3 of Chapter IB.

theme, then, is **the continuing development of linguistic forms in use** throughout childhood (and well into adolescence). It is our conviction that any given linguistic form or construction acquires new functions — and new relations with other forms and constructions — as the child builds a complex and interactive system of form/function relations for purposes of producing extended discourse. (And although our study is limited to elicited narration, we take this as but one instance of the broad range of speech activities which every child comes to master.)

As a consequence of this discourse-oriented view of the endstate, our approach differs from work on language acquisition which puts linguistic form and syntactic and/or semantic principles on center stage. However, our work also differs from approaches which center on the pragmatics of discourse, in that we believe that a finegrained analysis of linguistic form — within a typological framework — is essential to an understanding of the child's acquisition and use of language. Thus we focus both on the **proficient speaker** and the **native speaker**. That is, in the course of development, the child learns to use the expressive options of a particular native language to carry out general discourse functions. Further, those general functions are, to some extent, shaped and channeled by features of individual languages (and — though not considered here — by cultures as well). For us, then, knowledge of forms — while critical in itself — is only part of what is involved in language acquisition and development. It is our hope that the present study will contribute to an understanding of what **other** kinds of knowledge play a role, and how these interact with and impinge on the acquisition of grammatical forms.

In examining the several ways of "relating events in narrative" across the five languages of our study, we have been impressed with the ways in which each of the languages represents a particular set of rhetorical options. After reading many frog stories in many languages, one comes to recognize an "English type" or a "Turkish type" of narration. That is, the various formal options available in a particular language, when taken together — as a system — orient speakers to particular patterns of information selection and information flow. In *VB* we summarize such "rhetorical types" and suggest that these patterns may reflect underlying processes of "thinking for speaking" in a particular language.

At the same time, in reading frog stories produced by narrators of different ages — across languages — one comes to recognize patterns of narration characteristic of specific age groups. In *IIA* we have attempted to specify those narrative patterns that are a function of age, rather than language (and such patterns are also summarized in *IVA*). In the following chapter, *VA*, we attempt to ground these patterns in a developmental framework.

The picture that emerges from our study is complex, dealing with orthogonal dimensions of age and native language, within the context of interacting dimensions of form and function. This is not an approach that lends itself to modeling or implementation at our current stage of theoretical and technological sophistication. But we believe it is a realistic approach, in that it attempts to pay due attention to the several interacting and developing systems that are involved in the processes of becoming both a proficient and a native speaker.

Chapter VA

BECOMING A PROFICIENT SPEAKER

---

0. Introduction
1. Development of Linguistic Form
2. Forms Acquire Functions
3. Functions Acquire Forms
4. Integrating Linguistic Knowledge in Narration

---

0. INTRODUCTION

We embarked on this study by making certain assumptions about the development of linguistic forms: that individual forms would take on more functions with development (Prediction 5), that new forms would emerge in order to meet the narrative functions involved in telling the frog story (Prediction 6), and that the interrelated development between form and function would be expressed most particularly in what we have called syntactic packaging (Prediction 7). Our study has made it possible to examine these assumptions against the background of shared findings for the developmental route of overall narrative abilities (Part II) and in light of the different paths taken by children en route to becoming proficient speakers/narrators in different languages. The complex developmental path taken en route to mature, proficient syntactic packaging is detailed for each language in the sections on connectivity in Part III and re-evaluated from a functional perspective in *IVC*. This chapter focuses on the more general issue of forms and functions in developing abilities to tell the frog story. We aim to show that while the findings from our study strongly confirm all three of our predictions about general linguistic development, the overall picture which emerges is more complex, and more multifaceted, than we had originally envisaged.

"Becoming a proficient speaker" means being able to use linguistic forms to meet specific discourse needs in a way which is appropriate from at least three points of view: (1) **structural**, as determined by the morphosyntax of the native language; (2) **rhetorical**, as determined by the way in which texts are typically constructed in a particular native language (*VB*); and (3) **discursive**, as suited to the particular task at hand — in our case narrating the contents of a picturebook adventure-story. Here, we start out by considering the development of linguistic structures, with particular attention to forms which are relatively late to emerge (Section 1). We then return to the Leitmotif of this study, that form and function interact in development, to examine the development of certain linguistic forms and of certain discursive functions — focusing on those used in the expression of temporality (Sections 2 and 3). We conclude by proposing that "being a proficient speaker" requires fully integrated knowledge of the **overall** resources of the linguistic system and the cognitive ability to maintain a fully updated representation of the **listener's** current state of knowledge (Section 4).

1. DEVELOPMENT OF LINGUISTIC FORM

We began this study with the assumption that younger children would avail themselves of fewer expressive options, that is, they would make use of a more restricted range of "forms" — in the very broad sense that we assign this term (*IB-1*) — than would children at more advanced stages of development. We suggested three reasons for why this would be the case (*IA-3.3*). First, younger children **cognitively**, cannot conceive of the full range of encodable perspectives. This claim is demonstrated, for instance, in *IVC*, which documents the increasing abilities to shift perspective and to analyze and integrate event components.

A second reason is that **communicatively**, young children cannot fully assess the listener's viewpoint. For example, for speakers to be able to deploy relative clauses for the discourse function of REIDENTIFICATION (*IVB-2.1*) — providing old information about an old referent, typically when a speaker believes a particular discourse entity has become "inactive" — it is necessary to maintain a continually updated assessment of the listener's needs. (This is a point we return to in Section 4.)

A third reason, of course, is that, **linguistically**, young children do not command the full range of formal devices. The broad range of ages, and the different structural domains which we examined, yield a rather complex picture in this regard. On the one hand, even the youngest children in our sample show a good command of a wide range of forms across the morphosyntactic systems in their language. On the other hand, some forms occur only in the texts of older, more proficient speakers (this section), while others are used only restrictedly by younger, or less proficient speakers (Section 2). With regard to the first observation, across our sample the youngest children can construct simple clauses which are well-formed in terms of the word-order constraints, casemarkings, and inflectional systems of their particular native language. For example, among the 3-year-olds, English speakers make use of present and past tense (*IIIA-1.1*), adverbial particles and prepositional phrases (*IIIA-2.2.1, 2.2.2*), and passive voice (*IIIA-3.2*); Spanish children use verb inflections to mark no fewer than six tense and aspect distinctions (*IIIC-Table 1*), and they use null subjects as required by their grammar (*IIIC-4;3*); and Hebrew-speaking 3-year-olds mark verbs with the correct inflections for number and gender agreement as well as for grammatical tense (*IIID-1.1*), and they use appropriate casemarking prepositions to construct oblique noun phrases (*IIID-2.1*). The chapters in Part III thus leave one with an overall sense that the availability of grammatically encoded distinctions in the target language leads children, early on, to exploit them in discourse. In our texts, children younger than age 5 make use of almost the full range of morphological and syntactic patterns involved in the four domains considered in Part III (tense/aspect, event conflation, perspective, and connectivity — as defined in *IIIo*).

As against this early emergence of structural proficiency, there are some forms in each language which do not occur at all in the texts of the younger children, being confined to occasional appearances among the 9-year-olds, or to strictly adult usage. These "late acquisitions" include: the past perfect form of verbs in the four languages in our sample which possess such a form (except for Hebrew); nonfinite forms used with adverbial or other subordinate-type functions — gerunds, participles, and/or nominalizations, depending on the language — except for Turkish, where these are the major means of subordination (*IIIE-4;2*); and multiple marking of aspectual notions within a single verb phrase (e.g., *And then the deer **went running off** with the little boy* [*E20i*]; see *IIIA-1.3.4*). Two other domains of linguistic expression which set the adult speakers off from even the older children are: (1) increased lexical diversity in the range of forms deployed within a particular subsystem — e.g., the much greater variety of time-expressions used by adults compared with children across the sample or the broad range of locative prepositions and temporal conjunctions found exclusively in the adult texts in the Hebrew sample (*IIID-2;3, IVA-5.2.2*); and (2) across the sample, the relatively large stretches and internal complexity of syntactic packaging in the adult narratives (*IVC-2.1*).

In line with our general view of language acquisition and language development, we assume that a variety of factors act in concert to contribute to late rather than early acquisition of a particular linguistic form. These include factors which have been touched on only marginally in this study, such as: frequency in input, acoustic salience, and pragmatic functions relating to social cognition. Two other factors which have been considered here as impinging on relative ease or delay of acquisition are morphosyntactic processing complexity and narrative functions relating to discourse cognition. The latter form the core of our analysis of developing form/function relations in becoming a proficient speaker (Sections 2 and 3, below). With respect to the former, we have found that constructions which apparently impose a heavy processing load are used less frequently in a language — such as relative clauses in Turkish and German (*IVB*) or passives in German (*IVC*).

Frequency and complexity together account for the fact that such constructions will be learned later and used less frequently than comparable constructions in other languages where they are less demanding — such as relative clauses in Spanish and Hebrew, and passives in English. However, "complexity" per se is not an adequate index of age of acquisition. If a system is transparently organized, as the Spanish tense/aspect system, preschoolers explore almost all of the many options and are probably stimulated to make early use of forms that fit the system, such as the present perfect. At the same time, even if a system is formally quite transparent, some options will not be used until school age, due to their conceptual and/or discursive complexity, such as the "circumstantial" converb *-erek* in Turkish and the perfective progressive in Spanish.

A moral to be drawn from these proposals is that it is misleading to make generalizations about the acquisition of a particular type of grammatical construction on the basis of its use in a single language (and type of discourse).

2. FORMS ACQUIRE FUNCTIONS

Considering the emergence of linguistic forms in and of themselves, as in Section 1, goes counter to the Leitmotif of our undertaking — **that form and function interact in development**. The design of our study — using elicitation materials which allow us some control over the content of the expression without determining its form (*IB-1*), with children of different ages compared with adult native speakers of five different languages — has provided us with powerful evidence for the claim that, regardless of the acquisition point of a linguistic device, it acquires new functions with age. In other words, acquisition of the structural mechanics of a particular linguistic form is only the beginning of the story. This point was clearly demonstrated by analysis of how superficially similar forms, all classifiable as **relative clause** constructions, both extend and change the range of general discourse as well as specifically narrative functions which they serve across different age groups (*IVB*). And it was discussed with respect to numerous different forms in the chapters in Part III, including such diverse phenomena as prepositionals like *in* and *after* in English, the connective 'and' in different languages, and use of null subjects in Hebrew. Here, we examine the development of forms from the domain of **tense/aspect** systems in our five languages, in order to demonstrate the implications of the claim that forms acquire broader and more discourse-motivated functions across different developmental phases.[1]

---

[1] Development does not necessarily involve a **broadening** of the functions of a particular form. Children must also learn to abandon the use of forms for functions which are discursively unconventional, inappropriate, or overly general. Examples noted in our study are the immature marking of simultaneity by such expressions as German *auch*, Hebrew *gam*, and

The use of **progressive aspect** in English was taken as "a mini case-study" to demonstrate this point at the outset of our study (*IA-1*). The developmental picture was enriched and expanded by our findings for the distribution and use of the *-ing* form in the English frog stories: from being the default case of encoding immediate present in simple clauses, to serving as an early means for indicating simultaneity with physical event and perception verbs in the preschool-age texts (*IVA-5.2.3*), and on to performing syntactically more complex functions in different types of complement clauses, each with its own developmental history. For example, the presentative function in expressions like *there's an owl coming out* emerges earlier than the function of expressing extended aspect with verbs like *start* or *go on*. Eventually, in adult discourse these same forms are used in modifying contexts of nonfinite adverbial and relative clauses, serving the discursive function of backgrounding (*IIIA-1.2.1*).

A major finding, then, which emerges from this study in the domain of temporality is that while 3-year-olds in all our languages use past and present tense as well as local marking of clause-level aspectual distinctions (in the languages where these are available), the functions associated with these forms become discursively-motivated rather later in development, revealing a stepwise developmental progression. Consider, for example, the area of **tense/aspect shifting**. This can be considered as discursively functional only once a dominant narrative tense becomes established (*IIA-4.2.2*), beyond the stage where moving from one tense and/or aspect form to another is motivated at the most local level of individual predicate-semantics or the pictured situation.[2] Whatever tense is chosen, the fact that the speaker uses one tense as an anchor seems to go together with presentation of a plot-oriented narrative, as defined in *IIA*. In all five languages we see a developmental change from "perceptually-motivated" choice of tense/aspect forms to "narratively-motivated" choice. That is to say, once a given tense is established as the carrier of plot-advancing clauses, contrasting tense/aspect forms can be used to serve narrative functions, rather than reflecting the visibly evident characteristics of individual pictures. For example, one factor contributing to "mixed" usage at early ages is a tendency to use the present tense to describe events pictured as ongoing, and to use a different tense form (typically past, perfect, or nonwitnessed modality) for events that are not pictured but can be inferred from visible endstates or consequences. With the

---

Turkish *de* all meaning roughly 'also, too', as well as by the expression *o zaman* 'at that time' in Turkish, and certain nonproficient aspectual contrasts in Spanish (*IVA-6*).

[2] For those languages with 4-year-old data (English, Spanish, Hebrew), a dominant narrative tense tends to be established at this age, and by age 5 in German and Turkish.

establishment of an anchor tense, however, such contrasts can be dealt with by distinctions of aspectual marking within a given tense. Compare, for example, the following two English versions of the same scene:

(1) *And he's* [=dog] **running** *through there and he* [=boy] **fell off.** [*E3e-3;8*]

(2) *And the dog was still running with the bees after him, and the boy fell.* [*E5c-5;3*]

The 3-year-old narrator of (1) uses PROGRESSIVE *'s running* to describe the event pictured as in progress, switching to PAST for the completed event that can be inferred from the transition between Picture 11 (boy in tree) and Picture 12 (boy on ground). The 5-year-old narrator of (2), anchoring her story in the past, is able to switch aspect while maintaining tense: *was running* versus *fell*.

In most instances, however, our five languages do not provide systematic aspectual contrasts in each tense (or, in the case of Hebrew, in any tense). For example, Turkish provides a PROGRESSIVE-NONPROGRESSIVE distinction in the past tense, but not in the present. Accordingly, the two events of Picture 12 can be contrasted in the narrative past (M.PAST), as in (3), but not in the present, as in (4):

(3) *Arılar **uçuyormuş** köpeğin ardından. ... Ağbisi hemen yere **atlamış**.*

'The bees **were.flying**:M.PAST.PROG after the dog. ... His master immediately **jumped**:M.PAST to the ground.' [*T5g-5;2*]

(4) *Sonra köpek **kaçıyor, adam düşüyor**.*

'Then the dog **is.running.away** / **runs.away**:PRES, the man **is.falling** / **falls**:PRES.' [*T5c-5;1*]

In Hebrew, where the only way to mark the temporal overlap of a completed and ongoing event is to juxtapose past and present, tense shifting is used for this purpose even by proficient narrators, as in (5):

(5) *Eyze yanshuf **yaca** lo mehaxor ba'ec ve **hipil** oto, ve hakelev, bediyuk hadvorim **rodfot** axarav.*

'Some owl **came.out**:PAST at him from the hole in the tree and **threw**:PAST him, and the dog, just then the bees **chase**:PRES after him.' [*H20a*]

But even this type of simple-tense shifting between present and past for the narrative purpose of backgrounding is confined to more mature narrators. Hebrew-speaking 5- and 9-year-olds use the alternation between present and past tense in more complex syntactic and semantic functions than do younger children, for example to express relative tense and the notion of anteriority between matrix and complement clauses. But only our adult narrators deploy these structurally simple forms for the discursively-motivated narrative function illustrated in (5).

Thus, knowledge of tense/aspect in one's native language includes shifting these structural devices for discursive functions of backgrounding and foregrounding, beyond the level of a single clause or even for marking grammatical sequence of tenses across clauses. Moreover, comparison of these formal systems in our five languages demonstrates that narrative functions of tense and aspect cannot be considered without taking into account the range of options available in each language, both for aspectual contrast in general and for aspectual contrast within a given tense (*IIIo-Table 2*, and see, further, Section 4 of this chapter, and *VB*).

Linguistic forms are thus shown to have extended and quite complex developmental histories, both when a particular grammatical construction, such as **relative clause**, is analyzed from a discourse-functional perspective (as in *IVB*), and when a type of process, such as tense and aspect shifting is examined in extended narratives (as in this section). With age, forms acquire an extended range of functions across the five languages, although the languages themselves differ in the extent to which a structural option is exploited by speakers. In this respect, as for the other morphosyntactic systems analyzed in this study, development in knowledge of both the structure and use of linguistic forms, qualitatively as well as quantitatively, is critically dependent on the development of general discourse abilities — being able to construct a coherent and cohesively organized text, and of specifically narrative skills — being able to construct a narrative which is hierarchically organized and evaluatively motivated.

3. FUNCTIONS ACQUIRE FORMS

An assumption underlying our study has been that the emergence of new functions motivates the acquisition of new forms to serve those functions. Here we have been guided by an old principle in developmental psychology, stated succinctly by Werner and Kaplan many years ago (1963, p. 60):

> [W]herever functional shifts occur during development, the novel function is first executed through old, available forms; sooner or later, of course, there is a pressure towards the development of new forms which are of a more function-specific character, i.e., that will serve the new function better than the older forms.

Again, we use the domain of temporality to illuminate how, in becoming proficient speakers, children learn to deploy already-acquired forms for new discourse functions. In a narrative context, there are three plotline temporal functions: the neutral or "default" instance of **sequentiality**, in which each succeeding predication expresses the next event in time; the case of **simultaneity,** in which two or more events co-occur or overlap in time, as analyzed from both a developmental and a crosslinguistic perspective in *IVA*; and **anteriority** or **retrospection,** in which speakers refer back to a prior event in time at some later point in the discourse. (In addition, the narrator can move away from the temporal axis of the plotline to make timeless and irrealis comments — by using forms such as habituals, conditionals, hypotheticals, and counterfactuals.)

One might think that children could not give overt linguistic expression to the function of retrospection without the use of temporal markers. However, a close examination of early frog texts shows that this function is already present, expressed by "old, available" means. A 3- or 4-year-old who refers to 'the frog's jar' when describing the dog's predicament in Pictures 4-6, **is** taking a retrospective perspective on events, looking back mentally to that particular object in a prior state. However, this **referential** function of retrospection is not yet integrated with a more mature **discourse** function of retrospection, namely, to interrupt the onward flow of action to introduce an extended comment about a relevant past situation in one or more clauses. Compare, for example, 'the dog got stuck in the frog's jar' with 'the dog got stuck in the jar that the frog had been kept in'. We suggest that the "pressure towards the development of new forms" in such instances finds expression in the growing ability to construct and monitor hierarchically-organized narrative.

As another "mini case-study," consider the recruitment of tense/aspect shifts to carry out functions of retrospection. In the preceding section we noted that across all the languages, tense shifts perform discursive functions by age 5; that is, choice of tense is determined not only by event characteristics (ongoing process versus state or inferred antecedent process) but also by narrative considerations. The most important narratively-motivated temporal functions to develop in the 5-9 age range are **retrospection** (discussed below) and the encoding of **simultaneity** (discussed in *IVA).* On the level of narrative organization, retrospection involves reference to an earlier event which is reinvoked because of its relevance to the current point in plot development. The precursors of retrospection on the level of interclausal relations are locally-determined temporal readjustments employed to mention an immediately prior circumstance, typically causal. These are rare in all of the 3- and 4-year-old texts, which almost always move inexorably forward in time. When causal factors are invoked, they tend to be mentioned in iconic order, as in (6), rather than in temporally reversed order, as in (7) — although the latter order is more typical of children's early use of causals for argumentation and justification (Ervin-Tripp, 1989; Kyratzis, 1991, 1992):

(6) *Und da ist das Bienenhaus runtergefallen. Und da erschreckt sich der Hund.*

'And there the beehive has fallen down. And there the dog gets scared.' [*G3c-3;11*]

(7) *Und der hat sich da versteckt weil er Angst vor den beiden hat.*

'And he [=little frog] has hidden himself there because he's afraid of the two of them [=boy and dog].' [*G3k-3;7*]

Contexts such as (7) are probably the preparatory ground for the linguistic devices that are used to refer back to nonimmediate temporal antecedents on a more-embracing level of narrative organization. This echoes an earlier theme (noted at various points in *IVc*), that forms which eventually become recruited for narrative purposes may have antecedents earlier on in other types of discourse settings — as pointed out, for example, in studies by Kyratzis (1991) and Kyratzis, Guo, and Ervin-Tripp (1990) of interactive conversational usages of very young children.

Once children start expressing retrospection as a narrative function, this can be coded by switching from a present to a past tense, as in (8), or, when available in the language, by switching within the past to a prior past, as in (9). The first type of switch can be performed by various forms, depending on the language (to simple past, present perfect, perfective, evidential past). The second type of switch, in these languages, generally requires the past perfect. The following examples show that both types of retrospection are available by age 5 in each language where they are provided by the grammar. The examples in (8) are drawn from present-tense texts and those in (9) from past-tense texts.

Present → Past

(8a) **English:** *There's frogs. They **were waiting** there for them.* [*E4c-4;8*]

(8b) **German:** *Hier ist der Frosch drin. Den **haben** die **gefangen, haben** die **mitgenommen** und in das Glas **gesteckt.***

'Here **is** the frog inside (of the jar). They **have caught** it, **have taken** it with them and **put** it in the glass.' [*G5f-5;1*]

(8c) **Spanish:** *Y cuando se **despierta** el niño, se encuentra que se **ha ido**.*

'And when the boy **wakes.up**, he discovers that (the frog) **has gone away**.' [*S5c-5;4*]

(8d) **Hebrew:** *Ve kan hayeled **ro'e** she hacfardea **barxa** mi kan.*

'And here the boy **sees** that the frog **ran.away** from here. [*H4f-4;3*]

(8e) **Turkish:** *Kurbağa kaybolmuş görüyor.*

'He **sees**:PRES (that) the frog **got.lost**:M.PAST [nonwitnessed].' [*T5c-5;1*]

Past → Prior Past

(9a) **English:** *And then they saw the frog had married another frog.* [*E5c-5;3*]

(9b) **German:** *Und dann lief der Hund davon. Er hatte auch ein ganz großen Schrecken bekommen.*

'And there the dog **ran away**. He **had** also **gotten** a big scare.' [*G5a-5;7*]

(9c) **Spanish:** *El niño buscaba a ver si se había metido por ahí.*

'The boy **looked**:IPFV to see if (the frog) **had hidden** herself over there.' [*S5h-5;9*]

(9d) **Hebrew:** *Ve ra'u she ha-cfardea ne'elma.*[3]

'And (they) **saw** that the frog **disappeared**.' [*H5k-5;9*]

(9e) **Turkish:** *Bir baktılar, kavanozun içinden kurbağa kaçmıştı.*

'They **looked**:D.PAST, the frog **had.escaped**:PAST.PERF from inside the jar.' [*nT5g-5;7*][4]

Thus it is evident that, regardless of particular tense-aspect forms provided by the language, they are recruited to perform the function of narrative retrospection in the preschool period. The past-tense forms used in PRESENT → PAST switches are available long before they are needed for narrative retrospection. This is a clear instance of Werner and Kaplan's generalization, or what Slobin (1973, p. 184) formulated as the principle that: "New forms first express old functions, and new functions are first expressed by old forms."

It is more difficult to discern the precursors of the past perfect forms used in the PAST → PRIOR PAST switch, however, and it is possible that, in some languages, these forms may develop together with the kinds of temporal organization required for narrative. The only possible examples of an antecedent to the past perfect are rare instances of narrative retrospection

---

[3] Only one past-tense form is available in Hebrew, so that anteriority is inferrable when the verb of the complement clause is in the past tense. That is, in both (8d) and (9d), if the verbs *barxa* 'escaped' and *ne'elma* 'disappeared' had been in the present tense, they would be interpreted as simultaneous with the matrix verbs meaning 'sees' and 'saw' respectively.

[4] This example comes from the data gathered by Küntay (see *IB*), since there are no instances of the past perfect in the smaller sample gathered by Aksu-Koç.

marked in English by use of the PAST PROGRESSIVE or PAST HABITUAL *used to*, and in Turkish by the M.PAST (nonwitnessed), as in the following three examples:

(10) *I think they **swam** out so far and they **came** right back to see their mom cause I think they **were missing** their mom.* [=had been missing their mom?] [*E3g-3;9*]

(11) *And he **takes** one of them, and they **said**, "This one **used to be** ours."* [cf. indirect discourse: and they said that that one had been theirs] [*E5f-5;8*]

(12) *Ondan sonra aşağıya **baktılar**. Kurbağa da çocuğu **doğmuş**.*
'Then they **looked**:D.PAST [witnessed] down. The frog **gave.birth**:M.PAST [nonwitnessed] to a child.' [=it seems that the frog had given birth] [*T5a-5;4*]

In many cases, however, children may simply not have available means for the expression of narrative retrospection in the past until they acquire the past perfect. If this is the case, some uses of the past perfect may represent the emergence of a "new form" to serve a "new function." Only in Spanish, with its abundance of verbal morphology, are there instances of early uses of the past perfect, used to contrast two events in the past, without a clear retrospective interpretation, as in (13).

(13) *Y el ubo **estaba** en el agujero que **había subido** el niño.*
'And the owl **was**:IPFV in the hole that the boy **had.climbed**:PAST.PERF to.' [*S4k-4;10*]

In Spanish, then, the extension of the past perfect to reinvoke a nonimmediate past situation for narrative purposes may be a case of an "old form" performing a "new function." It may be that the richness and systematicity of the Spanish tense/aspect system encourages children to explore the functions of the past perfect at an early age. In other languages, alternative forms may be pressed into service to express retrospection in past-tense narratives before the past perfect has been mastered (as in the English and Turkish examples in (10), (11), and (12)). In German, where this kind of narrative, at least, is almost always told in the present tense, the issue does not arise. And, in a language like Hebrew, with no grammatical equivalent of the past perfect, this function may be left to inference from context.

This discussion shows that the range of expressive options for the same function broadens **and** becomes conventionalized with age. This applies across the different dimensions which make up narrative discourse, including those of simultaneity and retrospection, of cohesion and connectivity, of describing locative trajectories, of taking undergoer perspective, as well as in expressing evaluative commentary. In this process, the proficient speaker comes to function as a proficient narrator, able to relate events in narrative as well as in real time, and to take the perspective of narrator in addition to that of the protagonist.

4. INTEGRATING LINGUISTIC KNOWLEDGE IN NARRATION

It appears that no language has a specialized grammatical system devoted to narrative alone. Rather, all available sets of grammatical devices are coordinated for this purpose (tense, aspect, voice, word order, subordination, and so forth). One task of becoming a "proficient narrator," then, is to learn to coordinate these various components into a single system. Further, as children build up knowledge about the forms available in their language, these become coordinated and reorganized within more complex, interacting systems. As Karmiloff-Smith has shown in her work on linguistic development (as well as in other cognitive domains), "children first consolidate each of the systems (the morphophonological, the syntactic, and the semantic) separately; only later does one system constrain another" (1992, p. 181).

Eventually, proficient speakers of a language have at their disposal a rich array of "rhetorical options" which can be alternated to express a full range of discourse functions in such activities as conversing, describing, arguing, or narrating. This means, for example, that children must learn that a function like retrospection can be met by using past perfect relative tense or sequence of tenses, and also by relative clauses (e.g., 'the jar in which the frog had been kept'), though these two forms are associated with quite distinct systems of the grammar, and may serve other discursive functions apart from retrospection. Similarly, connectivity can be achieved, with some variation from one language to another, by such diverse means as coordination, subordination, nonfinite participles, subject elision, and/or overt markers of temporal relations between clauses like those meaning 'meanwhile' or 'afterwards'. Or, both within and across languages, changing perspective from, say, agent to undergoer, can be achieved by such varied formal devices as word-order shifts, topicalizations, middle and passive voice, impersonal constructions, as well as verb morphology. Another instance is demonstrated in Sections 2 and 3, above: We see that the narrative functions of tense and aspect cannot be considered without taking into account the range of options available in each language, both for aspectual contrast in general and for aspectual contrast within a given tense. That is, the type of rhetorical options afforded by a given language within and across its systems of morphosyntax has **expressive** implications for what speakers choose to say and how they will say it.

It is thus not surprising that acquisition of a full range of linguistic forms (Section 2) and of discourse functions (Section 3) has a fairly lengthy developmental history, extending well into school age. Our findings indicate that development of proficient command of form-function interactions continues at least through adolescence. The cognitive task involved is extremely complex. Being a proficient speaker means knowing what to mark explicitly, and what to leave the listener to infer. This can only be achieved once children have acquired (1) knowledge of the overall resources of the linguistic forms and rhetorical options of their native language, and (2) the ability to work with all these various systems and keep all of them active simultaneously, within a continuing, and continually updated, representation of the listener's current state of knowledge, the already completed discourse, and the planned continuation. This must be based on a "theory of the listener" combined with awareness of what constitutes shared information (either from sources prior to the current discourse or constructed as part thereof — as well as, in the case of the frog-story task, from the pictures in the storybook).

Our findings yield clear instances of a U-shaped pattern of development with respect to these interrelated requirements of the proficient speaker (Strauss, 1982). Young children tend either to **omit** information that is necessary to the listener or to **overuse** available devices. At the phase where children have just gained mastery of a particular system, they tend to use the relevant devices quite redundantly; that is, they have not yet learned what they can leave to the listener to infer. Only proficient speakers, and narrators, tell as much as is necessary and no more, adhering to the Gricean maxims of relevance and informativity. Where children exhibit either of these two patterns, of telling too much or too little, it suggests that they are engaged in monitoring their output more for themselves as speakers/narrators than for the listener. That is, they are not yet constructing and updating what we have termed "a representation of the listener."

Examples of redundant overmarking of distinctions, and overuse of available devices, abound across the texts — mainly of the children in the late preschool or early school-age period. These include excessive use of temporal adverbs such as *ya* 'already' in Spanish (unnecessary in view of the availability of perfect aspect for marking current relevance) and, also in Spanish, overmarking of locative information to yield the equivalent of 'he exited out', or 'entered inside'. Another example, in several languages, is the occurrence of repeated NP reference and use of pronouns in place of null subjects in conjoined, subordinate, or adjacent clauses, supporting Hickmann's (1991, p. 181) observation that "it is not until after seven years that children stop reintroducing referents across utterances as they go from picture to picture, and that they rely maximally on presuppositions established within discourse." Perhaps the clearest example in our data is the excessive marking of sequence by the use of 'and' alone or 'and then' across the languages (Berman, in press-c). The finding that adults in all languages use 'and then' or its equivalents, as well as other markers of continuity, far more sparingly than children highlights another facet of what it means to be a proficient speaker. While children use such expressions to move each step of the action forward, adults — recognizing that sequentiality is the default temporality for narrative — rely on sequencing of clauses as the implicit encoding of sequences of actions in the narrative, and use explicit marking to move the action from one episode to the next or to meet the discourse function of reinstantiation (*IVD*). The generalization which emerges, then, is that the course of developing a mature "syntax of discourse" means that not only do linguistic forms acquire more specialized functions (the burden of Section 2 above), but they also lose more local syntactic and referential functions — which can be dispensed with in the hierarchical organization of ongoing text construction.

The result of these many interwoven strands of development is a **proficient speaker** who has mastered the demands of textual cohesion. Cohesion is generally approached as a phenomenon of **text**, as clearly stated, for example, by Hickmann (1991, p. 157):

> [C]ohesion is created by the conjoined use of linguistic devices which in various ways link together utterances in discourse and thereby create a 'co-text' necessary for the unfolding of discourse. The ontogenesis of discourse cohesion corresponds to the development of children's ability to 'anchor' speech in co-text and thus to use language as *its own context.*

To this we would add the developing ability of the child to create and attend to "co-text" in the process of **speaking**, thus viewing cohesion as the consequence of flexible, online access to a set of integrated systems. Indeed, as Fleischman has concluded, in her study of tense and narrativity, the "textual component" of a linguistic system can be characterized in terms of "the strategies speakers use for controlling the rate of information flow in a discourse, for partitioning of a discourse into smaller subunits, and marking the boundaries between them, and for signaling levels of saliency or information relevance — for creating texture within text" (1990, pp. 5-6). In short, "co-text" and "cohesive texture" are the products of goal-directed communicative activity, based on mature knowledge of the integrated subsystems of the native language.

Chapter VB

BECOMING A NATIVE SPEAKER

In Chapter IA we presented the themes of **filtering** and **packaging** that run throughout the book:

- **Filtering**: The world does not present "events" to be encoded in language. Rather, experiences are filtered — (a) through choice of perspective and (b) through the set of options provided by the particular language — into verbalized events.

- **Packaging**: A skillful narrative does not simply consist of a linear chain of successive events located in time and space. Rather, events must be packaged into hierarchical constructions.

These themes have been repeatedly demonstrated with data from individual languages in Part III and in discussions of form-function relations in Part IV. We have also suggested, at various points, that filtering and packaging are differentially shaped by each language. In becoming a **native** speaker of a given language, the child learns to attend to particular aspects of experience and to relate them verbally in ways that are characteristic of that language. Becoming a native speaker thus involves not only the acquisition of the phonology and morphosyntax of a given language; it also requires attention to the grammaticized semantic distinctions of the language and to the ways in which grammatical forms are deployed in the construction of connected discourse. Each language, and each type of language, represents a different constellation of such factors. As a consequence, a **proficient native speaker** selects and organizes information in ways that result in a language-specific **rhetorical style**.

In this chapter we explore some of the ways in which frog stories are distinctly different when told in each of the five languages of the study. These
differences contribute to what Myhill (1992) has called "typological discourse
analysis," which he describes as "the crosslinguistic study of the factors
affecting the choice of one construction or another in a given language, taking
the surrounding discourse context into consideration as having a crucial effect
on this choice" (pp. 1-2).

We propose, further, that such differences have important cognitive
implications. Language-specific patterns of "telling the frog story" suggest
that the native language directs one's attention, while speaking, to particular
ways of filtering and packaging information. In making this proposal, we
present a modified form of the Sapir-Whorf hypothesis — attending only to
the mental processes that are accessed **in the course of constructing linguistic messages**, and making no claims with regard to the effects of language on
other kinds of mental processes.[1] In so doing, we are following formulations
of Boas and Sapir that emphasized the role of language in "expression" —
that is, speaking:

> [I]n each language only a part of the complete concept that we have
> in mind is expressed, and ... each language has a peculiar tendency
> to select this or that aspect of the mental image which is conveyed
> by the expression of the thought. (Boas, 1911/1966, pp. 38-39)

> [The forms of each language] establish a definite relational feeling
> or attitude towards all possible contents of expression and, through
> them, towards all possible contents of experience, in so far, of
> course, as experience is capable of expression in linguistic terms.
> (Sapir, 1924/1958, p. 152)

Slobin (1987, 1990, 1991, in press-a) has applied this orientation to a
typological discourse analysis of frog stories, proposing a particular kind of
language-cognition interface (1991, p. 12):

> The expression of experience in linguistic terms constitutes **think-
> ing for speaking** — a special form of thought that is mobilized for
> communication. ... We encounter the contents of the mind in a spe-
> cial way when they are being accessed for **use**. That is, the activity
> of thinking takes on a particular quality when it is employed in the
> activity of speaking. In the evanescent time frame of constructing

---

[1] For current discussions of these broader issues, see Gumperz and Levinson (in press) and
Lucy (1992).

utterances in discourse one fits one's thoughts into available linguistic frames. "Thinking for speaking" involves picking those characteristics of objects and events that (a) fit some conceptualization of the event, and (b) are readily encodable in the language. **I propose that, in acquiring a native language, the child learns particular ways of thinking for speaking**.

In this chapter, we review the evidence that becoming a native speaker involves becoming a native "thinker-for-speaking" in the terms of a particular language. We first offer examples on the level of event description and then go on to characterize the rhetorical styles that are typical of frog stories in the five languages.

1. CHANNELING OF ATTENTION

The picture-story method makes it possible to compare the ways in which the identical picture is described by speakers of different languages. Consistent crosslinguistic differences cannot be attributed to the stimulus, and therefore must reside in the speakers. If particular aspects of the pictured situation are regularly encoded in a language, we can conclude that those aspects attract the attention of speakers in the course of constructing a verbalized expression of their perceptions. Our data present a number of instances in which there seem to be clear differences between languages with regard to the event components which are encoded by their speakers. We propose that such differences are due to the channeling of attention in the course of thinking for speaking. We offer examples from the domains of temporal and spatial description.

1.1. Aspectual Contrasts

In the frog story — thanks to the overlapping activities of the several protagonists — there are many instances in which two kinds of events occur in the same temporal-spatial frame. The encoding of simultaneity is examined in detail in *IVA* with regard to the use of various kinds of interclausal connectives. Here we focus on contrasts between the temporal contours of two simultaneous events, looking for cases in which an event of brief duration takes places within the time frame of an event that is more extended in time. Clear examples are provided by Picture 12 (boy falls — dog runs) and Picture 2 (frog escapes — boy and dog sleep). In both of these scenes, it is evident that the two events do not overlap completely in time, and that the duration of the first is bounded and contained within the duration of the second. This temporal distinction, however, is not noted by all of our narrators; furthermore, those narrators who do take note of the distinction tend to be speakers of languages with grammaticized aspect.

Consider, first, narrations of Picture 12. English allows for an opposition between an aspectually neutral verb form and a progressive. This aspectual contrast is already available to 3-year-olds:

(1) *He's [=dog] **running** through there. And he [=boy] **fell** off.* [*E3e-3;8*]

A similar contrast is available in Turkish (though only in the past tense), and it is used by 4-year-olds in Küntay's sample:

(2) *Yere düştü.* [...] *Köpeğe yakalıyorlardı.*

> '[Boy] **fell**:D.PAST to the ground. [...] [Bees] **were.chasing**:D.PAST:PROG the dog.' [*nT4c-4;10*]

As has been repeatedly noted in this book, Spanish provides the most elaborated set of aspectual contrasts in our sample, with either a progressive or an imperfective for durative events, contrasting with a perfective for bounded events or a perfect for completed events. That is, experience with the language should channel children's attention to a number of ways of conceptualizing the temporal contours of situations. The various types of oppositions are available to 3-year-olds. The youngest example of a perfective-progressive contrast comes from the Chilean sample:

(3a) *Se cayó.* [...] *El perro está corriendo.*

> '[Boy] **fell**:PFV. [...] The dog **is running**:PRES.PROG.' [*cS3g-3;4*]

A perfect-progressive contrast is also used by 3-year-olds (3b), as well as a perfective-imperfective contrast (3c):

(3b) *Se **ha caído** el niño.* [...] *Los mosquitos **estaban saliendo** de las ramas de detrás.*

> 'The boy **has fallen**:PERF. [...] The mosquitoes **were exiting**:PAST.PROG from the branches behind.' [*S3d-3;8*]

(3c) *Se cayó. **Corría** el perro.*

> '[Boy] **fell**:PFV. The dog **ran**:IPFV.' [*aS3f-3;7*]

German and Hebrew differ from these three languages in that they lack distinctive grammatical marking of either pole of the aspectual contrast. The available options for marking the aspectual distinction are to present the boy's fall in the past tense, contrasted with the action of the dog and bees in the present tense, or to use some lexical means to contrast the two events (such as verb repetition or adverbial marking to indicate the durativity of the latter event). There are examples of such options but, as we will see, they are quite rare. In both languages, some speakers make use of contrasts; e.g.:

(4) **German:**

*Und der ist vom Baum **runtergefallen** und der Hund **läuft** schnell weg.*

'And he [=boy] **has fallen**:PRES.PERF down from the tree and the dog **runs**:PRES away quickly.' [*G5k-5;4*]

(5) **Hebrew:**

*Ha-yeled **nafal**. [...] Ve ha-kelev **boreax**.*

'The-boy **fell**:PAST. [...] And the-dog **runs.away**:PRES.' [*H5j-5;7*].

There are occasional attempts to indicate the durativity of running by stretching out or repeating the verb, such as the Hebrew:

(6) *Uri **nafal** ve kibel maka xazaka. Ha-kelev **barax, ve racccc**.*

'Uri [=boy] **fell**:PAST and got hurt. The-dog **ran.away, and rannnnn**.' [*H5h-5;5*]

Similar elaborations are used by only a few, older, German narrators, such as:

(7) *Und er **rannte schneller und immer schneller** [...] und der Junge fiel vom Baum auf den Boden.*

'And he **ran faster and ever faster** [...] and the boy **fell** from the tree to the ground.' [*G9l-9;5*]

What is most common, however, is that speakers of Hebrew and German simply do not distinguish the temporal contours of the two events of Picture 12, but rather use two simple verbs in the same tense. The following examples are from 3-year-olds, but, as we will see, they are typical of all age groups.

(8) **Hebrew:**

*Hu **nafal**. Hu **barax**.*

'He **fell**. He **ran.away**.' [*H3j-3;9*]

(9) **German:**

*Da **fällt** der Junge hin. [...] Und der **läuft** da weg.*

'There the boy **falls**:PRES down. [...] And he **runs**:PRES away there.' [*G3a-3;9*]

Looking across the entire sample of ages and languages, there is a striking contrast between the two groups of languages. Table 1 presents figures on the percentage of narrators who use the **same** tense/aspect form for both verbs in describing Picture 12 ('fall' versus 'run/chase'). The last column gives overall figures, across ages.

In the three languages that provide aspectual marking to contrast durative with nondurative or punctual events, only a minority (20-35%) of the narrators do not make use of these options. In other words, two-thirds or more of

TABLE 1
Percentage of Narrators Using Same Tense/Aspect Form
for 'Fall' and 'Run' for Picture 12

| Language | Age Group | | | |
	Preschool (3-5)	School (9)	Adult	OVERALL
Spanish	23	18	21	21
English	26	22	27	27
Turkish	38	40	29	35
German	54	80	78	71
Hebrew	71	100	63	78

the speakers **do** note the aspectual contrast. In marked contrast, in the two languages that do not provide inflectional marking of the contrast, only about one-quarter of the speakers seek alternate means to do so. As we have found repeatedly in this study, speakers seem to pay special attention to the semantic categories that are grammatically marked in the language.

However, it is critical for our proposal of thinking for speaking that some speakers **do** go beyond the set of grammaticized distinctions in the language. If the figures for Hebrew and German were uniformly 100%, and for Spanish, English, and Turkish 0%, we could only conclude that speakers strictly adhere to the formal contrasts provided by their language, and it would not be possible to separate thinking from speaking. The deviations from these extremes show (contra Whorf's [1940] strong determinism) that it is, indeed, possible to try to mark aspectual notions that are not part of the regular system of verb morphology in one's language. (And, on the other hand, that one is not compelled to make use of the full array of distinctions available in verbal morphology.) But what is most striking in Table 1 is the finding that speakers so rarely make use of options that differ from the norm. Narrators of all ages, across languages, certainly know, on a conceptual level, that the boy's falling is punctual and completed with regard to the simultaneous, ongoing chasing and running of bees and dog. But they generally do not seem to be inclined to express **linguistically** any more of this knowledge than fits the available distinctions in their language.

It is striking that children as young as 3 already show the channeling of attention favored by the native language. There is essentially no developmental picture in the three aspectual languages. The youngest children, by and large, behave like the adults. In Hebrew, however, there is a U-shaped curve, in which the school-age children are most extreme in adhering to the pattern of the language. This reflects the general stereotypy of performance of this age group, as discussed in *IIA*.

The overall figures in Table 1 also nicely mirror the range of aspectual distinctions in these languages. Spanish, with the most options, has the smallest percentage of narrators who do not make use of aspectual contrasts. Turkish speakers, whose language only provides a progressive-nonprogressive distinction in the past tense, pay less attention overall to this contrast. That is, when not telling a past-tense narrative, they are less inclined to use other means to mark the distinction. English stands in between Turkish and Spanish, having a progressive in all tenses, but no perfective-imperfective distinction. We suggest that distinctions which have to be accessed more frequently become more salient. We will return to this issue after examining narrations of Picture 2.

In this picture, again, we have two overlapping events which differ in durativity and boundedness: the frog escapes while the boy and dog are sleeping. As in this English description, the two events can be contrasted by use of progressive and nonprogressive verb forms. In addition to the set of options available for the contrast in Picture 12, this scene also allows for a stative-active contrast, e.g., *the boy and dog are asleep and the frog escapes*. And in Spanish past-tense narrations, the state is encoded as imperfective and the action as perfective. However, Picture 2 differs from Picture 12 in that both its events are depicted as ongoing. That is, Picture 2 shows the frog halfway out of the jar and the boy and dog asleep on the bed. Therefore, the two events cannot be differentiated simply by a tense contrast (such as *the boy and dog are asleep and the frog ran away*). Whereas the three aspect-marking languages provide a range of inflectional contrasts, the only options in German and Hebrew are: (1) to use verb repetition to mark the durativity of sleeping ('slept and slept'), (2) to mark sleeping as inceptive ('they went to sleep and the frog ran away'), or (3) to mark the escape as sudden or inceptive ('they lie in bed and suddenly the frog runs away'). Picture 2 thus gives us an opportunity to see if Hebrew and German speakers attempt to "compensate" for the lack of the relevant aspectual distinctions in their verbal morphology. Again, there are no discernible developmental patterns, and so we present data on all of the child narrators, ages 3-9, as one group, as shown in Table 2.

As in the previous analysis, German and Hebrew speakers tend not to contrast these two events aspectually; Spanish speakers almost always do (i.e., 82% of the time); and English and Turkish speakers lie in between, though tending to use an aspectual contrast over half the time. Again, there is no strong evidence for "compensation" in German and Hebrew. Table 2 differs from Table 1 in that the difference between English and Turkish is not present. In the prior analysis, we noted that English makes aspectual

TABLE 2
Percentage of Child Narrators
Using Same Tense/Aspect Form
for 'Sleep' and 'Escape' for Picture 2

Spanish	18
English	44
Turkish	47
German	92
Hebrew	71

distinctions across the tenses, whereas the corresponding distinction in Turkish exists only in the past tense. In the present analysis, however, Turkish speakers also have ready access to another device for marking this kind of contrast, that is, by the use of **converbs** to contrast the temporal contours of the two events. As discussed in *IIIE-4.2*, this clause-combining device is highly **accessible** in Turkish. By this we mean that the form is morphologically transparent, perceptually salient, regular, and frequent — that is, easy to process and therefore also easy to acquire. Three-year-olds can mark the contrast using the converb -*ken*, which indicates that the action in the first clause is durative with respect to that of the second clause, e.g.:

(10) *Uyurken de, ordan çıkıyor uslu uslu.*

     sleep-*ken* PARTICLE, there.from **exit**:PRES quietly quietly

     'While (they) (are) sleeping, (the frog) exits from there quietly quietly.'
     [T3i-3;11]

Again, as we saw with regard to tense/aspect in Spanish, the availability of a grammatical contrast seems to lead speakers to pay more attention to the corresponding semantic contrast.

     One might expect that if a language does not provide aspectual markers to distinguish an ongoing state from a simultaneous punctual event, then speakers might be sure to use some sort of temporal conjunction — such as 'when' or 'while' — to mark the temporal contrast. But this is not the case, either. Table 3 shows that German- and Hebrew-speaking children are quite unlikely to link the two clauses with a temporal conjunction. Interestingly, only Spanish-speaking children are comparably low in this regard. Here we suggest that the aspectual contrasts are so clearly and regularly marked in Spanish that there is little danger of misinterpreting the two verbs as encoding two sequential, rather than simultaneous events.

TABLE 3
Percentage of Child Narrators
Relating 'Sleep' and 'Escape' with a
Temporal Conjunction for Picture 2

Spanish	24
English	66
Turkish	47
German	13
Hebrew	24

Our analyses of Pictures 2 and 12 give strong evidence for language-specific thinking for speaking. As suggested above, not only do speakers tend to limit their attention to those semantic distinctions marked in the grammar, but they may even **over**attend to such distinctions in early phases of development. One piece of evidence comes from a comparison of the languages with regard to perfect aspect. Here the division is different. Madrid Spanish makes widespread use of perfect aspect, and it is acquired early, as discussed in *IIIC*. The North German perfect has lost many of its classical functions as a perfect, but is frequently used in our present-tense narrations to contrast an immediately completed change of state with a current situation in the story. By contrast, Hebrew and Turkish have no marking of perfect aspect, and it is also largely absent in the speech of our American English narrators. We have searched for uses of adverbs with perfect meanings in our preschool texts — again looking for evidence of compensation. For example, do English-speaking children use *already* and *anymore* at points in the narration where Spanish-speaking children would use the present perfect? Table 4 shows that there is absolutely no evidence for such compensation. And, on the other hand, it shows that Spanish-speaking preschoolers, as discussed in *IIIC-1.3.3*, **over**use *ya* 'already', redundantly combining it with the present perfect. It appears that frequent use of the present perfect — in the input language and in their own speech — has sensitized these children to the notion of an enduring effect of a recently completed process.

Additional evidence for **grammatically-induced channeling of attention** is provided by the perfective use of the reflexive in Spanish, where children use it to mark a kind of present-tense perfectivity. As suggested in *IIIC-1.3.2*, the central role of perfectivity in the Spanish inflectional system might make that notion more available for discourse purposes, attracting additional means of indicating perfectivity even in a present-tense narrative. In a similar

TABLE 4
Percentage of Clauses with a Perfect Adverb
in Preschool Texts (ages 3-5)

Spanish (*ya*)	2.1
German (*schon, noch nicht*)	0.7
English (*already, anymore*)	0.2
Hebrew (*kvar*)	0.4
Turkish (*artık, henüz*)	0.0

vein, Aksu-Koç and von Stutterheim suggest in *IVA* "that explicit marking of aspectual distinctions in the morphology of a language contributes positively to or facilitates the child's differentiation of similar temporal notions embodied in the lexical forms of the language." In their analysis, temporal subordinating constructions emerge earlier in the three aspectual languages — Spanish, English, and Turkish — than in German and Hebrew.

We suggest, as a generalization from these and other findings, that **a rich repertoire of grammaticized notions leads the child to explore the corresponding semantic/pragmatic domain.** As discussed below, with regard to rhetorical style, such exploration has consequences for the pacing of development of form-function relations and for the resulting patterns of use of the language in connected discourse.

1.2. Locative Movement

In *III0-3* the five languages of our study are grouped differently with regard to the encoding of temporal and locative distinctions. When we turn to verbs of movement, German and English provide compact and elaborated descriptions of trajectories by means of their satellite-framed typology. By contrast, the verb-framed typology of Spanish, Hebrew, and Turkish provides speakers with a small set of inherently directional verbs, that must be combined with other verbs and adverbs for similar purposes. (Compare, for example, *fly down from out of the hole* and *salir del agujero volando hacia abajo* 'exit from the hole **flying towards downwards**'.) The five language-specific chapters in Part III show considerable crosslinguistic differences in the degree to which narrators present elaborated descriptions of trajectories. Here we bring the languages together for a typological comparison with regard to thinking for speaking. Table 5 summarizes child data from the three events in which a protagonist falls or is thrown downward: the fall from the window (Picture 6), the fall from the tree (Picture 12), and the fall from the cliff

(Picture 17). At issue is whether the verb occurs alone or with some kind of locative addition — a particle, adverb, or locative phrase (prepositional or inflectional) indicating downward direction, source, or goal of motion. The figures in the table are based on all of the verbs used to describe these three events — mainly versions of 'fall' and 'throw'.

TABLE 5
Percentage of Downward Motion Descriptions
Using Only a Verb (Pictures 6, 12, 17)

Language	Age		
	3 yrs	5 yrs	9 yrs
English	4	27	13
German	15	2	0
Spanish	68	37	54
Hebrew	68	72	45
Turkish	61	44	33

First consider the 3-year-olds. It is evident that — for the youngest subjects — the satellite-framed languages form one group and the verb-framed languages another. (Note that this typological division is independent of of the division with regard to "aspect-marking languages" presented in the previous section.) Three-year-olds in the first group hardly ever use a verb of motion without some locative elaboration, whereas those in the second group use bare verbs of motion about two-thirds of the time. This clear difference holds up across age as well. Although there are different developmental patterns, at each of the three ages, the contrast between the two types of languages is maintained.

There seems to be a U-shaped curve in the case of Spanish, as discussed in *IIIC-2*. Some Spanish 4- and 5-year-olds seem to attempt to provide more information about paths of motion than is generally found in the language, using directional adverbs redundantly or elaborating descriptions of source or goal. It might appear that such children are attempting to compensate for the limited options for movement description in their language, thereby contradicting our claim in the previous section that compensation generally does not occur. However, there is an important difference between the phenomena considered in these two sections. In the case of aspectual morphology, "compensation" requires the child to lexically express notions that are **not** grammatically marked in the language. This, we suggest, hardly ever occurs —

giving support to the analysis of thinking for speaking. In the case of movement descriptions, the additions made by preschoolers are **redundant**, reinforcing what is already expressed in the verb (e.g., *sube arriba* 'ascends upwards'). These children seem to be seeking means to express directionality in separate lexical items (incipient satellites?) — but they are not attempting to mark notions that are absent in the grammatical system of the language. Earlier, with regard to verbal aspect, we found only rare instance of attempts in German and Hebrew to **add** distinctions of punctuality or durativity that are not marked grammatically in the language. Here, by contrast, speakers sometimes make attempts to be more explicit, using tools that are part of their grammar. We continue to argue, therefore, that children's attention is heavily channeled in the direction of those semantic distinctions that are grammatically marked in the language. (For related claims, see Bowerman, 1985; Choi & Bowerman, 1991.)

2. RHETORICAL STYLE

The phenomena reflected in Table 5 are part of a larger picture, falling in the domain of "typological discourse analysis" (Myhill, 1992) or "contrastive rhetoric" (Bar-Lev, 1986). Redundant elaboration of paths of motion is a short-lived phenomenon in Spanish, to be replaced by a more typologically-consistent rhetorical style. Examples were given in *IA-3.1* of 9-year-old descriptions of the fall from the cliff in the five languages. By this age, clearly different narrative strategies can be recognized in the two types of languages, as was shown in examples (9)-(13) in *IA-3.1* (p. 11) and in further discussions of motion and location in the chapters in Part III. The following are additional examples of these contrasting strategies in English and Spanish:

(11a) *He pushed him off the side of the cliff into water.* [*E9e-9;7*]

(11b) *They fall off the edge into a pond.* [*E9b-9;3*]

(11c) *El ciervo frena delante de una montañita que da a un río y entonces los dos caen en el río.*

'The deer brakes in front of a little mountain that faces a river and then the two of them fall in the river.' [*S9l-9;11*]

(11d) *Y le tira desde un barranco. Hay un lago, y se cae encima.*

'And he throws him from a cliff. There's a lake, and he falls on.top.' [*S9j-9;11*]

The satellite-framed languages — English and German (and Russian, in ongoing research) — allow for compact presentation of a path of motion, clustering around a single verb, as in the case of *push* in (11a) and *fall* in (11b). This means of expression is already available to some preschool-age children — as, for example, the following source-goal description given by an English-speaking 5-year-old, where the satellites *over* and *into* are associated with the verb *throw*:

(11e) *He threw him over a cliff into a pond.* [*E5j-5;10*]

By contrast, in verb-framed languages, where the verb indicates only directionality, the narrator is faced with the task of providing enough "stage-setting" information for the details of the trajectory to be inferred, as in the Spanish examples in (11c) and (11d). Hardly any preschool-age narrators show this level of proficiency in these languages.

Table 6 shows the percentages of 5- and 9-year-olds who provide the kind of extended locative elaboration exemplified in the Spanish examples given above — that is, descriptions of the static locations of landmarks, such as cliff and water, enabling the listener to infer the source and goal of movement. It is evident that this sort of locative elaboration is rare in the preschool texts in Spanish, Hebrew, and Turkish, but that it develops in school age. By contrast, it is not an option that is exploited in English and German, where satellite-framed devices are available from early on.

TABLE 6

Percentage of Narrators Providing Extended Locative
Elaboration in Describing the Fall from the Cliff

Language	Age Group	
	5 yrs	9 yrs
English	8	8
German	0	17
Spanish	8	42
Hebrew	0	42
Turkish	10	42

What we see here is an impact of grammatical typology on rhetorical style. Children learning verb-framed languages must develop procedures of scene-setting which allow directional verbs of motion to be more precisely interpreted in context. It apparently takes time to develop such procedures — no doubt due, in part, to the factors involved in becoming a proficient speaker, as discussed in the preceding chapter.[2] Elaborated scene-setting requires both

---

[2] Hoiting and Slobin (1993) have proposed that all natural sign languages should tend to be verb-framed, because verbs of motion are inherently directional in signing space. Prelim-

an appreciation of the needs of the listener and the capacity to background such information syntactically. A major device for this purpose is the relative clause, as in (11b): 'a place, where below there was a river' (and compare the Hebrew example in *IA-3.1*, 'a cliff that had a swamp underneath').

Here we see a subtle interplay of the development of narrative and syntactic abilities. Relative clauses have a higher functional load in Spanish and Hebrew, and speakers of those languages use relative clauses more frequently and at younger ages. (The options for relative clause use are different in a verb-final language like Turkish, as discussed in *IVB*.) Dasinger and Toupin (*IVB*) propose a number of factors that make this construction more accessible in Spanish and Hebrew, in addition to its frequency: transparent morphology, consistent pattern of information flow, etc. A generalization that emerges from our study is that **if a linguistic form is highly accessible, its functional development may be accelerated**. That is, it may be used at an earlier age for more advanced functions. This is evident in the earlier emergence of the PRESENTATIONAL and CONTINUATIVE uses of relative clauses in Spanish and Hebrew, in comparison with the other languages. In addition, the present analysis suggests that the discourse need to provide locative settings — motivated by the verb-framed typology of these languages — provides another stimulus for the development and use of relative clauses. These several factors combine to produce a particular rhetorical style for each language.[3] Spanish, for example, with its widespread use of relative clauses, past participles, and gerunds, seems to have a "taste" for subordination and stage-setting. And with its flexible word order and null subjects, along with person/number morphology and clitic object pronouns, it allows for easy

---

inary examination of narrative development in children acquiring both ASL and Netherlands Sign Language suggests that, as in spoken verb-framed languages, it is not until school age that children devote sufficient attention to locative stage-setting in narrative. That is, although younger children already command verbs of motion, they are less proficient in referentially specifying sources and goals of motion events.

[3] Slobin (in press-c) has found that the contrasts between English and Spanish analyzed here, with respect to motion descriptions in the frog stories, can also be found in novels written in the two languages. Novelists writing in English devote more attention to paths of movement, whereas novelists writing in Spanish pay more attention to settings and present much less information about paths. Similar contrasts can be found with regard to manner of movement. English verbs of movement often conflate manner (e.g., *dash, crawl, shove, drag*), and English-writing novelists use such verbs abundantly. Manner must be provided in separate expressions in Spanish (e.g., *salir corriendo* 'exit running', *cerrar con un empujón* 'close with a push'), and Spanish-writing novelists use such expressions more sparingly. Similarly, English- and German-speaking preschoolers make abundant use of MOTION+MANNER verbs, whereas narrators in the verb-framed languages pay far less attention to manner of movement (Berman & Slobin, 1987).

tracking of participants across different types of clauses. German, by contrast — probably due to morphosyntactic complexity — makes limited use of relative clauses and passives, and has restricted possibilities of word-order variation, due to an eroded case-inflectional system. As a consequence, German narratives have more chained clauses and use more dynamic predicates, along with analytic descriptions of event components (e.g., 'put his head in and couldn't get it out').

As a graphic demonstration of language-specific rhetorical style, compare the following two 9-year-old frog stories — the first in English and the second a translation from Turkish. Particular typological and rhetorical features of the two languages are given in boldface (to the extent, of course, that a translation can convey such features).[4] Comments about these features are given in italics in square brackets. It is evident, even from this limited exercise, that by age 9, children have become not only proficient speakers, but native speakers with particular directions of attention and narrative organization.

(12) There's a boy **who has a pet frog and a pet dog** [*background information in postposed relative clause*]. And one night after he goes to bed the frog sneaks out. And he wakes up and it's gone. So he and his dog look all over the place for it. So then they go outside and **start calling** [*participial complement*] for it. The dog **had got the jar stuck on his head** [*get-passive; retrospective past perfect*], and he **falls out of the window** [*satellite-framed trajectory*] and it breaks and the little boy picks it up. And they **start calling** [*participial complement*] after the frog. And the dog **starts sniffing** [*participial complement*] some bees. And then he **looks** in a hole and the dog's **looking** at this beehive [*aspectual contrast*: looks/looking]. Then some little gopher **comes up** [*satellite-framed*]. And then the dog's **still looking** [*continuative progressive*] at that beehive. So then the beehive falls and all the bees **start chasing** [*participial complement*] after him. The little boy **climbs up a tree** and looks into a hole and an owl **flies out** and he **falls off the tree** [*satellite-framed*], and the bees **are chasing** after the dog [*aspectual contrast*: PRES/PRES.PROG]. So the owl **flies up**. And then he **stands up on the rock** and hangs onto some branches. Then it turns out they're a deer's

---

[4] The translation from Turkish in (13) loses many Turkish features, such as the verb-final word order, the use of null-pronouns and verbal inflections, the absence of definite articles, the use of focus particles, etc. What is intended is a rough view of some of the typological features that are characteristic of Turkish narrative style, by contrast with English. The two stories happen to be told in different tenses, but the sorts of typological characteristics revealed by the comparison are not obscured by this fact.

antlers, so- and **he gets-** [*attempt at* get-*passive*] he lands on his head and he **starts running** [*participial complement*]. And he **tips him off over a cliff into the water** [*satellite-framed elaboration of trajectory*]. And he lands. But they're both OK. So then he says to his dog "shh." And they **peek over the log** [*satellite-framing of perception verb*] and there's two frogs. And then there's a little family of frogs. And I guess one frog is his, so he gets one of the frogs — one of the little baby frogs. [*E9k-9;11*]

(13) [*The entire story is told in the narrative past* — M.PAST.] 'One day a boy found a frog. He put it in a jar. Then it got to be night. He went to sleep. The frog **exited** the jar [*verb-framed*]. The boy, **on waking up, seeing the jar empty,** [*chaining of nonfinite verbs (converbs)*] got very scared. He quickly started to look for his frog. He looked in his boots. It wasn't there. The boy had a dog. Then the dog's head **entered** the jar [*verb-framed*]. The boy opened the window. The dog **ascended to the window** [*verb-framed + goal phrase*]. After that they looked for the frog again. The dog fell to the ground. And the boy, he **jumped** [*verb-framed: source/goal implicit*] and got very angry at his dog — **that he entered the jar, his head** [*nominalized clause*]. Then they **exited to.outside,** [*verb-framed + goal adverb*] looked for their frog everywhere. They saw a beehive, they saw a squirrel nest. They **were calling** [*aspectual contrast*: PAST/PAST.PROG] its name, the frog's, but it was really too bad that they **weren't being able to find** it. The bees and the squirrel got very angry at the children. Then the boy looked in tree holes. The bees, **exiting their nest,** [*converb (-erek) (cf.* CONT *relative clause function)*] flew right for the boy's dog. After that the boy started to look for his frog again. Then **he got caught on a deer** [*agentless passive*]. The deer ran. He **threw the on-the-hill boy to the ground** [*scene-setting by preposed relative clause, describing source*] together with his dog. **On the ground there was a lake** [*scene-setting*]. They **fell to the lake** [*motion follows scene-setting*]. **Holding onto a tree trunk** [*converb (-erek)*], they **exited** [*verb-framed; source/goal implicit*]. Behind the tree trunk they saw frogs. There was a frog couple, they had babies. One of their babies was the boy's frog.' [*T9c-9;1*]⁵

---

⁵ *Bir gün bir çocuk bir kurbağa bulmuş. Onu kavanoza koymuş. Sonra gece olmuş. Uyumuş. Kurbağa kavanozdan dışarı çıkmış. Çocuk uyandığında, kavanozu boş görünce, çok korkmuş. Kurbağasını telaşla aramaya başlamış. Çizmelerinin içine bakmış. Yok. Çocuğun bir köpeği varmış. O zaman köpeğin başı kavanozun içine girmiş. Çocuk pencereye çıkmış. Daha sonra yine kurbağayı aramışlar. Köpek yere düşmüş. Çocuk da atlamış ve köpeğine çok kızmış. Kavanoza girdi diye başı. Sonra dışarı çıkmışlar, her yerde kurbağalarını aramışlar. Ve arı kovanı görmüşler, bir sincap yuvası görmüşler. İsmini*

Consider these two stories in the light of the four major topics guiding out analyses in Part III.

- **Tense/aspect:** Both texts make free use of aspectual contrasts with a single tense. The **English** story moves along in present tense, using the progressive to take an "internal," ongoing perspective on events, in contrast to the simple present for events or states presented as totalities. Compare, for example, *climbs up...flies out...falls off* with *are chasing*. The beginning of a continuing activity is marked with an inchoative verb: *start calling, start chasing, starts running*. And the past perfect is used for a retrospective shift *had got the jar stuck on his head*. The **Turkish** story is told in the narrative past, using the M.PAST form (*-miş*). Continuing states are presented by adding the PROGRESSIVE morpheme (*-iyor*) to this form ('were.calling', weren't.being.able.to.find'). Preparatory states are given in converbs ('seeing the jar empty', 'exiting their nest').

- **Event conflation:** English uses the familiar satellite-framed means of presenting locative trajectories (e.g. *tips him off over a cliff into the water*). **Turkish** either uses an isolated verb of motion (e.g., 'jumped', 'exited'), or devotes attention to scene-setting, as in the final description of the locale in which the fall from the cliff occurs.

- **Perspective:** The **English** text moves on primarily in a series of SV(O) clauses in active voice. At one point, the narrator attempts a *get*-passive to keep the boy — topic and patient — in subject position, but fails (*...and he gets - he lands...*). By contrast, the **Turkish** text exploits various word-order alternations which are, unfortunately, not evident in the translation. Additionally, the passive is successfully used for the same event in which the English narrator backtracked ('he got caught on a deer').

- **Connectivity:** The **English** narrator uses a variety of clause-initial connectives, breaking the narration in segments (*and, so then, and then, then*). Subject ellipsis is rare, except for coordinated, same-subject clauses (e.g., *he stands up on the rock and Ø hangs onto some branches*). The **Turkish** narrator also uses clause-initial connectives

---

bağırıyorlarmış kurbağanın, fakat ne yazık ki bulamıyorlarmış. Arılar ve sincap çok kızmış çocuklara. Sonra çocuk ağaç kovuklarına bakmış. Arılar yuvalarından çıkarak çocuğun köpeğinin üstüne doğru uçmuşlar. Daha sonra çocuk yine kurbağasını aramaya başlamış. O zaman bir geyiğe takılmış. Sonra geyik koşmuş. Tepesindeki çocuğu yere atmış, köpeğiyle birlikte. Yerde de göl varmış. Göle düşmüşler. Bir ağaç kovuğuna tutunarak çıkmışlar. Ağaç kovuğunun arkasında kurbağalar görmüşler. Bir çiftmiş kurbağalar, yavruları da varmış. Yavrularından biri de çocuğun kurbağasıymış.

('then', 'after that'), but additionally uses converbs and nominalization to join clauses. Compare *And he wakes up and it's gone* with 'The boy, on waking up, seeing the jar empty, got very scared.' There are no subject pronouns. Zero pronouns are the norm for continuing topics, and reference shift is accomplished by use of a noun, sometimes with the focus particle *de*.

We have spent some time on these two examples in an attempt to make the issue of language-specific rhetorical style more clear to the monolingual reader. In the concluding section of the chapter we provide impressionistic summaries of these overall patterns for each of the five languages. We hope that these examples demonstrate the extent to which learning a language entails more than acquiring a set of forms and corresponding functions.

3. CONTRASTIVE RHETORIC

In order to complete our portrayal of "becoming a native speaker," we have attempted to create composite sketches of the rhetorical styles of proficient frog-story narrators in each of the five languages. These are not data summaries, but rather impressions of what seems to be typical in each language, especially in the texts of proficient 9-year-olds and of adults. Non-English examples are given only in English glosses, in order to facilitate reading. We offer this final section as a crosslinguistic and developmental exercise in typological discourse analysis.

3.1. Telling the Frog Story in English

In narrating the frog story in English, choice of an anchor-tense, whether present or past, has a strong effect on the overall temporal flavor given to a text. Where present tense is selected, narrators deploy progressive aspect contrastively, as a means of emphasizing durativity or for expressing simultaneity of events construed as backgrounded to others, e.g., *When he gets to the top of the rock, he holds onto something that he thinks are branches, and calls to the frog, **while the dog is whimpering and scowling and sulking back**.* (Young children, in contrast, exploit progressive forms as the default case for relating the events as situated in the immediate, speech-time present.) English speakers can also use present perfect for expressing anteriority (although its "present relevance" function has been largely taken over by the simple past tense in American English, the native language of our narrators), e.g., *The boy and frog are in his bedroom looking at a frog **they've just found***; or *Early the next morning, they discover that the frog **has escaped**.* Thus, the present-tense narratives of most of our English-speaking adults alternate quite naturally between a simple-present backbone plotline and an occasional shift to perfect for relative tense or to progressive for contrastive aspect.

Past-tense narratives rely similarly on alternations between simple and progressive aspect, where the latter serves to background situations ongoing at the time some plot-advancing event took place, e.g., *To the dog's amazement, he knocked the beehive off the tree while the boy **was searching** the trunk*; and later in the same text, *The dog **was running** away from the bees, while the boy was frightened by an owl in the treetrunk in which he **was looking**. The owl chased him far and wide.* On the other hand, even our adult speakers of American English make little use of past perfect forms to express anteriority or in grammatical sequence-of-tense contexts.

Another means for varying the temporal flow of simple past-tense description is through use of nonfinite verbs as complements to aspectual or modal past-tense forms, e.g., *The owl **kept bothering** the boy, but then he left him alone*; *The deer **went running off** with the little boy and the doggie ran along the side*; *The dog didn't like all those bees **bothering** him.* Indeed, a major means used by our English narrators for breaking up a monotonous flow of verbs in simple present or simple past is through the multifunctional *-ing* form of verbs. Examples of other uses of this form, from four different adult texts, are the following: *He lifted his head up, **carrying** the boy with him*; *The boy, **searching** frantically for his frog, was bit in the nose by a gopher*; *The dog seems interested in the beehive, with all the bees **flying** out, while the boy is sitting in a tree; ...**looking** in a hole in the tree, **thinking** maybe the lost frog is there....*

Textural layering is also achieved in English through **voice** alternations, with past participles being used in adjectival passives, in *get*-passives, and in full syntactic passives, e.g., *but luckily for the dog he **was unharmed**, however, the boy **was quite perturbed**; the boy **gets his nose either bitten or sniffed at by some little animal**; The boy is also in danger now that the owl **has been disturbed**.* That is, flexibility of event description is attained by alternating the internal shape of verb-phrases and through use of auxiliaries and modals rather than by changing the position of the verb relative to the subject which precedes and the objects or complements which follow it.

The general flow of the English narratives is strongly right-branching, in the form SVXY, where XY constitutes some elaboration of the post-subject predicate element. It is extremely rare for a proficient English text to end with a "bare" verb. Rather, the verb is always filled out by some further information. In the most tightly packaged, complex chunking of strings of predications, the postverbal positions are filled by clauses with different internal syntax, e.g., *and reprimands him + for being so hasty + to which the dog tries to make up + by licking his face*; or, more linearly, from a 9-year-old, *Then the dog's running away + cause the bees were all chasing him, and he had fell down + cause an owl poked him out of the tree, and ... he bumped his head +*

when he fell.

More typically, and very clearly from age 5 years up, English narrators make rich use of verb-satellite elements (particles) and prepositional phrases to elaborate on **locative** facets of events, often incorporating both source, manner, and goal within a single descriptive package, e.g., *an owl flew out of the hole in the tree and knocked him down out of the tree*; *the deer picks him up and pushes the boy and dog off the cliff into the water*; or *the deer takes the boy over in the direction of a ravine, and deposits him off the side of the ravine into the creek.* Even among younger English narrators, and even where vocabulary is limited to a fairly simple stock of basic, Germanic verbs, these satellites and associated phrases provide a descriptive richness well-suited to this particular story.

In addition, English narrators rely on a large number of lexically specific verbs which encode **manner** of motion. Use of expressions like *crash, bump, pop, splash, swoop, tumble* — with or without additional particles — provide speakers with a colorful descriptive mechanism appropriate to quite everyday colloquial usage.

The standard SV linear laying out of events in sequence is further modified in the more proficient English narratives by various devices for textual cohesiveness. One such form is syntactic coordination with same-subject elision, e.g., *The boy has climbed a tree and Ø is looking into a hole*; *The owl came out of the hole and Ø scared the boy.* Interestingly enough, several narrators also employ **topic elision**, by omitting the subject across strings of same-topic clauses, e.g., *In the morning, the boy wakes up and sees that the jar is empty. Ø Decides to look in...*; *He's looking for his frog, and he's not there, and he gets - he's really upset, looks like he's about to cry. And then he looks everywhere, Ø looks in his boots, Ø calls out the window...* However, as is to be expected in a highly subject-requiring language like English, this is an occasional stylistic device selected by only a few narrators.

Another, less linear means for packaging events, which we noted earlier, is through use of nonfinite, participial verb forms — predominantly with -*ing.* Our texts reveal this as a major backgrounding and subordinating device for organizing the ongoing flow of events in proficient English narratives. In contrast, even older speakers make comparatively little use of relative clauses as an option for continuing the narrative flow, e.g., *The dog has found something new to look at which is a beehive, which he starts barking at*; although they do use relative clauses a fair amount for the temporal effect of retrospection, e.g. *The dog has a jar on top of his head, which was where the frog was originally located.* Again, the flow of an English narrative in our sample seems better served by verb-phrase expansion and nonfinite subordination, rather than by stringing of two or more finite subordinate clauses. Where speakers

feel the need to express some overt semantic relation between or within propositions — whether temporal, logical, or attributive — they tend to rely on
lexical connectives and modifiers, e.g., *But the boy did not give up his search,
and he called "frog! frog!" while on top of a rock. / However, while holding
onto supposed branches, he accidentally ran into a deer*. This is not merely a
personal predilection on the part of an individual narrator, nor is it confined to
those who favor high-register Latinate vocabulary (although it is rare among
even the older children in our American English sample). For example,
another narrator says *That [=the beehive] was a really dangerous thing to
play with. And pretty soon, well the little boy went and looked in the tree, he
better be careful*; while a third, rather more self-consciously elaborate style is
revealed by another adult in the following terms: *The dog, being the rambunctious animal that he is, found a beehive and decided to have some fun, while
the boy, searching frantically for his dog, was bit in the nose by a gopher [...]*

In sum, although the adult English narrations differ in length, in degree
of elaborative detail, and in level of stylistic register, they all manifest the following features: variation of the basic simple-tense (present or past) temporal
contour by use of progressive aspect, combined with cohesive packaging
through reliance on nonfinite participial forms of verbs (preferred throughout
these narratives to Latinate nominalizations, possibly favored for expository
prose); rich elaboration of locative trajectories through verb-modifying prepositional phrases and particles; and lexical diversity to express manner of
activity as well as temporal, causal, and attributive relations between events.

3.2. Telling the Frog Story in German

With almost no exceptions, German narrators choose to tell the frog
story in the present tense. The only available tense/aspect contrast is to the
perfect, in either its past or present forms. Perfect forms are used to break the
onward temporal flow of narration in order to look back or ahead, marking
event boundaries or interrupting the flow to comment on a relevant prior
situation. Retrospection can be marked by present perfect (e.g., 'When they
wake up, they discover that the frog has run away.'), or by past perfect (e.g.,
'The dog, who had earlier disturbed the wasps, is now chased by the wasps.').
In its prospective narrative function, the present perfect functions to complete
one phase of the action in order to move on to the next (e.g., 'The dog has
leaned so much against the tree that the beehive has fallen down and now all
the bees swarm out.'). Event boundaries are also marked by a variety of verb
satellites, encoding inception and completion; similar means are used to mark
recurrent events. Otherwise, temporal contours or phases of events tend not to
be explicitly marked. Our narrators make only rare use of adverbial and periphrastic means available in German for indicating progressivity. Temporal

relations between events are indicated by temporal conjunctions and adverbs, as in English (though terms for 'meanwhile' are not used until age 9, and are only frequent in the adult texts).

Much attention is devoted to path and manner of movement, using a diversity of verbs that conflate manner and motion, along with a wide range of satellites encoding directionality and deixis (e.g. 'falls downwards into the sea thither', 'creeps outwards out of the jar'). German verbs of motion often convey additional features of intensity, suddenness, and the like ('shove', 'hurl', 'tumble', 'plop'), sometimes reinforced by onomatopoeic elements such as *schwupp, schuppdiwupp, plattsch, husch.*

There is relatively little word-order variation, beyond that which is syntactically required. Passives are infrequent, and are used by adults for topic continuity when a protagonist becomes an undergoer (e.g., 'Then the boy is attacked by the owl.'). Topic shift is often carried out by a noun followed by a pronoun copy ('And the dog, he shakes the tree.').

Relative clauses are not used very frequently in the rather informal style of our narrators. And they tend to be used for a narrower range of functions than in Spanish or Hebrew. For example, rather than introducing participants with a relative clause, as 'This is a story about a boy and a dog who have a frog in a jar', German narrators prefer simple clauses for introductions, as 'It's about a frog, a boy, and a dog to begin with, and the boy has a frog in a jar.'

As a result of these various factors, the narration tends to move forward along the backbone of the plot, with little backgrounding. Sequences of the following type are typical even of adult narrators. Note the "action-packed," seemingly rapid sequence of relatively short and simple clauses: 'And the deer probably can't see anything, because the boy has his legs over his eyes. And all of them race to the terrible abyss. And the deer manages to brake in time — maybe he knows the terrain instinctively better than the boy and the dog — and throws the boy off, *husch*, in one swing.' This sort of "analytic" narrative style is also evident in less dramatic parts of the story. For example, in the head-in-jar event, German narrators tend to say things like 'The dog sniffs in the glass. He can't get it off of his head anymore.' (Contrast this with English *get*-passives, such as *the dog's head got stuck in the jar.*)

In sum, the German narrators elaborate phases of events and movement in space far more than they elaborate temporal contours of events. That is, there is much attention to the beginning- and end-points of events, to the components that make up complex events, and to details of locative trajectories. There is also attention to recurrence and repetition. But, by contrast to the detailed description of spatial trajectories, "temporal trajectories" are quite unelaborated in German.

3.3. Telling the Frog Story in Spanish

The dominant tense for frog stories in Spanish is the present, used by the majority of 9-year-olds and adults (although past tense is preferred by 4- and 5-year-olds). However, in both tenses, aspectual contrasts of several types are marked on the verb. The tense/aspect system is highly elaborated in Spanish, and its variety is flexibly used by narrators. Tense/aspect switches are used for presenting background information — prior events or continuing states — against which the foreground stands out in either present progressive or past perfective, depending on the dominant tense of the narrative.

In present-tense narratives, the action moves forward with verbs in the simple present, with continuous activities in the present progressive. Switches to the present perfect are used to give information about a currently relevant prior event ('He looks in the jar where he normally keeps:PRES his frog, but something has happened:PRES.PERF, and it is that the frog has escaped:PRES.PERF.'). Past perfect is used for more distant, completed events ('He finds:PRES his frog, who had met:PAST.PERF a male frog.'). A switch to the past imperfective can also be used to refer to a prior state ('There are:PRES many frogs, and one assumes that they take:PRES one; what one doesn't know is if it is the same one they had:IPFV.'). Past-tense narratives move the action forward in perfective aspect, with shifts to past perfect to refer to prior situations, and against a background of both imperfective and past progressive verbs. The past progressive can be used with an auxiliary that is either perfective or imperfective, thus allowing narrators to present an ongoing situation as either bounded or unbounded. In brief, the Spanish verb-inflectional system provides a rich set of options for marking a number of features of temporality.

In addition, proficient narrators make use of a collection of aspectual verbs, consistent with the verb-framed typology of the language. Some of these verbs mark the temporal regions associated with event boundaries — about to happen, having just happened, about to end, having just ended; others indicate if an ongoing event is in progress, protracted, continuing, or repeated. Clearly, then, Spanish narratives provide detailed information about movement and overlap of events in time. In addition, the set of tense/aspect distinctions is mirrored in the subjunctive and conditional moods, which project a similar range of contrasts onto the irrealis plane.

By contrast, movement in space receives little attention in this verb-framed language. Generally, the verb simply indicates the direction of the path ('enter', 'exit', etc.), and although source and goal can be indicated by prepositional phrases, narrators prefer to mention neither, or — at most — only one of the landmarks of a path ('fell', 'fell from the cliff' or 'fell to the water' — but not 'fell from the cliff to the water'). Perhaps in order to render such minimal path descriptions interpretable, proficient Spanish narratives devote a good deal of attention to scene-setting, that is, static descriptions of the locations of landmarks. These, then, provide the background against which one or more verbs are used to trace out the path ('They approach a cliff, below which flows a river. He gives a push and throws him, and he falls. He remains seated in the center of the river.').

Such descriptions make frequent use of two characteristic devices: relative clauses and past participles, as in the above example, often with an aspectual verb indicating durativity ('below which flows a river', 'remains seated'). Relative clauses serve a range of purposes, both for introducing and situating objects and protagonists, and for moving the action forward. Typically, a participant is introduced in a presentative construction, followed by a relative clause indicating the new participant's action ('(There) exited a gopher that bit him on the nose.').

The use of relative clauses is also part of the general order of information flow in Spanish. This is a topic-dominant language, in which new participants are introduced into the narrative in nonsubject position, as in presentational constructions. A continuative relative clause thus allows the action to move forward without the use of a pronoun. The latter constraint is due to the "pro-drop" typology of the language. Subject information is carried by person/number marking on the verb, and pronouns are used for contrastive reference. Thus, 'there exited a gopher and **he** bit him on the nose' would switch reference from the gopher to another participant. Subject pronouns are virtually nonexistent in our sample. These various typological factors — verb-framing, topic-dominance, null subjects — all contribute to the importance of relative clauses in Spanish.

Although null-pronouns are the preferred option for subjects, clitic object pronouns play an important role, carrying the action on when topics become undergoers or recipients. Pre-verbal position of object clitics and object phrases makes it possible to shift perspective from actor to undergoer without the use of passive constructions, which are quite rare in the narratives ('and then (to the boy) him threw the deer'; rather than 'and the boy was thrown by the deer').

Nonfinite constructions also perform important discourse functions in Spanish. In addition to past participles, used for stative descriptions ('seated in the water', 'hung from a branch'), present participles are used for backgrounding ('the boy, who was mounted in a tree looking for her [=frog]', 'they continue exploring, looking for the frog'). This form is also used for expressing manner, in association with a main verb of movement ('he carried the boy on his head, running towards a precipice', 'the dog exited running').

(Manner of movement, however, is rarely indicated in the Spanish narratives.)

Temporal, causal, and concessive relations between events are marked with a variety of conjunctions, as in other languages of this type.

All of these factors taken together contribute to a narrative style that is rich in subordination and embedding, with flexible use of word order and a high rate of event packaging, along with nuances of tense/aspect shifting. The following is typical of adult narratives: 'But Pepito had not noticed:PAST.PERF that his dog had broken:PAST.PERF a beehive, and he (=Pepito) didn't do:IPFV more than to look in all of the holes that Ø found:IPFV in order to see where the frog was:IPFV. But suddenly Ø realized:PFV that his dog exited:IPFV running at full speed and that behind him came:IPFV many bees that wanted:IPFV to punish him for having broken their house; and from the hole exited:PFV an owl.'

3.4. Telling the Frog Story in Hebrew

In talking about events, Hebrew speakers have no grammatical means for expressing aspectual contours or relative aspect, nor do they seek to compensate for this lack — for instance, by analytical means such as adverbials like *kvar* 'already' for perfect or *kol ha-zman* 'all the-time' for durativity. Instead, they tend to distinguish between **who** performs an event, since number- and gender-marking on the verb show whether an activity is performed by, say, the boy alone or the boy and the dog together. And proficient narrators can shift temporal frames by switching from present to past tense to indicate anteriority, and by embedding past tense plot-advancing events in more neutral present-tense backgrounded states and circumstances.

How, then, do Hebrew narrators provide aspectual flavoring to their narratives? They use a variety of rhetorical devices, which are optional rather than grammaticized, and as such tend to differ from one age group and one narrator to the next. School-age children mark new or noteworthy events by inchoative adverbials, mainly the word for 'suddenly'; some adults use lexical and other types of repetition to express protractedness of events and reiteration of activities. A related rhetorical device is that of using parallel constructions which prove extremely useful in establishing and reinstantiating narrative threads in this particular story — of searching and not finding, of climbing and falling and moving from one place to another. Narrators also make use of verb-initial constructions for introducing new characters in presentative contexts, so breaking up the monotonous SV(O) flow of their discourse and indicating that a new participant is going to appear or has appeared on the scene.

Hebrew narrators can and do shift perspectives on events by alternations in verb-pattern morphology, which enables them to express a patient perspective through use of middle-voice intransitive change-of-state verbs compared with an agentive perspective with activity verbs or a resultant endstate with passive participials. The fact that causativity is morphologically marked in verbs provides Hebrew narrators with another highly accessible device for distinguishing between, say, a person or object that falls, and someone or something that makes.fall this person or object, or between the dog getting into the jar and inserting his head into the jar. These verb-alternations supply Hebrew narrators with considerable flexibility for encoding events as construed from differing perspectives.

On the other hand, Hebrew speakers rely minimally on verb morphology to express aspectual distinctions. Older narrators rely on the analytic device of separate verbs, in this story those meaning 'begin' and 'continue' to express the "extended" aspects of inchoativity and protraction.

In describing locative trajectories, Hebrew narrators can make use of prepositional phrases and other adverbial expressions for describing both source and goal — but they do this relatively seldom. Instead, they distinguish movement in terms of directionality as encoded directly in the verb itself, and find little need to elaborate further on locative properties of event complexes with verbs of motion. Or else they express the source and goal in separate clauses, e.g., 'The deer makes.fly the boy (from the cliff). The boy, together with his dog, plunges into the water'. Hebrew narrators may, however, focus on locative elements by fronting them to sentence-initial position — e.g., the equivalents of 'In one of the trees he finds', 'On top of the tree sits an owl'.

In organizing the flow of narrative discourse, Hebrew speakers rely on relative clauses in presentative contexts, particularly in setting the scene at the start of a narrative. And they use them, too, in locating objects on a scene, e.g., talking about 'the hole that was in the tree', 'a cliff that has a marsh underneath it'. Elsewhere, Hebrew narrators use coordination with 'and' to package together sequentially or causally related events relating to the same protagonist(s) by deletion of the repeated subject — e.g., 'An owl came out **and** frightened the boy'. Or they may use verbless (copula) clauses to express event-simultaneity and cohesiveness, e.g., 'The dog fled, and/with the bees after him'. An important means of achieving narrative cohesion is by topic elision, relying on null subjects (combined with gender- and number-marked verbs noted earlier) to package together events undergone or activities perpetrated by the same participant(s). These two devices combined with verb-initial presentatives serve to alternate between topic maintenance and topic shifting in a flexible fashion.

In establishing temporal relations between events, Hebrew narrators make use of overt lexical forms, such as sentence-modifying adverbs like 'meanwhile' or expressions like 'in the course of' compared with those meaning 'later on' or 'afterwards' to express relations of simultaneity or anteriority. These combine with subordinated adverbial clauses or derived nominal constructions — e.g., 'in the time that he fell', 'in the course of his flight' — or to present different phases of complex events or sequences of distinct events, as temporally (and/or logically) interconnected in the ongoing flow of discourse.

This range of expressive options combines in the adult Hebrew frog stories with (a) availability of markedly different stylistic registers, ranging from more normative and formal or self-consciously literary style to everyday colloquial usage and (b) individual construals of the narrative task and personal stylistic preferences. These factors together yield several different narrative profiles, along the following lines: (1) medium-length narratives built up along a sequential chaining of short, clipped clauses strung together in a series of mainly SVO structures; (2) matter-of-fact, prosaic texts which also follow SVO order with little elaboration or evaluation, but with more cohesive chunking of clauses into tightly-packed units of discourse; (3) a compact, highly cohesive type of text, achieved by heavy reliance on syntactic subordination and/or subject ellipsis, sometimes combined with deliberate repetition of syntactically or lexically parallel constructions; and (4) self-consciously literary style, achieved through high-register, often slightly archaic lexical usage combined with VS sentence structure and bound morphology.

3.5. Telling the Frog Story in Turkish

The dominant tense for frog stories in Turkish is the present, though some narrators at every age tell past-tense stories, particularly using the past of indirect experience (M.PAST) which is characteristic of fairy-tale narrative. In the present tense, a single, neutral aspectual form is used to move the action forward, sometimes contrasting with the M.PAST to present a completed earlier situation that is currently relevant ('They look:PRES and see:PRES the frog. [...] Probably he chose:M.PAST freedom, escaped:M.PAST from the jar.'). In the past tense there are contrasts between progressive and nonprogressive aspect, especially to juxtapose a simultaneous durative and bounded event ('The dog was still looking: M.PAST.PROG at the beehive and knocked.down: M.PAST the beehive. Meanwhile, the boy was looking: M.PAST.PROG into holes in the trees.'). And there are also switches to past perfect for narrative retrospection ('In the morning, when Osman woke up, he found: D.PAST an empty jar, because the frog had.escaped: D.PAST.PERF.').

However, the main tools for providing aspectual contrast, as well as various other sorts of temporal and causal subordination, are morphological, represented by the nonfinite verb forms called converbs. This method of clause-linking, in which only the final clause has a finite verb, is one of the most characteristic features of connected discourse in Turkish. Without going into the details of the various converbs, the following gives some idea of this type of narrative flow (using *-ing* to represent a range of converb morphemes): 'Taking his frog, the boy — waving to the mother, father, and other sibling frogs, walking through the water, set off for home.' This pattern is consistent with the information flow of a verb-final language, and is reinforced by the use of prenominal relative clauses (something like 'the owl-fearing boy climbed up onto a rock' — or, more literally 'owl.from fear:REL boy one rock's top.to climbed'). Converbs and relative clauses are woven together by proficient narrators in dense clause-packages, finally ending in the main, finite verb, such as: 'The boy, being afraid, falling downwards, the dog:TOPIC.SWITCH quickly running past, because all the bees that were in the hive he knocked down were after the dog' (more literally: 'Boy, fearing inside, downwards falling, dog:TOPIC.SWITCH quickly from.side running passed, because his.knocked.down beehive.being.inside all bees dog's trail were on.'). Conjunctions are rare, and clauses are typically either mentioned in succession or reduced to nonfinite forms, as indicated above. (Complement clauses are also typically reduced, becoming deverbal nominalizations, such as 'the frog's escaping:NOMI. surprised them'.)

The long example given above also demonstrates Turkish means of marking and shifting referents in discourse. There are no definite articles, and the numeral 'one' serves as a definite article. Topic switches are marked by a postnominal particle. Null subject pronouns are the norm, with person/number marking on the verb; but object pronouns are used to maintain reference to a topical participant who becomes an undergoer or recipient ('Deer comes, him picks.up.'). Word order is flexibly used for upgrading and downgrading, with the preverbal slot used for focus and the postverbal slot for old information. In the following example, the object pronoun, referring to the dog, is placed after the verb, rather than in its canonical preverbal position. This makes it possible for the narrator to maintain the boy as continuing subject and topic: 'Boy behind.him goes, picks.up him.'

It is characteristic of Turkish to avoid redundancy. Generally it is sufficient to string along finite clauses, if they all encode forward-moving, foreground information ('Deer him picks.up. Carries. Throws.'). It is also a feature of the grammar to mark a semantic category only once in a phrase — e.g. '**two** dog:∅ is.running' vs. 'dogs is.running' vs. '∅ **are**.running'. This economy, combined with null pronouns and the many nonfinite forms (converbs, nominalizations, relative clauses) contribute to a lean and compact narrative style.

Consistent with the verb-framed typology, paths of motion are encoded in monomorphemic verbs ('enter', 'exit', etc.). Some narrators build up the landmarks in a scene, while using the verbs simply to convey the path: 'Then the deer came right to the edge of a cliff. There was a lake there. He threw them to there.' However, many narrators provide compact source and goal information by the use of casemarked nouns associated with the verb: 'cliff:ABL water:DAT fell' (=fell from the cliff to the water).

Casemarking and word-order flexibility allow narrators to foreground or background various arguments of a verb. In addition, frequent use is made of the agentless passive for the several situations in the story in which a patient is foregrounded ('got.caught', 'got.broken', etc.). Clearly, morphology and word-order patterns are the dominant characteristics of connected discourse in Turkish.

4. CONCLUSIONS

Finally, we return to Predictions 8-10 from *IB*. Prediction 8 deals with grammatical forms that are both **accessible** and **obligatory**. We proposed that these two factors operate in concert to draw the learner's attention not only to the forms themselves, but to the conceptual distinctions that must be made in order to use those forms appropriately — both referentially and in connected discourse. We have defined accessibility in terms of features that aid detection and acquisition: acoustic salience, frequency, transparent form-function mapping, regularity of paradigm, few competing forms, and the like. These are features that can be modeled in connectionist networks, which may aid in providing more precise definitions of accessibility.

We also propose that those distinctions which are obligatory play a special role in channeling the attention of the learner. Obligatory distinctions have several important characteristics for the language-user. Typically they are arranged in small sets, by contrast with optional forms. Compare, for example, the relatively small number of tense/aspect distinctions within a language with the much larger, though still limited set of aspectual verbs and aspectual/temporal adverbials. In addition, grammatically-marked distinctions of the sort considered here divide a domain **exhaustively** according to **a small number of distinctions**, (e.g., perfective / imperfective, progressive / nonprogressive, active / middle / passive), requiring the learner to rather neatly divide up the domain according to criteria that must be quickly and automatically accessed, online, for nearly every utterance. Such distinctions, therefore, are repeatedly reinforced through use.

We have proposed, further, that frequent use of forms directs attention to their functions, perhaps even making those functions (semantic and discursive) especially salient on the conceptual level. That is, by accessing a form frequently, one is also directed to the conceptual content expressed by that form. Since such content is organized, by language, into compact systems — devoted to some types of distinctions and excluding others — particular conceptual domains come to be organized in the speaker's mind, becoming the basis of thinking for speaking. The crosslinguistic findings reported in this chapter lend support to these proposals.

Prediction 9 gives a developmental thrust to the sort of modified linguistic determinism offered here. We have found evidence — presented at various places in the book — that the acquisition of a form to express a particular function may also serve as an opening wedge for the acquisition of more advanced functions carried out by that form. Thus a form that is highly accessible, in the terms defined above, can lead the learner to the expression of more mature discourse functions, using that already acquired form. For example, Spanish- and Hebrew-learning 9-year-olds use relative clauses —

which are highly accessible in their languages — for adult-like functions which are not present at this age in the other languages.

Our final prediction was not confirmed. We began the study with an expectation that there was a basic set of semantic notions that all children would try to express by some means or other, whether or not grammatically-marked in their language (Slobin, 1985a). Before our data had taught us to attend to the quite different ways in which frog stories are told from language to language, we expected that German- and Hebrew-learning children would attempt to compensate for the lack of grammaticized aspect, that Spanish-learning children would attempt to elaborate the details of locative trajectories, and so forth. We were repeatedly surprised to discover how closely learners stick to the set of distinctions that they have been given by their language.[6] To be sure, a minority of narrators do use lexical means to fill in temporal or locative detail that is sparsely encoded or absent in the input language, but this seems to be a transient and sporadic phenomenon, and not as widespread as we had expected when formulating Prediction 10.

We are left, then, with a new respect for the powerful role of each individual language in shaping its own world of expression, while at the same time representing but one variant of a familiar and universally human pattern.

---

[6] Choi and Bowerman (1991) have come to similar conclusions with regard to the early learning of lexicalization patterns for the expression of motion events in English and Korean, suggesting that children "are influenced by the semantic organization of their language virtually from the beginning" (p. 83).

Coda

Telling the Frog Story in Academia

Once upon a time there were two researchers who had a theory that they kept in a jar. And one night, while they were asleep, the theory ran away. When they woke up, and found that they had no theory anymore, they went out on a search in the Grove of Academe. First they looked in a hole in the ground. A gopher popped out and said: "I am a syntactician, tending the deep structures. Your theory had no deep structures, so it couldn't be here." Then they saw a black box hanging on a tree, and it fell down when they shook the tree. All of the hidden units swarmed out and said: "We were happy up there, hard at work in our connectionist network. Your theory couldn't fit into our closed world. Go away and don't bother us." Then they climbed a tree and an owl flew out and said: "I am a pragmatist. I sleep during the day and eat other theories at night, when I fly through the air. Your theory couldn't be here, because you don't know how to fly." Finally they were picked up by a deer, who was hard to distinguish from other things in the Grove. He said: "I am a functionalist. I know where you can find your theory." And he threw them down into a swamp, where they found a lot of little theories hopping around. They weren't sure which one was the right theory, but they picked a lively one and hoped for the best. They went back home to write a book.

Appendices

Appendix I

Frog, where are you?[1]

_____
[1] Pictures reproduced from Mayer (1969), with permission of the author/artist and publisher. Original format: 25 cm x 14.5 cm, sepia-tone, one single panel or one-half double panel per page, no text; page numbers added.

-6-

-7-

-8-

−15−

−16−

−17−

−18−

−19−

−20−

−21−

Appendix II

GLOSSING AND TRANSCRIPTION CONVENTIONS

1. GLOSSING

All examples from the transcripts, in any language, are given in italics. Boldface (both roman and italic) is used for authors' emphasis. Words in capitals indicate intonational emphasis, based on the tape recordings. Glosses are given in single quotes, e.g., *kurbağa* 'frog'. Where an item would normally be obligatory in English but is omitted grammatically in the source-language, the "missing" element is given in parentheses, such as pronouns in "pro-drop" languages, e.g., *cayeron* '(they) fell'. In some contexts, the symbol ∅ is used to represent a zero-morpheme. Where necessary for interpretation, references of pronouns are indicated by an equal sign in square brackets, e.g., *Er fällt runter* 'He [=boy] fall down'.

The following conventions are used for glossing grammatical morphemes:

- Elements in the gloss which are expressed by a single lexical item in the original are separated in the gloss by a period, e.g., *hipil* 'made.fall', as are names for grammatical elements, e.g., PRES.PERF = present perfect.

- Grammatical morphemes are appended after a colon, e.g., *cayó* 'fell:PFV'. The same convention is used for combinations of grammatical morphemes, e.g., *düşürüyor* 'fall:CAUS:PRES'.

- In examples for which morphological segmentation is relevant to the discussion, morphemes are separated by hyphens, corresponding to hyphens in the gloss, e.g., *geç-ir-iyor* 'get.on-CAUS-PRES.

- If an example has both a morpheme-by-morpheme and a more colloquial gloss, the latter is given in single quotes, using the following format:

  Baykuş düşürüyor onu, köpek de kaçıyor.

  owl fall:CAUS:PRES him dog TOPIC run.away:PRES

  'The owl knocks him [=boy] down; and as for the dog, he runs away.'

Grammatical categories are abbreviated and given in small caps. The following abbreviations are used:

ABL = Ablative
ACC = Accusative
ART = Article
ASP = Aspect
AUX = Auxiliary
CAUS = Causative
CL = Clitic
COMPL = Completive
CONTIN = Continuous, Continuative
COP = Copula
DAT = Dative
DEF = Definite
DO = Direct Object
D.PAST = Direct Experience Past
EVID = Evidential
FEM = Feminine
FIN = Finite
FUT = Future
GEN = Genitive
HAB = Habitual
INCH = Inchoative
INF = Infinitive
INFER = Inferential
INSTR = Instrumental
INTRANS = Intransitive
IO = Indirect Object
IPFV = Imperfective
IRR = Irrealis
ITER = Iterative
LOC = Locative
MASC = Masculine
MOD = Modal
M.PAST = Modal/Indirect Experience Past
N = Noun
NOML = Nominalization

NEG = Negative
NOM = Nominative
NONPAST = Nonpast
NUM = Numeral, Numeric
OBJ = Object
OPT = Optative
PART = Participle
PASS = Passive
PAST = Past
PAT = Patient
PERF = Perfect
PFV = Perfective
PL = Plural
POSS = Possessive
PP = Past Participle
PREP = Preposition
PRES = Present
PRO = Pronoun
PROG = Progressive
PTL = Particle
PURP = Purposive
RECIP = Reciprocal
REFL = Reflexive
RC = Relative Clause
REPET = Repetition
RES = Resultative
SG = Singular
SIM = Simultaneity
STAT = Stative
SUBJ = Subject
TNS = Tense
TOP = Topic
TRANS = Transitive
V = Verb
VN = Verbal Noun

Narrator identification. Every example from a narrative is followed by a narrator identifier in square brackets, indicating the language, age group, specific narrator, and specific age. For example, [E4c-4;6] denotes an

English-speaking 4-year-old who was the third child (*4c*) in the sample, aged 4;6. Any linguistic example without such an identifier is an invented example.

2. TRANSCRIPTION

A uniform format was applied across the sample for transcribing the texts. The basic unit of analysis is the **clause**, defined for this study as "any unit that contains a **unified** predicate" by which we mean "a predicate that expresses a **single** situation (activity, event, or state), including finite and nonfinite verbs as well as predicate adjectives" (Berman, et al., 1986, p. 37; and see Chapter IB, Section 2.3). Each clause was entered on a new textline, as in the example reproduced below of the text of an English-speaking 5-year-old (*E5d-5;6*). (To aid researchers who might want to use our definition of the clause in their own transcriptions, this Appendix ends with the extended instructions to coders from our coding manual [Berman, et al., 1987.)

Transcripts, in this form, are available for public use in the CHILDES archive (MacWhinney, 1991; e-mail *info-childes@andrew.bitnet* or *info-childes@andrew.cmu.edu*). Each clause in a transcript is preceded by an ID code which identifies the subject, the picture to which the utterance refers, and a clause number. The prefix of the ID consists of six digits for children and four digits for adults, and specifies the subject's age and position in that age group (for each particular language). The data portion of the ID specifies the picture that the subject was looking at when s/he produced the utterance entered on that textline and the number of the clause in that text. Thus, for example, in the text reproduced below, the string **05;06D 03b005** refers to a child aged 5 years and 6 months who is the fourth child in that age group (in the English sample), talking about picture 3b, and the textline is the fifth clause out of the total 24 in that text. An example of an adult ID would be **20j 11a095**, standing for the tenth adult talking about picture 11a, in the 95th clause in that text, and assigning an arbitrary age of 20 to all adult subjects.

The first three digits in the data portion refer, as noted, to the **page** in the picturebook which the subject was referring to when producing that line of the text. Unlike the consecutive numbering we have used for the frog-book pictures throughout this study, from 1 to 24, the original transcriptions list the pages as from 01- to 15-, with a hyphen (-) standing for a picture that fills two facing pages, the letter **a** specifying a lefthand picture and **b** a righthand picture on pages which have two separate pictures. In order to identify the picture the subject was referring to for every piece of the recording, the investigator would lightly tap on the microphone when the subject moved his or her eyes to the next part of the page, or turned the page. When the subject did not refer to each page consecutively, but either skipped or turned back one or more pages, this was noted down by the investigator and so indicated on the transcript.

A new textline was used for each clause, even if this was not a complete sentence or a well-formed subordinate or nonfinite clause — as in clause #1 in this sample transcript. However, a single clause might contain more than one verb, when one of the verbs expresses an aspectual or modal specification of the main verb, rather than an independent event or state — as in clauses 2, 3, and 11, *and then they* **were going to sleep,** *and then he's* **gonna go out** *the window, and they* **start calling.**

All text was entered in lowercase letters, using conventional orthography and spelling, except where potentially relevant for morphosyntactic or semantic analysis. (Following German orthographic convention, German nouns were capitalized.) For example, the *-ing* form of the verbs *looking* and *calling* in the sample text would be transcribed as such even if the child pronounced them as *lookin, callin.* Another example is of initial *h* in Hebrew, which is quite typically elided in everyday adult as well as child speech, but which was always indicated so as to ensure consistency of lexical forms.

In the case of Hebrew, the only language in our sample with a non-Roman script, texts were entered in broad phonetic transcription (see Chapter IIID).[1]

Material in square brackets indicates interviewer comments to the child and remarks on the situation (e.g., what page is being described in unclear or nonconsecutive references, as in clauses 7 and 16 in this text). Curly brackets indicate false starts or repairs (e.g., clause 24), uninterpretable strings (e.g., clause 8), and other material which was not included in our coding system (Chapter IB, Section 2.3). Thus, all material, except what occurs between square brackets, represents the subject's output as recorded by the investigator. Text length in clauses (*IB-Table 3*) is based only on clauses **not** totally enclosed in curly brackets. (Thus the sample in 2.1, below, has 23 codable clauses, excluding 008.)

---

[1] The main departures from fairly standard English distinctions in the Hebrew transcriptions are: *c*, which stands for the Hebrew letter *cade*, pronounced as *ts*, as in the loan English word *tsetse*, and *x*, which stands for the voiceless velar fricative (and also the historical pharyngeal *chet*), pronounced like the final consonant in words like *Bach, loch*. These occur in the Hebrew frog story, in words like *cfardea* 'frog', *cincenet* 'jar', and *rac* 'run' or *xipes* 'searched', *baxa* 'cried'. The glottal stop *alef*, where needed to represent a historical root (it is typically not pronounced in normal speech in word-initial or word-final position) is represented by a question-mark, and the apostrophe represents the historical pharyngeal *ayin* for roots, and otherwise is used to indicate a modified glottal stop between two vowels, e.g., *ne'elam* 'disappeared', *le-he'alem* 'to-disappear'.

The following standardized conventions were used to indicate (minimal) prosodic features of the text:

Default (no indication) = steady or sustained intonation
A dash (-) = a short pause
Three dots (or more if needed) = a longer pause
Comma (,) = partially falling intonation
Period (.) = fully falling intonation, end of utterance
Question-mark (?) = end of question-type utterance
Single slash (/) = rising intonation or other indication of marked emphasis
Double slash (//) = exaggeratedly marked emphasis
Exclamation-mark (!) = on both sides of a word or series of words,
    indicates excited delivery (e.g., ! Look !)
Colon (:) = lengthening of a vowel (e.g., ru:n stands for a long drawn-out
    pronunciation of the English verb 'run' and ra:c stands for
    something like raaaac in its Hebrew equivalent
Three exes (xxx) = an unintelligible string
Parentheses ( ) = uncertain, but possible interpretations of a string.

Other comments on paralinguistic features such as speech quality are indicated in square brackets, e.g., [whispering], [child laughs]. As noted in various connections throughout the book (e.g., in Chapter IB-Section 2.4, Chapter IIA, Chapter IVC, Section 2), this level of transcription does not allow for in-depth analysis of the role of prosodic (or other paralinguistic features) elements in telling the frog story.

2.1. Sample Transcript

05;06D	01-001	looking in [uhhuh]
05;06D	02a002	and then {he - } they were going to sleep,
05;06D	02a003	and then he's - gonna - go out the window [singsong] [he's gonna go out the window / oh.]
05;06D [uhhuh/]	03a004	and then he - he had - a jar stuck on his head, ...
05;06D	03b005	and then they were - calling for the frog. [umhm/]
05;06D	04-006	and then he - breaks - the jar. [oh.]
05;06D	05-007	there's a - beehive. [yep.] and a gopher. [from page 6a]
05;06D	06-008	{ xxx }
05;06D	07-009	and ... the beehive fell down. [umhm/]
05;06D	07-010	and they look in the tree,
05;06D	09-011	and they ... and they start calling. [umhm/]
05;06D	09b012	and they think
05;06D	09b013	that's sticks,

05;06D	10a014	but it's a d - um - an antler. [antlers - ah.]
05;06D	10b015	and then they run,
05;06D	11-016	and then they - go in the water. [oh.] [also page 12]
05;06D	13-017	and behind that log is frogs. [oh, really / aha.]
05;06D	14b018	there's some more frogs. [yeah /]
05;06D	15-019	and there's another frog.
05;06D	15-020	[What about the boy?] he gocs in the water ... [uhhuh/]
05;06D	15-021	and they look ...
05;06D	15-022	and watch.
05;06D	15-023	oh there's one // ...
05;06D	15-024	{ they can't get - } he can't get up .

2.2. Definition of "Clause" as Unit of Transcription[2]

Each clause should be transcribed on a new textline. We define a clause as any unit that contains a unified predicate. By unified, we mean a predicate that expresses a single situation (activity, event, state). Predicates include finite and nonfinite verbs, as well as predicate adjectives. In general, clauses will be comprised of a single verbal element; however, infinitives and participles which function as complements of modal or aspectual verbs are included with the matrix verb as single clauses, e.g., *want to go, started walking.* These matrix verbs plus modifiers should not be confused with utterances that clearly express two "situations," as in subordinate complement clauses, e.g., *I thought that I would go.* As illustration, each of the following phrases would be analyzed as a single clause with a unified predicate: *running through the woods; taken by surprise; (in order) to help his friends; was angry.*

In general, then, treat as a single clause those utterances that have two verbs but one subject, and treat as two separate clauses cases when each verb has a different subject, e.g., *I want to go* vs. *I want you to go.* Predicates that are clearly narrator-comments are kept with the matrix verb in a single predicate, e.g., *I assume that the boy is happy; it appears that the dog is going to fall.* These phrases constitute one clause.

2.2.1. Single Clause Examples

Single clause with two verbs and one subject: *he stopped running; they had begun to search all over.*

Single clause with different subjects (Narrator Comments): *I think the boy misses the frog; it appears that the frog is happy.*

---

[2] This section is taken directly from our coding manual (Berman, et al., 1986); therefore, "clause" is defined in terms of instructions to coders.

2.2.2. Two Clause Examples

Subordinate Complements — Same Subject NP:

> he thought
> he could get the bees .

> he said
> he would find the frog .

Subordinate Complements - Different Subject NP:

> he decided
> that it was an owl .

> he told the dog
> to be quiet .

2.2.3. Special Cases

Verbless Clauses: While a clause is defined by the presence of a "unified" predicate, a clause need not contain an overt verb. For example, copular sentences in Hebrew and Turkish which have zero-expression of the copula in the present tense are coded as a separate clause.

Ellipsis and Gapping: Treat as separate clauses strings in which the verb is lacking due to grammatical reductions such as gapping and where the verb semantics is fully recoverable from the text, or structures which can be analyzed as clauses where the copula has been deleted.

> the boy looked in his boots
> and the dog in the jar .

> with the frog not there
> the boy felt very upset .

> he began searching for the frog
> and the dog too .

Crucial Plot Information: Verbless clauses that are critical to the story-line should be coded on a separate line.

> and then he climbs over ,
> and ! little ! baby frogs .

Do not code separately as a clause speech that would otherwise be con-sidered part of another utterance if not for considerations of intonation or the subject's orientation to the picture book (i.e., the page at which the subject is currently looking). ($ indicates page turn in middle of utterance.)

[pg. 5] there were bees . $ [pg. 6] and a gopher .

Do not code speech strings that are not elaborated in adjacent utterances and that do not appear to be part of the storyline. Enclose these portions of text in curly brackets and omit from coding.

{ boy } [mhm /] { dog. }[mhm /] { frog.}

[mhm /] [looking at pg. 2]

{ ! bees ! } [looking at pg. 5]

2.2.4. Center-Embedded Clauses/Discontinuous Constituents

In order to have a constant measure of story length in number of clauses, and to allow for potential coding of each clause separately, center-embedded relative clauses are enclosed in curly brackets { } on the original textline (i.e., not coded), displaced from their original location, and coded on a new line after the associated main clause. Indicate that the clause has been displaced from its original location by enclosing it in angle brackets < > on the textline where it is coded.

the owl { who pushed the boy } flew away .
< who pushed the boy >

little Moritz { who I just call little Moritz } sits in front of his bed .
< who I just call little Moritz >

Some adverbial clauses may be separated from their associated main clause by an introductory adverbial phrase which sets the temporal anchor for the main clause, e.g., *in the middle of the night, one day, at night*. Because these adverbial phrases are syntactically associated with the main clause and not the subordinate adverbial clause, they should be enclosed in curly brackets { } on the original textline — i.e., not coded — displaced to the clause line containing the main clause, placed in angle brackets < > , and coded with that main clause.

{ in the middle of the night } , after they had gone to sleep
< in the middle of the night > the frog escaped from the jar .

{ and after that } when they had gotten to the other side
< and after that > they saw a whole lot of little frogs .

Subordinate clauses or other embedded phrases that do not have adverbial anchors are treated normally and coded in order of the surface predicates.

> after they woke up
> they realized
> that the frog was gone .

> while they were sleeping
> and the moon was shining brightly
> the little frog jumped out .

2.2.5. Additional Coding Conventions

Task Comments: Asides which are not part of the type of text under study in the frog stories, such as task-oriented questions to the interviewer or expressions that are used to engage the listener, are not included in the clause count and are not coded.

> { I think we could be finished now . }
> { what's that called / }

> { is that a gopher / }
> { should I turn the page now / }
> { ! look ! }
> { lookit what happened . }
> { see / }
> { I don't know . }
> { do you know what that is / }
> { isn't it /}
> { right / }

or parts of utterances which are formulaic with respect to the story-telling situation are not counted or coded.

> { once upon a time }
> { and they lived happily ever after }
> { the end }
> { and that's all . }

Unintelligible Speech: Clauses or parts of clauses that contain a substantial portion of unintelligible speech should not be coded, especially if an accurate interpretation of the temporal quality of the clause or the predicate in general is jeopardized.

Reformulations/False Starts: The fullest version is coded in clauses containing reformulations and false starts. The repaired portion is enclosed in curly brackets { }.

{ and then he starts } ... then a gopher pops out of the hole.

{ he - the dog } - the dog was barking at the deer.

Appendix III

Research Using *Frog, where are you?*, by Mercer Mayer

FIRST LANGUAGE

THE BERKELEY PROJECT

English, German, Hebrew, Spanish, Turkish

Papers listed below can be found in the **References** *to this volume. Language(s) dealt with in each paper are indicated by the letters* **E, G, H, S, T,** *following each citation in boldface.*

Aksu-Koç (1988a, 1991, 1992b: **T**)
Bamberg (1985, 1987, 1990, 1992: **G**; 1991b: **E**; 1993a: **E, G**);
  Bamberg, Budwig, & Kaplan (1991: **G**); Bamberg & Damrad-Frye
  (1991: **E**); Bamberg & Marchman (1990, 1991: **E, G**)
Berman (1988, 1990, 1993, in press-c: **H**); Berman & Slobin
  (1987: **E, G, H, S, T**)
Marchman (1989: **E**)
Renner (1988: **E**)
Sebastián (1989: **S**)
Slobin (1987, 1991, in press-a: **E, G, H, S**); Slobin (1988, 1993a: **T**);
  Slobin, (1989, 1990: **E, G, H, S, T**); Slobin (1993b: **E, G, S, T**);
  Slobin (in press-c: **E, S**); Slobin & Bocaz (1988: **E, S**)

OTHER PROJECTS

American Sign Language

Ursula Bellugi, Laboratory for Language and Cognitive Studies, The Salk
  Institute for Biological Studies, P.O. Box 85800, San Diego, CA
  92186-5800 (*bellugi@crl.ucsd.edu*) (**with** Edward S. Klima, Judy
  Snitzer Reilly)

Dennis Galvan, Dept. of Psychology, Gallaudet University, 800 Florida Ave.,
  N.E., Washington, DC 20002 (*dbgalvan@gallua.gallaudet.edu*) [**Age
  range:** 3, 5, 7, 9 (native ASL), 5, 9, adult (late signers)] (**Ref.:** Galvan,
  1988, 1989)

Arabic (Moroccan)

Michèle Kail, Laboratoire de Psychologie Expérimentale, CNRS, 28 rue Serpente, 75006 Paris, France (*labexp@frmop22.cnusc.fr*) (**with** Mohammed Bamhamed, Abdelkébir Drissi) [**Age range:** 3, 4, 5] (**Ref.:** Kail & Drissi, 1990)

Arandic Languages (Australia)

David P. Wilkins, Dept. of Linguistics, SUNY at Buffalo, Buffalo, NY 14260 (*lindavid@ubvmsc.cc.buffalo.edu*) **Languages: Mparntwe Arrernte, Western Arrernte, Alyawarre** [**Age range:** adult]

Bulgarian

Krzysztof Olszewski, Dept. of General Linguistics, Jagiellonian University, Mickiewicza 9/11, Kraków, Poland (**with** Magdalena Smoczyńska, *ulsmoczy@if.uj.edu.pl*) [**Age range:** child, adult]

Dutch

Karin Dijkhuis, Marja Roelofs (*mroelofs@alf.let.uva.nl*), Carla Zijlenmaker: Dept. of Linguistics, University of Amsterdam, Spuistraat 210, 1012 VT, Amsterdam, Netherlands (**with** Anne Mills, *aemills@alf.let.uva.nl*) [**Age range:** 4-9, adult] (**Ref.:** Dijkhuis, in prep.; Zijlenmaker, 1992, 1993)

English (American)

Carolyn Cowan, Philip Cowan, Institute of Human Development, University of California, Berkeley, CA 94720 (*bafanaly@cmsa.berkeley.edu*) [**Age range:** child]

Mavis Donahue, College of Education, m/c 147, Box 4348, University of Illinois, Chicago, IL 60680 (*u18353@uicvm.bitnet*) [**Age range:** adult (mother-child)]

Morton Ann Gernsbacher, Dept. of Psychology, University of Wisconsin, Madison, WI 53706 (*morton@macc.wisc.edu*) [**Age range:** adult (comprehension test)] (**Ref.:** Gernsbacher, 1985)

Debra A. Harkins, Dept. of Psychology, Suffolk University, Beacon Hill, 41 Temple St., Boston, MA 02114-4280 [**Age range:** adults (mothers to 4-5-year-olds)] (**Ref.:** Harkins, 1992)

Lowry Hemphill, Projects in Language Development, 306 Larsen Hall, Harvard Graduate School of Education, Cambridge, MA 02138 (*hemphilo@hugse1.bitnet*) [**Age range:** 5-8] (**Ref.:** Hemphill, Wolf, Camp, & Griffin, 1993; Miranda, Camp, Hemphill, & Wolf, 1992)

Margaret Barzilay, Elite Olshtain, School of Education, Tel Aviv University, Ramat Aviv, Israel 66978 [**Age range:** adult (special condition: native Americans compared with American immigrants in Israel; study of language attrition)] (**Ref.:** Olshtain & Barzilay, 1991)

Judy Snitzer Reilly, Department of Psychology, San Diego State University, 6363 Alvarado Court #221, San Diego, CA 92120-4913. (*q300022@calstate.bitnet*) [**Age range:** 3-4, 7-8, 10-11] (**Ref.:** Reilly, 1992)

Tom Trabasso, Dept. of Psychology, University of Chicago, 5848 S. University Ave., Chicago, IL 60637 (*tsqd@midway.uchicago.edu*) (**with** Camille Baughn, Margret Park Munger, Margaret Nickels, Philip C. Rodkin, Nancy Stein) [**Age range:** 3, 4, 5, 9 (data of Renner), adult (data of Marchman)] (**Ref.:** Trabasso & Nickels, 1992; Trabasso, Stein, Rodkin, Munger, & Baughn, 1992)

Joan Manhardt, Lowry Hemphill, Helen Tager-Flusberg (*see below, under* **Language / Developmental Impairment**)

English (Australian)

Gillian Wigglesworth, Department of Applied Linguistics, University of Melbourne, Parkville, Victoria 3052, Australia (*Gillian_Wigglesworth@muwayf.unimelb.edu.au*) [**Age range:** 4, 6, 8, 10 adult] (**Ref.:** Wigglesworth, 1992)

Julie Hebert (*see below, under* **Second Language/Bilingual**)

English (British)

Elena Lieven, Dept. of Psychology, University of Manchester, Manchester M13 9PL, U.K. (*lieven@psychology-a.manchester.ac.uk*) [**Age range:** 3-5]

J. R. Martin, Dept. of Linguistics, University of Sydney, Sydney, Australia [**Age range:** 6-7, 8-9, 10-11] (**Ref.:** Martin, 1977, 1983)

Finnish

Lisa Dasinger, Dept. of Psychology, University of California, Berkeley, CA 94720 (*dasinger@cogsci.berkeley.edu*) [**Age range:** 3-9, adult]

Christer Laurén, Karita Mård, Swedish Immersion Research Project, Dept. of Scandinavian Languages, University of Vaasa, P.O. Box 297, SF-65101 Vaasa, Finland (*karita.mard@macpost.uwasa.fi*) [**Age range.:** 6-8]

Jorma Toivainen, Dept. of Finnish and General Linguistics, University of Turku, 20500 Turku, Finland (*toivainen@sara.cc.utu.fi*) (**with** Reetta Jokinen, Kati Juhola, Elisa Koskinen, Annikka Kotiranta, Susanna Leveelahti, Sirpa Niiniviita, Liisa Ollila, Risto Palttala, Marja Raukola, Henna Seppä, Kirsti Toivainen) [**Age range:** 3, 5, 7, 9-10, adult] (**Ref.:** Toivainen, 1989, 1992)

Finno-Permic Languages

Jorma Toivainen, Dept. of Finnish and General Linguistics, University of Turku, 20500 Turku, Finland (*toivainen@sara.cc.utu.fi*): **Estonian** — Paul Alvre, Ago Kunnap, Tiina Mihailov (Dorpat), **Finnish** (Sweden) — Raija Kangassalo (Umea), **Komi** (or **Zyrian**) — Jevgeni Igushev (Syktyvkar), **Mari** (or **Cheremis**) — Valentin Vasiljev (Joshkar-Ola), **Mordvinian** — Mihail Mosin (Saransk), **Udmurt** (or **Votyak**) — Alexandr Sutov (Izhevsk), **Veps** — Nina Zaiceva (Petrozavodsk) [**Age range:** 3, 5, 7, 9]

French (France)

Maya Hickmann, Michèle Kail, Laboratoire de Psychologie Expérimentale, CNRS, 28 rue Serpente, 75006 Paris, France (*labexp@frmop22.cnusc.fr*) (**with** Françoise Roland) [**Age range:** 6, 9, 11] (**Ref.:** Hickmann, Kail, & Roland, 1989; Hickmann, Kail, & Roland, 1993; Kail & Hickmann, 1992)

Harriet Jisa, Centre de Recherches Linguistiques et Semiologiques, Université Lumière — Lyon 2, 69500 BRON, France (*crlslyon@cism.univ-lyon1.fr*) (**with** Sophie Kern) [**Age range:** 3-12, adult] (**Ref.:** Jisa & Kern, 1993)

Galician

José Ramón García Soto, Dept. of Developmental and Educational Psychology, University of Santiago de Compostela, Campus Universitario, 15707 Santiago, Spain (**with** Miguel Pérez-Pereira, Urzáiz 77, 2° B, 36201 Vigo, Spain; *pezzs018@seins.usc.es*) [**Age range.:** 4-2, adult] (**Ref.:** García Soto, 1993)

Ana Rodríguez-Trelles, Patio de Madres 16, Santiago de Compostela (La Coruña), Spain (**with** Miguel Pérez-Pereira, Urzáiz 77, 2° B, 36201 Vigo, Spain; *pezzs018@seins.usc.es*) [**Age range:** 4, 5, 7, 9, 11, adult] (**Ref.:** Rodríguez-Trelles, 1991)

Guugu Yumithirr (Pama-Nyungan: Australia)

Stephen Levinson, Cognitive Anthropology Research Group, Max-Planck-Institute for Psycholinguistics, PB 310, NL-6500 AH Nijmegen, Netherlands (*lĕvinson@mpi.nl*) [**Age range:** adult]

Icelandic

Hrafnhildur Ragnarsdóttir, University College of Education, v/Stakkahlíd, 105 Reykjavik, Iceland (*hragnars@ismennt.is*) [**Age range:** 3-4, 5, 7, 9, adult] (**Ref.:** Ragnarsdóttir, 1987, 1988, 1991a, 1991b)

Italian

Margherita Orsolini, Istituto di Pedagogia e Psicologia, Via Madonna degli Angeli 30, 66100 Chieti, Italy; Clotilde Pontecorvo and Franca Rossi, Dip. Psicologia n. 38, Via de Marsi 78, 00185 Rome, Italy [**Age range:** 4, 5, 6, 8, 10, adult] (**Ref.:** Orsolini, Rossi, & Pontecorvo, 1993; Rossi, 1993)

Piero Bottari, Anna Maria Chilosi, Paola Cipriani, Elisabetta Lanzetta, Lucia Pfanner: Laboratory for the Study of Normal and Pathological Child Language Acquisition, Stella Maris Foundation and Institute of Child Neuropsychiatry of the University of Pisa, Viale del Tirreno 331, 56018 Calambrone - Pisa, Italy (*beppe@icnucevm.cnuce.cnr.it / bottari@ipgcuic.bitnet*) [**Age range:** 4-11]

Japanese

Keiko Nakamura, Dept. of Psychology, University of California, Berkeley, CA 94720 (*nakak@cogsci.berkeley.edu*) [**Age range:** 3, 4, 5, 7, 9, adult] (**Ref.:** Küntay & Nakamura, 1993; Nakamura, 1992, 1993)

Kazumi Takahashi, 550 N. Harvard Ave., Claremont, CA 91711 (*ktakahashi@pomona.claremont.edu*) [**Age range:** adult] (**Ref.:** Takahashi, 1993)

Nobuko Uchida, Bunkyoiku Gakbaku, Ochanomizu Women's University, 2-1-1 Otsuka, Bunkyo-yo, Tokyo 112, Japan [**Age range:** 3-5] (**Ref.:** Uchida, 1982, 1983)

Seiko Yamaguchii Fujii, Dept. of East Asian Languages and Cultures, and Dept. of Linguistics, 608 S. Matthews Ave., University of Illinois, Champaign-Urbana, IL 61801 (*fujii@lees.cogsci.uiuc.edu*) [**Age range:** adult] (**Ref.:** Fujii, 1992, 1993)

Kgalagadi (Bantu: Botswana)

Sabine Neumann, Cognitive Anthropology Research Group, Max-Planck-Institute for Psycholinguistics, PB 310, N-6500 AH, Nijmegen, Netherlands (*sneumann@mpi.nl*) [**Age range:** adult]

Kickapoo

Jule Gomez de Garcia, Campus Box 295, Department of Linguistics, University of Colorado, Boulder, CO 80309 (*garcia_jm@cubldr.Colorado.edu*) [**Age range:** child, adult]

Kilivila (Austronesian: Trobriand Islands, Papua New Guinea)

Gunter Senft, Cognitive Anthropology Research Group, Max-Planck-Institute for Psycholinguistics, PB 310, NL-6500 AH Nijmegen, Netherlands (*senft@mpi.nl*) [**Age range:** 12 - adult]

Lakhota

Robert D. Van Valin, Jr., Dept. of Linguistics, SUNY at Buffalo, Buffalo, NY 14260 (*linvan@ubvms.bitnet*) [**Age range:** adult]

Longgu (Austronesian: Solomon Islands)

Deborah Hill, Cognitive Anthropology Research Group, Max-Planck-Institute for Psycholinguistics, PB 310, NL-6500 AH Nijmegen, Netherlands (*dhill@mpi.nl*) [**Age range:** 12, 16, adult]

Malay

Yap Siew Peng, 64 Pinngir Zaaba, Taman Tun Drive, Ismail 6000, Kuala Lumpur, Malaysia [**Age range:** 5, 7, adult] (**Ref.:** Peng, 1992)

Mandarin (Peoples Republic of China)

Jiansheng Guo, Dept. of Psychology, University of California, Berkeley, CA 94720 (*guo@cogsci.berkeley.edu*) [**Age range:** 3, 4, 5, 9, adult]

Mopan (Mayan: Belize)

Eve Danziger, Cognitive Anthropology Research Group, Max-Planck-Institute for Psycholinguistics, PB 310, NL-6500 AH Nijmegen, Netherlands (*danziger@mpi.nl*) [**Age range:** child, adult]

Myene (Bantu: Gabon)

Pierrette Andrée Ogouamba, Centre de Recherches Linguistiques et Semiologiques, Université Lumière — Lyon 2, 69500 BRON, France [**Age range:** 6, 8, 9, 10, 11, 12]

Nilotic Languages

Edith Bavin, Dept. of Linguistics, La Trobe University, Bundoora, Victoria 3083, Australia (*linel@lure.latrobe.edu.au*) **Western Nilotic Languages: Acholi, Alur, Dhopodhola, Lango** [**Age range:** adult]

Norwegian

Elizabeth Lanza, Dept. of Linguistics, University of Oslo, Post Box 1102, Blindern, 0317 Oslo, Norway (*elizabeth.lanza@ilf.uio.no*) [**Age range:** 4-8]

Polish

Magdalena Smoczyńska, Długa 50-5, 31-146 Kraków, Poland (*ulsmoczy@if.uj.edu.pl*) [**Age range:** child, adult]

Portuguese

Isabel Hub Faria, Departamento de Linguística, Faculdade de Letras, Universidade de Lisboa, 1699 Lisboa codex, Portugal [**Age range:** child, adult]

Russian

N. V. Durova, Institute of the National Problems of Education, Moscow, Russia; N. M. Yurieva, Institute of Linguistics, Russian Academy of Sciences, ul. Semashko, dom 1/12, 103009 Moscow K-9, Russia (*sham@iling.msk.su*) [**Age range:** 3-6] (**Ref.:** Durova & Yurieva, 1993)

Dan I. Slobin, Dept. of Psychology, University of California, Berkeley, CA 94720 (*slobin@cogsci.berkeley.edu*) (**with** Yana Mirsky) [**Age range:** 4-10, adult]

Tatiana Ushakova, Institute of Psychology, Russian Academy of Sciences, Moscow (**with** Michèle Kail: see above under **French**) [**Age range:** 5, 9, 11, adult]

Sign Language of the Netherlands

Nini Hoiting, Royal Institute for the Deaf "H. D. Guyot," Rijksstraatweg 63, 9752 AC Haren, Netherlands (**with** Dan I. Slobin) [**Age range:** child, adult] (**Ref.**: Hoiting & Slobin, 1993)

Spanish (Argentina, Chile)

Aura Bocaz, (Universidad de Chile), Versailles 2977, Depto 94, Las Condes, Santiago, Chile (**with** Dan I. Slobin)

[**Age range:** 3, 4, 5, 7, 9, 11, adult] (**Ref.**: Bocaz, 1989a, 1989b, 1989c, 1991a, 1991b, 1991c, 1991d, 1992a, 1992b; Slobin & Bocaz, 1988)

Spanish (Mexico)

Rosa Graciela Montes, Instituto de Ciencias Sociales y Humanidades, Universidad Autónoma de Puebla, Apdo. Postal 1356, 72001 Puebla, Pue, Mexico (*rmontes@cca.pue.udlap.mx*) [**Age range:** child, adult]

Spanish (Spain)

Susana López-Ornat, Dpto. Psicología Cognitiva, Campus de Somosaguas, Universidad Complutense de Madrid - 28223, Spain (*pscog09@sis.ucm.es*) (**with** Javier del Castillo; Michèle Kail, Maya Hickmann: see above under **French**) [**Age range:** 3, 4, 5, 6, 7, 8, 9, 10, 11, adult]

Maria D. Sera, Institute of Child Development, University of Minnesota, 51 East River Rd., Minneapolis, MN 55455 [**Age range:** 3, 4, 5, 9, adult (data of Sebastián)] (**Ref.:** Sera, 1992)

Swedish

Christer Laurén, Karita Mård (*see above, under* **Finnish**) [**Age range.:** 11-12]

Sven Strömqvist, Dept. of Linguistics, University of Göteborg, S-412 98 Göteborg, Sweden (*sven@ling.gu.se*) [**Age range:** 14-15 (videotaped oral stories and computer-logged written stories)]

Tamil (Dravidian: India)

Eric Pederson, Cognitive Anthropology Research Group, Max-Planck-Institute for Psycholinguistics, PB 310, NL-6500 AH Nijmegen, Netherlands (*pederson@mpi.nl*) [**Age range:** 10, adult]

Totonac (Totonacan: Mexico)

Paulette Levy, UNAM, Seminario de Lenguas Indígenas, Instituto de Investigaciones Filológicas, Circuito Mario de la Cueva, 04510 México, D.F., Mexico [**Age range:** adult]

Turkish

Aylin Küntay, Dept. of Psychology, University of California, Berkeley, CA 94720 (*kuntay@cogsci.berkeley.edu*) [**Age range:** 3, 4, 5, 7, 9, adult] (**Ref.:** Küntay, 1992; Küntay & Nakamura, 1993)

Tzeltal (Mayan: Mexico)

Penelope Brown, Cognitive Anthropology Research Group, Max-Planck-Institute for Psycholinguistics, PB 310, NL-6500 AH Nijmegen, Netherlands (*pbrown@mpi.nl*) [**Age range:** 5, 6, 7, 12, adult]

Tzotzil (Mayan: Mexico)

Esteban Gutiérrez, Linguistics Dept., Reed College, Portland, OR 97202 (*esteban@reed.edu*) (**with:** John Haviland, Lourdes de León) [**Age range:** child, adult]

Lourdes de León, Linguistics Dept., Reed College, Portland, OR 97202 (*deleon@reed.edu*) [**Age range:** 3, 5, 8, 10] (**Ref.:** de León, 1992)

Warlpiri (Australia)

Edith Bavin, Dept. of Linguistics, La Trobe University, Bundoora, Victoria 3083, Australia (*linel@lure.latrobe.edu.au*) [**Age range:** 3-4, 6-7, 11-13, adult]

Yiddish (USA)

Dan I. Slobin, Dept. of Psychology, University of California, Berkeley, CA 94720 (*slobin@cogsci.berkeley.edu*); Judith L. Slobin, Norval L. Slobin, 22801 Essex Way, Apt. 511, Southfield, MI 48034 [**Age range:** child, adult]

Yucatec Mayan (Mexico)

John Lucy, Suzanne Gaskins, Dept. of Anthropology, University of Pennsylvania, Philadelphia, PA (*jlucy@sas.upenn.edu*)

Yupno (Papua New Guinea)

Jürg Wassmann, Cognitive Anthropology Research Group, Max-Planck-Institute for Psycholinguistics, PB 310, NL-6500 AH Nijmegen, Netherlands (*cogant@mpi.nl*) [**Age range:** adult]

SECOND LANGUAGE / BILINGUAL

Arabic (Moroccan) - Dutch

Ludo Verhoeven, Linguistics Department, Universiteit Brabant, PB 90153, NL-5000 LE Tilburg, Netherlands (*t170ludo@kub.nl*) (**with** Petra Bos) [**Age range:** 4-12] [**Language of narration:** Arabic, Dutch] (**Ref.:** Verhoeven, 1993)

Finnish - Swedish

Christer Laurén, Karita Mård (*see above, under* **Finnish**) [**Age range.:** 11-12 (Finnish L1)]

German - Russian

Jeannette Dittmar, FB-16, Germanistik, Freie Universität Berlin, Germany [**Age range:** 5;1 - 6;5 (one child, longitudinal)] [**Language of narration:** German, Russian]

Greek - English

Calliope Haritos, Katherine Nelson: Developmental Psychology, City University of New York Graduate Center, 33 W. 42nd St., New York, NY 10036 [**Age range:** adult]

Guugu Yimithirr - Australian Aboriginal English

Lourdes de León, Dept. of Linguistics, Reed College, Portland, OR 97202 (*deleon@reed.edu*) [**Age range:** 6-14, adult] [**Language of narration:** Guugu Yimithirr, Australian Aboriginal English]

Norwegian-English

Elizabeth Lanza, Dept. of Linguistics, University of Oslo, Post Box 1102, Blindern, 0317 Oslo, Norway (*elizabeth.lanza@ilf.uio.no*) [**Age range:** 4-8] [**Language of narration:** Norwegian, English]

Spanish-Basque (Spain)

Hernán Urrutia Cárdenas, Fac. de Ciencias de la Communicación, Universidad del País Vasco, Bilbao, Spain; Carmen Silva-Corvalán, Dept. of Spanish and Portuguese, University of Southern California, Los Angeles, CA 90089 (*silva@vm.usc.edu*) [**Age-range:** 5-6] [**Language of narration:** Spanish, Basque] (**Ref.:** Urrutia Cárdenas, 1992)

Spanish-English (U.S.A.)

Carmen Silva-Corvalán, Dept. of Spanish and Portuguese, University of Southern California, Los Angeles, CA 90089 (*silva@vm.usc.edu*) [**Age range:** 5-7] [**Language of narration:** Spanish, English] (**Ref.:** Silva-Corvalán, 1992)

Spanish-English, Turkish-English (Australian)

Julie Hebert, 18 Evans St., Moonee Ponds 3039, Australia [**Age range:** 6-8] [**Language of narration:** English (English L1, Spanish L1, Turkish L1)] (**Ref.:** Hebert, 1990)

Christine Howell, Adult Migrant Education Service, Melbourne, Victoria, Australia [**Age range:** adult] [**Language of narration:** English (English L1, Spanish L1, Turkish L1)] (**Ref.:** Howell, 1993)

Turkish-Dutch

Ludo Verhoeven, Linguistics Dept., Universiteit Brabant, PB 90135, NL-5000 LE Tilburg, Netherlands (*tl70ludo@kub.nl*) (**with** Jeroen Aarssen) [**Age range:** 4-12] [**Language of narration:** Turkish, Dutch] (**Ref.:** Verhoeven, 1993)

Turkish-French (France)

Harriet Jisa, Centre de Recherches Linguistiques et Semiologiques, Université Lumière — Lyon 2, 69500 BRON, France (*crlyslyon@cism.univ-lyon1.fr*) (**with** Sophie Kern) [**Age range:** 6-11, adult] [**Language of narration:** French (Turkish L1)]

LANGUAGE / DEVELOPMENTAL IMPAIRMENT

English (American)

Elizabeth Bates, Center for Research in Language, C-008, University of California at San Diego, La Jolla, CA 92093 (*bates@crl.ucsd.edu*) (**with** Virginia Marchman, Judy Snitzer Reilly, Joan Stiles, Beverly Wulfeck) [**Type of impairment:** specific language impairment, early focal brain injury] (**Ref.:** Reilly, Marchman, & Bates, in press)

Ursula Bellugi, Laboratory for Language and Cognitive Studies, The Salk Institute for Biological Studies, P.O. Box 85800, San Diego, CA 92186-5800 (*llcs@salk-sci.sdsc.edu*) (**with** Edward S. Klima, Judy Snitzer Reilly) [**Type of impairment:** Down Syndrome, Williams Syndrome] [**Age range:** 10-18] (**Ref.:** Reilly, Klima, & Bellugi, in press)

Robin Chapman, Department of Communicative Disorders, University of Wisconsin, 1975 Willow Dr., Madison, WI 53706 (*chapman@waisman.wisc.edu*) [**Type of impairment:** Down Syndrome] [**Age range:** child, adolescent]

Heidi Feldman, Child Development Unit, Children's Hospital of Pittsburgh, Pittsburgh, PA 15213 (*hf0a+@andrew.cmu.edu*) [**Type of impairment:** perinatal brain injury]

Jonathan Fine, Dept. of English, Bar-Ilan University, Ramat-Gan, Israel (*f24054@barilan.bitnet*) [**Type of impairment:** reading disability] [**Age range:** 10-12] (**Ref.:** Fine, 1985, in press)

Lowry Hemphill, Graduate School of Education, Harvard University, Roy E. Larsen Hall, Appian Way, Cambridge, MA 02138 (**with** Linda Camp and Dennis Palmer Wolf) [**Type of impairment;** mildly mentally retarded (and nonretarded)] [**Age range:** 11 (retarded), 7 (nonretarded)] (**Ref.:** Wolf, Hemphill, & Camp, 1991)

Joan Manhardt, Dept. of Human Development, Bryn Mawr College, Bryn Mawr, PA 19010 (*jmanhard@cc.brynmawr.edu*) (**with** Leslie A. Rescorla) [**Type of impairment:** specific expressive language delay] [**Age range:** 8 (compared with 8 normally developing children)] (**Ref.:** Rescorla & Manhardt, 1993)

Janis Oram, School of Communication Sciences and Disorders, McGill University, Montreal, Quebec, Canada H3G 1AB (*inmc@musicb.mcgill.ca*) (**with** Martha B. Crago, Myrna Gopnik) [**Type of impairment:** familial specific language impairment] [**Age range:** 13-43]

Helen Tager-Flusberg, Dept. of Psychology, University of Massachusetts, Boston, MA 02125-3393 (*htagerf%umbsky.dnet@ns.umb.edu*) (**with** Lowry Hemphill, Nancy Picardi) [**Type of impairment:** mildly mentally retarded (and nonretarded), autistic] [**Age range:** 10;11 (mean age, retarded), 7;8 (mean age, nonretarded)] (**Ref.:** Hemphill, Picardi, & Tager-Flusberg, 1991; Tager-Flusberg, 1993)

Robert D. Van Valin, Jr., Dept. of Linguistics, SUNY at Buffalo, Buffalo, NY 14260 (*linvan@ubvms.bitnet*); David P. Wilkins, Dept. of Linguistics, SUNY at Buffalo, Buffalo, NY 14260 (*lindavid@ubvms.bitnet*); Nina Dronkers, University of California at Davis and VA Medical Center, Martinez, CA (*dronkers@garnet.berkeley.edu*); Jeri Jaeger, Dept. of Psychology, SUNY at Buffalo, Buffalo, NY 14260 (*linjeri@ubvms.bitnet*) [**Type of impairment:** aphasia] [**Age range:** adult]

Dutch

Claudia Blankenstijn, Annette Scheper: Department of General Linguistics, University of Amsterdam, Spuistraat 210, 1012 VT Amsterdam, Netherlands (**with** Anne Mills, *aemills@alf.let.uva.nl*) [**Age range:** 4-9] [**Type of impairment:** psychiatric disturbance]

French

Michèle Kail (see above under **French**) [**Type of impairment:** mentally retarded (and non-retarded)] [**Age range:** 17 (retarded), 9 (non-retarded)]

Hebrew

Rachel Schiff, Dept of Education, Bar-Ilan University, Ramat Gan, Israel. [**Type of impairment:** reading disability (proficient and nonproficient readers)] [**Age range:** 10-13 (oral and written stories)] (**Ref.:** Schiff, 1991)

Italian

Piero Bottari, Anna Maria Chilosi, Paola Cipriani, Elisabetta Lanzetta, Lucia Pfanner (*see above, under* **Italian**) [**Type of impairment:** Down Syndrome, Williams Syndrome, SLI, dysphasic] [**Age range:** 4-16]

Turkish

Dan I. Slobin (**with** Dr. Öget Öktem-Tanör, Dept. of Neurology, Çapa Medical School, Istanbul University, Istanbul, Turkey) [**Type of impairment:** aphasia] [**Age range:** adult]

REFERENCES

Abbeduto, L., & Rosenberg, S. (1985). Children's knowledge of the presuppositions of *know* and other cognitive verbs. *Journal of Child Language, 12*, 621-641.

Aksu, A. A. (1978). The acquisition of causal connectives in Turkish. *Papers and Reports on Child Language Development, 15*, 129-139.

Aksu-Koç, A. A. (1988a). Simultaneity in children's narratives: The development of cohesion in discourse. In S. Koç, (Ed.) *Studies on Turkish linguistics* (pp. 55-78). Ankara: Middle East Technical University Press.

Aksu-Koç, A. A. (1988b). *The acquisition of aspect and modality: The case of past reference in Turkish.* Cambridge: Cambridge University Press.

Aksu-Koç, A. A. (1991). *A developmental analysis of temporality in narratives.* Unpublished manuscript, University of Istanbul.

Aksu-Koç, A. A. (1992a). *Eğitim düzeyi ve cinsiyetin anlatı yapısına etkisi* [The effect of level of education and gender on narrative structure]. Paper presented at the 7th National Congress of Psychology, Hacettepe University, Ankara.

Aksu-Koç, A. A. (1992b). *The development of complement constructions.* Paper presented at the 6th International Conference on Turkish Linguistics, Anadolu University, Eskişehir, Turkey.

Aksu-Koç, A. A. (1993). Anlatı yapısının kavramsal ve dilsel gelişimi [Conceptual and linguistic development of episodic structure]. *Dilbilim araştırmaları* (pp. 51-60). Ankara: Hitit Yayınevi.

Aksu-Koç, A. A. (in preparation). *The interaction of tense, aspect and modality in Turkish.* (Paper originally presented at conference on "Tense-aspect," Cortona, Italy, Oct. 10-13, 1993).

Aksu-Koç, A. A., & Slobin, D. I. (1985). The acquisition of Turkish. In D. I. Slobin (Ed.), *The crosslinguistic study of language acquisition: Vol. 1. The data* (pp. 839-878). Hillsdale, NJ: Lawrence Erlbaum Associates.

Amidon, A., & Carey, P. (1972). Why five year olds cannot understand "before" and "after." *Journal of Verbal Learning and Verbal Behavior, 11*, 417-423.

Ammon, M., & Slobin, D. I. (1979). A cross-linguistic study of the processing of causative sentences. *Cognition, 7*, 3-17.

Anderson, L. B. (1982). The "perfect" as a universal and as a language-specific category. In P. J. Hopper (Ed.), *Tense-aspect: Between semantics and pragmatics* (pp. 227-264). Amsterdam: John Benjamins.

Anderson, L. B. (1986). Evidentials, paths of change, and mental maps: Typologically regular asymmetries. In W. Chafe & J. Nichols (Eds.), *Evidentiality: The linguistic coding of epistemology.* Norwood, NJ: Ablex.

Antinucci, F., & Miller, R. (1976). How children talk about what happened. *Journal of Child Language, 3,* 169-189.

Applebee, A. N. (1978). *The child's concept of a story.* Chicago: University of Chicago Press.

Aske, J. (1989). Path predicates in English and Spanish: A closer look. *Proceedings of the Annual Meeting of the Berkeley Linguistics Society, 15,* 1-14.

Astington, J. W. (1990). Narrative and the child's theory of mind. In B. K. Britton & A. D. Pellegrini (Eds.), *Narrative thought and narrative language* (pp. 151-171). Hillsdale, NJ: Lawrence Erlbaum Associates.

Astington, J., & Gopnik, A. (1991). Theoretical explanations of children's understanding of the mind. *British Journal of Developmental Psychology, 9,* 7-31.

Bäuerle, R. (1979). *Temporale Deixis, Temporale Frage* [Temporal deixis, temporal question]. Tübingen: Gunter Narr Verlag.

Bamberg, M. (1985). *Form and function in the construction of narratives: Developmental perspectives.* Unpublished doctoral dissertation, University of California, Berkeley.

Bamberg, M. (1986). A functional approach to the acquisition of anaphoric relationships. *Linguistics, 24,* 227-284.

Bamberg, M. (1987). *The acquisition of narratives: Learning to use language.* Berlin: Mouton de Gruyter.

Bamberg, M. (1990). The German perfekt: Form and function of tense alternations. *Studies in Language, 14,* 253-290.

Bamberg, M. (1991a). Conceptualization via narrative: A discussion of Donald E. Polkinghorne's "Narrative and Self- Concept." *Journal of Narrative and Life History, 1,* 155-167.

Bamberg, M. (1991b). Narrative activity as perspective taking: The role of emotionals, negations, and voice in the construction of the story realm. *Journal of Cognitive Psychotherapy, 5,* 275-290.

Bamberg, M. (1992). Binding and unfolding: Establishing viewpoint in oral and written discourse. In M. Kohrt & A. Wrobel (Eds.), *Schreibprozesse - Schreibprodukte: Festschrift für Gisbert Keseling* (pp. 1-24). Hildesheim, Germany: Solms.

Bamberg, M. (1993a). Actions, events, scenes, plots and the drama: Language and the constitution of part-whole relationships. *Language Sciences, 15.*

Bamberg, M. (1993b). Communication and internal states: What is their relationship? *Behavioral and Brain Sciences, 16.*

Bamberg, M., Budwig, N., & Kaplan, B. (1991). A developmental approach to language acquisition. *First Language, 11,* 121-141.

Bamberg, M., & Damrad-Frye, R. (1991). On the ability to provide evaluative comments: Further explorations of children's narrative competencies. *Journal of Child Language, 18,* 689-710.

Bamberg, M., & Marchman, V. (1990). What holds a narrative together? The linguistic encoding of episode boundaries. *Papers in Pragmatics, 4,* 58-121.

Bamberg, M., & Marchman, V. (1991). Binding and unfolding: Towards the linguistic construction of narrative discourse. *Discourse Processes, 14,* 277-305.

Banguoğlu, T. (1974). *Türkçenin grameri* [Grammar of Turkish]. Istanbul: Baha Matbaası.

Bar-Lev, Z. (1986). Discourse theory and "contrastive rhetoric." *Discourse Processes, 9,* 235-246.

Barrie-Blackley, S. (1973). Six-year-old children's understanding of sentences adjoined with time adverbs. *Journal of Psycholinguistic Research, 2,* 153-165.

Bates, E., & Devescovi, A. (1989). Crosslinguistic studies of sentence production. In E. Bates & B. MacWhinney (Eds.), *Crosslinguistic studies of sentence processing* (pp. 225-253). Cambridge: Cambridge University Press.

Bauman, R. (1986). *Story performance and event: Contextual studies of oral narrative.* Cambridge: Cambridge University Press.

Bavin, E. (1987). Anaphora in children's Warlpiri. *Australian Review of Applied Linguistics, 10,* 1-111.

Behrens, H. (1993). *Temporal reference in German child language: Form and function of early verb use.* Zutphen, Netherlands: Koninglijke Wöhrmann b.v. (Doctoral dissertation, University of Amsterdam)

Berman, R. A. (1978). *Modern Hebrew structure.* Tel Aviv: Universities Publishing.

Berman, R. A. (1979a). Form and function: Passives, middles, and impersonals in Modern Hebrew. *Proceedings of the Annual Meeting of the Berkeley Linguistics Society, 5,* 1-27.

Berman, R. A. (1979b, August). *Repetition as a property of Hebrew usage.* Paper presented at the Twelfth Annual Conference of the European Linguistics Society, Hebrew University, Jerusalem.

Berman, R. A. (1980). The case of an (S)VO language: Subjectless constructions in Modern Hebrew. *Language, 56,* 759-776.

Berman, R. (1981). Dative marking of the affectee role. *Hebrew Annual Review, 6,* 35-59.

Berman, R. (1984, December). *Immature and adult perceptions of even-sequences in story-telling.* Paper presented at Cognitive Aspects of Discourse Conference, Tel-Aviv.

Berman, R. A. (1985). The acquisition of Hebrew. In D. I. Slobin (Ed.), *The crosslinguistic study of language acquisition: Vol. 1. The data* (pp. 255-371). Hillsdale, NJ: Lawrence Erlbaum Associates.

Berman, R. A. (1986a). A crosslinguistic perspective: Morphology/syntax. In P. Fletcher & M. Garman (Eds.), *Language acquisition* (2nd ed., pp. 429-447). Cambridge: Cambridge University Press.

Berman, R. A. (1986b). *Expression of simultaneity in Hebrew narratives.* Workshop notes, University of California, Berkeley.

Berman, R. A. (1986c). A step-by-step model of language acquisition. In I. Levin (Ed.), *Stage and structure: Reopening the debate* (pp. 191-219). Norwood, NJ: Ablex.

Berman, R. A. (1987a). A developmental route: Learning the form and function of complex nominals. *Linguistics, 25,* 1057-1085.

Berman, R. A. (1987b). Al ha-be'atiyut be-xeqer ha-ivrit ha-xadasha [Issues and problems in Modern Hebrew research]. *Praqim, 7,* 84-96.

Berman, R. A. (1988). On the ability to relate events in narrative. *Discourse Processes, 11,* 469-497.

Berman, R. A. (1990). Acquiring an (S)VO language: Subjectless sentences in children's Hebrew. *Linguistics, 28,* 1135-1166.

Berman, R. A. (1993). The development of language use: Expressing perspectives on a scene (pp. 172-201). In E. Dromi (Ed.), *Language and cognition: A developmental perspective.* Norwood, NJ: Ablex.

Berman, R. A. (in press-a). Crosslinguistic perspectives on native language acquisition. In K. Hyltenstam & A. Viberg (Eds.), *Progression and regression in language.* Cambridge: Cambridge University Press.

Berman, R. A. (in press-b). Developmental perspectives on transitivity: A confluence of cues. In Y. Levy (Ed.), *Other children, other languages: Issues in the theory of language acquisition.* Hillsdale, NJ: Lawrence

Erlbaum Associates.

Berman, R. A. (in press-c). Form and function in developing narrative abilities. In D. I. Slobin, J. Gerhardt, A. Kyratzis, & J. Guo (Eds.), *Social interaction, social context, and language: Essays in honor of Susan Ervin-Tripp*. Hillsdale, NJ: Lawrence Erlbaum Associates.

Berman, R. A. (in press-d). Marking of transitivity by Hebrew-speaking children. *Journal of Child Language*.

Berman, R. A. (in press-e). Modern Hebrew. In R. Hetzron (Ed.), *The Semitic languages*. London: Routledge.

Berman, R. A., & Dromi, E. (1984). On marking time without aspect in child language. *Papers and Reports on Child Language Development, 23*, 23-32.

Berman, R. A., & Slobin, D. I. (1987). *Five ways of learning how to talk about events: A crosslinguistic study of children's narratives* (Berkeley Cognitive Science Report No. 46). Institute of Cognitive Studies, University of California, Berkeley.

Berman, R. A., Slobin, D. I., Bamberg M., Dromi, E., Marchman, V., Neeman, Y., Renner, T., & Sebastián, E. (1986). *Coding manual: Temporality in discourse (rev. ed.)*. Institute of Cognitive Studies, University of California, Berkeley.

Berman, R. A., & Weissenborn, J. (1991, May). *Early grammatical development: A crosslinguistic study*. Final report submitted to the German-Israel Foundation for Research and Development (G.I.F.), Jerusalem.

Bloom, L. (1973). *One word at a time*. The Hague: Mouton.

Bloom, L., Lifter, K., & Hafitz, J. (1980). Semantics of verbs and the development of verb inflections in child language. *Language, 56*, 386-412.

Boas, F. (1911). Introduction to *Handbook of American Indian Languages*. Bulletin 40, Part I, Bureau of American Ethnology. Washington, D. C.: Government Printing Office. [Reprinted in P. Holder (Ed.), (1966). F. Boas *Introduction to Handbook of American Indian Languages* / J. W. Powell, *Indian linguistic families of America North of Mexico*. Lincoln: University of Nebraska Press.]

Bocaz, A. (1989a). Desarrollo de la referencia temporal adverbial [Development of adverbial temporal reference]. *Lenguas Modernas* (Santiago, Chile), *16*, 23-39.

Bocaz, A. (1989b). Estudio evolutivo de la marcación aspectual de los sucesos en la producción de discurso narrativo [Developmental study of aspectual marking of events in the production of narrative discourse]. In

Actas del III Congreso Internacional sobre el Español de América (pp. 1311-1320). Salamanca, Spain: Gráficas Varona.

Bocaz, A. (1989c). Los marcadores de expresión de la simultaneidad en el desarrollo de estructuras sintácticas y textuales complejas [Markers of the expression of simultaneity in the development of syntactic structures and textual complexes]. *Revista de Lingüística Teórica y Aplicada* (Concepción, Chile), *27*, 5-22.

Bocaz, A. (1991a). Desarrollo de construcciones sintácticas temporales y sus funciones en el discurso narrativo [Development of temporal syntactic structures and their functions in narrative discourse]. In *Actas del Primer Simposio sobre Cognición, Lenguaje y Cultura: Diálogo Transdisciplinario en Ciencia Cognitivas* (pp. 169-176). Santiago, Chile: Editorial Universitaria.

Bocaz, A. (1991b, September). *El caso de 'estar subido': ¿Una antesala en el desarrollo del perfecto?* [The case of *estar subido* ('to be ascended'): A waiting room in the development of the perfect?]. Paper presented at the IX Seminario Nacional de Investigación y Enseñanza de la Lingüística, Universidad de Concepción, Chile.

Bocaz, A. (1991c). Esquematización espacial y temporal de escenas narrativas y su proyección lingüística en el español [Spatial and temporal schematization of narrative scenes and their linguistic projection in Spanish]. *Lenguas Modernas* (Santiago, Chile), *18*, 47-62.

Bocaz, A. (1991d). Marcación de la organización secuencial de los sucesos en la producción de discurso narrativo [Marking of sequential organization of events in the production of narrative discourse]. In *Actas del VIII Seminario Nacional de Investigación y Enseñanza de la Lingüística* (pp. 249-255). Santiago, Chile: Universidad de Santiago de Chile.

Bocaz, A. (1992a, December). *Funciones de las claúsulas relativas en la producción de relatos en dos variedades del español de América* [Functions of relative clauses in the production of stories in two varieties of American Spanish]. Paper presented at the IV Congreso Internacional sobre el Español en América, Pontificia Universidad Católica de Chile.

Bocaz, A. (1992b). Procesos inferenciales abductivos en la interpretación de escenas narrativas complejas [Abductive inferential processes in the interpretation of complex narrative scenes]. *Lenguas Modernas* (Santiago, Chile), *19*, 99-106.

Boeschoten, H. E. (1990). *Acquisition of Turkish by immigrant children.* Wiesbaden: Otto Harrassowitz.

Borer, H. (1984). *Parametric syntax: Case studies in Semitic and Romance languages*. Dordrecht: Foris Publications.

Borer, H., & Grodzinksy, Y. (1986). Lexical cliticization vs. syntactic cliticization: The case of Hebrew dative clitics. In H. Borer (Ed.), *Syntax and semantics: Vol. 19*. New York: Academic Press.

Bornens, M.-T. (1990). Problems brought about by "reading" a sequence of pictures. *Journal of Experimental Child Psychology, 49*, 189-226.

Bowerman, M. (1974). Learning the structure of causative verbs: A study in the relationship of cognitive, semantic, and syntactic development. *Papers and Reports on Child Language Development, 8*, 142-178.

Bowerman, M. (1977). The acquisition of rules governing "possible lexical items": Evidence from spontaneous speech errors. *Papers and Reports on Child Language Development, 13*, 148-156.

Bowerman, M (1982a). Evaluating competing linguistic models with language acquisition data: Implications of developmental errors with causative verbs. *Quaderni di Semantica, 3*, 5-66.

Bowerman, M. (1982b). Reorganizational processes in lexical and syntactic development. In E. Wanner & L. R. Gleitman (Eds.), *Language acquisition: The state of the art* (pp. 319-346). Cambridge: Cambridge University Press.

Bowerman, M. (1984, July). *Event segmentation*. Paper presented to Workshop on Temporality, Max-Planck-Institute for Psycholinguistics, Nijmegen, Netherlands.

Bowerman, M. (1985). What shapes children's grammars? In D. I. Slobin (Ed.), *The crosslinguistic study of language acquisition: Vol. 2. The data* (pp. 1257-1320).

Bowerman, M. (1990, March). *When a patient is the subject: Sorting out passives, anticausatives, and middles in the acquisition of English*. Paper presented at the symposium on Voice, University of California, Santa Barbara.

Braine, M. D. S. (1976). Children's first word combinations. *Monographs of the Society for Research in Child Development, 41*(1, Serial No. 164).

Brinton, E. J. (1988). *The development of English aspectual systems: Aspectualizations and post-verb particles*. Cambridge: Cambridge University Press.

Brislin, R. W. (Ed.). (1976). *Translation: Applications and research*. New York: Gardner Press.

Bronckart, J.-P., & Sinclair, H. (1973). Time, tense, and aspect. *Cognition, 2*, 107-130.

Brown, R. (1970). *Psycholinguistics*. New York: Free Press.

Brown, R. (1973). *A first language: The early stages*. Cambridge, MA: Harvard University Press.

Brown, R. L., Jr. (1976). *Language acts in context: An intentional theory of discourse*. Unpublished doctoral dissertation, University of Michigan, Ann Arbor.

Brown, G., & Yule, G. (1983). *Discourse analysis*. Cambridge: Cambridge University Press.

Bruner, J. (1986). *Actual minds, possible worlds*. Cambridge, MA: Harvard University Press.

Budwig, N. (1989). The linguistic marking of agentivity and control in child language. *Journal of Child Language, 16*, 263-284.

Budwig, N. (1990). The linguistic marking of non-prototypical agency: An exploration into children's use of passives. *Linguistics, 28*, 1221-1252.

Budwig, N. (Ed.). (1991). *Functional approaches to child language*. Special issue of *First Language, 11*.

Burke, K. (1968). *Counter-statement* (2nd ed.). Berkeley: University of California Press.

Burke, K. (1969). *A grammar of motives*. Berkeley: University of California Press.

Bybee, J., & Slobin, D. I. (1982). Rules and schemes in the development and use of the English past tense. *Language, 58*, 265-289.

Casparis, C. P. (1975). *Tense without time: The present tense in narration*. Bern: Francke Verlag.

Cassell, J. (1991). *The development of time and event in narrative: Evidence from speech and gesture*. Unpublished doctoral dissertation, University of Chicago.

Cassell, J., & McNeill, D. (1990). Gesture and ground. *Proceedings of the Annual Meeting of the Berkeley Linguistics Society, 16*, 57-68.

Catford, J. C. (1965). *A linguistic theory of translation: An essay in applied linguistics*. London: Oxford University Press.

Chafe, W. L. (1976). Givenness, contrastiveness, definiteness, subjects, topics, and point of view. In C. N. Li (Ed.), *Subject and topic* (pp. 25-55). New York: Academic Press.

Chafe, W. L. (Ed.). (1980). *The pear stories: Cognitive, cultural, and linguistic aspects of narrative production.* Norwood, NJ: Ablex.

Chafe, W. (1987). Cognitive constraints on information flow. In R. S. Tomlin (Ed.), *Coherence and grounding in discourse* (pp. 21-52). Amsterdam: John Benjamins.

Chatman, S. (1978). *Story and discourse: Narrative structure in fiction and film.* Ithaca: Cornell University Press.

Chi, M. (1978). Knowledge structures and memory development. In R. S. Siegler (Ed.), *Children's thinking: What develops?* (pp. 73-96). Hillsdale, NJ: Lawrence Erlbaum Associates.

Choi, S., & Bowerman, S. (1991). Learning to express motion events in English and Korean: The influence of language-specific lexicalization patterns. *Cognition, 41,* 83-121.

Chung, S., & Timberlake, A. (1985). Tense, aspect, and mood. In T. Shopen (Ed.), *Language typology and syntactic description, Vol. 3. Grammatical categories and the lexicon* (pp. 202-258). Cambridge: Cambridge University Press.

Chvany, C. V. (1984). Backgrounded perfectives and plot-line imperfectives: Towards a theory of grounding in text. In M. S. Flier & A. Timberlake (Eds.), *The scope of Slavic aspect* (pp. 247-273). Columbus, OH: Slavica Publishers.

Clahsen, H. (1988). *Normale und gestörte Kindersprache* [Normal and impaired child language]. Amsterdam/Philadelphia: Benjamins.

Clancy, P. M., Jacobsen, T., & Silva, M. (1976). The acquisition of conjunction: A cross-linguistic study. *Papers and Reports on Child Language Development, 12,* 71-80.

Clark, E. V. (1970). How young children describe events in time. In G. B. Flores d'Arcais & W. J. M. Levelt (Eds.), *Advances in psycholinguistics* (pp. 275-284). Amsterdam: North-Holland.

Clark, E. V. (1971). On the acquisition of the meaning of "before" and "after." *Journal of Verbal Learning and Verbal Behavior, 10,* 266-275.

Clark, E. V. (1978). Discovering what words can do. In D. Farkas, W. M. Jacobsen, & K. W. Todrys (Eds.), *Papers from the Parasession on the Lexicon* (pp. 34-57). Chicago: Chicago Linguistic Society.

Clark, E. V. (1985). The acquisition of Romance with special reference to French. In D. I. Slobin (Ed.), *The crosslinguistic study of language acquisition: Vol. 1. The data* (pp. 687-782). Hillsdale, NJ: Lawrence Erlbaum Associates.

Clark, E. V. (in press). *The lexicon in acquisition.* Cambridge: Cambridge University Press.

Clark, E. V., & Carpenter, K. L. (1989). On children's use of *from, by* and *with* in oblique noun phrases. *Journal of Child Language, 16,* 349-364.

Clark, E. V., & Carpenter, K. L. (1991). The notion of source in language acquisition. *Language, 65,* 1-32.

Clark, H. H. (1992). *Arenas of language use.* Chicago: University of Chicago Press & Center for the Study of Language and Information.

Comrie, B. (1976). *Aspect: An introduction to the study of verbal aspect and related problems.* Cambridge: Cambridge University Press.

Comrie, B. (1981). *Language universals and linguistic typology.* Chicago: University of Chicago Press.

Comrie, B. (1985). *Tense.* Cambridge: Cambridge University Press.

Comrie, B. (1986). Tense in indirect speech. *Folia Linguistica, 20,* 265-296.

Contreras, H. (1978). *El orden de las palabras en español* [Word order in Spanish]. Madrid: Cátedra.

Coste, D. (1989). *Narrative as communication.* Minneapolis: University of Minnesota Press.

Coseriu, E. (1976). *Das romanische Verbalsystem* [The Romance verb system]. Tübingen: TBL Verlag Gunter Narr.

Croft, W. (1990). A conceptual framework for grammatical categories. *Journal of Semantics, 7,* 245-279.

Croft, W. (1993). Voice and the conceptual autonomy of events. In B. Fox & P. J. Hopper (Eds.), *Voice: Form and function.* Amsterdam: John Benjamins.

Cromer, R. F. (1968). *The development of temporal reference during the acquisition of language.* Unpublished doctoral dissertation, Harvard University.

Cromer, R. F. (1971). The development of the ability to decenter in time. *British Journal of Psychology, 62,* 353-365.

Cromer, R. F. (1974). The development of language and cognition: The cognition hypothesis. In B. Foss (Ed.), *New perspectives in child development.* Harmondsworth, England: Penguin Books.

Dahl, O. (1985). *Tense and aspect systems.* Oxford: Basil Blackwell.

Dasinger, L. K. (1990). *Towards a functional approach to the acquisition of language: The crosslinguistic development of the functions of relative clauses in narrative.* Unpublished second-year paper, Department of

Psychology, University of California, Berkeley.

de Beaugrande, R. (1980a). Text and discourse in European research. *Discourse Processes, 3*, 287-300.

de Beaugrande, R. (1980b). *Text, discourse, and process: Toward a multidisciplinary science of texts.* Norwood, NJ: Ablex.

Declerck, R. (1990). Sequence of tenses in English. *Folia Linguistica, 24*, 513-544.

Declerck, R. (1991). *Tense in English: Its structure and use in discourse.* London/New York: Routledge.

De Lemos, C. (1981). Interactional processes in the child's construction of language. In W. Deutsch (Ed.), *The child's construction of language.* London: Academic Press.

de León, L. (1992). *Observations on the use of directionals by Tzotzil children in the frog stories.* Unpublished draft manuscript, Cognitive Anthropology Research Group, Max-Planck-Institute for Psycholinguistics, Nijmegen.

DeLoache, J. S., Cassidy, D. J., & Carpenter, C. J. (1987). The three bears are all boys: Mothers' gender labeling of neutral picture book characters. *Sex Roles, 17*, 163-178.

Demonte, V. (1991). *Detrás de la palabra: Estudios de gramática del español* [Behind the word: Studies of Spanish grammar]. Madrid: Alianza Editorial.

Demuth, K. (1989). Maturation and the acquisition of the Sesotho passive. *Language, 65*, 56-80.

de Villiers, J., & de Villiers, P. (1985). The acquisition of English. In D. I. Slobin (Ed.), *The crosslinguistic study of language acquisition: Vol. 1. The data* (pp. 27-139). Hillsdale, NJ: Lawrence Erlbaum Associates.

Dijkhuis, K. (in preparation). *Coherentie in vertellingen en taalvaardigheid: Een onderzoek met psychisch gestoorde kinderen* [Coherence in narratives and linguistic capacity: An investigation of mentally disturbed children]. Unpublished master's thesis, General Linguistics, University of Amsterdam.

Dilaçar, A. (1974). Türk fiilinde "kılınış"la "görünuş" ve dilbilgisi kitaplarımız [Aktionsart and aspect in the Turkish verb and our grammar books]. *Türk dili araştırmaları yıllığı* (pp. 159-171).

Dowty, D. (1979). *Word meaning and Montague grammar.* Dordrecht: Reidel.

Dromi, E., & Berman, R. A. (1986). Language-general and language-specific in developing syntax. *Journal of Child Language, 14,* 371-387.

Durova, N. V. & Yurieva, N. M. (1993). *Sostavlenie rasskaza po serii illjustracij det'mi doškol'nikami* [Production of a story according to a series of illustrations by preschoolers]. Unpublished paper, Institute of Linguistics, Russian Academy of Sciences, Moscow.

Ehrich, V. (1992). *Hier und jetzt: Studien zur lokalen und temporalen Deixis im Deutschen* [Here and now: Studies of local and temporal deixis in German].

Eisenberg, P. (1986). *Grundriß der deutschen Grammatik* [Outline of German grammar]. Stuttgart: Metzlersche Verlagsbuchhandlung.

Ekmekçi, O. (1986a). The developmental errors in the pre-school Turkish children's speech. In A. Aksu-Koç & E. Erguvanlı-Taylan (Eds.), *Proceedings of the Turkish Linguistics Conference* (pp. 249-268). Istanbul: Boğaziçi University Press.

Ekmekçi, F. O. (1986b). The significance of word order in the acquisition of Turkish. In D. I. Slobin & K. Zimmer (Eds.), *Studies in Turkish linguistics* (pp. 265-272). Amsterdam: John Benjamins.

Erguvanlı, E. E. (1984). *The function of word order in Turkish grammar.* Berkeley: University of California Press.

Erguvanlı-Taylan, E. (1987). Tense variation in Turkish narratives. In H. E. Boeschoten & L. T. Verhoeven (Eds.), *Studies on modern Turkish* (pp. 177-188). Tilburg, Netherlands: Tilburg University Press.

Erguvanlı-Taylan, E. (1988). The expression of temporal reference in embedded sentences in Turkish. In S. Koç (Ed.), *Studies on Turkish linguistics* (pp. 333-351). Ankara: Middle East Technical University Press.

Erguvanlı-Taylan, E. (1992, August). *On the parameter of aspect in Turkish.* Paper presented at the Sixth International Conference on Turkish Linguistics, Anadolu University, Eskişehir, Turkey.

Erguvanlı-Taylan, E. (1993). Türkçede -dık ekinin yan tümcelerdeki işlevi üzerine [On the function of the suffix -*dik* in subordinate clauses in Turkish]. *Dilbilim Araştırmaları* (pp. 161-171). Ankara: Hitit Yayınevi.

Erlich, V. (1965). *Russian formalism: History, doctrine* (2nd ed.). The Hague: Mouton.

Ervin-Tripp, S. (1989). *Speech acts and syntactic development: Linked or independent?* (Berkeley Cognitive Science Report No. 61), Institute of Cognitive Studies, University of California, Berkeley.

Fernández-Ramírez, S. (1986). *Gramática española: Vol. 4* [Spanish grammar]. Madrid: Arco/Libro, S.A.

Ferreiro, E., Othénin-Girard, C., Chipman, H., & Sinclair, H. (1976). How do children handle relative clauses? A study in comparative developmental psycholinguistics. *Archives de Psychologie, 44*, 229-266.

Ferreiro, E., & Sinclair, H. (1971). Temporal relationships in language. *International Journal of Psychology, 6*, 39-47.

Fillmore, C. (1987). *Relative clauses.* Unpublished manuscript, Linguistics Department, University of California, Berkeley.

Fine, J. (1985). Cohesion as an index of social cognitive factors: Oral language of the reading disabled. *Discourse Processes, 8*, 91-112.

Fine, J. (in press). *How language works: Cohesion in normal and nonstandard communication.* Norwood, NJ: Ablex.

Fivush, R., & Slackman, E. (1986). The acquisition and development of scripts. In K. Nelson (Ed.), *Event knowledge: Structure and function in development* (pp. 71-96). Hillsdale, NJ: Lawrence Erlbaum Associates.

Fleischman, S. (1990). *Tense and narrativity: From medieval performance to modern fiction.* Austin: University of Texas Press.

Fletcher, P. (1979). The development of the verb phrase. In P. Fletcher & M. Garman (Eds.), *Language acquisition: Studies in first language development* (pp. 261-284). Cambridge: Cambridge University Press.

Fletcher, P. (1981). Description and explanation in the acquisition of verb-forms. *Journal of Child Language, 8*, 93-108.

Flier, M. S., & Timberlake, A. H. (Eds.). (1985). *The scope of Slavic aspect.* Columbus, OH: Slavica.

Flores d'Arcais, G. B. (1978). The acquisition of the subordinating constructions in child language. In R. N. Campbell & P. T. Smith (Eds.), *Language development and mother-child interaction* (pp. 349-393). New York: Plenum Press.

Foley, W. A., & Van Valin, R. D., Jr. (1984). *Functional syntax and universal grammar.* Cambridge: Cambridge University Press.

Fox, B. (1987). The noun phrase accessibility hierarchy reinterpreted: Subject primacy or the absolutive hypothesis? *Language, 63*, 856-870.

Fox, B., & Thompson, S. (in press). Discourse and cognition: Relative clauses in English conversation. *Cognitive Linguistics.*

French, L. A. (1986). The language of events. In K. Nelson (Ed.), *Event knowledge: Structure and function in development* (pp. 119-135). Hillsdale, NJ: Lawrence Erlbaum Associates.

Fujii, S. Y. (1992). The use and learning of temporal clause-linkage in Japanese and English. In B. Kettermann & W. Wieden (Eds.), *L2 acquisition research in Europe: Selected papers from the 1991 European Second Language Association Conference*. Tübingen: Gunter Narr.

Fujii, S. Y. (1993). *The use and learning of clause-linkage: A case study of conditionals in Japanese and English*. Unpublished doctoral dissertation, University of California at Berkeley.

Galvan, D. B. (1988). *The acquisition of three morphological subsystems in American Sign Language by deaf children with deaf or hearing parents*. Unpublished doctoral dissertation, University of California, Berkeley.

Galvan, D. (1989). A sensitive period for the acquisition of complex morphology: Evidence from American Sign Language. *Papers and Reports on Child Language Development, 28*, 107-114.

García Soto, J. R. (1993). *Evolución da cohesión nos relatos infantís*. Unpublished doctoral dissertation, University of Santiago de Compostela, Spain.

Gardner, H. (1974). *The shattered mind*. New York: Random House.

Gathercole, V. C. (1986). The acquisition of the present perfect: Explaining differences in the speech of Scottish and American children. *Journal of Child Language, 13*, 537-560.

Gee, J. (née Gerhardt) (1985). An interpretive approach to the study of modality: What child language can tell the linguist. *Studies in Language, 9*, 197-229.

Gencan, N. T. (1975). *Dilbilgisi* [Linguistics]. Türk Dil Kurumu Yayınları. Istanbul: Murat Matbaası.

Gerhardt, J. (1988). From discourse to semantics: The development of verb morphology and forms of self-reference in the speech of a two-year-old. *Journal of Child Language, 15*, 337-393.

Gerhardt, J. (1990). The relation of language to context in children's speech: The role of HAFTA statements in structuring 3-year-olds' discourse. *Papers in Pragmatics, 4*, 1-57.

Gernsbacher, M. A. (1985). Surface information loss in comprehension. *Cognitive Psychology, 17*, 324-363.

Geva, E., & Olson, D. (1983). Children's story retelling. *First Language, 4*, 85-110.

Giora, R. (1981). Seder ha-milim be-mishpat ve-yaxaso la-tekst: nituax funkciyonalisti shel mishpatim memukadim [Word order in the sentence in relation to the text: A functionalist analysis of topicalized sentences].

In S. Blum-Kolka, Y. Tobin, & R. Nir (Eds.), *Iyunum be-nituax ha-siax* (pp. 263-302). Jerusalem: Akademon.

Giora, R. (1983). Segmentation and segment cohesion: On the thematic organization of the text. *Text, 3,* 155-182.

Giora, R. (1985a). What's a coherent text? In E. Sozer (Ed.), *Text connexity, text coherence: Aspects, methods, results* (pp. 16-35). Hamburg: Buske.

Giora, R. (1985b). Towards a theory of coherence. *Poetics Today, 6,* 699-716.

Giora, R. (1986). *On the organization of information in texts.* Unpublished doctoral dissertation, Tel-Aviv University.

Giora, R. (1990). On the so-called evaluative material in informative text. *Text, 10,* 299-320.

Giora, R., & Shen, Y. (in press). Degrees of narrativity and strategies of semantic reduction. *Cognitive Development.*

Givón, T. (1976). On the VS order in Israeli Hebrew: Pragmatics and typological change. In P. Cole (Ed.), *Studies in Modern Hebrew syntax and semantics* (pp. 153-182). Amsterdam: North-Holland.

Givón, T. (1977). The drift from VSO to SVO in Biblical Hebrew: The pragmatics of tense-aspect. In C. N. Li (Ed.), *Mechanisms of syntactic change.* Austin: University of Texas Press.

Givón, T. (1979). *On understanding grammar.* New York: Academic Press.

Givón, T. (1980). The binding hierarchy and the typology of complements. *Studies in Language, 4,* 333-377.

Givón, T. (1982). Tense - aspect - modality: The creole prototype and beyond. In P. Hopper (Ed.), *Tense-aspect* (pp. 115-163). New York: Plenum Press.

Givón, T. (1990). *Syntax: A functional typological introduction. Vol. 2.* Amsterdam: John Benjamins.

Givón, T., & Yang, L. (1993). The rise of th English GET-passive. In B. Fox & P. J. Hopper (Eds.), *Voice: Form and function.* Amsterdam: John Benjamins.

Goldsmith, J., & Woisetschlaeger, E. (1982). The logic of the English progressive. *Linguistic Inquiry, 13,* 79-89.

Gopnik, A. (1993). How we know our minds: The illusion of first-person knowledge of intentionality. *Behavioral and Brain Sciences, 16,* 1-14.

Green, J. N. (1990). Spanish. In B. Comrie (Ed.), *The world's major languages* (pp. 236-259). New York/Oxford: Oxford University Press.

Grice, H. P. (1975). Logic and conversation. In P. Cole & J. L. Morgan (Eds.), *Syntax and semantics, Vol. 3: Speech acts* (pp. 41-58). New York: Academic Press.

Grimes, J. E. (1978). *The thread of discourse*. The Hague: Mouton.

Grimshaw, J. (1987). Unaccusatives - an overview. In J. McDonough & B. Plunkett (Eds.), *NELS 17, Vol. 1* (pp. 244-258). (GLSA, Dept. of Linguistics, University of Massachusetts, Amherst)

Grundzüge einer deutschen Grammatik [Foundations of a German grammar]. (1981). (under editorial direction of K. E. Heidolph). Berlin: Akademie Verlag.

Gumperz, J. J. (1982). *Discourse strategies*. Cambridge: Cambridge University Press.

Gumperz, J. J., & Levinson, S. (in press). *Rethinking linguistic relativity*. Cambridge: Cambridge University Press.

Halliday, M., & Hasan, R. (1976). *Cohesion in English*. London: Longman.

Hammer, A. E. (1971). *German grammar and usage*. London: Edward Arnold.

Harkins, D. A. (1992). Parental goals and styles of storytelling. In J. Demick, K. Bursik, & R. Dibiase (Eds.), *Parental development* (pp. 61-74). Hillsdale, NJ: Lawrence Erlbaum Associates.

Hatav, G. (1985). Criteria for identifying the foreground. *Theoretical Linguistics, 12*, 265-273.

Hatav, G. (1989). Aspects, *Aktionsarten*, and the time line. *Linguistics, 27*, 487-516.

Hatcher, A. G. (1951). The use of the progressive form in English. *Language, 27*, 254-280.

Hausendorf, H., & Quastoff, U. M. (1992). Patterns of adult-child interaction as a mechanism of discourse acquisition. *Journal of Pragmatics, 17*, 241-259.

Hawkins, J. A. (1985). *A comparative typology of English and German: Unifying the contrasts*. Austin: University of Texas Press.

Hebert, J. (1990). *Language-specific differences in the encoding of events in narrative discourse*. Unpublished B. A. Honours Thesis, Department of Linguistics, La Trobe University, Melbourne, Victoria, Australia.

Hemphill, L., Picardi, N., & Tager-Flusberg, H. (1991). Narrative as an index of communicative competence in mildly mentally retarded children. *Applied Psycholinguistics, 12*, 263-279.

Hemphill, L., Wolf, D., Camp, L., & Griffin, T. (1993, March). *Narrative competence: Local patterns of usage.* Paper presented at the Biennial Meeting of the Society for Research in Child Development, New Orleans, LA.

Herring, S. C. (1985). *Marking and unmarking via the present tense in narration: The historical present redefined.* Unpublished manuscript, University of California, Berkeley.

Herring, S. (1990). Information structure as a consequence of word order type. *Proceedings of the Annual Meeting of the Berkeley Linguistics Society, 16*, 163-174.

Hickmann, M. (1980). Creating referents in discourse: A developmental analysis of linguistic cohesion. In J. Kreiman & E. Ojeda (Eds.), *Papers from the Parasession on Pronouns and Anaphora.* Chicago: Chicago Linguistic Society.

Hickmann, M. (1982). *The development of narrative skills: Pragmatic and metapragmatic aspects of discourse cohesion.* Unpublished doctoral dissertation, University of Chicago.

Hickmann, M. (1991). The development of discourse cohesion: Some functional and cross-linguistic issues. In G. Piéraut-Le-Bonniec & M. Dolitsky (Eds.), *Language bases...discourse bases: Some aspects of contemporary French-language psycholinguistics research* (pp. 157-185). Amsterdam: John Benjamins.

Hickmann, M., Kail, M., & Roland, F. (1989, July). *The referential organization of children's narrative discourse as a function of mutual knowledge.* Paper presented at the Tenth Biennial Meeting, International Society for the Study of Behavioural Development, Jyväskylä, Finland.

Hickmann, M., Kail, M., & Roland, F. (1993, July). *Cohesive anaphoric relations in French children's narratives as a function of mutual knowledge.* Paper presented at the Twelfth Biennial Meeting, International Society for the Study of Behavioural Development, Recife.

Hickmann, M., & Liang, J. (1990). Clause-structure variation in Chinese narrative discourse: A developmental analysis. *Linguistics, 28*, 1167-1200.

Hickmann, M., Liang, J. & van Crevel, M. (1989, July). *The given/new distinction in children's narratives: A cross-linguistic analysis.* Paper presented at the Tenth Biennial Meeting of the International Society for the Study of Behavioral Development, Jyväskylä, Finland.

Hickmann, M. & Roland, F. (1992, October). *Déterminants sémantiques et pragmatiques dans l'acquisition du temps et de l'aspect: étude comparative du français, de l'allemand et de l'anglais* [Semantic and pragmatic determinants in the acquisition of tense and aspect: a comparative study of French, German and English]. Unpublished manuscript, Réseau Européen de Laboratoires sur l'Acquisition des Langues. Lyon.

Hicks, D. (1986). *Children's encoding of simultaneous events in narrative discourse.* Unpublished manuscript, Harvard University.

Hicks, D. (1991). Kinds of narrative genre skills among first graders from two communities. In A. McCabe & C. Peterson (Eds.), *Developing narrative structure* (pp. 55-88). Hillsdale, NJ: Lawrence Erlbaum Associates.

Hinds, J., Maynard, S., & Iwasaki, S. (1987). *Perspectives on topicalization: The case of Japanese 'WA'.* Amsterdam: John Benjamins.

Hoiting, N., & Slobin, D. I. (1993, July). *Reference to movement in speech and sign.* Paper presented at the Sixth International Congress for the Study of Child Language, Trieste, Italy.

Hoppe-Graff, S., Schöler, H., & Schell, M. (1981). Kinder erzälen Geschichten: Eine entwicklungspsychologische Untersuchung an 4-8 järigen [Children tell stories: A developmental psychological investigation of children aged 4-8]. In R. Michaelis (Ed.), *Bericht über den 32. Kongress der deutschen Gesellschaft für Psychologie* (pp. 439-444). Göttingen: Hogrefe.

Hopper, P. J. (1979). Aspect and foregrounding in discourse. In T. Givón (Ed.), *Syntax and semantics: Vol. 12. Discourse and syntax* (pp. 213-242). New York: Academic Press.

Hopper, P. J. (1982). Aspect between discourse and grammar: An introductory essay for the volume. In P. Hopper (Ed.), *Tense-aspect* (pp. 3-17). Amsterdam: John Benjamins.

Horgan, D. (1978). The development of the full passive. *Journal of Child Language, 5,* 65-80.

Hough, R. A., Nurss, J. R., & Wood, D. (1987). Tell me a story: Making opportunities for elaborated language in early childhood classrooms. *Young Children, 43,* 6-12.

Howell, C. (1993). *Aspects of second language narratives.* Unpublished master's thesis, Department of Linguistics, La Trobe University, Melbourne, Victoria, Australia.

Hudson, J. A., & Nelson, K. (1986). Repeated encounters of a similar kind: Effects of familiarity on children's autobiographic memory. *Cognitive Development, 1,* 253-271.

Hyams, N. (1987). Parameter theory and syntactic development. In T. Roeper & E. Williams (Eds.), *Parameter setting* (p. 1-22). Dordrecht: Reidel.

Hyams, N. (1989). The null subject parameter in language acquisition. In O. Jaeggli & K. Safir (Eds.), *The null subject parameter* (pp. 215-238). Dordrecht: Kluwer.

Jacobsen, T. (1981). *Tense and aspect in Spanish acquisition: A study in early semantic development.* Unpublished manuscript, University of California, Berkeley.

Jaeggli, O. (1982). *Topics in Romance syntax.* Dordrecht: Foris Publications.

Jisa, H. (1987). Sentence connectors in French children's monologue performance. *Journal of Pragmatics, 11,* 607-621.

Jisa, H., & Kern, S. (1993). *La cognition, la langue elle aime ça: Développement cognitif et langagier chez l'enfant* [Cognition — language loves it: Cognitive and language development in the child]. Unpublished paper, Université Lumière, Lyon.

Johanson, L. (1971). *Aspekt im Türkischen: Vorstudien zu einer Beschreibung des türkeitürkischen Aspektsystems* [Aspect in Turkish: Preliminaries to a description of the Turkish aspectual system]. Uppsala: Acta Universitatis Upsaliensis, Studia Turcica Upsaliensia 1.

Johnson, C. J. (1985). The emergence of present perfect verb forms: Semantic influences on selective imitation. *Journal of Child Language, 12,* 325-352.

Johnson, N. S. (1983). What do you do if you can't tell the whole story? The development of summarization skills. In K. E. Nelson (Ed.), *Children's language: Vol. 4.* Hillsdale, NJ: Lawrence Erlbaum Associates.

Johnston, J. R., & Slobin, D. I. (1979). The development of locative expressions in English, Italian, Serbo-Croatian and Turkish. *Journal of Child Language, 6,* 529-545.

Joos, M. (1964). *The English verb: Form and meanings.* Madison: University of Wisconsin Press.

Kail, M., & Drissi, A. (1990). Acquisition des indices linguistiques et temporels du traitement: Recherches interlangues [Acquisition of linguistic and temporal indices of processing: Crosslinguistic investigation]. In Z. Zavialoff (Ed.), *La lecture: De la neurobiologie à la pédagogie. Vol. 1* (pp. 348-352). Paris: Editions L'Harmattan.

Kail, M., & Hickmann, M. (1992). French children's ability to introduce referents in narratives as a function of mutual knowledge. *First Language, 12,* 73-94.

Kamp, H., & Rohrer, C. (1982). Tense in texts. In R. Bäuerle, C. Schwarze, & A. von Stechow (Eds.), *Meaning, use, and interpretation of language* (pp. 250-269). Berlin: de Gruyter.

Kaplan, R. B. (1966). Cultural thought patterns in intercultural education. *Language Learning, 16,* 1-20.

Karmiloff-Smith, A. (1979). *A functional approach to child language: A study of determiners and reference.* Cambridge: Cambridge University Press.

Karmiloff-Smith, A. (1980). Psychological processes underlying pronominalization and non-pronominalization in children's connected discourse. In J. Kreiman & E. Ojeda (Eds.), *Papers from the Parasession on Pronouns and Anaphora.* Chicago: Chicago Linguistic Society.

Karmiloff-Smith, A. (1981). The grammatical marking of thematic structure in the development of language production. In W. Deutsch (Ed.), *The child's construction of language.* London: Academic Press.

Karmiloff-Smith, A. (1983). Language development as a problem-solving process. *Papers and Reports on Child Language Development, 22,* 1-23.

Karmiloff-Smith, A. (1984). Children's problem-solving. In M. Lamb, A. L. Brown, & B. Rogoff (Eds.), *Advances in cognitive psychology: Vol. 3.* Hillsdale, NJ: Lawrence Erlbaum Associates.

Karmiloff-Smith, A. (1985). Language and cognitive processes from a developmental perspective. *Language and Cognitive Processes, 1,* 61-85.

Karmiloff-Smith, A. (1986a). From meta-processes to conscious access: Evidence from children's metalinguistic and repair data. *Cognition, 23,* 95-147.

Karmiloff-Smith, A. (1986b). Stage/structure versus phase/process in modelling linguistic and cognitive development. In I. Levin (Ed.), *Stage and structure: Reopening the debate* (pp. 164-190). Norwood, NJ: Ablex.

Karmiloff-Smith, A. (1987). Function and process in comparing language and cognition. In M. Hickmann (Ed.), *Social and functional approaches to language and thought.* London: Academic Press.

Karmiloff-Smith, A. (1992). *Beyond modularity: A developmental perspective on cognitive science.* Cambridge, MA: MIT Press.

Katzenberger, I. (1992). *Ha-yaxas beyn ha-mucag be-sidrat tmunot le-veyn ha-sipur ha-mesupar al pihen: hebetim kognitiviyim u-leshoni'im shel ha-yexolet ha-narativit* [Use of pictures in mediating between cognitive and linguistic aspects of narrative abilities]. Unpublished manuscript, Tel Aviv University.

Keenan, E. L. (1985a). Passive in the world's languages. In T. Shopen (Ed.), *Language typology and syntactic description: Vol. 1. Clause structure* (pp. 243-282). Cambridge: Cambridge University Press.

Keenan, E. L. (1985b). Relative clauses. In T. Shopen (Ed.), *Language typology and syntactic description: Vol. 2. Complex constructions* (pp. 142-170). Cambridge: Cambridge University Press.

Kemper, S. (1984). The development of narrative skills: Explanations and entertainments. In S. A. Kuczaj (Ed.), *Discourse development* (pp. 99-124). New York: Springer-Verlag.

King, L. D. (1983). The semantics of tense, orientation, and aspect in English. *Lingua, 59*, 101-154.

Kintsch, W. (1977). On comprehending stories. In M. Just & P. Carpenter (Eds.), *Cognitive processes in comprehension* (pp. 33-62). Hillsdale, NJ: Lawrence Erlbaum Associates.

Klein, W. (1981). Knowing a language and knowing to communicate. In A. Vermeer (Ed.), *Language problems of minority groups* (pp. 75-95). Tilberg: Tilberg Studies on Language and Literature, 1.

Klein, W. (1992). The present perfect puzzle. *Language, 68*, 525-552.

Klein, W. (in press). *Time in language*. London: Routledge.

Kononov, A. N. (1956). *Grammatika sovremennogo tureckogo literaturnogo jazyka* [Grammar of the contemporary Turkish literary language]. Moscow/Leningrad: Izdatel'stvo Akademii Nauk SSSR.

Kozminsky, E. (1986). "Hayo hayta yalda xaviva...": havanat sipurim al ydey yeladim ["There was a little girl ..."]: Children's comprehension of stories]. *Iyunim BeChinuch, 45*, 83-104.

Kuczaj, S. A. (1978). Why do children fail to overgeneralize the progressive inflection? *Journal of Child Language, 5*, 167-171.

Küntay, A. (1992, August). *Developing referential cohesion in elicited Turkish narratives*. Paper presented at the Sixth International Conference on Turkish Linguistics, Anadolu University, Eskişehir, Turkey.

Küntay, A., & Nakamura, K. (1993, July). *Evaluative strategies in elicited Turkish and Japanese narratives*. Paper presented at the Sixth International Congress for the Study of Child Language, Trieste, Italy.

Kyratzis, A. (1991). Pragmatic determinants of subordination and coordination in children's causal constructions. *Papers and Reports on Child Language Development, 30*, 47-54.

Kyratzis, A. (1992, February). *Beyond semantic meaning: Expressive and textual meanings of causal and temporal connectives*. Paper presented at the Fourteenth Annual Meeting of the American Association for Applied Linguistics, Seattle.

Kyratzis, A. (1993). *Discourse markers and discourse structure.* Unpublished paper, Department of Psychology, University of California, Berkeley.

Kyratzis, A., Guo, J., & Ervin-Tripp, S. (1990). Pragmatic conventions influencing children's use of causal constructions in natural discourse. *Proceedings of the Annual Meeting of the Berkeley Linguistics Society, 16,* 205-214.

Labov, W. (1972). *Language in the inner city: Studies in the Black English vernacular.* Philadelphia: University of Pennsylvania Press.

Labov, W. (1984). Intensity. In D. Schiffrin (Ed.), *Meaning, form, and use in context: Linguistic applications (Georgetown University Round Table on Language and Linguistics).* Washington, DC: Georgetown University Press.

Labov, W., & Waletzky, J. (1967). Narrative analysis: Oral versions of personal experience. In J. Helms (Ed.), *Essays on the verbal and visual arts* (pp. 12-44). Seattle: University of Washington Press.

Lambrecht, K. (1987). Sentence focus, information structure, and the synthetic-categorical distinction. *Proceedings of the Annual Meeting of the Berkeley Linguistics Society, 13,* 366-382.

Lambrecht, K. (1988). There was a farmer had a dog: Syntactic amalgams revisited. *Proceedings of the Annual Meeting of the Berkeley Linguistics Society, 14,* 319-339.

Langacker, R. (1985). Observations and speculations on subjectivity. In J. Haiman (Ed.), *Iconicity in syntax* (pp. 109-150). Amsterdam: John Benjamins.

Langacker, R. (1987a). Nouns and verbs. *Language, 63,* 53-94.

Langacker, R. (1987b). *Transitivity, case, and grammatical relations: A cognitive grammar prospectus.* Reproduced by Linguistic Agency University of Duisburg, Series A., Paper No. 172.

Langacker, R. (1987c). *Foundations of cognitive grammar: Vol. 1. Theoretical prerequisites.* Stanford, CA: Stanford University Press.

Langacker, R. (1990). *Concept, image, and symbol: The cognitive basis of grammar.* Berlin/New York: Mouton de Gruyter.

Langleben, M. (1981). Latent coherence, contextual meaning, and the interpretation of a text. *Text, 1,* 279-313.

Lehmann, C. (1988). Towards a typology of clause linkage. In J. Haiman & S. A. Thompson (Eds.), *Clause combining in grammar and discourse* (pp. 181-225). Amsterdam: John Benjamins.

Levelt. W. J. M. (1989). *Speaking: From intention to articulation.* Cambridge, MA: MIT Press.

Levin, B. (1989). *Towards a lexical organization of English verbs.* Evanston, IL: Northwestern University.

Levin, B., & Rappaport, M. (1990). The lexical semantics of verbs of motion: The perspective from unaccusativity. In I. Roca (Ed.), *Thematic structure: Its role in grammar* (pp. 247-269). Berlin: Walter de Gruyter.

Lewis, G. L. (1967). *Turkish grammar.* Oxford: Oxford University Press.

Li, C. N., & Thompson, S. A. (1976). Subject and topic: A new typology of language. In C. N. Li (Ed.), *Subject and topic.* New York: Academic Press.

Li, C. N., & Thompson, S. A. (1981). *Mandarin Chinese: A functional reference grammar.* Berkeley: University of California Press.

Löbner, S. (1989). German 'schon' - 'erst' - 'noch': An integrated analysis. *Linguistics and Philosophy, 12,* 167-212.

Longacre, R. (1981). A spectrum profile approach to discourse analysis. *Text, 1,* 337-359.

Lucy, J. A. (1992). *Language diversity and thought: A reformulation of the linguistic relativity hypothesis.* Cambridge: Cambridge University Press.

Lyons, J. (1968). *Introduction to theoretical linguistics.* Cambridge: Cambridge University Press.

Lyons, J. (1977). *Semantics: Vol. 2.* Cambridge: Cambridge University Press.

Mackie, J. L. (1980). *The cement of the universe: A study of causation.* Oxford: Clarendon Press.

MacWhinney, B., & Bates, E. (1989). *Cross-linguistic studies of sentence processing.* Cambridge: Cambridge University Press.

MacWhinney, B. (1991). *The CHILDES project: Tools for analyzing talk.* Hillsdale, NJ: Lawrence Erlbaum Associates.

Mandler, J. M. (1982). Some uses and abuses of story grammar. *Discourse Processes, 5,* 305-318.

Mandler, J. M., & DeForest, M. (1979). Is there more than one way to recall a story? *Child Development, 50,* 886-889.

Mandler, J. M., & Johnson, N. S. (1977). Remembrance of things passed: Story structure and recall. *Cognitive Psychology, 9,* 111-151.

Mann, W., & Thompson, S. (1986). Relational propositions in discourse. *Discourse Processes, 9,* 57-90.

Mapstone, E. R., & Harris, P. L. (1985). Is the English present progressive unique? *Journal of Child Language, 12*, 433-441.

Marchand, H. (1955). On a question of aspect: A comparison between the progressive form in English and that of Italian and Spanish. *Studia Linguistica, 9*, 44-52.

Marchman, V. (1989). *Episodic structure and the linguistic encoding of events in narrative: A study of language acquisition and performance.* Unpublished doctoral dissertation, University of California, Berkeley.

Marchman, V., Bates, E., Burkardt, A., & Good, A. (1991). Functional constraints on the acquisition of passive: Toward a model of the competence to perform. *First Language, 11*, 65-92.

Martin, J. R. (1977). *Learning how to tell: Semantic systems and structures in children's narratives.* Unpublished doctoral dissertation, University of Essex.

Martin, J. R. (1983). The development of register. In J. Fine & R. O. Freedle (Eds.), *Developmental issues in discourse* (pp. 839-878). Norwood, NJ: Ablex.

Maslov, Yu. S. (Ed.). (1976). *Voprosy sopostavitel'noj aspektologii.* Leningrad: Izd-vo Leningradskogo Universiteta. [English translation by J. Forsyth (1986): *Contrastive studies in verbal aspect in Russian, English, French and German.* Heidelberg: Julius Groos Verlag.]

Mayer, M. (1967). *A boy, a dog, and a frog.* New York: The Dial Press.

Mayer, M. (1969). *Frog, where are you?* New York: Dial Press.

Mayroz, O. (1988). *Rexishat ma-arexet shmot ha-pe'ula be-ivrit ha-xadasha* [Acquisition of action nominals in Modern Hebrew].

McCabe, A., & Peterson, C. (Eds.). (1991). *Developing narrative structure.* Hillsdale, NJ: Lawrence Erlbaum Associates.

McCawley, J. D. (1971). Tense and time reference in English. In C. J. Fillmore & D. T. Langendoen (Eds.), *Studies in linguistic semantics* (pp. 97-114). New York: Holt, Rinehart & Winston.

McCawley, J. D. (1981). The syntax and semantics of English relative clauses. *Lingua, 53*, 99-149.

McCawley, J. D. (1988). *The syntactic phenomena of English: Vol. 2.* Chicago: University of Chicago.

McCoard, R. W. (1978). *The English perfect: Tense-choice and pragmatic inferences.* Amsterdam: North-Holland.

McConaughy, S. H., Fitzhenry-Coor, I., & Howell, D. C. (1983). Developmental differences in schemata for story comprehension. In K. E.

Nelson (Ed.), *Children's language: Vol. 4.* Hillsdale, NJ: Lawrence Erlbaum Associates.

McGann, W., & Schwartz, A. (1988). Main character in children's narratives. *Linguistics, 26,* 215-233.

McKeon, R. (Ed.). (1947). *Introduction to Aristotle.* New York: Modern Library.

McNeill, D. (1992). *Hand and mind: What gestures reveal about thought.* Chicago / London: University of Chicago Press.

Merritt, D. D., & Liles, B. Z. (1986). Narrative analysis: Clinical applications of story generation and story retelling. *Journal of Speech and Hearing Disorders, 54,* 438-447.

Miller, P. J., & Sperry, L. L. (1988). Early talk about the past: The origins of conversational stories of personal experience. *Journal of Child Language, 15,* 293-315.

Mills, A. E. (1985). The acquisition of German. In D. I. Slobin (Ed.), *The crosslinguistic study of language acquisition. Vol. 1. The data* (pp. 141-254). Hillsdale, NJ: Lawrence Erlbaum Associates.

Miranda, A., Camp, L., Hemphill, L., & Wolf, D. (1992, October). *Developmental changes in children's use of tense in narrative.* Paper presented at the Boston University Conference on Language Development, Boston, MA.

Moore, C., & Davidge, J. (1989). The development of mental terms: Pragmatics or semantics? *Journal of Child Language, 16,* 633-641.

Myhill, J. (1992). *Typological discourse analysis: Quantitative approaches to the study of linguistic function.* Oxford UK / Cambridge, MA: Blackwell.

Nakamura, K. (1992). *The acquisition of referential structure: The development of the usage of* wa *and* ga *in Japanese oral narratives.* Unpublished manuscript, Department of Psychology, University of California, Berkeley.

Nakamura, K. (1993). Referential structure in Japanese children's narratives: The acquisition of *wa* and *ga.* In S. Choi (Ed.), *Japanese/Korean Linguistics 3.* Stanford, CA: Center for the Study of Language and Information.

Nelson, K. (Ed.). (1989). *Narratives from the crib.* Cambridge, MA: Harvard University Press.

Nelson, K. (1991). Remembering and telling: A developmental story. *Journal of Narrative and Life History, 1,* 109-127.

Nelson, K. (1992). Emergence of autobiographical memory at age 4. *Human Development, 35*, 172-177.

Nelson, K., & Gruendel, J. (1981). Generalized event representations: Basic building blocks of cognitive development. In A. L. Brown & M. E. Lamb (Eds.), *Advances in developmental psychology: Vol. 1* (pp. 131-158). Hillsdale, NJ: Lawrence Erlbaum Associates.

Nezworski, T., Stein, N., & Trabasso, T. (1982). Story structure versus content in children's recall. *Journal of Verbal Learning and Verbal Behavior, 21*, 196-206.

Nida, E. A. (1964). *Toward a science of translating, with special reference to principles and procedures involved in Bible translating.* Leiden: E. J. Brill.

Ninio, A. (1988). The roots of narrative: Discussing recent events with very young children. *Language Sciences, 10*, 35-52.

Nussbaum, N., & Naremore, R. (1975). On the acquisition of present perfect 'have' in normal children. *Language and Speech, 18*, 219-226.

Ochs, E. (1979). Planned and unplanned discourse. In T. Givón (Ed.), *Syntax and semantics: Vol 12. Discourse and syntax* (pp. 51-80). New York: Academic Press.

Olshtain, E., & Barzilay, M. (1991). Lexical retrieval difficulties in adult language attrition. In H. W. Seliger & R. M. Vago (Eds.), *First language attrition* (pp. 139-150). Cambridge: Cambridge University Press.

Orsolini, M., Rossi, F., & Pontecorvo, C. (1993). *Re-introduction of reference in Italian children's narratives.* Manuscript submitted for publication.

Palmer, F. R. (1974). *The English verb.* London: Longmans.

Partee, B. H. (1984). Nominal and temporal anaphora. *Linguistics and Philosophy, 7*, 243-286.

Payne, D. L. (1987). Information structuring in Papago narrative discourse. *Language, 63*, 783-804.

Peng, Y. S. (1992). *Developmental study of aspects of Malay narratives.* Unpublished B. A. honours thesis, Department of Linguistics, La Trobe University, Melbourne, Victoria, Australia.

Perner, J. (1992). Grasping the concept of representation: Its impact on 4-year-olds' theory of mind and beyond. *Human Development, 35*, 146-155.

Peterson, C., & McCabe, A. (1983). *Developmental psycholinguistics: Three ways of looking at a child's narrative.* New York: Plenum.

Peterson, C., & McCabe, A. (1991). Linking children's connective use and connective macrostructure. In A. McCabe & C. Peterson (Eds.), *Developing narrative structure* (pp. 29-54). Hillsdale, NJ: Lawrence Erlbaum Associates.

Piaget, J. (1960). *Die Bildung des Zeitbegriffs beim Kinde.* Zürich: Rascher. [Translation of (1946), *Le développement de la notion du temps chez l'enfant.* Paris: Presses Universitaires de France.]

Pinker, S. (1989). *Learnability and cognition: The acquisition of argument structure.* Cambridge, MA: MIT Press.

Pinker, S., Lebeaux, D. S., & Frost, L. A. (1987). Productivity and constraints in the acquisition of the passive. *Cognition, 26,* 195-267.

Pitcher, E. G., & Prelinger, E. (1963). *Children tell stories: An analysis of fantasy.* New York: International Universities Press.

Poulsen, D., Kintsch, E., Kintsch, W., & Premack, D. (1979). Children's comprehension and memory for stories. *Journal of Experimental Child Psychology, 28,* 379-403.

Preece, A. (1992). Review of M. Bamberg *The acquisition of narratives: Learning to use language. Journal of Child Language, 19,* 481-486.

Prince, E. (1981). Toward a taxonomy of given-new information. In P. Cole (Ed.), *Radical pragmatics* (pp. 223-255). New York: Academic Press.

Propp, V. (1968). *Morphology of the folktale.* Austin, Texas: University of Texas Press. [Original work published in 1928 in Russian]

Pye, C., & Quixtan Poz, P. (1988). Precocious passives (and antipassives) in Quiche Mayan. *Papers and Reports on Child Language Development, 27,* 71-80.

RAE [Real Academia de la Lengua Española] (1982). *Esbozo de una nueva gramática de la lengua española* [Outline of a new grammar of the Spanish language]. Madrid: Espasa-Calpe.

Ragnarsdóttir, H. (1987, November). *The development of narrative structure and its relation to the use of tenses and aspects in Icelandic children's stories.* Paper presented at the conference of the Icelandic Linguistic Society in honor of the 200th anniversary of Christian Rask, Reykjavik.

Ragnarsdóttir, H. (1988, January). *Söguprádur og setningagerdir í sögum barna og fullordinna* [Narrative structure and sentence types in children's and adults' stories]. Paper presented at the conference on Icelandic in the primary school, organized by the Icelandic Institute of

Educational Research, Reykjavik.

Ragnarsdóttir, H. (1991a). Episodic structure and interclausal connectives in Icelandic children's narratives. *Proceedings of Colloquium Paedolinguisticum Lundensis 1991*. Lund, Sweden.

Ragnarsdóttir, H. (1991b, June). *What does it take to tell a story?* Paper presented at the Scandinavian Congress of Logopedics and Phoniatrics, Reykjavik.

Rau, M. L. (1979). Die Entwicklung von Vergangenheitsstrukturen in der Sprache eines Dreijährigen [The development of past structures in the language of a 3-year-old]. *Folia Linguistica, 13*, 357-412.

Ravid, D. (in press). *Language change in child and adult Hebrew: A psycholinguistic perspective.* New York: Oxford University Press.

Reichenbach, R. (1947a). *Elements of symbolic logic.* New York: The Macmillan Co.

Reichenbach, H. (1947b). *Symbolic logic.* Berkeley, CA: University of California Press.

Reilly, J. S. (1992). How to tell a good story: The intersection of language and affect in children's narratives. *Journal of Narrative and Life History, 2*, 355-377.

Reilly, J., Klima, E. S., & Bellugi, U. (in press). Once more with feeling: Affect and language in atypical populations. In D. Cicchetti (Ed.), special issue of *Development and psychopathology.* Cambridge: Cambridge University Press.

Reilly, J., Marchman, V., & Bates, E. (in press). Discourse in children with anomalous brain development or acquired brain lesions. *Brain and Language.*

Reinhart, T. (1984). Principles of gestalt perception in the temporal organization of narrative texts. *Linguistics, 22*, 779-809.

Renner, T. (1988). *Development of temporality in children's narratives.* Unpublished doctoral dissertation, University of California, Berkeley.

Rescorla, L., & Manhardt, J. (1993). *Narrative competencies of children with a history of specific expressive language delay.* Unpublished ms, Department of Human Development, Bryn Mawr College.

Rizzi, L. (1982). *Issues in Italian syntax.* Dordrecht: Foris Publications.

Rizzi, L. (1986). Null subjects and the theory of *pro. Linguistic Inquiry, 17*, 501-557.

Rohrer, C. (Ed.). (1980). *Time, tense, and quantifiers.* Tübingen: Max Niemayer Verlag.

Rodríguez-Trelles Astruga, A. (1991). *Expresión de las relaciones temporales y aspectuales en los relatos: Una perspectiva evolutiva* [Expression of temporal and aspectual relations in stories: A developmental perspective]. Unpublished doctoral dissertation, University of Santiago de Compostela, Galicia, Spain.

Rossi, F. (1993). *Forms and functions of reference in spoken and written narratives.* Unpublished manuscript, Department of Developmental and Social Psychology, University of Rome, Italy.

Roth, F. P., & Spekman, J. J. (1986). Narrative discourse: Spontaneously generated stories of learning disabled and normally achieving students. *Journal of Speech and Hearing Disorders, 51*, 8-23.

Rumelhart, D. E. (1975). Notes on a schema for stories. In D. G. Bobrow & A. Collins (Eds.), *Representation and understanding: Studies in cognitive science* (pp. 211-236). New York: Academic Press.

Rumelhart, D. E. (1977). Understand and summarizing brief stories. In D. LaBerge & J. Samuels (Eds.), *Basic processes in reading: Perception and comprehension* (pp. 265-304). Hillsdale, NJ: Lawrence Erlbaum Associates.

Sachs, J. (1983). Talking about the there and then: The emergence of displaced reference in parent-child discourse. In K. E. Nelson (Ed.), *Children's language: Vol. 4* (pp. 1-28). Hillsdale, NJ: Lawrence Erlbaum Associates.

Sachs, J., Goldman, J., & Chaille, C. (1984). Planning in pretend play: Using language to coordinate narrative development. In A. D. Pellegrini & T. D. Yawkey (Eds.), *Advances in discourse processes: Vol. 13. The development of oral and written language in social contexts* (pp. 119-128). Norwood, NJ: Ablex.

Sandbank, A. (1992). *Hitpatxut ha-ktiva shel tekstim ecel yeladim ba-gan u-ve-xita alef: ha-tahalix ve ha-tocar* [The development of text writing in preschoolers and first graders: The writing process and the written product]. Unpublished master's thesis, Tel Aviv University.

Sapir, E. (1924). The grammarian and his language. *American Mercury, 1*, 149-155. [Reprinted in D. G. Mandelbaum (Ed.). (1958). *Selected writings of Edward Sapir in language, culture and personality.* Berkeley/Los Angeles: University of California Press.]

Savaşır, I. (1983). *How many futures? A study of future reference in early child language.* Unpublished master's thesis, University of California, Berkeley.

Savaşır, I. (1986). Habits and abilities in Turkish. In D. I. Slobin & K. Zimmer (Eds.), *Studies in Turkish linguistics* (pp. 137-146). Amsterdam: John Benjamins.

Schank, R. C. (1975). The structure of episodes in memory. In D. G. Bobrow & A. Collins (Eds.), *Representation and understanding: Studies in cognitive science*. New York: Academic Press.

Schiff, R. (1991). *Hashva'a beyn ha-yexolot ha-morfologit, ha-taxbirit ve ha-narativit ecel kor'im tovim le'umat mitkashim* [A comparison of the morphological, syntactic, and narrative ability of proficient and poor readers]. Unpublished master's thesis, Tel Aviv University.

Schiffrin, D. (1981). Tense variation in narratives. *Language, 57,* 45-62.

Schmidt, W. (1967). *Grundfragen der deutschen Grammatik: Eine Einführung in die funktionale Sprachlehre* [Basic questions of German grammar: An introduction to functional linguistics]. Berlin: Volk und Wissen.

Scholnik, E. K. & Friedman, S. L. (1987). The planning construct in the psychological literature. In S. L. Friedman, E. K. Scholnik, & R. R. Cocking (Eds.), *Blueprints for thinking: The role of planning in cognitive development* (pp. 3-38). New York: Cambridge University Press.

Schuetze-Coburn, S. (1984). On the borders of subordination: Signaling relative clauses in spoken German. *Proceedings of the Annual Meeting of the Berkeley Linguistics Society, 10,* 650-659.

Schwenter, S. A. (in press). The grammaticalization of an anterior in progress: Evidence from a Peninsular Spanish dialect. *Studies in Language.*

Sebastián, E. (1989). *Tiempo y aspecto verbal en el lenguage infantil* [Verbal tense and aspect in child language]. Unpublished doctoral dissertation, Universidad Autónoma de Madrid.

Sera, M. D. (1992). To be or not to be: Use and acquisition of the Spanish copulas. *Journal of Memory and Language, 31,* 408-427.

Shen, Y. (1985). On importance hierarchy and evaluation devices in narrative texts. *Poetics Today, 6,* 681-698.

Shen, Y. (1988). The X-Bar grammar for stories: Story grammar revisited. *Text, 9,* 415-467.

Shen, Y. (1990). Centrality and causal relations in narrative texts. *Journal of Literary Semantics, 19,* 1-29.

Shen, Y., & Berman, R. A. (in press). Me-ha-irua ha-boded le-mivne pe'ula: shlabim ba-hitpatxut ha-narativit [From isolated event to action structure: Stages in the development of narrative]. In Y. Shimron (Ed.), *Mexkarim ba-psixologiya shel ha-lashon*. Haifa: Haifa University Press.

Shibatani, M. (1985). Passives and related constructions. *Language, 61*, 821-848.

Silva, M. (1991). Simultaneity in children's narratives: The case of *when, while*, and *as. Journal of Child Language, 18*, 641-662.

Silva-Corvalán, C. (1983). Tense and aspect in oral Spanish narrative: Context and meaning. *Language, 59*, 760-780.

Silva-Corvalán, C. (1992). Algunos aspectos de la gramática de los niños bilingües de Los Angeles [Some aspects of the grammar of bilingual children of Los Angeles]. In H. Urrutia Cárdenas & C. Silva-Corvalán (Eds.), *Bilingüismo y adquisición del español* (pp. 227-239). Bilbao, Spain: Instituto Horizonte.

Sleight, C. C., & Prinz, P. M. (1985). Use of abstracts, orientations, and codas in narrative by language-disordered and nondisordered children. *Journal of Speech and Hearing Disorders, 50*, 361-371.

Slobin, D. I. (1973). Cognitive prerequisites for the development of grammar. In C. A. Ferguson & D. I. Slobin (Eds.), *Studies of child language development* (pp. 175-208). New York: Holt, Reinhart & Winston.

Slobin, D. I. (1982). Universal and particular in the acquisition of language. In E. Wanner & L. R. Gleitman (Eds.), *Language acquisition: The state of the art* (pp. 128-170). Cambridge: Cambridge University Press.

Slobin, D. I. (1985a). Crosslinguistic evidence for the Language-Making Capacity. In D. I. Slobin (Ed.), *The crosslinguistic study of language acquisition: Vol. 2. Theoretical issues* (pp. 1157-1256). Hillsdale, NJ: Lawrence Erlbaum Associates.

Slobin, D. I. (Ed.). (1985b). *The crosslinguistic study of language acquisition* (Vols. 1-2). Hillsdale, NJ: Lawrence Erlbaum Associates.

Slobin, D. I. (1986). The acquisition and use of relative clauses in Turkic and Indo-European languages. In D. I. Slobin & K. Zimmer (Eds.), *Studies in Turkish linguistics* (pp. 273-294). Amsterdam: John Benjamins.

Slobin, D. I. (1987). Thinking for speaking. *Proceedings of the Annual Meeting of the Berkeley Linguistics Society, 13*, 435-444.

Slobin, D. I. (1988). The development of clause chaining in Turkish child language. In S. Koç (Ed.), *Studies on Turkish linguistics* (pp. 27-54). Ankara: Middle East Technical University. [Circulated as Berkeley Cognitive Science Report No. 55, Institute of Cognitive Studies, University of California, Berkeley, 1989.]

Slobin, D. I. (1989, July). *Factors of language typology in the crosslinguistic study of acquisition.* Paper presented at the Tenth Biennial Meeting of the International Society for the Study of Behavioural Development, Jyväskylä, Finland. [Circulated as Berkeley Cognitive Science Report No. 66, Institute of Cognitive Studies, University of California, Berkeley, August 1990.]

Slobin, D. I. (1990). The development from child speaker to native speaker. In J. W. Stigler, G. Herdt, & R. A. Shweder (Eds.), *Cultural psychology: Essays on comparative human development* (pp. 233-256). Cambridge: Cambridge University Press.

Slobin, D. I. (1991). Learning to think for speaking: Native language, cognition, and rhetorical style. *Pragmatics, 1,* 7-26.

Slobin, D. I. (1993a). Converbs in Turkish child language: The grammaticalization of event coherence. In M. Haspelmath & E. König (Eds.), *Converbs (adverbial participles, gerunds) in cross-linguistic perspective.* Berlin York: Mouton de Gruyter.

Slobin, D. I. (1993b). Passives and alternatives in children's narratives in English, Spanish, German, and Turkish. In B. Fox & P. J. Hopper (Eds.), *Voice: Form and function.* Amsterdam: John Benjamins.

Slobin, D. I. (in press-a). From 'thought and language' to 'thinking for speaking'. In J. J. Gumperz & S. Levinson (Eds.), *Rethinking linguistic relativity.* Cambridge: Cambridge University Press.

Slobin, D. I. (in press-b). Talking perfectly: Discourse origins of the present perfect. In W. Pagliuca & G. Davis (Eds.), *Perspectives on grammaticalization.* Amsterdam: John Benjamins.

Slobin, D. I. (in press-c). Two ways to travel: Verbs of motion in English and Spanish. In M. Shibatani & S. A. Thompson (Eds.), *Essays in semantics.* Oxford: Oxford University Press.

Slobin, D. I., & Aksu, A. A. (1982). Tense, aspect and modality in the use of the Turkish evidential. In P. Hopper (Ed.), *Tense-aspect: Between semantics and pragmatics* (pp. 185-200). Amsterdam: John Benjamins.

Slobin, D. I., & Bocaz, A. (1988). Learning to talk about movement through time and space: The development of narrative abilities in Spanish and English. *Lenguas Modernas* (Santiago, Chile), *15,* 5-24. [Circulated as Berkeley Cognitive Science Report No. 55, Institute of Cognitive Studies, University of California, Berkeley, January 1989.]

Slobin, D. I., & Talay, A. (1986). Development of pragmatic use of subject pronouns in Turkish child language. In A. Aksu-Koç & E. Erguvanlı-Taylan (Eds.), *Proceedings of the Turkish Linguistics Conference,*

August 9-10, 1984 (pp. 207-228). Istanbul: Boğaziçi University Publications No. 400.

Smith, C. S. (1980a). The acquisition of time talk: Relations between child and adult grammars. *Journal of Child Language, 7*, 263-278.

Smith, C. S. (1980b). Temporal structures in discourse. In C. Rohrer (Ed.), *Time, tense, and quantifiers* (pp. 355-374). Tübingen: Max Niemayer Verlag.

Smith, C. S. (1983). A theory of aspectual choice. *Language, 59*, 479-501.

Snell-Hornby, M. (1988). *Translation studies: An integrated approach.* Amsterdam/Philadelphia: John Benjamins.

Snow, C. E. (1977a). Mothers' speech research: From input to interaction. In C. E. Snow & C. A. Ferguson (Eds.), *Talking to children: Language input and acquisition.* Cambridge: Cambridge University Press.

Snow, C. E. (1977b). Mothers' speech to children learning language. *Child Development, 43*, 549-565.

Snow, C. E., & Dickinson, D. K. (1990). Social sources of narrative skills at home and at school. *First Language, 10*, 87-104.

Snow, C. E., & Ferguson, C. A. (Eds.). (1977). *Talking to children: Language input and acquisition.* Cambridge: Cambridge University Press.

Sprott, R. (1990, August). *Cognitive and social effects on children's use of justifications.* Paper presented at the Congress of the International Pragmatics Association, Barcelona.

Stein, N. L. (1983). On the goals, functions, and knowledge of reading and writing. *Contemporary Educational Psychology, 8*, 261-292.

Stein, N. L., & Glenn, C. G. (1979). An analysis of story comprehension in elementary school children. In R. O. Freedle (Ed.), *New directions in discourse comprehension: Vol. 2: Advances in discourse processes.* (pp. 53-120). Norwood, NJ: Ablex.

Stein, N. L., & Levine, L. (1987). Thinking about feelings: The development and organization of emotional knowledge. In R. E. Snow & M. Far (Eds.), *Aptitude, learning, and instruction. Vol 3: Cognition, conation, and affect* (pp. 165-197). Hillsdale, NJ: Lawrence Erlbaum Associates.

Stein, N. L., & Levine, L. (1989). The causal organization of emotion knowledge: A developmental study. *Cognition and Emotion, 3*, 343-378.

Stein, N. L. & Levine, L. (1990). Making sense out of emotional experience: The representation and use of goal-directed knowledge. In N. L. Stein, B. Leventhal, & T. Trabasso (Eds.), *Psychological and biological approaches to emotion*. Hillsdale, NJ: Lawrence Erlbaum Associates.

Stein, N. L., & Policastro, M. (1984). The concept of a story: A comparison between children's and teacher's viewpoints. In H. Mandl, N. L. Stein, & T. Trabasso (Eds.), *Learning and comprehension of text*. Hillsdale, NJ: Lawrence Erlbaum Associates.

Stein, N., & Salgo, D. (1984, November). *The relationship between the story concept and the development of story-telling skill*. Paper presented at Psychonomic Society Meeting, San Antonio, Texas.

Stein, N. L., & Trabasso, T. (1982). Children's understanding of stories: A basis for moral judgment and dilemma resolution. In C. J. Brainerd & M. Pressley (Eds.), *Verbal processes in children: Progress in cognitive development research*. New York: Springer-Verlag.

Stephany, U. (1981). Verbal grammar in modern Greek early child language. In P. S. Dale & D. Ingram (Eds.), *Child language: An international perspective*. Baltimore, MD: University Park Press.

Stephany, U. (1986). Modality. In P. Fletcher & M. Garman (Eds.), *Language acquisition* (2nd ed., pp. 375-400). Cambridge: Cambridge University Press.

Stern, C., & Stern, W. (1928). *Die Kindersprache* [Child language]. Leipzig: Barth.

Sternberg, M. (1978). *Expositional modes and temporal ordering in fiction*. Baltimore: Johns Hopkins Press.

Strauss, S. (Ed.). (1982). *U-shaped behavioral growth*. New York: Academic Press.

Suñer, M. (1990). Sintaxis y semántica del español en la década de los ochenta: El modelo de principios y parámetros [Spanish syntax and semantics in the 80s: The model of principles and parameters]. *Lingüística, 2*, 86-120.

Szagun, G. (1976). *A cross-cultural study of the acquisition of tense forms and time concepts in young children*. Unpublished doctoral dissertation, University of London.

Szagun, G. (1977). Time concepts and tense forms in children's speech. In B. A. Geber (Ed.), *Piaget and knowing: Studies in genetic epistemology*. London: Routledge and Kegan Paul.

Szagun, G. (1979). *The development of spontaneous reference to past and future: A cross-linguistic study*. Forschungsbericht Nr. 79-4. Institut für Psychologie, Technische Universität Berlin.

Tager-Flusberg, H. (1993, September). *Once upon a ribbit: Stories narrated by autistic children.* Paper presented at the Developmental Section of British Psychological Society, Annual Meeting, Cambridge.

Takahashi, K. (1993). *Tense variation in Japanese narrative.* Unpublished manuscript, University of California at Los Angeles.

Talmy, L. (1985). Lexicalization patterns: Semantic structure in lexical forms. In T. Shopen (Ed.), *Language typology and syntactic description: Vol. 3. Grammatical categories and the lexicon* (pp. 36-149). Cambridge: Cambridge University Press.

Talmy, L. (1991). Paths to realization: A typology of event conflation. *Proceedings of the Annual Meeting of the Berkeley Linguistic Society, 17.* [Supplement in *Buffalo Papers in Linguistics 91-01* (pp. 182-187).]

Talmy, L. (in press). The windowing of attention in language. In M. Shibatani & S. A. Thompson (Eds.), *Essays in semantics.* Oxford: Oxford University Press.

Tannen, D. (1982). The oral/literate continuum in discourse. In D. Tannen (Ed.), *Spoken and written language: Exploring orality and literacy* (pp. 1-16). Norwood, NJ: Ablex.

Thieroff, R. (1992). *Das finite Verb im Deutschen: Tempus - Modus - Distanz* [The finite verb in German: Tense - Mode - Distance]. Tübingen: Gunter Narr Verlag.

Thompson, S. A. (1978). Modern English from a typological point of view: Some implications of the function of word order. *Linguistische Berichte, 54,* 19-36.

Timberlake, A. (1982). Invariance and the syntax of Russian aspect. In P. J. Hopper (Ed.), *Tense-aspect: Between semantics and pragmatics* (pp. 305-334). Amsterdam: John Benjamins.

Toivainen, J. (1989, July). *Situationally determined linguistic differences between narratives produced by a five-year-old Finnish child: Demonstratives and tenses in face-to-face and telephone narratives.* Paper presented at the Tenth Biennial Meeting of the International Society for the Study of Behavioural Development, Jyväskylä, Finland.

Toivainen, J. (1992). Vieri- ja puhelinkerronan erot erään viisivuotiaan kuvakirjakertomuksessa: Demonstratiivit ja tempukset [Differences between face-to-face and telephone narratives in the picturebook stories of a 5-year-old: Demonstratives and tenses]. *Virittäjä, 96,* 60-71.

Tolchinsky-Landsmann, L., & Sandbank, L. (in press). Text production and text differentiation: Developmental changes and educational influences. In S. Strauss (Ed.), *Learning environments and psychological development*. Norwood, NJ: Ablex Publishers.

Tomlin, R. S. (Ed.). (1987). *Coherence and grounding in discourse*. Amsterdam: John Benjamins.

Toolan, M. (1988). *Narrative: A critical linguistic introduction*. London: Routledge.

Torrego, E. (1984). On inversion in Spanish and some of its effects. *Linguistic Inquiry, 15*, 103-130.

Toury, G. (1986). Translation: A cultural-semiotic perspective. In T. A. Sebeok (Ed.), *Encyclopedic dictionary of semiotics: Vol. 2* (pp. 1111-1124). Berlin York: Mouton de Gruyter.

Trabasso, T., & van den Broek, P. (1985). Causal thinking and the representation of narrative events. *Journal of Memory and Language, 24*, 612-630.

Trabasso, T., van den Broek, P., & Suh, S. (1989). Logical necessity and transitivity of causal relations in stories. *Discourse Processes, 12*, 1-25.

Trabasso, T., & Nickels, M. (1992). The development of goal plans of action in the narration of picture stories. *Discourse Processes, 15*, 249-275.

Trabasso, T., Secco, T., & van den Broek, P. (1984) Causal cohesion and story coherence. In H. Mandl, N. L. Stein, & T. Trabasso (Eds.), *Learning and comprehension of text* (pp. 83-111). Hillsdale, NJ: Lawrence Erlbaum Associates.

Trabasso, T., & Sperry, L. L. (1985). Causal relatedness and importance of story events. *Journal of Memory and Language, 24*, 595-611.

Trabasso, T., & Stein, N. L. (in press). Using goal/plan knowledge to merge the past with the present and the future in narrating events on-line. In M. M. Haith (Ed.), *The development of future oriented processes*. Chicago, IL: University of Chicago Press.

Trabasso, T., & Suh, S. (in press). Understanding text: Achieving explanatory coherence through on-line inferences and mental operations in working memory. *Discourse Processes*.

Trabasso, T., Stein, N. L., Rodkin, P. C., Munger, M. P., & Baughn, C. (1992). Knowledge of goals and plans in the on-line narration of events. *Cognitive Development, 7*, 133-170.

Trabasso, T., van den Broek, P., & Suh, S. (1989). Logical necessity and transitivity of causal relations in stories. *Discourse Processes, 12*, 1-25.

Tracy, R. (1991). *Sprachliche Strukturentwicklung* [Development of linguistic structure]. Tübingen: Narr.

Tura, S. S. (1986). *Dır* in modern Turkish. In A. Aksu-Koç & E. Erguvanlı-Taylan (Eds.), *Proceedings of the Turkish Linguistics Conference* (pp.

145-158). Istanbul: Boğaziçi University Press.

Uchida, N. (1982). Yooji wa ika ni monogatari o tsukuru ka? [How do children make narratives?]. *Kyooiku Shinrigaku Kenkyuu, 30(3)*, 212-222.

Uchida, N. (1983). Kaiga sutorii no imiteki tougouka ni okeru mokuhyoo koo-zoo no yakuwari [The role of goal structure in the semantic synthesis of picture stories]. *Kyooiku Shinrigaku Kenkyuu, 31(4)*, 302-313.

Umiker-Sebeok, D. J. (1978). Preschool children's intraconversational narratives. *Journal of Child Language, 6*, 99-109.

Underhill, R. (1976). *Turkish grammar*. Cambridge, MA: MIT Press.

Urrutia Cárdenas, H. (1992). Competencia léxica y sintáctica en niños monolingües y bilingües en el País Vasco [Lexical and syntactic competence in monolingual and bilingual children in the Basque Country]. In H. Urrutia Cárdenas & C. Silva-Corvalán (Eds.), *Bilingüismo y adquisición del español* (pp. 17-26). Bilbao, Spain: Instituto Horizonte.

van Dijk, T. A. (1972). *Some aspects of text grammars: A study in theoretical linguistics and poetics*. The Hague: Mouton.

van Dijk, T. A. (1980). *Macrostructures*. Hillsdale, NJ: Lawrence Erlbaum Associates.

van Dijk, T. A., & Kintsch, W. (1983). *Strategies of discourse comprehension*. London: Academic Press.

Van Valin, R. D., Jr. (1990). Semantic parameters of split intransitivity. *Language, 66*, 221-260.

Van Valin, R. D., Jr. (1993). A synopsis of role and reference grammar. In R. D. Van Valin, Jr. (Ed.), *Advances in role and reference grammar*. Amsterdam: John Benjamins.

Vendler, Z. (1967). *Linguistics in philosophy*. Ithaca, NY: Cornell University Press.

Verhoeven, L. (1993). Acquisition of narrative skills in a bilingual context. In B. Kettemann & W. Wieden (Eds.), *Current issues in European second language acquisition research* (pp. 307-232). Tübingen: Gunter Narr Verlag.

von Stutterheim, C. (1986). *Temporalität im Zweitspracherwerb* [Temporality in second-language acquisition]. Berlin: de Gruyter.

von Stutterheim, C. (1987). *Simultaneity in discourse*. Unpublished manuscript, University of Heidelberg.

von Stutterheim, C., & Klein, W. (1989). Referential movement in descriptive and narrative discourse. In R. Dietrich & C. F. Graumann (Eds.), *Language processing in social context* (pp. 39-76). Amsterdam: North

Holland.

Vygotsky, L. S. (1962). *Thought and language.* Cambridge, MA: MIT. Press. [Edited translation by E. Hanfmann & G. Vakar of *Myšlenie i reč'*. Moscow: Sotsekgiz, 1934.]

Vygotsky, L. S. (1978). *Mind in society: The development of higher psychological processes.* (M. Cole, V. John-Steiner, S. Scribener, & S. Souberman (Eds.)). Cambridge, MA: Harvard University Press. [Original work published 1934 in Russian.]

Warden, D. (1981). Learning to identify referents. *British Journal of Psychology, 67,* 101-112.

Warren, W. H., Nicholas, D. W., & Trabasso, T. (1979). Event chains and inferences in understanding narratives. In R. Freedle (Ed.), *New directions in discourse processing, Vol. 2. Advances in discourse processes.* Hillsdale, NJ: Lawrence Erlbaum Associates.

Weissenborn, J. (1991). Null subjects in early grammars: Implications for language acquisition theories. In J. Weissenborn, H. Goodluck, & T. Roeper (Eds.), *Theoretical issues in language acquisition: Continuity and change in development* (pp. 269-300). Hillsdale, NJ: Lawrence Erlbaum Associates.

Weist, R. M. (1986). Tense and aspect. In P. Fletcher & M. Garman (Eds.), *Language acquisition: Studies in first language development* (2nd ed., pp. 356-374). Cambridge: Cambridge University Press.

Weist, R. M. (1990). Time concepts in language and thought: Filling the Piagetian void from two to five years. In I. Levin & N. Zakay (Eds.), *Time and human cognition: A lifespan perspective* (pp. 54-109). Amsterdam: North-Holland.

Weist, R. M., Wysocka, H., Witkowska-Stadnik, K., Buczowska, E., & Konieczna, E. (1984). The defective tense hypothesis: On the emergence of tense and aspect in child Polish. *Journal of Child Language, 11,* 347-374.

Wells, C. G. (1985). Language development in the pre-school years. Cambridge: Cambridge University Press.

Werner, H. (1957). The concept of development from a comparative and organismic point of view. In D. B. Harris (Ed.), *The concept of development: An issue in the study of human behavior.* Minneapolis: University of Minnesota Press.

Werner, H., & Kaplan, B. (1984). *Symbol formation.* Hillsdale, NJ: Lawrence Erlbaum Associates. [Original work published in 1963. New York: Wiley]

Wertsch, J. V. (Ed.). (1985). *Culture, communication, and cognition: Vygotskian perspectives.* Cambridge: Cambridge University Press.

Whorf, B. L. (1940). Science and linguistics. *Technology Review, 42*(6), 229-231, 247-248. [Reprinted in J. B. Carroll (Ed.), (1956). *Language, thought, and reality: Selected writings of Benjamin Lee Whorf* (pp. 246-270). New York: Technology Press of M.I.T. and John Wiley & Sons.

Wigglesworth, G. (1990). Children's narrative acquisition: A study of some aspects of reference and anaphora. *First Language, 10,* 105-126.

Wigglesworth, G. (1992). *Investigating children's cognitive and linguistic development through narrative.* Unpublished doctoral dissertation, Department of Linguistics, La Trobe University, Bundoora, Victoria, Australia.

Williamson, S. (1978, April). *English in parallels: A study of Arabic style.* Paper presented at the Sixth Annual Meeting of the California Linguistics Association, University of California, Riverside.

Wilss, W. (1982). *The science of translation: Problems and methods.* Tübingen: Gunter Narr.

Wolf, D. P., Hemphill, L., & Camp, L. (1991, May). *A contrastive analysis of narrative performance in a child with mild mental retardation and a nonretarded child.* Paper presented at the Gatlinburg Conference on Language Disorders, Key Biscayne, FL.

Wolfson, N. (1982). *CHP: The conversational historical present in American English narrative.* Dordrecht: Foris Publications.

Yavaş, F. (1980). *On the meaning of the tense and aspect markers in Turkish.* Unpublished doctoral dissertation, University of Kansas.

Ziv, Y. (1988). Word order in children's literature: FSP and markedness. In Y. Tobin (Ed.), *The Prague School and its legacy* (pp. 123-144). Amsterdam: John Benjamins.

Zijlenmaker, C. (1992). *Het gebruik van referentie in het vertellen van een verhaal "The frog story" bij kinderen en volwassenen* [The use of reference in telling a story "The frog story" by children and adults]. Unpublished master's thesis, General Linguistics University of Amsterdam.

Zijlenmaker, C. (1992). *Anafoorgebruik van kinderen in een narratieve setting* [Use of anaphora by children in a narrative setting]. Unpublished doctoralscriptie, Institute of General Linguistics, University of Amsterdam.

Zorriqueta, M. E. (1988). *The acquisition of relative clauses in Spanish.* Unpublished doctoral dissertation, State University of New York, Buffalo.

Subject Index

Categories entered in the index refer to discussions of developmental, linguistic, or narrative issues in one or more of the five languages in the sample: (American) English, German, Hebrew, (European) Spanish, and Turkish. These languages are not further specified in the index, except for references to geographical or historical alternants (e.g., British English, Biblical Hebrew, Argentinian Spanish). References to other languages are entered as such in the index (e.g., French, Icelandic).

321-322, 331n, 364, 375, 432, 479, 480

Estonian, 668

evaluation, evaluative clauses, 7, 10, 13n, 45, 57, 73-74, 80, 231, 233, 234-237, 339, 402, 492, 493, 517n, 539-540, 546

event(s) (*see also* scenes), 1, 44, 46, 51

event complexes, 552-554

event-component (*see also* episode, scenes), 51-57, 545-546, 613

event conflation (*see* conflation)

event time (*see* time, event)

evidential past (*see* tense, past of direct experience)

existential(s) (*see also* presentative), 270, 312n, 335, 338, 365, 462, 464

expletive subject, 172n, 173, 266-267, 270

exposition (*see* plot components),

expressive options (*see* options)

extended aspect (*see* aspectual adverbs; aspectual verbs; lexical aspect)

F

fairytale (*see* genres)

fall, falling (*see also* scenes), 305-307, 347-350, 620-522

false starts (*see* disfluency)

fantasy (*see* genres)

fiction, fictive (*see* genres)

film, movie, 11, 32, 41, 335

filter(ing), 9, 12, 35, 390, 515-538, 611

finite (*see* verbs, finite)

Finnish, 668, 674

Finno-Permic Languages, 668

five-year-olds (*see* age groups)

flow (*see* information)

focus (*see also* topic-focus), 19, 33, 361

folk story (*see* genres)

foreground (*see* grounding)

foreshadowing, 35, 344, 555-595

forestalling, 580

form, linguistic (*see also* form/function relations), 4, 15, 17, 18, 81-82, 109-125

form/function relations (*see also* form, linguistic), 4-6, 17-20, 27, 32, 33, 34, 80-81, 160, 174-175, 183-184, 186, 194, 206, 275-276, 293-294, 317-318, 370-371, 381-382, 389-390, 409, 481, 509-512, 516-517, 554, 594, 600-603, 603-608, 640-641

formal options (*see* options)

formulaic, 148n, 267

four-year-olds (*see* age groups)

free relatives (*see* relative clauses, headless)

French, 10, 45n, 486n, 668, 675, 677

function (*see* form/function)

functionalism, functionalist, 2, 3

future tense (*see* tense, future)

mother(s) (*see* parents)

motherese, 194n

motion verbs (*see* verbs, motion)

motivation (*see* causality; evaluation)

movement (*see* locative trajectory; verbs, motion)

movie (*see* film)

Mparntwe Arrernte, 666

multifunction(ality) (*see* function)

Myene, 671

myth (*see* genres)

N

naming, 463-464, 472-473, 481-483, 499-500

narrative stance (*see* individual style; rhetoric; task-construal)

narrative structure (*see* action-structure; evaluation; plot components; plotline)

narrativity, degrees of, 44, 58

negation, negative, 423n

nesting, 565, 567-568, 580

network (*see* causal)

new (*see* information)

Nilotic languages, 671

nine-year-olds (*see* age groups)

nominal sentence, 287

nominalization, nominalized forms (*see also* converbs; verbs, nonfinite), 19, 33, 81, 322-323, 371, 378, 403, 404, 405, 446, 447, 454-455, 478

nonfinite (*see* verbs, nonfinite; *see also* converbs)

nonrestrictive (*see* relative clauses, nonrestrictive)

nonwitnessed past (*see* tense, past of indirect experience)

normative usage (*see* register)

norms, narrative (*see* convention)

Norwegian, 671, 674

noun modification, 390, 459, 460n, 487-488, 509-512

novel(ist) (*see* genre, fiction)

null subject (*see also* ellipsis), 125, 177, 181-182, 221, 225-226, 244n, 280-283, 323-325, 540, 540n, 544, 598, 609, 636, 638-639

O

obligatory, 33, 34, 640

ongoing (*see* aspect)

onset (*see* plot components)

options, expressive (*see also* selectivity), 2, 12, 15, 109-110, 144, 187, 313, 479, 509-512, 594, 607-608

order of clauses, mention/occurrence, 6, 13, 195, 209-210, 277, 399-400, 441, 470n, 483, 484, 505-506, 546, 604-605

order, word (*see also* dislocation), 7, 18, 19, 111, 121-122, 167, 168-173, 190, 209, 213, 226-227, 266-271, 311-315, 324, 361-366, 406, 477-478, 479, 487-490, 509, 517, 520, 521, 531, 533-534, 573, 598, 629-630, 632, 635, 638, 639

resolution (*see* plot components)

restrictive (*see* relative clauses, restrictive)

resultative (*see* aspect)

resumptive pronoun, 320, 478, 480

retardation, mental, 676, 677

retrospection, retrospective (*see also* aspect), 3, 72, 196, 254-252, 259-260, 279-280, 336, 337, 389, 398, 426, 435, 443, 604-607, 608, 609

rhetoric(al norms), (*see also* contrastive rhetoric; individual style; options), 10, 12, 19, 32, 76-78, 183-184, 220, 265, 325-326, 448, 513-514, 527, 531, 622-628

rhetorical options (*see also* options; selectivity), 608-609

rhythm, 19, 539, 542

Russian, 8, 10, 240, 671

S

saliency, 61-62

Sapir-Whorf hypothesis, 612, 616

satellite (*see also* particle), 19, 158-159, 219-220, 261, 577, 584, 630

satellite-framed, 111, 118-121, 261, 354, 512, 620, 621

scaffold(ing) (*see also* parents; prompting), 23, 60, 105

scene(s) (*see also* episodes; plot components), 391

bees after dog, 8, 21, 123, 165-168, 269-270, 516, 518-522, 614-616

broken jar, 516, 527-533

deer picks up boy, 121, 144n, 168, 308-309, 358-360, 516, 522-526

deer's antlers, 15-16, 21, 54-57, 144n, 522-526

discovery frog is missing, 52-54

dressing, 572-573

entry into jar, 168, 308, 357-358, 516, 526-527

escape from jar, 153-154, 215-217, 354-355, 617-619

fall from cliff, 5, 11-12, 21, 144n, 155n, 162-164, 233, 265, 270, 294-295n, 353-354, 620, 622-624

fall from tree, 13-14, 233, 348-350, 620-622

fall of beehive, 347-348

leave-taking, 215, 217-218

school setting, 75

schoolchildren (*see* age groups)

script, 41, 203

segmentation, 34

selectivity (*see also* rhetorical options), 54n, 135, 186-187, 272-273

semantics, inherent (*see* Aktionsart)

semi-modals (*see also* modal; verb, modal), 27, 129

Semitic languages (*see also* Arabic), 183n, 303n

sequence, sequentiality (*see also* chaining; clause, sequence of; temporality), 3, 7, 10, 21, 32, 45, 58, 66-67, 177-181, 207-

Name Index

Numbers in italics indicate pages with complete bibliographic information.